HERCULES AT THE CROSSROADS

HERCULES AT THE CROSSROADS

The Life, Works, and Thou

Ronald G. Witt

Duke Monographs in Medieval and Re
DUKE UNIVERSITY PRESS   Durh

The author would like to thank the following for permission to republish parts of the following articles:

Fordham University Press: "Coluccio Salutati, Citizen of Lucca, 1370–72," *Traditio* 25 (1969): 191–216.

Istituto Nazionale de Studi sul Rinascimento: "Coluccio Salutati and the Political Life of the Commune of Buggiano," *Rinascimento*, ser. 2, 6 (1966): 27–55.

Nuova Rivista Storica: "The *De Tyranno* and Coluccio Salutati's View of Roman History and Politics," *Nuova Rivista Storica* 53 (1969): 434–76.

Library of Congress Cataloging in Publication Data

Witt, Ronald G.
  Hercules at the crossroads.

  (Duke monographs in medieval and
Renaissance studies ; no. 6)
  Includes bibliographical references and
index.
    1. Salutati, Coluccio, 1331–1406.
  2. Authors, Latin (Medieval and modern)—
Biography. 3. Statesmen—Italy—Biography.
  I. Title. II. Series.
  PA8420.S15Z95 1983 878'.0409 [B] 82–9572
  ISBN 0-8223-0527-5

To Myron Piper Gilmore *in memoriam*

Nam quod Herculem Prodicus dicit, ut est apud Xenophontem, cum primum pubesceret, quod tempus a natura ad deligendum, quam quisque viam vivendi sit ingressurus, datum est, exisse in solitudinem atque ibi sedentem diu secum multumque dubitasse, cum duas cerneret vias, unam Voluptatis, alteram Virtutis, utram ingredi melius esset. . . .

Cicero, *De off.*, I, 32, 118

Tenere autem viam mediam, veram, rectam, tanquam inter sinistram desperationis et dextram praesumptionis, difficillimum esset nobis, nisi Christus diceret, "Ego sum," inquit, "via, et veritas, et vita." . . . Securi ergo ambulemus in via: sed insidias timeamus iuxta viam. Inimicus insidiari non audet in via, quia Christus est via.

Augustine, *Sermo* 142, 1: P.L. 38
(Paris, 1845), p. 778.

CONTENTS

viii

ABBREVIATIONS

A.C.B.	Archivio comunale, Buggiano
A.C.F.	Archivio comunale, Fucecchio
A.C.M.C.	Archivio comunale, Massa Cozzile
A.C.Mons.	Archivio comunale, Monsummano
A.C.Mont.	Archivio comunale, Montecatini
A.S.B.	Archivio di Stato, Bologna
A.S.F.	Archivio di Stato, Firenze
A.S.L.	Archivio di Stato, Lucca
A.S.T.	Archivio di Stato, Todi
A.S.V.	Archivio segreto, Vaticano
Akad. Z.	Jugoslavenska Akademija Znanosti i Umjetnosti, Zagreb
B.A.V.	Biblioteca apostolica, Vaticano
B.C.P.	Biblioteca comunale, Pescia
B.C.R.	Biblioteca corsiniana, Roma
B.C.Rav.	Biblioteca classense, Ravenna
B.C.S.	Biblioteca colombina, Sevilla
B.C.Siena	Biblioteca comunale, Siena
B.E.M.	Biblioteca estense, Modena
B.G.L.	Biblioteca governativa, Lucca
B.L.F.	Biblioteca laurenziana, Firenze
B.L.O.	Bodleian Library, Oxford
B.M.L.	British Museum (now the British Library), London
B.M.F.	Biblioteca marucelliana, Firenze
B.Marc.V.	Biblioteca marciana, Venezia
B.N.F.	Biblioteca nazionale, Firenze
B.N.Mad.	Biblioteca nacional, Madrid
B.N.P.	Bibliothèque nationale, Paris
B.R.F.	Biblioteca riccardiana, Firenze
B.Triv.Milan	Biblioteca trivulziana, Milano

FONTI

Unless otherwise cited, all *fonti* will refer to holdings in the Archivio di Stato of Florence (A.S.F.)

AGN	Arti, Guidici e Notai
Balie	Balie
Cap.	Capitoli
Capitano	Atti del capitano del popolo
Delib. (ord. autor.)	Deliberazioni dei signori e collegi, fatte in forza ordinaria autorità
Delib. (spec. autor.)	Deliberazioni dei signori e collegi, fatte in forza speciale autorità
Dipl.	Diplomatico
Dipl., Arch. gener.	Diplomatico, Archivio generale
Dipl., Monte comune	Diplomatico, Monte comune
Dipl., Riform.	Diplomatico, Riformagioni
Giud., App. e Null.	Guidice degli Appelli
Libro delle età	Libro delle età dei cittadini fiorentini
Man.	Manoscritti
Miss.	Signoria, Iᵃ Cancelleria, Missive
M.C.	Monte comune
Notarile	Notarile antecosimiano
Provv. reg.	Provvisioni registri
SCS	Statuti comuni soggetti
Tratte	Tratte
A.S.L., Con. gen. Riform. pubbl.	A.S.L., Consiglio generale, Riformagioni pubblici
B.A.V., Capp.	B.A.V. Fondo capponiano
B.A.V., Ottob.	B.A.V., Fondo ottoboniano latino
B.A.V., Urb.	B.A.V., Fondo urbinate latino
B.A.V., Vat. lat.	B.A.V., Vaticani latini
B.L.F., Ashb.	B.L.F., Ashburnham
B.L.F., Ed.	B.L.F., Edile
B.L.F., Mar.	B.L.F., Marciano
B.L.O., Auct.	B.L.O., Auctarium
B.M.L., Add.	B.M.L., Additionals
B.N.F., Conv. sopp.	B.N.F., Conventi soppressi
B.N.F., Magl.	B.N.F., Fondo magliabechiano
B.N.F., Naz.	B.N.F., Fondo nazionale

B.N.F., *Palat.*   B.N.F., Fondo palatino
B.N.F., *Panc.*   B.N.F., Fondo panciatichiano
B.N.P., *Lat.*   B.N.P., Latins
B.N.P., *Lat. nouv. acq.* B.N.P., Latins, nouvelles acquisitions

GENERAL

Epist.   *Epistolario di Coluccio Salutati*, ed. Francesco
                        Novati, Fonti per la storia d'Italia, vols. 15–
                        18 (Rome, 1891–1911)
Petrarca, *Opera*   Petrarca, *Opera omnia que extant*, 4 vols. in 2
                        (Basel, 1554)
PL   *Patrologia Latina*
RIS   *Rerum Italicarum Scriptores*
ST   Aquinas, *Summa Theologica*
sci. mor. e lett.   classe scienze morali e lettere

PREFACE

With two brief references in his *De vita solitaria* to the dilemma of Hercules at the crossroads, Petrarch reintroduced into Western Europe a long-forgotten episode in the ancient cycle of myths surrounding the demigod.[1] Fascinated by the same anecdote, Coluccio Salutati devoted his most ambitious scholarly work, the *De laboribus Herculis*, to celebrating in elaborate allegorical analyses the hero's election of the path of virtue and the courageous pursuit of good which earned him divinity. Before he could complete the writing, however, Salutati's commitment to the task of orienting nascent Italian humanism toward Christian goals became so impelling that it forced him to redefine the nature of the choices at the crossroads and to reassess the capacity of the *viator* to choose the proper way. When that occurred, the value of humanistic studies themselves came into question. A major objective of the following study is to describe the evolution of this Christian conception of the human predicament in Salutati's thought and its effects on his humanism.

A second objective of the analysis, one intimately connected with this evolution, is to situate Salutati's work within the context of the Italian rhetorical tradition. This involves defining the relationship of Salutati's humanism to *ars dictaminis*, protohumanism, and Petrarchan humanism, as well as to the humanistic pursuits of his immediate followers. I will deal more generally with the problem of the origins of Italian humanism and medieval rhetorical movements in a subsequent study, but some of the lines of development already become visible here.

Originally my intention had been to include in the present volume an analysis of Salutati's contribution to institutional rhetoric and political theory. Given the amount of detail necessary in treating Salutati's missive production for the Florentine *Signoria*, however, it seemed wiser to publish a separate monograph on these subjects. That monograph, *Coluccio Salutati and His Public Letters*, Travaux d'Humanisme et Renaissance, 151 (Geneva, 1976), had as its central focus Salutati's role in the evolution of institutional rhetoric in thirteenth- and fourteenth-century Italy. Nevertheless, its results have been incorporated here together with

---

1. Theodore E. Mommsen, *Medieval and Renaissance Studies*, ed. Eugene F. Rice, Jr. (Ithaca, 1959), pp. 181–82. In his brilliant study, *Hercules am Scheidewege und andere antike Bildstoffe in der neueren Kunst*, Studien der Bibliothek Warburg, vol. 18 (Leipzig and Berlin, 1930), p. 155, Erwin Panofsky had identified Salutati as responsible for reviving the story.

a fuller description of Salutati's work as chancellor of the Florentine state.

More is known of the life of Coluccio Salutati than of that of any other European thinker before the sixteenth century, yet this study represents the first full-length biography. Late in the last century the Italian scholar Francesco Novati produced a slim volume devoted to the early life of Salutati,[2] but his treatment of the maturity of the humanist was limited to the copious notes accompanying his superb edition of Salutati's private correspondence, an edition which was to become a model for subsequent editors of the correspondence of Renaissance humanists.[3] So extensive in fact was the amount of information found in Novati's notes, arranged as they were chronologically with the letters, that the edition probably served to discourage formal biographical treatment. In 1910 Demetrio Marzi, in *La cancelleria della Repubblica fiorentina* (Rocca S. Casciano, 1910), pp. 113–52, further increased the total of biographical data by adding extensive archival material pertaining to Salutati's tenure as chancellor.

Since the time of Novati and Marzi scholars have edited other of Salutati's works and explored in great detail various aspects of his humanistic interests. Yet a synthesis of this material has yet to be made. While selective in its range, the little study of Salutati by Armando Petrucci, *Coluccio Salutati*, Bibliotheca biographica, vol. 7 (Rome, 1972), comes perhaps the closest of any recent study to presenting an integrated analysis of both Salutati's life and humanism. Although in my opinion Petrucci generally tends to underestimate Salutati's contribution to humanism, my own interpretation recognizes a significant debt to Petrucci's work at a number of points.

In the course of researching and writing this book I have received generous financial assistance from a variety of sources. Harvard University provided me with a Sheldon Graduate Fellowship in 1962–63, two Canaday Grants for the Humanities for summer study in 1965 and 1969, a Tosier Fellowship in the summer of 1966 and over the years since 1968 the use of the library of Villa I Tatti and the company of fellow Renaissance scholars. I was also the recipient of an Italian Government Fulbright in 1962–63 and a grant from the Old Dominion Trust for I Tatti in 1968–69. The Duke University Research Council awarded me Faculty Summer Fellowships in 1973 and 1977, and since 1971 has generously paid for the typing of various drafts of the manuscript and other

---

2. *La giovinezza di Coluccio Salutati (1331–1353)* (Torino, 1888).
3. *Epistolario di Coluccio Salutati*, ed. Francesco Novati, Fonti per la storia d'Italia, vols. 15–18 (Rome, 1891–1911).

expenses involved with research. The American Philosophical Society and the Folger Library furnished me financial support in 1973, and in 1975 I was the recipient of a summer grant from the National Endowment for the Humanities.

I am grateful for the aid and counsel I received in the various libraries and archives in Europe and America where I worked and especially to the personnel of the Archivio di Stato and the libraries of Florence, of Widener Library of Harvard, and of Perkins Library at Duke.

Sections of the manuscript at various stages of preparation have been read and criticized by Ricardo Fubini, Richard Greenbaum, John Headley, Andrew McCormick, and Charles Trinkaus, while Ann Carmichael went carefully over an intermediate draft and made many excellent suggestions. Dr. Gino Corti of Florence checked a number of the transcriptions.[4] I am grateful to Francis Newton for his advice on problems connected with Salutati's Latin. My wife, Mary Ann Frese Witt, read each of the versions, and partially edited a number of chapters. Frequently confronted with an almost illegible page, Dorothy Sapp, who typed the whole manuscript, skillfully deciphered my meaning and occasionally improved on it. Janet Whitehead and Betty Cowan helped prepare the final version for the press. Esther Sperry was willing to undertake the laborious task of checking the galleys. Daniela De Rosa prepared the index.

I would particularly like to single out three scholars. Berthold Louis Ullman did not live to see my book, but his influence on it is unmistakable. In the last stages of work I was also able to check my notes on Salutati's library with his, and this saved me from more than one error. Edward P. Mahoney, editor of this series of monographs, has not only afforded me over the years an example of the highest standards of scholarship but, painstakingly going twice over the manuscript, he commented on style, significantly enriched the bibliography, and improved the text in matters of substance, particularly in the philosophical sections. Hans Baron's *The Crisis of the Early Italian Renaissance* originally inspired me to study Salutati and since that time, through his personal letters and conversation, he has shared with me his profound erudition and remarkable intuitive understanding of Italian humanism.

I began the study of Coluccio Salutati as a Harvard dissertation, under the direction of Myron P. Gilmore, on Salutati's early life and edu-

---

4. Throughout the manuscript when citing unpublished source material I have retained the original spelling.

cation. It was in Prof. Gilmore's company in the Archivio di Stato di Lucca that I made my first discoveries regarding Salutati's earlier life. Not only did I receive from him the training essential for a Renaissance historian but, more than this, an appreciation of the moral and aesthetic disposition that gives eloquence to words, balance to judgment, cogency to truth, and dignity to life. Although already stricken by the disease that was to prove fatal within months, he read the manuscript closely and gave me the benefit of his penetrating criticism. As I intended to dedicate this book to him in his year of retirement from Harvard, so now I dedicate it to his memory.

Hillsborough, N.C.
Fall, 1980

PART I. THE FORMATIVE YEARS

CHAPTER 1. STIGNANO AND BOLOGNA

The valley known as the Valdinievole runs along the southern foothills of the Pescatine Alps in the region between the towns of Lucca and Pistoia, and in the first decades of the fourteenth century the little communes that overlook this valley's low-lying, swampy plain became pawns in the foreign policy of their two great neighbors, Guelf Florence and Ghibelline Lucca. The Guelf-Ghibelline struggle, conceived in broadest terms as a papal-imperial conflict, reflected at the local level a complicated rivalry of interests and traditions and had the effect of poisoning the internal political life of these communes. In 1328 the hastily assembled dominion of the imperial duke of Lucca, Castruccio Castracani, included the Valdinievole and Pistoia, but the duke's sudden death that year provided an opportunity for the resurgence of Guelf power under Florentine aegis in this area. Florence quickly asserted its hegemony over Pistoian territory, and later, on June 21, 1329, a military league was established between the Republic and the communes of the Valdinievole.

The Guelf victory, however, was not complete. Less than a month after the formation of the league local Ghibellines, aided by Lucchese soldiers, took over the hilltop town of Montecatini, the strongest fortress in the valley. Timely action by the Florentine army prevented the reinforcement of the defenders by Ghibellines who were secretly on their way from neighboring Montevettolini. For almost a year the defenders held out. The desperate attempts of the new lord of Lucca, Gherardino degli Spinoli, to break through the immense network of ditches and walls thrown up by the besieging Florentines were, however, unavailing, and finally on July 19, 1330, the starving garrison surrendered.

But if the Guelf population of the Valdinievole expected the recapture of Montecatini to put them behind the battlelines by permitting an advance of Florentine troops into the *contado* of Lucca, they were disappointed. Despite the presence of a Florentine garrison, on the night of September 19 the Ghibellines of Buggiano, a commune of the Valdinievole directly bordering on Lucchese territory, betrayed the communal castle to Spinoli's forces. Three of the four rural settlements making up the rural commune, Buggiano, Stignano, and Colle, appear to have fallen immediately with the castle. Only Borgo-a-Buggiano, that part of the commune at the foot of Buggiano's hill, remained in Florentine hands. But after five months of suffering the assaults of their enemy from the heights, the remnants of the Florentine garrison were forced to abandon this position as well. For the next eight years, until the peace treaty between Florence and Venice with Mastino della Scala in 1339, the commune of Buggiano remained in Ghibelline hands.[1]

On February 16, 1331, in the very month when the Florentine soldiers withdrew completely from the area, Coluccio Salutati was born in Stignano on the hillside overlooking their positions. We know little of the origins of the Salutati family. In the early fourteenth century at least two branches of the family were living in Pescia, but their degree of relationship with those of Stignano is unclear. There are also traces of a fourth branch resident in Buggiano in the same period.[2] Of Coluccio's maternal grandfather we know only that his first name was Lino, while the one document so far discovered relating to the paternal grandfather, Coluccio, merely mentions him in 1321 as a resident of Stignano holding property in Buggiano.[3]

The political tradition of the Salutati was Guelf, and like other members of their faction in the commune they had lived through years of repression. Their memory of the persecution of the local Guelfs by Castruccio in 1323 would have been particularly vivid. Discovering a plan to deliver Buggiano to the Florentines, the lord of Lucca promptly seized the plotters and hung twelve of them.[4] Although we have no

---

1. A summary of the political events in the Valdinievole between 1329 and 1339 is found in Giuseppe Calamari, *I comuni di Valdinievole dalla pace con Firenze alla loro definitiva sottomissione, 1329–1339* (Pistoia, 1927), pp. 12–13. See also, *Storie Pistoresi*, ed. Silvio A. Barbi, R.I.S., vol. 11, pt. 5 (Città di Castello, 1914–27), pp. 139–44.

2. *Epist.*, IV, 381–427, discusses the genealogy of the Salutati at length. A study of the notarial register of ser Ludovico di Barone Barelli of Pescia (*Notarile*, B 549, 1350–57), who seems to have been the notary of the Riccomi and Lupori Salutati, would greatly add to the genealogical tables of these branches. For example, whereas Novati shows Puccino Riccomi as having had only one son, Simone (*Epist.*, IV, 423, n. 3), he had in fact four living in 1352 (*Notarile*, fol. 49ᵛ).

3. Augusto Mancini, *Sulle traccie del Salutati* (Lucca, 1920), p. 14, suggests that the great grandfather's name might have been Andrea. The *Estimo del Castello di Stignano* on which this information is based can no longer be located in the state archives at Lucca. For the names *Coluccio* and *Lino* see n. 6 below. The reference to Coluccio's paternal grandfather is found *Dipl., Borgo a Buggiano*, 10 Sept. 1321, in a list of property of the late Simo di Stignano, a local doctor of medicine: "Item unam petiam terre in dicto campo Buggiani in loco dicto Savognane, que fuit Curradi Folchepti et cohabet ab una parte terre Coluccii Salutati et ab alia terre heredum Cepti Martini."

4. *Cronica di Giovanni Villani*, ed. Francesco Dragomanni, 4 vols. (Florence, 1844–45), II, 273.

other details, concomitant with the hangings there was doubtless other punitive action taken against the Guelf community as a whole. Nevertheless, the Salutati survived as a family, and with the assumption of power by the Guelfs in 1328, Piero Salutati, Coluccio's father, emerged as a local leader of the party. Because of his prominence, therefore, the successful rising of the Ghibellines on September 19 was especially threatening to Piero Salutati. Taking refuge in Borgo-a-Buggiano protected by Florentine troops, he was forced to abandon his pregnant wife, Puccina, in Stignano. Very probably he followed the Florentine army in their withdrawal in February, ignorant of the fate of his wife and the expected baby.[5]

In Piero's absence Puccina and her mother-in-law quarreled over the name to be given the infant, probably the first born. Puccina wished to call him Lino after her father, while his grandmother insisted that he be called Coluccio after her own husband. The result was a compromise and when the two presented the baby to be baptised in S. Maria di Pescia, the baptismal church of Stignano, he was given the name Lino Coluccio.[6] According to the custom of the area, the wives and young children of political exiles were allowed to remain unmolested. Piero's wife, however, resolved to join her husband as soon as she was strong enough to travel and, two months after Coluccio's birth, accompanied by her mother-in-law, she set out to meet her husband in Florentine territory.[7]

The whereabouts of the family for the next few years is uncertain, but, because Piero appears to have had military talents, he probably did not remain unemployed for long. In some manner he came to the attention of Taddeo dei Pepoli, who, as *signore* of Bologna after August 1337, was interested in building a retinue of faithful supporters. If we are to

5. "Pater autem, cui Piero nomen erat, qui tunc crudelitate nequiciaque gebelline factionis cum suis omnibus exulabat . . . " (*Epist.*, IV, 149). Berthold L. Ullman, *The Humanism of Coluccio Salutati*, Medioevo e umanesimo, vol. 4 (Padua, 1963), p. 3, discovered the name of Salutati's mother in an unpublished family tree made by Sincero da Lamole in 1665.

6. "Contentione quidem matris et avie de imponendo michi nomine pertinaciter oborta, quarum illa patris sui nomen, quod Linus fuerat, michi volebat imponi, hec autem coniugis sui, avi mei paterni, vocamen, quod Colucius fuerat, me referre cupiebat; tandem in concordiam devenerunt quod sub Lini Coluciique nominibus baptizarer" (*Epist.*, IV, 149). Throughout most of his life, Salutati preferred the name *Coluccio di Piero Salutati*. The name of the baptismal church for Stignano is found in Francesco Novati, *La giovinezza di Coluccio Salutati* (Turin, 1888), p. 12, n. 1.

7. Salutati writes: "Postquam ad ipsum ab oppido Stignani, natalis mei loco, nondum exacto etatis mee bimestri, delatus in exilium fui" (*Epist.*, IV, 149). The grandmother died later in Bologna (ibid., IV, 11).

believe Coluccio's friend, Domenico Bandini, "learning that he [Piero] was well known for his military ability and wise in council," Taddeo brought him to Bologna with the promise of "a large salary."[8] The archives of Bologna containing documents relative to the Pepoli household and the commune for the years 1331–51 never mention Piero, yet the apparent intimacy of the Salutati family with the Pepoli after Piero's death suggests that he occupied a post of some trust in the retinue of the powerful Bolognese. Once settled in Bologna, the Salutati returned to the Valdinievole only for visits. After 1339, when that area became part of the Florentine Republic, the property of the Guelf exiles was restored and Piero Salutati maintained his interests there through his brother, Paccino.[9] Presumably, during these years the family more than once took the three- or four-day journey south from Bologna to spend the hottest weeks of the summer on the shaded hillsides. On these occasions the young Coluccio had the chance to play with his cousins and to trap and fish in the Swamp of Fucecchio, which then came almost up to the walls of Borgo-a-Buggiano. Long before he celebrated the Stagnipesce, the little stream that flows through the valley between Stignano and Buggiano, he had learned its habits by following the thin ribbon of water up through the olive groves and vineyards to the place in the highlands behind Massa where it begins.

Had Salutati spent the whole of his boyhood years in the little Tuscan border town, he might not have received even a rudimentary education in Latin.[10] In Bologna, on the other hand, he found himself in one of the greatest educational centers of Europe, one which for a number of decades had been caught up in an intellectual current promising to change

8. Novati incorrectly writes that Salutati spent twenty instead of fifteen years in Bologna (*La giovinezza*, p. 24, n. 1). In a letter to Bernardo da Moglio, son of his former teacher in Bologna, Salutati writes that his love of Bologna stems from "trilustri nutritione incolatuque domestico" (*Epist.*, IV, 10–11). In the chapter on Salutati edited by Novati, *Epist.*, IV, 502, from Domenico Bandini's *Fons memorabilium universi*, pt. 5, lib. 1, "de viris claris virtute aut vitio," Bandini specifically says that the father of Salutati was called to Bologna by Taddeo dei Pepoli: "ubi orta dudum partialitatis discordia, ut frequenter assolet inter Tuscos, Pierus, veluti caput partis guelfe, pellitur, bonis eius famelicis hostibus ad predam datis. Hunc ergo Tadeus de Pepolis, tunc Bononiensis dominus, largo stipendio ad se traxit, edoctus eum fore armis clarum nec minus consilio prepollentem." Pepoli became lord of Bologna on August 28, 1337. Because the Salutati family left Bologna at the end of 1350 or early in 1351, this makes approximately fifteen years of residence in the city.

9. On February 20, 1346, in Borgo-a-Buggiano ser Giovanni di ser Ugolino di Bonaccio of Buggiano recorded the repayment of a debt owed to Piero Coluccio of Stignano (*Notarile*, C 468, fol. 11). In Piero's absence his brother, Paccino "quondam Coluccii de Stignano asserens se . . . procurator Pieri, germani sui, et quondam dicti Coluccii . . ." collected the money.

10. See below, chap. 2, n. 13.

the character of Italian intellectual life. Beginning in Padua with Lovato dei Lovati in the 1280s, a renewed interest in classical studies, or, more particularly, a new approach to ancient writings, manifested itself and almost immediately thereafter appeared in other Northern Italian cities.[11]

Neither Lovato nor his far more illustrious intellectual heir, Albertino Mussato, elegant defender of poetry and author of the first Renaissance drama, can be said to have been the leaders of the widely scattered movement.[12] In effect what seems to have occurred in the decades around the turn of the fourteenth century is that, whether individually or severally, certain scholars simply abandoned an aesthetic standard of modernity that had dominated European rhetoric since at least the beginning of the thirteenth century. Demonstrating an intense concern for understanding ancient Latin writings in their integrity, they strove to imitate the ancients both in the form and content of their own work. Admittedly, outstanding literary men and teachers of rhetoric like Thomas of Capua, Boncompagno, and Bene di Firenze, indicated in their work an appreciation, if limited, of the stylistic difference between ancient and contemporary prose and poetry, but, motivated by the pur-

11. For Lovato dei Lovati, see Guido Billanovich, "Il preumanesimo padovano," in *Storia della cultura veneta*, vol. 1 (Vicenza, 1976), pp. 19–110, with its rich bibliography. On the Paduan circle and its relationship with other contemporary groups with classical interests, consult Rino Avesani, "Il preumanesimo veronese," Luciano Gargan, "Il preumanesimo a Vicenza, Treviso e Venezia," and Girolamo Arnaldi-Lidia Capo, "I cronisti di Venezia e della Marca Trevigiana," in the same volume, pp. 111, 142–46, 276–85 respectively, but see "Indici" of this rich volume for other references. See as well Remigio Sabbadini, *Le scoperte dei codici latini e greci*, ed. anast, with corr. and add. by E. Garin, 2 vols. (Florence, 1967), I, 1–22 and II, passim; L. Lazzarini, *Paolo de Bernardo e i primordi dell'umanesimo in Venezia* (Geneva, 1930), pp. 4–14; E. Franceschini, *Studi e note di filologia latina medioevale*, Pubblicazioni dell'Università cattolica del Sacro Cuore, 4th ser., vol. 30 (Milan, 1938), pp. 12–18; Roberto Weiss, *The Dawn of Humanism* (London, 1947); Giorgio Petrocchi, "Cultura e poesia del Trecento," in *Il Trecento*, Storia della letteratura italiana, vol. 2 (Milan, 1965), pp. 561–72. John Hyde, *Padua in the Age of Dante* (Manchester-New York, 1966), provides an excellent description of the society in which the Paduan scholars lived and wrote.

12. The bibliography on Mussato is enormous. For editions and secondary treatments see Guido Billanovich, "Il preumanesimo padovano." On the new classical interests in Tuscany see Roberto Weiss, "Geri d'Arezzo," in *Il primo secolo dell'umanesimo*, Storia e letteratura, vol. 27 (Rome, 1949), pp. 53–56. Dante's Latin eclogues testify to his participation in this early pre-Petrarchan humanist movement. Of the many editions of his exchange of poems with Giovanni Virgilio the best is *La corrispondenza poetica di Dante e Giovanni del Virgilio e l'ecloga di Giovanni al Mussato*, ed. G. Albini and G. Pighi, Studi pub. dall'Istituto di Filologia classica, vol. 18 (Bologna, 1965). On Dante's view of Roman history and culture, see Charles T. Davis, *Dante's Idea of Rome* (Oxford, 1957); Nicolai Rubinstein, "Marsilius of Padua and the Italian Political Thought of His Time," *Europe in the Middle Ages*, ed. J. Hale, R. Highfield, and B. Smalley (Evanston, 1965), pp. 50–59, and 62; and Davis, "Ptolemy of Lucca and the Roman Republic," *Proceedings of the American Philosophical Society*, 118 (1975), 30–50.

suit of originality and a concern for keeping rhetoric abreast of the times, they preferred artistic conceptions and models of their own creation.[13] The classicizing movement beginning at the end of the century, consequently, did not derive from a "discovery" of ancient prose and poetry but rather from a new standard of taste and perhaps an unstated confidence in the appropriateness of ancient aesthetic principles for contemporaries.

Of course, the more intensive focus on ancient models produced deeper comprehension of these principles along with increased facility in applying them in contemporary writing. In the elementary distinction between the ancient poets and the moderns appearing in his *Compendium moralium notabilium*, Geremia da Montagnone illustrates the significance of the aesthetic shift by developing an incipient sense of historical perspective.[14] Greater appreciation of stylistic differences together with closer examination of context also led to scholarly achievements like the rejection of the attribution of the *De quattuor virtutibus* to Seneca and the distinction between the two Plinys.[15]

But the achievements of the movement by the 1330s, if impressive, were nonetheless restricted by continuing allegiances to the tradition of instructing grammar and rhetoric established in the previous century.

13. The sizeable literature on the issue of the *moderni* and *antiqui* does not address itself directly to this problem. See chap. 9, n. 35, below. Thomas of Capua very clearly differentiated between the salutatory form used by the ancients in their letters and those utilized by modern writers: Emmy Heller, *Die'Ars dictandi'des Thomas von Capua*, Sitzungsberichte der Heidelberger Akademie der Wissenschaften, Phil. Kl., 1928–29, vol. 4 (Heidelberg, 1929), p. 19. Boncompagno in his *Tractatus virtutum* distinguished between Latin styles of authors writing before Christ and those writing after: Karl Sutter, *Aus Leben und Schriften des Magisters Boncompagno* (Freiburg, 1894), p. 63; while Bene di Firenze was capable of lucidly distinguishing the *stilus Tullianus* based on quantity from one based on accentuated rhythm: Charles Baldwin, *Medieval Rhetoric and Poetic* (New York, 1928), pp. 216–17. At the time of writing, the edition of the first five books of Bene's *Candelabrum* by G. Vecchi, "Temi e momenti d'arte dettatoria nel *Candelabrum* di Bene da Firenze," *Atti e memorie della deputazione di storia patria per le provincie di Romagna*, n.s., 10 (1958–9), 113–68, was not available to me. Cf. Helene Wieruszowski, "Rhetoric and the Classics in Italian Education of the Thirteenth Century," *Politics and Culture in Medieval Spain and Italy*, Storia e letteratura, vol. 121 (Rome, 1971), pp. 598 and 600. On Padua and its scholars in the arts generally in this period, see Nancy G. Siraisi, *Arts and Sciences at Padua: The Studium at Padua before 1350* (Toronto, 1973), pp. 33–65; and R.G.G. Mercer, *The Teaching of Gasparino Barzizza with Special Reference to his Place in Paduan Humanism*, MHRA Texts & Diss., vol. 10 (London, 1979), pp. 1–15.

14. Roberto Weiss, "Geremia da Montagnone," *Il primo secolo*, pp. 22–47, and Berthold L. Ullman, "Hieremias de Montagnone," *Studies in the Italian Renaissance*, Storia e letteratura, 2nd. ed., vol. 51 (Rome, 1973), pp. 79–81.

15. Roberto Weiss, "Geremia da Montagnone," p. 28, and Weiss, *The Dawn*, pp. 13–14. For the critical powers of Benzo d'Alessandria in writing his *Chronicon*, see Joseph R. Berrigan, "Benzo d'Alessandria and the Cities of Northern Italy," *Studies in Medieval and Renaissance History*, 4 (1967), 135–36. Also consult Avesani, "Il preumanesimo veronese," pp. 116–21.

Above the elementary level, courses in grammar provided the student with training in literature, primarily through reading the poets, and in composition, largely in poetry. While ancient prose works were studied, the formal structure of education centered on the *auctores*, usually understood as the ancient poets, particularly Virgil, Statius, Ovid, and Lucan. Medieval manuals of *ars poetria* and poetic works like the *Anti-Claudianus* of Alain de Lille guided students in their own creative endeavors.[16]

Rhetoric was the domain for prose but, especially in Italy, the courses did not afford much opportunity for reading ancient prose literature. Rather, courses in rhetoric were devoted largely to the practical goal of instructing students in the rules of *ars dictaminis*. If, as increasingly happened in the last half of the thirteenth century, such instruction was accompanied by commentaries on Cicero's *De inventione* and the pseudo-Ciceronian *Ad Herennium*, the lessons aimed at perfecting the student's talents in composing in a nonclassical way following models drawn from prose writings of past masters in *dictamen*, eminent *dictatores* like Guido Faba and Pietro delle Vigne.[17]

16. The classic division of Quintilian, which left prose to the rhetor and poetry to the grammarian, largely broke down throughout Europe in the twelfth century, the grammarian becoming responsible for teaching both forms: Philippe Delhaye, "L'enseignement de la philosophie morale au XIIe siècle, *Mediaeval Studies*, 11 (1949), 90–91. On the preponderance of instruction of ancient poetry in schools, see J. de Ghellinck, *L'essor de la littérature latine au xiie siècle*, 2 vols. (Brussels-Paris, 1946), II, 86–87. For the term *auctores* as essentially referring to the poets, Giuseppe Billanovich, "Auctorista, humanista, orator," *Rivista di cultura classica e medievale*, 7 (1965), 147–48. Paul O. Kristeller, "Humanism and Scholasticism in the Italian Renaissance," *Studies in Renaissance Thought and Letters*, Storia e letteratura, vol. 54 (1956), pp. 568–69, points to the increasing interest in the study of ancient poetry and in poetic composition in thirteenth-century Italy, especially after the mid-part of the century. Helene Wieruszowski, "Rhetoric and the Classics," pp. 604–5, while agreeing with Kristeller on the increasing diffusion of interest in ancient poetry, considers it to have had greater prominence in education in the first half of the century than Kristeller grants. Both, however, see French influence at work in arousing Italian interest in the classics. Berthold L. Ullman, "Some Aspects of the Origin of Italian Humanism," *Studies*, pp. 27–40, emphasizes French intellectual influence on Italian humanism right into the fourteenth century. Kristeller, "Humanism and Scholasticism," pp. 568 ff., views Italian humanism as a fusion of "novel interest in classical studies imported from France toward the end of the thirteenth century and the much earlier traditions of medieval Italian rhetoric" (p. 571). Cf. Jerrold Siegel, *Rhetoric and Philosophy* (Princeton, 1968), pp. 200 ff., for an emphasis on the position of the *dictatores* in the origins of humanism. My analysis in the text above is largely descriptive rather than causal. I intend to treat the issue of the origin of humanism in detail in a later work.

17. On this trend in the late thirteenth and early fourteenth centuries, see J. R. Banker, "The *Ars Dictaminis* and Rhetorical Textbooks at the Bolognese University in the Fourteenth Century," *Medievalia et humanistica*, n.s., 5 (1974), 153–68; and Sandra Karaus Wertis, "Commentary of Bartolinus de Benincasa," *Viator*, 10 (1979), 283–86, with its rich bibliography. John O. Ward, "From Antiquity to the Renaissance: Glosses and Commentaries on Cicero's *Rhetorica*," in *Medieval Eloquence: Studies in the Theory and Practice of Medieval*

The orientation of the new scholarship beginning with Lovato's generation reflected these pedagogical traditions in its obvious predilection for poetry. Because the ancient poets had been regularly taught as literature in the schools, they were better known as a basis for imitation to those members of the movement with creative abilities. The common belief, so brilliantly articulated by Mussato, that poetry was akin to theology because of its concealment of religious truth, moreover, bestowed an aura of the sacred on poetry denied to prose.[18] Not coincidentally a favorite of the new rhetorical movement was Seneca's poetical drama.[19]

One prose genre significantly affected by the concern for imitating the ancients was history. Historical narrations of contemporary events by Albertino Mussato and Ferreto dei Ferreti are marked by the authors' acquaintance with Sallust and Livy.[20] But as long as *ars dictaminis* dominated prose composition, general reform in the area of prose was difficult to achieve. Surviving correspondence of these early classically oriented writers is in poetry because they had no alternative prose style to substitute for the traditional *dictamen*.[21]

Partially institutional necessities barred the way to reform here. The

---

Rhetoric, ed. James J. Murphy (Berkeley-Los Angeles-London, 1979), p. 38, identifies two periods, 1080 to 1225 and 1290 to the age of printing, as the "principal foci of medieval rhetorical interest." Whereas commentaries on the *De inventione* and the *Ad Herennium* in the earlier period were largely produced in Northern Europe, those after 1290 were primarily Italian. See now Paul O. Kristeller's concise summary of the evolution of *dictamen* in his *Renaissance Thought and its Sources*, ed. Michael Mooney (New York, 1979), pp. 228–42.

18. On Mussato's defense of poetry, see my "Coluccio Salutati and the Conception of the *Poeta Theologus* in the Fourteenth Century," *Renaissance Quarterly*, 30 (1977), 540, n. 8.

19. For the reading of Seneca in the fourteenth century, see E. Franceschini, *Studi e note*, pp. 8–105; Roberto Weiss, "Notes on the Popularity of the Writings of Nicholas Trevet O. P. in Italy," *Dominican Studies*, 1 (1948), 262, n. 8; and Billanovich, "Il preumanesimo padovano," pp. 56–66.

20. Mussato's style in his historical writings is described by Antonio Zardo, *Albertinus Mussato: Studio storico e letterario* (Padua, 1884), pp. 256 ff. His treatment involves a comparison between the style of Mussato and that of Ferreto dei Ferreti. Compare Manlio Dazzi, "Il Mussato storico," *Archivio veneto*, 5th ser., 6 (1929), 386–88. For a less favorable judgment of Mussato's prose style see Billanovich, "Il preumanesimo padovano," pp. 83–84.

21. The one exception known to me is Geri d'Arezzo, who tried to break with *ars dictaminis* and whose letter collection was popular throughout the fourteenth century. See below, n. 23. If Dante is considered one of the classicizing reformers, then, of course, we have in his letters other examples of the epistolary style of the movement: *Epistole* in *Le opere di Dante. Testo critico della Società dantesca italiana* (Florence, 1921), pp. 413–51. However, the fact that he wrote following the rules of *dictamen* proves the basic point that *dictamen* dominated letter writing almost absolutely in the early fourteenth century. Of the rich literature on Dante's Latin, see particularly Gudrun Lindholm, *Studien zum Mittellateinischen Prosarhythmus: Seine Entwicklung und sein Abklingen in der Briefliteratur Italiens*, Studia Latina Stockholmiensia, vol. 10 (Stockholm, 1963); and Ettore Paratore, "Il latino di Dante," *Cultura e scuola*, 4, nos. 13–14 (1965), 94–124, with its rich bibliography.

If the correspondence of others in this reforming group is subsequently discovered, presumably this too will be marked by the medieval method.

formulae, the *cursus,* and the divisions of the letter, had over the centuries become universally adopted as required modalities for communication between states and individuals alike. So rigid were the rules, that deletion of an element could easily be ascribed to intentional discourtesy or ignorance.

To an extent, however, the enormous success of *dictamen* derived from its flexibility. At the lowest level it afforded the expert a series of formulae for rapidly expediting official business. At the highest level, the most expressive form, the *stilus rhetoricus,* allowed the writer to present his thoughts dramatically with force and passion like the orator haranguing the senate. Indeed *stilus rhetoricus* with its oratorical character provided enough antique echoes that it proved largely invulnerable to transformation by classical reformers.[22]

The most important area in prose style where basic reform could be made without threatening over much the elaborate code of diplomacy and courtesy was in private communication between friends. Geri of Arezzo was perhaps the first to initiate reforms in the private letter in the opening decades of the fourteenth century, but in his own generation they seem to have had no effect.[23] By the middle of the century, however, when his models were exercising an influence at the local level in Tuscany, his work was overshadowed by one far greater than he. Partially inspired by his discovery of Cicero's correspondence in 1345, Petrarch established reforms in prose style which in a few decades revolutionized prose writing throughout Italy and served to alter the relative literary standing of prose vis-à-vis poetry. While *ars dictaminis* continued to dominate official correspondence down to the end of the fifteenth century, a new age in the composition of private letters began with Petrarch.

The new classicizing movement in the generation of Lovati and Mussato remained true to its medieval Italian roots, moreover, in its almost wholly secular tendency. Italian rhetorical schools in the thirteenth century were consciously designed to respond to the practical needs of students interested in becoming doctors, lawyers, or notaries with the re-

22. For bibliography on the *stilus rhetoricus,* see my *Coluccio Salutati and His Public Letters* (Geneva, 1976), pp. 35–38.

23. Weiss, "Geri d'Arezzo," pp. 109–33. Of the six prose letters published by Weiss, five are strikingly novel in their relative freedom from the rules of *dictamen.* Their violations of the rules of the *cursus* can only be intentional. Geri (c. 1270–late 1320s) was a product of the schools of Arezzo, the leading intellectual center in Tuscany in the last half of the thirteenth century: ibid., p. 54, and Helene Wieruszowski, "Arezzo as a Center of Learning and Letters in the Thirteenth Century," *Politics and Culture,* pp. 387–474. For possible influence on Salutati, see below, chap. 3.

sult that the traditional concern of rhetoric for moral questions was neglected.[24] More significant is the fact that when the rhetoricians of this century dealt with ethical problems, they did so in a context only superficially Christian.[25] Although most were doubtless sincere Christians, none of these writers gave a distinctly Christian orientation to ethics.

Possibly this was intentional, a product of the strict division between different courses of study in the universities. The *ars dictaminis*, secular rhetoric—official ecclesiastical documents included—was clearly distinguished from *ars predicandi* or religious eloquence. But the consistency with which the professional rhetoricians of this century observed this restriction both in their private as well as in their institutional writings suggests that unconscious elements were also involved. While they

24. Helene Wieruszowski, "Ars Dictaminis in the Time of Dante," *Politics and Culture*, p. 373; see also *The Earthly Republic. Italian Humanists on Government and Society*, ed. B. Kohl and R. Witt (Philadelphia, 1978), p. 5.

25. The remarks of Wieruszowski, *Politics and Culture*, pp. 607–10, on the secular orientation of the rhetoricians at the court of Frederick II can be extended to apply to those in the Bolognese tradition as well. In the late twelfth century the Bolognese-trained Henry of Settimello composed his self-consciously pagan *Elegia* (ed. G. Cremaschi [Bergamo, 1949]), which enjoyed an enormous success in the thirteenth and fourteenth centuries. As Cremaschi, in "Enrico da Settimello e la sua *Elegia*," *Atti dell'Istituto veneto di scienze, lettere ed arti*, cl. sci. mor. e lett., 108 (1949–50), 193, describes Henry's conception of death in the fourth part of the poem, it is not the door to Christian Paradise but "la fine dei mali e la liberazione dell'anima imprigionata, secondo la concezione socratico-platonica nel carcere del corpo." Where personal expression of moral views occurs in the work of other Bolognese *dictatores* like Boncompagno and Guido Faba, they lack a Christian orientation. Two of Boncompagno's three specifically moral tracts can be said to manifest his Christian faith, but the integration of his Christianity with his ideas does not go far. His *Amicitia*, ed. Sarina Nathans, in *Miscellanea di letteratura del medio evo*, vol. 3 (Rome, 1909), pp. 46–88, presents friendship as divided into two genera, heavenly and earthly, God being the origin of the first and Satan of the second (p. 79). The essay, moreover, concludes with an appeal to readers to put their faith in the "heavenly friend," who shines his light on good and evil" quia fragilitati subiacet omnis amicitia mundanorum" (pp. 88). Yet there is nothing specifically Christian about his description of either of the two varieties of friendship. In his treatise on old age, *De malo senectutis et senii*, published by Francesco Novati in *Reale Accad. dei Lincei, Rendiconti*, cl. sci. mor., ser. 5, 1 (1892), 50–59, Christian sentiment is only found in the concluding passage when he writes: "Deprecemur denique omnipotentem Deum ut animas nostras prius evocet de vite presentis exilio et de hoc ergastulo carceris, antequam in senium tam horribile ac miserabile dilabamur et concedat nobis de sue gratie munere, ut armis vere penitentie premuniti, pervenire ad infinibilia paradisi gaudia mereamur" (p. 59). So ambiguous is Boncompagno's approach to the Bible and Christian teachings in general that Georg Misch, *Geschichte der Autobiographie*, vol. 3, pt. 2 (Frankfort a. M., 1962), p. 1123, feels compelled to cite the isolated examples which prove "dass er fest im Kirchenglauben stand."

Hans M. Schaller, "Die Kanzlei Kaiser Friedrichs II. Ihr Personal und ihr Sprachstil," *Archiv für Diplomatik-Schriftgeschichte, Siegel- und Wappenkunde*, 4 (1958), 288, notes, however, the decidedly paganizing tendencies exhibited by members of the southern *stilus rhetoricus* tradition in the second half of the thirteenth century. Brunetto Latini's *Li livres dou Tresor*, ed. F. J. Carmody (Berkeley-Los Angeles, 1948), written in the same period, while not "pagan," nonetheless, is not specifically Christian either. See below, chap. 3, n. 67.

sought originality in their work, the *dictatores* did not ignore ancient literature, looking to it both for some stylistic guidance and for its *sententiae*.[26] Although largely superficial, their reading of ancient pagan poetry and prose was sufficient to suggest problems which they as rhetoricians and descendents of the ancients could appropriately address. When confronting favorite moral issues such as the power of fortune, the nature of friendship, old age or death, they easily fell into a naive Stoic posture in what they felt to be imitation of their ancient sources. Consequently, the program of education by its very nature insulated both teacher and student from the need to confront the issue of the relationship between pagan eloquence and Christian culture. On the whole the secular quality of thirteenth-century Italian rhetoric derives from this failure to examine critically its heritage from ancient times and to effect some kind of integration between it and Christian culture.

Despite the increasing philological interests of the late thirteenth- and early fourteenth-century group of Northern Italian scholars, their production indicates a similar absence of Christian orientation. Where an author like Giovanni del Virgilio introduces a reference to Christ amidst a long series of mythological references, one senses immediately its inappropriateness and judges it a misguided striving for literary effect.[27] Mussato's various efforts to justify the study of ancient poetry for Christians so assimilates Scripture to poetry that the inspiration and truth content of the two appear almost identical.[28] Without questioning the depth of their personal faith, we can affirm that these writers, like their immediate predecessors, the *dictatores*, were unconscious of a serious problem involved in reconciling Christian beliefs with their classical interests and their effort to attain Latin eloquence. This awareness was to play a major role in Petrarchan humanism.

Salutati would encounter these new currents of culture as a young

26. Wieruszowski, pp. 596–605.

27. Cesare Foligno, "Epistole inedite di Lovato de'Lovati e d'altri a lui," *Studi medievali*, 2 (1906/7), 45 and 53.

28. See summaries of Mussato's position in Alfredo Galletti, "La 'ragione poetica' di Albertino Mussato ed i poeti-theologi," in *Scritti varii di erudizione e di critica in onore di Rudolfo Renier* (Turin, 1912), pp. 331–58; Ernst R. Curtius, *European Literature and the Latin Middle Ages*, trans. Willard R. Trask (New York, 1963), pp. 214–21; and my "Coluccio Salutati and the Conception of the *Poeta Theologus*," pp. 540–41. Michele Minoia, *Della vita e delle opere di Albertino Mussato* (Rome, 1884), p. 192, writes of Mussato's effort at composing religious poetry: "È sempre il letterato, il dotto latinista che tenta di vestire dell'antica e classica veste il pensiero nuovo del Christianesimo. . . . Lo scopo letterario in queste poesie religiose pare che vi predomini, e lo studio e l'artifizio, più che all' empireo, spingon la mente alla bella aiuola di questo mondo." Though in nineteenth-century fashion, Minoia considers Mussato's treatment of religion as characteristic of future humanism, it is more accurate to see him as a part of the thirteenth-century rhetorical tradition.

teenager, but for the moment, as an elementary school pupil in one of the schools maintained by the commune in each of the quarters of the city, his program of education was not much different from what it would have been a hundred or two hundred years earlier.[29] *Donatus* and the *Psalter*, as the first textbooks, provided both the elements of Latin grammar and an introduction to the Christian religion. Parts of the *Psalter* had to be recited from memory. Giovanni di Conversino, who attended elementary school in Bologna a decade after Salutati, illustrated the cruelty of the masters by referring to the brutal punishment meted out to one of his classmates, an eight-year-old boy from the country who failed to retain a certain verse from the *Psalter*. Brutally beaten, stripped naked, feet bound together, and hung for hours down a well, the boy almost perished.

At a more advanced level, the "second order"—the phrase is Conversino's—the pupils read Aesop, "Eva columba fuit" (The *Ditochaeon* of Prudentius), "Tres leo naturas" (the *Physiologus*), the *Distichs* of Cato, Boethius, Prosper's *Epigrams*, which gave the basic principles of St. Augustine in verse, and perhaps the versification of the Scriptures called the "Aethiopam terras." Giovanni Dominici seems to have followed an almost identical program in his early schooling in Venice a decade after Conversino himself.[30]

Unlike Conversino, who provided vivid details of his earliest schooling, Salutati almost never discussed it. He mentioned only one teacher and then with both affection and admiration—Pietro da Moglio, whose school he entered at fourteen or fifteen.[31] In this period Pietro da Moglio conducted a secondary school of grammar with the assistance of his

---

29. Francesco Cavazza, *Le scuole dell'antico studio bolognese* (Milan, 1896), pp. 131–32.

30. Remigio Sabbadini, *Giovanni da Ravenna, insigne figura d'umanista (1343–1408)* (Como, 1924), p. 132, compares the curriculum of the school attended by Giovanni di Conversino with the program outlined by Giovanni Dominici in his *Regola del governo di cura familiare* (Florence, 1860), pp. 133–36. The anecdote on cruelty occurs in Sabbadini, *Giovanni da Ravenna*, pp. 130–31. Neither Giovanni mentions Donatus as a text, but see Guido Zaccagnini, "L'insegnamento privato a Bologna e altrove nei secoli xiii e xiv," *Atti e memorie della r. deputazione di storia patria per le provincie di Romagna*, 4th ser., 14 (1924), 280. Charles H. Haskins, *The Renaissance of the Twelfth Century* (Cambridge, Mass., 1927), pp. 131–32, describes a similar course of readings for the grammar schools of the twelfth century.

31. Salutati describes da Moglio as "meus in adolescentia . . . premonitor" (*Epist.*, I, 115). In the law *adolescentia* began at fourteen. In the *De laboribus Herculis*, ed. Berthold L. Ullman, 2 vols. (Zurich, 1951), II, 267, Salutati writes: "Usque ad initium adolescentie tempus, quod est in masculo quando quatuordecimus annus impletus fuerit. . . ." In later years he speaks of Pietro as "doctor meus" (*Epist.*, II, 182) and of himself as Pietro's "discipulus" (ibid., p. 319). One of Salutati's earliest extant letters was written to Pietro (ibid., I, 3). Giovanni di Conversino felt much the same about Pietro's character and intelligence: "Mores probavi, scienciam credidi" (Sabbadini, p. 141).

younger brother. The location of their school in 1345 and 1346, when Salutati first attended classes, is unknown but it was probably in one of the many school buildings concentrated in the via Porta Nuova, behind the *Palazzo Comunale* where classes in medicine were also held. In Salutati's second or third year (1347) the da Moglio brothers rented a building in this same street from the heirs of one Giovanni di Bono da Soncino, recently deceased. There was a high desk at the front of the hall with benches along the walls for the students, with room for more in the balconies overhead. The area in the center was left open for recitation or disputation. Connected with the school was a dormitory, an orchard, storage rooms and quarters for the master and his family. In 1347, however, the Soncino heirs reserved the right to these quarters and the da Moglios must have lived elsewhere in the city.[32]

Through da Moglio Salutati was introduced into the new age of scholarship.[33] In all probability a student of Giovanni del Virgilio, leader of the new movement in Bologna in the previous generation,[34] Pietro became known as the greatest teacher of rhetoric in the mid-fourteenth century. Besides Salutati he counted among his pupils Giovanni di Conversino, Francesco Piendibeni da Montepulciano and Francesco da Fiano. Da Moglio's renown as a teacher at the secondary level finally led to a professorship in the Paduan *Studio* in 1362. However, by 1368, Bologna managed to lure him back and he held the chair of rhetoric in the *Studio* there until his death in 1383.[35]

Despite the identification of portions of his writings, Pietro remains a shadowy figure. His 249 line lament of Anna, Dido's sister, links him directly to the poetic tradition of Mussato and del Virgilio, as does his

---

32. For a map of the *Studio* area, see Cavazza, map facing p. 3. The contract for the school is published in Luigi Frati, "Nuovi documenti su Pietro da Muglio," *Studi e memorie per la storia dell'Università di Bologna*, 12 (1935), 87. A succession of teachers including Benvenuto da Imola in 1369 rented the school from the Soncino brothers: Lodovico Frati, "I *Flores veritatis Grammaticae* di maestro Bertoluccio," *Archivum romanicum*, 8 (1924), 321–22.

33. For a detailed list of bibliography on the life of da Moglio see, Giuseppe Billanovich, "Giovanni del Virgilio, Pietro da Moglio, Francesco da Fiano," *Italia medioevale e umanistica*, 6 (1963), 204.

34. On Giovanni del Virgilio, ibid., 6 (1963), 206; and Augusto Campana, "Guido Vacchetta e Giovanni del Virgilio (e Dante)," in *Studi in onore di Alfredo Schiaffini, Rivista di cultura classica e medioevale*, 7, no. 1 (1965), 252–65. On his epistolary exchange with Dante, see above, n. 12. On the authenticity of the exchange, see Enzo Cecchini, "Giovanni del Virgilio, Dante, Boccaccio: Appunti su un'attribuzione controversa," *Italia medioevale e umanistica*, 14 (1971), 25–56; and John Larner, "Boccaccio and Lovato Lovati," *Cultural Aspects of the Italian Renaissance: Essays in Honour of Paul Oskar Kristeller*, ed. Cecil H. Clough (Manchester-New York, 1976), pp. 22–32. Armando Petrucci, *Coluccio Salutati*, Bibliotheca biographica, vol. 7 (Rome, 1972), p. 11, stresses Bologna's traditionalism as contrasted with other centers of learning.

35. Billanovich, "Giovanni del Virgilio," *Italia medioevale e umanistica*, 6 (1963), 206.

Like his own teacher, Giovanni del Virgilio, who coupled his new approach to literature with traditional instruction in *ars dictaminis* (in this case utilizing his own manual),[41] da Moglio in the early decades of his teaching, when Salutati was one of his pupils, relied on an incongruous combination of old and new. Paradoxically, Salutati's only direct discussion of da Moglio's classroom focuses solely on his teacher's skill in imparting the rules of *dictamen*. In a poem dedicated to da Moglio in 1360–61, more than ten years after leaving da Moglio's classroom, Salutati writes of the teacher and the lessons.[42] After confessing himself unable to praise da Moglio sufficiently, Salutati reviews the things he has learned from his venerated master. What stands out in the former student's memory is the instruction in *ars dictaminis* with its division of the letter into the standard five parts (the *salutatio*, the *exordium* or *benivolentie captatio*, the *narratio*, *petitio*, and the *conclusio*), the *flores rhetorice*, the *cursus*, and punctuation. Da Moglio, he writes, had taught him the "power" of the letter. One can surmise that Salutati emerged from this classroom with at least the basic skills for composing in *stilus rhetoricus* which were to make him the greatest chancellor in Europe in his day.

In his letter the thirty-year-old Salutati says nothing of da Moglio's teaching of literature or of any aspects of instruction relevant to humanistic reform. Even later, when he specifically traced the origins of his interests in various areas of humanistic learning, he never credited his early schooling with having given him the initial inspiration.[43] Yet whether or not he recognized it, Salutati's life-long interest in Seneca doubtless came from his teacher, who gave that author such a prominent place in the curriculum. In fact, the only extant manuscript in Salutati's library written in his own hand is a copy of the tragedies.[44] It must have been added early to his collection at a time when, anxious to have the work and unable to pay a scribe, he undertook the laborious task of copying it himself. This link with pre-Petrarchan humanism

41. Giovanni's *ars dictaminis* is published by Paul O. Kristeller, "Un 'ars dictaminis' di Giovanni del Virgilio," *Italia mediovale e umanistica*, 4 (1961), 193–200. Also see Kristeller's introduction, pp. 181–92.

42. Ullman, *Studies*, p. 298, publishes the poem. Like Conversino's teacher ten years later, Pietro da Forli, Pietro da Moglio may have used Bonandrea's popular *Brevis introductio ad dictamen* as his textbook: James Banker, "Giovanni di Bonandrea's 'Ars dictaminis' Treatise and the Doctrine of Invention in the Italian Rhetorical Tradition of the Thirteenth and Early Fourteenth Centuries" (Dissertation, Rochester, 1972), pp. 267–68. On the other hand, he may have utilized Giovanni's manual.

43. See below, chap. 3.

44. For a discussion of this manuscript, see chap. 3.

Looking back on the period of his life spent in da Moglio's classroom, Coluccio characterized it as one of "the happier times."[49] Nevertheless, Piero Salutati considered his son's training with da Moglio only a preparation for notarial school.[50] Both law and medicine were in that period as now more remunerative than the arts and, given the boy's talents at rhetoric, he was marked out for the law rather than medicine. Roman and Canon Law, however, required long years of study, and the Salutati were not well-to-do. Following the notarial course lasting two years meant that within a short time he would be ready to practice, and the help of the Pepoli, his father's patrons, could materially advance his career.

Piero Salutati did not live to realize his plans for Coluccio's future. In 1347 Bologna was struck first by a severe food shortage and then by a pestilence. Piero's employer, Taddeo dei Pepoli, fell victim to the disease and Piero himself probably perished at the same time.[51] Of his not less than ten children, four are known to have died in Bologna and perhaps some were killed by the epidemics that raged in the city over a period of three years.[52] Salutati never forgot how at this juncture Giovanni dei Pepoli, the tyrant's son and one of his successors, stepped in to help Puccina and her young family. Coluccio, the eldest of the children, was probably a favorite of Giovanni: the mutual affection of the two men ended only with Giovanni's death in 1367. Long after leaving Bologna, Salutati journeyed from the Valdinievole to Pavia to see his

---

the role of disputation in early Italian humanism, see Neal W. Gilbert, "The Early Italian Humanists and Disputation," in *Renaissance Studies in Honor of Hans Baron*, ed. A. Molho and J. Tedeschi (Dekalb, 1971), pp. 201–26. For da Moglio's relationship to Salutati's later love of poetry, see below, chap. 3.

It may be that his consistent refusal in later life to flee the plague derived from Pietro's example. See Petrarch's letter to da Moglio praising the latter's refusal to leave Bologna during the epidemic of 1374: *Seniles* (XV, 10) in *Opera*, II, 1040–41.

49. *Epist.*, I, 115.

50. Filippo Villani, whose 'de Coluccio Piero, poeta,' was corrected by Salutati himself, mentions that Salutati studied for the notary "volente patre" (ibid., IV, 490).

51. Alfonso Corradi, *Annali delle epidemie occorse in Italia dalle prime memorie fino al 1850, compilati con varie note e dichiarazioni*, 5 vols. (rep. ed., Bologna, 1973), I, 188–89, considers the disease as probably a *febbre tifica*. The Black Death struck Bologna 1348–50. Salutati writes that he was "pene adolescens" when his father died (ibid., I, 36). Since this age lasted from fourteen to twenty-five, we might assume his father died when he was between fourteen and perhaps sixteen. Piero was still alive early in 1346, as is shown by the notarial document, above n. 9. Bandini's statement, accepted by Novati and others, that Piero Salutati "anno undecimo sui exilii clausit feliciter vite terminum" (ibid., IV, 502–3), if taken literally, is in error. Very probably, however, Bandini was referring to the length of Piero's residence in Bologna and out of Florentine territory.

52. Ibid., IV, 384–86.

former benefactor broken in health and awaiting death. On receiving news of his demise, Coluccio expressed his grief for the loss of a person he described as "more than parent."[53]

In the fall of 1348, in accord with Piero Salutati's original intentions, Giovanni Pepoli encouraged his young protégé to enroll in the notarial program in the *Studio*.[54] Preparation for the notarial profession in the Bologna schools was determined by the regulations laid down by the Guild of Notaries of Bologna. The 1336 guild statutes required that the candidate for admittance should have studied at least five years of grammar and have two or more years training in the notary from one or more doctors in this art in the city of Bologna.[55]

Generally speaking, the notary was a public person possessing the power to give official recognition to an action by means of a written instrument attesting to its performance. Prior to the thirteenth century the typical notary received his training through apprenticeship to a practicing notary. From this experience he acquired the ability to apply relevant legal formulae to the specific problem at hand. The reinstitution of the formal study of Roman law, starting at the end of the eleventh century, appears to have had little impact on the notariate for at least a hundred years. This was true even in Bologna where regular courses in the art of the notariate existed in the twelfth century.

The growing complexity of twelfth-century society and the accomplishments of Roman lawyers attempting to adapt the law of ancient Rome to another culture gradually forced a reform in both the education of the notary and the formulae he used.[56] The low esteem in which

---

53. Ibid., I, 37.

54. The limits of chronology here are given by our knowledge of Piero's death after 1346 (probably in the plague of 1347) and of the fact that, although Salutati finished the notarial course, he had not yet matriculated in the Bolognese notarial guild by early 1351 (see below, n. 61). Given the two years *et ultra* required for completion of the notarial course, we may assume that he began that program in the fall of 1348. Salutati tells us, moreover, that after his father's death Giovanni dei Pepoli conducted himself as "michi hortatorem . . . me iubens in litterarum militare gignasio" and that Giovanni "quasi iam tunc presagiret ingenioli mei vires, ad sacrarum legum studia compellebat")*Epist.*, I, 36–37). I interpret these phrases to mean that after the father's death Giovanni encouraged Salutati to continue his education with da Moglio (1346 or 1347) and then in 1348 advised him to enter the notarial school.

55. A.S.B., *Società d'Arti, cod. min. 11, Statuto dei notai,* 1336, requires that the candidate "studuerit spatio quinque annorum in grammatica ad minus. Item quod studuerit spatio duorum annorum et ultra in documentis notarie sub ordinario doctore uno vel pluribus ipsius artis, cive Bononie" (fol. 19). See Lauro Martines, *Lawyers and Statecraft in Renaissance Florence* (Princeton, 1968), pp. 35–38, for some general remarks on the training of notaries elsewhere in Italy.

56. Luigi Sighinolfi, "Salatiele e la sua *Ars Notariae,*" *Studi e memorie per la storia dell'Università di Bologna,* 4 (1920), 65–149, dates the beginning of the shift in notarial edu-

the notarial art was held is reflected by the fact that until the mid-thirteenth century teachers of this subject at Bologna were only given the title of *magister*. The introduction of the word *doctor* around 1240 to apply to teachers of the *ars notarie* in the *Studio* was a mark of the prestige acquired by the profession as a result of educational reforms.[57] By this decade not only had more relevant notarial formulae been worked out but, more important, a general theory of the notariate had been developed, one which required systematic training in the civil law. The work of Rolandino Passaggeri (†1300) represented the culmination of these reforms. His great collection of works, the *Summa totius artis notarie*, the *Aurora*, the *Tractatus notularum*, and the *Tractatus de officio tabellionatus in castris et villis exercendo*, together with the commentaries of Pietro Boattieri and Pietro da Anzola on the *Summa*, formed the nucleus of the reading material for the *ars notarie* down to the seventeenth century.[58]

The training Salutati received in his two years of study in the art reflected the reforms brought about in the previous century. The course of study followed by Salutati under his teacher, conte Francesco di Giordano Benintensi, between 1348 and 1350 would not have differed much from that taken by Giovanni di Conversino, whose study of the *ars notarie* took place in Bologna ten years later.[59] In his autobiography Giovanni writes that his teacher first treated the *Summa totius artis notarie* of Rolandino and then took up Justinian's *Institutes*.[60] In other words,

---

cation as occurring in the mid-thirteenth century. More recently Gianfranco Orlandelli, "Appunti sulla scuola bolognese di notariato nel secolo XIII per una edizione della *Ars Notarie* de Salatiele," *Studi e memorie per la storia dell'Università di Bologna*, n.s., 2 (1961), 3–54, convincingly argues that it takes place in the opening decades of that century.

57. Anselmo Anselmi, *Le scuole di notariato in Italia* (Viterbo, 1926), p. 8; Sighinolfi, pp. 112–13; and discussion of Orlandelli on Ranieri da Perugia as the innovator of the reforms: "Appunti," pp. 7 and 10 ff. Salatiele was called *doctor* as early as 1244 (not 1249 as Anselmi suggests): Arturo Palmieri, *Rolandino Passaggeri* (Bologna, 1933), p. 54.

58. Orlandelli, "Appunti," p. 14.

59. Giovanni Alidosi, *I dottori bolognesi di teologia, filosofia, medicina, e d'arti liberali* (Bologna, 1623), p. 55, mentions "conte Francesco di Giordano Benintensi," as teaching the notarial art in the *Studio* in 1348. In what appear to be fairly complete rolls for the readers in the *Studio* for 1351–53, published by Albano Sorbelli, *La Signoria di Giovanni Visconti a Bologna* (Bolgna, 1901), pp. 294 and 296, the name of Francesco Giordani occurs in 1352 and 1353 in the same post. There is no mention of any other reader in this field between 1348 and 1353 in these sources. Also see Novati, *La Giovinezza*, p. 55, n. 1. Did Giovanni have Salutati's teacher? Sabbadini assumes this to be the case (Giovanni da Ravenna, p. 25) but Alidosi (p. 57) lists a "Conte di Francesco Bruntasi de'Malavolti" as teaching *ars notarie* in 1356: *Li dottori bolognesi di legge canonica e civile* (Bologna, 1620), p. 57. See also, Serafino Mazzetti, *Repertorio de'Prof. della Università di Bologna* (Bologna, 1847), p. 131. Anselmi (p. 10) believes conte Francesco di Giordano Benintensi, Francesco Giordano and Conte di Francesco Brunatasi de'Malavolti to be three different people, but in the case of the first two we are obviously dealing with the same person.

60. "Quippe summam notarie primum atque Institutam, ita persuasum extitit, doctore Comite Francesco, audivi et iudicio docentis auditorumque proficere supra videbar" (Sab-

in the first year the class studied Rolandino's work, presumably with commentaries, while the second year was devoted principally to the *Institutes*. Since the commentaries to the *Summa* contained a good many references to Roman law in explaining the principles involved in the formulae, the first year served as a preparation for the more difficult study of the law itself.

One seminal influence of the *ars notarie* on Salutati's intellectual development was the experience with the Roman law it afforded. The primary intention of the glossators and postglossators of Bologna was to apply the Roman law, so magnificently formulated in the *Institutes*, to their own world. Very often, however, in the course of their comments it was necessary to refer to the history of the society that produced this law: for example, in elucidating an ambiguous passage it was found useful to determine the original reason for the particular law in question. Therefore, the various commentaries together with the historical sections of the *Institutes* themselves offered, potentially at least, a massive impression of Roman history as it related to the law. At the same time the contemporary importance of the law furnished proof of the continuity between the two ages.

The extent to which lawyers and notaries counted among the ranks of the humanists in the fourteenth century was due not only to the fact that they formed the core of the educated public. To a degree their interest in the ancient world was derived directly from their schooling in the law. Petrarch himself, who felt that his years in Bologna in the 1320s studying civil law were "wasted rather than spent," was nonetheless clear that he abandoned its study "not because I was displeased by the majesty of the law, which is unquestionably great and full of Roman antiquity in which I delight but because the use of the law is depraved by man's iniquity."[61] By contrast Salutati loved the law as a source of knowledge of Roman history and society and because he saw it as the cornerstone of both social order and human freedom. He was thrilled as he passed within inches of some of the greatest lawyers of his age on the crowded streets of Bologna. Years later he proudly remarked that

---

badini, *Giovanni da Ravenna*, p. 141). The same kind of instruction was given in Florence. If there Rolandino was not used, some sort of notarial manual was studied and commentaries were offered to students on the *Institutes: Statuti della Università e Studio fiorentino dell'anno MCCCLXXXVII*, ed. Alessandro Gherardi, Documenti di storia italiana, vol. 7 (Florence, 1881), p. 65.

61. "Poseritati," *Prose*, ed. Guido Martellotti, La letteratura italiana, Storia e Testi, vol. 7 (Milan, 1955), p. 10. For an important analysis of the relationship between students of law and humanism, see William Bouwsma, "Lawyers and Early Modern Culture," *American Historical Review*, 78 (1973), 309–27.

"I have seen Giovanni Andrea," whom he regarded as supreme above all other lawyers. His frequent citations from the *Institutes* in later life are evidence that he assiduously prepared his lessons in the class-room.[62]

His notarial course finished in August 1350, Salutati had yet to pass the entrance examination administered by the Bolognese Guild of Notaries later in the year. Once admitted to the guild he would be permitted to practice his profession anywhere in the city and territory. With three or four months before his examination he perhaps took advantage of the weeks of the wine harvest, the longest of the student holidays, to enjoy the scholar's vacation for the last time. He was, however, never to present his candidature.[63] Political events intervened to thwart his plans and to change the course of his life.[64]

When Taddeo dei Pepoli, doctor of civil law and *signore* of Bologna, died in September 1347, his power passed without difficulty to his sons, Jacopo and Giovanni. These two, lacking their father's political astuteness, proved themselves incapable of conserving their patrimony and on October 16, 1350, sold the dominion of the city to the archbishop of Milan for a large sum of money and a guarantee of their right to retain a few castles. Distrusting the strength of his hold over the city while the Pepoli were at liberty, the archbishop within months had the Pepoli in prison.

Unable to maintain herself and her children in the city without the patronage of the Pepoli, Puccina Salutati thought of returning to the Valdinievole. Piero had left her lands and a house in Stignano; her own family probably lived in the area and her brother-in-law Paccino was

62. In the margin of Filippo Villani's first edition of the *Liber de civitate Florentiae famos. civib.*, B.L.F., *Ashburnham*, 942, fol. 28ᵛ, opposite the life of Giovanni d'Andrea, Salutati wrote: "De postmortem sum dubius. Nam Henricus obiit anno 1313 et Io. An., quem vidi, decessit 1347 vel 48 proxime et ideo hanc supputationem puto corrigendam." When praising famous lawyers in history, Salutati, in his *De nobilitate medicine et legum: De verecundia*, ed. Eugenio Garin, Edizione nazionale dei classici del pensiero italiano, vol. 8 (Florence, 1947), p. 72, refers to Giovanni d'Andrea who "quanta super omnes fulget gloria."

63. The school year for the arts ran from mid-October to the end of August: Albano Sorbelli and Luigi Simeoni, *Storia dell'Università di Bologna*, 2 vols. (Bologna, 1944–47), I, 214. Sorbelli bases his observation on later statutes of the *Studio*, but Giovanni di Conversino indirectly confirms at least the beginning date for classes when he writes (Sabbadini, pp. 140–41) that he retired to the country for the *vindemia* and returned, while at the *Studio*, to Bologna to resume his studies *hieme*. The entrance records of the Guild of Notaries, which are complete for this period (A.S.B., *Arti, Sentenze di creazione dei notai, 1300–1385*, vol. 1), show no matriculation for Salutati.

64. For the fall of the Pepoli, see *Corpus chronicorum bononensium*, ed. Albano Sorbelli, R.I.S., vol. 18, pt. 1.2 (Città del Castello, 1911–14), pp. 604–12; Sorbelli, *La Signoria*, pp. 1–36; and Nino Valeri, *L'Italia nell'età dei principati*, Storia d'Italia, vol. 5 (Verona, 1949), pp. 117–22.

there to help.[65] Perhaps late in 1350 or the following spring with the return of good weather, the family of Piero Salutati returned to its homeland. Coming to manhood in close contact with a ruling tyrant family, Coluccio Salutati, at twenty, became a member of the small commune of Buggiano in Florentine territory, and thereafter his biography forms a part of the history of that republic.

65. Paccino was alive in 1373 according to an act rogated by Salutati on February 24 of that year: Armando Petrucci, *Il protocollo notarile di Coluccio Salutati, 1372–73* (Milan, 1963), p. 131.

Chapter 2. THE PROVINCIAL NOTARY

I

At mid-century the Valdinievole was politically a part of the Florentine Republic and constituted the major portion of the province known as the Valdinievole and Valdariana. A frontier province, the area was protected on its western border by a line of fortresses stretching from Sorana, four miles to the north of Pescia on the Pescia River, to Ponte Buggianese, five miles to the south on the edges of the Swamp of Fucecchio. These nine miles of fortifications, joined to those of the adjacent province of the Lower Valdarno further to the south, formed the first line of defense of the Florentine Republic against Pisa and Lucca. Besides several independent castles, each under the command of a castellan and a small detachment of troops, the province consisted of eight communes whose combined population in 1350 was roughly seven thousand.[1] In addition to Pescia, the provincial capital, three of the communes were on the frontier: Vellano, less than a mile south of the fortress of Sorana; Uzzano on the hillside a half-mile above and to the south of Pescia; and the complex of Buggiano another mile beyond in the same direction. In the interior behind Buggiano was Massa with its mountain fortress, Cozzile; while east of Buggiano was the powerful stronghold of Montecatini Alto with its thriving suburb, Montecatini Basso, and the smaller hilltop towns of Monsummano and Montevettolini.

As with scores of other Tuscan communes in the fourteenth century, the communities of the Valdinievole had been absorbed into the Florentine state as subject communes. While the eastern part of the region was incorporated into the Republic in 1330–31, it was not until January 20, 1339, that Mastino della Scala ceded the western part of the Valdinievole to the Florentines in the Treaty of Venice.[2] The official cession of the communes by the officials of Mastino was followed by a formal oath

---

1. Ronald G. Witt, "Coluccio Salutati and the Political Life of the Commune of Buggiano," *Rinascimento*, 6 (1966), 31, n. 1. A comparison with the administration of Pisa's *contado* in the fourteenth century suggests some interesting differences in policies between the two powers: Koichiro Shimizu, *L'amministrazione del contado pisano nel trecento attraverso un manuale notarile* (Pisa, 1975). See also my review in *Speculum*, 52 (1977), 1045–46.

2. A. Torrigiani, *Le castella della Val di Nievole* (Florence, 1865), pp. 154–55.

of submission sworn by the individual communes themselves. Accordingly their relationship to Florence was not one of equality but rather of subject to master. Buggiano, for instance, submitted itself unconditionally (*sine aliquo pacto*).[3] Following its usual policy of integrating a commune into its dominions, Florence created a division of responsibilities between its local representative, the *podestà*, and the communal government, an arrangement that left the latter important powers.

While the Florentine *podestà* of Buggiano was recognized as possessing full jurisdiction over civil and criminal cases, the statutes of the commune indicate that the local government was assigned a share in the administration of civil justice.[4] Whereas the *podestà* was charged with keeping the peace, he relied heavily on the communal administration for the actual defense organization. Taxes, moreover, whether collected to satisfy obligations to Florence or to defray the commune's ordinary expenses, were in the citizens' control. The citizens of the commune were also responsible for the maintenance and construction of bridges, roads, and fortifications and for supervising the local market. To enforce its commands, the commune had the power to exact fines.[5]

To insure that the local administration carried out its functions satisfactorily and in accord with their wishes, the Florentines required the *podestà* to be present at all deliberations of the various governing bodies of the commune. If he was unable to attend, his notary, who could not be a citizen of a commune within the province, was designated to take his place.[6] But of far greater importance in communal politics was the vicar of the Valdinievole. In regular contact with the *Signoria*, the vicar was charged with communicating its will to the communes under his

3. Placido Puccinelli, *Memorie dell' insigne e nobile terra di Pescia* (Milan, 1664), p. 449. Giuseppe Calamari, *Lo statuto di Pescia del MCCCXXXIX* (Pescia, 1927), analyzes the statutes of that commune written immediately after the subjection to Florence.

4. *Dipl., Pescia, Privilegi a quaderno*, April 14, 1339, fol. 2. Also *Cap.*, 65, fols. 128–31. Although this is a copy of the *capitoli* given to Pescia, those of Buggiano undoubtedly contained a similar proviso. The Pescia *capitoli* provide in three separate paragraphs (ibid., fol. 3ᵛ) for *podestà* and their staffs for Pescia, Buggiano, and Uzzano. This was probably the only point upon which the *capitoli* of the three communes differed, and in making out the individual copies for the communes the notary merely wrote the whole section into each instead of omitting the parts pertaining to the other two. See also my "Coluccio Salutati," p. 33. The commune was responsible for seeking out and punishing those who inflicted damage on private property. A special commission was appointed by the communal government for this purpose (*SCS*, 102, *Buggiano, 1366–1572*, fol. 91).

5. See first complete statutes of Buggiano (1378) in *SCS, Buggiano*, where the index to the various rubrics at the beginning of the statutes gives an idea of the scope of the communal government's activities. The statutes of 1366 bound with these are merely *additiones et correctiones* to previous statutes now lost.

6. The presence of the *podestà* or of his notary is recorded at the beginning of the minutes of the meetings of the communal council recorded in A.C.B., *Deliberazioni*.

jurisdiction. The representatives of Buggiano were summoned as many as two or three times a week to meetings at the vicar's palace in Pescia to hear a command of the *Signoria* or to give advice on various projects.

One of the most interesting aspects of current research on Florentine history is the attempt to describe and explain the progressive centralization of the Florentine state in the last half of the fourteenth and early part of the fifteenth centuries, centralization which involved the growing power of the Florentine government over the people and the economic resources of the subject communes. At the end of the third quarter of the fourteenth century, however, this process was only in its early stages. Before the great war with the Church and Milan necessitated merciless taxation of the subject communes, the military and financial obligations owed to Florence by Buggiano and other communes of the area seem to have been comparatively light. If the commune frequently appealed a new levy and sought devious means to avert it, this was only natural. When the sum had been fixed by both parties, there appears to have been no great difficulty in collecting the money. A loan was usually imposed on a number of residents who were reimbursed when the communal revenues came in. As a result, during these years Buggiano was capable of satisfying the claims of its overlord while conserving most of its resources for local projects.

The vigor and intensity of local politics reflected in the public deliberations of the communes of the Valdinievole stemmed in large part from another source, the continued threat of a revolt of local Ghilbellines coordinated with an attack from Lucchese territory. In normal times there were less than one hundred and fifty soldiers in the whole province, and in the event of a sudden uprising these would have been helpless without the aid of the communal militia.[7] Besides insuring the

7. This figure is an estimate based on the number of soldiers each *podestà* in the province must bring, scattered indications of the number of soldiers stationed in frontier castles, and the size of the troops under the command of the vicar of the province. For instance, the *podestà* of Buggiano brought with him four men-at-arms (Pescia, *Privilegi*, fol. 3ᵛ). The garrison of the castle of Buggiano in the third quarter of the fourteenth century was about ten men (see lists of these soldiers, *Delib.*, 5, fol. 93ᵛ, and 7, fol. 131). Even the vicar of the province had only a handful of regular troops; in 1354 he had twenty-three at his disposal (*Provv. reg.*, 41, fol. 14).

 • Giorgio Chittolini, *La formazione dello stato regionale e le instituzioni del contado: Secoli XIV e XV* (Torino, 1979), pp. 318–21, discusses the evolution of Florentine policy toward the Valdinievole in the fourteenth and fifteenth centuries. The growth of the Florentine territorial state was a major theme of Marvin Becker's *Florence in Transition*, 2 vols. (Baltimore, 1967–68). Among recent work I would like to single out Giorgio Chittolini, "La formazione dello stato regionale e le instituzioni del contado: ricerche sull'ordinamento territoriale del dominio fiorentino agli inizi del secolo XV" in *Egemonia fiorentina ed autonomie locali nella Toscana nord-occidentale del primo Rinascimento: Vita, arte, cultura, Settimo convegno*

preparedness of its citizen army, each commune, by a ruthless system of regulation, tried to insure the impotency of the local Ghibellines. Since Guelfism was a way of life, the institution of the commune was responsible for its preservation on a day-to-day basis. Because of the Ghibelline threat, the commune of Buggiano, along with others in this frontier region, was able to command an unusual degree of obedience and sacrifice from its Guelf citizens who saw the future of the commune vitally connected to their own. At least until 1369, when Lucca became Guelf, Ghibellinism was an imminent threat to the political regime of the region.

Although communal politics preserved its vital character in these border communities in the decades after 1350, we must also presume that, like the Florentine territory generally, the long term demographic decline in the Valdinievole was sharply accentuated by the plague. The immediate, severe loss of life caused by the first onslaught of the Black Death in 1348–50 was probably followed here as elsewhere in the provinces by a continuing diminution of population. The persistently adverse demographic trend stemmed both from recurrent attacks of plague and the rapid contraction of Tuscan agriculture, oriented as it was to urban markets. The fiscal oppression, which became apparent by the last years of the century, only exaggerated the demographic decline already in progress.

The mortality rate between 1348–50 was appalling. Enrico Fiumi estimates, for example, that forty-five percent of the population of the countryside around San Gimignano lost their lives in the two-year period.[8] No such exact figure can be adduced for the Valdinievole but, judging from what appears to have been the death rate among the notaries, Fiumi's estimate is probably accurate for Buggiano as well. The notarial protocol of ser Giovanni di ser Ugolino of Buggiano for 1346–47 mentions the names of fifteen notaries in the commune who were either involved in the acts recorded by him or appeared as witnesses. Since none of them was designated as coming from Colle-a-Buggiano, the fourth fraction of the commune and the third most populous, it is likely that there were others practicing in that community as well. A decade later, when the *Deliberazioni* begin and we have fairly definite information about the number of men in the profession, there are nine

internazionale (Pistoia, 1975), pp. 17–70, and David Herlihy, "Le relazioni economiche di Firenze con le città soggette nel secolo XV," in the same volume, pp. 79–109.

8. Enrico Fiumi, *Storia economica e sociale di San Gimignano* (Florence, 1961), p. 171; David Herlihy, *Medieval and Renaissance Pistoia* (Princeton, 1967), pp. 55–73.

or at the most ten notaries practicing in Buggiano, but only four of these are also found in the protocol of 1346–47.[9] While it is possible that some of those not reappearing had moved away in the interval, no trace is found of them anywhere in the archives of the Valdinievole, Pistoia, Florence, or Lucca. The likely explanation is that many of the eleven died in the Black Death along with the writer of the protocol himself, ser Giovanni, who perished in 1348.[10] If the number of notaries was determined by demand, it might be assumed that the nine or ten notaries in Buggiano in 1356–57 were serving a community about half the size of that served by double their number a decade before.

Perhaps never before in human history had there been an experience so universally shared as the Black Death of 1348–50. Responses were various yet all derived at least partially from the general realization of helplessness before a phenomenon that struck individuals without apparent discrimination. The Salutatis did not escape the plague, but in their case the suffering caused by the loss of family members was compounded, in 1350, by the collapse of the Pepoli regime. Within the space of a few months the family's pattern of life and their expectations altered drastically. Forced to leave Bologna, Puccina with her surviving children had to create a new life in rural Stignano. Having lost his father, confronted with the vastly diminished prospects for a career in the provinces, the young Salutati had cause to accuse fortune, whose wiles he would expose at length in his first known letters.

II

If the young man can be described on the basis of portraits and accounts of the old man, Salutati at twenty was moderately tall and raw-

9. *Notarile*, G 468. The fifteen names are found on the following pages of the protocol: fols. 1ᵛ, 4ᵛ, 6ᵛ, 7, 9, 10, 12, 28, 30ᵛ, 37ᵛ, and 75. The four notaries who survived the plague were ser Niccolò di ser Cecco, ser Giovanni Lemmi, and ser Domenico Cenci of Buggiano and ser Francesco Righi of Stignano. In 1357–58 there were in addition to the four mentioned, ser Mazzeo Delli, ser Jacopo Rigozzi, ser Sardo di ser Niccolò, Salutati, and perhaps ser Andrea di ser Conti. In the next decade ser Giovanni Lemmi died and his place was taken by his son, ser Francesco, but three of the area's notaries were expelled for being Ghibellines during the Pisan War or just before its outbreak (ser Sardo, ser Domenico, and ser Andrea). *Delib. (ord. autor.)*, 12, fol. 39, mentions a ser Giannellino Cosi of Buggiano as secretary of the commune of Figline on June 21, 1364, but he does not seem to have been a resident of Buggiano.

10. The last documents written in his hand were in December 1347. Subsequently, alterations and cancellations were made in the protocol, but, at least from November 13, 1348 (fol. 67ᵛ), these entries were by ser Giovanni Lemmi to whom the records of the deceased notary must have been entrusted.

boned with none of the personal beauty and litheness that so distinguished Petrarch. While the projecting lower lip of the septuagenarian was the sign of lost teeth and advancing age generally, the prominent, high-bridged nose had been a permanent feature of the face.[11] Endowed with a physical frame well-suited to the active life he was to lead, Salutati seems rarely to have suffered serious illness throughout his seventy-five years.

Having grown up in a large family, one closely associated with a minor princely court, Salutati felt at home amidst a crowd. He was to thrive best in the bustle of public life, and even in later years, when he could have afforded to retire, his occasional yearnings for leisure and solitude went unsatisfied, primarily because he had an unerring sense of the atmosphere in which he could be most creative. He enjoyed the panoply of religious festivals and solemn public occasions, and he relished the relaxed discussions at banquets and parties. Because of his lively conversation infused with humor, he proved a delightful guest and companion.[12] Despite the scars left by the misfortunes of recent years, therefore, the young Salutati probably adjusted easily to the permanency of his situation in the narrow world of the Valdinievole, renewing old friendships and making new ones.

One of the first concerns of Salutati in the early days after his arrival in Stignano was to obtain authorization to practice his profession. As a product of the *Studio* of Bologna, the young man had received an education far superior to that of most of the other notaries in the region. Since local schoolmasters employed by these rural communes often did not know Latin, the general instructional level was low and notarial training normally consisted of an apprenticeship with a practicing no-

11. Francesco Novati has published a number of existing portraits of Salutati: *Epist.*, I, facing p. 3; III, facing p. 3; IV, facing p. 168. He has also edited (IV, 500–501) a description of Salutati written about 1405 by the unknown translator of Filippo Villani's short biography of Salutati: "Fu et anchora è di statura un pocho più che mezana, ma alquanto chinato, con hossa larghe, colore quasi biancho, faccia tonda, larghe et pendente mascelle, et con labbro disotto alquanto più eminente: pronuntiatione modesta, ma tarda. L'aspetto suo è alquanto orido et malinchonicho, ma cominciando a parlare è giocondo." The iconographic problems involved in the various pictorial representations of Salutati are discussed by Novati, ibid., IV. 557–65. Cf. Pieter Meller, "La Capella Brancacci," *Acropoli*, 1 (1960–61), 277–78 and 308–9, n. 20. I have been unsuccessful in finding Meller's "Nuovi appunti per l'iconografia di Coluccio Salutati" which was to be published subsequently.

12. Two contemporary sources describe the ease with which Salutati conducted himself in company: Leonardo Bruni, *Ad Petrum Paulum Histrum Dialogus*, in *Prosatori Latini del Quattrocento*, ed. Eugenio Garin, La letteratura italiana, Storia e testi, vol. 13 (Milan, 1952), pp. 44–98; and the *Paradiso degli Alberti*, see below, chap. 10.

tary.[13] Even in Florence during this period the standards of education for a notary were inferior to those in Bologna. Although prospective candidates for the guild were examined for their knowledge of Latin, there was no specific requirement for formal training in the language, nor did the organization require proof of attendance in a notarial school: several years of apprenticeship were regarded as sufficient preparation for the examination.[14] Given his systematic training not only in notarial formulae but also in civil law, the young Salutati was regarded as a wonder of learning by his fellow citizens, a reputation that no doubt helped advance his career.

His family connections, moreoever, were also to prove of assistance in this regard. The Salutati family, though in relatively moderate circumstances by Florentine standards, belonged to the upper class of this rural area. Coluccio's father had been a political leader in the commune and the Lupori-Salutati in Pescia were prosperous. Ser Luporo, a contemporary of Piero Salutati, was a successful notary, and one of his sons obtained a doctorate in civil law. While Coluccio's salary was necessary to support his mother and a large household of younger children, he could still find enough money to purchase books. The four manuscripts he bought in 1355, for example, cost him four florins, equivalent to about two months of his salary as a communal secretary.[15]

To understand how Salutati entered practice in Buggiano and to establish the nature of his early career is at the same time to appreciate the extent to which the organization of crafts and professions at the local level remained in this period relatively independent despite the formal subjection of the communes to the Florentine state. The 1344 statutes of the Florentine Guild of Judges and Notaries were categorical in prohibiting anyone not a guild member from practicing either in Florence or in the district.[16] However, the *capitoli* or basic laws govern-

13. Regarding the schoolmaster, the statutes of Buggiano in 1372, *SCS, Buggiano*, fol. 119ᵛ, provide that "possit pro eius salario sibi stantiare, si docebit gramaticam, libros quinquaginta et, si non doceret gramaticam, libros vigintiquinque. . . ."

14. *AGN*, 749, fols. 39–40, contains the requirements and describes the examination. See discussion of this point, Lauro Martines, *Lawyers and Statecraft in Renaissance Florence* (Princeton, 1968), pp. 34–35. See also Santi Calleri, *L'arte dei guidici e notai di Firenze nell'età comunale e nel suo statuto del 1344* (Milan, 1966), pp. 32–34.

15. Berthold L. Ullman, *The Humanism of Coluccio Salutati*, Medioevo e umanesimo, vol. 4 (Padua, 1963), p. 167. The notarial protocol of ser Ludovico di Barone (above, chap. 1, n. 2) suggests that the Riccomi and Lupori Salutati were prosperous and involved in many business dealings.

16. *AGN*, 749, fol. 40ᵛ. Alfred Doren, *Studien aus der Florentiner Wirtschaftsgeschichte*, 2 vols. (Stuttgart, 1901–8), II, 186–87, is the only previous writer to deal with the relation-

ing the relationship between Florence and newly admitted territories in effect contravened this provision. For instance, when the various communes of the Lower Valdarno and Valdinievole were incorporated into the state in the 1330s and 1340s, the Florentine government allowed members of the local guilds, including the notaries, to join the respective Florentine guilds free of charge and without examination, within the two years following the commune's admission.[17] After that those wishing to join would have to follow the normal procedure. Presumably, those exercising their art only within the boundaries of their own commune could still continue to do so without Florentine guild membership: the *capitoli* of Massa e Cozzile in fact specifically state this.[18]

In this way the Florentine government implicitly recognized the right of individual communes to license their own notaries. How this was done varied with the locality. In a commune such as Pescia, with an active guild system of its own, the authorization was acquired through membership in the local Guild of Notaries.[19] In Fucecchio, in the neighboring province of the Lower Valdarno, the communal government seems to have regulated the notaries within its jurisdiction.[20] By contrast with these two communes, Buggiano had no guild organization, nor did the

---

ship of the Florentine guilds to the communes of the Valdinievole, and his few observations are in fact not very helpful. The only book on the legal profession in Florence, Martines's *Lawyers and Statecraft in Renaissance Florence*, is not concerned with the problem of the contact between notaries and judges in the territories and the guild in the capital. Francesco Novati, *La giovinezza di Coluccio Salutati* (Torino, 1888), p. 64, n. 1, believed that Salutati received his authorization to practice either at Lucca or Florence. Ullman, *The Humanism*, p. 6, n. 2, opts for Florence and Armando Petrucci, *Il protocollo notarile di Coluccio Salutati, 1372–73* (Milan, 1963), p. 15, believes it was "quasi sicuramente a Firenze, e non a Bologna, intorno al 1350." Because so little is understood about the nature of the notarial profession in the Florentine territories in the Trecento, it is necessary to go into some detail in order to understand Salutati's career during this period of his life.

17. This specific provision is contained in the *capitoli* of nine out of the thirteen communes in the two provinces: Montecatini (1330), *Cap.*, 2, fol. 45ᵛ; Montevettolini (1331), ibid., fols. 28ᵛ–29; Monsummano (1331), ibid., fol. 31; Massa e Cozzile (1339), ibid., fols. 20–20ᵛ; Castelfranco (1330), ibid., fol. 63ᵛ; Fucecchio (1331), ibid., fol. 73; Santa Croce-sul-Arno (1331), ibid., fols. 97ᵛ–98; Santa Maria-a-Monte (1349), ibid., fols. 118–18ᵛ; Montopoli (1349), ibid., fols. 112ᵛ–13. The *capitoli* for Vellano are not recorded and those of Pescia, Buggiano, and Uzzano are incomplete: *Dipl., Pescia, Privilegi a quaderno*, April 14, 1339. Also *Cap.*, 65, fols. 128–31. There is, however, no reason to believe that the guild privilege found in the *capitoli* of nearby Massa e Cozzile dated December 11, 1339, was not also granted to the other four with which it became a part of Florence in the same year.

18. *Cap.*, 2, fols. 20–20ᵛ.

19. B.C.P., *Statuti 1340*, fol. 8, where the oath of *podestà* contains a promise to uphold the local Guild of Notaries: " . . . et consules communis et matriculam notariorum favorare et eorum iura et dicte matricule manutenere." For a list of officers of this guild and that of other guilds of *Pescia*, see B.C.P., 1-A 58 (102), *Priorità pesciatino*, passim.

20. A.C.F., *Deliberazioni 1373–1388*, fol. 102, where the commune approves the petition of an outside notary to practice in Fucecchio.

communal government exercise much control over the guilds aside from its supervision of the market and of weights and measures. Salutati might simply have begun to practice without any official authorization but it is more likely that the members of the local notariate met with the young candidate and, after an interview, consented to recognize him as one of their number.

In considering his prospects for employment Salutati was not limited to Buggiano. In fact, the average notary in Buggiano would have found difficulty in earning a living entirely from private practice in a rural commune of fifteen hundred people. Even when he had clients further afield in towns such as Massa and Uzzano, his income might still be inadequate. Some notaries, like the late ser Cecco Lemmi and his son, ser Niccolò, had found ways to increase their earnings through dealing in real estate or money lending, but the normal source of extra money came from one of the many short-term official appointments available in the provinces. This, of course, raises the question of how a young notary without membership in the Florentine guild—Salutati did not join it until 1366—would have been able to consider employment outside the bounds of his own commune. The answer to this question suggests the capacity of the Florentines for adjusting laws to the realities of life.

In regulating the status of the local guilds, the *capitoli* imposed unrealistic limitations on the freedom of the various crafts and professions. At least in the case of the notaries, membership in the Florentine guild would have been both expensive and troublesome, yet, at the same time, most members of the profession often needed to work outside their home communes. Although the only mention of the arrangement so far identified occurred in 1365, it is fair to assume that the use of a special license, called the *pactum*, had been introduced decades earlier to cover this situation. The *pactum* was a permit extended by the state to an individual notary allowing him to work both in Florence and the environing territory without guild membership. It was available to members of the profession who lived outside the old Florentine territory in those areas more recently annexed.[21]

There were two types of official appointments available to the notary in the Valdinievole: as notary of the Florentine vicar or *podestà* and as an

21. *AGN*, 28, June 21, 1365, fols. 138–38ᵛ, refers to notaries in outlying territories who "exercent artem et offitium in comitatu Florentie et habere dicuntur pacta cum communi Florentie per que possunt in civitate et comitatu Florentie dictam autoritatem notarie et officium libere exercere. . . ." See below, n. 83.

employee of a commune. With significant exceptions, each commune in a province had not only its own local administration but also a *podestà* sent out from Florence with his official family on six-month assignment. The *podestà*'s duties were primarily to execute the *Signoria*'s wishes and to administer criminal and civil justice. A third governmental unit, that of the provincial governor and his staff, was located in the capital of each province. This governor, called the vicar, seems to have been occupied chiefly with coordinating the defense and military organization in the various communes under his control, but he also exercised judicial powers in the most important cases. Primarily to insure the loyalty of its provincial administration but also to render it independent of local interests, Florence required vicars and *podestà* to be Florentine citizens and the members of their staffs to come from areas outside their place of employment.

Francesco Novati has painted in vivid detail the life of the notaries who made up the retinues of these *podestà* and vicars.[22] Usually far from home, completely dependent for the necessities of life on their immediate employers, these officials often led a miserable existence. Many *podestà* and vicars regarded their offices as a means for enriching themselves and found various ways of reducing the operating expenses of their households to a minimum. Common are the complaints of bad food, short rations, and cold rooms from those who served in such official families. Terms of employment, moreoever, were short, normally only six months, and often there would be periods of unemployment between appointments.

The other type of official post open to the notary, one neglected by Novati's study, was that of the communal secretary. Each commune had its own government and accordingly required a secretary to record the deliberations of the councils, to maintain the correspondence and to notarize the various acts connected with its operations. In every one of these government units the secretary of the commune was forced to perform minor judicial functions. In certain communes, such as Vellano which lacked a *podestà*, these duties could be quite extensive. The emoluments and honor connected with this type of work obviously depended on the importance of the commune. The residence requirement for the post of communal secretary was that he not be a citizen of the commune that employed him.

22. Novati, *La giovinezza*, pp. 94 ff.

Although the officials coming from Florence had some choice in selecting the suite they brought with them, the usual method for filling the notarial posts in the communal administration was by a combined system of drawing lots and election. The commune concerned required all notaries wishing to apply for a particular appointment to submit their names. These were written on slips of paper and placed in a special purse. At six-month intervals a number of names were drawn from the purse and the communal council voted on the names extracted. The notary who received the most votes was then notified of his election. As the statutes of Buggiano show, however, if a large majority of the communal council wished to summon or retain a particularly popular notary, they had the authority to dispense with this procedure.[23]

On the whole, the working conditions of a communal secretary seem to have been more favorable than those of a notary to a *podestà* or vicar. Usually employed closer to home, perhaps located in a neighboring commune, the notary was not cut off from his family and often he was well known in the commune where he worked. Under such circumstances he might even be able to maintain his private clientele. Although the appointments lasted only six months at a time, proximity minimized dislocation. If often subject to the whims of the communal councils, the communal secretary appears generally to have enjoyed a greater degree of freedom under many masters than his counterpart under a *podestà* or vicar.

At the age of twenty Salutati would have been considered young for a communal secretary. In Pescia, in fact, the statutes of the commune required holders of the post to be at least twenty-five.[24] Even where not barred by law, he would have found it difficult to compete with older, more experienced candidates. That in the first few months of residence in the Valdinievole he received any sort of official position, was perhaps the result of his Bolognese degree and the influence of his relatives in Pescia. The appointment was an ideal one for a young notary without practical experience and the only one of its kind in the province. As *officialis* of the commune of Pescia, a sort of assistant secretary to the communal notary, he was able to gain experience in dealing with the

23. A. C. Mons., *Statuti 1372*, fols. 4–5, for description of the usual procedure of election. The election in Vellano was more complicated than elsewhere, *SCS, 920, Vellano 1367–1738*, fol. 2. For power of General Council on matter of election of notary in Buggiano see, A.C.B., *Delib. 6*, fols. 301 and 303.
24. B.C.P., *Statuti 1340*, fol. 82.

daily affairs of a commune and at the same time was close enough to home (less than an hour's walk over the hillside road) to be able to begin building a private clientele in his spare time.[25]

For the next sixteen years a score of public and private documents record Salutati's movements from one official post to another in the Valdinievole and other provinces of the Florentine Republic. The intervals of months and sometimes years between appointments were usually spent in Stignano, where, when not occupied in politics or study, he earned his living doing notarial work for his own commune or for private clients in the neighborhood. This departure from and return to Stignano was a recurrent pattern in Coluccio's life until his definitive move to Florence in 1374. Although he traveled a good deal between 1351 and 1374, he never lost touch with Stignano for long. Accordingly, his life had a continuity which the following account of his notarial career does not suggest.

Salutati's first appearance in a document after August 1351 occurs sixteen months later in Monsummano, about a three hours' walk to the east of Buggiano. There on December 31, 1352, as secretary of the commune, Salutati notarized an act recognizing the presence of the new *podestà*, Como Federighi of Florence, in his charge.[26] Salutati had just started his term, probably right after Christmas, and as salary he was to receive 40 lire (roughly thirteen or fourteen florins) for the six-month period, in addition to a house and the right to have private clients to augment his income.[27] As elsewhere in the Valdinievole his movement as secretary of the commune was restricted: in Monsummano he could not be absent from the commune more than three days in any month without special permission.[28] This restriction meant that often it was

---

25. *Guid., App. e Null.*, Fa 10a. First cited, Demetrio Marzi, *La cancelleria della Repubblica fiorentina* (Rocca San Casciano, 1910), p. 114, n. 3. The various existing editions of the statutes of Pescia do not mention this office, but in the first surviving book of deliberations for the communal council, A.C.P., *Partiti e Delib.*, 1373–75, fol. 252ᵛ, the secretary of the commune appears to have an assistant.

26. *Dipl, Arch. gener.*, ad an.; Marzi, p. 114, n. 5.

27. This remark is based on the assumption that the statutes of Monsummano of 1372 reflect the situation twenty years earlier (A.C. Mons., *Statuti 1372*, fols. 4ᵛ–5ᵛ). Prior to Salutati the post had probably been held by ser Cambio Giani di Montevettolini: A.C.M.C., *Diverse Scritture Antiche*, fols. 44ᵛ–45. The document mentions a procuration drawn up by ser Cambio authorizing a certain Filippo di ser Niccolò to represent Monsummano at a meeting with the vicar of Pescia on January 12, 1353. Because procurations were often drawn up some time before they were used, it is very likely that ser Cambio had been communal secretary before Christmas 1352.

28. A. C. Mons., *Statuti 1372*, fol. 5. Compare *SCS, Vellano*, fol. 2ᵛ; ibid., *Buggiano*, fol. 57; ibid., 904, *Uzzano*, 1339, fol. 3. This should resolve difficulty raised by Francesco No-

easier for his clients from home to come to him in Monsummano than for him to go to them. This explains why a contract between three citizens of Buggiano was written by Salutati on May 9, 1353, in Monsummano.[29]

Monsummano was a small commune and the burden of work was not very heavy, but Florence, in an effort to economize, had stipulated that, rather than bring a notary with him to the post, the *podestà* should make use of the services of the communal secretary. This regulation doubtless increased the latter's responsibilities.[30] Salutati must have performed these tasks to the satisfaction of the communal council because in June 1353, at the expiration of his first term, he was reconfirmed. On August 27 he attested to the presence of Federighi's successor for the following six months[31] and there is a record of his having drawn up a procuration in the fall of that year for a certain Andrea Vanni charged with going to Florence on behalf of Monsummano.[32]

After leaving his post there at the end of 1353 Salutati disappears from our view for about two years. When we next find mention of him, it is as notary of an act of October 18, 1355, testifying to the arrival of the new *podestà* of Santa Maria-a-Monte in the province of the Lower Valdarno. Five days later he purchased the four manuscripts already mentioned, which had belonged to a deceased notary.[33] Because of the disappearance of most of the records for this diminutive commune, there is no way of proving conclusively that Salutati was the communal secretary, but it is likely. Like Monsummano the commune of Santa Maria-a-Monte had no notary attached to the *podesteria*, and the communal secretary did the work of both.[34] Located eighteen or nineteen miles from Stignano, moreover, it is improbable that this commune would have commissioned him to rogate an act of presentment had he not been an official of the government.

Over the next ten years the documents suggest that Salutati held an

---

vati, *Epist.* I, 33, n. 2, and Ullman, *The Humanism*, pp. 7–8, n. 4, as to Salutati's place of residence while employed in Vellano in 1366.

29. Novati, *La giovinezza*, p. 64.

30. A. C. Mon., *Statuti 1372*, fols. 4–5, where vicar's staff is mentioned and duties of communal secretary outlined.

31. *Dipl., Arch. gener.*, ad an.; Marzi, p. 114, n. 6.

32. A. C. Mont., 186 (*Contratti 1330–1393*), fol. 39ᵛ. Presumably Salutati's two terms ran from late December to June and from June to late December.

33. *Dipl., Arch. gener.*, ad an.; Marzi, p. 114, n. 7.

34. *Cap.*, 2, fol. 117ᵛ, does not mention a notary among the staff of the *podestà*. Also see *SCS*, 816, *Santa Maria-a-Monte, 1391–1592*, fol. 4.

appointment as communal secretary in Uzzano in the fall of 1356[35] and in Pescia in the first half of 1358.[36] His tenure of a similar office in the first six months of 1360 in Montecatini is certain,[37] and he is known to have had some kind of official appointment in Empoli in the last half either of 1359 or 1361.[38] It is possible, moreover, that he held an office in Uzzano in the first six months of 1361, but this conjecture is based solely on the fact that he appears to have written a letter from there during this period.[39] In February 1363 and again three months later Salutati was at Peccioli in what had recently been Pisan-held territory.[40] In August 1362 the area had been seized by the Florentines and for almost two years, until the Peace of Pescia on August 28, 1364, when it was definitely ceded to Florence, the settlement was in constant danger of recapture by the Pisans. Salutati was probably among the first regular officials to serve there under Florentine control. Because the notarial act of February was a document testifying that the new *podestà*, Stefano Piero di Altoviti, had arrived in Peccioli, it is probable that Salutati was again serving as secretary of the commune. When his term of office began is not known, but a deed drawn up by him in Stignano on July 8 of the same year proves that he had returned home by that time.[41]

At least from the middle of 1363 until he moved to Vellano to assume the office of secretary there in late June of 1366, Salutati seems to have remained almost continuously in residence at Stignano, engaging in private practice in Buggiano and neighboring communities. Depending on the circumstances, he would receive his clients in his study at home or

35. On September 22, 1356, he notarized the consignment of the castle to the new castellan and another document notifying the *Signoria* of the arrival of the new *podestà* on November 23 (*Dipl.*, *Arch. gener.*, ad an.; Marzi, p. 114, n. 8). See also the notarization of a private document on September 11, 1357 (*Dipl.*, *Badia di Firenze*, ad an.).

36. B.C.P., *Priorista*, fol. 53.: "E perchè ser Coluccio di Piero Salutati de Stignano e ser Simone di Martini, stati notari et offiziali del comune di Pescia, avevano finito il loro offizio, furon eletti per sindicarli l'infrascritti (two names follow)." Which communal office Salutati held there is unspecified, but because of his previous experience it was probably that of the communal secretary. Also see mission of Salutati to Florence, presumably for Pescia, fol. 53ᵛ.

37. *Camera fiscale*, March 9, 1360; Marzi, p. 114, n. 9. Salutati signs as "notarius et scriba communis Montis Catini ad offitium reformationum deputatus."

38. For the Empoli appointment, see chap. 3.

39. Novati, *Epist.*, I, 5–6, publishes a letter from Uzzano dated January 25, 1361? It is unlikely that Salutati at Uzzano, a little over a mile from Stignano, would have addressed a letter from there unless he were detained in the commune for some reason and expected his correspondent to direct the reply to Uzzano.

40. *Dipl.*, *Arch. gener.*, ad an. Also in the same commune, *Dipl.*, *Riform.*, May 4, 1363; Marzi, p. 115, n. 2.

41. A.C.B., *Delib.*, 7, fol. 20.

would meet them outside. From a brief summary of facts written hastily during the conversation he would later draw up the legal documents on fine white parchment. Before delivering the acts, he was required to record their contents in a register which he kept for his files. Many times he must have been called to the nearby church of St. Andrea in Stignano to rogate acts of donation. In addition to the deed of land written by him for St. Andrea on July 8, 1363, there is mention of one rogated years before on July 4, 1358, and another written on November 4, 1364.[42]

Salutati seems to have continued the life of a private notary during 1365 and the first half of 1366. We have two letters sent from Stignano to friends in 1365 and a third dated January 18, 1366.[43] Also in 1366 Salutati was one of the authors of the new compilation of statutes written at the end of February.[44] The only official appointment he seems to have held outside Buggiano during these four years was that of syndic for the commune of Pescia, charged with reviewing the books of the commune's outgoing public officials, but this required only a few weeks. One of the motives for staying so close to home, at least in 1365 and early 1366, was that he was courting a wife. His marriage to Caterina di Tomeo di Balducci, daughter of one of the richest men in the commune, took place sometime in the late winter of 1366. Celebrated in part with the distribution of three thousand oranges ordered from Lucca, the wedding was probably the most elegant social event of the year.[45]

For nine years, probably during his twenties and early thirties, Salutati had been madly infatuated with a local girl: "For nine years I was not myself," he later confessed. Neither a Beatrice or a Laura for Salutati, he had kissed and fondled his beloved a thousand times (*cum millies in amplexus iverim suos*). That they were never "befouled by any disgraceful act" was not from lack of desire.[46] Despite the extent of his sexual involvement, in his now lost *Bucolics* Salutati was to make the sweetheart of his youth into an allegorical representation of "the grace of God."[47] If the liason had not already been concluded by 1365, presumably Salutati's marriage to Caterina ended it.[48] And, although hardly

42. Ibid., fol. 19.
43. *Epist.*, I, 7–15. Novati, *Epist.*, I, 345, corrects his dating of letters, pp. 15 ff.
44. *SCS, Buggiano*, fol. 1.   45. *Epist.*, I, 15.
46. Ibid., III, 17.   47. Ibid.
48. Ibid., I, 15. The name of Salutati's first wife is established by A.C.B., *Delib.*, 8, fols. 333ᵛ–34. These pages relate to Caterina's mother's rich dowry. The extent of Tomeo Balducci's business enterprises is suggested by ibid., fols. 78ᵛ, 176, and 182.

a love-match, the arranged marriage proved to be a successful one. A good husband, endowed with a strong sexual desire but exempt from extravagant passions, rarely troubled by periods of melancholy, Salutati found it possible, despite his initial doubts, to harmonize marriage and philosophy.[49]

Salutati's election by the communal council of Vellano in June of 1366 as communal secretary temporarily interrupted his residence in Stignano.[50] Sometime toward the end of June, he and his new wife moved north to take up residence in the small commune on the hill overlooking the confluence of two branches of the Pescia River. Because Vellano was without a *podestà*, the duties of the secretary of the commune were much heavier than usual.[51] That the salary was not commensurate with the responsibilities did not make the burdens of office any more bearable. Only two years after Salutati finished his term of office the salary of the communal secretary was raised from 50 to 80 lire (from approximately 17 to 27 florins) for the six months because of the onerous nature of the duties.[52]

The latter part of Salutati's term was spent in drafting a completely new set of communal statutes. Although in Florentine territory additions were frequently made to a particular set of statutes, a complete revision was an infrequent and time-consuming undertaking. The task of revising the Vellano statutes was left to three of its citizens, who must have relied heavily on the experience of their communal secretary.[53] The original copy written on now yellowing parchment in the clear and even cursive of Coluccio Salutati and bound together with folios of *correctiones* and *additiones* from subsequent decades reposes at present in the municipal library of Pescia. Approved on December 31, 1366, the rough draft was probably taken back to Stignano by the departing notary in order to be recopied in its present form. In any case, at least by mid-February 1367, Salutati and Caterina had returned home.[54]

49. Salutati himself initially felt such a harmony impossible. A few months after his marriage he reported how distracted he had been and confirmed the truth of Cicero's words that one cannot serve both woman and philosophy (*Epist.*, I, 32). He refuted Petrarch's criticism of marriage, ibid., II, 372–73. But see below, chap. 7.

50. Ser Piero di Guerruccio of Montevettolini was secretary of Vellano in the first half of 1366 (*Dipl.*, *Arch. gener.*, ad an., April 29, 1366) and ser Gabriello di Michele Orlandi held that position in the spring of 1367 (ibid., March 16, 1367).

51. The Vellano statutes of 1367 (*SCS*, *Vellano*, and B.C.P., *Statuti di Vellano 1367*) never mention a *podestà*.

52. *SCS*, *Vellano*, fol. 51ᵛ.

53. Salutati signed the original B.C.P., *Statuti*, fol. 25. See also Ullman, *The Humanism*, pp. 7–8, n. 4.

54. A.C.B., *Delib.*, 5, fol. 11.

III

Despite prolonged absences from Buggiano caused by his notarial appointments in other communes, the official records of Buggiano indicate
that by 1367 Salutati had attained a position of political leadership in his
community. However, his ascendancy in Buggiano was not exceptional.
Intense political activity was a characteristic common to the careers of
many provinicial notaries in Florentine territory. Both by education and
experience the notary was eminently suited for a leading role in local
politics. Since by profession he dealt constantly with legal problems, he
felt at home as a legislator. From his training he knew how to draw up
regulations using the most binding legal formulas and, in negotiating
with neighboring communes, he was in the best position to achieve his
own commune's goals. Besides these political assets, the official posts
held in the secretariats of other governments gave the notary a mastery
of administrative detail and made him aware of the problems confronting his own locality and of possibilities for their solution. Unlike the
tradesmen and landowners of the community, moreover, the notary
was less tied to a daily routine and was often able to devote days to an
assignment without severely damaging his private interests. Ultimately,
he was in the best position to profit financially from communal service.
The salaries of public office were insignificant, but participation in government opened opportunities to do notarial work for the commune
and to go on embassies which paid relatively well. Patriotism and private interest become exceedingly difficult to distinguish in such cases.

The *Deliberazioni* of the commune of Buggiano do not begin early
enough to show the first entry of Salutati into local politics. Nor does
the first volume of this series, that dated 1357–61, contain the records
of the meetings of the communal councils. It consists rather of an incomplete collection of audits drawn up by a succession of syndics, who
were called in periodically to examine the accounts of officials charged
with receiving and disbursing public funds over a four-and-a-half year
period. Only five of the seven existing audits, covering a period of forty-
two months, include the names of the members of the ten-man college
that headed the communal government.[55] This body, referred to as the

55. Although the series of *Deliberazioni* in the communal archives at Borgo-a-Buggiano
runs almost without interruption down to the present day, the relevant volumes are listed
in the inventory as follows: *Deliberazioni, 1357–1361* (4), *1367–1373* (5), *1370–1372*(6), *1373–*
(6), *1373–*(6), *1373–1376*(7). Until 1978 these volumes had the numbers 11–14 respectively
and were cited accordingly in my prior writings. Volumes 5 and 7 also are paginated dif-
ferently from the original pagination (which I followed in my previously published ar-

Ten Defenders of the Commune, was elected four times a year. All of the audits, on the other hand, omit the names of the twenty or twenty-five men called Councillors, who were charged with ratifying the actions of the Ten Defenders.

Despite these lacunae the earliest list of communal officials found in this volume of audits shows Salutati as one of the Ten Defenders of the Commune for the trimester December 1356–February 1357.[56] Moreover, less than two years later, the audit for the period June-November 1358 mentions him as a Defender for the trimester September-November of that year.[57] Another source tells us that in August 1358, together with ser Giovanni Lemmi of Buggiano, he appeared before the vicar of the province, Pazzino Strozzi, to plead the case of Buggiano in its border dispute with Uzzano and the latter's dependency, La Costa.[58] That Salutati was already recognized as an important member of the local Guelf party is confirmed by the fact that in 1360 he was one of the eight Guelfs of Stignano allowed by the vicar to carry arms when traveling outside Buggiano.[59]

The absence of *Deliberazioni* from the last half of 1361 to the beginning of 1367 makes it difficult to say anything definite about Salutati's political career during these years. We have already seen that he seems to have been almost continually in residence in Stignano from mid-1363 to mid-1366, when he went to Vellano, and the set of revisions made to

ticles). The first volume marked *Deliberazioni, 1357–1361*, contains deliberations only in the first five detached folio pages, and these are for the years 1373 and 1375. Folios 6–74ᵛ contain audits made of the accounts of the communal officials during the years designated on the cover. From fol. 75 on there are hundreds of loose sheets all relating to the sale of the gabelles of the commune from 1367 up to the second decade of the fifteenth century. At the very end of the volume, in nine folio pages (in mediocre condition), are the remains of the *Statutes of 1367* relating to the sale of gabelles. The volume marked *Deliberazioni, 1367–1373*, records the first real deliberations. They probably began in January 1367 (the first legible date is February 8, fol. 4, and end with November 1369, fol. 263ᵛ). The deliberations from fol. 264 to the end concern meetings held in November and December 1372. The *Deliberazioni, 1370–1372* and *1373–1376* are in order except that the latter volume terminates with deliberations of 1375. Of the audits in volume 4, those for part of 1357, all of 1359, and half of 1361 are missing.

This is not the first time these registers have been used for the study of Salutati. Augusto Mancini used *Delib.* 8 and 10 in writing his *Sulle tracce del Salutati* (Lucca, 1920), but oddly enough the Lucchese historian did not investigate the first four volumes of the series or systematically examine those he did use.

56. A.C.B., *Delib.*, 4, fols. 73ᵛ–74.   57. A.C.B., *Delib.*, 4, fol. 32.

58. The document in the hand of ser Jacopo di ser Tuccio of Castelfranco is found in the office of the Mayor of Uzzano in a cabinet to the right of the door on entering from the council chamber. Of the sixteen parchments it is the ninth.

59. B.C.P., *Priorista pesciatino*, fol. 74. For the variety of notarial tasks he performed for Buggiano between 1358 and 1361, see my "Coluccio Salutati," pp. 42–43, n. 6.

the communal statutes of Buggiano in February 1366 gives a fair indication of the political position which Salutati had attained by that time. These statutes provided for a reorganization of the communal government: the Ten Defenders were reduced to six and a new body, the Captains of the Guelf party, was created to supervise the communal military organization, hitherto controlled by the Defenders.[60] In addition to the Defenders and the Captains, the General Council of the Commune was to consist of eight men, called the Councillors of the Guelf party, and sixteen others with the simple title of Councillors. As before, all these officials were to be chosen by lot. In the case of the new college of the Captains the statutes stipulated that thirty-six men from the commune were to be chosen as candidates for the office, eighteen of these to be from Buggiano and six each from Stignano, Colle, and Borgo. The names of these men were to be placed in a special purse from which six names would be drawn every three months. These six were to be the holders of the office for the coming trimester. Of six seats Stignano and Buggiano had two apiece and one each went to Colle and Borgo. Membership in this new executive body was, therefore, highly restricted. While the method of choosing the other new body, the Councillors of the Guelf party, was not specified in the document itself, the frequent appearance of communal leaders in both the new colleges strongly suggests that similar limitations applied to it. Given the incomplete nature of the audits for the years 1356–61, it is impossible to determine whether this represented any innovation. Probably the provisions were refinements of already existing techniques designed to concentrate power.

As for Salutati himself, the arrangement is extremely interesting. Because the ratio of population was three to four, it is understandable that Stignano was assigned the same number of seats in the college of the Captains as was Buggiano.[61] But the important point is the relation of the number of men eligible in the four settlements to the number of seats assigned to each. Whereas eighteen men were to be nominated from Buggiano for two seats and six for one seat in both Colle and Borgo, in Stignano six men were put up for two places. What was the justification for such a distribution since the number of men eligible in a particular settlement had nothing to do with the ratio of power between that settlement and the others? It was obviously a means of concentrating the political power of Stignano in the hands of fewer people

60. *SCS, Buggiano*, fol. 2.   61. See my "Coluccio Salutati," p. 31, n. 1.

and thereby of increasing the chances that the leading men from this settlement would be able to participate more regularly in the General Council of the Commune. Salutati, the only major political figure in the communal government from Stignano, probably had great influence in devising this particular scheme. His almost continual presence in the assembly, most frequently as Captain or Councillor of the Guelf party, during his periods of residence in the commune between 1367 and 1374, proves that the device served him well.

Only in 1367, when for the first time we have the actual minutes of the meetings of the communal councils, can we observe the political role of Salutati on a day-to-day basis. As the records begin, Buggiano appears confronted with the problem of improving its military defenses. The commune had been lax in maintaining its military organization and now, following a visit of inspection by Bardo de' Altoviti, one of the Officials of the Castles in Florence, it had to take steps to repair its defenses and reform its militia.

On February 12, a committee of five was set up to supervise the operations and to make certain that every able-bodied man in the commune had the required military equipment. Forty specially designated citizens, including Salutati and his brother, Currado, were ordered to equip themselves with armor (probably a breastplate) within three days or suffer a penalty. All were to be ready for an inspection to be called at the will of the *podestà*.[62] On the same day various officials were elected for overseeing the building of new fortifications in the four settlements (fol. 4ᵛ). Two days later, acting on ser Niccolò di ser Cecco's motions, the commune voted to pay for the work by providing one hundred lire from the communal treasury and on February 17 the secretary of the commune, ser Luca Grazia of Serravalle, went to Pescia to arrange for the purchase of the necessary materials (fol. 11). The most expensive reconstruction required, however, was on the castle of Buggiano and the council hoped to induce the Florentines to pay for this work.

Salutati, who had been in Vellano for part of the first trimester of 1367 (December-February) was on February 28 chosen by lot as one of the eight Councillors of the Guelf party for the next period (fol. 15). During the following three months he took charge of the commune's negotiations with Florence (fol. 21ᵛ). On March 16 he and Giuntino Dogi were delegated to make the first recorded embassy concerning this matter to the Officials of the Castles in Florence. The embassy did not leave

62. A.C.B., *Delib.*, 5, fols. 4ᵛ–5 and 8ᵛ.

until March 28 and returned after three days to report to the Ten Defenders. According to the ambassadors the commission ordered the commune to repair the roofs of the fortress at its own expense (fol. 24ᵛ). The matter was debated by the assembly on April 4 and finally, on a motion by Giuntino, Salutati was given full authority to deal with the commission in Florence. The General Council hoped that Florence could at least be convinced to share the cost (fol. 25). Salutati took with him Mingo Turini and on the 10th, after an absence of five days, the two men returned to disclose the results of the assembly (fol. 25ᵛ).

The Florentines remained adamant. A letter brought from the Executor of Florence, one of the high executive officials of the Republic, ordered the commune to bear the financial burden and, admitting defeat, the Council decided that an assessment would have to be levied (fol. 27). It then commissioned Salutati and Turini to return to Florence to complete the arrangements for the area's defense organization. Thus, Salutati took the road to Florence for the third time in a month. This trip consumed five days, one spent in Pescia and four in Florence, and with that the matter drops out of the register.[63]

During the spring and summer Salutati undertook a number of other missions. The *Deliberazioni* recorded no less than six one-day trips to the court of the vicar in Pescia between May and July.[64] On April 21, moreover, he was sent to Uzzano to obtain a list of the lands held by citizens of Uzzano and La Costa in Buggiano territory.[65] This was connected with the problem of forcing those living outside the communal jurisdiction but owning land within it to pay taxes—a recurring preoccupation of the communal government. It was probably this situation that Salutati had in mind when, on July 22 (he had been elected Captain of the Guelf party for June-August), he proposed a law designed to compel all the "foreign" landowners to pay their taxes within fifteen days or face penalties.[66] One month later he returned to this matter in a speech, this time asking the General Council to decree that all "foreigners" who had not satisfied their obligations on land held within the commune be forbidden the privilege of sowing crops on that land.[67] The

---

63. Ibid., fols. 26–26ᵛ. According to the statutes of 1366, *SCS, Buggiano*, fol. 6, for any embassy traveling to a place twelve miles or more from Buggiano the ambassador was to receive twenty *soldi* (one lira) per day. If, however, the embassy lasted over four days only fifteen *soldi* were paid per day for the additional time. A local assignment between March 1 and October 1 earned the ambassador six *soldi* if a notary, or five if not; at other times of year the rate was five and four respectively (fol. 16).

64. Ibid., fols. 33ᵛ, 35ᵛ, 38ᵛ, 41, 49, and 51.   65. Ibid., fol. 28.

66. Ibid., fol. 53ᵛ.   67. Ibid., fol. 59ᵛ.

"foreign" tax delinquents in this year seem mainly to have been the people of Uzzano but Buggiano was also having difficulties with another neighbor, Massa e Cozzile.

Initially, the people of Massa appear to have taken control of the road that ran along the boundary of the two communes. Certain citizens of Massa began, in fact, to take down the posts marking the communal boundaries.[68] On May 3 Salutati proposed that the Defenders and Captains be given full authority to deal with the matter. They, in their turn, appointed a ten-man committee including Salutati to inspect the boundary line.[69] The problem was not easily settled and on May 27 another trip to the borders was ordered while embassies were sent to the vicar on the 26th and again on the 30th. At least this latter meeting was attended by delegates from Massa.[70] Also on the 30th Buggiano decided to send to Lucca to obtain documents to support its case. The former dominant power in the valley, Lucca was believed to have in its archives records which would establish the true boundaries. The ambassador selected for this task was Andrea Mini.[71] Mini left Buggiano carrying with him a letter from Salutati addressed to ser Andrea ser Conte, a Ghibelline notary who sometime before had fled Buggiano and who now was probably serving in the chancery of Lucca. In the letter Salutati asked Conte to aide Andrea Mini in his effort to obtain proof of Buggiano's claim. Apparently, ser Andrea refused and on July 8 Salutati sent off a second letter, this time bitterly upbraiding the former resident of Buggiano for his lack of feeling for his country.[72] Similarly, years later, when he was Chancellor of Florence, Salutati would use such personal letters to reinforce his official attempts to achieve a particular end.

During the third trimester of 1367 Salutati was extremely active in the assembly.[73] June was the month when the gabelles, the indirect taxes placed by the commune on wine, bread, oil, and other commodities were put up for sale for the coming year. Elaborate regulations sur-

68. *Dipl.*, *Massa*, May 23, 1367. According to the document, the vicar ordered the posts restored.

69. *Delib.*, 5, fols. 31ᵛ, and 32ᵛ.   70. *Ibid.*, fols. 38ᵛ, 39ᵛ, and 41.

71. Ibid., fol. 42.

72. Novati, *Epist.*, I, 20–21 and 26–29. By July Andrea Mini was able to see the archives after paying one *lira* to an employee. On July 22 the commune paid "Andree Mini quos de suo solvit quando ivit Lucam pro communi, Bartolomeo, filio olim ser Bonagiunte Guarzonis, pro videndo cartas et scripturas confinium et terminorum territorii communis Buggiani et Masse—solidos viginti" (A.C.B., *Delib.*, 5, fol. 51).

73. Ibid., fol. 38. He held the office of Captain of the Guelph Party for June through August. During this time he also was a member of an unpaid committee of five in charge of weights and measures in the territory (ibid., fol. 48ᵛ).

rounded both the gabelles themselves and the method of farming them. Each one was to be sold individually at auction to the highest bidder. On June 11 Salutati nominated ser Jacopo Rigozzi and Giunta Lani to supervise the sale of contracts for the coming year.[74] That afternoon and in the following days he also attended the bidding and, in addition to witnessing a number of the sales, acted as bondsman for several of the buyers.[75] There is no indication, however, that he personally purchased or bought interest in a gabelle either at this time or in later years.[76] Two days after the nomination of the commissioners for these sales, on June 13, eight men including Salutati were chosen by the General Council to correct the statutes of the gabelles. The completed work was ready for ratification on July 22.[77]

Other matters appearing in Salutati's speeches before the assembly in these summer months are local ones such as the new baptismal font to be placed in the Abbey of Buggiano and the payment of a notary for work done for the commune.[78] The meeting of August 19, however, was an important one for him personally. During the discussion four motions were proposed, three by Salutati.[79] The fourth, offered by his friend, ser Jacopo Rigozzi, concerned Salutati himself. From Rigozzi's motion it appears that Salutati had been elected Chancellor and Notary of Legislation for the Commune of Todi (*cancellarius et notarius reformationum communis Tuderti*), and, prior to confirming him in the office, Todi demanded a promise from Buggiano that it would never grant Salutati the right of reprisal against Todi or its citizens for any matter arising from the administration of his office.[80] Rigozzi moved that the promise be given and the assembly agreed unanimously. On August 23, Salutati appeared in the General Council for the last time and within the week he was at Todi, not to return to Stignano for two and a half years.[81]

---

74. Ibid., fol. 43.

75. Apparently one or more of the gabelles had already been sold before June 11, because the final clauses of a contract dated June 7, 1367, appear at the top of A.C.B., *Delib.*, 4, fol. 75. This gabelle was sold to a "Niccolò . . . " and Salutati went bond for him. He also acted in the same capacity on June 20 (fol. 75ᵛ). On June 11 he witnessed a sale (fol. 76).

76. His brother, Currado, however, was a purchaser of gabelles (marginal note, June 16, 1370, fol. 77ᵛ).

77. A.C.B., *Delib.*, 5, fol. 44ᵛ. The nine loose sheets of the statute are found at the end of volume 4.

78. Ibid., fols 53ᵛ and 45ᵛ.   79. Ibid., fols. 59–60ᵛ.

80. Ibid., fol. 59.

81. Ibid., fol. 63ᵛ. Not coincidentally with the departure of Coluccio his brother Currado began to appear frequently in the *Deliberazioni*. On the same date he was elected a Defender. After Salutati's definitive departure from the Valdinievole in 1374 Currado played a major role in local politics. He also held various appointments in the Florentine provin-

IV

Salutati's appointment in Todi represented a successful conclusion to his efforts, evident at least as early as January 1366, to leave the Valdinievole. Sometime between January 26 and 29, just before his marriage to Caterina, Salutati became a member of the Guild of Judges and Notaries in Florence.[82] In so doing he was taking advantage of a law passed by the Florentine government in 1364 or 1365 offering guild membership to certain groups of provincial notaries under very attractive conditions. Although one can only guess at the motive behind this new statute, it probably represents an effort on the part of the Republic to define the relationship between the guilds of the capital and the crafts and professions of areas newly acquired under the terms of the Treaty of Pescia. One section of the law contained a provision allowing men practicing an art in the recently annexed territories to enter the appropriate guild of the capital without paying an entrance fee. At the same time, however, the privilege appears to have been extended to areas

---

cial government through his brother's influence. He was Castellan of Montopoli in 1377; that of Mangone in 1378 (Marzi, pp. 133–34, n. 8); that of Montecatini in 1381 (*Epist.*, IV, 409); and Captain of Pistoia in 1383 (*Epist.*, II, 65). Coluccio arbitrated a dispute between the communes of the Valdinievole in June 1386 in which Currado served as procurator for Buggiano (ibid., IV, 448–52). Currado died in the same year (A.C.B., *Delib.*, 8, fols. 229 and 249).

The second brother of Coluccio, Giovanni, followed in the footsteps of his elder brothers in politics. The Buggiano registers are replete with information on him and his branch of the family. He died sometime after March 5, 1423 (*Delib.*, 13, fols. 52ᵛ–53) after having most of his extensive property holdings confiscated for communal debts. The third brother of Salutati, Andrea, died comparatively young. Alive in the summer of 1370 (ibid., 6, fol. 67ᵛ), when drawn for his first office in the General Council on May 28, 1375, he was marked *mortuus* (ibid., 7, fol. 275).

82. AGN, *Libri d'atti e d'entrata*, 90–93, contain an incomplete record of new matriculations for the years 1350–74. Sometime in the seventeenth century when the collection was more complete a *spoglio* was made of matriculation for the years 1349–1414. Those for the period May 1365–December 1369 are found in B.N.F., *Naz.*, II, IV, 399, *Spogli di Cosimo della Rena*, pp. 359–91. A copy of the list of new members is found in ibid., 393, pp. 234–36. Under January 1366, the writer of the *spoglio* included the name of Salutati as one of the new members, ibid., 399, p. 362: "Ser Coluccius quondam Petri Coluccii de Stigniano, com(m)unis Buggiani, provincie Vallis Nebula, mata. 107" (the page in the missing *Libro d'atti* where this notice was found). His enrollment occurred between January 26 and 29. On the first date a provision was passed by the guild (AGN, 748, *Provv. e delib. del Proconsolo*, fol. 5ᵛ) allowing a mass admission of new members in accordance with guild legislation of the previous year (see next note). On January 29 along with other guild members Salutati posted his bond for the coming year (AGN, 606, *Comparse ed altri atti avanti al Proconsolo del 1365 e 1366*, ad an.): "Ser Coluccius Pieri de Stigniano, notarius, comparuit et promisit et cavit ut supra (pro quo, eius precibus et mandatu, fideiuxit ut supra)— Tomasius Bernardi Viviani su(b)mit(t)ens se et ser Arrighus Dominici Pauli, notarius et ut supra quilibet eorum insolidum—approbatum per supradictos approbatores per unum annum."

such as the Valdinievole and the Lower Valdarno. Why this second group was included is unclear, but the offer was quite similar to the one contained in the original *capitoli* granted these communes at the very beginning of their subjection to Florence.

Perhaps the Florentine government hoped by means of this grant to bind individuals in the outlying areas more closely to the city. In the case of communes in the Valdarno and Valdinievole the privilege might have been regarded as a reward for their loyalty and courage during the Pisan War (1362–64) when these regions had taken the brunt of the enemy attacks. No one was apparently coerced into joining the respective Florentine guilds: the pacts that had permitted these provincial notaries to practice outside their own communes—both in Florence and in the territories—seem to have remained in effect.

What we know of this new legislation affecting the guilds comes from the registers of the Guild of Judges and Notaries. On June 21, 1365, the guild records indicate that the guild's council discussed the matriculation of new members. The provision resulting from this discussion described the arrangement for admitting candidates requesting admission on the basis of the exemptions extended by the statute.[83] Eager to increase their enrollment, even on the basis of the generous terms offered to the candidates, the guild council took advantage of the situation to allow any and all worthy candidates to become members after passing only one examination rather than the usual two—actually, on this occasion the two examinations were to be combined in some way. Those

---

83. The section relevant to the Valdinievole is as follows (AGN, 28, *Provv. e delib. del Proconsolo*, June 21, 1365, fol. 138–38ᵛ): "Et cum nonulli sint de infrascriptis terris et locis que venerunt sub iurisdictione communis Florentie, videlicet, Bibiena, Soci, Romena, Gello, Ragiuolo, Montaione florentino, Prato, Montecatino, Castrofranco Vallis Arni Inferioris, Sancta Cruce, Ficechio, Santa Maria ad Montem, Montetopolis, Sancto Geminiano, Staggia, Colle Vallis Else, Cerbaria, Montecarello, Alpibus Ubaldinorum, Valle Nebula et eius partibus, Valle Ambre, et aliis locis que de novo venerunt sub iurisdictione communis Florentie seu venient in futurum; qui notarii exercent artem et offitium in comitatu Florentie et habere dicuntur patta cum communi Florentie per que possunt in civitate et comitatu Florentie dittam artem notarie et offitium libere exercere; et cum per formam statuti Florentie notarii existentes de locis supra dittis debeant ad dittam artem recipi et admitti sine aliqua solutione; quod domini proconsul et consules ditte artis presentes et qui pro tempore fuerint, possint eisque liceat recipere et admittere in dittam artem et collegium et in matriculam ditte artis describi ad primam et secundam examinationes simul et semel uno et eodem tempore omnes et sing(u)los de dittis terris et locis et cuiuslibet alterius terre vel loci que vel quod de novo venirent seu venerint sub jurisdictione communis Florentie in notarios ditte artis. Dummodo illi qui reciperentur, si tempore submissionis erant seu essent notarii vel benefitium seu privilegium haberent a communi Florentie tale quod admitti deberent absque ulla solutione, solvant et solvere teneantur et debeant ditte arti in totum florenos auri tres. Et illi qui non fuissent seu non essent tempore submissionis notarii vel huiusmodi benefitium seu privilegium non haberent, solvant in totum ditte arti florenos quinque."

wishing to take the examination and enter the guild could do so at the normal rate set by guild statutes. For individuals already notaries in the newly annexed areas and in those newly privileged by the communal statute the same examination was required but they were to pay a fee of only three florins, while candidates in the same areas who were not yet notaries but who wished to join the Florentine guild had to pay five.

For those provincial notaries with "pacts," it is not at all clear what advantages they hoped to derive from membership. There was certainly the honor of belonging to one of the greatest guilds in the capital at a reduced expense of time and money; yet membership was still not free and required some effort. Since the pacts allowed notaries holding them to work throughout the Florentine dominion, what did a notary possessing one stand to gain? In fact, the response of the majority of the notariate in the Valdinievole seems to have been negative. Among the few who did join at this time was Salutati.[84]

An examination of the careers of the notaries from the Valdinievole who joined the guild prior to June 1365 supplies a probable motive for his action. Ser Gabriello di Michele Orlandi of Pescia was a member of the guild and in 1365 was assistant to ser Pietro di ser Grifo, *Notaro delle Riformagioni* of Florence.[85] The previous year another guild member from the province, ser Naddo di ser Nepo of Montecatini, had been among ser Pietro's assistants and in 1365 had become a Florentine citizen along with his brother, ser Jacopo, also a member of the guild and interested in working in Florence.[86] By contrast, ser Antonio di Andrea of Monte-

---

84. Ser Niccolò di Jacopo of Montecatini joined the guild in September 1365 (B.N.F., *Naz.*, II, IV, 399, p. 365), Coluccio and Paolo di Paganello Renuci of Pescia in January 1366 (ibid., p. 362). Ser Niccolò (January 26, 1366), ser Coluccio and ser Paolo (January 29) posted their bonds for the coming year (*AGN*, 606, *Comparse*, ad an.). Ser Simone Martini of Monsummano is listed in the same register as posting a bond on January 14, but his name is then crossed out. *Naz.*, II, IV, 399, p. 385, shows him joining the guild in 1368.

In addition to the three new members, the *Comparse* gives five other notaries designated as coming from communes in the Valdinievole. These must have matriculated prior to 1365. Ser Antonio Nesini of Uzzano (January 24) never appears anywhere in the documents regarding the Valdinievole in the third quarter of the century and was probably a resident of Florence. The other four are: ser Jacopo and ser Naddo di ser Nepo of Montecatini (January 14 and 16), ser Gabriello di Michele of Pescia (January 12), and ser Antonio Andrea of Montecatini (August 4—late because of absence). Perhaps there were other members from the Valdinievole who did not post bond in that year, but there could not have been many judging from an examination of other registers of the guild. Ser Manno di Dominico of Vellano was listed as paying dues in 1368 (AGN, 92, *Libri d'Atti*, fol. 125) but is not listed as joining the organization 1365–68.

85. *Provv. reg.*, 53, fol. 28.

86. Ibid., 52, fol. 10ᵛ. He becomes a citizen (fol. 111) along with his brother ser Jacopo, but restrictions were placed on their holding offices for twenty-five years.

catini held an important post outside Florentine territory in 1365 as notary of the *podestà* of Bologna and the following year also received a notarial appointment abroad.[87]

The obvious conclusion to be drawn from this list of men from Salutati's province who had, prior to mid-1365, become members of the Florentine Guild of Judges and Notaries is that, while the pacts insured the provinicial notary the right to practice throughout the Republic, they were insufficient to permit him to hold a position of importance in the capital or in a foreign state. When no legal requirement existed, guild membership certainly facilitated one's admission to the lucrative posts available in the major cities.

In joining the Florentine guild Salutati probably had this goal in mind. The opportunity was offered by the Florentine statute of 1364–65 but Salutati's grasping of it, when so many others let it pass, stemmed from his desire to leave the Valdinievole for a wider world. By 1366 he had been working as a provincial notary for fifteen years. During that time he had practiced in a number of provinces and might even have rogated some private acts in Florence itself. In the 1360s he had spent a good deal of time in the capital on business for his commune and, having established a number of friendships with intellectual and political leaders in the city, apparently felt that his talents were recognized by them.

Had Salutati remained in Stignano for the rest of his life, he might have looked forward to a relatively comfortable existence. His notarial practice was probably large, he was certain of official appointments from time to time and his future wife's dowry would be a new source of income. But by late 1365 Stignano had become too small. Salutati was not interested in ease; he sought fame. He was a master of the Latin formulae of the notarial documents and understanding how, from the perspective of the provinces, the Florentine state functioned, knew how to get things done. But the round of petty official appointments was too confining. He thought himself a talented *dictator*, yet in these provincial offices he had no chance to compose in Latin. Official correspondence at this level had to be in Italian. Already in middle age, unless he found a way out of this narrow circle, he would die within it, unknown.

Perhaps it was his imminent marriage which served to crystallize feelings that had been working in him for a long time. The application for membership in the Florentine Guild of Judges and Notaries in Janu-

87. B.N.F., *Naz.*, II, IV, 399, p. 369.

ary 1366 was in fact only the initial step. Once matriculated he was able
to submit his name for office not only in Florence but also in other cities
outside the Republic. It was a common practice for the name of a city
to be drawn at random and then for a candidate to be elected from a
list of notaries from that city who had expressed an interest in the position. He had doubtless hoped that something in Florence would ma-
terialize, but either through influence of friends or the luck of the draw,
the strife-torn commune of Todi in papal territory offered him his first
important post. He was too eager not to seize an opportunity to win
glory.

CHAPTER 3. INTELLECTUAL BEGINNINGS (FROM STUDENT YEARS TO 1367)

I

To advance one's knowledge of ancient literature in the Valdinievole in the mid-fourteenth century required an interest in learning and a force of will far beyond the ordinary. Books were available in Florence, only a day's ride away, but the young notary knew no one in the city who might lend them, and manuscripts were exceedingly expensive. Salutati probably brought a few volumes with him from Bologna and occasionally borrowed one from a local notary, the schoolmaster, or a priest. Since men like ser Giovanni di Lemmi of Montecatini, Maestro Jacopo da Uzzano, and the priest Michele of Stignano doubtless had modest libraries, the opportunities for reading were increased by mutual exchange.[1] In time he could compile a collection both through occasional purchases and by copying borrowed texts in his own hand, but the process was a slow one.

In Salutati's case the lack of codices in the Valdinievole was not the only obstacle to his undertaking a regular program of reading. Caught up in a new life, he was faced with the problem of building up a private clientele and of mastering the intricacies of an official notarial post. Nevertheless, in his new situation he maintained his interest in ancient literature. Whether he came to Florence expressly for that purpose or was there on an official assignment for Pescia or another commune, Salutati was present in the cathedral in 1351 or early in 1352 when Zanobi da Strada, still a teacher of rhetoric in the city, presented a long public lecture on the allegorical interpretation of portions of the sixth book of Virgil's *Aeneid*. He might even have taken notes on the lecture, so detailed was the account of Zanobi's words included in the *De laboribus Herculis* forty or fifty years later.[2]

---

1. For ser Giovanni see, *Epist.*, I, 35–39. Salutati in a letter of 1370 (ibid., I, 128) written to Maestro Jacopo observed how strange it was to write a letter to him "quo prius in domestico atque patrio, ut ita loquar, pulvere desudarem, quam in hoc eloquentie gignasio forinsecus experirer." Salutati characterized Michele of Stignano in 1365 as interested in "bonarum artium studia" (ibid., I, 8).

2. Berthold L. Ullman, *The Humanism of Coluccio Salutati*, Medioevo e umanesimo, vol.

What had been an interest, however, became a passion after 1354 or 1355. Many years later Salutati described what happened in the terms of divine intervention. There was first of all his reading of Ovid, whom he doubtless knew from his school days in Bologna. Now suddenly, "as if by divine intervention," Ovid inflamed him with a new love of poetry and he was led, "as if by God's gift," to read all the ancient poets.[3] It was in all probability this reading of Ovid which influenced him in October 1355, while working in Santa Maria a Monte, to spend the substantial sum of four florins for four manuscripts: Priscian's *Institutiones grammaticae* and the writings of Virgil, Lucan, and Horace.[4] The inspiration from Ovid perhaps came to Salutati through reading the *Metamorphoses*, and in 1357 he was able to add to his collection of the poet's work by purchasing a copy of the *Fasti* in Florence.[5]

As an old man, Salutati gave no credit to his early training in Bologna for preparing the ground for this compelling attraction to poetry. He mentioned only the text of Ovid and the presence of God. In much the same way Salutati in his sixties looked back on his long interest in orthography. Again he felt he had come to realize the importance of proper spelling without a teacher, guided only by his own intelligence and the hand of Providence. Writing these remarks in 1391, oddly enough to the son of his former teacher, Pietro da Moglio, Salutati noted that this concern first began thirty-five years before, or, about the time he purchased Priscian's textbook.[6]

Da Moglio had not neglected poetry in his classroom. (See chap. 1.) Indeed, Salutati had probably encountered there for the first time the very text of Ovid that later provoked the sudden intense feeling for

---

4 (Padua, 1963), pp. 42–43. The passage in question is in *De laboribus Herculis*, ed. Berthold L. Ullman, 2 vols. (Zurich, 1951), II, 483–86.

3. "Multa quidem sibi (Ovid) debeo, quem habui, cum primum hoc studio in fine mee adolescentie quasi divinitus excandui et accensus sum, veluti ianuam et doctorem. Etenim nullo monitore previo nullumque penitus audiens a memet ipso cunctos poetas legi et, sicut a deo datum est, intellexi, postquam noster Sulmonensis michi venit in manus" (ibid., I, 215). See Ullman, *The Humanism*, pp. 44–45.

4. Ullman, *The Humanism*, p. 167 and above, chap. 2.

5. Ullman, *The Humanism*, p. 199.

6. "In qua tamen re prefari volo me grandem natu Dei digito et ingenio, quod michi dederat, duce, in hec studia et harum rerum vestigationem intrasse rudem, sine magistro et ferme sine principio; nec tamen adhuc, licet diutius laboraverim, errores puericia conceptos et adolescentia connutritos triginta quinque annorum cura potuisse diligentiaque purgare" (*Epist.*, II, 279). Eleven years after writing this passage dated June 7, 1391, Salutati again referred to the origins of his interest in spelling as occurring over forty-six years before (ibid., III, 609). Ullman was the first to link these statements with the purchase of Priscian in October 1355 (Ullman, *The Humanism*, pp. 108–9).

poetry. At least the teacher seems to have aroused enough interest in the young adolescent so that in the year of his return to Tuscany Salutati took the trouble to attend Zanobi's lectures on Virgil in the Duomo. Moreover, even decades after his contact with Petrarchan humanism, Salutati continued to manifest views, especially in regard to poetry, that tied him closely to the older variety of classical interests which guided da Moglio's teaching.

Still, he viewed his intense love of literature as self-generated, as it probably was. Guided by a father lacking literary tastes and who was eager to see his son follow a practical career, Salutati as a youth passed through da Moglio's classroom intent on mastering *dictamen*, the key to success in the notariate. He gratefully acknowledged his master's role in helping attain his skill here. The family's increasingly precarious situation, first with Piero Salutati's demise and then the fall of the Pepoli, made him even more his father's son, bent on professional success. That desire never left him, but by his mid-twenties he suddenly awakened to the needs of his own aesthetic impulses and surrendered to the beauties of a poem. From that point on literature became the major interest of his life.

A brief examination of one of the oldest manuscripts in Salutati's library, BM *Add.* 11987, indicates how Salutati went about educating himself after the mid-1350s.[7] Already mentioned as the only known volume in his library to be copied by Salutati himself, the manuscript containing the complete *Tragedies* of Seneca and Mussato's *Ecerinis* and *Somnium* (the latter in fragmentary condition) mirrors the interests and achievements of pre-Petrarchan humanism. Although the numerous marginalia and interlinear variants could have been added at different times over the years, doubtless some of them belong to this earlier period.

The most obvious concern of the marginal notes is with orthography, etymology, and definition. Proper names are usually duplicated in the margins in the nominative case and often etymologies are supplied. When *Cerberus* appears in the text (fol. 2ᵛ; *Hercules furens*, 60) Salutati notes: "Cerberus, canis inferni a creos. caro et beros comedo. carnem vorans." Or again opposite *strigis* (fol. 11ᵛ; *H.f.*, 688) he writes: "Stix. gis, palus inferni. a sto. quia ad penam stet. vel a statim quia pota statim occidat. vel a stigeto greco. l. tristicia." In the case of other interest-

---

7. Ullman, *The Humanism*, p. 197, describes the manuscript.

ing words, the marginal notations serve as a kind of thesaurus. Anno-
tating the verb *laxari* (fol. 8; *H.f.*, 476), Salutati comments: "laxo. solvo.
amplio. scil. lasso, fatigor, infirmor, et est activum." On fol. 2ᵛ(*H.f.*, 43)
for the word *thyranni* in the text, the marginal note reads: "Tirannus.
ni. per duo. N. olim rex erat a tiros fortis. hodie a tiro. i. angustia dicitur tirannus. qui in re p(ublica) non iure principitur." The sources for
most of this information were medieval lexicographers like Isidore, Papias, Balbus, and Hugutio.

Stylistic interests are reflected in his frequent bracketing of memo-
rable lines. At times he reinforces this marking with a "No." (Nota) or
draws a hand with a long index finger pointing out the choice passage.
For example, taken by the line (fol. 6ᵛ; *H.f.*, 362): "Si eterna semper odia
mortales agent (sic)," he designates it with a bracket and a pointing finger. The only stylistic technique he seems interested in isolating is *comparatio*, and repeatedly the term *comparatio* or *co*, appears in the margins
opposite the examples. Toward the end of the *Tragedies* (fol. 168ᵛ) he
comments on the meter of the plays: "saphycum dactilicum constans
ex trocheo spondeo dactilo et duobus trocheis."

Where the text only alludes to known incidents, persons, places, or
things, Salutati often identifies them in the margins. When in a certain
context the word *torrens* is used, Salutati appropriately writes the name
of the river *Sperchyus* in the margin (fol. 5ᵛ; *H.f.*, 288). He follows the
same procedure of identification where the text alludes to the various
labors of Hercules. The margins also serve to store up useful material
found in the text. When the names of the judges of the dead in Hell
occur in the play (fol. 12; *H.f.*, 732), Salutati remarks in the margin:
"Nota tres inferni iudices." He is also sensitive to chronological errors
by the author. Commenting on Megara's curses of Lycus and her recalling the sad fate of Oedipus and others, Salutati notes (fol. 7; *H.f.*, 387–
95): "Hic Statio videtur contradicere. Nam secundum eum iam Hercules mortuus erat et deus."

Inclusion of frequent interlinear variants suggests that Salutati made
a serious effort to collate his manuscript with others. He may have had
an opportunity to do this while still in the Valdinievole.

A text like that of Seneca was a mine of information and a bounteous
source of imagery and quotation for a young writer. The manuscript
especially afforded him an opportunity to develop his vocabulary, improve his spelling, and test his critical powers. In a sense the pages of
the *Tragedies* represent a sort of dialogue between the developing scholar

and his favorite author but one which has none of the intimacy found in Petrarch's marginalia. Lacking the extensive and often very personal comments which make Petrarch's manuscripts such interesting reading, Salutati's notations appear primarily those of a technician.

Although these silent interchanges with ancient writers played a major role in his education, Salutati also sought the acquaintance of contemporaries with similar interests in poetry and scholarship. When, serving in various official capacities, he moved around the Valdinievole and neighboring provinces in the Florentine domain, he maintained contact with his friends by letter. Ser Tancredi Vergiolesi of Pistoia and Maestro Rolfo da Samminiato were two of his earliest intellectual companions and correspondents.[8] At some point, however, perhaps in 1359 but most likely in 1361, Salutati reached out for contact with greater minds.

By 1350 Petrarch's reputation rested on the tidbits of his Latin writings in circulation and second-hand reports. Certainly, some of the glamor surrounding this son of an exiled Florentine family who grew up in Southern France was associated with his Italian poetry. Moreover, the secrecy with which Petrarch guarded much of his work and the exotic style of his life excited the imagination of the age and created a public eager to read his Latin works and to share his vision. Yet there was substance to this fame. What so thrilled two generations of scholars was the sense of antiquity his words conveyed.

Sometime in the years immediately preceding the Black Death a small group of Florentines, drawn together by their common love of Latin literature and their admiration for Petrarch, began to meet informally to discuss these interests. The two great events in the history of their association were Petrarch's visits made to Florence in October 1350, on his way to Rome from Parma, and in December of the same year on his return trip.[9] By the time of these visits Bruno Casini, one of the bright young men of the group who had sent Petrarch an *epistola metrica*, had already been dead two years, but Francesco Nelli, Boccaccio, Zanobi da Strada, Lapo Castiglionchio, and Forese Donati were there to meet the poet. Francesco Bruni, another member of the circle, was employed by

8. See his letters to them, *Epist.*, I, 5–6 and 31–33.
9. Giuseppe Billanovich, *Petrarca letterato. Lo scrittoio del Petrarca*, Storia e letteratura, vol. 16 (Rome, 1947), pp. 93–96; Fortunato Rizzi, *Francesco Petrarca e il decennio parmense* (Turin, 1934), pp. 426–34 and 443–46. Billanovich's study gives an intimate description of this Florentine group, although he assumes Salutati's presence in it at too early a date (p. 191).

the Carrara in Padua and had to wait ten years to receive a personal letter from Petrarch.[10] On the other hand, the latter exchanged letters with all the other members of the Florentine circle during that decade and received personal visits from Boccaccio and Forese.

Curiously, Salutati did not establish contact with the leading members of this group until relatively late, either in 1359 or 1361. He introduced himself by dispatching a number of his odes to Francesco Nelli, Petrarch's closest Florentine friend, in the spring of one of those years. Although the first letter accompanying the poetry to Nelli is lost, the second one of July 20 and a third written on August 19 give some idea of how Salutati entered the inner circle of Florentine intellectuals.[11] The letters are plainly exultant that Nelli, whom he had never met, has agreed to acknowledge him as a friend.[12] If originally urged to send the odes to Nelli by another member of the group, Salutati was accepted into the circle following this sanction by the Prior of Santi Apostoli.

Presumably, Salutati's praise of Nelli and Petrarch was based on at least some knowledge of their writings.[13] The letter of July 20 begins with an expression of joy at Nelli's favorable reception of his poetry and continues with praise of Nelli's own eloquence, which Salutati characterizes as incomparable to that of anyone save Petrarch.[14] The letter concludes with a request for any writings of Petrarch that Nelli might have as well as for one of the Prior's succinct works. While the July

10. Ullman, *The Humanism*, p. 42. Nelli apparently tried early to bring Bruni to Petrarch's attention. In his second letter to Petrarch of January 20, 1351, he wrote of the meeting of the circle "ad cenam splendidam extollendi viri Francisci Bruni de Florentia": Henri Cochin, *Un amico di Francesco Petrarca* (Florence, 1901), p. 52.

11. The two letters to Nelli are dated July 20 (*Epist.*, IV, 619–21) and August 19 (ibid., IV, 241–45). Novati dated them as written sometime between 1351 and 1363 (pp. 619 and 241). The earlier letter refers to a group of Salutati's odes read by Nelli (p. 619). For the dating of these letters see my "Toward a Biography of Coluccio Salutati," *Rinascimento*, 2nd ser., 16 (1976), 20–25.

12. Salutati writes on 19 August: "me non parum arbitror esse felicem, quem sic secundo celo natale solum produxit, quod tuam amiciciam me ignotum acquisivisse conspicio" (*Epist.*, IV, 245). "Ignotum" could of course refer to the fact that Salutati was a humble notary, but it is most likely that this should be taken to mean that the two had never met or had done so only recently (see ibid., n. 1, for Novati's similar interpretation).

13. No definite reference to Petrarch's work exists in Salutati's writings before 1367 (*Epist.*, I, 35) when Salutati echoes Petrarch's *Variae*, 2, in arguing for the use of the singular second person. From 1368 on (ibid., I, 57) he frequently mentions Gnato (Ter., *Eunuchus*). This probably derives from *Var.* 29 (as emended by Cochin, *Un amico*, p. 3 ff.). As Ullman wisely suggests in *The Humanism*, p. 242, the fact that Salutati mentions a number of Petrarch's works in his letter on the humanist's death in 1374 does not mean that he possessed or even read the works themselves. There is, moreover, no way of dating Salutati's Latin versions of two of Petrarch's sonnets, published by A. Zardo, *Il Petrarca e i Carraresi* (Milan, 1887), pp. 306–7. See Appendix I.

14. *Epist.*, IV, 620.

letter exalts the eloquence of Petrarch and Nelli, that of August deals primarily with their lofty moral lives: "Among so many shipwrecks, therefore, I consider that Petrarch and you alone have reached safe ports." Already in this very early correspondence Salutati makes the connection between eloquence and virtue, a theme that comes to dominate his writings.

Francesco Bruni's inclusion of one of these letters to Nelli in his copybook in 1363 or 1364 is proof of the strong impression Salutati's style made on the group.[15] A comparison of this letter with others in Bruni's collection written by Zanobi, Lapo Castiglionchio, Nelli, and Bruni himself shows that the young notary was less bound by the tradition of the *ars dictaminis* and had a better understanding of ancient Latin syntax than the older men.

While the July letter to Nelli contains a few exotic words like *prothogrammate* and *subsannasse*, it follows the ancient use of *tu* for the second person singular and avoids set phrases typical of medieval *dictamen*. The basic structure of Salutati's Latin sentences is unclassical in that the clauses are juxtaposed rather than integrated into an harmonious periodic construction. Introductory words to clauses like *et, nam, sed* tend more to demarcate than to join the parts into a whole. But, while beginning in the Middle Ages, such a fragmentation of the classical period remained a prime characteristic of linguistic development in both Latin and *volgari* in the Renaissance.[16]

15. Francesco Bruni's *copialettere* forms the first part of B.N.F., Magl. VIII, 1439, fols. 1^v–14^v. Although Novati never saw the actual manuscript, he published (*Epist.*, IV, 619–21) Salutati's letter of 20 July to Nelli from it (fols. 4^v–5^v). Zanobi's letter is found fols. 6^v–7, but the manuscript also contains letters to Bruni from, among others, Lapo da Castiglionchio (fols. 10^v–11), Nelli (fols. 2^v–3), and Luigi Gianfigliazzi (fols. 3^v–4), as well as a number of Bruni's own private letters and several official ones written by him during the first years of his office as papal secretary. This correspondence is extremely enlightening for a number of aspects of early humanism and it will be published in the near future. In his letter Zanobi urges his correspondent to come to Avignon to imitate his own example by making his fortune at the papal curia. One passage reads: "Habes multorum exempla, qui relictis propriis laribus hoc in loco clari evaserunt. Et si non vis ad preterita respicere, ante oculos tuos ego sim, quem ex humili loco eo provexit divina largitas quo tu vides." The best biographical sketch of Zanobi is Paola Guidotti, "Un amico del Petrarca e del Boccaccio," *Archivio storico italiano*, ser. 7, 13 (1930), 249–93.

16. Novati, *La giovanezza di Coluccio Salutati* (Turin, 1888), p. 76, stresses the extent to which Salutati preserved the old elements in his style. Th. Zielinski, *Cicero im Wandel der Jahrhunderte* (Berlin, 1908), p. 224, endorses this view while E. G. Parodi in his review of Francesco Ercole's edition of the *De Tyranno* (Berlin, 1914), in the *Bull. Soc. dantesca*, 21 (1914), 278, indicates that in the *De tyranno* most of Salutati's periods close with a velox. Also see Remigio Sabbadini, *Storia del Ciceronianismo* (Turin, 1885), pp. 11–12; Alfredo Schiaffini, *Tradizione e poesia nella prosa d'arte italiana*, Storia e letteratura, vol. 1 (Rome, 1943), p. 130; Gudrun Lindholm. *Studien zum mittellateinischen Prosarhythmus*, Studia latina stockholmiensia, vol. 10 (Stockholm, 1963), pp. 124–40; my *Coluccio Salutati and His Public*

On the other hand, heavy reliance on the *cursus* links this letter with traditional medieval rhetoric. Eighteen of twenty periods are terminated in the preferred prose meters of the Italian thirteenth-century *dictatores—planus*, *velox*, and *tardus*. Yet Salutati's attitude to the by now traditional *cursus* here seems uncertain. He cannot be unaware that four of these eighteen meters are incorrect according to the rule of *ars dictaminis* governing the arrangements of words employed to produce the meter. While the music of the *cursus* still pleases him, Salutati seeks variety both in having a few periods which lack a meter and others which, while conveying the sound, are irregular in failing to follow the rule that the final meters must be composed of words of three or four syllables or equivalent combinations of one and two syllable words.

Pietro da Moglio, who seems to have modified his own *dictamen* style only late in life, could not have been the model for this innovative style.[17] By the late 1350s, even if not yet in contact with the Petrarchan circle in Florence, Salutati may of course have utilized copies of Petrarch's correspondence as his guide. However, possibly Salutati's earliest master in the new style was the shadowy Geri d'Arezzo, who in the early decades of the fourteenth century appears to have been the first to make significant modifications in the *ars dictaminis* tradition.

That twice in later life Salutati credited Geri along with Mussato as the first representative of the new rhetorical movement may reflect both a Tuscan bias and a personal experience. Whereas he brought with him from Bologna first-hand knowledge of the widely disseminated poetical works of Mussato, he probably encountered Geri's epistolary prose for the first time only on returning to Tuscany, where it may already have played a role in modifying the style of Boccaccio's generation prior to the advent of Petrarch's work.[18] The breadth and artistry of Petrarch so

---

Letters (Geneva, 1976), pp. 23–41; and especially the excellent pages of Berthold L. Ullman, *The Humanism*, pp. 106–8, and Armando Petrucci, *Coluccio Salutati*, Biblioteca biografica, vol. 7 (Rome, 1972), pp. 93–101. On the tendency to paratactic structure in the medieval and renaissance periods see Luigi Malagoli, "Forme dello stile mediolatino e forme dello stile volgare," *Studi letterari. Miscellanea in onore di Emilio Santini* (Palermo, 1956), pp. 57–86; Raffaele Spongano, "Un capitolo di storia della nostra prosa d'arte," *Due saggi sull'Umanesimo* (Florence, 1964), pp. 39–78; and *The Earthly Republic, Italian Humanists on Government and Society*, ed. Benjamin Kohl and Ronald Witt (Philadelphia, 1978), pp. 13–14. Armando Petrucci, *Coluccio Salutati*, pp. 14–15, comments directly on the style of these letters to Nelli.

17. See chap. 1.

18. In a letter to Bartolomeo Oliari in 1395 (*Epist.*, III, 84), Salutati writes: "Emerserunt parumper nostro seculo studia litterarum: et primus eloquentie cultor fuit conterraneus tuus Musattus Patavinus, fuit et Gerius Aretinus, maximus Plinii Secundi oratoris, qui alterius eiusdem nominis sororis nepos fuit, imitator." A bit below (ibid., p. 88) he makes

far surpassed the achievements of Geri that the Aretine jurist was soon forgotten. But Salutati, surveying humanism at the end of the Trecento and perhaps recalling the chronology of development both in himself and in Tuscany generally, assigned Geri a pioneering role in the movement. While the earliest surviving letters of the brilliant young writer from the Valdinievole doubtless reflect some contact with Petrarch's correspondence, Petrarch's was a supervenient—rather than the original—influence on Salutati's private prose style.

His letter of 1360–61 to his former teacher (the letter accompanied the poem praising da Moglio's teaching of *ars dictaminis*) was patently designed to impress da Moglio with his own innovative personal style. The abrupt reference to the traditional dictum that a letter requires a conclusion served both as a closing device and as a means of bringing out the author's degree of liberation from the manuals of the *dictatores*.[19] Perhaps the master's reluctance to correspond with his former student (about which Salutati complained repeatedly) was not so much an indication of a lack of affection as it was the older man's embarrassment at being unable to match his disciple's epistolary style.

Geri the direct predecessor of Petrarch: "fecit et hoc idem seculi nostri decus, Franciscus Petrarca; fecerat et ante eum Gerius Aretinus." In 1400 he again combines Geri's name with that of Mussato in writing to Francesco Zabarella (ibid., pp. 408–9): "Duos doctores memini, vir insignis, extra gregem inter iuris consultissimos numerande, qui stilo et eloquentia hoc quartodecimo seculo claruerunt: unus, scilicet, compatriota tuus Albertinus Mussatus, cuius admiramur hystorias et habemus poemata; alter fuit Gerius aretinus, cuius versus et epistolas satirasque prosaicas non mediocriter commendamus." While Salutati perhaps knew of Mussato's historical works when still a student in Bologna, it is unlikely that he read them there. Although he mentions Geri's satires and poetry along with his letters, the epistolary style would have had the most distinctive effect on Salutati's writing. Roberto Weiss, "Geri d'Arezzo," *Il primo secolo dell'umanesimo*, Storia e letteratura, vol. 27 (Rome, 1949), p. 66, suggests: "Ma forse il lato più importante degli scritti di Geri è la rivelazione che ci forniscono circa l'esistenza di un gruppo umanistico a Firenze durante la prima metà del Trecento non dissimile dal cenacolo padovano. Gli scambi di epistole metriche con Cambio da Poggibonsi, la corrispondenza con Gherardo da Castelfiorentino, il dialogo inviato a Francesco da Barberino, i contatti con la corte di Carlo di Calabria, tutto ciò è prova dell'esistenza a Firenze di un cenacolo letterario che troverà poi continuatori tra i contemporanei del Boccaccio, tra i quali troveremo il figlio stesso di Geri, Federigo, e la cui influenza si ripercuoterà sulla Napoli angioina." My opinion is that Geri's break with strict adherence to the rules of *ars dictaminis*, while too innovative for his contemporaries—see the remnants of Francesco da Barberino's correspondence: A. Thomas, "Lettres latines de Francesco da Barberino," *Romania*, 16 (1887), 73–91—nonetheless probably helped mold the prose style of Florentine literati in Boccaccio's group before the influence of Petrarch had its effect. Lapo Castiglionchio knew Geri's work: Weiss, *Il primo secolo*, p. 108. Cf. Petrucci, *Coluccio Salutati*, p. 16. Furthermore, my assumption is that the development of the young provincial's prose style, given the greater accessibility of Geri's writings compared with those of Petrarch in the last half of the 1350s, followed the same pattern of development.

19. *Epist.*, I, 3–5. He alludes to the fifth part of the letter according to the rules of *ars dictaminis* (p. 5): "et ut epistole morem reddam, vale, mei memor. . . ."

It is not clear why Salutati delayed so long in establishing contact with the men in the Petrarchan circle. As a provincial notary without important friends in the capital, he probably had to search for a way to obtain an introduction. His own uncertainty about the value of his talents, moreover, may have hindered him in his determination to make the acquaintance of members of the group. Although Nelli later departed for Naples, Salutati became closely linked with those of the Petrarchan circle who remained in Florence. Over the next eight or nine years his letters from the Valdinievole, from Todi, and from Rome reveal that he had established close friendships not only with Boccaccio, Bruni, and Lapo but also with politically important, if less intellectually distinguished men, such as ser Niccolò Monachi, the Florentine chancellor, and the lawyers Luigi Gianfigliazzi and Filippo d'Antella.[20] On his many trips to Florence during these years he found himself welcome in their discussions and had access to their libraries. With such relationships as these he began to think seriously of breaking out of his rural existence; sensing his promise, his Florentine friends doubtless encouraged him in this ambition. Perhaps not coincidentally, in 1365–66 Salutati also began to save copies of his letters, a sign that he was starting to look on himself as a historically significant person.[21]

II

From Salutati's correspondence of the 1360s, it is difficult to detect distinctly Christian tendencies in his thought. Not that he considered himself a pagan—in 1365 he characterized Roman religion as more a "blindness and poisonous superstition" than a religion.[22] He doubtless attended church regularly and, in late 1367, already at Todi, he asked one

20. Letters to these three men are found ibid., I, 9–12, 29–31, and 39–41.
21. Salutati made copies of the letters he wished to preserve in quires: *Epist.*, III, 511, and Ullman, *The Humanism*, p. 275, n. 1. On the basis of surviving manuscripts Ullman convincingly argues that at some point in later life Salutati arranged his own correspondence into ten groups according to number, length, and chronology (pp. 272–78). Whatever letters exist apart from the ten groups were probably either stolen from Salutati's files or were conserved by his correspondents. B.N.P., *Lat.* 8572 contains the first group of letters, chronologically speaking, consisting of fifty-one letters written during the period 1365–72. Only five other letters are known for this period (Novati published four and for the fifth, see below, chap. 4, n. 115. I would assign all four in Novati to 1360–61, the two to Nelli and the first two found in *Epist.*, I, 3–6. To my mind the reason for the survival of these letters is that they were kept by their recipients and that only in 1365 did Salutati himself begin to keep his letters carefully.
22. Ibid., I, 10.

of his correspondents, a priest, to remember him in the mass.[23] During these years, however, he gives no indication that he had any acquaintance with the writings of the Church Fathers, and the only quotation from the Bible found in those letters is the proverbial "many are called but few are chosen."[24] The general impression is that his Christianity, if sincere, was not very important to his thought and had not been integrated into his preoccupation with learning.

The philosophical writings of Aristotle and those of the scholastics were equally unimportant to him at this time. The main concern of his letters was ethics, and his reading seems to have been limited to Roman poets and rhetoricians. Never systematically presented, his basic conception of ethics focused on the conflict between fortune and virtue. Superficially Stoic in its tendencies, Salutati's thought had a dramatic element that stimulated his aesthetic as well as his moral sense. But it is difficult to say how much of that element came from Cicero, Seneca, and Valerius Maximus, and how much was drawn from popular and more traditional literary currents of his own century.

The predominate feature of his thought at this time was the concept of fortune. Variously described by Salutati as envious, cruel, treacherous, and deceptive, there is no way for man to discipline her. Now raging, now enticing, she endeavors to destroy his control over the emotions.[25] As long as one leads life according to the passions, one's existence is forever agitated and futile because it is dependent on fortune's whims.[26] Salutati never analyzed his notion of fortune during these years, but clearly for him the word was more than a poetic way of describing the vicissitudes of human life. Having grown up in a century in which belief in fortune was almost universal, Salutati continued to

23. Ibid., I, 35.
24. Ibid., IV, 244. Cicero's dictum "non posse simul uxori et philosophie servire," quoted by Salutati in 1367 (ibid., I, 32), although found as Novati notes in Jerome's *Adversus Iovinianum*, I, 48 (316) (*PL*, vol. 23 [Paris, 1883], p. 291), was probably well known and its use does not indicate direct contact with Jerome. He referred once to figures from the *Old Testament* as illustrations proving that prosperity was not good for man (*Epist.*, I, 30).
25. He calls her "invidiosa" (ibid., p. 7), "truculentissima" (p. 19), and speaks of "illius perfidi prestigiosique monstri" (p. 41). In a letter of consolation written to Ugolino Orsini on the death of his father, Coluccio equates fortune with nature: "Incipe ergo ludum fortune, imo, ut verius loquar, nature fragilem condicionem agnoscere." The equation must be taken in the specific sense that, because the human body is mortal, the father's death in old age was natural. Immediately before this, however, he speaks of fortune in a general sense: "Desine igitur illi dolere; optime, crede michi, cum ipso natura egit; nescimus an malis subtractus sit. Iam videbis forte sevire fortunam, inquietare rempublicam, perturbare Italiam, regna transferre . . . " (p. 112).
26. In his second letter to Nelli (ibid., IV, 243–44) Salutati describes life lived according to the passions. His psychology of the affections is most clearly presented in a letter to Ercolano da Perugia (ibid., I, 59–61).

accept the idea without feeling any need to analyze it. Furthermore, he found justification for his acceptance in Seneca, not realizing that this fervent believer in ineluctable fate had used the term primarily for rhetorical purposes.[27]

While the essential moral combat of the individual lay for Salutati in his efforts to resist fortune, a second force impinging on human action, the stars, had to be recognized. As a young man Salutati consulted the Florentine astrologer, Dagomar, whenever he happened to be in Florence,[28] but from his scattered remarks it is difficult to determine the extent of his belief in astrology. He appears, however, to have looked on them primarily as furnishing signs to man as to whether the times were propitious or inauspicious for particular actions. Someone properly trained to interpret their message, like his friend Dagomar, might render indispensable service not merely to private individuals but to the political community.[29] Again, as in the case of fortune, Salutati probably absorbed the notion of fate or belief in the power of the stars from the general cultural climate in which he grew up, thus feeling no need either to integrate it into a scheme consistent with his conceptions of virtue and fortune or to define it in Christian terms.

Of the four major ancient ethical schools he later identified in the *De laboribus Herculis*—the Stoic, Peripatetic, Academic, and Epicurean—the Stoics had the greatest influence on Salutati through most of his life.[30] Despite the assaults of fortune and the influence of the stars, he held that man had control over his inner realm. For man the only true evil was vice and the only true good virtue: "For as that Ciceronian Platonic Socrates says, no evil of any sort can befall the good man living or dead nor is he ever forsaken by the Gods."[31] A man's wealth lay in the virtues

27. Klaus Heitmann, *Fortuna und Virtus. Eine Studie zu Petrarcas Lebensweisheit*, Studi italiani, vol. 1 (Cologne-Graz, 1958), p. 37. For analysis of fortune as a popular notion, see pp. 25–39. Also see Erhard Lommatzsch, *Beiträge zur älteren italienischen Volksdictung. Unterschungen und Texte*, Deutsche Akademie der Wissenschaften zu Berlin, Inst. für Roman. Sprachwissenschaft, Veröffenlichungen, vol. 2 (Berlin, 1951), pp. 65–102. For detailed bibliography on concepts of fate and fortune in ancient, medieval, and early modern world, see Heitmann, pp. 25–26. On Seneca and Petrarch, see Aurelia Bobbio, "Seneca e la formazione spirituale e culturale del Petrarca," *Bibliofilia*, 43 (1941), 224–91.

28. *Epist.*, I, 17.

29. Ibid., I, 15–16.

30. *De lab.*, I, 311–12. Salutati believed with the Stoics that an individual must have all the virtues to be deemed virtuous. See Cicero, *Tusc. disp.*, II, 14; Seneca, *Epist. ad Lucil.*, LXVII, 10. For Salutati, *Epist.*, I, 113, and III, 348.

31. *Epist.*, I, 19. From Cicero and Seneca he learned that wealth and honor were *commoda* not to be sought but neither to be rejected: Cicero, *De officiis*, I, 8, 25; Seneca, *Dial.*, VII, 21, 4 and 23, 1. Also *Epist. ad Lucil.*, LXXIV, 16 ff. For Salutati's expression of this view, see *Epist.*, II, 449.

he possessed; these being his own creation, fortune could neither add nor detract from them. He who possessed virtue, from whatever level of society he came, was truly free and noble.

He shared the Stoics' contempt for the ignorant mob, balloted in all directions according to the whims of fortune. As he wrote Nelli in 1361, the mass of mankind stood in subjection to this inconstant force; led by her blandishments or driven by her threats they rushed to destruction.[32] Only the man of virtue realized that the things of this world were unimportant. He feared neither the afflictions of the body nor even death itself. Rather, since the body was but the prison of the soul and this life an exile, he understood that death might even be desirable. To the virtuous man, death, fortune's final weapon against him, was not an evil: "If death is an evil, then our whole life is really evil because it leads to death."[33] Citing the *bon mot* of Silenus, probably taken from Cicero (*Tusc. disp.*, I, 48, 114), he wrote in 1365: "It is best for man by far not to have been born, and second best, to die as soon as he is born."[34] In 1374 he admitted mourning Petrarch's death day and night but characterized it as "a blind error of the mind."[35] Beyond the grave the wise man looked forward to eternal life. The Stoic confidence in virtue as its own reward was here supplemented by a vague conception of an afterlife.

He was sometimes willing, however, to concede that even the sage could not stifle all emotions. At the first onslaught of good or bad fortune a sage might be momentarily caught off balance.[36] The distinction between the philosopher and other men was that the former regained control of himself immediately after the first moments of upset. But until his last years Salutati remained ambivalent about the Stoic goal of impassivity. In the same passage he could remark that there was no true virtue without passions to prevail against and refer approvingly to the opinion of "many philosophers" who considered wise those, "who holding themselves within, are not affected by anything that happens."[37]

32. *Epist.*, IV, 243–44. On Stoic conception see Max Pohlenz, *Die Stoa. Geschichte einer geistigen Bewegung*, 4th ed., 2 vols. (Göttingen, 1970), I, 154–58.

33. Ibid., I, 317. Also see I, 19, 111–12, 163; and II, 125.

34. Ibid., I, 11.

35. Ibid., I, 199. Also see description of the wise man (ibid., I, 47): "Qui sibi ipsi sufficiat et intra se mentis presidio sit contentus atque beatus." For Salutati's early dependence on the Stoics, see Luigi Borghi, "Dottrina morale di Coluccio Salutati," *Annali della R. Scuola Normale Superiore di Pisa, lett. stor. e filosofia*, ser. 2, 3 (1934), pp. 87–88. Borghi, however, exaggerates the change which Salutati undergoes in later life. See below, chap. 13.

36. Ibid., I, 98; II, 55, 73, and 267. Cicero guided Salutati in this attack. See *De amic.*, XV, 48.

37. *Epist.*, II, 55–56. After stressing the importance of the passions he writes: "Quod si, ut plurimi philosophorum voluerunt, sapientes sunt qui, se ipsi contenti, nullis extra

A problem that perplexed him throughout his life was the relationship of virtue to glory. Both in youth and old age Salutati admitted that like others he loved to hear himself praised.[38] From his earliest letters, however, he condemned the pursuit of popular acclaim and warned his correspondents against paying heed to flatterers.[39] The praise of wise men, on the other hand, was valuable as a spur to virtue. Inspired by Cicero, he wrote: "If you remove glory and praise, you immediately destroy and extinguish zeal for the virtues."[40] A virtuous life and literary achievements would serve as a fitting basis for lasting fame, which even the sage wanted. After his "conversion" to Christianity in 1369, however, the conflict between humility and the desire for fame became problematic.[41]

Another source of ambiguity was the question of the nature of nobility. Although Salutati insisted repeatedly that true nobility was not a matter of birth or blood, but virtuous behavior, he recognized that some men had a natural disposition to virtue.[42] Without this natural gift one could perhaps do virtuous acts, but perfect virtue required a continuous disposition to do good works. Accordingly, nobility of character did not

contingentibus afficiuntur, nonne insipientia est obicere, cum aliquem voluerimus consolari? Non igitur, frater optime, cum te putem in illum status mentis evectum, unde omnes adversantis fortune casus et blandientis oblectamenta infra te videas, insistendum supervacuis arbitror." For his mature views, see chap. 13.

38. Ibid., I, 20, and III, 89.

39. Ibid., I, 8, and 69.

40. Cicero expressed the view in *Tusc. disp.*, I, 1, 4: "Honos alit artes, omnesque incenduntur ad studia gloria, iacent que ea semper, quae apud quosque improbantur." For Salutati's position, see *Epist.*, I, 70, and II, 406.

41. Ibid., I, 105, 109–10, 336–37. His way of coping with the problem of glory is detailed in chap. 10. For other citations on glory, see Alfred von Martin, *Coluccio Salutati und das humanistische Lebensideal* (Berlin, 1916), pp. 116–21; and Alberto Tenenti, *Il senso della morte e l'amore della vita nel Rinascimento (Francia e Italia)* (Torino, 1957), pp. 27–33.

42. On nobility as a matter of attainment, not birth or fortune, see *Epist.*, I, 57: "Non ego vel fortunam tuam admiror vel sanguinis nobilem fomitem, quorum unum benigne sortis, aliud seu Dei seu nature munus tes; sed tuam virtutem, qua cunctis excellis, que non alterius hominis indulgentia est, sed tuum opus conspicuum: virtutem, inquam, cui non dignitatis tue gradus luminis est, sed que in illo clariori luce refulget." Cf. Cicero, *Nat. deorum*, III, 36.87–88. Most "nobles" do not act nobly because they are given to passions (*Epist.*, I, 56–57). Also see ibid., II, 288; III, 270 and 647, and B.N. *Mad.* 17652 (formerly Gayagos 736), fol. 164. This manuscript contains nine letters (fols. 161ᵛ–171), six of which remain unpublished. A seventh not found in Novati has been published by Giuseppe Billanovich (chap. 9, n. 117 below), who intends to edit the remaining six. Some men are born with a noble nature "que semper virtutibus adest" (ibid., III, 651). Also I, 79. Again as in his discussion of virtue he seems ambivalent about the importance of struggle in the attainment of virtue. He argues (ibid., III, 652) that "difficile quidem est naturaliter incontinenti prestare castitatem vel avaro largitatem; imo, cum virtus sit circa difficile, dispositionem naturalem ad vitium certum est posse difficile removeri. Quod si dispositio foret de facili mobilis, nec tantum esset virtutis meritum nec haberet circa difficile fundamentum." Cf. Seneca's belief that virtue strengthened in hard times (*Dial*, I, 3, 2, and 5, 10).

appear to be completely within the power of the individual. He was even prepared to grant that nobility of blood provided a kind of "energy, a certain trait and inborn ethical propensity" which made the noble more fit for virtuous actions than others.[43] Yet, if a necessary condition for perfect virtue, a noble nature was only a predisposition of virtue itself: "For all virtue consists in actions."[44]

The virtuous life involved the full realization of one's essence as a human being. In distinguishing the peculiar attributes setting human beings apart from other animals, Salutati usually emphasized man's power of speech as peculiarly human, and his power of intelligence or reason as shared only with higher beings: "For if intelligence and reason, by which the human race has some common property with superior beings, are a source of beauty; if men are clearly distinguished from other living creatures because they can use words; how much more excellent than other men is he who, relying on his reason, stands forth with brilliant eloquence?"[45] If men differ from other beings in their use of words, the man who uses words best is the most human among his fellows, i.e., he who best realizes the essence of *humanitas*, the condition of truly being a man.[46] But this eloquence must be grounded in truth and therefore is intimately tied to intelligence.

At different times Salutati characterized eloquence now as a power of the will, now of the intellect.[47] In 1402, he viewed eloquence as "subordinate to wisdom and contained in it as in the sum of all things which can be known, so that whoever pursues wisdom necessarily pursues eloquence at the same time."[48] The problem of assigning eloquence either

43. *Epist.*, III, 389.
44. Ibid., I, 65, and III, 651–52.
45. Ibid., I, 79. Also see ibid., I, 77, and II, 204.
46. Speech is referred to as the "human property" in the *De nobilitate legum et medicinae: De verecundia*, ed. E. Garin (Florence, 1947), pp. 282–84.
47. *Epist.*, IV, 223. Actually he does so by implication when he writes here: "Et ad rhetoricam, que cum voluntate congreditur, veniamus." On the other hand, he makes intelligence the central human attribute, ibid., II, 204.
48. Ibid., III, 599, characterizes eloquence and wisdom as the distinguishing properties separating men from other animals. Salutati, however, then writes: "Subicitur eloquentia sapientie et in ipsa, quasi toto quodam, quod cuncta scibilia possideat, continetur, ut qui sapientie studium profitetur, simul et eloquentie profiteatur necesse sit. Quia tamen ea ratione, qua duo hec per intellectum ab invicem separantur, eloquentia rarior sapientia est, difficiliorem eam esse sapientia non inconvenienter possumus arbitrari, quoniam quidem in his habitibus, qui studio industriaque parantur quosque laboribus adipiscimur, raritas argumentum est certissimum difficultatis. Accedit ad hec, quod intentio, studium facultasque bene dicendi calcar est ut sapere concupiscamus; ut huius eloquentie studium capessende sapientie sit etiam instrumentum. Neque etiam aliquid bene dicitur quod perfectissime non sciatur. Possumus multa scire, que tamen eloqui distincte debitoque cum ornatu sermonisve maiestate nescimus; ut maxime studendum sit eloquentie, cui et sapientie studium annexum est" (p. 602). Even as presented here, how-

to the will or to the intellect, however, stemmed from the fact that it was learned through study and experience but only reached perfection in an individual possessing the highest moral character: "Eloquence is the embellishment of virtue."[49] It was to serve as a vital force in society, stirring men who were neglectful of virtue and borne down by bad habits and concern for the body to seek a better life.

The foregoing statements suggest that, despite ambiguities, Salutati's nobleman, his ethical ideal, was the orator, whose eloquence reflected the highest development of man's intellective and volitional powers. Natural talent and a disposition for virtue were prerequisites for the great orator, but intensive training was necessary to develop these gifts. Acquainted with Cicero's dictum (De orat., II, 1, 5) that the orator must know all things human and divine, Salutati from his early letters repeatedly subscribed to this proposition.[50] Usually, however, he had a narrower range of studies in mind: the artes liberales or the studia humanitatis. Liberal studies were so called in his view "not only because they are the concern of free men, not those of servile condition, but because they free mortal minds that they might more easily be drawn to virtue."[51] In practice he appeared to identify them roughly with the trivium and quadrivium.[52] At least he clearly differentiated these artes from philosophy, poetry, and theology.[53] Certainly used in such a restricted sense, the term artes liberales was insufficient to cover the range of disciplines Salutati felt necessary for training the orator. The term studia humanitatis, on the other hand, was much more satisfactory for this purpose. Although Salutati used humanitas normally in the sense of humane,[54] he frequently gave it a broader meaning. In a letter of 1401, humanitas is defined in both moral and intellectual senses:

ever, it would be difficult to rank one more important than the other, and usually he linked wisdom and eloquence together as equals (ibid., III, 79, 411, 598–99, 604; IV, 192).

49. Ibid., I, 76. He seems undecided as to whether it should be called a faculty or a power (ibid., I, 79, and 309). Normally, however, he refers to it as a faculty (ibid., I, 180; III, 411 and 506). In later years he emphasized the superiority of the will over the intellect but never clearly identified eloquence as a power or faculty of the will: see above, n. 47.

50. Ibid., I, 309; III, 411 and 605. Also see De laboribus Herculis, ed. Berthold L. Ullman, 2 vols. (Zurich, 1951), II, 419. The specific Ciceronian definition of wisdom is found in Tusc. disp., IV, 26, 57.

51. Ibid., II, 274. He considered it significant to note, in praising Giangaleazzo Visconti for removing his uncle, Bernabò, from power, that under Bernabò the "liberalium artium scole" languished (ibid., II, 150).

52. Ibid., IV, 215 ff.   53. Ibid., I, 178 and 309; IV, 186.

54. Ibid., III, 506–7. He first used the term humanitatis studia in 1369 (ibid., 106). See also, ibid., I, 229–30 and 248, for early references. He referred to Florence in 1405 as the "studiorum humanitatis . . . domicilium" (ibid., IV, 119).

For not only does this word mean that virtue which is usually called "kindness," but also experience and learning. Thus, *humanitas* signifies more than is commonly thought. Indeed the best authors, both Cicero and many others, used this word to mean learning and moral science; nor is this strange. No animal except man can learn. So that, since it is the characteristic of man to be taught and the learned are more men than the unlearned, the ancients appropriately referred to learning as *humanitas*.[55]

Again as with *artes liberales* Salutati was not very precise about the specific subjects included in the *studia humanitatis*. In a letter written about the same time as the one just mentioned, he distinguished *studia humanitatis* from *studia rationis* and *studia secretorum nature*, presumably logic and natural sciences.[56] The most definite outline of a program of study for the orator appeared in a letter of 1402 which began by rejecting Cicero's demands on the orator for total knowledge as impossible. Rather, Salutati advised the aspiring student of eloquence to acquire knowledge of the moral writings of Cicero, Seneca, and Aristotle, the works of history, and finally of that "which promises to teach the natures, the passions, and the motions of things and men." Under this last category he evidently intended to include subjects ranging from poetry to zoology, the latter an area presumably within the *studia secretorum nature*.[57]

Personally Salutati never gave up the Ciceronian ideal and his writings reflect an extensive acquaintance with all fields of learning in his own day. Yet, the range of references to authors from his earliest letters indicates that he intended the orator to focus on a central set of disciplines including the *trivium, quadrivium,* moral philosophy, history, and poetry. For training in these disciplines, moreover, he was convinced that the ancients furnished the fundamental guidance.

Taking counsel with Cicero rather than Seneca, Salutati believed that vital to character building was diligent study of great writings in prose and poetry. The ancients were the masters:

For who, I ask, without the writings of the ancients, with nature alone as a guide, will be able to explain with sufficient reason what is hon-

55. Ibid., III, 536. See the excellent *explication de texte* of this passage dealing with *humanitas* by Eckhard Kessler, *Das Problem des Frühen Humanismus. Seine Philosophische Bedeutung bei Coluccio Salutati* (Munich, 1968), pp. 44 ff. He also deals in these pages with the classical antecedents for the term.

56. Ibid., III, 586–87.   57. Ibid., III, 605.

est, what useful and what is the meaning of this battle of the useful and honorable? Doubtless nature makes us fit for virtues and secretly impels us to them but we are made virtuous not by nature but by works and learning.[58]

These men of great soul and mind discovered the way and delineated it eloquently in their works. The writings of the pagan authors not only instruct us in the art of living, but through beauty of speech their works touch our souls with the truth they contain, thereby effecting a moral reform. Repeatedly Salutati urged his correspondents to continue their studies that they might become better men. So intense was Salutati's belief in the value of study for the acquisition of virtue that he declared such study "a broad road to the summit virtue."[59] How was it possible, he asked at one point, for evil to be present where there was knowledge of the arts?[60] Thus, while the orator effectively set forth the truth in compelling words, he testified to it by the conduct of his life and served as an example to others. Believing that the first duty of every man was to serve the good of the community, Salutati considered the orator in the best position to maximize virtue in his life.

This faith in the power of ancient writings to effect the moral development of the individual helps explain why Salutati described such studies as *studia sacra*. He was not in the least embarrassed to use this phrase, normally applied to theology, to characterize the study of secular letters, and the term continued to appear in his writings until the late 1370s when, sensing its impropriety, he ceased to employ it.[61]

Naturally, Salutati doubted that many men could ever attain an extensive knowledge of the *studia sacra* and thereby reach a high level of moral development. However, among those few seriously working toward this goal mutual attraction was irresistible. Salutati himself admitted that whenever he heard of someone applying himself to these studies, a feeling of love for that person arose within him, even though he had never looked on the individual.[62] Such a common interest in studies and virtue was the only basis for true friendship. All other human relationships, that of husband to wife, son to parent, parent to child, and the like, were products of nature and inherently selfish. More precious than all these was true friendship because it alone sprang from free choice and was founded on mutual love of virtue. It was the fitting relationship for free men.[63] Salutati regarded his correspondence as the

58. Ibid., I, 106.
59. Ibid., I, 122.
60. Ibid., I, 8.

61. Ibid., I, 55, 95, and 208.
62. Ibid., I, 77.
63. Ibid., I, 47 and 117.

means by which this widely scattered community of like-minded men communicated with one another, now giving, now receiving encouragement in their common pursuit of moral excellence through *studia sacra*.

As the chronology of Salutati's writings utilized for this analysis of the model orator and his education indicates, the humanist's solution to the human predicament represents not merely a position taken in his early maturity but a lifelong view. Yet a continuity exists only in the most general fashion. The relationship of eloquence to knowledge and of both to virtue appears in very different contexts in the years before and after the development of his genuine Christian commitment. After that time his moral ideas are inseparable from theological conceptions of grace and original sin. On the other hand, in the earlier years Salutati conceived of the ethical problem primarily as a conflict of the individual with fortune and, to a degree, with fate. At this stage he was in no way working out a "layman's morality." Unlike his own followers early in the next century, he was not consciously presenting a "natural ethic" for men living without Christian Revelation, thus recognizing by implication the existence of a corresponding Christian morality. His ethical ideas seem totally determined by a reading limited to the Roman writers and to contemporary currents of thought lacking any distinctly Christian orientation.

Consequently, the early letters reveal the extent to which Salutati was still committed to the ethical tendencies of the *dictatores* and pre-Petrarchan humanists. Almost certainly the development of specifically Christian intellectual concerns in his later thought was a product of deeper understanding of Petrarch's work, more extensive reading, and personal experience. That Petrarch and Boccaccio had undergone a similar spiritual evolution reveals a fundamental characteristic of rhetorical education in early fourteenth-century Italian society. Although individual idiosyncrasies must certainly be taken into account, it was largely the fault of the aims and orientation of contemporary schools of rhetoric that these gifted and learned men, educated in important centers of culture, remained for so long largely unaffected by the categories with which Christian thinkers had previously discussed moral questions.[64]

The nineteenth-century notion that the humanists initiated a return to paganism has been repeatedly rejected in favor of the view that religious concerns played a determining role in the movement, at least in

64. See chap. 1.

its first century. In itself a correct evaluation, this later interpretation does not do justice to the extent of the humanists' contribution.[65] Rather than continuing the "religious" concerns of the thirteenth century, humanism's Christian orientation, at least in the field of rhetoric, represented an innovation. With Petrarch, first of all, began an attempt not only aggressively to reclaim for rhetoric the field of ethics, largely abandoned by the *dictatores* and of secondary concern to pre-Petrarchan humanists, but more important, an effort to re-Christianize rhetorical studies. This integration demanded a transcendence of the goals of the contemporary educational system. Petrarch seems to have achieved this by his early forties.[66] Partly with his example as a guide, both Boccaccio and Salutati developed deep religious commitments by middle age.[67] Yet Salutati's remarks on moral questions in his earliest surviving corre-

65. For a cogent summary of the four major trends of interpretation in Renaissance humanism, see Donald Weinstein's "Interpretations of Renaissance Humanism" *Journal of the History of Ideas*, 33 (1972), 165–76. My position on the religious nature of fourteenth-century humanism differs from that of a scholar like Charles Trinkaus, *In our Image and Likeness*, 2 vols. (London, 1970), primarily in my stress on religion being a *new* concern for Italian rhetoricians.

66. As noted in *Il 'De otio religioso' di Francesco Petrarca*, ed. Giuseppe Rotondo, Studi e testi, vol. 195 (Città del Vaticano, 1958), p. 71, Petrarch himself confessed: "Sic inter ecclesiasticos et religiosos viros secularibus literis delector, que et prime et aliquandiu michi sole fuerunt. . . ." Petrarch's interest in Augustine's writings, of course, began in his mid-twenties: G. Billanovich, "Nella biblioteca del Petrarca, I; Il Petrarca, il Boccaccio e le *Ennarrationes in Psalmos* di S. Agostino," *Italia medioevale e umanistica*, 3 (1960), 1–27. The saint's works were on Petrarch's two lists of *Libri mei peculiares* drawn up in 1333 and about 1335 respectively: Francisco Rico, "Petrarca y el 'De vera religione'," *Italia medioevale e umanistica*, 17 (1974), 335. The *De otio religioso* of 1347, however, is the first datable writing of Petrarch in which he seems to come to grips with the relationship of his humanism and his interest in pagan literature. On the probable dating of the first edition of the *Secretum* also in 1347, see Francisco Rico's analysis, *Vida u obra de Petrarca. I: Lectura del Secretum*, Studi sul Petrarca, vol. 4 (Padua, 1974), pp. 452–71. Hans Baron is preparing an extensive critique of Rico's position. My position should in no way be confused with that of Giuseppe Toffanin, *Storia dell'Umanesimo*, 3 vols. (Bologna, 1952); *History of Humanism*, Engl. trans. with augmented bib. by E. Gianturco (New York, 1954). Toffanin sees humanists from the late thirteenth century (including the Paduan humanists) as orthodox Catholics combatting the individualistic, mystical, and philosophical tendencies of the *Duecento*. My thesis speaks only of the evolution within the field of Italian rhetoric in the thirteenth and fourteenth centuries and stresses the development in the thought of the humanists themselves.

67. On Boccaccio's spirituality after 1360, see Carlo Muscetta, "Giovanni Boccaccio e il novellieri," *Il Trecento*, Storia della letteratura italiana, vol. 2, (Milan, 1965), pp. 362–67; and Millard Meiss, *Painting in Florence and Siena After the Black Death* (New York, 1951), pp. 160–64. Vittore Branco, *Boccaccio, The Man and His Works* (New York, 1976), stresses the influence of Petrarch for Boccaccio's religious development, p. 108. Also see pp. 128–30. Salutati for his part admits in later life to having had a preference for the teachings of the ancient pagans in his younger days, when he writes (*Epist.*, III, 416) of the "moralia Gentilium . . . precepta . . . quibus adolescens et iunior delectatus sum." For Salutati's changed outlook, see below chaps. 5, 11, and 13.

spondence reveal the extent to which the ethical attitudes characteristic of the previous Italian rhetorical tradition still prevailed in his thought into the late 1360s.[68]

Closely related to Salutati's ideas on virtue was his conception of patriotism. Four of the fifteen letters still extant from the period before his departure for Todi in August 1367 have patriotism or civic duty as one of their themes.[69] Inspired by Cicero (*De officiis*, I, 17, 57), he holds no love (*caritas*) comparable to that for one's homeland. The individual has ties and duties to parents, wife, children, relatives, and friends, but the deepest respect and love are owed to the *patria*, because it contains all these relationships, all things dear to the individual, including himself. The *patria*'s gift is justice: by a chain of law it joins together not only citizens but even foreigners who live within its frontiers, and it is essentially the awareness of cohesion through law which gives rise in the citizen to a deep sense of duty and love.[70] So strong is this patriotism that "not only while we live do we wish to serve the state, but even for an infinity of centuries and, if it were possible, even for eternity."[71] "If it would serve to defend or extend the homeland, we should not consider it a distasteful and hard task to thrust an axe into one's father's head, mangle our brothers and deliver the unborn child from one's wife's womb with a sword."[72]

It is, of course, difficult to reconcile an ethical ideal which teaches the individual to free himself from attachment to the gifts of fortune with a teaching that places the highest value on love of country. Just as difficult is the accommodation of patriotism with a belief that a relationship of nature or necessity is inferior to one founded on free choice. Nor were

68. Karl Hampe, *Beiträge zur Geschichte der letzten Staufer. Ungedruckte Briefe aus der Sammlung des Magisters Heinrich von Isernia* (Leipzig, 1910), pp. 46, 134, and 137; and Eugen Müller, *Peter von Prezza, ein Publizist der Zeit des Interregnums* (Heidelberg, 1913), pp. 115, 117, 118, 120, 124, 128, illustrate conceptions of fate and fortune similar to those expressed by Salutati. Henry of Settimello's popular *Elegia* (see above, chap. 1, n. 25) was devoted to the struggle of the poet with fortune. For a dramatic representation of the same conflict in an example of *dictamen* around 1200, see Karl Hampe, "Zur Auffassung der Fortuna im Mittelalter," *Archiv für Kulturgeschichte*, 17 (1927), 33–34. Cf. Müller, *Peter von Prezza*, p. 114.

69. Letters, 1, 6, 7, and 10.

70. *Epist.*, I, 21.

71. Ibid., p. 27. Just before this passage Salutati writes: "Illa [patria] nos creavit, illa nos tuetur; ab illa, quod primum est, originem trahimus; qua re pre cunctis nobis esse cure debet." Cicero, *De leg.*, II, 2, is probably the source of the idea.

72. Ibid., p. 28: "Si pro illa tutanda augendave expediret, non videretur molestum nec grave vel facinus paterno capiti securim iniicere, fratres obterere, per uxoris uterum ferro abortum educere. . . ."

the ancient writers who partly inspired these ideas conspicuously successful in resolving that contradiction.[73] As in the case with his dramatic diatribes against fate and fortune and his unqualified statements
committing himself to the ideal of friendship, Salutati's expression of
patriotism suggests an attempt to achieve eloquence by shouting. Yet
as in these other cases, this fervent rhetoric about love of country represents basically sincere sentiments. Contrary to Ernest Kantorowicz's
contention that his was a "type of scholarly blood-lust and overheated
desk patriotism,"[74] beneath Salutati's inflated formulation of the patriotic idea lay a genuine devotion attested by a long record of service in
Buggiano.

Although such sentiments ran counter to the Augustinian tendency
to deprecate love of the earthly *patria* when compared with that of the
heavenly (*De civ. Dei*, V, 12 ff.), patriotism as a legitimate Christian sentiment had some precedent in the thought of the Church Fathers.[75]
From the twelfth century especially, Christian thinkers began stressing
the obligation owed by the individual to the homeland. In the work of
theologians like Aquinas and Henry of Ghent patriotism came to be
interpreted as one aspect of the theological virtue *caritas* and therefore
as an element in Christian conduct.[76] Aquinas, however, was careful to
specify that the pagan *caritas patriae* was imperfect, lacking as it did an
orientation toward the highest end of man.[77]

73. Gaettano Righi, *La filosofia civile e giuridica di Cicerone* (Bologna, 1930), pp. 154 ff.,
presents Cicero as reconciling the opposing currents of thought with difficulty. For a brief
cogent assessment of Cicero's political thought, see Charles McIlwain, *The Growth of Political Thought in the West* (New York, 1932), pp. 106–18. On the political thought of the Stoics
in general, see Max Pohlenz, *Die Stoa*, 2 vols. (Göttingen, 1948–49), I, 139–41, 204–7, 282–
90, and 313–16. Seneca is not unmindful of the sage's political duties but he emphasizes
them less: Concetto Marchesi, *Seneca* (Milan, 1944), pp. 287–300.

74. Ernst Kantorowicz, *The King's Two Bodies. A Study in Mediaeval Political Theology*
(Princeton, 1957), p. 246. Alfred von Martin, *Coluccio Salutati*, pp. 125–26, makes a similar
criticism of Salutati's patriotism.

75. For Augustine's view of the Roman's love of glory and patriotism, see Volkmar
Hand, *Augustin und das klassisch römische Selbstverständnis*, Hamburger Philologische Stu-
dien, vol. 13 (Hamburg, 1970), pp. 16–27. On the other hand, another Church Father, St.
Ambrose, attempted to reconcile Christian charity with Cicero's sense of the individual's
duty to the state: Hélène Pétré, *Caritas. Etude sur le vocabulaire latin de la charité chrétienne*,
Spicilegium sacrum lovaniense. Etudes et documents, fasc. 22 (Louvain, 1948), pp. 75–77.
Cf. R. Thamin, *Saint Ambroise et la morale chrétienne au IVe siècle* (Paris, 1895), p. 230.

76. Kantorowicz, *The King's Two Bodies*, pp. 232–49 and especially 243–44. Also see for
Ciceronian origin of phrases, Hélène Pétré, *Caritas*, pp. 34–40. For the relationship be-
tween *caritas* and the state—in addition to Kantorowicz—see Gaines Post, *Studies in Medieval
Legal Thought, Public Law and the State, 1100–1322* (Princeton, 1964), pp. 434–53, and refer-
ence to other relevant notes in the same volume, p. 285, n. 92. Cf. Halvdan Koht, "The
Dawn of Nationalism in Europe," *American Historical Review*, 52 (1947), 265–80.

77. *ST*, IIa IIae, 23, 7, *ad resp.* and comment by Etienne Gilson, *Le Thomisme: Introduc-*

Thirty years after Aquinas the Florentine Dominican friar Remigio de' Girolami, while insisting that the citizen make enormous sacrifices for the *patria* and justifying his position in terms of Christian duty, nonetheless presented *caritas patriae* as a virtue within the capacity of natural man.[78] The general tendency of the late thirteenth and fourteenth centuries, moreover, was to write of patriotism outside a theological context, making no distinction between the exercise of *caritas patriae* by pagans and that by Christians.[79] Nor did Salutati, in the passages cited above, intend to use *caritas* in a specifically theological sense, although religious associations with the term added force to his statements.

If, surrounding Salutati's assertions of the value of patriotism in his early letters, there is an aura of republican fervor, this derives not from any specific statement in the text but from the local political context in which he was writing and the examples he utilized, usually taken as they were from the history of republican Rome. In fact his first explicit affirmations of a republican conception of history and politics did not appear until the period of the conflict between Florence and the Church between 1375 and 1378, and they emerged only under the temporary stresses of the war.[80]

Despite Salutati's republican experience and his obvious sympathies with some form of popular constitution, a hierarchical conception of political authority remained with him throughout his life. He had been trained in Roman law with its glorification of empire. This law gave the basic legal structure to the universal society, legitimizing the particular

---

tion à la philosophie de Saint Thomas d'Aquin, 6th ed., Etudes de philosophie médiévale, vol. 1 (1965), p. 416: "Il y a, dirions-nous aujourd'hui, le sacrifice des Decius, et il y a le sacrifice de Jeanne d'Arc."

78. "Il *De bono communi* di Remigio de' Girolami," ed. Maria C. De Matteis, in *Annali dell'Università degli Studi di Lecce*, Facoltà di lettere e filosofia e di magistero, 3 (1965–67), 74: "Et ideo homo naturali amore magis sequitur bonum sui superioris, idest sui communis, quam bonum proprium, et supernaturali amore caritatis magis sequitur quod est Dei, quam quod est sui communis, si commune faciat Dei contraria, iuxta illud Exod. 23: 'non sequeris turbam ad faciendum malum.'" Cf. comment of Charles T. Davis, "Remigio de'Girolami and Dante," *Studi danteschi*, 36 (1959), 115–16. On Remigio's political thought, see Davis, "An Early Florentine Political Theorist: Fra Remigio de'Girolami," *Proc. Am. Philos. Soc.*, 104 (1960), 662–76.

79. Kantorowicz, pp. 245–46. On *caritas* in Ptolemy of Lucca, see Charles T. Davis, "Ptolemy of Lucca and the Roman Republic," *Proc. Am. Philos. Soc.*, 118 (1974), 33. In Dante, see *Convivio*, IV, 5, 13. While recognizing pagan *caritas patriae* as imperfect love (*De viris illustribus*, ed. Guido Martellotti, Edizione nazionale delle opere di Francesco Petrarca, vol. 2, pt. 1 [Florence, 1964], p. 275), Petrarch does not allow for a specifically Christian patriotism.

80. See my *Coluccio Salutati and His Public Letters* (Geneva, 1976), pp. 53–56; and below, chap. 5.

statutes of each of the states of the empire. To someone knowledgeable in the law, it must have seemed an awesome vision, a great chain of power leading from the emperor, lord of the secular world and font of law, down through various degrees of lesser authority until ultimately they reached that corner of Tuscany where Salutati acted as imperial notary and public official. Allegiance to such a conception of descending authority seriously deterred expression of genuine republican ideas.

Salutati was also a Guelf, and while he never defined theoretically the relationship between the imperial and pontifical powers, what he wrote regarding political institutions must be understood in the context of his basic acceptance of a universal order ruled mutually by pope and emperor. In the spring of 1369, for instance, he experienced one of the most thrilling moments of his life. He was a witness to the crowning of Charles IV at Rome by Urban V, recently returned from Avignon. "Oh, good Jesus," Salutati wrote at that time, "what a spectacle it was, when the two greatest princes of the whole world, nay rather the only monarchs, the one lord of souls, the other of bodies, met together in such peace, with such concord, with such eagerness, with so much good will!" He was completely overwhelmed by the significance of the event: "I was so filled with joy that I was hardly able to keep control of myself, for I was seeing what in the memory and times of our fathers was unseen and perhaps unhoped for."[81]

The fact that Salutati felt not only an intense local patriotism but also a sense of belonging to a greater whole as a citizen of the Empire made it easier for him to look beyond Buggiano and the Florentine Republic in planning for the future. For almost a decade after his experience with Ovid the satisfactions of his notarial work, the excitement of his studies and political activities, and his uncertainty regarding his own capacities were probably enough to make him reasonably well satisfied with his life in the Valdinievole. The more his studies advanced, however, the more ambitious he became. If he had any hope of becoming a great rhetorician, he needed more leisure for reading and writing and a larger stage on which to act. While he saw certain parallels between the Roman Republic and the small subject communes of the Valdinievole, he could not deceive himself as to the importance of political decisions taken by the General Council of Buggiano for the world at large. Once having accepted the challenge to become great, he had to find a means

81. *Epist.*, I, 86–87.

to extricate himself from his present way of life. Only after leaving Tuscany behind was he able to express these feelings clearly in his letters. What he sought was the opportunity "to rise and stand forth" (*emergere*),[82] and to achieve this goal he needed to enjoy a "quiet and free life" (*quietam et liberam vitam*) with ample opportunity to study and write.[83]

82. Ibid., p. 78.   83. Ibid., p. 49.

Chapter 4. THE WANDERING YEARS (1367–74)

In 1344 at thirteen Salutati had gone to Venice and in the early 1360s had visited his former benefactor Jacopo dei Pepoli in Pavia, but he had never before been south of Tuscany.[1] By August 31, 1367, after a trip of three or four days, he was already at Todi ready to take up his office.[2] The political situation in Todi, as in the other cities of Central Italy under papal suzerainty, was, in these months, highly unstable.[3] Urban V had just returned from Avignon, thereby ending six decades of exile from the See of Peter. Now, with the pope again in Rome, the cities of the Patrimony were suspicious of possible papal designs on their liberties. In September Viterbo revolted against the Church, and during his entire term of office Salutati lived in fear that Todi would follow suit.

The office of chancellor of Todi was the most prestigious position that Salutati had so far held, and the salary of eighty florins per year plus

1. *De laboribus Herculis*, ed. Berthold L. Ullman, 2 vols. (Zurich, 1951), I, 173 (cited in Berthold L. Ullman, *The Humanism of Coluccio Salutati*, Medioevo e umanesimo, vol. 4 (Padua, 1963), p. 4, n. 4. On his trip to Pavia, see *Epist.*, I, 37.

2. Novati, *Epist.*, I, 34, n. 1, refers to a procuration written by Salutati as chancellor on August 31, 1367. He gives no indication where it is located in the Todi archives. There is, however, a parchment, dated April 14, 1368 (A.S.T., Sala I, arm. I, cass. VIII, n. 394 bis), which refers to a procuration "manu Colucci quondam Pieri Colucii de Stignano communis Buggiani et Luchanensis diocesis, publici notarii et tunc cancellarii communis Tuderti," dated September 7, 1367, which concerns the same matter as the procuration reported by Novati. Also see Lorenzo Boselli, *Zibaldone di notizie storiche todine*, fol., 74ᵛ (Sala II, arm. I, palch. I, n. 27). The register of *Riformagioni* written by Salutati during his term of office is missing. In the early part of the nineteenth century another document in the hand of Salutati must have been in the archive. The *Libro d'oro* compiled at this time (ibid., Sala I, arm. VI, cass. VIII, n. 3, fol. 22) mentions under the months July and August 1367, an instrument containing the list of the priors for that period "ex instrumento ser Petri Colucii, not." In addition to the inaccuracies in the name of Salutati, the chronology of the *Libro d'oro* for this period is incorrect. The author erroneously assumed that the terms of the Chancellor of the Commune began in the first and seventh month of the year rather than in the third and ninth. For example, for January and February 1368 (when we know Salutati to have been chancellor) under the heading "ex libro ser Nicolai Balducii de Aretio, Cancellarii" we have the list of priors who actually held office in April and May of that year (A.S.T. *Riform.*, vol. 48, ad an., fol. 1). Although there is no way of checking the assumption because of loss of the book of the *Riformagioni* written by Salutati, it is probable that the instrument recorded by the *Libro d'oro* as in the hand of Salutati was written by him in September or October of 1367. I should like to thank Roberto Abbondanza, Superintendent of the Archives of Umbria, whose expert assistance during my researches in Todi was responsible in large part for the few relevant documents discovered.

3. Lorenzo Leonij, *Cronaca dei vescovi di Todi* (Todi, 1888), p. 88, referred to by Novati, I, 46.

meals would have been highly favorable had the commune allowed him an additional income from private practice. Its prohibition against such supplementary income, however, seriously reduced his potential earnings; the elaborate dress it required him to purchase and maintain necessitated significant additional expenditure.[4] Confronted with these financial drawbacks and the unsettled political conditions of the town, he was disillusioned almost from the beginning. Nonetheless, he had come a long way and would return to Tuscany only as a last resort. It was probably then for the first time that he had serious thoughts of going to Rome to join the Curia. A potential source of wealth and honor, positions in the papal chancery were not overly demanding, and he could expect extensive periods of leisure for study. He had, moreover, a powerful contact at the Curia in Francesco Bruni, papal secretary. Although no correspondence to Bruni before this time survives, it it almost certain that after Bruni's departure for Avignon at the very beginning of 1363 the men had exchanged a few letters.[5]

The four letters sent to Bruni in the fall of 1367 and the spring of 1368 reflect Salutati's desperation during these months. Behind the obsequiousness, the contradictions and hypocrisy, there is an anxious, wheedling petitioner who at all costs must obtain his request. It is difficult to recognize in this pitiful figure the controlled and forceful personality of only a few months before. Salutati had resolved to make a new beginning, but the disappointment of his initial venture outside of Tuscany had been a blow to his confidence. Bruni's prolonged silence and then his lukewarm reaction to Salutati's Roman project were hardly reassuring. The anger of an exasperated man lies just below the surface of Salutati's carefully phrased letters to a person he dared not alienate.

Already before November 3, the date of the first letter, Salutati had sent a poem to his friend lauding the return of the pope to the Eternal

---

4. *Epist.*, I, 46.

5. Ibid., I, 42 (Nov. 3, 1367), refers to the long lapse of time (*tandiu tacitus*) since he has written Bruni. Had Salutati considered Rome a likely possibility while still in Stignano, he would have written Bruni before this. Enough material now has been identified to warrant a small monograph on Bruni. Gene Brucker, "An Unpublished Source on the Avignonese Papacy: The Letters of Francesco Bruni," *Traditio* 19 (1963), 351–70, has brought together in his notes a rather complete bibliography of published material concerning Bruni's career and has himself edited seven of his letters found in A.S.F., *Carte Del Bene*, 49, 50, and 51. The notarial protocols of ser Albizzo di M. Filippo di Albizzi (*Notarile*, A 208–9–10–11–12–13–14–15), who seems to have been Bruni's principal notary throughout his adult life, contain a wealth of information on Bruni, his family, and their relationship with Florentine society. Bruni's *copialettere* mentioned in the last chapter provides a second new source of information about the papal secretary and some additional letters from the *Carte del Bene*, 49, can be added to those published by Brucker: *Carte Del Bene*, 49, fols. 102–2ᵛ; 337–37ᵛ, and 338 (Brucker, p. 368, published the last paragraph of this letter from fol. 338ᵛ).

City, apparently in the hope that Bruni would show it around the Curia and thereby make him known to the powers there. Although Salutati had probably given his messenger instructions to inform the papal secretary of his whereabouts, Bruni had thus far failed to notify him of the receipt of the poem. In writing this first letter Salutati had thus to assume that the work had never been delivered, even though he suspected otherwise.

Not having written his friend for a long time, Salutati begins, he would surely be blamed if, only a day's journey from Rome, he did not send congratulations on Bruni's return to Italy.[6] After announcing his new appointment at Todi, he comes to the real motive for writing: his desire to be in Rome and to have Bruni's help in obtaining employment there.[7] He mentions the poem which Bruni has perhaps received and then asks his correspondent to forward him the names of the cardinals with their formal titles[8]—apparently he intended a letter-writing campaign once he procured such a list. Salutati was clearly embarrassed: he had not been a good correspondent in recent years, and now, in his eagerness to leave Todi, he was forced simultaneously to re-open contact and to request a favor. Unsure of Bruni's feelings, he alternated between the formal second person and familiar expressions (*mi Francesce* or *Francescum meum*). Certainly some of his insecurity came from what he felt was an initial rebuff of his poem.

Two weeks passed following this first appeal but no answer came from Rome. Finally, on November 19, Salutati swallowed his pride and wrote again. After reassuring Bruni that he understands perfectly the reason for the secretary's delay in replying to his letter, Salutati returns to the attack: "If you are able, take me away from this place!" An account of his miseries at Todi follows the plea along with a second request for the names of the cardinals.[9] Yet Salutati was left in his wretched state of suspension for almost a month before receiving an answer. When it came, it was friendly but noncommital.[10] Nor did Bruni send Salutati the cardinal's names.

The third letter to Bruni on December 20 is anguished. Salutati rejoices that his friend could take time from his busy round of duties to write him. This leads to a long panegyric on friendship. All he desires is to be in the Curia near his friend. Seemingly unaware of the inconsis-

---

6. *Epist.*, I, 43.   7. Ibid., I, 44.

8. Ibid., I, 44–45. He alludes to the poem he has sent: "feci quedam carmina de adventu domini pape in urbem Romam; nescio si habuistis" (pp. 44–45).

9. Ibid., I, 45–46.

10. This is seen by the nature of Salutati's third letter to Bruni, ibid., I, 46–48.

tency, he mentions near the close of the letter that he knows of an opening in the chancery of Viterbo and would like to have it. The same day
he sent off a second letter, this time to Boccaccio, who was in Rome on
a diplomatic mission for Florence. After revealing that he intends to
come to Rome he asks Boccaccio to do what he can to aid his petition,
meaning, by implication, that Boccaccio should plead his case to Bruni.[11]

Salutati's term of office was to expire on the last day of February 1368
and, according to a clause in his contract, he had to notify the commune
by the end of December were he interested in renewal. So firm was his
resolve to leave Todi that, even without any assurance of a post in
Rome, he let the deadline pass without requesting reappointment. Although he was asked to stay on for the month of March, probably so
that the government of Todi could find a suitable replacement, he had
determined to leave for Rome by the first week of April.[12] He had no
idea what sort of reception awaited him there since Bruni, his supposed
sponsor, had never encouraged his coming. In his final letter from Todi
to the papal secretary on March 8, he tried to do as much as possible to
insure a cordial welcome. He begged the secretary to bear in mind that
he would not be exigent: Bruni should treat him as one of his servants.
In order to make rejection more difficult he added that everyone at
home knew of his plans and that all were delighted (*letantur immen-
sum*).[13]

Nevertheless, Salutati had not cut off all paths of retreat. He had left
open the possibility of returning to Stignano and resuming his old life.
Indeed, not until the end of 1368 did he notify Buggiano that he was
not returning. Although his name had not been drawn for communal
office during the six-months duration of his service in Todi or in the
subsequent trimester (March-May), beginning in June 1368 it was
drawn three times in succession.[14] While replacements were found for
each of these terms, the commune was apparently expecting his return
and, until definitely notified of his intentions, continued to elect him to
communal office every trimester. That his failure to request exemption
from public office was intentional is corroborated by the fact that Salutati took pains to maintain his membership in the Florentine Guild of
Judges and Notaries, a precaution presumably unnecessary had he in-

11. Ibid., I, 49.
12. Ibid., I, 53. That he was still employed in Todi in March is shown not only by the
address of his letter of March 8 (ibid., I, 53) but also by the record of his salary for this
month: A.S.T., *Riform.*, 48 (1368), fol. 119ᵛ.
13. *Epist.*, I, 54.
14. A.C.B., *Delib.*, 5, fols. 127ᵛ, 140ᵛ, and 162ᵛ.

tended to remain working in the papal chancery.[15] On May 31, 1368, Salutati, together with ser Giovanni Balducci of Uzzano, was listed in the guild records as having paid his annual dues.[16] Either from Todi or Rome Salutati had probably sent instructions to ser Giovanni to do this for him when the notary from Uzzano went to Florence to make his own payment.

Bruni, however, did not disappoint his expectations of assistance. In April 1369, a year later, Salutati wrote to Boccaccio telling him that he was working under Bruni in the Curia.[17] A general kind of specialization existed in the chancery whereby each papal secretary was concerned with the affairs of a major geographical area.[18] Appropriately Bruni handled correspondence with Northern Italy, and it is likely that some of his assistants were also from that area. In addition to Salutati, one of Bruni's sons, Mariotto, worked for him.[19]

These were exciting days in Rome; for sixty-three years, while its absent successive masters raised up a new if more modest Rome on the banks of the Rhone, the ancient city had languished. Now, with the return of Urban V Rome became again the capital of Christendom. On all sides new construction was in progress to render the city worthy of that honor. At the Lateran a new church was rising on the ruins of the two which had been consumed successively by fire since the death of Boniface VIII. St. Paul's, destroyed by an earthquake, was also being rebuilt and repairs were underway on the roof of St. Peter's.[20] Along with an interest in rebuilding the city, Urban had initiated a moral re-

---

15. After his return from Rome Salutati altered his manner of subscribing to notarial documents in order to indicate that he had received authorization from the pope to act as a notary. Prior to going to Rome he signed his documents "publicus imperiali auctoritate notarius et judex ordinarius." After Rome he combined his papal and imperial authorization as follows: "apostolica auctoritate notarius imperialique auctoritate iudex ordinarius et scriba publicus." He had probably been examined by Francesco Bruni, who in 1368 was charged with passing judgment on candidates for the notariate at the *Curia*: Paul M. Baumgarten, *Von der apostolischen Kanzlei*, Görres-Gesellschaft zur Plege der Wissenschaft im katholischen Deutschland, Section für Rechts-und Sozialwissenschaft, vol. 4 (Cologne, 1904), p. 59. On the role of the papal secretary in the Avignon period, see Friedrich Bock, "Einführung in das Registerwesen des Avignonesischen Papsttums," *Quellen und Forschungen aus italienischen Archiven und Bibliotheken*, 31 (1941), 39–85.

16. *AGN*, 92, fol. 123ᵛ.   17. *Epist.*, I, 88.

18. Inventories at the beginning of *Registri vaticani* for this period arrange letters under the names of various papal secretaries who were responsible for writing them.

19. In letter of March 8 Salutati sent his regards to *dominus Mariottus* (*Epist.*, I, 54). Novati suggests that this was probably Mariotto del Conte (n. 2), but almost certainly it was Bruni's son; see Bruni's testament in *Notarile*, A 213, fols. 117ᵛ–21. A document drawn up by Salutati as an official of the *Curia* is published by G. Savino, "Una carta rogata a Roma da Coluccio Salutati," *Bollettino storico pistoiese*, 3rd ser., 1 (1966), 54–57.

20. *Epist.*, I, 81.

form. He had ambitious plans for disciplining the Roman clergy, the most licentious in the world according to common report.[21]

Life in the papal household itself, however, was anything but harmonious. The large French contingent of the Curia's prelates had consistently opposed Urban's decision to return to Italy. Uncomfortable in their new makeshift quarters, living amidst an alien and at times unruly populace, they longed for their own country and the conveniences of modern Avignon. Outspoken in their discontent, they moved in their discussions from specific complaints to a general criticism of Italy and the Italians. While prepared to admit the former greatness of Italy, they maintained that in their own time France was the superior nation. This, of course, brought protests from the Italian faction. The dispute became so widespread that finally the pope declared that he himself would hear the merits of both cases and render judgment.[22] Very probably, in the midst of such debates, Salutati first had occasion to recognize and express his own Italian prejudices. He left the Curia with a firm conviction of French fickleness (levitas), which he retained throughout his life.

While at Todi, in spite of the many harrassments, the new chancellor managed to persevere in his intellectual work. He had finished at Stignano the Conquestio Phyllidis and perhaps the declamation De Lucretia as well,[23] but, as he related in his letter to Boccaccio, during his months at Todi he produced a wealth of different types of poems: odes, satires, and comic verse.[24] In the midst of his worries and fears, his literary labors doubtless furnished him a refuge. In the service of the Curia he had looked forward to long leisure hours, and in this he was not disappointed. At no time since his student days did he have so much time

---

21. Ibid., I, 81–82.   22. Ibid., I, 74–76.

23. Ibid., I, 41, for the Conquestio and also Appendix I, this volume. Salutati's friend, Domenico Silvestri, composed a reply to the Conquestio, entitled Consolatio missa per Dampnem ad Phillidem conquerentem de suis infortuniis, ed. Richard C. Jensen, Domenico Silvestri: The Latin Poetry (Munich, 1973), pp. 34–50. Silvestri also wrote a companion piece for another of Salutati's works. Silvestri's Fabula cancri is a reply to Salutati's Fabula de vulpe et cancro (ibid., pp. 55–64, and below, chap. 4, n. 14). The Fabula cancri was also published by Novati, "Per una novella del Sacchetti," Rassegna bibliografica della letteratura italiana, 13 (1905), 76–82. For the De Lucretia, see Appendix I, this volume. Hans Galinsky, Der Lucretia-Stoff in der Weltliteratur (Breslau, 1932), pp. 44–46, discusses the work. Georg Voigt, "Die Lucretia-Fabel und ihre literarischen Verwandten, "K. Sächs. Ak. d. Wiss. zu Leipzig, Berichte über die Verhandlungen, Phil.-lit. cl., 35 (1883), 25, assigns a date for composition in Salutati's youth: "Gegen den Selbstmord an sich wird von Vater und Gatte nicht das mindeste eingewendet. Das hätte Salutato, der Stoiker nach antiken Zuschnitt, sicher auch in seinen späteren Jahren nicht gethan, in deren er sich mehr als Philosoph wie als Dichter fühlte." In my opinion the work was written before his religious conversion in 1368. Because both this work and the Conquestio deal with the theme of suicide, they could have been written in the same period around 1367.

24. Ibid., I, 48–49.

free for study as during these two years in Rome. But something happened there that rendered him unable to profit from a liberty he had so eagerly desired but a short time before. As he wrote Boccaccio:

> However, I have had time to write, I must confess, nor is a subject ever wanting. But a certain lethargy and disgust at this labyrinth of Acheron has not permitted me to do so. As soon as I conceived of something, behold, another topic more worthy to be treated presented itself; and thus, uncertain as to which I would rather choose, I have remained for a long time with pen suspended.[25]

No doubt Salutati was genuinely disgusted with the immorality of the Curia, but his description of his mental state suggests other causes for his depression. His feeling stemmed in part from his failure to find quick advancement in Rome. He had wanted leisure, but he also craved immediate recognition and the financial rewards that would bring. As the months passed and the possibility of obtaining a lucrative appointment in the near future receded, he became disillusioned and restless. A third and perhaps most cogent reason for Salutati's pervasive lethargy was the new-found leisure itself. His mind, grown accustomed to literary creation under the stress of a hectic public life, simply could not function properly without the stimulus of outside pressures compelling it to discriminate among possible projects. Always forced to make the most of those brief hours snatched from the demands of his official and civic duties, Salutati demonstrated at Rome that compulsive activity had for him become a constitutive part of the creative process.

Consequently, in the midst of his longed-for freedom he found himself wishing for another kind of life, that of the citizen-scholar, devoting part of his time to domestic duties, part to friends, part to the service of his homeland, but the most important part to study.[26] However, although this routine might have fulfilled both his ethic of civic obligation and his pursuit of virtue through the cultivation of eloquence, it would not have provided the fame Salutati now also sought.[27] By the winter of

25. Ibid., I, 85–86.
26. Looking back on his Roman experience from Lucca, Salutati wrote: " . . . cum pridem in curie romane sentinam omnium vitiorum olentissimam incidissem, et quasi apud inferos, fato quodam meo, biennio remansissem, ipse mecum cogitans tenorem vite, etsi non omnino quietum, saltem statui meo satis accomodabilem disponebam, ita michimet ipse constituens: hoc domui, hoc amicis reique publice tempus impertiar; hanc optimam dierum particulam studio deputabo" (ibid., I, 130–31).
27. He continued the above: "Sed fallimur omnes, nec de nobis ipsis nobis licet quod volumus. Imminent enim preter exspectatum occupationum turbe; imminent siquidem et

1368 he was importuning Bruni to exert his influence to obtain some post for him in one of the cities ruled by the Church.[28] For the moment, however, these efforts were unsuccessful.

For Salutati, one of the most exciting events of his Roman period was Petrarch's recognition of him as a friend and correspondent, although the relationship ended almost as quickly as it began. Salutati had written Petrarch without receiving an answer and now, in 1368, he attempted to establish a correspondence by indirect means. He requested Bruni to include greetings from him in one of the papal secretary's letters to Petrarch and when, in response to Bruni, Petrarch referred to Salutati as a friend, the door was open for direct communication.[29] Between September 11, 1368, and August 21, 1369, Salutati sent the older scholar five letters; the first was answered in October, but, apparently conscious of the burden involved in responding to the stream of letters from his eager correspondent, Petrarch wrote no more.[30] Had Petrarch been intending a delayed response to the others, Salutati's fifth letter, that of August 21, 1369, probably caused him to give up the idea. Aware that the relationship was going nowhere and chagrined that Petrarch had not kept a promise to come to Rome, Salutati attacked him for accepting the invitations of tyrants while ignoring those of the pope. Petrarch, who by this time probably found the whole relationship tiresome, felt little need to defend himself from the chidings of a man he barely knew.

Despite his abortive "friendship" with the leading European humanist, these two years at Rome, even if Salutati himself disparaged them, were vitally important to his intellectual development. Prior to his departure for Todi, his Christianity had no discernible effect on his intellectual life. In Rome there was no sudden shift, no quasi-mystical experience comparable to the one he had had with Ovid. Nonetheless unquestionably, in the years after 1368, Salutati's thought became gradually permeated by Christian ideas, and a number of citations, first from the Bible and then from the Fathers, began to appear alongside refer-

---

subito quasi de latebris emergunt que tum necessitate quadam, tum honorantie splendore ordinem vite nostre pervertunt statumque commutant."
   28. Ibid., I, 78.   29. Ibid., I, 62, n. 1.
   30. Ibid., I, 61–62, 72–76, 80–84, 95–96, and 96–99. Petrarch's *Sen.* XI, 4, dated October 4: Ernest H. Wilkins, *Petrarch's Correspondence*, Medioevo e umanesimo, vol. 3 (Padua, 1960), p. 102. From his first letter Salutati avoided the adulatory tone found in Nelli's correspondence with Petrarch. This treatment from a relative unknown perhaps estranged Petrarch.

ences to Seneca, Ovid, Livy, and Cicero. This process began in Rome; its earliest manifestations are found in Salutati's letters of 1369.

It was during this year that the first unambiguous reference to the Bible and certain other surprising phrases appeared in his remarks on ethics. In a letter dealing with the liberation of Lucca, written to Niccolosio Bartolomei and dated April 26, 1369, Salutati, for the first time in his correspondence, consciously paraphrased a biblical verse.[31] In itself this is not particularly significant but, taken together with segments of other letters written during these months, it is indicative of the changes that were slowly occurring in his thinking. In January 1369, for example, writing to Bartolomeo di Jacopo, Salutati spoke of the latter's having attained his mastery of eloquence by divine aid (*gloriosam hanc exercitationem cuius te Deus compotem fecit*),[32] and, in another of April, carried away by thought of the imperial coronation, he made the first mention of Christ's name to appear in the letters.[33]

Another instance occurred in a letter of consolation to Ugolino Orsini de'Conti di Manupello (September 31, 1369): here Salutati not only stated that Ugolino's deceased father had rendered up his soul to Christ but also described the Christian heaven with the saints and the Trinity.[34] Three quotations from the Bible heighten the Christian character of the discourse.[35] A theme that enjoyed a long life in Salutati's writings, the often close agreement between Christian truth and the ideas of pagan philosophers, was casually expressed here for the first time: "We maintain, however, that there is a soul and it is eternal, which is not only Christian but philosophical, and that it will return again to the body. . . ."[36] Moreover, he introduced a new formulation of his essentially pagan ethical doctrine of virtue, the implications of which were not to be developed for decades to come:

31. *Epist.*, I, 91: Psalms 102:19–21. He compares the liberation of Lucca to biblical events like the freeing of Israel from bondage in Egypt (p. 89). Von Martin observes the development of Salutati's religious interests but does not offer a chronology: *Coluccio Salutati und das Humanistische Lebensideal* (Berlin, 1916), pp. 71–72.

32. Ibid., I, 80.

33. Would that the union of pope and emperor, he wrote (ibid., 87), lead to a universal concord: "Unicum in uno orbe Christi nomen veneraretur et coleretur!" He had of course already used the name of Christ in an address ("Reverendo in Christo patri et domino," p. 46); in referring to the pope as "Christi vicarius" (p. 75); and to Rome in a figurative way as "christicolarum sidus" (p. 62). The statement of April 1369, however, was the first to demonstrate a truly religious feeling behind the usage.

34. Ibid., I, 105. The description of heaven here should be compared with that pictured in the letter on the death of Dagomar (ibid., pp. 15–20).

35. Ibid., I, 111–12.   36. Ibid., I, 111.

We live with the indulgence of nature and this is common to us and other animals; however, to live well is peculiar to a human being and is the mark of a good and virtuous man. This capacity is not within our power alone but is acquired by us through the cooperating grace of God (*cooperante gratia Dei*), the virtues, and a good disposition of mind.[37]

Curiously, this letter, written in consolation of the death of an unknown man and probably out of hopes for patronage, contrasted in its Christian character with that sent to Lapo Castiglionochio earlier in the month on the death of Simone, Lapo's nephew and Salutati's dear friend.[38] One of the tenderest and most sincere letters of condolence Salutati ever wrote, it contained no traces of Christian influence and ended with an exhortation to Lapo to steel himself against fortune. The letter to Ugolino belongs to a traditional genre and draws some of its Christian sentiment from that fact. Yet, in the text, Salutati so pointedly established the connections between grace and virtue and the Christian and philosophic positions on the soul, that he gave evidence of taking a new personal interest in such problems. On the other hand, Salutati's profound but non-Christian expression of grief for the death of his dear Simone suggests that at this stage his Christianity was primarily on the intellectual level. In a time of genuine sorrow Christianity was not yet a source of comfort for him.

Fourteen months later, in January 1371, in a letter to Francesco Bruni on the death of Urban V and the election of Gregory XI, Salutati reveals the degree to which his approach to ethics and history had become Christianized.[39] About the death of Urban, Salutati's feelings are clear; the pope deserted Italy and has been struck down by divine justice— man cannot play with God! Salutati then takes up the election of the new pope connecting it with the theme of the Christian theory of Providence. While virtue and fortune are often responsible for raising a man to high station, in the matter of Christ's vicar, divine Providence alone is at work. Whereas most ancient philosophers were prepared to concede God's control of the human race as a whole, he continues, they tended to deny it in the lives of individuals and groups. The Christian believes, however, that everything is governed by the will of God. In the election of Peter's successor a special providence is at work. If the

37. Ibid., I, 110.
38. Ibid., I, 100–103.

39. Ibid., I, 140–44.

man chosen is not virtuous, God will make him so; if he is already virtuous, he will become better "since it is right to believe that the Providence of God works more effectively in those matters which are more
important and by it we are strongly impelled to desire good things and
are effectively assisted in doing them."[40] By opening his discussion with
the statement that we might attain honors and offices either by virtue,
by fortune or by the gift of God, Salutati showed that he probably had
not yet reexamined the virtue-fortune formula but had merely complicated it by his intrusion of the Christian concepts of grace and God's
Providence.

No certain explanation can be offered for Salutati's gradual introduction of Christian texts and ideas into his letters in the course of 1369. In
spite of his criticism of the Curia as a labyrinth of vice and luxury, he
seems to have been impressed by the scenes of devotion, the splendid
rituals, the richly appointed churches and other Christian monuments.
He surely found some men, virtuous and learned in theology, with whom
he could talk, and never before had he had such easy and wide access
to theological works. Perhaps in Bruni's library he first encountered
writings of Petrarch which, with their religious character, inspired him
to think more seriously about his own faith. Possibly, however, the primary effect of Petrarch was to demonstrate that eloquence was not inherently linked to pagan attitudinizing.

No matter how it may be explained, there was a noticeable change in
Salutati's correspondence in the course of 1369, and afterward, a new
tone: the sharp conflict between virtue and fortune became blunted by
the active presence of a third force, the Christian God. Man was no
longer alone in his struggle with fortune as he had seemed to be in
Salutati's earlier ethical pronouncements. He had traveled an enormous
distance from 1367 when he published his Ovidian *Questio Phyllidis*, to
1369–70 when he conceived and began work on his bucolic poems. While
he intended the *Questio* to serve as a companion piece for Ovid's *Nux*
and as a warning to young girls of the dangers of loving too much, the
first poem of the *Bucolics* was an allegorical treatment of the salvation
of man by the grace of God.[41]

Salutati's efforts to find employment outside the papal Curia became
almost frenzied after Urban V definitely decided to return to Avignon.
On August 31, 1369, the pope sent a *breve* to Lucca recommending ser

40. Ibid., I, 144.
41. For the *Questio*, see above, n.23, and for the bucolic poetry of Salutati, see Appendix I.

Coluccio Salutati di Stignano as a man notable for his knowledge and morals, suggesting that the commune of Lucca find some honorable office for him.[42] Less than five months before, on April 8, 1369, the Emperor had declared Lucca free of Pisan domination. Since 1342 the city had been under Pisan control, and now, with the expulsion of the enemy, the whole structure of communal government had to be revamped in order to fit its newly independent status. In the course of this reform Salutati could expect that many offices would become available because some members of the communal administration who had cooperated with the former Pisan overlords would surely be ousted.

The temporary vicar of the city, Cardinal Guido Porto, could be expected to support the request of the pope, and Salutati was also not without friends in that city, less than a half-day's ride from Stignano.[43] Most important, Bruni, Salutati's patron at the Curia, had doubtless requested the letter from the pope; his section of the chancery had drawn it up; and he would use his great influence in Lucca to push for Salutati's appointment. The Lucchese considered Bruni one of the principal champions of Lucchese independence at the Curia. Promised a thousand florins by city leaders in exchange for his influence "apud Papam," Bruni was officially granted the money on June 3, 1371.[44]

Bruni was also in contact with the commune in his own name. On November 1, 1370, Urban V wrote to the *Anziani*, the supreme governing council of Lucca: " . . . that we follow your community with sincere love and we labor and we intend to labor in its behalf in so far as we will be able with God's help, just as our beloved son, Master Francesco Bruni, our secretary, who strives sincerely for your honor and position, will be able to reveal more extensively through his letters according to our command to him."[45] We may assume, therefore, that Salutati was fairly confident his formal recommendation from the pope would be reinforced by a personal recommendation from one whom the city regarded as its protector.

42. A.S.L., *Dipl. Tarpea*, ad an.; see printed version, *Epist.*, IV, 431.
43. See the names on the guest list for a banquet given in Buggiano on March 11, 1369: Ronald Witt, "Coluccio Salutati, Chancellor and Citizen of Lucca (1370–1372)," *Traditio*, 25 (1969), 192, n. 8. Major members of the noble faction in Lucca were present.
44. A.S.L., *Con. gen., Riform. pubbl.*, reg. 2, fol. 156ᵛ. This was to be paid at fifty gold florins per year. On March 23, 1373, Bruni wrote a letter thanking the *Anziani* for their gift of one hundred florins: A.S.L., *Anziani al tempo della libertà, Registrum quarundam literarum*, 529, fol. 78. We have another indication of Bruni's intervention in the matter of the *breve*: it was written by ser Mariotto (see n. 19 above).
45. A.S.L., *Dipl. Tarpea*, ad an. Also see personal letter of Bruni to *Anziani* written on August 22, 1370: A.S.L., *Anziani al tempo della lib., Lettere originali*, 1370–1400, no. 439).

Salutati did not, however, wait for the papal *breve* to bring himself to the attention of the rulers of Lucca. Only two weeks after the Pisans were formally deprived of their control over the city, on April 26, 1369, he wrote a letter from Viterbo to Niccolosio Bartolomei, one of the leaders in the movement for Lucchese independence. In it he expressed his happiness at Lucca's liberation by the Emperor and added that: "I have already begun a new panegyric in heroic verse about this, although it be in uneven style, and with God's aide I shall finish it."[46] Not only did he intend to praise Charles IV as liberator, but Niccolosio and several others were to be celebrated in the panegyric for their "diligence and labors" in freeing their homeland. The inspiration for this poem doubtless came in part from Salutati's sincere joy at the liberation of the long-suffering city, but its composition was at least partly motivated by his attempt to win the favorable attention of the commune.

Since, by statute, many of the public offices in Lucca were forbidden to noncitizens, Salutati had to apply to become a citizen. Only a few weeks after the arrival of the papal request of August 31, he along with his brothers and a number of other men who had been proposed for citizenship in the commune were admitted to that honor. The Salutati family was, however, accorded a special privilege: whereas the others became citizens only on condition "that they remain and live in the city of Lucca or its suburbs and swear an oath of fealty according to the custom within the next fifteen days," the Salutati were allowed to become citizens "from the day on which he [Salutati?] comes to live in the city of Lucca" (*a die quo venerit ad habitandum in civitate Lucana*).[47] Despite this the commune took no action on a possible post for Coluccio.

This delay apparently resulted from the fact that all the major notarial offices had already been filled for the six months or a year beginning the first of August, a month before the papal letter had arrived.[48] A second cause for delay was the contemplated reorganization of the chancery. Early within the first year of Luccan independence (1369) it had become obvious that the current organization of the chancery under a single chancellor, contrary to usual Tuscan practice, was ineffi-

46. *Epist.*, I, 89.
47. A.S.L., *Con. gen., Riform. pubbl.*, 1, fol. 55, September 27, 1369.
48. Cardinal Guido on July 2, 1369, had been made imperial vicar for Tuscany. He chose the *Anziani* and the *podestà* in July and they subsequently filled the other offices. The cycle of offices, consequently, would have run from July to July: Girolamo Tommasi, "Sommario della storia di Lucca dall'anno MIV all'anno MDCC," in *Archivio storico italiano*, 10 (1847), 237 ff. For the state of Lucca in 1369, see Christine Meek, *Lucca 1369–1400: Politics and Society in an Early Renaissance City-State* (Oxford, 1978), pp. 19–30.

cient and that the office would have to be divided.[49] But imperial command barred the way to reform. On July 12, 1369, ser Pietro di Tomeo di Beato di Bologna, who had become part of the emperor's *familia* perhaps as recently as February 24,[50] was appointed chancellor of Lucca at the enormous salary of twenty-five florins per month in addition to much of the income of the chancery and other perquisites.[51] The chancery was to be completely under his control,[52] and his appointment was without limit of time. To insure that ser Pietro would encounter no obstacles from the communal government, moreover, the emperor added that Lucca was to accept him as "our [the emperor's] notary and official." Thus, until the commune's power to make basic reforms in its statutes was restored in February 1370 by the imperial vicar, Cardinal Porto, any attempt to reorganize the chancery was impossible.[53] Even then, Lucca could not afford to offend one of the emperor's intimates. Accordingly, an additional condition of the reform was that ser Pietro would accept it.

The dispatch of a second letter from the Curia on February 9, 1370, the very month in which Lucca regained the right to rule herself, proves that the reorganization was being contemplated months before July 17, 1370 (the date of the formal change), and that it was recognized as dependent on the resumption of sovereignty by the commune. This letter specified that, since Lucca had not yet provided Coluccio Salutati with an honorable office, the *Anziani*, the leading executive body of the commune, should elect him chancellor.[54] Although a number of basic laws were enacted beginning in February, the *Anziani*, probably in agreement with ser Pietro and in conformity with the cycle of appointments, took no action on this second request until July. Salutati meanwhile had already made preparations to leave Rome.

But he did not intend to go to Lucca. Rather he had decided to return to the Valdinievole until he learned the effect of the second papal *breve*.

49. Demetrio Marzi, *La cancelleria della Repubblica fiorentina* (Rocca San Casciano, 1910), p. 11.

50. *Con. gen., Riform. pubbl.*, 1, fol. 6.

51. Ibid., fol. 5. He was given the salary "cum omnibus aliis juribus, proventibus, comodis, comoditatibus et honoribus consuetis habendis, tolendis et precipiendis et in usus tuos [i.e., ser Pietro] convertendis."

52. Ibid., fol 5. Charles IV declared that the chancery was to be directed "per te vel coadiutores tuos quos tu elegeris et nominaveris in casu ubi fueris aliis occupatus." The assistant was ser Pietro Saraceni, who continued in this post after the reforms of July 17, 1370.

53. This grant of power was preparatory to the investiture of the *Anziani* with the prerogatives of the imperial vicarship by the Cardinal on March 12, 1370 (Tommasi, p. 241).

54. A.S.L., *Dipl. Tarpea, ad an.*

On February 27, 1370, in a letter to Gaspare Squaro dei Broaspini, he speaks of returning to Stignano in the near future.[55] He does not seem to have arrived in the Valdinievole, however, much before the end of April.[56] He had reason to believe that his stay in Stignano would be brief, but to all appearances he simply took up his old life where he had left it over two and a half years before. In his three months at home he represented Buggiano on a number of missions lasting thirty-five days in all, of which he spent seven in Florence.[57] In addition, he made almost three-quarters of the motions made in the communal assembly during May, June, and July.

Although politics took a good share of his time during these months, a procuration dated February 28 indicates that he also resumed his notarial work.[58] Nor did he abandon his beloved studies. His last letter from Stignano, on July 27, addressed to Master Jacopo da Uzzano, suggests that he spent many hours at his books.[59] Whereas at the *Curia* he had complained of "a certain lethargy and disgust" and of his pen's remaining idle for months,[60] back in Tuscany a tremendous burst of activity succeeded this torpor. Doubtless the expectation of the brilliant future awaiting him as the chancellor of a great city significantly contributed to this change. It was with high hopes that Salutati left for Lucca.[61]

The act of July 17, 1370, which appointed Salutati chancellor of Lucca, also decreed the new organization of the Lucchese chancery.[62] There were in fact to be two chancellors: the Chancellor of the *Anziani* was to handle all work connected with the *Anziani*, acting independently, while the Chancellor of the Commune of Lucca was responsible for all matters with which the several councils together with the *Anziani* were concerned. Each chancellor had a notary to assist him with his duties.

---

55. *Epist.*, I, 121.
56. Letters dated from Rome, ibid., I, 122–24, March 30, 1370.
57. A.C.B., *Delib.*, 6, fol. 48 (four days); fol. 50 (three days); fol. 82; fol. 87 (four days); fol. 93ᵛ (six days); he was also paid in July for unrecorded trips lasting a total of ten days (fol. 87). The Florentine missions were of four (ibid., 6, fol. 58) and three days (fol. 58ᵛ).
58. On February 28, 1370, in Pescia a certain Parente Paganelli of Porcari named Salutati, together with two others, as his procurator (B.G.L., *Note di contratti di compre e vendite, alluogazioni, ec., estratte dal Can. Vinc. Gius. Baroni da pergamene e da altri documenti 1370–99*, 6, fol. 7ᵛ). This document is copied in vol. 920, ad an. in the same library. Because a procuration could be given months before it was to be exercised, there is no basis for believing that Salutati returned to the Valdinievole briefly at the end of February only to journey back to Rome in March to conclude his affairs there.
59. *Epist.*, I, 128.   60. Ibid., I, 85–86.
61. For a discussion of the erroneous belief that Salutati was employed by the Florentine chancery in 1370, see my "Coluccio Salutati, Chancellor," p. 196, n. 27.
62. A.S.L., *Cons. gen., Riform. pubbl.*, I, fol. 223ᵛ; cf. transcription, *Epist.*, IV, 433–37.

Ser Pietro di Tomeo was henceforth to be known as Chancellor of the *Anziani* with ser Pietro Sarceni, already his notarial assistant in the preceding year, as coadjutor. Salutati, as Chancellor of the Commune of Lucca, had as his assistant first ser Niccolò Sartoi and later, after ser Niccolò resigned, Niccolò di Opizo Dombellinghi.[63] Tomeo's salary was generous: he received two hundred florins per year, one-third of the profit from notarizing documents in his chancery and, if he wished, he could share the table of the *Anziani*. His assistant had six florins per month, one-sixth of the profit of the chancery and obligatory meals. On the other hand, the compensation of the Chancellor of the Commune shows that his status was decidedly inferior to that of the emperor's protégé. He received eight florins per month and one-third of the profits from his department of the chancery but no board.[64] His coadjutor was to receive five florins per month and one-sixth of the income of the chancery of the commune.

Salutati's duties began on August 1, 1370, and the first entry in his register of the *Riformagioni*, i.e., the record of the deliberations of the General Council, was made on August 3.[65] Although the introduction specifies the coadjutor as one of the writers of the register, in his entry on July 27, 1371, Salutati wrote: "all things contained in the present book have I written with my own hand and published from my office of the chancellorship."[66] This volume of *Riformagioni* consists of final copies of the minutes of the regular meetings of the General Council. The rough drafts, taken down in haste at the meetings themselves (also in what appears to be Salutati's hand), were collected in a register called *Minute delle Riformagioni*.[67] At the meetings, in addition to keeping a

63. A.S.L., *Cons. gen., Riform. pubbl.*, 2, fol. 44. The change occurred on Sept. 4, 1370. Novati incorrectly calls Salutati chancellor of the *Anziani* both in the title he gives to the document containing Salutati's election (*Epist.*, IV, 433) and in his biography (p. 388). Ser Pietro di Tomeo is clearly appointed the *cancellarius dominorum Antianorum* (p. 434).

64. See n. 62 above. See also record of Salutati's salary for five months with gabelle deducted (A.S.L., *Camerlingo Gen., Cam. Int.-Esito*, 82, fol. 63ᵛ, under the date August 1, 1371).

65. A.S.L., *Cons. gen., Riform. pubbl.*, 2, fol. 18.

66. Ibid., fol. 186ᵛ: "Omnia in presenti libro contenta manu mea propria scripsi et ex meo cancelleriatus officio publicavi."

67. A.S.L., *Anziani al tempo della libertà, Minute delle riform.*, 2. Only the notes for the period April 16–July 30, 1371, are extant. Part of these notes of the deliberations are written in a simple cipher: fols. 39 and 44. Although these deliberations were transcribed in the *Riform. pubbl.*, it is impossible to determine whether if what was actually said (represented by the sections of the rough draft in cipher) was faithfully reported in the final copy. L. Fumi, who first noted these passages, suggests in his introduction to the *Il carteggio degli Anziani, Registri del reale archivio di stato in Lucca*, 2 vols. (Lucca, 1903), II, pt. 2, p. ix, that this use of cipher was only the first of a series to be found in the *Minute*. However, after examination of subsequent registers, I was unable to find proof that any chan-

record of the proceedings, Salutati collected the ballots used in voting, counted them, and announced the results.[68] He was also required to keep a list of all the decrees passed by the Council, which list forms part of the *Indici dei Decreti*.[69] As specified by the statute creating his office, he was to be responsible for all affairs in which the General Council and the *Anziani* acted together: this included all relations between the commune and its officers and soldiers in the *contado*. He also was responsible for swearing in communal officials.[70] The loss of all the records of his chancery except those already indicated unfortunately makes it impossible to determine the full extent of Salutati's responsibilities or the manner in which he shared them with his coadjutor. Neither the signature of Sartoi nor that of Dombellinghi appears anywhere in the surviving documents.

When Salutati's one-year appointment expired, it was not renewed. Instead, on July 22, 1371, Pietro Saraceni, coadjutor of Pietro di Tomeo, became Chancellor of the Commune for the succeeding twelve months.[71] In explaining the cause for his rejection, Salutati vaguely spoke of himself as the victim of a factional struggle: "The Lucchese Republic, where I was content to fill the office of the chancellorship, has rejected me because of the opposition of a faction."[72] Once before, during his youth

---

cellor after Salutati used cipher in the *Minute*. My suggestion would be that this was an unsuccessful and unique experiment by Salutati to keep secret certain deliberations that the commune desired to conceal even from those who were trusted enough to have access to the official registers. G. Costamagna, "Scritture segrete e cifrari della cancelleria della serenissima Republica, *Bollettino ligustico*, 9 (1957), 12, points to a passage in cipher in a Venetian notarial document of 1263. See by the same author, *Tachigrafia notarile e scritture segrete medioevali in Italia*, Fonti e studi del corpus membranarum italicarum, vol. 1 (Rome, 1968), pp. 40–48. A. Luzio, *L'archivio Gonzaga di Mantua*, 2 vols. (Mantua, 1920–22), II, 89, mentions the presence of cipher in diplomatic documents in Mantua and Neapolitan documents from 1368. Also see G. E. Santini, "Dispacci in cifre del r. archivio di stato di Firenze," *Archivio storico italiano*, 14 (1871), 473–76. I am grateful to Prof. Vincent Iliardi for some of these references. Cf. *La correspondance de Pierre Ameilh, Archêveque de Naples puis d'Embrun (1363–1369)*, ed. Henri Bresc, Sources d'histoire médiévale, vol. 6 (Paris, 1972), pp. xxi-xxv. For Salutati's relationship to ciphers or codes, see R. Witt, *Coluccio Salutati and His Public Letters*, p. 21. Cf. for fifteenth century, Paul M. Kendall and Vincent Iliardi, *Dispatches with Related Documents of Milanese Ambassadors in France and Burgundy, 1450–1483*, vol. 1 (Athens, Ohio, 1970), pp. xvii-xviii.

68. See, for example, A.S.L., *Con. gen., Riform. pubbl.* 2, fol. 18ᵛ.

69. This register is entitled *Cons. gen., Indici di Decreti* 1369–1488: Salutati's part begins fol. 15. It bears the title *Rubrice actorum Reformationum manu Colutii de Stignano Cancellarii Communis Lucani anno n. D. MCCCLXX, Ind. VIII.*

70. See, for example, A.S.L., *Con. gen., Riform. pubbl.*, 2, fol. 44.

71. This is the only deliberation of the General Council during Salutati's time as chancellor that is not recorded in his register. It is found written in the hand of ser Pietro di Tomeo at the end of the register of the *Riformagioni* ser Tomeo had kept the previous year (ibid., 1, fol. 244ᵛ).

72. *Epist.*, I, 147.

at Bologna, Salutati had seen his own future compromised by the defeat of a regime to which his family's fortunes were tied. Now, twenty-five years later, his career was again blighted by the fall from power of the faction that had sponsored him.

The letter of April 1369 to Niccolosio Bartolomeo, one of the members of the aristocratic party in Lucca,[73] is the first clue to the existence of a relationship between Salutati's appointment and that group. A second and more definite sign appears in the composition of the guest list for the feast held at Buggiano in March of that same year shortly before the liberation of Lucca. The presence of Niccolosio, Niccolò Diversi, Nino degli Opizi, and one of his sons, Giovanni, all important leaders of the Lucchese aristocracy, indicates that a special bond existed between the commune of Buggiano and these men who, after years of exile, were shortly to be at the head of the newly liberated republic.[74] Although there is no conclusive proof that Salutati was a protégé of this faction, the surviving evidence points in that direction.

This relationship in itself would have made him an object of attack for the popular party, disgusted as it was with a regime in which the aristocratic families were, by law, granted privileges and offices distinguishing them from the mass of the people. As far as the popular party was concerned, Lucca had not shaken off the Pisan tyranny in order to replace it with a domestic one, exercised by a local oligarchy. Salutati's appointment was made on July 17, 1370; only a few weeks later, on July 31, a minor revolution took place in the communal assembly. On that day the popular opposition finally felt strong enough to force through measures abolishing the aristocrats' political privileges. When the motion was proposed, it was Nino degli Opizi, the head of the Opizi family, who rose and voiced the opposition of the aristocratic faction. But the popular element had not underestimated its strength and when the vote was taken, the motion passed. Everyone, including the nobles, was forced to swear "to support the people in the name of the people and to uphold the common and popular government."[75] Although it did not destroy the nobles as a power in the assemblies, the reform put them in a definite minority.

An uneasy truce between the two parties ensued. Then, in February 1371, the aristocratic faction tried to overthrow the regime of July 31 by an overt act of revolution. Giovanni degli Opizi was subsequently accused of treason, and Niccolò Diversi and Tommaso degli Opizi were

---

73. Ibid., I, 88–91 and n. 43, above.   74. See n. 43, above.
75. See the document published by Tommasi, "Documenti," p. 40.

forced to go surety for him.[76] By the summer of 1371, when it came time to discuss the renewal of Salutati's contract, all the Luccan leaders on the Buggiano guest list of 1369 had disappeared from the assembly and with them Salutati's assurance of reappointment.[77]

It is impossible to be sure to what degree Salutati suffered because of his associations. Very possibly his failure to obtain reappointment for a second year was partly the result of more positive activity on his part. His intense participation in the government of Buggiano both before his departure for Todi and after his return from Rome might have induced him, once a citizen of Lucca, to enter actively into its political life. Judged by the optimism and energy displayed during the preceding summer at Buggiano, Salutati was at least psychologically prepared for a career in Lucchese politics. Although the decree of July 31, 1370, constituted a palpable setback for the aristocratic party, Salutati might have considered it merely a temporary one and, in the course of his year in office, might have worked somewhat too openly for a restoration of their power.

Regarding his failure to be reappointed, however, a secondary motive could have been financial: Salutati was probably considered too expensive. At least, his successor received a lower salary. The new chancellor, Saraceni, had the same title but his salary was kept at six florins per month, the stipend he had received as Pietro di Tomeo's coadjutor. It is certainly possible that the move to dismiss Salutati found support among some economy-minded councillors, who, conscious of the opportunity to cut expenses and of the presence of a replacement prepared to work for less, considered Salutati an unnecessary luxury.

But Salutati had powerful friends in the city. Within a week or ten days of completing his term as chancellor on July 27, Salutati was chosen to the newly created post of judge and chief consul of the Merchants' Court of Lucca.[78] Since the liberation of the city this court, which

---

76. *Croniche di Giovanni Sercambi*, ed. Salvestro Bongi, Fonti per la storia d'Italia, vols. 19–21 (Rome, 1892), I, 204–6.

77. Although Niccolosio Bartolomei cannot be linked directly with the events leading to the attempt of Giovanni to capture Lucca by force, he seems to have disappeared from the councils of the Republic during 1371. He reappears in 1372: P. Paganini, *Due lettere di F. Petrarca a N. Bartolomei da Lucca* (Lucca, 1869), pp. 21–22, which includes a biography of Niccolosio. Novati, *Epist.*, I, 147, n. 1, emphasizes this link between Salutati and the noble faction as the probable reason for Salutati's dismissal. Oddly enough, twenty years later in his summary of Salutati's life Novati writes: "Dal 3 agosto 1370 al 27 luglio 1371 egli resse e con lode l'uffizio . . . quindi, opponendosi gli statuti ad una sua riconferma, forza gli fu riparare a Stignano dove represe ad esercitare per suo conto il notariato" (*Epist.*, IV, 388). There is nothing to substantiate this latter assertion of such a statutory prohibition.

78. See my "Coluccio Salutati, Chancellor," appendix 1, pp. 212–14.

regulated the various guilds of the Lucchese *contado* and adjudicated all disputes connected with the commerce of the Republic,[79] had consisted of seven consuls and one chief consul, elected to bi-monthly terms. No change in this organization was being contemplated as late as November 1370, when the list of court officials was drawn up for the coming year, nor was there any alteration of the succession as late as the middle of 1371. Yet by the first week of August the structure of the court had been altered. It now had a new official, the judge and chief consul, with much greater powers over the administration of the court than those possessed formerly by the chief consul.[80] Simone Bonagiunta, who in the previous November had been designated to fill the latter position for July and August, was still on the court bench but now was merely one of the seven consuls. Surely Salutati's friends, in an effort to compensate him for his loyalty, had exerted pressure on the general council of the Merchant's Court to bring about the restructuring and to name their protégé to the new office.

The duties of the new officer are difficult to determine. The first extant statute of the court, written in 1376, refers to a body composed of seven consuls, one of whom is called the chief judge (*giudice maggior*). Elected by the general council of the Merchants' Court together with the consuls, he had to be a foreigner. His term of office was for one year while that of the consuls was for two months. As head of the court, he was responsible for the regulation of the industries and commerce of the Republic. He could judge infractions of the rules and statutes either by himself or in conjunction with other consuls. For the discharge of these functions he received two hundred and fifty florins per year for himself and three men-at-arms.[81] Very probably, although the salary, length of term, and other details of the appointment may have been different, the main functions of the president of the court, whether called judge and chief consul or chief judge, remained much the same. This would mean,

79. Ibid., p. 201, n. 46.
80. Evidence for this is that, while before Salutati's appointment there had been examples of the court sitting on a case without the presence of the chief consul, Salutati was always present in the court when the names of the judges are given in the documents. In one case, he sat alone (October 8), a situation that suggests a power analogous to those outlined for the chief judge (*giudice maggior*) discussed below in text.
81. Under Pisan control the court apparently was headed by a doctor of laws called the *avocatus* (A.S.L., *Corte de'Mercanti, Cause civili*, 136, fol. 1). Moreover, although after Salutati the office of judge and major consul seems to have been abolished (*Cause civili*, 138, for July-December 1372, does not list any such official in the court), it was restored at least by April 1, 1373 (ibid., 139, fol. 1), and another doctor of laws is listed as holding the post. The fact that this work was usually done by such a specialist indicates the importance of the assignment.

therefore, that Salutati, after July 1371, still occupied an important position in Lucca; as head of the Merchants' Court, he was able to exercise considerable control over the commercial life of the city.

Since no records exist after October 1371, when Salutati was still on the court, until July 1372, when he was back in Stignano, the length of his term is unknown but perhaps the appointment was made for the period August 1371–January 1372.[82] Whether because of the statutes of the court or a shift in power in the general council of the court, the appointment was not renewed and in his last months in Lucca Salutati eked out a living working as a private notary. On February 13, 1372, in a letter to Giovanni di Montecalvo, he complains that his body is "dulled by leisure."[83]

The two years spent in Lucca, begun with such enthusiasm and high expectations, were perhaps the bitterest of Salutati's life. He had hoped to acquire glory and fortune from this appointment. While he knew in advance that his moments of free time would necessarily be fewer than they had been as a clerk in the Curia, he probably reasoned that the post of chancellor would give him greater opportunity to unfold his talents before the public. But in the sequel Salutati was deeply disappointed. Almost immediately he found himself overwhelmed by his official duties. He rose early to attend the meetings of the *Anziani* and worked at the *palazzo comunale* until twilight, having only enough free time to return home briefly for lunch. As he wrote to his friend, ser Tancredi Vergolesi, on October 24, 1370:

> Hardly have I finished my sleep when another morning comes and the same group of *Anziani* calls me by lictor, ready to load me down with anxious cares. If I had the time I would place before your eyes one day; but so busy am I, that I hardly am able to relate these things.[84]

While not allowing him sufficient time for his beloved studies, the post offered him no chance to develop his rhetorical abilities: the *Anziani* had no interest in eloquence. At least it seems that he was referring to his

82. The court in this period was unstable. The 1373 register of the *Cause civili*, for example, gives the term of the judge and chief consul as nine months: ibid., 139, fol. 1. His remark to Giovanni di Montecalvo cited below implies an even shorter term of appointment than six months.

83. *Epist.*, I, 159: "Provide tu, si qua via est, ut hinc me coneris honoranter evellere. Adhuc valet corpus et laboribus, licet hebetatum ocio, scio quod abunde sufficiet, et si forsan horreat, illudetiam invitum assuescere cogam."

84. *Epist.*, I, 133.

work as chancellor when he complained that in writing letters he was compelled to "unlearn" (*dediscere*).[85]

It is difficult, however, to say what Salutati's public letters during this period were like. There is no record of a register of letters kept by the Chancellor of the Commune either in Salutati's time or in that of his successors. Besides, according to practice, all foreign correspondence of the commune was sent in the name of the *Anziani* alone; if the organizational arrangement created by the provision of July 17, 1370, was observed, this would have meant that the Chancellor of the *Anziani* was responsible for such correspondence. The register of the letters of the commune for this and later periods, written as it was by the Chancellor of the *Anziani* or his assistant, suggests that the rule was followed. Where, then, are the letters which Salutati was incessantly called upon to write for the *Anziani*? The only extant letters of the commune to its officials in the *contado*, letters which we might expect Salutati's chancery to handle, are those found recorded from time to time in the *Deliberationi* of the *Anziani* in the hand of the assistant to their chancellor, ser Pietro Saraceni.[86] Were the letters of Salutati merely notes dispatched to local officials and not important enough to be registered? Did he perhaps write some of the letters which are recorded in the registers kept by the other chancery?[87]

In spite of the inconveniences of his appointment in the chancery, the lack of free time to devote to his studies,[88] and the indifference of his employers to reforming chancery style, Salutati would gladly have accepted a renewal of his contract had it been offered. But probably very early in his term he began to realize that tremendous forces were building up in opposition to his reappointment. He felt himself surrounded

85. Ibid.

86. A.S.L., *Anziani al tempo della libertà, Delib.*, 132, *passim*.

87. I am somewhat more reluctant now than in my article, "Coluccio Salutati, Chancellor," pp. 204–7, to make Salutati the author of the document that appears as A.S.L., *Con. gen., Riform. pubbl.*, 2, fols. 79–79ᵛ, and published as appendix 2 of the article, pp. 214–16. There is still a good possibility, however, of his authorship. Although this does not affect the attribution, I should observe that, despite Salutati's assertion at the end of the register that he had written the whole (see above, n. 66), I am now certain that the pages containing this document were copied by another hand, probably that of his coadjutor Dombellinghi, whose calligraphy I have not been able to identify.

88. Nevertheless, in this first year he seems to have been able to spend some time with his books. In the course of that year he might have begun work on what appears to be his first long piece of prose, *De vita associabili et operativa* (*Epist.*, I, 156), while his production of poetry continued (he probably devoted some time to his *Bucolica* [ibid., I, 157]). Moreover, he was busily engaged in exchanging books with his friends and copying volumes for his own library (ibid., I, 134 and 157).

by enemies. It is this unvoiced insecurity that lay beneath the discontent articulated in his letter to Vergolesi of October 24, 1370.[89] Lured by the promise of honors, Salutati writes, man is prompted to abandon well-laid plans. In his own case, he complains that he is always changing, reversing himself, always just beginning to live. Nor can he abide by the Stoic ethics; he has never learned to bear with equanimity the loss of loved ones, illness, fears of disgrace or poverty, and other external threats to self-mastery. What he did not express was his growing apprehension that the honors he had sought would prove chimerical, that all his efforts to perform well in the service of the Republic would not gain his reappointment. His subsequent employment on the Merchants' Court could have given only a temporary and superficial surcease to his anxiety. He knew that he could not remain in Lucca and wearily began to look for an escape. At least as early as the summer of 1371, he had alerted his numerous correspondents to his situation.[90]

Plagued by self-doubts, depressed by his professional failure, Salutati suffered an even greater blow. In February 1371 his wife, Caterina, had given birth to their first child, a son whom they baptized Bonifazio.[91] Sometime that fall, while pregnant with a second child, she was carried off by a sudden illness (*morbi impetu*), probably the plague, which struck the city early in September of that year.[92] During the six years of their marriage Salutati came to care for Caterina deeply. This had been a difficult period of moving from place to place, first to Todi, then to Rome, and finally to Lucca. Salutati's professional disappointments probably bound him ever closer to his wife. Now, overwhelmed by grief, Salutati lapsed into utter despondency. He abandoned his work on the *De vita associabili* never to resume it; friends' letters lay forgotten and unanswered on his desk.[93] Not until the end of January 1372 had he recovered sufficiently to be able to resume work again.[94] Yet, as late as

89. *Epist.*, I, 130–34.
90. His friend, ser Giovanni Cambini, had spoken of his case to the bishop of Arezzo, who expressed an interest in hiring Salutati as soon as the ailing chancellor ser Jacopo Magrini died. But Magrini recovered and held on to his post. The whole negotiation must have taken place over a number of months in the period before October 8, 1371, when Salutati wrote to the bishop and Cambini thanking them for their attempt to help him (*Epist.*, I, 145–49). Salutati announced in the letter to Cambini that he had written a poem against a certain "ser Santi de Valiano" (p. 149), who had defamed Lucca in a poetic invective: see Guiseppe Billanovich, "Giovanni del Virgilio, Pietro da Moglio, Francesco da Fiano," *Italia medioevale e umanistica*, 7 (1964), 307–21.
91. *Epist.*, I, 144.
92. Sercambi, I, 206.
93. *Epist.*, I, 156.
94. The letter to Boccaccio is dated January 21, 1372 (ibid., I, 156): Salutati is at least able to speak of his poetry (p. 157).

mid-February in his letter to Giovanni di Montecalvo, he described his sorrow as boundless and his weeping as uncontrolled.[95]

In these letters written after Caterina's death, as before in his sorrow at the death of Simone, nephew of Lapo Castiglionchio, he offered no sign of Christian sentiment and no indication that he derived any consolation from his religion.[96] Rather, he identified fortune as having robbed him both of his beloved wife and of the little child growing in her womb.[97] Nor were the philosophers of any help in this time of need. In fact, their teachings had proved wrong. They said that nothing dried more quickly than tears, yet experience said the opposite. But there was no time at this point to philosophize. For Salutati, it was a question of survival and that meant getting out of Lucca: "If it happens that I stay here longer, perhaps, although willingly, I shall accompany the bier of my wife."[98] Sometime in the second half of February or early in March 1372, a desperate, still mourning Salutati departed Lucca for the last time.

In Lucca Salutati had lived only thirteen miles from his home in Stignano, and this proximity had permitted him to return there on a number of occasions during the course of his nineteen months in the city. On some of these trips he found time to represent Buggiano and to add the prestige of the chancellor of Lucca to its embassies. On April 20, 1371, while on vacation from his official duties, he was appointed the representative of Buggiano in its negotiations before the vicar of the Valdinievole over a local dispute with Uzzano, and again in June he went to Pescia twice for the same reason.[99] In these last two missions he acted as a member of the Buggiano government: his name had been drawn as Defender at the end of May 1371 for the trimester June-August.[100]

The infant Bonifazio had probably been sent back to Stignano on his

95. *Epist.*, I, 158–59: "mens quidem mea . . . nedum dolet, sed insaniat"; his sorrow "transcendit enim omnem modum et mole sua nixum nec minui patitur nec augeri."

96. See above, p.

97. *Epist.*, I, 159: "et ne putes hoc solo fortune sevientis pondere me confractum, scito et cum illa conceptum iam ad quintum mensem in utero puerulum interisse." A little further below he mentions fortune again: "et quoniam istic videtur nescio quid deliberare fortuna. . . ." In his letter to Lapo on the death of Simone he had used the idea of fortune as a form of consolation: "quodque ipse facere nescio, fortior contra fortunam, quasi Antheus contra Herculem, ex huiusmodi prostratione resurgas, et eo tutior ad congressum, quod nunc minus habes in quo sit illi ius sevire (ibid., I, 103). There is no sign of such an effort in the letters of 1372.

98. Ibid., I, 159.

99. A.C.B., *Delib.*, 6, fols, 190, 208ᵛ, and 212.

100. Ibid., fol. 201, but his brother, Currado, seems to have served in his place in the council.

mother's death to stay with Salutati's family, but the first sign of Salutati's presence in the commune after his ambassadorial work in June
1371 came on February 2, 1372, when he notarized a document there.[101]
Nevertheless, his stay in the valley lasted only a few days. As mentioned above, he sent a letter to Boccaccio from Lucca on January 21 and
another from there to Giovanni di Montecalvo on February 13. What
happened to him in the following months is uncertain. He was in Buggiano on March 7 and 30 when he made the second and third entries in
his notarial register, but the fourth was dated July 4, more than three
months later.[102] Moreover, on May 27, when his name was drawn as
Defender for the period June-August 1372, his brother, Currado, took
his place because "now ser Coluccio is absent from the territory of Buggiano so that he is not able to fulfill the said office."[103] Yet he must have
spent some of April and May in Buggiano because on June 1 he was
paid twenty *soldi* for his work in reforming the communal statutes.[104]

Since there is ample evidence from the *Deliberazioni* that Salutati was
in Buggiano from July 4, 1372, until February 1374, only some three
months are in question. It is unlikely that during this time he remained
in Lucca, the city where he had suffered so much. Most probably, he
spent some weeks during this period in Florence visiting friends he had
not seen for years. Perhaps he also tried unsuccessfully to arrange an
appointment for himself in the Florentine chancery. This would not
have been an easy task since few notarial posts in the Florentine Republic, or anywhere else for that matter, were suitable for an ex-chancellor
of Lucca. Salutati had become too important to continue the pattern of
office-holding he had followed before leaving for Todi. If he was in Florence during part of the spring and early summer of 1372, he very probably paid his annual dues to the Guild of Judges and Notaries on May
26 in person.[105]

July 4, the date of the first entry in his notarial protocol after those in

101. *Il protocollo notarile di Coluccio Salutati (1372–1373)*, ed. Armando Petrucci (Milan,
1963), pp. 52–54.

102. Ibid., pp. 54–59 and 59–61. The last date given for a document in the protocol is
April 4, 1373 (ibid., pp. 147–50). By a strange coincidence Roberto Abbondanza has located a transcription of an act notarized by Salutati on April 6, 1373, which might have
been among the first to be written in a new protocol (A.S.F., *Archivio della Badia, Boiani*, T.
VI, 280, fols. 31–32).

103. A.C.B., *Delib.*, 6, fols. 296ᵛ. His brother is substituted, fol. 299.

104. Ibid., fol. 299ᵛ.

105. AGN, *Libri d'atti e d'entrata*, 93, fol. 121ᵛ. Salutati had kept up his ties with the
Florentine guild while in Lucca. On February 27, 1371, he had paid half a fine of ten *lire*
because of failure to send in his *imbreviatura* of notarial records for the previous year (*AGN*,
603, ad an.).

March, also marked Salutati's first appearance in the Buggiano assembly. On that day he and three other citizens were delegated to go to Pescia on unspecified business.[106] A week later he was sent to Florence to discuss various matters with the central government.[107] High on the list of topics was probably the perennial question of the Usciana. The communes along the Arno had again resorted to damming the Usciana River, which, flowing across the lowlands of the Valdinievole, emptied into the Arno. This allowed them to utilize the river for water mills and fishing ponds. Obstructed as it was, the Usciana overflowed its banks, flooding the plain and making a marshland of the low-lying areas belonging to citizens of the communes of the Valdinievole. On August 9 Salutati acted as one of the four citizen-captains who led a communal army of 181 men on a three- or four-day expedition to destroy the dikes and weirs.[108] Oddly enough, forty years later Salutati's son Arrigo, during his six-months term of office as *podestà* of Buggiano, led the forces of the same commune against the dikes on the river.[109]

Nineteen months passed between his return home and his departure for Florence in February 1374 to assume the office of notary of the *Tratte*, the official entrusted with supervising Florentine elections. In that interval Salutati served in the General Council of Buggiano in every trimester except those of December 1372–February 1373 and June-August 1373.[110] Over the whole nineteen-month period he made approximately thirty percent of all the recorded speeches in the assembly. Unfortunately, because of the summary fashion in which the debates in the General Council were recorded, it is impossible to know more than the general tenor of most of Salutati's speeches during the period. In transcribing his notes the communal secretary usually only summarized the remarks of the speakers either by repeating the wording of the original proposal or by presenting in a few lines the speaker's reasoning.

---

106. A.C.B., *Delib.*, 6, fol. 310ᵛ.

107. Ibid., fol. 312. An embassy of eleven days.

108. Ibid., fol. 318. The expedition lasted three or four days (fols. 323–24ᵛ). If we are to believe his later reminiscences, he had seen considerable military service as a young man (*Epist.*, II, 179).

109. The battle and subsequent victory of Arrigo Salutati's forces were commemorated by pairs of chains, some of those used by the enemy to bar the way to the men of Buggiano, still to be seen suspended on the facades of S. Pietro Apostolo in Borgo-a-Buggiano and of S. Andrea in Stignano.

110. Salutati was not originally elected to office during the trimester September-November 1372 (ibid., 6, fols. 328ᵛ–29) but must have been appointed after the drawing as a substitute. The first mention of him as a member of the General Council during this term comes on September 29 (ibid., 6, fol. 351ᵛ). In the cases of the trimesters December 1372–February 1373 and June-August 1373 mentioned in the text, even though he did not hold an official post in the government, he still served on a number of embassies.

Nevertheless, on September 29, 1372, a topic was debated which evoked Salutati's eloquence and something of his delivery echoed in the terse description written by the communal secretary. The issue involved the abolition of the land contract known as the perpetual lease (*affictus perpetuus*) whereby those taking up a lease on land obligated themselves and their heirs to work the holding and pay the rent forever.[111] The resolution called for a law which would make such leases illegal in the future and would allow for the redemption of existing leases "at the original price of the land."

Salutati placed the proposal before the assembly in the form of a motion. He urged passage of the law "for reasons of obvious utility and the good and pacific state of the men and persons of the commune of Buggiano and for removing errors, scandals, wars, enmities, and difficulties which can occur and arise in the said commune because of the aforementioned perpetual lease and in order to lead men back to liberty, which is dearer than all things. . . ."[112] A comparison of the notary's summary of Salutati's remarks with the original proposition shows that, as usual, the notary merely stated in different words the content of the proposal. When, however, Salutati added a philosophical dimension to this utilitarian appeal, he used an argument not found in the original formulation: man was born to live in liberty. The perpetual lease, he presumably argued, bound not only the man originally making the agreement but also his children and their children. Thus, the actions of future generations were determined by a will not their own.

There is no way to develop his reasoning further, given the brevity of the summary. Nevertheless, we can say that in this concrete situation

111. Ibid., 13, fols. 349–49ᵛ. "Cum hoc sit quod affictus perpetui inducant in liberos homines quandam spem servitutis quod ex ipsis, quasi vassalli dominis ad certum redditum perpetuo prestandum, homines obligantur et videntur laborandis prediis tam ipsi quam eorum heredes ascripti et deputati; ex quibus in communi Buggiani multa actenus inconvenientia sunt secuta et secutura timentur fortius in futurum. Idcircho quid dicto consilio et hominibus dicti consilii videtur et placet providere, stantiare et reformare et legem at decretum validum et roboratum facere et ordinare, quod in futurum in communi Buggiani aut etiam extra dictum commune aliquis de Buggiano ibidem habitans non possit conducere suum aliquo titulo vel causa recipere ab aliqua persona, communi, collegio vel universitate aliquid predium rusticum vel urbanum . . . ad affictum perpetuum, in feudum seu in emphiteosim aut ad contractum."

112. Ibid., 6, fol. 351ᵛ: "Ser Coluccius Pieri unus ex hominibus dicti consilii surgens ad arengheriam consuetam et arengando et consulendo super dictam primam propositam et contentam in ea qua incipit 'in primis cum hoc et cetera,' et finit, 'derogata,' dixit et consulit quod sibi videtur et placet in quantum nutibus reliquorum sit conforme pro evidenti utilitate et bono et pacifico statu hominum et personarum communis Buggiani et ad extolendum errores, scandala, guerras, imicitias, et discrimina que in dicto communi et inter homines dicti communis nasci et oriri occasione dicti affictus perpetui possent et ad reducendum homines in libertate que omnibus aliis rebus carior prestitit. . . ."

Salutati saw the relevance of his political ideals and hoped, by articulating the problem in terms of those ideals, to strengthen his appeal for a practical solution. Whatever the examples used, the manner in which the theme was developed and the eloquence with which it was expressed, the speech must have so moved the secretary that, contrary to his general practice, he reported the outline of Salutati's remarks as actually spoken.

In addition to his army service and various assignments within the commune itself, Salutati spent more than eighty-three days on missions for Buggiano outside the communal territory, over half of the time on business in Florence.[113] As the result of a new method of keeping vicarial letters, instituted by ser Giovanni di Giuntavita da Montecarlo, who was appointed communal notary in August 1373, we also learn that Salutati acted occasionally as representative of the entire province in Florence.[114] Since the province paid for such service, the records were not kept by the commune and, consequently, we do not know how much additional time on behalf of the Valdinievole Salutati spent in Florence during these nineteen months.

To all appearances Salutati had returned to Stignano to take up his old life. After almost five years away, after the failures and tragedies that had afflicted him at Rome and Lucca, and perhaps after a brief and still unsuccessful search for a position in Florence, Salutati had returned to his homeland, where his modest earnings and relative obscurity were compensated for by the affection and respect of his compatriots. Another time, twenty-one years before, the *patria* had offered the notary and his family refuge. Now, the familiar surroundings received and sheltered the grief-stricken, insecure man in middle age. Just as he resumed his political activity, he went back to regular work as a notary. Only one of his notarial protocols for this period exists, but there were certainly others that have been lost. A note to Luigi Marsili, probably written during this period, indicates that he also continued his interest in collecting books.[115] In this instance the religious character of the

---

113. The reference to Florentine embassies are as follows: ibid., 6, fol. 312 (eleven days); ibid., 5, fol. 276ᵛ (six days); ibid., 7, fol. 3ᵛ (eighteen days), fol. 43 (six days), fol. 121 (four days "et ultra"); (Pescia), ibid., 6, fols. 310ᵛ, 318, 326, 340ᵛ, 344, 359ᵛ, and 366ᵛ; ibid., 7, fols. 15, 38, 39, 39ᵛ, 42ᵛ, 55, 55ᵛ, 64ᵛ, 73ᵛ, 81, 82, 87, 97 (two days), 101ᵛ, 106ᵛ, 114ᵛ, 119ᵛ, 121, 125ᵛ, 126, 128ᵛ, 136ᵛ; (Massa), ibid., 6, fol. 326 (two days); (Montecatini), ibid., 6, fol. 341 (two days); (Lucca), ibid., 7, fol. 58 (two days); (Castelfranco), ibid., 7, fol. 3ᵛ; and (Montevettolini), ibid., 7, fol. 72.

114. Ibid., 7, fol. 106ᵛ.

115. This brief note and Marsili's response are published by Agostino Sottili, "Postille all'epistolario di Coluccio Salutati," *Romanische Forschungen*, 79 (1967), 585–86. For the dat-

manuscripts he sought represents the influence of his Roman experience on his literary interests.

One can only guess his state of mind. The conclusion of his letter to
Marsili, whom he did not yet know well, was revealing: "Pray for me,
since I am in need of it and perish."[116] This was no formal pose of humility but reflected the inner turmoil of a man who, at this point in his
life, might well have felt he had reached a dead end, both spiritually
and professionally. Marsili, who appreciated the depths of Salutati's despair, replied: "I will pray; I believe you need it."[117] Yet these long
months in the Valdinievole must also have resulted in some degree of
recuperation. The presence of his friend Ugolino da Montecatini in Buggiano in 1373, where he functioned for a term as town doctor, also
greatly comforted him.[118] One almost certain sign of the recuperative
process was that he re-married, probably in 1373.[119] His second wife,
Piera, was the daughter of Simone di Puccino Riccomi, from one of the
branches of the Salutati family residing in Pescia.

At times Salutati might seriously have considered trying to realize the
plan of life he had thought ideal before leaving Rome, that is, a simple
existence divided among friends, family, public service, and study. But
he was still ambitious, if now more cautious, and although he might
have been unconscious of it, his own ambition coincided with the interest of a group of leading Guelfs in the capital. By means of an elaborate
project, these men hoped to rid themselves of a troublesome enemy, ser
Niccolò Monachi, the incumbent Florentine chancellor. Salutati was to
be introduced into the Florentine bureaucracy through the creation of a
new position, that of notary of the *Tratte*, and, once established in it, he
would be ready to take ser Niccolò's place when the time was ripe.

On January 24, 1374, Salutati was chosen to go to Pescia to consult
with the vicar on an unspecified matter.[120] Subsequently, on February 1
and 3, he was listed as absent from the meetings of the General Coun-

---

ing of the letter, see Ronald Witt, "Toward a Biography of Coluccio Salutati," *Rinascimento*,
16 (1976), 25–28. Marsili's use of a brief phrase in Greek in his response to Salutati appears
to qualify Roberto Weiss's assertion that "il Marsili il greco non cercò mai d'apprenderlo":
"Lo studio del greco a Firenze," *Medieval and Humanist Greek, Collected Essays by Roberto
Weiss*, ed. R. Avesani, G. Billanovich, and G. Pozzi, Medioevo e umanesimo, vol. 8 (Padua,
1977), p. 232.

    116. Sottili, "Postille," p. 586.   117. Ibid.
    118. A.C.B., *Delib.*, 7, fol. 24ᵛ. See below, chap. 10.
    119. For the second wife, see *Epist.*, IV, 390. The couple's first child, Piero, was born in
1375 (see below, chap. 7).
    120. A.C.B., *Delib.*, 7, fol. 136ᵛ.

cil.[121] His name did not occur again in the *Deliberazioni* until April 3 when it appeared in a petition offered by ser Rigozzi asking that Salutati be henceforth exempted from paying all taxes in the commune of Buggiano save his share of the *estimo*, the annual general tax levied on the territory by Florence.[122] Although by this time, having exercised his new office in the *Tratte* for only six weeks, he must have felt certain enough of his official position, or at least of his own intentions, to make a request for tax exemptions which he had never done when at Todi, Rome, or Lucca. From this point on, although paying the *estimo* on his property in the commune, he was no longer a full citizen of Buggiano, and his conception of the *patria* expanded to include the entire state of which Buggiano was but a minor part.

121. Ibid., 7, fols. 138ᵛ and 142.   122. Ibid., 7, fol. 157ᵛ.

PART II. THE FLORENTINE CHANCELLOR

CHAPTER 5. THE CHANCELLOR'S WORLD (1375–82)

The *Palazzo della Signoria*, three stories of roughened stone block surmounted by an immense tower looming three hundred and five feet over its piazza, was one of the great engineering feats of medieval Italy.[1] The official residence of the Florentine *Signoria*, the supreme executive body of the Republic which consisted of eight priors and the standard-bearer of justice, the building also housed many of the other state offices and the assembly halls for the great councils of the Republic. By 1374 the palace had changed very little since the completion of the original structure in 1302. To someone standing in the unpaved piazza before the warm brown facade, the front entrance was over on the far right of the principal surface. From the left side of this door a stone platform ran the length of the front and around the corner where it encountered another door into the palace. Fenced by a balustrade, the long platform, the *ringhiera*, was higher than a man's head and in good weather served as the stage for much of the public drama of Florentine life. Here important visitors were officially welcomed, the highest officials of the commune took their oath of office, and the Florentines were lectured on the benefits of justice and good government. The platform also provided a good vantage point from which dignitaries could comfortably view the frequent processions and celebrations occurring in the piazza. Some of this activity, especially on rainy days, was to be transferred to the *Loggia dei Lanzi* after its completion in 1382.

Once through the front portal of the palace one entered a large interior courtyard, which covered more than half the space on the ground floor. Occupying the rest of this floor was the *Camera d'Arme*, where the utensils and goods pertaining to the operation of the priors' household jostled machines of war and stores of salt for the *contado* under the high painted vaults.[2] A stairway set against the wall of the inner courtyard toward the piazza led to the floors above. On the second was the *Sala del Gran Consiglio*, the meeting place for the large popular assemblies.[3]

---

1. This paragraph is based on the work of Alfredo Lensi, *Palazzo vecchio* (Milan-Rome, 1929), pp. 8, 24, 28, and 38.

2. Demetrio Marzi, *La cancelleria della Repubblica fiorentina* (Rocca S. Casciano, 1910), pp. 446–54, discusses the function of the *Camera d'Arme*.

3. Lensi, pp. 14–15.

The offices of the chancellor and the notary on legislation were probably on this floor, but the present chancery is a later construction.[4] As for other departments of the government, long before Salutati's appointment to the *Tratte* they had spilled out of the original structure and were partially housed in buildings behind the palace.

The priors and the standard-bearer of justice (*gonfaloniere di justitia*) lived on the third floor, which housed their audience hall, their chapel, and the dormitory where until the fifteenth century the top officials of the state slept together during their two months' term, their beds separated from one another by wooden partitions, their bedlights nestling in niches in the wall. Such arrangements provided ample opportunity for the priors to play practical jokes with bed clothing and chamber pots, which became famous throughout the city.[5] Also on the same floor was a large room where the *Signoria* met with the other two executive colleges, the Twelve (*dodici buon uomini*) and the Sixteen (*gonfalonieri delle companie*).[6] First as notary of the *Tratte* and then as chancellor, Salutati was to spend a good part of the last thirty-one years of his life in this massive edifice, which housed most of what scholars generally have regarded as the Florentine "bureaucracy."

I

A bureaucratic institution is by nature vertical, hierarchical; the Florentine public administration was horizontal and relatively egalitarian.[7] The

4. A document attests to the fact that Salutati on June 21, 1380, took his yearly oath of office "in the chancery of the palace of the lord priors of the arts and the Standardbearer of Justice where he resides for the purpose of exercising the duties of his chancery," but it only proves that Salutati worked somewhere in the building (*Epist.*, IV, 443–44).

5. Lensi, p. 12, describes the dormitory. For humor among government officials see Franco Sacchetti, *Il trecentonovelle*, ed. Emilio Faccioli (Torino, 1970), pp. 213–18 and 344–46.

6. *Statuta Populi et Communis Florentiae publica auctoritate collecta castigata et praeposita, anno salutis MCCCCXV*, 3 vols. (Freiburg, 1778–83), II, 547.

7. There is a tendency among modern scholars to speak of the Florentine administrative organization as a bureaucracy without reminding the reader that the term can only be used with qualification: Marvin Becker, *Florence in Transition*, 2 vols. (Baltimore, 1967–68), II, 214, 216; Gene Brucker, *Florentine Politics and Society 1343–1378* (Princeton, 1963), p. 60. Lauro Martines, *Lawyers and Statecraft* (Princeton, 1968), avoids this term. This problem of correct terminology was first brought to my attention in conversation with Hans Baron. Unfortunately the work done by Federico Chabod on the Milanese bureaucracy is largely irrelevant to a study of the Florentine administration. His analysis focuses primarily on the sixteenth century and even for the earlier period he is dealing with a principality

efficiency of a bureaucracy derives from continuity of experience and specialization; in Florence the emphasis was on massive and regular turnover in officeholding. Florentine terms of public office were short, usually lasting for a few months and rarely exceeding a year. As a rule consecutive terms were forbidden. The short tenure in office made it difficult for the average officeholder to become well-acquainted with the powers of his office. While the mass of citizen officials were amateurs, the notaries were professional administrators.[8] Acting as secretaries to the various collegial governing bodies, the notaries constituted a class of legal men with special education fitting them for administrative work.

Until the second quarter of the fourteenth century notaries appeared frequently among the lists of those holding essentially political positions in the government. But beginning in the second quarter of the century the share of the notariate in high government political posts dropped sharply.[9] This diminution was, of course, partially the result of the rising educational level of the Florentine citizenry as a whole. While the notary still possessed a special kind of knowledge, his literacy was not as unique as it had been and no longer merited political privilege. But an important cause was the gradual extension from the 1320s of the practice of electing by lot on the basis of a prior scrutiny to determine those

---

where administrative offices as a whole—not merely notarial appointments—were generally awarded without limitation on tenure. In such a situation the notaries together with other ducal officials developed a corporate feeling to a degree unknown in Florence. See his *Lo stato e la vita religiosa a Milano nell'epoca di Carlo V*, Opere di Federico Chabod, vol. 3, pt. 1 (Milan, 1971), pp. 169–82. Also see his more general remarks based primarily on the Milanese experience in "Y a-t-il un état de la Renaissance," *Actes du colloque sur la Renaissance* (Paris, 1958), pp. 71–72. The work by Caterina Santoro, *Gli offici del comune di Milano e del dominio visconteo-sforzesco, 1216–1515* (Milan, 1968), pp. 209–13, creates the impression that the Milanese chancery was considerably larger in the fifteenth century than the Florentine one. The extensive literature on the papal chancery in this period, moreover, appears to have little relevance to the Florentine situation. For the administrative organization of the Kingdom of Naples in the early seventeenth century, see Vittor I. Comparato, *Uffici e società a Napoli (1600–1647)* (Florence, 1974). Also see his excellent general biographical essay, pp. 5–38.

8. Anthony Molho, "Politics and the Ruling Class in Early Renaissance Florence," *Nuova rivista storica*, 52 (1968), 407, estimates there to have been roughly 3000 public offices to fill annually. See, however, Gene Brucker, *The Civic World of Early Renaissance Florence* (Princeton, 1977), p. 253.

9. The statistics of this reduction in the number of priorate seats are provided by Martines, *Lawyers*, pp. 49–50: 1282–1328, 72 places; 1328–48, 10 places; 1348–78, 9 places; 1378–98, 12 places; 1398–1418, 7 places; 1418–38, 5 places. For Martines by the fifteenth century the lawyers have superseded the notaries as leading political figures. "The special skills of the lawyer," Martines writes (p. 55), "in strict connection with the political needs of the Florentine Republic," and the more "'aristocratic' tenor of public life" explain the ascendancy of the lawyers. This explanation, however, cannot apply to the sharp drop in priorate seats which already occurs in the second quarter of the fourteenth century.

eligible for particular offices.[10] Approaching the task of coordinating the whole system of elections, the body of men assigned to place the names of citizens in the purses tended to set the notaries off as a separate category with a monopoly on a particular set of offices. Furthermore, in the last quarter of the fourteenth century this tendency to segregate notaries as a special group of citizens was reinforced by the evolution of what might be considered a professional ethic among them.[11]

As a class even the Florentine notaries would not fit the modern notion of bureaucrats. The majority of notarial offices in Florence were part-time. Only a handful of top notarial posts in Florence and a few dozen assignments on the staff of territorial vicars or *podestà* furnished full-time employment. Secondly, the methods of choosing notaries for official posts made the turnover in notarial personnel only slightly less than that for other citizens. Some notarial posts, including many of the full-time ones, were elected by lot. Some of these offices were renewable but most were not. In the case of many other notarial appointments an elected commission or official was empowered to choose a notary to serve as secretary but only for the duration of its or his own term.[12] These methods of election made any regular system of promotion impossible and often created significant discontinuity in officeholding for individual notaries.

What made the Florentine system of rapidly changing public officials work in the case of the notaries was that, while differentiated, the functions of most notarial positions did not vary greatly from one to another. Although regulations governing particular jurisdictions and operational procedures were different, the basic procedures, the recording of delib-

10. See Guidubaldo Guidi, "I sistemi elettorali del Comune di Firenze nel primo Trecento. Il sorgere della elezione per squittino (1300–1328)," *Archivio storico italiano*, 130 (1972), 392–407.

11. The increasing number of notarial posts in the government in the fourteenth century would further have helped establish the notaries as separated from other citizens. The growing tendency to keep official records, beginning around the end of the thirteenth and the early years of the fourteenth century, enhanced the public character of the notary's office in the government. Geoffrey Barraclough, *Public Notaries and the Papal Curia* (London, 1934), pp. 124–25, after noting that the initiation of public record keeping begins about the same time all over Europe, ascribes the development to the "rise to maturity of the notarial system." To an extent Barraclough is not exaggerating when he remarks "private *Imbreviaturen* of notaries of an earlier day became transformed into official registers" (p. 125). Cf. *Das Formelbuch des Henrich Bucglant*, ed. Jakob Schwalm (Hamburg, 1910), p. xxxviii.

12. For notarial positions awarded by the scrutiny procedure, see *Statuta*, II, 725–27. For examples of offices elected by the official body concerned, see ibid., II, 92; III, 273 and 352. The popular councils chose the notaries charged with cancellation of condemnations (I, 62).

erations, keeping accounts of money passing through the office, etc., were fairly standarized throughout the government. For this reason notaries, who had a basic knowledge of Florentine statutory law and administrative practices, could move into a new post and within a matter of days have the office running smoothly.[13]

Within this professional class, however, a number of individual notaries in every generation appeared almost permanently in official notarial positions. For instance, in the last quarter of the fourteenth century a check of notarial signatures on a wide variety of documents of different date issued by dozens of official bodies of the government creates the impression that notaries like ser Domenico Silvestri and ser Antonio Chelli spent their mature lifetime in the offices and corridors of the palace.[14] Despite the impermanence of the immediate function and the uncertainty about the nature of the next appointment, notaries in this situation formed something like an inner corps of administrators with a real cohesiveness.

Because of the tendency to retain the same person in office year after year and the specialized nature of the functions, two notarial offices of the Republic stand out as exceptions to the general character of notarial appointments in the Florentine Republic. These two officials were the notary of legislation and the chancellor of the Republic. The first was concerned with internal affairs and the second with supervising the notarial tasks related to foreign relations. Election to these offices was not by lot but rather by the vote of the *Signoria* together with the two other executive councils, the Sixteen and the Twelve. Although subject to annual election, the incumbents were normally reconfirmed year after year, so that tenures of twenty or thirty years in the same office were not unusual. The exceptional nature of the position of these two notar-

13. Martines, *Lawyers*, p. 170.
14. For Silvestri's biography see, Piero Ricci, "Per una monografia su Domenico Silvestri," *Annali della Scuola Normale Superiore di Pisa: lettere, storia e filosofia*, 19 (1950), 13–24, and in the same year and publication, Roberto Weiss, "Note per una monografia su Domenico Silvestri," pp. 198–201. Silvestri's work has been published in part. See Steven P. Marrone, "Domenico Silvestri's Defense of Poetry," *Rinascimento*, 13 (1973), 125–32; and Richard Jensen, *Domenico Silvestri, the Latin Poems*, ed. Richard C. Jensen (Munich, 1972). Silvestri, for example, was one of Salutati's assistants in 1377 (*Dipl. Riform.*, Aug. 28, 1377) and served as notary of the *Signoria* in 1378, 1387, and 1406: Marzi, pp. 492, 493, and 495. Antonio Chelli was another of Salutati's assistants in 1377 (ibid., Oct. 15, 1377), as well as in 1378 (ibid., Nov. 16, 1378), 1381 (ibid., Apr. 5, 1381), and 1382 (ibid., Aug. 8, 1382). He served as notary of the *Signoria* in 1380, 1383, and 1404 (Marzi, pp. 493 and 495). Some of his other elections to notarial office are found in *Miscellanea repubb.*, vol. 30, fols. 114^v, 142^v, 163^v, 176, 182, 200, 215^v, and 216. For references to Chelli's correspondence on the plague see below, chap. 10, n. 32.

ies stemmed from the Republic's need to have highly qualified men with long experience in these key administrative posts.

The basic function of the notary of legislation was to serve as secretary for the two great councils of the Republic, preparing the material for their meetings, counting their votes, and drawing up the laws they passed.[15] Yet the range of his office's jurisdiction was so broad that this notary was easily the chief official for internal affairs. Among his other duties were those of writing concessions of reprisal against foreign merchants, orders of exile and recall, licenses permitting Florentines to accept foreign posts, and a variety of other instruments. He frequently administered the oath of office to foreign officials and citizens and certified the act so that they might legally take up their duties. Until 1374 he was principally responsible for the hundreds of purses involved in the Florentine system of election including the supervision of the drawings for offices.[16] Perhaps his major function, one which could not be formulated specifically among his list of duties, was to furnish guidance to legislative and executive bodies throughout the state. Present at the deliberations of the legislative councils, keeper of the registers of *provvisioni*, having on request to locate a specific law either for public officials or private individuals, the notary of legislation with his long years of service knew the statutory law of the Florentine Republic better than any other person. He was also equal to none in his understanding of the unwritten rules and practices of government. When there was doubt about jurisdiction, specific powers, legal precedents, and the like, the notary of legislation was expected to have the answer or know where to find it in the maze of registers. Because of the extreme sensitivity of this position, it was originally regarded as necessary for the notary to be a foreigner, that is, a citizen of a territory outside Florence and its district.

The counterpart of the notary of legislation in foreign affairs was the chancellor. Because of the nature of his assignment, it was necessary for the chancellor to be a citizen of either Florence or its territory.[17] One of

15. Marzi treats the duties of this office in detail together with the careers of those who held office, pp. 17–19, 29–34, 52–56, 69–71, 74–79, 82–91 (for the period up to 1375).

16. Guidi, "I sistemi electorali," pp. 399 ff., indicates the important role of this official in the election process from the very introduction of use of lots.

17. Marzi analyzes the duties of the office in terms of the careers of those who held it, pp. 19–23, 34–47, 56–65, 68–69, 71–73, 77–82, 91–105. Although in fact the chancellors in the thirteenth and fourteenth centuries were all notaries, in the fifteenth some like Accolti and Scala were lawyers while two, Bruni and Marsuppini, were neither. Alison Brown, *Bartolomeo Scala, 1430–1497, Chancellor of Florence: The Humanist as Burocrat* (Princeton, 1979),

this official's most frequent designations, *dictator litterarum*, suggests his principal function. His task was to write letters to foreign powers abroad, to Florentine administrative officials in the territory, and to the Republic's subject communes. He was also responsible for all written exchanges between the Republic and its ambassadors on mission. Private citizens who wished to have official testimony of their citizenship or of their professional status had recourse to the chancery along with merchants in trouble with subjects of other powers or with a foreign government itself. Usually the merchants sought letters expressing the *Signoria's* sympathy for their case and its concern that foreign rulers do justice to the bearers. Together with the notary of legislation, moreover, the chancellor also had the task of delivering public orations to visiting dignitaries. In view of the character of these central functions, the *Signoria* sought not only a skilled notary for the post but one who had literary abilities as well.

Although not a daily task, a time-consuming assignment of the chancellor was the work of keeping the records of the *Consulte e Practiche*, consulative groups made up of the three leading executive colleges and leading citizens called together from time to time to advise the government on important matters. Since the majority of topics discussed concerned foreign affairs, the chancellor was the natural secretary for this body. Often called on to compose letters embodying conclusions reached in these discussions, the chancellor, with the notes of the meeting before him, was able to express the consensus of the members of the *Consulte* with relative accuracy. While officially only a secretary, the chancellor with his daily involvement in the foreign affairs of the Republic was a major expert on foreign policy issues confronting the government, and he frequently exercised an important unofficial role in the determination of policy but one leaving no trace in the records of official deliberations.

The office of the notary of the *Tratte*, which Salutati was called to fill, was the first indication that the Florentines were willing to create other less important notarial offices where the incumbent could expect a fairly extensive tenure of office. The four successive reappointments of ser Stefano Becchi to be notary of the *Otto di Balìa* in 1375–78 and the regular tenure of Benedetto Fortini as notary of the *Dieci di Balìa* from 1384 to 1406, also suggest that the Florentines were beginning to recognize the

---

p. 162, is somewhat misleading on this point. Also only one (Accolti), and not "several," of Scala's predecessors was a lawyer (p. 173).

advantages of continuity such lengthy tenure afforded.[18] This trend appears to have continued in the next century.[19]

The notary of legislation in 1375 was the Sienese notary ser Piero di ser Grifo, better known, on account of his long hold on the office, as ser Piero of Legislation. Born in the Casentino, ser Piero had been appointed to his office in 1348, after years of experience in the chanceries of the counts of Poppi and the commune of Arezzo. During his decades of service as notary of legislation, he had become renowned for his expertise in legal and administrative matters and for his cleverness at manipulating the statutes for the benefit of the state. It was he, for instance, who suggested the means for tripling the interest paid on the Florentine *Monte* in order to attract investors without directly contravening the iron restrictions prohibiting changes in *Monte* regulations.[20]

His talents, however, were not totally devoted to the public weal. Although earning a modest salary of 250 l. per annum, the notary of legislation had traditionally been able to augment his income by charging private individuals for transcribing copies of laws, rogating grants of reprisals, procurations, and a host of other documents. Ser Piero availed himself of every opportunity to make money out of his office, and over the thirty years of his tenure became a very rich man. He also managed to find lucrative employment in notarial posts for a host of brothers, sons, and nephews.[21]

18. Stefano di ser Matteo Becchi became notary of the Otto on August 17, 1375 (*Balie*, 12, fol. 2), and he remained in office until that body's authority lapsed in 1378. See Becchi's third appointment to the *Otto: Delib. (ord. autor.)*, 20, fol. 48. Fortini's biography is given by Marzi, pp. 153–55. On the *Dieci*, Marzi, pp. 176–78. The position of notary of the *Specchio* established in 1389 also belongs to the category of "bureaucratic" offices. Because of the complicated nature of the operations of this office, this notary enjoyed a long tenure (ibid., pp. 169–76). Also see Ronald Witt, *Coluccio Salutati and His Public Letters* (Geneva, 1976), pp. 16–17, and 40–41.

19. Nicolai Rubinstein, "Machiavelli and the World of Florentine Politics," in *Studies on Machiavelli*, ed. Myron P. Gilmore (Florence, 1972), p. 8, suggests that this was the trend in the fifteenth century. Also see Riccardo Fubini, "Note machiavelliane e para-machiavelliane a proposito della relazione di N. Rubinstein," ibid., pp. 373–87. I owe these references to Hans Baron. For an excellent analysis of the evolution of the chancery under Bartolomeo Scala, see Alison Brown, *Bartolomeo Scala*, pp. 135–92.

20. Marzi (p. 82) describes ser Piero as born in Pratovecchio but Marchionne di Coppo Stefani, *Cronica fiorentina*, ed. Niccolò Rodolico, R.I.S., vol. 30, pt. 1 (Città di Castella, 1903–55), p. 350, speaks of him as coming from Poppi. Anecdotes regarding ser Piero's cleverness are found in Marzi, p. 89.

21. An incomplete list of notarial offices held by ser Piero's relatives is given by Marzi, p. 91, n. 5. Most income from these posts was derived from service charges on the users. In 1371 there was a general protest against the high fees government notaries were demanding (Stefani, p. 278). Ser Piero himself used his large income to buy up lands in the area around Poppi and become "almost a minor lord of all that province" (Stefani, p. 350). Matteo Villani remarks on his hypocrisy: *Cronica*, ed. Francesco G. Dragomanni, 2 vols. (Florence, 1846), I, 371.

While he seems to have held no other notarial position in the communal government, the fact that his relatives were found frequently in important posts suggests that ser Piero was in the habit of resigning in their favor notarial posts for which he was drawn. Despite appearances, the Florentines of the fourteenth century had not developed an unambiguous conception of the administrative post as a public office. Notaries drawn for a particular position were recognized as enjoying something akin to a property right in the office. If the individual elected did not choose to serve, he could transfer the right to exercise the office to another qualified person. Whereas this right had commercial value, ser Piero evidently preferred to use his easy access to such employment to furnish members of his family with a livelihood.

Since ser Piero was not a citizen, he was excluded from holding a wide-range of communal offices primarily political in nature. Besides official positions in the Guild of Judges and Notaries, the only other appointment he seems to have held during these three decades was that of secretary of the Guelf party in 1373.[22] Nonetheless, his lack of political rights did not keep him from playing politics. Ser Piero's link with the Guelf party hierarchy became especially strong in the 1370s. The angry mobs who in July 1378 burned ser Piero's house and drove him out of the city along with leaders of the party were motivated as much by his association with the party as by his reputation as a robber of the poor. Nor did the destruction of the *Ciompi* bring an end to the old man's exile after September 1378. Soured by their experience with the Sienese notary, the Florentines altered the proviso requiring that the notary of legislation be a foreigner and named an honest, experienced apolitical local notary, ser Viviano di Neri, as ser Piero's replacement.[23] Henceforth that office could be filled by either a citizen or a foreigner.

The second of the two great chancery officials, ser Niccolò di ser Venturi Monachi, Florentine chancellor from 1348–75, resembled his colleague ser Piero in his greed but lacked the latter's capacity for hypocrisy.[24] Son and coadjutor of the preceding chancellor, ser Niccolò easily moved into the office on the death of ser Ventura Monachi in the terrible year of 1348. While not an outstanding *dictator*, he was competent and enough of a scholar to meet mid-Trecento standards of learning. He was, however, a difficult personality who never forgot his enemies

22. Marzi, p. 91. Marzi incorrectly writes that ser Piero was a prior in 1374.
23. Ser Viviano's background is discussed, ibid., pp. 128–29.
24. Marzi, pp. 91–105.

and who made many of them—especially among the leadership of the Guelf party. He narrowly escaped being branded a Ghibelline in 1366, but the arm of the party was long and its memory of enemies as good as that of ser Niccolò.

Unlike his father, who held major political offices in the commune during his tenure as chancellor, ser Niccolò had little time for nonremunerative duties. His goal was to accumulate as many lucrative notarial offices as possible. Some of these he exercised directly; others he sold outright; and still others he permitted an associate to fill while sharing in the total profits of the office. His own secret record of personal earnings over the years indicates that the chancellor was not above accepting bribes (or should they be considered fees?) for matching notaries seeking jobs with suitable appointments in the government.

Ser Niccolò's rapacity was well-known in the city, but he probably would have held on to his post until his death had it not been for the continued hostility of the Guelf party. The failure of the *Signoria* to reappoint ser Niccolò to another term in April 1375 occurred not surprisingly at the time when the Guelf party leader and ser Niccolò's personal enemy, Bonaiuto Serragli, was Standardbearer of Justice.[25] The new chancellor's impartial conduct of the position and his self-imposed restraints on manipulating his powers for personal gain were to contrast starkly with the greedy, quarrelsome behavior of his predecessor.

Indeed, the appointment first of Salutati as chancellor and then of ser Viviano di Neri as notary of legislation placed men in the leading notarial positions of the Republic who insisted on high ethical as well as intellectual standards for members of their profession. By their conduct they provided examples of public servants, concerned with serving what they considered the common good as opposed to that of a faction. Their actions as public administrators were both conducive to and symptomatic of the decrease in overt factionalism in the very last decades of the fourteenth century.[26] While they were not directly involved

25. Ibid., pp. 102–3 and below, chap.

26. The evolution of a conception of "public" administration in Florentine history is presented in most graphic detail by Marvin Becker, *Florence in Transition*. In his *Florentine Politics*, p. 95, Brucker also stresses the growth of a concept of impersonal government in the last half of the fourteenth century. Commenting on Brucker's statement, Riccardo Fubini in his review of Berthold L. Ullman's *The Humanism of Coluccio Salutati*, and Armando Petrucci's *Il protocolo notarile di Coluccio Salutati*, (*Rivista storica italiana*, 77 [1965], 974), ties Salutati's career in with this development: "Non si può negare che il S. col suo richiamo eloquente al civismo e patriottismo dei Romani, con la sua identificazione di libertà e legge, con la sua lunga practica e continuità della carica, col prestigio stesso della sua persona, abbia saputo impersonare tali aspirazioni, dando all'affermazione di una più moderna coscienza pubblica un contributo importante così ideale come pratico." Cf. Daniela De Rosa,

in teaching the notarial art, the careers of Salutati and Viviani doubtless influenced Goro Dati's assertion in the early fifteenth century that "the source of doctors of the law is Bologna and that of doctors of the notary is Florence."[27] Such a statement, credible if open to debate in Dati's time, would have appeared a ridiculous boast in Salutati's youth sixty or seventy years before.

II

According to the wording of the *provvisione* of February 21, 1374, creating the new post of notary of the *Tratte*, the government acted in response to the appeal of ser Piero of legislation.[28] The elderly notary had informed the priors that he was no longer able to discharge all the duties of his office alone. The salary of the newly created office reflects its dignity—up to one hundred and fifty florins, half again that paid the chancellor. The financial status of the new notary, however, was decidedly inferior both to that of the chancellor and the notary of legislation. Whereas the holders of these offices could increase their income in many ways, the *provvisione* of February 21 restricted the new notarial official solely to his salary.

The notary of the *Tratte* was primarily concerned with drawing up the lists of candidates for public office, extracting the names at election time, and swearing in those chosen. From the first years, however, he added other tasks including the custody of the communal archives. Within time the *Tratte* also did notarial work for the commission entrusted with approving the statutes and statutory revisions of subject communes.[29]

Coluccio Salutati. Il cancelliere e il pensatore politico, Biblioteca di storia, vol. 28 (Florence, 1980), pp. 72ff.

27. "La fonte de' dottori delle leggi è Bologna e la fonte de' dottori della noteria è Firenze . . . ": *L'istoria di Firenze di Gregorio Dati dal 1380 al 1405*, ed. Luigi Pratesi (Norcia, 1902), p. 141. One cannot be clear as to whether Dati is speaking specifically of professional teachers of the law and the notarial art or of great lawyers and notaries who inspire students of these disciplines.

28. *Provv. reg.*, 61, fols. 238ᵛ, and 249ᵛ; Marzi, p. 577. The new notary was said to be a "sotium et collegam."

29. *Statuta*, II, 722, refers specifically to Salutati's election to the *Tratte* in February 1374, but the actual document seems to have disappeared. A month after his election he referred to himself (*Dipl. Riform.*, Mar. 17, 1374) as "scriba scrutiniorum et extractionum omnium officialium commuis Florentie" and "scriba extractionum communis Florentie." On June 6, 1374 (*Delib. [spec. autor.]*, 2, fol. 17) he signed as "scriba communis Florentie ad extractiones et scrutinia necnon computanda et notanda juramenta omnium officialium forensium civitatis et communis Florentie et alia plura per ipsum commune specialiter deputata. . . ." This description might suggest that his duties were primarily con-

Ser Piero's request for a colleague is puzzling. Although the *provvisione* mentioned no specific duties of the new official, apparently he was to relieve ser Piero of the burden of the *Tratte*, whose records the old man had been handling for twenty-five years. There is no indication, however, that the amount of work required by the *Tratte* had recently increased. Was ser Piero merely growing tired? If so, why request a colleague? Why not simply add another assistant—perhaps another relative—to help him? This would not have required a petition to the government and would have been far less costly to him personally because, in any case, ser Piero, not the government, was obligated according to the terms of the *provvisione* to pay the appointee.

Most probably ser Piero's complaint of overwork was for public consumption and formed part of the Guelf party's scheme to ruin the incumbent chancellor, ser Niccolò Monachi. To prepare the way for Monachi's ouster, the Guelfs apparently had decided to have a suitable replacement ready in the wings, and Salutati, with his impeccable Guelf credentials and his recent experience as chancellor of the commune of Lucca, was an ideal candidate. His loyalty to the aristocratic Guelf faction which had cost him his post in Lucca also led Florentine Guelf leaders like Lapo Castiglionchio, whom Salutati had known for years, to view him as sympathetic to their interests.[30] They had first of all, however, to bring him into the *Palazzo della Signoria* so that he could demonstrate his worthiness for the high office of chancellor at first hand. Given the resistance of many citizens in the government to increasing the outlay for the palace staff, Salutati's appointment to the *Tratte* could only have been accomplished at the expense of ser Piero, who would have given up this substantial revenue in exchange for other considerations: for a man as avaricious as ser Piero, ill feeling against a colleague

---

fined to various operations involved in elections of foreign officials, but in this same register he specifically refers to himself on other occasions as "scriba extractionum officialium omnium" (ibid., fols. 13 and 19ᵛ–20). Also see *Tratte*, 341, fol. 1 (Sept. 30, 1374). As for his other duties, the renewal of Salutati's appointment as chancellor in 1376 (published by Marzi, p. 579) names him custodian of the archives. His assignment to be notary for the *Approbatores Statutorum et Ordinamentorum Communium* is found in *Statuta*, II, 722. Although these statutory provisions are found in the laws of 1415, they apply to an earlier period. See his signature as notary for the Approvers in the case of revisions of the statutes of Vellano in Berthold L. Ullman, *The Humanism of Coluccio Salutati*, Medioevo e umanesimo, vol. 4 (Padua, 1963), pp. 7–8, n. 4. Ullman misunderstands the context in which these signatures of Salutati after 1366 occur. As notary of the *Tratte* he was also charged with supervising the "presentationem cereorum floridorum" for the festival of San Giovanni: *Cap.*, 12, fol. 79, published in *I capitoli del comune di Firenze: Inventario e regesto*, ed. Cesare Guasti, 2 vols. (Florence, 1866–93), II, 178.

30. Salutati's letter to Lapo of 1369 (see above, Chap. 4) suggests a long prior relationship.

would not have been sufficient motivation to lose revenue. There is no more than circumstantial evidence for the existence of the plot, but ser Piero's petition of February 1374 resulted in fact in Salutati's coming to Florence as notary of the *Tratte* where he was available to become chancellor fourteen months later on Monachi's dismissal.

Several days before his official firing on April 15, 1375, Monachi had ceased to occupy his office; from April 13 Salutati began writing the records of the *Consulte e Practiche*, one of the chancellor's normal tasks.[31] If not directly involved in the plot against Monachi, Salutati must at the very least have known that such an intrigue was underway. Even the charitable Marsili in Paris, who received the announcement of the new appointment from Salutati himself, could not have believed his friend's protestation that he "had been ignorant of the whole matter."[32] Monachi himself never forgave Salutati and waited an opportunity to get revenge.

If Salutati had conspired with the Guelf party leadership, he seems to have become independent of it very quickly. While factionalism dominated the life of medieval Italian communes, men in these centuries had an abhorrence for parties and looked on divisions in the citizen body as unnatural and the work of evil men. From his first writings Salutati dwelt on the necessity of putting the interests of one's country before personal concerns or those of a party. Lucca had been a terrible lesson in politics for the ambitious notary. Too closely tied to the aristocratic faction, Salutati was engulfed in its ruin. He had a further seven months in Lucca and almost two years in Stignano to meditate on his mistakes. Even if relying on patronage to obtain the office, he had no intention of repeating the experience of 1370–71 in Florence. The international reputation he acquired within a few months of taking office enabled him to liberate himself from the status of a client to the Guelf party. At the same time so skillfully was this accomplished that he continued on friendly terms with the Guelf leadership.

Although the *provvisione* of April 19, 1375, naming Salutati chancellor said nothing of his retaining the *Tratte*, the records of that latter office indicate that until September 1375 he carried out the duties of both appointments concurrently. Once the war with the Church had actually begun, however, the pressures on the chancellor increased to the point

31. *Consulte e Pratiche*, 13, fol. 27; published in Armando Petrucci, *Il protocollo notarile di Coluccio Salutati (1372–1373)* (Milan, 1963), plate 5.
32. *Epist.*, I, 244–45. Also see his comment on his appointment made to Broaspini, I, 205–6.

where ser Piero di ser Grifo had to share the burdens of the *Tratte*.[33] By the fall his name alternates with Salutati in the documents pertaining to the office. This informal division of the functions of the *Tratte* received legal sanction in the *provvisione* of June 22, 1376, confirming Salutati in the office of chancellor for the second year.[34] By this *provvisione* the *Tratte* was joined to the office of chancellor as "one single office," but at the same time ser Piero was awkwardly described as having equal responsibility for the performance of its operations.

By early 1376 the *Signoria* and Colleges apparently had decided that the burden on the chancellor was still too great and they took steps to alleviate it by making an unprecedented division in the office, naming Salutati's coadjutor, ser Benedetto Fortini, the second chancellor. The decision was reached on February 4, and on the 10th ser Antonio di Michele Arrighi, who had been an assistant to Salutati in the chancery, swore in the new chancellor, whose term of office was to begin on June 22.[35] Ser Antonio himself was subsequently promoted to Fortini's old job as Salutati's coadjutor.[36] Salutati's section of the chancery monopolized correspondence with foreign powers while domestic communication seems to have been left to Fortini. The arrangement lasted only a year, but this division of the chancery foreshadowed the reform of 1437,

33. The two registers most relevant to this problem are *Tratte*, 341, and *Delib.* (*spec. autor.*), 2. As late as August 29, 1375 (*Delib.* 2, fol. 34), Salutati still referred to himself as "scriba extractionum officialium communis Florentie." On September 3 (*Tratte*, 341, fol. 61ᵛ) ser Piero first reappeared in the documents of the *Tratte*. On October 1 (*Delib.*, 2, fol. 38ᵛ) Salutati's title now included the phrase "quarundam extractionum," and in subsequent instances over the next few years when his title was written out, the same limiting adjective occurred, fols. 43ᵛ–44, 48, 70, 79ᵛ, and 80. Ser Piero di ser Grifo appears to have taken back supervision of the election of the *podestà*, castellans, and some other officials: after September 3, 1375, where these officers are involved, either ser Piero or one of his assistants presided over the election (*Tratte* 341, fols. 61ᵛ ff.; *Dipl.*, *Riform.*, Aug. 14, 1377; *Dipl.*, *Monte comune*, Dec. 24, 1376, and Nov. 13, 1377. Salutati kept control of the election of foreign officials as indicated by *Delib.* (*spec. autor.*), 2, which is devoted to the election of such officials. If the act naming him chancellor for third time on June 22, 1377, is assumed to describe the situation over the previous year and a half, Salutati also retained supervision over the election of the priors and the colleges: *Dipl.*, *Riform.*, ad an., where he is said to be "notarius extractionum dictorum dominorum et vexilliferi et collegiorum et aliorum dicti cancellariatus et extractionum offitiorum connex (orum)."

34. *Dipl.*, *Riform.*, under June 22, 1377; published in Marzi, pp. 578–79.

35. *Dipl.*, *Riform.*, Feb. 4, 1375 (6), published in Marzi, p. 578. For his taking oath see ibid., Feb. 10, 1375(6). Ser Benedetto had been Salutati's coadjutor in the *Tratte* since at least May 31, 1374, when his handwriting first appears in the registers of that department: *Delib.* (*spec. autor.*), 2, fol. 13ᵛ. He describes himself as coadjutor of Salutati in *Dipl.*, *Monte comune*, Dec. 4, 1374, and *Dipl.*, *Riform.*, May 14, 1375.

36. Ser Antonio's hand first appears in the *Tratte* registers on March 30, 1376: *Delib.* (*spec. autor.*), 2, fol. 48. His handwriting, however, is found in the first pages of *Missive* 16. See September 9, 1375, *Miss.*, 16, fol. 20ᵛ. His chancery cursive is discussed in Witt, *Coluccio Salutati*, pp. 16–17.

when a second office of chancellor was permanently created with responsibility for internal correspondence and many of the more pedestrian duties of the chancellorship.[37] In 1377, however, with the diminution of open hostilities the division no longer seemed necessary to the government, and from this point on to the end of his life Salutati exercised the undivided powers over the Florentine chancery.

Fortunately for Salutati's reputation as chancellor, the war of Florence with the papacy was largely fought on paper, and Salutati's missives were among Florence's most important weapons. Giovanni di Conversino in later years remarked that his first contact with Salutati's work came when he read the *Signoria's* response to the papacy in August 1375.[38] Possibly Conversino had seen the copy dispatched by Salutati to Padua in November of that year on Broaspini's request. By mid-1376 Salutati's missives were reported to be having a tremendous effect at the French court.[39]

From his very first public letters Salutati utilized *stilus rhetoricus* to present Florence's grievances and policies.[40] This thirteenth-century style took its name from the frequent use it made of exclamations and rhetorical questions characteristic of oratory. For its *cursus* it relied on the basic meters of *velox*, *planus*, and *tardus* as used by the Roman Curia. Employed in the Florentine chancery by Brunetto Latini in the second half of the previous century, the *stilus rhetoricus* had fallen out of favor with Latini's successors until revived by Salutati in 1375. Salutati, however, adapted the style to his own tastes. The rhetoric was shorn of some of its traditional formulae and vocabulary. Good humanist that he was, Salutati also structured his propaganda themes against a background of Roman and medieval history lacking in earlier writings in this style. At least partially because of his intensive study of Roman oratory, the new chancellor brought to the public correspondence a dramatic sense and an unrivaled ability to construct sequential lines of argumentation. For displaying these talents the *stilus rhetoricus* proved an ideal

37. Marzi, pp. 196–97. In *Miss.* 17, with public letters for the period March 8, 1376, to August 17, 1377, the vast majority of rough drafts of letters to foreign powers are in Salutati's hand. For identification of Fortini's letters in the *Missive*, see De Rosa, *Coluccio Salutati*, pp. 7–11.

38. *Epist.*, IV, 306: "Olim enim, duodeviginti annis ferme ante, ni fallor, dictata vestra ad Romanum antistitem, quibus animadversio publica in reum maiestatis monachum excusabatur, cum forte legissem, vestram mox in dilectionem exarsi, fierique vester optavi." The missive referred to here, which Novati was unable to identify, is B.A.V., *Capp.*, 147, pp. 316–19, written in August 1375.

39. *Epist.*, I, 245.

40. See Witt, *Coluccio Salutati*, pp. 23–41. See as well the excellent analysis given by De Rosa, *Coluccio Salutati*, pp. 16ff.

vehicle. The power of Salutati's missives derived from the fact that they reflected enough echoes of ancient rhetoric to excite a generation already stirred by the writings of Petrarch while basically remaining within the limits set for such correspondence by international chancery protocol.

III

Florence's war against its most traditional ally derived at least indirectly from the political decentralization in Northern and Central Italy, which by the last quarter of the fourteenth century had become institutionalized. Perhaps no authority had the power to reverse completely the process, yet the weakness of individual city-states and lordships invited not only petty aggression but also grand designs of conquest. Millions of inhabitants in the area which stretched from the Alps down to the Kingdom of Naples longed for a reign of peace and order, and this unrequited desire created in most regimes an element of instability. Although Venice, concerned with building an Eastern commercial empire, remained aloof, three major Italian powers profited from the situation. Milan, in the heart of the richest, most populous province of Italy, was the natural master of the Lombard plain. By 1375 the Visconti family's carefully accumulated territories, divided between two brothers, encompassed one half of the region. If one ruler was again to take control of these lands, he would have the potential of becoming the greatest prince in Italy. The largest state in Tuscany was Florence. Guided like Venice by commercial and industrial interests—it was the world's banking center—Florence was deeply committed to its business concerns. But unlike Venice, Florence was a city of the interior and its destiny was more closely tied to peninsular politics. Surrounded as it was by a welter of failing republics, Florence was understandably tempted to seek both economic and political domination of Tuscany.

The greatest territorial lord in central Italy was the pope. After decades of his residing in Avignon the papal states were by mid-century drifting toward anarchy, but by 1375 the expenditure of vast treasure and the activity of skillful papal generals had come close to bringing order out of chaos. So well in fact had the papal government succeeded, that Florence felt suspicious of its designs on Tuscany. Given the erosion of republican institutions in Florence's neighboring states, there would be no need of open aggression. The rising of a faction and the prearranged shouts from a mob in the piazza sufficed to have the pope elected to the lordship of a city.[41]

Overt opposition to the papacy was not easy for the Florentines. For almost a century since the triumph of the Guelf party in the commune, Florence had jealously guarded its heritage of Guelfism and its loyalty to the party's leaders, the pope and the Angevin king of Naples. Florence had of course fought numerous wars earlier in the fourteenth century acting independently of this leadership. The victory over Pisa in 1364 was only the most recent of such conflicts. Yet when Florentines thought of their international position, they saw themselves in terms of a configuration of powers dominated by the papal and Angevin powers. By 1375 such a conception was completely divorced from reality. On the one hand, Joanna I, a licentious and indolent queen, committed to bedroom intrigues and threatened by rival claimants to the throne, was patently unequal to the task of insuring Guelf hegemony in Italy in the tradition of her ancestors. On the other, the reestablishment of papal power in Italy and the intervention in Tuscany it made possible rendered Florence's traditional conception of international politics outmoded.

By the spring and summer of 1375 suspicion was building on both sides, and an open break between the papacy and Florence, still formally allies against Bernabò Visconti, seemed imminent. To Florentine accusations of plots against the Republic sponsored by papal officials, the pope responded with charges of Florence's betrayal of the war effort against Milan. In the very first months of his appointment, therefore, Salutati was confronted with one of the most difficult assignments of his career. He had to present the Florentine case to the pope so as to satisfy the papacy of Florence's continued good will while forcing Gregory XI to recognize the dangerous course on which his officials had embarked.[42]

---

41. Gene A. Brucker, *Florentine Politics*, pp. 410–11, gives a detailed bibliography of secondary studies relating to the war to which now should be added, Richard Trexler, *The Spiritual Power; Republican Florence under Interdict* (Leiden, 1974).

42. The letter of May 19 to the pope was only the first of four which Salutati himself designated in the register copies with numbers from one to four. Salutati's first three letters to the papacy contained in B.A.V., *Capp.*, 147, pp. 101–3, 77–78, and 316–19 (the letter of May 19 is also found in B.N.P., *Lat. nouv. acquis.*, 1151, fols. 15–17ᵛ) furnish hitherto unknown details on the early phases of the conflict. Salutati's *missive* of May 19, 1375, published in Witt, *Coluccio Salutati*, pp. 95–99, gives a summary of Florence's grievances against the papacy and a rebuttal of papal charges. The Pazzino and Manno mentioned in the text and identified by me as belonging to the Strozzi family (pp. 97 and 99) are certainly Pazzino and Manno Donati. I am grateful to Prof. Benjamin Kohl for bringing this error to my attention. On the latter see Ernest Hatch Wilkins, "Petrarch and Manno

Four missives to the Pope furnish evidence of the gradual disintegration of papal-Florentine relations. The fourth, dated October 30, while maintaining something of the reverent posture of the earlier letters, dismissed the most recent papal communication with barely concealed sarcasm. Summoned by Gregory XI to send an embassy to discuss a peace treaty with Milan, the *Signoria*, who had months before informed the pope of their alliance of July 24 with Milan, refused on the basis that "we are called upon to make peace with those with whom for a long time we have had an inviolable and firm peace. . . ." Compared with the previous three long, detailed missives, this one was relatively short. The time for negotiations was past.

One major objective of Florentine policy was to attract Tuscan allies by pointing out the threat posed to their liberty by Church aggrandizement. At the same time, however, they attempted to foster rebellion among the cities subject to the Church by recalling to these communes the advantages of their lost freedom. Throughout the fall of 1375 and winter of 1375–76, consequently, Salutati was kept busy composing letters directed to the cities of Tuscany and the Patrimony, extolling the virtues of liberty and the destructive influences of tyranny on a people. From mid-November on, one city of the Patrimony after the other rebelled, and by the following March the papacy had lost most of the cities north of Rome including Bologna.[43]

The papal response was to lay an interdict on Florentine territory on March 31, a move proving far more effective than the army of Breton soldiers sent into Italy in the same spring to lay waste the lands of his enemies. The Florentines were branded as outlaws, to be driven from every state in Christendom and their property and persons to be seized by anyone. Within the boundaries of the Republic all religious services were to cease, with a limited number of exceptions, and forty-nine citizens who had held the highest offices of state since June 1375 were excommunicated forthwith.[44]

Already before the interdict Salutati had been employed by the merchant community to write letters defending freedom of Florentine trade despite the city's struggle with the supreme spiritual power of Christendom. Once the interdict was actually operative, the incidence of general

Donati," *Speculum*, 35 (1960), 381–93. The fourth letter is found in B.A.V., *Capp.*, 147, p. 179.

43. The nature of the correspondence is discussed in Witt, *Coluccio Salutati*, pp. 43–56. Richard Trexler, "Rome on the Eve of the Great Schism," *Speculum*, 42 (1967), 489–509, provides a detailed account of Florentine efforts to foment rebellion in Rome.

44. Trexler, *The Spiritual Power*, pp. 39–43.

letters together with intercessions for private individuals increased decidedly. Trade was the source of life for Florence and, although Europe's rulers as a whole did not enforce the ecclesiastical prohibitions too assiduously, some Florentine merchants suffered severe financial losses both because of harassment abroad at the local level and because of their own reluctance to trade in such uncertain circumstances.

Despite his very recent entry into Florentine service, Salutati as chancellor "was admitted to the secret meetings of the city's leaders." "Daily," he wrote, "I intervene in the secret councils."[45] Present at these intimate discussions where policy was formulated, he was able not only to offer advice but also, aware of the real objectives of the government, to work out effective propaganda to fit the regime's desired goals. In fact, Giovanni di Conversino had Salutati's position specifically in mind when in 1395 as chancellor of Padua he lamented having to compose missives while excluded from the secret sessions where policy was made.[46] Given his access to secret information, Salutati could not delude himself in believing that his letters, as electrifying as they were, caused on their own the rebellions which rocked the Patrimony from November 1375. On March 6, 1376, for instance, in Salutati's presence the leaders of the rebellion of Città di Castello received a thousand florins from the *Otto di Balia*, the special college set up to direct the war, as reward for their activities.[47]

During the three years of war Salutati worked almost ceaselessly in the chancery. This was the exhilarating, bustling atmosphere he loved. Writing to Bernardo da Moglio about 1390 but describing a situation that was as true earlier as at this date, Salutati describes the circumstances in which he worked in the chancery:

> Consider a little, my beloved son, the size of this great city which, as it spreads out through almost the whole world, is compelled not only to fill the boundaries of Italy with letters but is forced to send letter after letter to all the princes of the world, wherever the Latin tongue and letters are known, both on account of public matters and because of the affairs of private individuals. Imagine me attempting to satisfy

45. *Epist.*, I, 217.
46. Akad. Z., II, C. 61, fol. 108/9: "Coluccius noster nichil omnino que gerenda sunt prorsus ignorat, ad omnia consilia agenda tractandaque semper admissus." Giovanni is quoting ser Piero da San Miniato. For date of letter, Remigio Sabbadini, *Giovanni da Ravenna, insigne figura d'umanista (1343–1408)* (Como. 1924), p. 79.
47. *Balie*, 12, fol. 65ᵛ. On the very same day that this money was paid, another hundred was given by the *Otto* for the services of a spy who had brought letters perhaps relevant to a similar plot to cause rebellion in another city elsewhere in the Patrimony.

everyone, surrounded unceasingly with citizens generally unable to state their problem. It is my task to discover from them what the nature of their business is so that, having understood the situation, I might work out what I must set forth in a letter and what is appropriate. Nor am I allowed to do this efficiently in peace but I am frequently interrupted by a call to come to the priors.[48]

In the few personal letters written during this period he constantly refers to the great demands of his office. He returns from the palace late in the evening and barely has time to eat and sleep. He seizes what moments he can to write to his friends.[49] Yet even among these supposedly "private" letters there are some which he clearly composed in the service of state policy. When in October 1375 fra Niccolò Casucchi da Girgenti wrote an appeal to Florence to make peace with the pope and enter into a general league with the Church and other major Italian powers, Salutati made a semiofficial reply to the friar rejecting his arguments. Florence could never trust its defense to such a general league, Salutati wrote, inasmuch as the pope, on the basis of his claim to *plenitudo potestatis*, could dissolve the agreement when it suited his purposes.[50]

A week before this letter to ser Niccolò, Salutati had written to an acquaintance in Perugia, ser Andrea Giusti, secretary of the hated Gerard de Puy, papal vicar general. A notarial post had recently been given to one of Salutati's childhood friends, ser Niccolò di ser Damo of Montecatini, on the strength of ser Niccolò's friendship with Salutati. Ostensibly flattered, Salutati wrote expressing his appreciation both to the secretary, who had been the prime mover in the appointment, and to his master: "Since he [ser Niccolò] is dearer to me than anything, recommend me, insignificant as I am, to him [de Puy] if you deem it appropriate."[51] Such obsequiousness can only be interpreted as a reinforcement of the unsuccessful official efforts during September and October to keep on friendly terms with de Puy. The harsh official letter to the pope of October 30, two days later, marked the end of such Florentine attempts. From that point on, personal contact with papal officials was regarded as collaboration with the enemy. On November 6,

48. *Epist.*, II 192–93. The date of the letter is established by Berthold L. Ullman, *Studies in Renaissance Humanism*, Storia e letteratura, vol. 51, 2nd ed. (Rome, 1973), p. 217.

49. *Epist.*, I, 190, 207, 209, 252, complain of the pressure.

50. Ibid., I, 216. On private letters written for political purposes see De Rosa, *Coluccio Salutati*, pp. 75–85.

51. Ibid., I, 213.

Francesco di Antonio degli Albizzi was fined three thousand lire for accepting the vicariate of Todi from de Puy and by late November Florentine propaganda branded de Puy, considered in Florence to have been a leading proponent for war on the papal side, as "that abominable monster."[52]

The petulant, disputatious attitude which sometimes appears in the humanist's mature correspondence reached its height in a letter written to his former benefactor at the Curia, Francesco Bruni. Bruni had returned to Tuscany in 1377 to spend the summer on his estates with the permission of the *Signoria*. Although contradicting its own policy by allowing a high papal official to reside in Florentine territory, the government was obviously anxious to keep on good terms with a man who might later prove useful in negotiations with Gregory XI. The papal secretary innocently wrote to Salutati expressing his joy at being in the countryside again. Doubtless irritated at Bruni's immunity while Florence waged war with Bruni's employer and eager to make political capital out of the opportunity, Salutati painted the simple leisures described by Bruni in the most lurid colors. Bruni's joy at being in the country was lascivious, caused him to 'enjoy', not 'use' nature and led him away from virtue. At the conclusion of an outrageous diatribe Salutati conceded that he found some cause for hope in Bruni's moral improvement in the latter's assertion that he was now beginning to be "less weighted down by the desire for the Curia and things curial."[53]

The dominant tone of the private letters is positive, even exuberant, during the first two years of the conflict. Salutati's religious scruples about warring against the papacy, like those of Luigi Marsili and Giovanni delle Celle, both devout Christians, were overcome by righteous anger at the Church, which utilized its spiritual powers for territorial aggression.[54] That the war was making the new chancellor's reputation doubtless strengthened his convictions. Only in the last year of the war did Salutati begin to show fatigue and signs of annoyance at the constant pressures of his office. Not only was the war going badly by then but Salutati was anxious over the outcome of the proceedings for heresy which Gregory XI had instituted in the spring of 1378 against him and two other Florentines, for their leading role in the struggle.[55]

52. *Miss.*, 16, fol. 56ᵛ.   53. *Epist.*, I, 275.
54. Felice Tocco, "I fraticelli," *Archivio storico italiano*, ser. 5, 35 (1905), 348–51.
55. Trexler, *The Spiritual Power*, pp. 155–56. Also see B.R.F., 786, fol. 88. The other two were Donato Barbardoro and Jacopo Folchi. Salutati's friend, Domenico Silvestri, by the spring of 1377 expressed his weariness with the war in his *Eryplois: Domenico Silvestri*, pp. 77–97.

At a distance of five years from the war, Salutati interpreted not only the Schism of 1378 but also the civil disorders in the Republic between 1378 and 1382 as punishments of God for the sins of both belligerents. The princes of the Church had the blood of the murdered masses of Faenza and Cesena on their hands, whereas the rulers of the Republic had grievously sinned first in laying "sacrilegious hands" on the possessions of the Church and then in forcing citizens to purchase and hold them not "without manifest injury to their souls and consciences." Nevertheless, he still maintained the essential justice of the Florentine cause: "without doubt" the Church intended to subvert Florentine liberty while the Florentines fought for that freedom "which we considered the greatest glory."[56]

Almost every Florentine lived to regret the war. In attacking the papacy the coalition of *gente nuova* and their patrician allies dominating the communal government had also declared war on the oligarchic faction centering on the Guelf party which had a monopoly of high church offices in the Republic. In essence the conflict involved those who wished to encourage a relatively wide participation in the Republic's political life and those favoring a narrow governing class of old established families. The war party fully realized that the continuation of the regime depended on a successful outcome to the war. As enthusiasm for the struggle waned in Florence in 1377 and early 1378, the oligarchic opponents of the regime became increasingly vociferous in their opposition to the fighting.[57] On the other hand, the pope insisted on terms for a settlement which in effect represented complete Florentine surrender. Fortunately for the government the death of Gregory XI enabled the Florentines to obtain somewhat more favorable terms from his successor, who had no strong commitment to the war. Nevertheless, when on July 28, 1378, a peace treaty was finally signed with Urban VI, the issue of the war for Florentines had already been pushed into the background by a civil conflict within the city itself.[58]

56. *Epist.*, II, 122. Salutati's authorship of the *De casu Cesene* has been decisively rejected by Francesco Novati, "Un umanista fabrianese del secolo xiv, Giovanni Tinti," *Archivio storico per le Marche e per l'Umbria*, 2 (1885), 135–46. It is the work of Ludovico Romani da Fabriano: Roberto Weiss, *Il primo secolo dell'umanesimo* (Rome, 1949), p. 94. Salutati's own account of the massacre, however, was extremely dramatic and may have inspired the *De casu: Miss.*, 17, fols. 91–92ᵛ, published in Johannes C. Lünig, *Codex Italiae diplomaticus*, 4 vols. (Frankfort-Leipzig, 1724–35), III, 1561–68; and Witt, *Coluccio Salutati*, pp. 101–3.

57. Brucker, *Florentine Politics*, pp. 319 ff. The general of the Order of Vallombrosa did not hesitate to write openly to Lapo Castiglionchio on June 7, 1378, lamenting Florence's hostilities against the papacy (B.N.F., *Conv. sopp.*, G. 6, 1502, fol. 4–4ᵛ).

58. Nino Valeri, *Italia nell' età dei principati*, Storia d'Italia illustrata, vol. 5 (Verona, 1949), p. 220, summarizes the peace terms. Salutati received absolution from all processes against

IV

The regime governing Florence in 1375 had been inaugurated in 1343 in the aftermath of the eleven-month dictatorship of Walter of Brienne and represented a compromise between the patrician families of the city and the "new men."[59] These latter, generally either sons of immigrants from the *contado* or immigrants themselves, had often become rich by trade and industry but up to 1343 had lacked sufficient political representation. The patricians, severely hurt by the collapse of the major Florentine banks and discredited by the results of their experiment with the one-man rule of Brienne, were forced to yield their monopoly of political power. While continuing the traditional Florentine policy of excluding the workers from all political power and restricting important segments of the citizen body in their access to public office, nevertheless, the new government, consisting of a coalition of "new men" and patricians, was the most democratic in the city's history to that point.

The evolution of Florentine political life in the decades after 1343 suggests that the compromise was on the whole successful. Among the patrician class, those who could claim hereditary wealth and a long record of family service to the Republic, a number of individuals and often an entire clan, like the Ricci, adhered to the conception that the city government should rest on the broad participation of the guild community. Because of their status, these patrician defenders of a widely based government acted as leaders of the "new men." Their motives are unclear, but genuine conviction as well as patrician rivalries and hope for political advantage were involved. The greater part of the Florentine patriciate, at least those who were *popolani* and endowed with full rights as citizens, seem to have accepted the regime.[60] Although not eager to sit elbow to elbow with the men of "Campi, Certaldo, and Figghine" at

him on October 26, 1378. The document certifying the absolution is published by Novati, *Epist.*, IV, 439–42. The treaty was never recognized by the new Avignon pope, Clement VII, and officially Florence remained at war with Avignon.

59. This account of the Florentine government from 1343 to 1378 is based on Brucker's *Florentine Politics*. Also see Marvin Becker, *Florence in Transition*, vol. 2.

60. The patrician class was divided into *popolani* and magnates. The latter constituted roughly the upper segment of the patriciate. Although many of the magnates originated from the feudal nobility of the countryside, others were members of old *popolani* families. Brucker, however, stresses that "the decisive criteria for magnate status were not antiquity and nobility; more important was the behavior pattern of the family, its reputation for violence and disorder . . . " (p. 29). What served to make the magnates a class was their common exclusion from the highest offices of state and by other limitations imposed by the Ordinances of Justice, the basic constititional statute of 1293 defining magnate status as a political category.

the council table, nevertheless, as long as the new order did not seriously threaten their wealth or exclude them from the high state offices, these patricians were reconciled to the situation.

The most important element of the "new men" in this amorphous alliance with members of the patriciate belonged to the major guilds. While as a group the "new men" agreed on the need for a large citizen body composed primarily of guildsmen and were of one mind regarding the disenfranchisement of the workers, those from the major guilds were also eager to limit the proportion of offices open to the minor guildsmen. Believing that the minor guildsmen would never unite with the despised workers, the major guildsmen felt free to join with friendly *popolani* patricians in assuring the ascendancy of the major guilds in the city government.

Decided opposition to the popular guild regime, however, came from some of the patrician *popolani* families who resented the power of the upstarts and longed for a return to the old days before the advent of Brienne. Like most Florentines of all classes they abhorred tyranny: the summoning of Brienne had been an error of judgment made in a moment of extreme crisis. What they wanted was a government of the rich, ancient, and respected families of the city. For them the pre-1342 period of patrician domination represented something of a golden age.

The natural allies of these *popolani* were the magnates. While the latter were by no means unanimously hostile to the regime established in 1343, the group resented any effort to enforce the provisions of the Ordinances of Justice restricting their freedom. If the magnates could not bring back the thirteenth century, at least they would have welcomed a reinstitution of the pre-1343 regime of the great *popolani* families which had looked sympathetically on magnate interests and given the Ordinances of Justice a less rigid interpretation.

The stronghold of oligarchic power and the institution which lent a degree of cohesion to what was essentially a tendency rather than a political party was the Guelf party structure. Established by a group of Guelf nobles in the mid-thirteenth century when the communal government itself had been only one of a number of competing authorities in Florence, the party had survived the commune's rise to political supremacy over the city, legally subordinate to communal institutions but in fact enjoying a measure of autonomy. The organization's prestige derived from the fact that Guelfism remained a vital force in Florence's political mythology long after domestic Ghibellinism had been laid to rest.[61] Although the party's mystique was not deeply ingrained in the "new men" and the workers, among the patriciate, save for a small body of irreverent individuals, Guelfism symbolized everything that was Florentine, while Ghibellinism encompassed all that was pernicious for the city and its people.

The party's chief weapon against its enemies was *ammoniziône*, the power of the Captains of the Guelf party to brand an individual a Ghibelline and to forbid him to accept public office on pain of judicial prosecution under the commune's anti-Ghibelline statutes. Because of the confused nature of their origins, the new men were particularly vulnerable to such a device. The commune's sometimes vigorous efforts in the 1350s and 1360s to control the party structure and especially to limit the practice of *ammonizione* enjoyed only temporary success. In 1375 the magnates and their *popolani* allies were still firmly entrenched in the party leadership and the *ammonizione*, although unpopular with most citizens, continued to drive the party's enemies from public office.

The outbreak of the war with the papacy momentarily set the party leaders in disarray, but within a year of the outbreak of hostilities it became obvious that the local party was not indissolubly linked in the popular mind with the papal cause. Despite the war, the organization felt able to resume its campaign of *ammonizione* and, as the Florentine war effort deteriorated, the chances of limiting the political power of the "new men" seemed increasingly favorable. The latter and their patrician allies had after all been the major sponsors of a fateful foreign policy that represented a break with Florentine political tradition.

Consequently, early in 1378, while the government desperately tried to reach an honorable accommodation with the pope, the party stepped up the process of *ammonizione* in an effect to terrorize its enemies. Attempts to reach a compromise involving a moratorium on *ammonizione* in exchange for a statutory modification in the procedure for designating *popolani* as magnates floundered on the refusal of the Captains of the party to accept the agreement.[62] In June as a reaction the anti-Guelf party forces led by Salvestro de'Medici, Standardbearer of Justice for

---

61. On the evolution of the conception of Guelfism in Trecento Florence, in addition to Brucker, *Florentine Politics*, pp. 101–4 and 346–51, see my "A Note on Guelfism in Late Medieval Florence," *Nuova rivista storica*, 53 (1969), 134–45; and Peter Herde, "Politische Verhaltensweisen der Florentiner Oligarchie, 1382–1402," in *Geschichte und Verfassungsgefüge: Frankfurter Festgabe für Walter Schlesinger*, Frankfurter Historische Abhandlungen, vol. 5 (Wiesbaden, 1973), p. 165.
62. Brucker, *Florentine Politics*, pp. 336 ff.

June and July, forced through the colleges and councils a statute reimposing in full the strictures of the Ordinances of Justice against the magnates.[63]

Convinced that only a violent expression of popular feeling would compel the government to take strong action against the party, Salvestro de'Medici probably encouraged a riot of the guildsmen on June 22.[64] Joined by many day laborers, the guildsmen burned, as if by design, a number of houses belonging to the leaders of the Guelf hierarchy.

The eruptions of June 22 were not punished; rather they resulted in a *balìa* which initiated effective action against the victims. A threat of more violence by the guilds on July 8 had the effect of forcing further restrictive measures out of the communal government.[65] The reaction of the regime to such shows of force encouraged these discontented elements in the city to plot a rebellion which would finally expel the oligarchs from their entrenched positions in both the government and society at large. On the morning of July 20, Florentines awoke to find houses burning and the *Signoria* isolated in their palace by a howling mob of woolworkers and lesser guildsmen. Within two days the old regime was abolished and a new one installed.

Although the government had a few hours notice that the uprising would occur on the morning of the 20th, Salutati apparently was at home when news of the event itself came. His first action was to flee to Santa Croce, the nearest church, to seek sanctuary.[66] He correctly estimated that the members of the communal bureaucracy would be special objects of mob vengeance. Ser Piero's house was burned and the notary would surely have been killed had he not left the city in time. Less fortunate, the chief of police, ser Nuto di Città di Castello was caught by the crowds and ripped to pieces.[67] Offices in the *Palazzo della Signoria* may have been ransacked, including the chancery.[68]

Salutati soon learned that he personally had nothing to fear. He was saved both by his reputation for fair administration of his office and by his identification with the war against the Church, a cause vigorously opposed by the Guelf party. His political propaganda was not merely a product of his professional duty as chancellor: Salutati really believed in the justice of Florence's cause and became something of a war hero.

63. Ibid., pp. 364–65.
64. Ibid., pp. 367–69.   65. Ibid., pp. 373–77.
66. Ser Nofri di ser Piero della Riformagioni, *Cronaca (1378–1380), Il Tumulto di Ciompi. Cronache e memorie*, ed. Gino Scaramella, RIS, vol. 18, pt. 3 (Bologna, 1917–34), p. 57.
67. Brucker, *Florentine Politics*, p. 385.
68. See below, chap. 7, n. 23.

True, he liked the company of men from old and wealthy families and his preferred political class was one heavily weighted with patrician elements. But the leadership of the Guelf party was clearly on a ruinous course. Secure in the knowledge that he had reached the height of his expectations with the chancellorship and fearing adverse change,[69] Salutati could only be critical of the extreme stands the Guelf leaders adopted in 1378 that pushed the Republic toward civil war. While he willingly composed the epithet for the tomb of Lapo Castiglionchio, who died in exile in Rome in 1381, Salutati considered the Guelf partisan unwise "to have bent his mind to the swollen desires of ambition."[70]

The new regime, headed by Michele di Lando as Standardbearer of Justice, had no intention of diminishing Salutati's position. On July 24, the day the new *Signoria* took power, he was recognized as official notary of the *balia* created late in June, whose original task of reform had enormously increased with the constitutional disruption caused by the civil war. On July 28 the *balia* once and for all removed the notary of legislation from any control over elements of the *Tratte* and assigned the whole to the chancellor.[71]

Despite the fact that the proletarian rioters succeeded in obtaining the creation of three new guilds, the wool carders (*Ciompi*), the dyers (*Tintori*), and the doublet-makers (*Farsettai*), the government which ruled after the riots of July 22 was hardly a radical proletarian regime.[72] Most of the new membership added to the reforming *balia* came not from the wage laborers but from the artisans and small shopkeepers. These elements were as frightened of the lowest classes as were their social superiors. In a melée in the piazza before the *Palazzo della Signoria* on the last day of August, the most violent and numerous group of the laborers, the *Ciompi*, were beaten and their leaders either killed or driven into exile by the forces of order. In the great *parlamento* or assembly of all the citizens called the following day, a new *balia* was created to deal with the altered political circumstances. Among the first acts of the *balia*

69. His letters exude confidence during the years 1375–78. After only a few months as chancellor, he feels that he is "powerful and famous," in that office (*Epist.*, I, 206). In a letter to Antonio degl Albizzi in 1377, he is barely able to conceal his newly found pride (ibid., I, 248): "nec magnitudo etiam mei nominis te a scribendo debuit deterrere. Hanc enim scio non te mirari, sed fingere. . . ."

70. Ibid., II, 219.

71. *Cap.*, 12, fol. 79; a summary of this provision is published in Cesare Guasti, *I capitoli*, II, 178.

72. For details of the Ciompi revolt and the immediate aftermath, see Gene Brucker: "The Ciompi Revolution," *Florentine Studies*, ed. Nicolai Rubinstein (Evanston, 1968), pp. 314–56, and his *Civic World*, pp. 41–46.

were the abolition of the Ciompi guild and the dismissal of all the employees of the commune with the exception of Salutati and the new notary of legislation ser Viviano.[73]

Effectively the same social groups which dominated the government in the weeks since July 22 continued to enjoy preponderance in the state after September.[74] Even after the reform of January 24, 1380, when the greater guilds, bastions of patrician power, received equal representation with the fourteen lesser guilds in the *Signoria*, the latter still gave the tone to the government's policies. Throughout its life this regime, which was to control the city until January 1382, was plagued by threats of violent overthrow. Outside the walls were the exiles to the right and left, created by the rapid succession of governments during the summer of 1378 and united by a common desire to return to the city as conquerors. Within the walls were some who covertly sympathized with these aspirations and participated in countless plots to destroy the present rulers. Demagogues like Giorgio Scali and Tommaso Strozzi found suspicion a useful tool for their own plans for domination. A charge of treason was an effective way of removing enemies and, if fears of treachery became sufficiently intense, the way would be open to establish a *signore* regime in the city.

Throughout his life Salutati had nothing but scorn for the lowest classes. In 1377 in reply to Francesco Bruni's remark that he was spending some of his summer hours teaching his servants and peasants to fish, Salutati sarcastically observed that the stomach was the best teacher of such people, "The same stomach which teaches the parrot to give his salutation, the crow to bow and the magpies to form our words."[75] When Florence was again threatened by a popular rebellion in 1383, Salutati recalled the short period of mob rule in the summer of 1378 when the city fell "into the hands of sordid men, whose quality of mind and amount of discretion is represented by their frightful rule of forty days in which this [human] plague raged."[76]

This was his honest judgment of the Ciompi, but throughout the three years' duration of the popular regime he said nothing. Both in his

73. *Balie*, 15, fol. 2ᵛ, revoked offices and fol. 3 made exception for the two notaries; published in Marzi as *Balie*, 16 (pp. 581–82).

74. For details of this regime, see Niccolò Rodolico, *La democrazia fiorentina nel suo tramonto (1378–1382)* (Bologna, 1905), and Brucker, *The Civic World*, pp. 46–59.

75. *Epist.*, I, 264.

76. Ibid., II, 84. Also see ibid., II, 179. Although he had sometimes found himself in mortal danger in battle, he writes years after the *Ciompi*, he never experienced anything so frightening as a popular revolt.

official and his private correspondence he tried to minimize the extent of the destruction. The missives of July and August assured other powers like Milan and neighboring Volterra that the change in regime entailed no alteration in Florence's foreign policy. In September the missives blamed the recent troubles in the city on "abandoned citizens."[77] The struggle all began when men like Lapo Castiglionchio tried to impose a tyranny on the city through abuse of their offices in the Guelf party. Throughout the next three years Salutati's primary task was to establish the legitimacy of the new government in the eyes of the rest of Italy and to prevail on other states to have nothing to do with the plotting exiles.

The crisis in the Church only intensified the atmosphere of insecurity. Two days after the signing of the peace of Tivoli on July 18, 1378, on the very day the Ciompi revolt burst on Florence, dissident cardinals led by the French members of the college openly proclaimed the election of Urban VI void. Why would Salutati not see this coincidence as a divine punishment levied on the two belligerents for their sins? A long official letter in the name of the *Signoria* to the dissident cardinals and a separate one to Pietro Corsini, a Florentine member of the group, begging them to restore unity to the Church, fell on deaf ears.[78]

To a degree Salutati's worries about the political state of Florence stemmed from his need to serve a regime whose continued existence seemed so problematical. Were he to become loyal to the present government he would have no future in the next. Still the regime continued to favor and trust him. Despite the endeavor of the government in August and September 1379 to exclude noncitizens from a wide range of offices both in the guild and the commune, Salutati and his then coadjutor ser Antonio Chelli, although provincials, were specifically exempted from the provision affecting notarial posts.[79] The former chan-

77. See Salutati's letter of August 4, 1378, to Bandini (ibid., I, 291). For public letters, see B.R.F., 786, fols. 135ᵛ–36; 136–36ᵛ; 150–50ᵛ; 151ᵛ–52; 159–61. On Lapo, fols. 152ᵛ–53. The phrase in the text is found 140ᵛ.

78. B.R.F., 786, fols. 170ᵛ–71 (Nov. 3, 1378). A second *missive* to Corsini, *Miss.*, 18, fols. 110–12 (Feb. 3, 1380), has been published in *Lini Coluci Pieri Salutati Epistolae*, ed. Giuseppe Rigacci, 2 vols. (Florence, 1741–42), I, 39–46. Corsini defended himself in a number of writings: B.C.R., 977, *De schismate*; B.A.V., *Vat. lat.*, 8497, *De electione Urbani VI et Clementis VII* (mentioned in Paul O. Kristeller, *Iter italicum*, 2 vols. [London, 1963–67], II, 106 and 345); and B.N.F., *Conv. sopp.*, G. 6., 1502, fol. 14. For other statements of Corsini on the origin of the Schism, see Louis Gayet, "Pièces justificatives," *Le grand schisme d'occident*, 2 vols. (Paris, 1889), II, 1–26 and 57–68.

79. The legislation on the notaries is found *Provv. reg.*, 68, fols. 109ᵛ and 121ᵛ. After listing the offices forbidden to those not meeting the qualifications, the text of August 17 adds: "Ita tamen quod hoc capitulum officiorum notariatus non preiudicet nec extendatur

cellor, ser Niccolò Monachi, had considerably augumented his income by holding similar offices concurrently with the chancellorship or selling to another the right to exercise them. In February 1381, moreover, for the only known time in his career, Salutati acted as Florentine ambassador on a mission to Lucca. He had the task of convincing the Lucchesi to join an alliance of Tuscan states with the Visconti. Not supprisingly he was unable to wait for the official reply because of "necessary and urgent business" back in Florence.[80] Three months later on May 5 the *Signoria* rendered him the signal honor of presenting his newborn son, Antonio, for baptism through their proctor ser Viviano.[81]

The extent of the chancellor's power of patronage over Florentine notarial appointments in the provinces is vividly illustrated in a letter of Lorenzo Ridolfi written in June 1380 to his preceptor Giovanni di Scolari, who had asked his student to obtain a Florentine notarial post for a friend. Ridolfi writes:

> As I am accustomed daily, I visited this same ser Coluccio [presumably in the *Palazzo della Signoria*]. With your letter foremost in mind I begged him, as far as the least important disciple could, to endeavor for my sake to propose [the name of your friend] to some rector for a notarial position. Whereupon we directly opened the register of drawings for external offices (*extrinsecarum electionum libellum*) in order to find someone ready to leave for his post. I confess there was none save the distinguished knight, Lord Pazzino Strozzi, who was about to take up the office of the same *podesteria* of Prato [where presumably Giovanni's friend already is serving as notary of the *podestà*]. I think it well known that the same man [the friend] can not remain there for the official who is coming [i.e., to hold a second term of office, this time with Pazzino as *podestà*]. Indeed because many are selected by lot and many of these are friends of Coluccio, I do not doubt that your wish will have support and I will try to do my best as I should do.[82]

---

ad presentem cancellarium communis predicti." Marzi, p. 132, n. 2, misinterprets this to mean that Salutati can hold political offices as well. Cf. *Statuta*, II, 749–50. On this legislation in general, see Julius Kirshner, "Paolo di Castro on 'Cives ex privilegio'," in *Renaissance Studies in Honor of Hans Baron*, ed. A. Molho and J. Tedeschi (Dekalb, 1971), pp. 239–42.

80. Francesco Landogna, "La politica dei Visconti in Toscana," *Bollettino della società pavese di storia patria*, 28 (1928), 111–112, publishes the letter of February 21 in which Lucca recognized Salutati's visit and excused his sudden departure: "Ipsum siquidem ser Colucium vidimus libenter atque recepimus gratiose, sed cura sicut demonstrabat necessaria et urgenti statim discessit a nobis nostrum determinatum consilium non expectans."

81. *Epist.*, IV, 444–46.

82. B.N.F., *Panc.*, 147, fol. 11: "Ut qualibet die solitus asto, vatem eundem Coluccium

Letters throughout Salutati's private correspondence over the years indicate that the chancellor served as a kind of employment agent for Florentine citizens seeking notarial work abroad as well as for foreigners looking for similar positions in the Republic.[83]

In the years immediately following the *Ciompi* Revolt, anyone in Florence risked ruin not only through a change in government but also from a false delation for treason. The judicial murder of the famous jurist Donato Barbadoro, reportedly the work of Tommaso Strozzi and Giorgio Scali, demonstrated that no one was safe.[84] As Salutati himself wrote to Francesco del Bene in April 1381: "You know how one lives today in Florence and how much danger is involved in quarreling." This was the final passage of Salutati's note to Del Bene, then vicar of the Valdinievole, urging him not to stir up trouble by supporting the knight attached to his suite who apparently infringed upon the jurisdiction of the notary of the *podestà* of Buggiano.[85] Not coincidentally Salutati's *De seculo et religione*, endorsing a life of monastic withdrawal, was a product of these years.

In the first days of January 1382 Salutati himself became the object of an accusation for treason by a member of the group around Giorgio Scali. Jacopo di Bartolomeo, a cloth shearer better known as Scatizza, had already denounced a merchant, Giovanni Cambi, to the *Signoria* which finished its term in December 1381. He then repeated the charge to the incoming priors, this time linking Salutati with the accusation:

> I was coming from eating with Nanni degli Asini and found in the Piazza of San Apollinario, Benedetto di Giovanni Michi, who told me

---

visitavi et tuis maxime epistulis introspectis, quantum valui et me scire possum tamquam minimus discipululus, suppliciter exoravi quatenus amore mei iusta posse totis conaretur habenis aliquo rectore pro tabellionatus offitio ponere. Unde confestim extrinsecarum electionum libellum aperuimus, cupientes aliquem reperire permigraturum. Et nullum fateor praeter inclitum militem dominum Pazinum de Strozorum proienie in eiusdem Pratensis potestariatus offitium accessurum. Et, ut credo notum constet, non est eodem possibilem (sic: possible) istic remanere venturo. Verum quia multi sedulo eliguntur et, quam sepius optimi preceptoris Colucci quam plurimum amicabiles, non ambigo quin quod desideras fulciaris et cunctis viribus conabor ut debeo." My translation of the last half of this Latin passage is an interpretation of a sometimes grammatically puzzling text. On this manuscript miscellany, see Eugenio Garin, *La cultura filosofica del Rinascimento* (Florence, 1961), pp. 29–32.

83. *Epist.*, II, 67, 140, 214–16, and 250–52, are examples of such letters. Also see *Epistolario di Pellegrino Zambeccari*, ed. L. Frati, Fonti per la storia d'Italia, vol. 40 (Rome, 1929), pp. 81–82.

84. Rodolico, pp. 393–94.

85. *Epist.*, II, 6. Salutati was a cousin of one of the people investigated by Del Bene for murder (ibid., p. 3, n.1). Salutati apparently brought all his influence to bear to end the investigation in Buggiano. He is really behind the "string-pulling" incident described by Brucker in *The Civic World*, p. 58.

secretly: "I was in the house of ser Paolo Ricoldi yesterday where it was said that while Coluccio held the office of chancellor there was no need for the enemies and opponents of those who run the present state to fear, because he was their champion." And it was said that in the house of Giovanni Cambi there were grouped certain soldiers and that with God's help the priors should take care of this matter.[86]

The accusation against Salutati was apparently dismissed out of hand by the trusting priors but Cambi was called to defend himself against Scatizza's statements. The supposed "soldiers" in his house, he explained, were certain foreigners who had brought and killed his pigs. Considering the charges against Salutati preposterous, the *Signoria* found it easier to believe Cambi's story. Accordingly, Scatizza was arrested by the captain and taken to prison where he confessed that together with Giorgio Scali, Tommaso Strozzi, and many others he had decided to fabricate the charges against the two men.[87]

In the records of the trial held before the captain, immediately after the summary of Scatizza's charge the text reads:

That all the words spoken by the said Jacopo in the aforesaid manner were not nor are they true but lacked and lack all truth. And they were said in a false, deceptive, and iniquitous manner for the purpose of bringing damage, injury, and danger to the said ser Coluccio and Giovanni in their persons and goods in so far as the aforesaid deed demanded and required, and that said ser Coluccio would be deprived absolutely and completely of the said office of the chancellorship.[88]

86. *Capitano*, 1392, fol. 69: "Signori, io venìa da dezenare cò Nanni de l'Asini e trovai ne la piazza de san Polenaro, Benedicto de Iohanni Michy, el quale me disse secretamente: 'Io me trovay geri sera en casa de ser Paulo Ricoldi, dove se disse che, mentro che ser Coluccio tenìa l'officio d'essere nostro cancellero, no' besognava de temere a li nemici et malivoli de quisti che regono el presente stato, perchè era loro campione. E fove dicto, che en casa de Iohanni Camby erano readunati certi fanti, e che per Dio sopra de ciò li dicti Signori remediassero." The text published in *Diario d'anonimo fiorentino dall'anno 1358–1389*, ed. Alessandro Gherardi, Cronache dei secoli xiii e xiv, Documenti di storia italiana, vol. 6 (Florence, 1876), 270, differs from mine in a few minor respects, but he gives no source for his passage. Brucker, "The Ciompi," p. 328, describes Scatizza's social status as above that of the lowest class worker.

87. Stefani, pp. 392–93; *Diario d'anonimo*, p. 434; and *Cronaca prima d'anonimo, Il tumulto dei Ciompi*, p. 96. *Cronaca terza d'anonimo*, ibid., p. 133, also summarizes the events briefly. Except for Stefani, p. 392, these sources do not mention the accusation against Salutati nor does Brucker, *The Civic World*, pp. 60–61, in his otherwise excellent account.

88. *Capitano*, 1392, fol. 69–69ᵛ: "Que omnia verba dicta per dictum Jacobum modo predicto non fuerunt nec sunt vera set omni veritate carebant et carent. Et dicta fuerunt falso, doloso et iniquo modo ad hoc ut dictis ser Colutio et Johanni dampnum, ingnuriam (sic)

Under torture Scatizza was forced to confess to a crime far more important than false delation: that he along with Scali, Strozzi, and others
was in league with Bernabò Visconti to give the city to the Lombard
tyrant.[89]

Whether or not the confessed plot actually existed, it is beyond question that ser Niccolò Monachi, motivated by hatred of Salutati, was involved in the Scatizza affair. In an effort to have their imprisoned accom-
plice released, Scali, Strozzi, Simone di Biagio, and others appeared
before the *Signoria* and colleges petitioning for his release. This body
consented and the order was issued. However, the captain, Opizzone
degli Alidosi of Imola, who held Scatizza, refused to comply, and so
desperate were Scatizza's friends that on the night of January 13 they
attacked the captain's palace and freed the prisoner by force. According
to the judicial proceedings of the next month concerning this attack,
among the group of attackers was the former Florentine chancellor.
Considering the assault an outrage, the captain in disgust went to the
Signoria and resigned his office. This action had the effect of bringing
the seven greater guilds to his defense and, after long hours of negotiations, on the 16th, with the sanction of the *Signoria* and supported by
the troops of John Hawkwood, the captain seized and executed Giorgio
Scali.[90] This was the signal for a general repression of the members of
Scali's group and a series of trials took place over the next few weeks.
On February 5 ser Niccolò was tried with eleven others accused in the
attack on the captain's palace.[91] He was punished by exile for six years
at a distance of at least fifty miles from Florence.[92]

The irresolution of the government in dealing with Scatizza's case revealed its weakness. In the face of imminent anarchy the seven major
guilds took the initiative. With their support the Priorate met the challenge, suppressed the mob, and executed its leaders. Nevertheless, the
victory of the forces of order led to a shift in the balance of power within

---

et periculum inferrent in eorum personis et bonis prout factum predictum postulat et re-
quirit. Et ut dictus ser Colutius dicto officio cancellariatus privaretur penitus et omnino."

89. B.N.F., *Panc.* 158, fol. 140[a].

90. Stefani, pp. 393–94, writes of all these events between the imprisonment of Scatizza and the death of Scali as occurring between January 8 and 13. The *Diario d'anonimo*,
pp. 434–35, dates them in more detail between the 7th and 16th. The *Cronaca prima d'anonimo*, p. 96, agrees with this latter account. B.N.F., *Panc.*, 158, fol. 140[a-b], and the *Cronaca
terza d'anonimo*, p. 133, relate the events substantially like the *Diario* except that Scali is
executed on the 17th and 18th respectively in the two chronicles.

91. *Capitano*, 1392, fol. 77–77[v] The *Diario d'anonimo*, p. 437, mentions only eleven men.
For details of the event and the trial, see *Atti del Podestà*, 3053, fols. 29–32[v], 34–35, 54–55[v],
131–38[v].

92. Stefani, p. 401, gives the punishment.

the state in favor of the upper classes. A series of street demonstrations decked out with the symbols of the Guelf party succeeded in cowing the divided minor guilds and in compelling the priors to convoke a *parlamento*, an assembly of the whole body of Florentine citizens. This assembly promptly approved the creation of a *balia* to reform the state.[93]

Burning for revenge, the horde of exiles of various persuasions created by the civil disturbances over the preceding three-and-one-half years now returned to the city. The great bulk of the Florentines, however, wanted compromise, and the legislation emerging from the *balia* of late January and February was surprisingly conciliatory. All exiles of all factions were permitted to return. The two guilds remaining of the three created in July 1378 were abolished and their membership put back as *sottoposti* under the rule of the wool guilds. Yet those among the *sottoposti* seeking entrance to the wool guild itself could be admitted with the approval of the Priorate and the wool guild consuls. Moreover, both the silk and the wool guilds were to have one and two consuls respectively on their governing boards taken from those who remained *sottoposti*.

On February 15 a coalition of extremists, Ciompi, former Guelf exiles, and Guelf sympathizers—men like Donato Acciaiuoli and Vanni Castellani—attempted to pack the reform *balia* by forcing the summoning of a *parlamento*, to add new members to the *balia*. After a short demonstration in the *Piazza della Signoria*, a mass meeting of members of a number of great patrician families and cloth workers in the *Mercato nuovo* decided on a list of forty-three men to be added to the existing *balia* with equal voting rights. Then, with messer Vanni Castellani holding the standard of the Guelf party in the lead, the crowd marched to the *Piazza della Signoria* to present their petition. Either through fear of the mob outside or from sympathy, the government decided to put the matter to the vote of a *parlamento*.[94]

Holding the proposal containing the forty-three names, Salutati read out its contents from the speaker's platform before the palace, and, having heard the expected roar of approbation, "si, si!", declared the proposal to be law. At this moment out of the crowd emerged three leaders of the mob, messer Donato del Ricco, Carlo Strozzi, and Buonaccorso di Lapo Giovanni, with a second petition to present. Having had their way

93. For notes to this and the next paragraph, see my "The Florentine Ruling Class, 1382–1407," *The Journal of Medieval and Renaissance Studies*, 6 (1976), 252.
94. Stefani, p. 403, and *Panc.*, 158, fol. 142[v-a].

with the first, they now endeavored to have the second petition passed by the assembly.[95] In all probability had the government seen the second text beforehand they would have been more reluctant to call the *parlamento* in the first place. Among the more objectionable articles in the petition were those demanding that the *Ciompi* be rearmed, that the returned exiles be reimbursed for all losses suffered in the burning of their possessions, that amnesty be given for all crimes committed up to that date, and that the *balìa* promise in advance to excuse all deeds perpetrated in the city on that same day up to midnight.

Confronted as he was by a mob eager for passage of the second petition, Salutati had no recourse but to read the petition chapter by chapter to the expectant throng. When he had finished, the crowd shouted its consent and, satisfied that the text had now become law, they began to disperse, "many to do the evil deeds for which no legal action could be taken." Their hopes, however, were to be frustrated by the courage of ser Viviano, who had stood near Salutati during the proceedings. When, after the voting and disbanding of the *parlamento*, messer Donato del Ricco came up to demand that the two notaries draw up the second petition in the form suited to a *provvisione* of the commune, ser Viviano flatly refused. He justified himself on the grounds that the *Signoria* had only given permission for the presentation of the first petition involving the forty-three names and that there was no official sanction for what had been done on the second. With this he walked off the platform into the palace to rejoin the priors.

The incident dramatically illustrates the difference between the personalities of the two leading notarial officials of the commune. Salutati intensely disliked such a direct confrontation. Had it not been for ser Viviano's resolve, it is difficult to predict what he would have done. Now, however, echoing his colleagues, Salutati answered: "I have read it to the people but I have not notarized it since without the antecedent deliberations of the priors I cannot do this." Nevertheless, in a gesture of compromise he took the document from the furious jurist's hands and retired into the palace while Donato hurried off to spread the word. On second thought, Salutati, apparently alarmed that new violence might break out, had him summoned back to the palace before he could go too far. "There [he] discussed with him at such length that he satisfied him that the *parlamento*'s action was not valid if everything that was

95. Stefani, p. 403.

proposed did not proceed from the command and deliberation of the *Signoria."*[96] Fortunately the failure of the second petition to become law gave the *balia* a definite bargaining position. On February 17 in return for a promise of the forty-three new members to resign from the *balia* at the end of the day, the body made certain of the less radical demands of the second petition of February 15 into law.[97]

When the work of the *balia* was completed at the end of February, the new order began to function. But on March 10 the extremists on both sides tried to cooperate with one another a second time. Again they forced the calling of a *parlamento* and had a series of petitions approved as law in the midst of a mob atmosphere. One of these, for instance, provided complete reimbursement for those whose houses had been burned in the riots of 1378, and another forbade those who had been branded as Ghibellines prior to 1378 from holding public office.[98] This show of force by the extremists, however, caused a general reaction in the city and resulted in the creation of a new *balia* which in a few days time revoked in substance the legislation approved by the *parlamento* of March 10. In the days after March 10 Donato Acciaiuoli and Vanni Castellani, who had supported the agitation of February 15, threw in their lot with the moderates.[99] The new regime was launched.

Salutati emerged from four years of intimate cooperation with a basically lower-middle class regime with his reputation enhanced. That government's mishandling of the false delation of Scatizza against Salutati was the immediate cause of its downfall. Salutati appeared as the innocent victim of a political situation that was intolerable and required change. Moreover, while lacking the decisiveness of ser Viviano, he probably saved the city from another civil war by adroitly sapping messer Donato's determination to have his way. Certainly the creation of Salutati and ser Viviano as honorary members of the patrician-dominated guild of the *Lana* in March 1383 reflects the gratitude felt by the propertied families of the city for their services during the turbulent period of transition the previous year.[100]

96. Ibid., p. 405.   97. Ibid., p. 406.
98. Ibid., p. 407, and *Panc.*, 158, fol. 144$^{v\text{-}a}$.
99. Stefani, pp. 408–11, and *Panc.*, 158, fol. 144$^{v\text{-}a}$.
100. *Epist.*, IV, 446–48.

CHAPTER 6. THE ELDER STATESMAN (1382–1406)

I

Although troubled by occasional conspiracies, including another abortive uprising of the Ciompi in 1383, the regime during the first years proved acceptable to most citizens. The extent to which the new order attempted to effect a compromise with the preceding regime is shown dramatically in the number of new families appearing in the lists of priors. The creation of a new set of purses in 1385, the so-called Scrutiny of Union, enabling more citizens to hold high public office, reflects the same effort to achieve a great degree of social harmony. Henceforth no one would be ineligible for the Priorate, the two advisory colleges—i.e., the Twelve and Sixteen—and the Captains of the Guelf party on the grounds that they were from a Ghibelline family.[1] This legislation implicitly favored the "new men." While the scrutiny did not begin to affect elections until the purses of 1382 were exhausted, the immediate psychological impact was to create a mood of cautious expectancy.

The first years of the new regime saw a reordering of Salutati's personal priorities. His reputation as first chancellor of Europe well-established, Salutati felt he could devote more time to his scholarship. Consequently, much of the energy he formerly invested in writing public letters became in the course of the eighties focused on his private work. His relationship with the Guild of Judges and Notaries indicates this new attitude. A member of the Guild since 1366, in 1381 he acted as councillor of the guild for the quarter of Santa Croce.[2] When, however, three years later in 1384 his name was again drawn for the same position for the four-month period September–December, Salutati refused the office and a replacement had to be made.[3] Such a renunciation was extremely rare for this guild: in the volume of elections from 1363 to 1385 Salutati's refusal was unique.

More significant of his determination to limit the amount of profes-

1. See my "The Florentine Ruling Class, 1382–1407," *The Journal of Medieval and Renaissance Studies* 6 (1976), 253–54; and Gene Brucker, *The Civic World of Early Renaissance Florence* (Princeton, 1977), p. 75.

2. *AGN*, 22, no official pagination but starting with the first folio Salutati's name is found on fol. 39.

3. Ibid., fol. 42.

sional responsibilities after 1382 was his reluctance to have his name included in the *Tratte* for a number of lucrative notarial posts in the administration. The provisions of August and September 1379 had made these posts available both to Salutati and his coadjutor, ser Antonio Chelli, even though neither was a citizen. In ser Antonio's case, the very next year his name was drawn for a two-months term of office as notary of the *Signoria*, a well-paying post he held again in 1383 and 1404.[4] Ser Niccolò Monachi had been notorious for snatching at every appointment to enrich himself. On the other hand, Salutati never held one of these additional offices in his lifetime. He is recorded as having been drawn as notary of the *Signoria* for May-June 1406, but this drawing was very likely a last-minute arrangement designed to give additional honor to the dying chancellor.[5] Apparently satisfied with his revenues from the chancery and *Tratte*, which were substantial, he preferred leisure for study to the scramble for appointments.

The political scandals which rocked Florence in the spring of 1387 and brought an end to the era of good feeling had little effect on Salutati's plan for spending more time with his studies. In April 1387 the name of Filippo Magalotti was drawn for the post of Standardbearer of Justice for May-June, even though he was not of legal age. His father-in-law, Benedetto degli Alberti, together with a large group of citizens, called on the priors and through pressure induced them to overlook the discrepancy. Because of the Alberti's collaboration with the regime of 1378–82, the clan was deeply hated by former Guelf exiles and their friends, but the angry reaction to Benedetto's audacity went beyond the narrow confines of this group. A popular family with the workers and the members of the minor guilds, the Alberti were easily suspected of plotting to set up a lordship resting on the support of the lower classes. The fact that Benedetto degli Alberti himself had been drawn for the advisory College of the Sixteen beginning in May only increased suspicion. Even if the Alberti had no immediate plans, the incident raised questions about the wisdom of the reform legislation of 1385. Throwing open the doors of high public office to citizens of dubious background made it ultimately possible for the Alberti to take over power through legal means.[6]

4. Demetrio Marzi, *La cancelleria della Repubblica fiorentina* (Rocca S. Casciano, 1910), pp. 493–95.
    5. See below, chap. 15.
    6. See Brucker, *The Civic World*, pp. 78–79; Anthony Molho, "Politics and the Ruling Class in Early Renaissance Florence," *Nuova rivista storica* 52 (1968), 418; and Witt, "The

The danger was considered sufficient to summon a *balia*. One of the extraordinary commission's major tasks was to exile most of the male members of the Alberti along with other prominent citizens including members of the Rinuccini and Del Bene families.[7] Once the *balia's* authority expired on May 7, the government acted to reduce the share of offices open to the minor guilds and to create a special purse which would contain the names of those "who had the very great confidence of their state."[8] At each extraction for the Priorate, two names would be chosen from the new purse, called the *borsellino*.[9] This new institution constituted primarily a response to the Scrutiny of Union of 1385.[10]

There was a good deal of pressure from the former Guelf exiles and their sympathizers to make further reforms and lengthen the list of exiles, but this tendency was resisted.[11] Oddly enough, the employment of the *borsellino* and the reduction of the share of the minor guilds in the highest state offices had little effect on the entrance of new families into the Priorate.[12] The prime target of this reform was obviously Florentine families previously elected to the Priorate but now considered politically unreliable.

Salutati was saddened by the exile of his friend and sometime correspondent Francesco del Bene, but probably like most upperclass Florentines he considered the *borsellino* a necessary reform in the light of the Alberti affair, one capable of blunting the democratic tendencies inherent in the Scrutiny of Union when its purses came to be used. He was not ignorant of the variety of forces interested in humbling the Alberti, but the fact remained that the family and their supporters had openly tried to break the law. No warm friend of the lower classes, Salutati

---

Florentine Ruling Class," pp. 254–55. Brucker suggests that the enemies of the Alberti had been plotting against them for months before the incident, yet he does not exempt Benedetto himself from blame (*The Civic World*, p. 78).

7. Ibid., p. 80.

8. *Cronica volgare di anonimo fiorentino dall'anno 1384 a 1409 già attribuita a Piero di Giovanni Minerbetti*, ed. Elina Bellondi, *RIS.*, vol. 27, pt. 2 (Città di Castello, 1915-), p. 35.

9. Brucker, *The Civic World*, pp. 80–82.

10. I am not persuaded that Bastari and other liberals spoke in favor of the borsellino because they "perhaps" wished to avoid trouble (ibid., p. 82). See Witt, "The Florentine Ruling Class," p. 255, n. 1.

11. *Cronica volgare di anonimo*, p. 34.

12. Witt, "The Florentine Ruling Class," p. 251, n. 23. My figures are for the whole period July 1387–October 1393. Brucker, *The Civic World*, pp. 88–89, shows a significant drop in eligibility in the scrutiny of 1391, but this would only have effect when these purses were used later. Through a year-to-year analysis of new families entering the Priorate in the fourteenth century based on A.S.F., *Man.* 226, John Najemy, "The Guilds in Florentine Politics, 1292–1394" (Ph.D. Diss., Harvard, 1972), was the first to demonstrate a significant drop in entrance of "new men" after October 1393.

used what influence he had to oppose a faction that presumably would not hesitate risking another *Ciompi* to attain political ascendancy. A political realist, in the interest of stability he doubtless supported official policy in the next crisis to trouble the regime.

There is a striking parallel between the immediate causes behind the *balia* of 1387 and those leading to that of 1393. In both cases the action to restrict political participation appears essentially a reaction to the threat to the *status quo*. Just as the earlier *balia* was related to a prior liberalization of requirements for public office and the supposed political ambitions of the Alberti, so that of 1393 had as its antecedents an effort to rehabilitate the Alberti along with those designated as their accomplices of 1387 and a series of laws doubtless motivated by fiscal necessities but also very attractive to the lower classes of the city.

A plot involving one of the Alberti had been discovered on the eve of the First Milanese War in March 1390, but the offender was dealt with lightly.[13] In the fall of 1391, with the period of exile imposed in 1387 nearly terminated, a concerted effort was made by the priors to restore political rights to most of the prominent exiles. Cipriano degli Alberti, now the head of the Alberti clan, was excluded from the recall, but his family, along with the Rinuccini, were called back in October, and the Del Bene in November. The more conservative of the two legislative councils, the Council of the Commune, nevertheless resisted further recalls.[14]

By August 1392, with the First Milanese War at an end, Giovanni Biliotti, then Standardbearer of Justice for the term July-August, sensed that the mood of the city was propitious for a recall of Cipriano himself. Not only was Biliotti successful in an endeavor which the year before had been blocked, but he was also able to have a number of proposals enacted altering the *Monte*, as the public debt was called, with a view to reducing the burden on the communal treasury. He postponed interest payments on the *Monte*, made steps for reducing the extent of communal indebtedness by paying off the principal, and reduced and postponed the regular payments to the Church for lands confiscated in the war with the papacy. This compensation to the Church had been a fundamental demand of the returning Guelfs in 1382.[15]

The full truth about the events surrounding the political crisis of October 1393, a year later, will perhaps never be known. On October 9,

13. B.N.F., *Panc.*, 158, fol. 158ᵃ.   14. Brucker, *The Civic World*, pp. 86–87.
15. Witt, "The Florentine Ruling Class," p. 256.

1393, three men were arrested and letters were found on their persons relating to a plot to create a rebellion in the city in the name of the "twenty-four arts." The latter phrase immediately evoked memories of the Ciompi demand for three new guilds in 1378, and upperclass demagogy. One of the three apprehended was an ironworker who had been among the citizens deprived of political rights in 1387 for supposed complicity with the Alberti. Under torture the three revealed that Cipriano and Alberto degli Alberti were leaders of the conspiracy. This information led to the arrest of the patricians and their examination. Although tortured, both insisted on their innocence. During the night of October 18, nine days after the original discovery of the plot, an apparently separate incident led to the collection of a crowd which quickly grew into an angry mob shouting for the punishment of the Alberti. The Standardbearer of Justice at the time was Maso degli Albizzi, bitter enemy of the Alberti, and he was naturally not unopposed to meeting this demand.[16]

A *balia* of eighty-five men, one of whom was Guidetto Guidetti, one of Salutati's sons-in-law, was charged with reforming the state.[17] The major acts of the new *balia* included exiling wide numbers of citizens, ordering the destruction of purses of the dreaded "Scrutiny of Union" pertaining to the Priorate, the Twelve, and the Sixteen, and providing for the careful screening of the names remaining from the scrutinies of 1382 and 1391. Henceforth in the election of the Priorate three rather than two priors would be selected from the *borsellino*. The *balia* also reclassified a number of magnate families as *popolani*, in an apparent attempt to weight the balance more in favor of conservativism, while it granted small economic and fiscal concessions to the lower classes, probably to attract their support. The overall effect of the *balia* of 1393 was decisively to restrict access to high communal office.[18]

If there was generally any doubt about Alberti guilt, their complicity was confirmed in the minds of many citizens by the popular riot which occurred on October 24 while the *balia* was still meeting to decide punishment for the Alberti. A number of artisans crying, "Long live the people and the arts!" rushed into the *Piazza della Signoria* in an attempt to seize the Banner of the People from the house of the captain. These men were set on by a large number of "good citizens" and were either

16. Brucker, *The Civic World*, pp. 90–91.
17. *Balie*, 19, fols. 22–23. See also chap. 10 below.
18. Witt, "The Florentine Ruling Class," p. 257; and Brucker, *The Civic World*, pp. 92–93.

killed or driven away. To pacify the population, Donato Acciaiuoli and Rinaldo Gianfigliazzi paraded through the city, the first carrying the Banner of the People and the other that of the Guelf party. Again on November 7 an attempt was made to start a riot when a group of artisans charged into the *piazza* shouting "Long live the arts!"[19]

Periodic exiling of substantial numbers of citizens and increasing control of election machinery became characteristic of the regime from 1393. Suspicion of a preeminent individual attempting to set up a popular tyranny combined with fear that Giangaleazzo Visconti was seeking to destroy the city from within led the ruling families of the city to seek concentration of political power within the hands of "reliable" families while stressing the need to share high office within the power group. The emphasis on collegiality of power, however, extended not only to the relationship between families but also to the relationship between members of the same family. With the rising fiscal burdens caused by the Milanese wars, family prosperity became integrally connected with a family's political power and the nature of public policy. The rash of political exiling after 1382 was eloquent testimony to the fact that the actions of one or two family members jeopardized the welfare of a whole clan. As a result of this experience, the membership of the diminishing number of families at the center of power demanded more and more of a role in political life. As opposed to the former situation where a family was represented by one or two members in the higher offices every generation, after 1382 more family members participated and family control of individuals increased.[20]

Politics between 1343 and 1378 can be described as a struggle between two rather informal parties, the new men and their *popolani* patrician allies against another group of *popolani* patricians in league with the magnates. After 1382, in contrast, there developed a politics of consensus, characterized by a willingness on the part of the majority of the

---

19. Witt, "The Florentine Ruling Class," p. 258.

20. Ibid., pp. 250–51. Brucker, *The Civic World*, p. 302, describes the change in Florentine government between 1382 and 1411 as basically a transformation from a corporate order to a regime controlled "by a stable, cohesive elite." He writes: "The intensity of this elite's commitment to the regime and the republican values that it symbolized distinguished it from earlier forms of civic leadership, which were usually linked to some party based on blood or ideology" (p. 283). Molho, "Florentine Politics," pp. 417–18, was the first to describe the political attitude of the leading Florentine statesmen as essentially a sense of collegiality. Where he differs from Brucker and myself is in his view that entrance to the governing class remained relatively open from 1382 to 1434 (ibid., p. 419). On the importance of extended family in fifteenth-century Florence, see Francis W. Kent, *Household and Lineage in Renaissance Florence* (Princeton, 1976). Cf. the critique of Kent's book by Richard A. Goldthwaite, *Speculum*, 53 (1978), 817–19.

political class to support government policies. A relatively large number of families held the center while factional fringes attempted to pull it in various directions. The primary goal of this large center group was political stability. Horror of the *Ciompi* still remained strong, and while the dangers of lower class revolt diminished after 1382, the fear of a patrician tyranny founded on lower-class support was an impelling force for civic unity.

As the circle of those exercising political power in the commune gradually narrowed between 1382 and 1400 largely in response to pressures from the left, the movement for Salutati had the appearance of power returning to its natural place. Although the policy of compromise imposed immediately after 1382 was acceptable to him, he was not surprised when it broke down. He remained unforgiving toward those patricians who sought popularity with the mobs for political advantage. Even if great men like Cypriano degli Alberti or Donato Acciaiuoli, whose confession of treason he formally recorded in 1396, were not guilty of conspiracy, they had at least been criminally irresponsible.[21]

A self-made man, he demonstrated the major strengths and weaknesses of the breed. In his more self-conscious moments he insisted that God deserved the credit for bringing him "born in a small but sunny village, to such a famous city" and for placing him "in such an honorable office beyond my merit."[22] But he also believed in a natural nobility and occasionally felt a rush of pride in his own accomplishments. At the same time he basked in the favor of patrician families and rejected much of the rest of humanity as inferior. The *Ciompi* and the regime of *mediocres* had confirmed his prejudice, causing him to yearn for the stability of a patrician-controlled regime.

He saw no inconsistency in his statements made in the first twenty years of public letters on the virtues of a government of merchants and artisans, and the focus of Florentine propaganda after 1393 on principles of legitimacy and order. No one in his generation had any definite ideas about how large the political class of a regime had to be for it to

---

21. *Epist.*, II, 13.

22. Witt, "The Florentine Ruling Class," pp. 259–60. Brucker, *The Civic World*, pp. 96–100. As Brucker writes: ". . . it [the regime] enjoyed more fervent support from Donato's enemies, and from those who longed for domestic peace and security, and who reacted violently against those who disturbed the status quo" (p. 99). Also cf. Molho, "Florentine Politics," pp. 417–18. On Salutati's role the *Signoria* wrote to Donato (B.N.F., *Panc.*, 158, fol. 186ᵃ): "Anche forse a dimentichato che per se medesimo al chanceliere nostro, il quale ridusse ogni cosa in iscrittura, e personalmente al coletterale del capitano nel palagio nostro liberamente confessò ogni cosa e che per lo suo prochuratore . . . pro tribunali sidendo ogni cosa confessò. . . ."

be considered a republic. His earlier letters presented republican ideas in the most abstract form, capable of application to a wide range of political circumstances. Although the motives for the later shift in themes were various, at one level Salutati was himself merely giving emphasis to principles he had always valued. Throughout his mature life he preferred a republican to a *signore* regime for a city-state but only if it was legitimately established and orderly. The chance of insuring at least stable republican government was for him greater where the upper classes dominated.

Salutati survived the various political reforms, therefore, partly because he agreed with them. Yet agreement was not enough. One could not know in the kind of environment prevailing after 1393 who would seize or be accused of seizing an occasion for betraying the city. Close association could mean ruin. Safety lay in conspicuous conformity and in avoiding making enemies. The latter endeavor was particularly difficult in Florence because as a people the Florentines were noted for the ease with which they felt insulted and for their passion for vengeance. Salutati, however, was a master of self-control. Both in Florence and abroad men recognized him as exempt from the two notorious vices of his compatriots, the love of money and personal vindictiveness. As the renowned Paduan canon lawyer Francesco Zabarella wrote to the aged chancellor:

> How often did you keep silent when harrassed not once but many times by injurious language as is frequent in all republics but in no other so much as in that one [Florence]. Immortal God! You kept silent, nay rather you dissimulated and appeared unharmed . . . never did you do injury for an insult but often gave favor and benefit.[23]

Both a religious commitment to humility and sound political instinct worked for his political survival.

Salutati was not always circumspect. Doubtless the occasions on which he availed himself of his high standing with the regime to make criticisms increased as he grew older. Government officials in Florence must have enjoyed a large measure of free speech. At least Salutati cannot have ignored the probability that his friend, the chancellor of Lucca, Antonio da Cortona, on state business in Florence in 1391, would report his words to the *Anziani* of Lucca: "This morning," ser Antonio wrote,

---

23. *Epist.*, IV, 355.

"when telling ser Coluccio how strange it was, all the problems having already been settled for six days, that they [the *Signoria*] do not elect a man [presumably as representative to Lucca]; he answered: 'It is a wonder that they do anything however small a matter it is.' "[24] Six years later the same official reporting on his mission to Florence repeated Salutati's judgment of the current *Signoria*. According to ser Antonio, Salutati remarked: "Florence will never have better news than that those [the present priors] will be leaving this palace."[25] Blunt comments like these permit glimpses of the humanity behind the mask of the pious, grave chancellor.

The political role of Salutati in making policy can never be precisely determined. Officially to the end of his days he remained a civil servant devoid of political power. In fact, comparison of the *Consulte e pratiche* and Salutati's state letters suggests that his role was limited to that of embellishing the basic ideas produced in the discussions. Yet his reputation for moderation, loyalty to the common good, and complete honesty in the administration of his office, together with his acknowledged wisdom could not fail to have exerted an influence in the Florentine councils of state.[26] Furthermore, although not formulating the ideas into a theory, he would have played a large role in the evolution of a political ethic of consensus, which seemed appropriate to the circumstances of political power in the city by the late fourteenth century.

II

Clearly this politics of consensus, reducing the concentration on internal political problems, favored Florentine territorial ambitions, rekindled after six years' dormancy by the purchase of Arezzo in 1384. The occupation of the Tuscan city lost to the Republic in 1343 marked the resurgence of Florence as an active international power and opened the way for Florentine expansion into the Valdichiana in the direction of

24. *Registri del reale archivio di stato in Lucca*, ed. Luigi Fumi, 2 vols. (Lucca, 1903), II, 410, n. 1883.

25. Ibid., II, 411–12, n. 1887.

26. Daniela de Rosa, *Coluccio Salutati. Il cancelliere e il pensatore politico*, Biblioteca di storia, vol. 28 (Florence, 1980), pp. 69–70. Her analysis, pp. 63–69, illustrates the degree to which Salutati followed the dictates of his employers in presenting arguments in the missives. On occasion they even provided him with the ideological themes. For a clear instance of Salutati's participation in politics, however, see below.

Siena.[27] Over the next few years the Republic incorporated a number of little communes and lordships in that area and in 1387 accepted the allegiance of Cortona, which thereby renounced its status as a Sienese dependent.[28] Furthermore, Florence appears to have initiated steps to bring strife-ridden territory on its northern border into its dominions. With Florence at the center of a power vacuum, the leaders of the Republic were obviously attracted by the prospect of easy territorial conquest.

Yet Florentine expansionist policy can also be justified in the name of self-defense. The very weakness which made Siena and Lucca potential victims of Florentine conquest made them susceptible to aggression by other powers. After 1385 Milan was finally reunited in the hands of one prince, Giangaleazzo Visconti, count of Virtù, and, if Florentines were in an imperialistic mood, Milanese designs were far more ambitious and pushed with greater consistency and energy.[29] Lombard poets like Francesco Vannozzo had taken to calling the Visconti prince Caesar and Messiah, and Giangaleazzo himself confessed his wish to become king of Lombardy.[30] As the Florentines observed Milan absorbing first Verona

27. Marchione di Coppo Stefani, *Cronica fiorentina*, ed. Niccolò Rodolico, *RIS.*, vol. 30, pt. I (Città di Castello, 1903–1955), pp. 428–31, recounts the details of the acquisition. When the report of the transaction reached Florence early on the morning of November 18, the city went wild with joy (B.N.F., *Panc.*, 159, fol. 148[v-b]: "A meza terza questo venerdì sonorono le canpane de' signiori priori a parlamento e in sulla piaza vene tutto il popolo fiorentino e andò il bando che tutte le botteghe si serassono e così si fè. E quivi venono alla ringhiera i signiori priori cho loro cholegi dodici e ghonfalonieri, tutti cho gli ulivi in capo e in su la ringhiera ser Choluccio chanceliere lesse le sopra nominate lettere." For an account of Florentine territorial acquisitions beginning with Arezzo, see Brucker, *The Civic World*, pp. 104 ff.

28. Daniel M. Bueno de Mesquita, *Giangaleazzo Visconti, Duke of Milan (1351–1402)* (Cambridge, 1941), pp. 90–91 and 95; and Brucker, *The Civic World*, pp. 104 ff.

29. De Mesquita, pp. 31–32, recounts the capture of Bernabò, uncle of Giangaleazzo, and gives the various sources for the event which led to the unification of Visconti lands. See the letter of Giangaleazzo to Florence of May 8, 1385, in which he announces the capture of Bernabò as a matter of self-defense: B.N.F., *Conv. Sopp.*, G. 6, 1502, fol. 55[v].

30. Ezio Levi, *Francesco di Vannozzo e la lirica nelle corti lombarde durante la seconda metà del secolo XIV* (Florence, 1908), pp. 257–65 and 274. For a bibliography on political poetry during the period of Giangaleazzo's rule, see Hans Baron, *The Crisis of the Early Italian Renaissance*, 1st ed., 2 vols. (Princeton, 1954), II, 451, n. 31. For Giangaleazzo's use of humanism for political purposes, see brief but cogent remarks by Nino Valeri, "L'insegnamento di Giangaleazzo Visconti e i 'Consigli al principe' di C. Malatesta," *Bollettino storico bibliografico subalpino*, 36 (1934), 461–63. On *pace* and *benessere* as a propaganda theme of the Visconti before the First Milanese War, see Valeri, *L'Italia nell'età dei principati*, Storia d'Italia illustrata, vol. 5 (Verona, 1949), pp. 259–61. No attempt has so far been made to analyze Milanese propaganda as subject to a development: cf. Valeri, *La libertà e la pace. Orientamenti politici del Rinascimento italiano* (Turino, 1942); and Eugenio Garin, "La cultura milanese nella prima metà del xv secolo," *Storia di Milano*, vol. 6 (Milan, 1955), pp. 554–56. *Cronica volgare*, p. 48, reports the words spoken by the count to the Florentine ambassadors after the fall of Verona in 1387: "A me ne cresce fatica, però che l'arò a reggere e

and then attacking Padua, they rightly suspected that the goals of Gian-galeazzo extended to conquest of Tuscany as well. Enlargement of the Florentine domain would increase the Republic's resources while add-ing depth to its defense against a future Visconti invasion.

To Florence's dismay, Siena, the object of Florentine advances, was not resigned to extinction at the hands of fellow republicans. In 1388, after the defection of Montepulciano, the city offered itself to Gianga-leazzo.[31] The Milanese lord, still gorged with his recent acquisition of Verona and deeply engaged in the war with Carrara, was reluctant to commit himself at this point to a step which could push him into im-mediate war with Florence. For this reason he willingly acceded to the appeals of the lord of Pisa, Pietro Gambacorta, for a general league to keep the peace. Territories of the cosigners would be guaranteed from aggression: Milanese influence would be excluded from Tuscany and Tuscan powers would promise not to meddle in Northern Italy. A series of agreements between Florence, Milan, Bologna, and Siena among others crowned Gambacorta's attempt with ostensible success in Oc-tober 1389.[32] Few believed, however, that the provisions had any real meaning.

Only a few weeks after the signing of the Treaty of Pisa on October 9, the count of Virtù expelled all Florentine and Bolognese citizens from Visconti lands. In a public letter on October 26, the count justified the step as taken in order to protect his own life from an assassination plot being organized in Bologna and Florence.[33] Giovanni de'Ricci, the Flor-entine civil lawyer, was accused of having publicly called for the murder of the Visconti lord in an official assembly with the *Signoria* and the *Dieci* present. Both states were quick to make a firm denial of a conspiracy.[34] The Romans, a missive of Salutati declared in rebuttal, had refused to

altro non ho intenzione di volerne da i Veronesi, nè dagli altri che quello Signore reggiate prima; e poi disse ch'egli aveva intenzione di mutar nome e lasciare in tutto il nome del tiranno, e non disse loro il nome che prendere volea; ma altra volta avea usato di dire ch'egli volea prendere nome di Re de' Lombardi."

31. The revolt of Montepulciano against Sienese authority in summer of 1388 and the unsuccessful attempt of the town to give itself to Florence brought matters to a climax: De Mesquita, pp. 90–97. Florence refused the offer of submission but sent troops to the re-bellious city to prevent the Sienese from punishing their vassals.

32. De Mesquita, pp. 108–10. Nevertheless, to impress the Florentines with his friend-ship for Siena, Giangaleazzo dispatched two hundred lances the next month to the south with the specious assignment of helping the Sienese fight the hordes of bandits infesting its territory (*Cronica di anonimo*, p. 76).

33. Ibid., p. 111. The Visconti letter is found in *Miss.* 22, fol. 1–1ᵛ.

34. Ibid., fols. 2–3, for Florentine answer. Pellegrino Zambeccari replied for Bologna: *Epistolario di Pellegrino Zambeccari*, ed. Lodovico Frati, Fonti per la storia d'Italia, vol. 40 (Rome, 1929), pp. 257–58.

resort to such weapons to gain victory and the Florentines, as their heirs, disdained them as well. If Ricci said such terrible things, then the minutes of the assembly would bear witness, but a check of the register showed no record of such a speech.[35]

Salutati's letter, while rhetorically moving, filled as it is with classical references and carefully constructed phrases, nonetheless presents a very weak case. Although Giangaleazzo, himself the murderer of his uncle, was unduly terrified of assassinations, he had reason to reject Salutati's argument as a lie. After all, despite its so-called Roman heritage, the Republic made no secret of its intention to murder the count's military commander in Siena who was ravaging Florentine territory. On April 26, 1390, ten thousand florins were promised to anyone who could commit the deed and a week later, in the face of continued depredations, four trumpeters went through the city promising additional benefits.[36]

The war began in earnest in the spring of 1390 with Giangaleazzo, Siena, the Gonzaga, the Este, the Savoy on one side and Florence and Bologna on the other. Francesco Carrara, Stephen of Bavaria, and the count of Armagnac allied with the Florentines at various points during the two-year struggle, but Bologna remained the Republic's most dependable partner.[37]

Salutati's missive style during this war represents a moderation in the exuberant *stilus rhetoricus* of official correspondence during the war against the Church. The letters on the whole are shorter and in the more important ones the sentence construction tighter. From the outset of the war Salutati worked out a propaganda campaign which played on the Visconti emblem of the snake, emphasizing Giangaleazzo's utter faithlessness and cruelty.[38] The chancellor made attacks against the lord of Milan in political poetry as well. Two of Salutati's compositions from these years survive. The first, in Latin, "Cur tenet infantem coluber crudelis in ore," was dedicated to Inghiramo Bracchi, an agent of the count in Pisa; and the second, which had an incredible success, was a particularly violent poem in *volgare*, "O scacciato dal ciel da Micael."[39] It was

35. *Miss.*, 22, fol. 10ᵛ. This missive of December 16, 1389, is published in my *Coluccio Salutati and His Public Letters* (Geneva, 1976), pp. 104–6.
36. B.N.F., *Panc.*, 158, fol. 158ᵇ–58ᵛ⁻ᵃ.
37. On the war, see de Mesquita, pp. 121–35.
38. Witt, *Coluccio Salutati*, pp. 58–63. Also see perceptive comments by Armando Petrucci, *Coluccio Salutati*, Biblioteca biographica, vol. 7 (Rome, 1972), pp. 84–87.
39. For the Latin poem entitled *Invectiva Florentinorum contra arma Domini Comitis Virtutum transmissa per ser Colucium Domino Henghiramo de Brachis*, see Appendix, I. It belongs to the first war with Milan because Giangaleazzo is still referred to as count, a title he

perhaps during this first Milanese war that the lord of Milan made the remark generally attributed to him that a letter of Salutati was worth a thousand horses.[40]

It was, however, not so much the effectiveness of the letters and poems as it was the personal nature of the verbal assaults which caused Giangaleazzo, the consummate plotter, to plan the destruction of the Florentine chancellor. Warned of the danger to his life Salutati announced in a letter to his informant, Filippo di Bartoletto, that he intended to do his duty despite the threat of death.

> If, as is the duty of my office, in my own name or in that of my country I have written about him that which disturbs and offends him, he should remember that he is the enemy of my homeland. Let him recall that he is a deadly enemy for each and everyone of us; nor should he deceive himself. We are Florentines and until he becomes friends again with the Republic, he cannot hope to receive anything in word or deed from any Florentine except what is hostile and unfriendly. Indeed! Does he think that I am going to restrict my pen when, if the opportunity were given, I would not hold back the sword.[41]

If attacked by an assailant, the doughty sixty-year old chancellor resolved to defend himself: "Although I am sixty years old, I have enough spirit and force not to recoil before an assailant but to defend my life with my hand and repulse him to the limit of my power." Salutati was not striking a pose here. He was angry.

Giangaleazzo, however, was more devious than Salutati realized. It seems logical to relate the undated account of a Visconti plot to have the chancellor convicted of treason to these threats against his life made in 1390–91. Present at the secret sessions of the inner war councils, Salutati was privy to mines of valuable information for an enemy. The count's plan was to exploit this fact by counterfeiting letters, containing

---

exchanged for duke in 1395. Inghirammo de'Bracci was Visconti agent at Pisa during the war: Brucker, *The Civic World*, p. 140. The Italian poem of Salutati almost certainly belongs to the first war. One manuscript of this very popular poem, B.N.F., *Naz.*, II, VIII, 40, fol. 236, follows the text with this date: "Finis, die sabati hora xviiii, v. februarii, Florentie degente causa pestis." This surely refers to the plague of late 1390–early 1391. The poem is published by Francesco Flamini, *La lirica toscana del Rinascimento anteriore ai tempi del Magnifico* (Pisa, 1891), p. 60. On pp. 732–33 Flamini supplies some of the codices where the text appears. This diatribe against the Visconti lord was answered by the sonnet, "O Cleopatra, o madre d'Ismael," perhaps by Antonio Loschi, also published by Flamini, p. 61.

40. *Epist.*, IV, 247–48 and 514, provide various versions of this statement supposedly made by the Milanese lord.

41. *Epist.*, IV, 252.

treasonous information, in the hand of Salutati. Once composed, the false letters conveniently fell into the possession of the *Signoria*, who immediately called in the chancellor to explain their meaning. The brief description of the incident summarizes Salutati's response: "and asked if it was in his handwriting, he answered: 'this is my hand but I never wrote it.'"[42] This was the second time in nine years that the charge of treason had been leveled against him, and, as in the earlier case in January 1382, the government was so convinced of his loyalty, that it needed only his own denial to discredit the charges as false. Salutati's correspondent and fellow chancellor, Pasquino de'Cappelli, despite his years of faithful service to Giangaleazzo, lacked such security, and a few years after this incident the powerful Visconti official perished on charges which were in all probability equally unfounded.

The Treaty of Genoa, which concluded the war in January 1392, was not a real settlement of the issues but merely a postponement of conflict. The Paduan state was divided, with Padua going to Francesco the Younger and Bassano, Feltre, and Belluno to Milan. Carrara, moreover, was to pay a crushing indemnity of ten thousand florins per year for fifty years. In Tuscany the status quo as of 1389 was restored with the exception that Siena took Lucignano, which it had lost by adjudication just before the war, and Florence was given Montepulciano.[43] Despite the fact that the agreement did not deceive the realistic Florentines, there was general rejoicing in the city at the news of the signing of the peace.[44] At least the danger was temporarily past and the tax burden would be lightened.

Writing in 1393, a year after the war, in circumstances where it is impossible to doubt his sincerity, Salutati unhesitatingly assigned the responsibility for starting the struggle to Florence's enemies. Giovanni da San Miniato, former poet, notarial official, recently become monk, found his conscience troubled by the memory of certain acts he had committed as a soldier during the recent struggle and appealed to Salutati for advice. Promising on his immortal soul to tell the truth, Salutati assured the monk that the recent conflict was a just war for the Florentines. Recounting the events leading up to its outbreak, the Florentine chancellor denied that Siena had any just motive for hating Florence and categorically stated that the Republic had done nothing to provoke

42. Ibid., IV, 248. By counterfeiting letters, the count had convinced the Lord of Mantua to execute his wife in 1391: *Cronica volgare*, pp. 116–17.
43. De Mesquita, p. 136, summarizes the terms of peace.
44. B.N.F., *Panc.*, 158, fols. 168[b] and 168[v-b].

either its Tuscan neighbor or Milan in the months after October 1389:
"Nor after the Pisan pact of concord I swear, was there anything publicly decreed which would give the enemy cause for war." Then, apparently with the Ricci matter in mind, he continued: "I do not excuse the
private feelings of a few, who, perhaps hoping for great things, very
passionately desired war; but, as you know, our Republic does not allow
such power to a few; nor, I pray God, ought these men be permitted to
push our commune into war, even if they try, or to incite it to do a thing
of such weight and danger."[45]

In his first personal letter to Milan after the war, despite his own firm
conviction of Florentine innocence, he was forced by circumstances to
imply that both sides shared responsibility. In his letter of July 4, 1392,
sent to Pasquino de' Capelli, he refers to the "errors of our lords" and
of the dangers of a war which could have destroyed them both: "I feared
that the madness of our lords would ruin the two pillars of Italy to the
exaltation of foreign peoples." The count (*communis dominus*) believed
too much in the anger and raving of our neighbors (the Sienese) and
too little in the peace-loving Pisans, and "perhaps my lords harbored
too much suspicion and too much hope." But throughout the conflict,
Salutati assured Capelli, "I was always mindful of you."[46]

This hypocrisy was, however, justified by the central purpose of the
letter. Salutati was negotiating through Capelli for the release of messer
Giovanni Ricci, whom the count had accused of openly advocating his
murder in 1389 and whom Giangaleazzo had seized at the battle of Alexandria in 1391. Dinozzo Stefani Lippi was coming to Milan on behalf
of Florence and Capelli was asked to show favor to the ambassador and
his mission.[47] Salutati's admission of mutual error was designed not
merely to win the good will of Capelli but also to make it easier for the
Milanese chancellor to work on behalf of Ricci.

Capelli's position in Milan was always a perilous one. Intimately involved in Giangaleazzo's secret councils, he was terrified of being sus-

45. *Epist.*, II, 467. On Giovanni da San Miniato, see Georg Dufner, *Die "Moralia" Gregors des Grossen in ihren italienischen volgarizzamenti* (Padua, 1958), pp. 31–80; and Berthold L. Ullman, *The Humanism of Coluccio Salutati*, Medioevo e Rinascimento, vol. 4 (Padua, 1963), pp. 59–64.

46. Ibid., II, 337–38. The only previous extant letter written to Capelli is a short letter of recommendation written, according to Novati, in the 1380s: ibid., II, 166–68. For No-vati's errors in dating the correspondence of Salutati with Loschi and Capelli during this period, see Berthold L. Ullman, *Studies in the Renaissance*, Storia e letteratura, vol. 51 (Rome, 1955), pp. 223–25.

47. *Epist.*, II, 338 and 377. De Rosa, *Coluccio Salutati*, p. 100, interprets Salutati's ac-knowledgement of errors on both sides as seriously intended.

pected of treasonous activities. Even before the war Capelli left many of Salutati's personal letters without response. Between July 4, 1392, and July 16, 1393, Salutati wrote six times without receiving an answer.[48] In his sixth and last extant letter to Capelli, that of July 16, Salutati brought the matter into the open. Capelli's failure to write did not stem from his lack of affection: Capelli had shown this in many ways and had given assurances of his feeling for Salutati through Capelli's assistant, Antonio Loschi. Rather Salutati ventured the explanation that he did not write because "it was your habit and a matter of caution to preserve the integrity of your position that you did not give cause for whispering or that something similar was involved." But certainly, Salutati complained, Capelli had nothing to fear in writing simply two words: "valeo; vale," for which his Florentine friend would be grateful.[49]

The terrified silence of the Milanese chancellor suggests the character of the atmosphere prevailing at the court of the obessively suspicious Giangaleazzo. Common report of the situation made Salutati's war propaganda of 1390–92 centering on the serpent theme eminently effective. Capelli's fate was almost predictable. When in December 1398 Salutati mentioned to a correspondent the fall and imprisonment of the former Milanese chancellor, he noted with a tone of sadness this glaring example of *utriusque fortune*, and, in reference to Loschi, who had replaced Capelli as Milanese chancellor, Salutati observed: "And our Loschi, when he rises, has before his eyes no less what frightens him than what causes him to rejoice and desire."[50]

Capelli's attitude was a much truer reflection of the real state of Florentine-Milanese relations in the postwar period than was the rosy assessment found in Salutati's letters to him. The League of Bologna consisting of Florence, Bologna, Carrara, the Gonzaga of Mantua, and the Este, was formed soon after the war in 1392, and the next four years were spent by both the League and Milan in searching out allies. Already linked with Pisa and Siena, in September 1395 Giangaleazzo, now Duke of Milan, signed a treaty with Genoa, thereby ignoring the claims of the French crown to sovereignty over the city. A Franco-Florentine alliance providing for the dismemberment of the Visconti dominions followed in September of the next year. The war began unofficially in January and February 1397 with sporadic raiding of Florentine and Lucchese territory by troops based at Pisa and Siena.[51]

48. Ibid., II, 340–41.   49. Ibid., II, 341–42.
50. Ibid., III, 330. On Capelli's fall, see A. Hortis, *M. T. Cicerone nelle opere di Petrarca e Boccaccio* (Trieste, 1876), p. 914.
51. The details of the interwar period are found in Francesco Cognasso, "Il Ducato

The main themes of Florentine propaganda after 1396 differ significantly from those found in both the war against the Church and the first Milanese War. Beginning in the fall of 1396 before the actual outbreak of fighting and continuing throughout the remaining ten years of his chancellorship, Salutati presented the struggle between Florence and Milan as another episode in the centuries-long battle between Guelfs and Ghibellines. Florence and her allies were repeatedly characterized as Guelfs, and the traditional associations of Guelfism and liberty were orchestrated. The Milanese tyrants, therefore became the enemies both of the Church and of the freedom of Italy. Within the medieval context of the struggle of the two parties, the classical tone was no longer appropriate. Accordingly, the ancient examples and allusions tended to disappear and to be replaced by references to medieval history. From 1396 and especially after 1401 the medieval conception of liberty as rule of law arising from a legitimate claim to power emerged as the dominant value in Florentine propaganda. The republican associations with liberty fell away.[52]

By stressing the Guelf heritage both of Florence and France Salutati hoped to make it more difficult for the Roman pope to contemplate an alliance with the Ghibelline Visconti. After 1399, when he had reunited most of the kingdom, Ladislaus, the Angevin ruler of Naples, also became an object of this appeal to Guelfism. Perhaps the tense domestic political situation in Florence itself as well as the international configuration of powers had an effect on the particular mode in which Salutati expressed Florentine foreign policy. Yet the resurrection of themes traditional in Florentine foreign policy before Salutati and abandoned almost totally by him from 1375 to 1396 was intimately related to the chancellor's own world of thought in the last ten years of his life.

The years between 1396 and 1400 saw the completion of three treatises, the first two of them extensive: the *De fato et fortuna*, the *De nobilitate legum et medicine*, and the *De tyranno*. The *De fato et fortuna*, written in 1396, presented the world as completely ordered by God in its cause and effect relations, yet remaining responsive to human decisions and actions. The focus of the discussion, therefore, fell on the nature of God's predestination and of man's free will. The concern of the *De nobilitate legum et medicine*, published in 1399, was to determine which life was better: that of the natural scientist, i.e., the physician, or that of the

---

visconteo da Gian Galeazzo a Filippo Maria," *Storia di Milano*, vol. 6 (Milan, 1955), pp. 3–32; de Mesquita, pp. 137–209; and Brucker, *The Civic World*, pp. 144 ff.
    52. Witt, *Coluccio Salutati*, pp. 64–72.

lawyer. In opting for the superiority of the lawyer's life, Salutati maintained that since no one would be saved without works and the law represented the measure of human action, the lawyer not only fostered earthly felicity but earned his personal salvation in the process. Eternal beatitude itself, moreover, was more properly linked with man's will than with his intellect. Finally in the *De tyranno* of 1400 Salutati viewed the fall of the Republic and rise of the empire in the perspective of the advent of Jesus Christ. In this work, which primarily constituted a defense of Dante's decision to place Cassius and Brutus in the depths of hell for the murder of Caesar, Salutati in true medieval fashion insisted that the establishment of the Roman monarchy was divinely ordained. Augustus had constituted the long era of peace needed for the diffusion of Christian doctrine.[53]

Within the narrowing Christian framework built up by these three successive works, ancient learning could play only an ancillary role. So in his approach to politics the important background against which to set the contemporary political struggle was not ancient Rome but medieval Europe. Banished from the earlier missives, the conception of Florence as member of a great, holy confederation against Ghibelline Milan informed the late public letters.[54]

Well might Florentines like Salutati dream of the protective mantle of a great confederation in the years after 1396. Despite the alliances formed by the city, there could be no doubt that the Florentines were the main stumbling block in Giangaleazzo's road to domination of Northern and Central Italy. The promised French army was still being collected a year after the outset of the second war, and Florence made the fatal mistake of drawing the Venetians into the struggle on its side in March 1398 under very limiting conditions. Venice insisted on preserving its right to make peace or continue the war independently of the allies. Less than two months later Giangaleazzo skillfully settled his differences with the *Serenissima*, stabilizing the situation in Lombardy but leaving all the problems of Tuscany and Umbria in the air. Suddenly confronted with this reconciliation, Florence could only ratify the truce under protest. The French regarded themselves as betrayed by the Florentines, thus dashing any hope of future aide from that quarter.[55]

The period after the Truce of Venice of May 1398 was merely an inter-

---

53. Separate chapters are devoted to these works below.
54. For illustrations of this Guelf ideology in the *Missives*, see my *Coluccio Salutati*, pp. 64–69.
55. On the war, see Cognasso, "Il Ducato," pp. 32 ff, and de Mesquita, pp. 206–38.

val for regrouping forces for another battle; and, when open war came again in March 1400, Giangaleazzo showed himself stronger than ever. By the summer of 1402, with the exception of Francesco Carrara Junior in Padua, all of Lombardy was either directly or indirectly under Visconti rule. Pisa, Siena, Perugia, Assisi, Spoleto, and Nocera had submitted voluntarily, and in the Romagna Florence's major ally Bologna fell that very summer. It must have appeared even to the Florentines that the years of struggle and the immense expenditure of resources had been in vain. Venice was stirring again but Florentine territory was almost completely surrounded.[56]

Throughout the long hot Tuscan summer Florence awaited the Milanese attack. The treasurer of the Romagna, who controlled some of the rough passes leading to the Adriatic still open, wrote directly on July 20 to Salutati promising access to the sea through his mountainous diocese. A missive from the *Signoria* in Salutati's hand amicably but firmly informed the friendly prelate that such an offer should have been sent not to the chancellor but to them directly as chief magistrates of the state.[57] The death of Giangaleazzo and the hasty retreat of his army, however, saved Florence from having to rely for long on such a slender connection with the world outside.

The perilous position of Florence which resulted from the resumption of hostilities in 1400 had made a tremendous impression on Salutati, as it must have on all residents of the city. As Giangaleazzo tightened the encirclement around the city, all Italy awaited the outcome. Salutati

---

56. The situation between the Truce of Venice and the fall of Bologna is described by Cognasso, "Il Ducato," pp. 34–64; de Mesquita, pp. 239–80; and Brucker, *The Civic World* pp. 165 ff.

57. B.C.S., 5.5.8, fol. 109ᵛ (photographs in Archivio di Stato, Florence). The Florentine response begins: "Vidimus ea que dignatio vestra scripsit spectabili viro, ser Colucio pieri de Salutatis, cancellario nostro, et qualiter dispositus estis cum Florentinorum mercantie portentur per castrum Penne et commune Sancte Agate que per vestram reverentiam gubernantur et etiam per vestrum oppidum Talamelli, quod libere transiant et ad solutionem alicuius passagii non cogantur et omnibus daretis auxilium, consilium et favorem. . . ." Cf. De Rosa, *Coluccio Salutati*, p. 76.

Salutati aided the prelate in late 1403: A.S.F., Dieci Balia, *Miss.*, 3, fol. 42 (December 1, 1403). The letter begins: "Reverende in Christo pater et amice karissime. Vir eloquentie singularis ser Colucius cancellarius florentinus nobis exposuit vestri parte qualiter prudentie vestre suggestum extiterat in hac civitate per quosdam obloqui contra vos propter victualia concessa Ubertinis et comitibus Balnei, hostibus nostri communis. Et quod in veritate a vestris nulla victualia receperunt et cetera. Quamobrem amicitiam vestram [*sic*] presentibus declaramus quod nobis relatum extitit dictos Ubertinos et comites victualia habuisse que per vestra territoria ferebantur et quod etiam aliquando a vestris subditis eisdem victualia clandestine et sine vestra conscientia prebebantur; sed quicquid in preteritum fuerit, nos continuo tenuimus et tenemus vos fuisse et esse cordialissimum et verum nostri communis amicum. . . ."

ceased his feverish production of scholarly treatises. Two years after the summer of 1402, Salutati expressed to Bernardo da Moglio, son of his former teacher, the intensity of his feelings during the darkest period. Excusing himself for not having communicated for a long time with the young man who himself had narrowly escaped death in the Milanese takeover of Bologna in June 1402, Salutati wrote on June 5, 1404:

> Such great sadness, such shame invaded my mind when I had to recall the misfortune of those times, that in no way could I remember the wounds of that stormy period without great heaviness of heart. So it happened that, since I was unable to break my silence without memory of those evils, it was too hard for me to begin, since I could not remove the sadness of such a great event from my mind. As many times as the memory came back to it, an unbearable grief arose, although your present felicity and ours ought to have changed everything.

Now, he continued, all that is gone so that it is even pleasing to think back on those dangerous times, which in the end had such a felicitous outcome for both Bologna and Florence.[58]

The salvation of the liberty which had seemed so near to destruction produced a swell of patriotic feeling in Florence. The buoyant mood of the Florentines was best reflected by a panegyric to the city, the *Laudatio urbis florentinae*, written by Salutati's disciple, Leonardo Bruni, late in 1403 or early in 1404.[59] In contrast with Salutati, who in his most enthusiastic moments during the war against the Church offered scattered elements of a republican conception of history and politics in a handful of his war missives, Bruni in 1403/4 presented an integrated and clearly articulated doctrine of the absolute superiority of republican government to any other form of constitution and a view of Florence as the heir to the republican freedom of ancient Rome.

Bruni's ability to synthesize ideas which had remained disparate in

---

58. *Epist.*, IV, 11–12. Salutati's correspondence makes no other mention of this harrowing period between 1400 and 1402, but it must have been constantly in the foreground of his thoughts. As Giovanni di Conversino wrote him in January 1400: "Finge vel me tecum deambulantem vel stantem inter libros rationari non de litteris studiove sapientie quo deflagras, sed de externis uti sepe mos ociosos implicat" (Akad. Z., II, fol. 105/6). Conversino had served as Paduan ambassador in January 1400 (B.C.S., 5.8.8., fol. 97ᵛ and *Epist.*, III, 375). In this letter Conversino berates the Florentines for their reluctance to take a more active stance against Giangaleazzo. For January 1400 date of letter, see Remigio Sabbadini, *Giovanni da Ravenna, insigne figura d'umanista (1343–1408)* (Como, 1924), pp. 80 and 218–219.

59. For the dating of this work, see Hans Baron, *From Petrarch to Bruni* (Chicago, 1968), pp. 102–37.

Salutati's work and to maintain consistency in presenting his republican views can be explained in a variety of ways. First of all, Bruni knew Tacitus while Salutati apparently remained ignorant of the second-century Roman historian almost to the end of his life. Tacitus' unambiguous account of the vices and corruption of Roman imperial society provided a solid basis for Bruni's republican arguments.[60]

Furthermore, Bruni reflected in his writing a fundamental change in the character of Florentine political life in progress from 1382. As has been seen, the years 1382–87 were guided by the desire of the majority of citizens to achieve civic reconciliation and to allow greater participation of citizens in public office in the name of harmony. The Alberti scandal of 1387 moved the center toward the right, but only after 1393 did the restrictive tendency definitely triumph. Still, for those who were within the ruling circle the ideals of equality between families and cooperation for the common good prevailed. Political equality between the ruling families, a stress on civic duty, and commitment to political consensus constituted the basic values implicit in the rule of this oligarchy. Bruni's *Laudatio* caught this situation and expressed it in theoretical and historical terms.[61]

More important, however, than this internal transformation as an explanation for the difference in the political mentality of the two humanists is the changed role of Florence in international politics in the last thirty years preceding the composition of the *Laudatio*. In these three decades Florence emerged as a major power in Italian politics. If in 1378 the Republic had little to show for the three years of war with the Church, nevertheless, the city had proven itself almost equal in strength to the enemy. Between 1389 and 1402 the long war with the Visconti, which ended in the temporary break-up of their empire, was a source not only of great prestige in the eyes of the rest of Europe but also of increased self-esteem for the Florentines themselves. From the 1370s on, therefore, the Florentines acted as if they sensed that the Florence of the Middle Ages, neatly tucked into the communal organization of

60. See Ronald Witt, "The *De tyranno* and Coluccio Salutati's View of Politics and Roman History," *Nuova rivista storica*, 53 (1969), 473–74; and Oliver P. Revillo, "The Second Medicean Ms and the Text of Tacitus," *Illinois Classical Studies*, 1 (1976), 195–96, who concludes that Salutati must have seen the manuscript of Tacitus by 1403. For additional historical background on the recovery of Tacitus, see Kenneth C. Schellhase, *Tacitus in Renaissance Political Thought* (Chicago and London, 1976), pp. 3–11.

61. Witt, "The Florentine Ruling Class," pp. 263–67. Although Brucker in his *The Civic World*, pp. 268 ff. makes this central ruling group somewhat smaller in size and correctly stresses the tensions and hostilities between various factions within the charmed circle, his account of the political development is not significantly different from mine.

Central and Northern Italy, living in the shadow of the papacy and the empire, had ceased to exist.[62]

Salutati's life spanned this age of transition. Both commitments to the old order and allegiances to the new struggled in him. He had grown up imbued with a deep respect for the empire and for its traditions; a Florentine subject, he also felt himself a subject of the emperor. When already middle-aged, he found himself a member of a people growing conscious of its political power and therefore of its identity. In his statements on politics Salutati reflected the various contradictions contained in the welter of his commitments. On the other hand, Bruni, born in 1370, belonged to the new age. For his generation the empire was a relic of the past. Growing up in the age of communal expansion, he was no longer limited to considering republican governments in Italy as subsystems of a larger system ruled by a monarchy.

Whereas Salutati's political propaganda from 1396 endeavored to conceptualize Florentine war aims in terms of the old Guelf ideals and a juristic conception of liberty which deemed any government ruled by law a government of free men, Bruni depicted any form of government short of a republican one as entailing subjection for its people. Within a decade the leaders of the regime would come to accept Bruni's republi-

62. This is a major thesis of Hans Baron, *The Crisis of the Early Italian Renaissance*, 2nd ed. (Princeton, 1966). Brucker, *The Civic World*, pp. 300–301, accepts Barons' interpretation of the significance of civic humanism as a vital force in early fifteenth-century Florentine political life but feels that internal developments were as important as external ones. My own view is that the external changes provided the catalyst for the transformation in political mentality which occurred. Quentin Skinner, *The Foundations of Modern Political Thought*, 2 vols. (Cambridge, 1978), I, 41, unfortunately confuses my position by ascribing to me the opinion that "no attempt was ever made to vindicate the superiority of republican liberty over monarchical forms of government before the work of the Florentine humanists at the end of the Trecento." Were this my thesis, he would be justified in presenting, as he does, quotations from authors in the thirteenth and fourteenth centuries as proof of earlier republican sentiments. But my thesis is very different. Prof. Skinner apparently bases his formulation of my position on pp. 175 and 192–93 of my article "The Rebirth of the Concept of Republican Liberty in Italy," in *Renaissance Studies in Honor of Hans Baron*, ed. Anthony Molho and John A. Tedeschi (Florence, 1971), pp. 173–99. I had hoped to make clear by the word *concept* in the title that I was concerned with establishing the first "clear articulation of a republican concept of *libertas*" (p. 172). My analysis in this article, in other articles cited by Prof. Skinner, and also in my detailed discussion in *Coluccio Salutati*, pp. 73–88 (which Prof. Skinner does not appear to know), proceeded by examining statements on republican liberty from the thirteenth and fourteenth centuries that might have some claim to be theoretical. My conclusion was that despite certain observations of earlier thinkers, especially Ptolemy of Lucca in the early fourteenth century, and despite the many theoretical statements made by Salutati, Bruni was the first at the beginning of the fifteenth century (not "at the end of the Trecento") to be "consciously aware of developing a specific conception of the term [*libertas*]" ("The Rebirth," p. 198). Bruni integrated consistently a theoretical conception of republican government with a historical justification of that form of rule.

can version of history and politics as their own.[63] Salutati, however, did not change. Until his death Guelfism remained the guiding ideal of Florentine war propaganda. In the very period when Bruni wrote his *Laudatio*, Salutati published his own long political tract, the *Invectiva contra Antonium Luschum*, directed against a vituperative anti-Florentine pamphlet of 1397 attributed to Antonio Loschi and left unanswered until this reply of 1403.[64] Echoing the official propaganda Salutati's work presented Florence and its allies as defenders of the rule of law and legitimate authority against Milan, which sought to overturn both established order and justice.

Most immediately, the pride of Florentines in the survival of their state produced two different attitudes regarding the future course of action for the Republic. One group, including Salutati, and the *Dieci di Balia*, charged with waging the Visconti war, believed that only the annihilation of the Visconti and the possession of Pisa as a port could prevent another 1402. So vital did the aged chancellor consider the acquisition of Pisa to the safety of the state, that he utilized the greater freedom of speech he had permitted himself for some years to advocate openly the conquest in the councils of state. The other group, tired of the burden of years of war and seeing the evident diminution of Visconti power, would gladly have negotiated with Giangaleazzo's heirs and settled for a small port on the coast as an outlet for Florentine trade. The *Signoria* elected for March-April 1404, dominated by those seeking a peaceful solution, even undertook covert negotiations for Porto Pisano, writing their own correspondence to keep it secret from Salutati and the Dieci.[65] As it was, events gradually pushed Florence toward a bellicose solution to the port issue. After a bitter and costly war, the Florentine Republic finally annexed its traditional Ghibelline enemy, Pisa, in July 1406—a triumph that Salutati did not live to see.[66]

III

The eventual consequences of a Visconti victory, alarming as it appeared to Salutati in these years, paled in significance when compared with the

---

63. Brucker, *The Civic World*, pp. 301 ff.

64. For the dating of this work, see chap. 13 below.

65. Lauro Martines, *The Social World of the Florentine Humanists* (Princeton, 1963), p. 148; and Anthony Molho, "A Note on the Albizzi and the Florentine Conquest of Pisa," *Renaissance Quarterly*, 20 (1967), 188.

66. On Pisan conquest the most recent account is Brucker, *The Civic World*, pp. 192–208.

possible effects of the continuing Schism within the Church on the eternal disposition of the human soul. Responding in August 1395 to a letter of Cardinal Oliari, who had written to urge him to prepare an edition of his correspondence, Salutati indirectly voiced his intense concern about the divided Church. He will not undertake the task of editing the letters himself, he writes, but will leave it to his followers "who avidly worship me and my works." There may be future letters more eloquent than the ones he would include were he to make the compilation now. Of all the letters he still wished to compose, he most wants to write one announcing to the princes and peoples of Christendom that the Schism has been concluded:

> O, if I had a chance to write of the schism! If it happened that this tear in the seamless robe were removed, what material there would be for writing to princes, for persuading peoples or even for discussing with the prelates themselves! What more fertile, what better, finally what more useful thing could one treat in letters?

Without this letter in his collection of correspondence, "it is better to die intestate than to leave an invalid and hastily considered will."[67]

Despite his deep interest from the beginning of the Schism in 1379 until a year before this letter to Oliari, Salutati had taken no active part in the campaign to reunite the Church. Like most other Christians he had watched helplessly as the intense desire of the rival claimants to the papacy overcame all pressures brought to bear by intelligence, prayer and righteous anger. But the election of a new Avignonese pope, Pietro de Luna, in September 1394, roused new hopes in Salutati, causing him to begin a personal campaign to work for reunification. The astute Aragonese, who took the name of Benedict XIII, had been a staunch supporter of reunion as a cardinal and on his election had taken a solemn oath to do everything in his power to end the Schism.[68] The newly elected pontiff began by making a great display of good intentions. Ambassadors furnished with letters were sent out in all directions carrying news of his commitment to reconciliation. When the papal representatives arrived in Florence, they brought with them letters directed not only to the *Signoria* but also to a number of key Florentines, among them Salutati.[69]

67. *Epist.*, III, 90.
68. Noël Valois, *La France et le grand schisme d'occident*, 4 vols. (Paris, 1896–1902), III, 14–15.
69. *Epist.*, III, 53–54, n. 1. Valois, III, 88–89.

Benedict XIII wrote at least twice to Salutati in the fall and early winter of 1394–95 and the Florentine chancellor doubtless wrote several times in reply. Only Salutati's two letters of January 20, 1395, however, are still extant. The first concerns a purely private interest of Salutati, the acquisition of a copy of the new pope's Latin translation of Plutarch's *Lives*. In return for permitting a copy to be made, Salutati promises his manuscript of Pilato's translation of the *Odyssey*.[70] The second contains a fervent plea to the pope not to fail in his intention to reunite the divided church: "Accomplish what you have set out to do; rebuild the temple of the Lord which for so many years now has been torn apart by the hands of schismatics. Work, I beg you, that we who are one in the rock (petra) not be many in Peter (Petro)."[71]

So frequent was Florentine official communication with Avignon in the course of 1395, that the *Signoria* was forced on December 4, 1395, to give the uneasy Roman pontiff unequivocal assurance of Florence's continued support for the Roman cause.[72] But by this time the ineffectiveness of Benedict's initial efforts had created doubts about his sincerity even in those countries officially supporting him. In France these suspicions gave added impetus to the efforts of an important group centered in the University of Paris working for a resolution of the Schism by way of the *via cessionis*.[73] It was the program of this group to abandon attempts to decide on the legitimate line of popes and to aim at either a voluntary abdication of both popes, or, if necessary, their forced abdication or deposition. Already in February 1395, half a year after the election of Benedict XIII, a royal council at Paris declared in favor of the *via cessionis*. In the spring of 1397 the German princes assembled a diet at Frankfort to discuss similar action on behalf of the empire, which up to this time had been pledged to support the Roman pope.[74] Although the Germans never reached an agreement, expectation during these years ran high throughout Europe that this kind of action would bring an end to the divided papacy in the near future.

Writing to the Margrave of Moravia, who had participated in the recent conclave of Frankfort, Salutati in August 1397 appears to have had

70. The two Salutati letters are found *Epist.*, III, 53–57, and IV, 264–66. See my "Salutati and Plutarch," *Essays Presented to Myron P. Gilmore*, ed. Sergio Bertelli and Gloria Ramakus, 2 vols. (Florence, 1978), I, 337 ff.

71. *Epist.*, III, 55.   72. *Miss.*, 24, fol. 172.

73. See the bibliography and summary statement of this position, Howard Kaminsky, "The Politics of France's Substraction of Obedience from Pope Benedict XIII, 27 July, 1398," *Proceedings of the American Philosophical Society*, 115 (1971), 367.

74. The attitude of the German princes and the emperor in 1397 is discussed by Valois, III, 124 ff.

hopes for an early settlement: "Now that you and the other princes of the Roman empire, whose duty it is to treat these things, are seen to meet together for the purpose of removing this Schism, praise be to God, who appears intent on judging his holy church and on vindicating its cause against an unholy people, freeing it from an unjust and deceitful man!"[75]

For the first time in discussing the Schism Salutati articulated his fears as to the effects it might have on the sacramental system of the Church.

> For if we do not have a legitimate pope on one side (which it is unquestionably necessary to confess), who does not know that from the defective side there can be no true bishops and as a result no true priests; and those who happen to have followed the corrupted faction will after a time not have true sacraments? For although the clerical character, once instilled, cannot be removed even through later heresy—which is so true that it is certain that publicly condemned heretics perform true sacraments—however, those things which pertain to jurisdiction perish with the right itself on account of heresy. So perhaps it is probable to affirm and believe that, after the death of Gregory XI of happy memory, on the side of the pope elected through corruption, no one has obtained the dignity of priest nor through these priests are sacraments legitimately able to be taken, in as much as the jurisdiction of conferring the elements of the priesthood has been lacking.[76]

It is a terrifying idea for a Christian: "What can be more criminal than this schism and what more abominable can be thought of?"

This letter to the German prince shows the Florentine chancellor well informed of the debates going on at the moment in Paris for the termination of the Schism. According to his analysis, the University of Paris saw three ways open for a settlement apart from the use of physical violence: the way of compromise, the way of a council, and the way of withdrawal of obedience. Salutati gives full support to the University's conclusion that only the third means is really workable. As Salutati explains the plan: "The cardinals of both obediences meet together and, as I understand it, with both colleges recognized, each of the pontiffs renounces his rights, so that a single pope is elected by everyone with

75. *Epist.*, III, 206–7. The last line is Ps. 74:1.
76. Ibid., III, 210.

the title of cardinal."[77] Just before this discussion, however, Salutati offers what appears to be his private plan for reunification:

> Each pontiff can recognize the other with his own rank and dignities unimpaired and, the one confirming the other, they divide the administration either along the lines of the obedience they now hold or along others, whichever way they find most agreeable. They would establish that no cardinals are to be made except perhaps by mutual consent and that, with one dying, the other, whom it pleased God to let live, would administer the whole.[78]

Nevertheless, making no comparison of his proposal with the way favored by the University of Paris, he strongly recommends to the Margrave the University's method than which "nothing more accessible, more just, more holy and more sincere can be conceived."[79] The princes of the empire, Salutati concludes, must give highest priority to the reunion of the Church (*negotium ante omnia*) for "never will you rule the empire unless first you regulate the papacy on which it is certain the empire depends."[80]

Salutati's information about discussions going on in Paris regarding the Schism might have come to him directly from informants there. Perhaps one of these was the chancellor of the French king, Jean de Montreuil, whom he had known since their first exchange of letters during the occupation of Arezzo by Enguerrand de Coucy in 1384.[81] When in the summer of 1393 the French court finally took the formal step of removing its obedience from Benedict XIII, Salutati must have been overjoyed.[82] That some of his own writings on the Schism—perhaps among them the letter to the Margrave of Moravia of the previous year—were circulating in the French court is clear from the royal letter of January 2, 1399, to the *Signoria*, concerning the withdrawal of obedience: "For you have numerous godfearing men of all ranks in whom

---

77. Ibid., III, 214. Compare Salutati's enumeration of the possibilities for solving the schism with the similar one found in the letter of Charles VI to Wenceslaus, *Veterum scriptorum et monumentorum historicorum dogmaticorum moralium amplissima collectio*, ed. Edmund Martène and Ursin Durand, 9 vols. (Paris, 1724–33), VII, 622–25.

78. *Epist.*, III, 211.   79. Ibid., III, 215.

80. Ibid., III, 217.

81. For the letter of 1384, see Giuseppe Billanovich and G. Ouy, "La première correspondance échangée entre Jean de Montreuil et Coluccio Salutati," *Italia medioevale et umanistica*, 7 (1964), 337–74. Two letters to Montreuil exist for the 1390s, *Epist.*, III, 71–76 and 143–47.

82. For a detailed treatment of France's revocation of obedience to Avignon see Kaminsky, "The Politics of France's Substraction of Obedience."

there is truth," one passage reads, "and among these Coluccio is recognized by us as virtuous because of his recent writings on this subject, just as everywhere, as fame attests, he is praised."[83] The monarchy obviously hoped to have in Salutati an advocate for the request presented in its letter. The Florentines by the treaty of alliance with France of September 29, 1396, had promised to withdraw support for the Roman pope were France to do the same for his Avignonese counterpart.[84] Now that France had taken this action, the king demanded Florence keep its part of the bargain. Unfortunately for French policy, the Florentine government was not as sanguine about this revolutionary method of settling the Schism as was its chancellor, and Salutati must have dictated with sadness the official response to the royal letter, a polite but evasive reply postponing definite action to a later date.[85] Within a few years the *via cessionis* showed itself to be as ineffective a means of obtaining Church reunion as all the others, but Salutati had not abandoned his efforts to end the division.

In his personal correspondence with the Roman pope, Boniface IX, it seems to have become his practice over the years to refer to the existing Schism regardless of the principal motive for writing.[86] But the election of Boniface's successor, Innocent VII, in November 1404, greatly increased his hopes for success, because the new pope, like his faithless Avignon rival ten years before, made the most binding promises to work for the union of Western Christendom if chosen.[87] Again Salutati was to be bitterly disappointed.

In the months before the death of Boniface IX in October 1404, the wily Benedict XIII had taken the initiative by sending representatives to Rome to offer possible methods by which their mutual differences could be solved. The Florentines had arranged for the safety of the Avignonese delegation in Rome and, when the death of Boniface interrupted negotiations, the emissaries of Benedict XIII returned to Florence to await the results of the election. One of Innocent's first acts was to invite the Avignonese representatives to return to Rome but he refused to furnish them a safe-conduct.[88] Salutati, close as he was to the negotiations,

---

83. *Amplissima Collectio*, VII, 629: "Habetis namque copiose viros potentes de omni plebe timentes Deum, in quibus est veritas, inter quos Colusius [sic!] per ea quae satis recenter scripsit in materia, apud nos sic virtuosus cognoscitur, sicut ubique etiam, fama teste, laudatur."

84. Ibid., VII, 628–29. The terms of the treaty of alliance are published in Johannes C. Lünig, *Codex Italiae diplomaticus*, 4 vols. (Frankfort-Leipzig, 1725–35), I, 1111–16.

85. B.A.V., *Capp.*, 147, p. 215 (March 20, 1399).

86. Witt, *Coluccio Salutati*, p. 27.

87. Valois, III, 381–82.   88. Ibid., III, 382.

could clearly see that the new pope, seduced like his predecessors by the glories of the papal office, was reluctant to execute his promises.

In December Salutati composed a strong letter aimed at strengthening the papal will. The Florentine embassy which left for Rome on January 25, 1405, charged among other things to obtain a safe conduct for Benedict XIII's emissaries, probably carried the message in its baggage.[89] Relatively harsh, the letter is indicative of the desperation Salutati felt at the succession of failures to reunite the Church over twenty-five years. Studiously avoiding flattery, Salutati repeatedly returns to the oath taken by Innocent along with the other cardinals prior to the election. Do not let the honor of being pope, Salutati urges, lead you to deny your obligation.[90] There have been many popes before you and many will come after but your singular glory could be to have ended the great Schism. Benedict XIII has offered to end the Schism but you will not even meet him. If you do not fulfill what you have promised God will accuse you of perjury at the hour of your death. He will say to you: "Why have you refused the way of discussion and justice? Why reject these and offer no way out acceptable to you unless you are unconcerned that my flock remains schismatically divided in these shadows?" You still vainly hope that the other side can be induced to recognize you.[91]

Regardless of the elevated status of his correspondent, Salutati could not withhold his anger and frustration. Official spokesman of a state which recognized the legitimacy of the Roman line of popes, Salutati had hitherto restrained himself from public criticism. But the blatant perjury of Innocent he would not tolerate. At seventy-four he could no longer afford to wait. He must speak not as a Florentine official but as a Christian, and there is a reckless passion in these words: "In my name and that of all the faithful I cry out and burning with love and zeal, do so loudly against the miseries of this schism. Let the whole world by means of this letter hear my voice produced by stout lungs! Let anyone heed who should and can! I call, I demand, I beg, I conjure: keep the faith! Do what you said you would!"[92] This letter marked the culmination of Salutati's ten-year personal struggle to heal the Schism. To give his opinion greater circulation, a copy of the letter was also dispatched to France, probably to the royal court.[93]

Salutati must have known that his frank statements would cause a

---

89. *Epist.*, IV, 43n.
90. *Epist.*, IV, 57.
91. Ibid., IV, 64–65.

92. Ibid., IV, 66.
93. Ibid., IV, 373.

scandal at the Curia. Leonardo Bruni, then working in Rome, confirmed these expectations when he reported in the spring that he had to defend Salutati against his critics.[94] Since the pope himself did not respond, Salutati took the occasion of Bruni's elevation to the rank of papal secretary in July 1405 both to mollify the pope indirectly and to provoke an answer. Devoting the body of the letter to praising Bruni's talents and Innocent's good judgment in making the promotion, he appended a brief concluding paragraph in which he ingenuously wrote that, while some think the pope angered by his letter, he personally believed the papal silence indicated that Innocent found no fault with its contents.[95]

But Innocent could no longer withhold a reply. Accordingly, he commissioned Vergerio, who had been at the Curia since the summer, to write a detailed refutation of Salutati's charges.[96] While superficially reassuring, there is no question that the papal letter in the autumn of 1405 bristles with anger. The pope clearly remembers his election and oath and intends to observe it. To assert, as Salutati does, that Benedict's representatives informed the Curia that their lord was ready to resign the papacy, is misleading. All these emissaries offered was a private meeting between the two popes and this offer was merely an effort to secure favorable public opinion for Avignon. Moreover, for Salutati to have dispatched a copy of his letter to France is merely to have given help to the enemy, "so that they might rejoice in their own lie and have new inventions to boast of."[97] Finally, as for Bruni's appointment, Salutati had no need to recommend him, "for by now we have such trust in him that, because of his own merits, he is in a position to recommend others to us."[98] But lest this seem too obvious an insult to Salutati, Innocent adds that it was of course with full knowledge of Salutati's high opinion of Bruni that the appointment was made.

Despite the political relevance, the intensity with which Florentine propaganda in Salutati's last years insisted on the theme of legitimacy represented in part the old man's fear of a world where authority, both temporal and spiritual, seemed corrupted from the top on down. An alcoholic emperor, deposed and replaced by a treacherous mercenary successor, had displayed the bankruptcy of imperial power. The French crown was disputed by the English king and the present Valois ruler afflicted with mental illness. A mass of claims and counterclaims made equitable settlement of the Angevin inheritance impossible. But more

---

94. Ibid., IV, 104.
95. Ibid., IV, 106–9.
96. Ibid., IV, 370–75.

97. Ibid., IV, 373–74.
98. Ibid., IV, 375.

important, a bitter conflict raged between two rivals for the supreme spiritual authority. Indeed, increasingly prone to interpret the secular within a religious context, Salutati could not but view the pervasive tendency to usurpation as stemming ultimately from the Schism. Could a just political order be established while the spiritual realm remained in such confusion? Even the religious credentials of a Guelf alliance were questionable so long as the papal title was contested. Nevertheless, while disquieted and vexed, Salutati made no effort to respond to Innocent's letter.

Instead he decided to make his best letters dealing with the Schism more accessible by bringing them together in one manuscript. Four in number, they included the long letter sent to the French cardinals in 1378 at the outbreak of the Schism; a letter of 1380 to Cardinal Corsini, the Florentine cardinal supporting Clement VII; and the letters sent to the Margrave of Moravia and Innocent VII in 1397 and 1405 respectively.[99] In January 1406 Salutati informed Bruni that as soon as he had a copy made from his own, he would send it to in Rome. Five months later he was dead.[100]

---

99. For letters to the French cardinals and Corsini, see *Lini Coluci Pieri Salutati Epistolae*, ed. Giuseppe Rigacci, 2 vols. (Florence, 1741–42), I, 18–39 and 39–46. The letters to the Marquess of Moravia and Innocent VII are discussed above. B.R.F., 1222C may be Salutati's own copy of the manuscript. Described at length in S. Morpurgo, *I manoscritti italiani della r. biblioteca riccardiana* (Rome, 1896–1900), pp. 293–94. For eighteenth-century copy, see B.C.Rav., 500, fols. 1–23.

100. *Epist.*, IV, 157.

PART III. THE HUMANIST

CHAPTER 7. PRIVATE LIFE AND LITERARY ACTIVITIES (1374–82)

I

That Salutati after 1375 continued to develop his humanistic interests, composing various treatises and maintaining a vast personal correspondence, is a tribute to his passionate concern for studies and his tremendous self-discipline. During periods of public crisis like the war with the Church his leisure time was severely limited, and even in normal times he had few full days completely free for scholarship. When a mild illness exempted him from having to go to work for a day in 1379, he writes of how he gave himself "licentiously" to his private writing and studies.[1]

At least by July 1378, when Salutati sought sanctuary in Santa Croce on the first day of the Ciompi Revolution, the chancellor and his family were in the rented house in the Piazza dei Peruzzi where they were to remain for the rest of Salutati's life.[2] The house in Stignano served as a retreat in those periods when Salutati could leave the chancery for a few days. The Florentine residence in the little piazza linking the Borgo dè Greci with the via dei Benci was convenient to his work only a few blocks away. Midway between the house and the Palazzo della Signoria were the baths where Salutati liked to stop to refresh himself on the way home from work in the evening.[3]

The house was large enough to hold the growing family and their servants. One of the latter was a female slave, probably of Circassian origin, who died in the plague of 1400 together with two of Salutati's sons.[4] Salutati's nephew, Giovanni, son of Currado, also lived with the

---

1. *Epist.*, I, 335: "Hac autem die, cum aliquantulo morbo correptus licentiose domi, rara dominorum indulgentia, longe felicior eger quam incolumis ociarer. . . ."

2. He is listed in the *estimo* of 1380 as residing in the quarter of Santa Croce, *gonfalone* of the *Carro* where the Piazza dei Peruzzi is located: *Epist.*, IV, 462, and again in the same *gonfalone* in the scrutiny of 1382: *Delizie degli eruditi toscani*, ed. Ildefonso di San Luigi, 25 vols. (Florence, 1770–1789), XVI, 145 and 252. The "Diario fiorentino di Bartolommeo di Michele Del Corazza. Anni 1405–1439," ed. G. O. Corazzini, *Archivio storico italiano*, 5th ser. 14 (1894), 241, describes the ceremonies that took place there during the celebration of Salutati's funeral. In 1401 Salutati referred to Antonio Mannini, who lived in the Piazza, as his neighbor (*Epist.*, III, 498–99).

3. See below, chap. 10.

4. *Grascia morti*, 2, ad an. Listed as buried on June 16, 1400, is "quedam sclava ser Colutii" [n. 1749]. On slavery in Tuscany, see Iris Origo, "The Domestic Enemy: The East-

family for many years.[5] By 1378 there were at least four and possibly five Salutati children. Bonifazio, product of Salutati's first marriage, had been born on February 16, 1371, and Salutati had by this time three or four by Piera, his second wife: Piero born in August 1375; Andrea probably in 1376; Dina in 1377; and Arrigo in 1378–80.[6] Subsequently the couple were to produce at least six more offspring.[7]

Salutati's occasional references to the size of his family suggest a father's pride in his virility. Domenico Silvestri's poem to his penis must have flattered his vanity.[8] He was already in his sixties when his last child, Lorenzo, was born and that there were no more babies may have been the result of Piera's age.[9] As an old man he confessed himself not

---

ern Slaves in Tuscany in the Fourteenth and Fifteenth Centuries," *Speculum*, 30 (1955), 321–66.

5. Giovanni's long residence in Florence with his uncle cannot be proven but is very probable. On Giovanni's father Currado, see above, chap. 2, n. 81.

6. On Bonifazio, see Demetrio Marzi, *La cancelleria della Repubblica fiorentina* (Rocca San Casciano, 1910), p. 133, n.7; and my "Coluccio Salutati, Chancellor and Citizen of Lucca (1370–72)," *Traditio*, 25 (1969), 208–9, n. 68. For Piero, see *Epist.*, I, 206. Andrea "qui Petrum sine medio sequebatur etate," (ibid., III, 415) was probably born the next year. For Dina see Notarile 81 (1392–99), fol. 14, Dec. 2, 1392, where arrangements for the dowry are discussed. B.N.F., *Poligrafo Gargani*, 1728, *Salutati*, refers to a lost record of the gabella for her marriage in 1391. Born after Andrea she was fourteen or fifteen when she was married. On 1378 and 1380 as the dates of Arrigo's birth, see *Epist.*, IV, 395.

7. The birth dates of only two of these six can be established with certainty: those of Antonio on May 1, 1381 (ibid., IV, 444–46) and Simone: ibid., IV, 390. Novati erroneously writes 1385 for 1386: cf. *Libro delle età (1429)*, S.M.Nov., Vip., fol. 31. When the remaining boys, Lorenzo, Leonardo, Filippo, and Salutato, were born is a matter of conjecture. Filippo was old enough to serve in the Council of the Commune in 1406, and Novati's date of 1383 for his birth is perhaps correct (Marzi, p. 133, n. 7, and *Epist.*, IV, 390). Although in his last years Salutati desperately tried to find a place in the Church for his sickly son, Salutato, his initial efforts to obtain ecclesiastical preferment were on behalf of Piero and Leonardo, a fact suggesting that Leonardo was older than Salutato: see chap. 10. Because Salutati is known to have had a set of twins, it seems likely that Filippo and Leonardo were those children. This would place the birthdate roughly in 1383. This event is mentioned in an epigram by ser Domenico Silvestri: *Epist.*, IV, 391. Silvestri's epigram is published in *Domenico Silvestri: The Latin Poetry*, ed. Richard C. Jensen (Munich, 1975), p. 177. In a letter dated August 4, 1383–89 (*Epist.*, II, 185), Salutati spoke of Bartolomeo di Riccomi, brother of his wife Piera, as "octo filiorum meorum avunculus." Because Bonifazio was not related to Bartolomeo the eight would have included Piero, Andrea, Dina, Arrigo, Antonio, Simone, Leonardo, and Filippo. My assumption here is that Salutati used *filii* to mean "children" rather than "sons." Salutati's eleventh child, Lorenzo, was still in tutelage in 1407 (Marzi, p. 148, n. 4) and was born after September 29, 1392, when Salutati wrote of his having "ten" children. Thus, almost certainly Salutato was born between 1384 and 1391. The *terminus post quem* for Salutato's birth depends on the date of the letter of 1383/89. The *terminus ante quem* is somewhat more precise. On February 27, 1391 (*Epist.*, IV, 251), July 23, 1392 (ibid., II, 360), and September 29, 1392 (ibid., II, 396), Salutati spoke of having ten children (*filii*). Novati incidentally rejects Lorenzo's existence (ibid., IV, 393–94). There is no proof of a tenth son called Coluccio (ibid., IV, 393).

8. See above, n. 7, for Silvestri's poem.

9. Novati describes Piera as "non ancora cinquantenne" (ibid., IV, 390) but without evidence. If we assume she was at least twenty when her first child was born in 1375, she would have been forty-one when she died in 1396 (see below, chap. 11).

immune to amorous passion, rebuking himself on one occasion with a sonnet which began: "Che farai tu, vecchio rugoso e bianco/mosso dalla virtù del terzo cielo?"[10]

Salutati's place of retreat in the busy house was his "studiolum."[11] Despite his modest descriptive term, there must have been space in the room for a desk, a few chairs and the chests in which the books were stored. In this room in his hours of leisure, Salutati wrote, read, and conversed with friends. His closest companions in the early Florentine years were notaries like ser Domenico Silvestri and ser Antonio Chelli, men of mediocre literary and intellectual abilities but devoted to their talented colleague. Lorenzo de'Ridolfi, the brilliant student of law at Bologna, was a younger member of Salutati's circle of friends. Describing a visit to Salutati in 1380, Ridolfi spoke of the study were there was "a plenitude of books" for teaching the art of poetry and where Salutati gave him instruction in Latin metric.[12]

If Salutati's collection by the end of his life actually reached the eight hundred and more volumes attributed to it, the library must eventually have spilled out of the study into other parts of the house. Many of these books were purchased during his first years in Florence, when for the first time earning plenty of money Salutati could indulge his passion for books. His extant letters in these years are replete with requests to his friends and acquaintances for authors like Gellius, Quintilian, Virgil, Jerome, and Claudian.[13] Petrarch's death on July 19, 1374, furnished a special incentive for book buying.

Within the space of a year and a half the world of Italian letters lost its two greatest lights, Petrarch and Boccaccio, the latter dying on December 21, 1375. Salutati knew and admired Boccaccio but he idolized Petrarch. A few months after Petrarch's death he started a long encomium on the dead poet.[14] At the same time in a letter to Count Roberto

10. The first lines are included in a Latin version (*Epist.*, III, 17–18). The actual poem has disappeared.

11. Ibid., I, 335. His word is *studiolum*.

12. B.N.F., *Panc.*, 147, fol. 11ᵛ: "Cum igitur die quodam optimo meo preceptore Colucyo in suo studio residerem, ubi tanta librorum copiam et iam circa metricalem scientiam satis erudisset ad plenum (non quin tamen aliquid puerili etate didicerim), tamquam verus magister ex mandato imposuit ut circa metricalem praticam aliquatenus me versarer."

13. Ibid., I, 203, 262, 300, and 312. The work of Jerome was the *De viris illustribus*. On the size of Salutati's library, see Berthold L. Ullman, *The Humanism of Coluccio Salutati*, Medioevo e umanesimo, vol. 4 (Padua, 1963), p. 129.

14. Although Salutati explained in December 1375 (ibid., I, 224) that the poem had grown longer than he originally intended and was not yet finished, there is no reason to doubt, as Novati does, that the work was not completed eventually. Even if Manetti's mention of the work (ibid., IV, 512) depended entirely on the Italian version of Villani's biography (ibid., IV, 500), it is arbitrary for Novati to dismiss the vulgarizer's reference to

da Battifolle, the grieving Salutati rendered a judgment on Petrarch's literary stature which, because of its sensational nature, became widely reported and subsequently criticized: in Salutati's judgment Petrarch had been greater in prose than Cicero and more gifted in poetry than Virgil.[15] In later, more objective moments this statement made him uncomfortable, but publicly until the end of his life he insisted on its validity while reinterpreting his meaning so as to weaken its import significantly.

The announcement of Petrarch's demise was the signal to scholars throughout Europe to seek copies of the humanist's writings, jealously guarded during his lifetime, and copies, if not the originals, of the other fabled treasures of Petrarch's library. Even while Petrarch lived Salutati had requested Benvenuto da Imola, an intimate of Petrarch,[16] to obtain for him copies of Petrarch's Propertius and Catullus, authors whom he knew only by name.[17] By March 1375, however, his more immediate concern was that the literary executors of Petrarch in Padua not carry out their reported intention to burn the uncompleted manuscripts of his work. He was especially afraid for the *Africa*. Petrarch's son-in-law, Francescuolo Brossano, had promised that Boccaccio could have the manuscript, and Salutati implored Benvenuto in a second letter to prevail on the heirs to execute the promise.[18] Apparently he had Boccaccio's consent to allow him to do the editing work.[19] Although burdened

the "della morte del Petrarcha" as "tutto vago." The title simply occurs in a list of Salutati's works and is not more "vague" than any of the other references. Mehus claimed to have seen the work, *De Petrarche interitu* in a Vallombrosa codex (ibid., I, 224). As planned, the poem pictured the Muses complaining the poet's death (ibid., I, 200–1 and 225). They were to be presented, however, in a novel way (ibid., I, 225). Novati suggests that the arrangement was doubtless echoed in the metric epistle he wrote later to Bartolomeo del Regno (ibid., II, 345).

15. Ibid., I, 181–82.

16. Salutati's letter of July 26, 1374, implies that he had previously asked Benvenuto to help him procure copies (ibid., I, 170). Cf. Nicola Festa, *Saggio sull'Africa del Petrarca* (Palermo, 1926), pp. 27–40, with the account of Salutati's negotiations with the Paduan circle about editing the *Africa*.

17. He writes for the work of the two authors (*Epist.*, I, 170): "In primis quidem votorum meorum diligentissimus executor dyomicenes Propertium Catullumque procuras, quorum michi nil pene nisi nomen innotuit."

18. Ibid., I, 198–201. Boccaccio had given Salutati the idea that the *Africa* as well as the *Trionfi* and the *De viris illustribus* were fated for destruction after Petrarch's death; Boccaccio expressed this fear in a letter to Brossano on November 3, 1374: *Opere latine minori*, ed. A. F. Massera, Scrittori d'Italia, 111 (Bari, 1928), pp. 222–27. See Festa, p. 20, and Giuseppe Billanovich and Elisabeth Pelligrin, "Una nuova lettera di Lombardo della Seta," *Studies in Honor of Berthold Louis Ullman*, ed. Charles Henderson, Storia e letteratura, vols. 93–94 (Rome, 1964), II, 219.

19. *Epist.*, I, 200: "Et quo te letiorem faciam, Franciscolus illam sub certis condicionibus

with official duties as notary of the *Tratte,* he longed to rescue the epic from oblivion and to earn "eternal fame" as its savior. Two months later he returned to the attack, imploring the aid of Benvenuto to rescue the manuscript from the hands of an inept editor who could destroy it (*Epist.,* I, 201–4).

By July Salutati was aware that his representations to Benvenuto were useless. Although a friend of Petrarch, Benvenuto was not closely connected with the literary heirs. Salutati's next move, therefore, was to write to Gaspare de'Broaspini, who was a friend of Brossano and Lombardo della Seta. Salutati had known Gaspare at the Curia and written a letter to Petrarch in 1369 expressing his admiration for the Veronese scholar.[20]

Benvenuto apparently had offered to contact Gaspare about the Propertius and Catullus manuscripts, but Gaspare had written Salutati recently without mentioning the matter. Salutati's letter to Gaspare was carefully worded so as not to appear importunate but nonetheless to get action. Benvenuto, he wrote, had promised to ask Broaspini to help in procuring the two poets' work, but Salutati "does not know if he has written." However, "I know I will find an advocate in you" (*Epist.,* I, 207).

Finding Gaspare compliant, over the next few months Salutati extended his requests to include Petrarch's *Africa* and his copy of the Veronese manuscript of Cicero's *Epist. ad Brut., Q.Fr., Octav., Att.* By mid-November 1375 Salutati knew he would receive Catullus from Gaspare but was unsure whether it would be copied for him in Padua or whether Petrarch's manuscript would be sent to Florence for copying there (*Epist.* I, 222). The B.N.P., Lat. 14137, may have been the copy prepared by Gaspare for Salutati from Petrarch's Catullus.[21] The same November

---

ad Boccacium nostrum transmissurum litteris suis pollicitus est. Qui prescripserit quasvis leges, si illa in iura nostra pervenerit, manus iniciam et perpetuam reddere conabor divinam Scipiadem." Boccaccio still had a half-year to live when this was written.

20. Ibid., I, 96. The letter does not appear to be, as Novati thought, a "presentazione" of Broaspini to Petrarch, who had known him possibly as early as 1360: see the article "Broaspini," E. Ragni, *Dizionario biografico degli Italiani,* vol. 14 (Rome, 1972), p. 379. In 1370 (Novati edition has misprint "1369") Salutati wrote to Gaspare in response to a letter from Gaspare in Padua (*Epist.,* I, 119–22). That the latter was closely linked at least to Lombardo della Seta is indicated by Salutati's letter of condolence to Lombardo on Gaspare's death (ibid., II, 53–56). Although Salutati described the deceased (who was murdered by a relative) as "mitis, innocuus, benignus" (ibid., II, 54), shortly before Gaspare's death he had personally had a sharp argument with him. Gaspare was badgering Salutati to return a codex of Cicero. See below, n. 27.

21. Novati (*Epist.,* I, 222, n. 2) was reasonably certain of this, while Berthold L. Ull-

letter shows him wanting Petrarch's own copy of Propertius but ready to settle for a transcription if necessary.[22] As for the Cicero, Salutati wanted to know the size of Petrarch's manuscript. Perhaps Gaspare would let him make a copy of the selection of sixty letters that had been taken from it. Furthermore, if he were to have the *Africa*, he assured his correspondent, it could only be through Gaspare's efforts.

Apart from the Catullus and the selection of Cicero's letters, Gaspare failed Salutati and forced him to focus his attention on the literary heirs themselves, men who were barely known to him.[23] Thus, in his first letter to Brossano of December 24, 1375, Salutati was plainly out to impress his correspondent with his qualifications for editing the *Africa* (*Epist.*, I, 223–28). He emphasized his "glorious office" in Florence, and, both as proof of his talent and his admiration for the dead poet, he informed Brossano that he was sending Lombardo a poem originally

man, *Studies in the Italian Renaissance*, Storia e Letteratura, 2nd ed., vol. 51(Rome, 1973), p. 208, and *The Humanism*, p. 196, expresses strong doubts. Salutati certainly owned the Vatican *Ottob. lat.* 1829 (Ullman, *The Humanism*, pp. 192–93). The Vatican manuscript, however, was not copied from the Paris one, but both derive from the same manuscript, Petrarch's lost copy: Berthold L. Ullman, "The Transmission of the Text of Catullus," *Studi in onore di Luigi Castiglioni*, 2 vols. (Florence, 1960), II, 1041. Apparently accepting Novati's identification in this earlier article, Ullman postulated that Salutati received the Paris Catullus "but not finding it completely to his liking, had R [i.e., the Vatican Catullus] made, probably in Florence" (p. 1049).

22. "Si prece vel precio Propertium de bibliotheca illius celeberrimi viri, Petrarce inquam . . . haberi posse confidis, vel ut meus sit vel ut exemplari queat" (*Epist.*, I, 221–22).

23. The date when Salutati received Broaspini's manuscript containing selections of the *Ad Atticum* is unclear. Salutati sent the manuscript back in July 1381 to its disgruntled owner (ibid., II, 9–10). He explained his tardiness in returning the book on the grounds that before copying the manuscript he had given it to another scholar, who kept it for a year and a half. Returned, the manuscript was subsequently lost "illo civilium rerum turbine." Salutati eventually found the manuscript but then had trouble getting it copied. Novati remarks in a note, but without evidence, that Broaspini sent the manuscript in 1375 (ibid., II, 9, n.1). He also identifies "ille turbo" as the *Ciompi* revolt of July 1378 (ibid., II, 10, n.2). In all, therefore, Salutati would have had the manuscript for about six years.

On the other hand, Novati offers no explanation of Salutati's request for the "epistolas Ciceronis" made to Broaspini in November 1377 (ibid., I, 278). Already in possession of the selection, was Salutati now trying to get the complete collection of the *Ad Atticum*? Ullman, *Studies*, p. 212, contends that Salutati received the Broaspini selection in 1377, but he does not explain the meaning of "ille turbo." He also assumes that Broaspini sent the manuscript almost immediately in reply to the November request. If this refers to the *Ciompi*, the scholarly friend of Saluati could not have kept Broaspini's manuscript a year and a half before returning it to Salutati. I would accept a date for Salutati's receipt of the Broaspini manuscript sometime in 1376 and to agree with Novati that the phrase "ille turbo" refers not generally to public affairs but specifically to the *Ciompi*. Thus, when in late 1377 Salutati asks for Cicero's letters he was still seeking Petrarch's copy of *Ad Atticum*.

Salutati did not, of course, have a manuscript of this latter work until the 1390s (see ibid., pp. 220–21). His copy of Petrarch's manuscript is B.L.F., *Plut.* 49, 18, but his manuscript of Broaspini's selections has disappeared.

designed to encourage Petrarch to publish the *Africa*.[24] As soon as it was completed, Brossano himself would receive the work on Petrarch he had been composing. (*Epist.*, I, 223–24). The month before, probably with an eye to publicizing his talents in Padua, he had happily complied with Gaspare's request for a copy of one of his major public letters.[25]

Throughout the following year he cultivated his contacts in Padua. At some point in 1376 he received a poetic response to his appeal to Petrarch to finish the *Africa*. Written by Master Anastasio di Ubaldo Ghezi da Ravenna, the poem purports to be sent to Salutati from the dead Petrarch.[26] After reporting on his present state in heaven, Petrarch outlines in brief the story of the *Africa* and explains why it was never finished. Rejecting Salutati's suggestion that he feared to publish it because of possible criticism, Petrarch explains that he hesitated to publish until he was sure that what he wrote was his own creation and not borrowed from other authors. Ultimately, Petrarch informs Salutati, before his *Africa* is published, it needs a "wise editor" (*Epist.*, IV, 284).

In early January Alberto degli Albizzi, then studying in Padua, eagerly wrote to Salutati informing him that he had been successful in prevailing on the executors to allow Salutati and Benvenuto to edit the *Africa* jointly. Salutati could hardly have been happy at Albizzi's great feat of persuasion. Swallowing his displeasure, he had no recourse but to reply: "Nothing could be more acceptable to my own inclination."[27]

24. *Epist.*, I, 228. He had already mentioned this poem as completed in the letter to Roberto di Battifolle in April 1374 (ibid., I, 184). He referred to it again in the November 1375 letter to Broaspini (ibid., I, 222). The poem is published in ibid., I, 231–41. See Billanovich-Pellegrin, "Una nuova lettera," p. 219, n.2, for a new manuscript of this work. Georg Ellinger, *Italien und der Deutsche Humanismus in der Neulateinishen Lyrik* (Berlin-Leipzig, 1929), p. 24, refers to this poem and to Salutati's later poem dedicated to Bartolomeo da Regno (*Epist.*, III, 345–54) as having "etwas Hartes, Ungelenkes, Prosaisches." Pleading for publication of the *Africa* served as the theme of another poetic work, "Versus Iohannis Boccatii de Certaldo pro Africa Petrarche in vulgus edenda": see Nicola Festa's introduction to *L'Africa*, Ed. nazionale delle opere di Francesco Petrarca, vol. 1 (Florence, 1926), pp. xlii–xliii.

25. Ibid., I, 223. Giovanni di Conversino first came to know of Salutati through reading this letter (ibid., IV, 306).

26. The poem is published, *Epist.*, IV, 278–84. Cf. Festa, pp. 34 ff., letter to Lombardo, Jan. 25 and June 4, 1376, in ibid., I, 229–43, and letters to Brossano, Jan. 28, 1377, in ibid., I, 250–54. Besides the *Africa* he asked only for the *Sine titulo* about which Boccaccio had told him (ibid., I, 242–43). He perhaps wanted it as a help in formulating antipapal propaganda.

27. Ibid., I, 249: "Scripsisti tandem, quo nichil acceptius meis sensibus fieri potest, te ut per manus meas et illius divini prorsus viri Benvenuti mei de Imola Africa, celeberrimi nostri Petrarce singularis labor et, auguror, singulare perpetuande sue fame presidium, publicetur obnixius procurare: de quo tibi solidas gratias refero. . . ."

But fortunately Antonio ser Chelli, who had brought Albizzi's letter from Padua and had been in contact with the same men, had better news. Not without a sense of uneasiness, Salutati added in his answer to Albizzi: "Ser Antonio has advised that he thinks that perhaps the whole task, whatever the burden and the honor, will surely be awarded me alone."[28]

Ser Antonio was proven right when the manuscript arrived in Florence in the final week of January, but Salutati was under strictest obligation not to publish anything. After three nights of reading through the eleven notebooks containing the work, Salutati's joyous expectation turned to depression. As he explained in his letter of appreciation to Brossano, he had hoped to edit the text and then send copies to Bologna, Paris, and England with one copy kept in a public place in Florence. A letter of his own praising the work would serve as its introduction. But this hope was now frustrated by the prohibition to diffuse the text. Moreover, vital portions of the work—perhaps never written—were missing, thus preventing any chance of publication. Accordingly, Salutati urged Brossano in consultation with della Seta to search for the missing sheets.[29] In the meantime he seems to have set about working on the manuscript as it was but having proceeded as far as the end of the second book, probably convinced that the missing part of the story would never be filled in, he laid the work aside.[30]

One might suspect from the relatively reserved praise Salutati made of the manuscript on the first reading that he found it of inferior artistic quality. He was, consequently, not eager to undertake an edition of the work as it stood. As he wrote to Brossano: "Astounded, I have read the elegance of the song, the majesty of the speech, the gravity of the thoughts and the organization and contents of the whole poem; and I confess that I have never studied anything more sober, more ornate, and finally more pleasing, but of this another time."[31] Such brief comments on the long anticipated *Africa* should be taken as less than en-

---

28. Ibid., I, 249.
29. Ibid., I, 253–54.
30. Ullman, *Coluccio Salutati*, pp. 243–44.
31. *Epist.*, I, 252. Later Vergerio, who considered publishing the poem worthwhile, admitted in his preface to the edition: "Constat quidem, et dictum est, iuvenem[eum] poema cepisse, et in brevi tempore, tanta fuit ingenii velocitas, complevisse. Quod, si ad extremam perduxisset etatem, quanto futurum fuerit excellentius nemo ambigit . . . " (*L'Africa*, ed. Festa, p. lvi, n.1). ". . . sed tamen [poema] est tale ut de eo et gloriari iuvenis debeat et pudere senem non possit" (ibid., n. 2). See the comments of M. Aurigemma, "Il 'Sermo de vita Francisci Petrarchae' di Pier Paolo Vergerio," *Studi filologici letterari e storici in memoria di Guido Favati*, ed. G. Varanini and P. Pinagli, Medioevo e umanesimo, vol. 28 in 2 pts. (Padua, 1977), I, 33–53.

thusiastic when compared with Salutati's usual manner of giving praise. If this is correct, Salutati's complaints about *lacunae* were essentially excuses for extricating himself from a time-consuming labor whose rewards he considered minimal.

His pursuit of Propertius, Cicero, and numerous writings of Petrarch continued over the next couple of years. His letter of July 13, 1379, indicates that by this time Lombardo had promised a copy of the *De viris illustribus* and Propertius (*Epist.*, I, 330–33). If at all possible, Salutati wanted the former written on parchment rather than paper to avoid the chance of errors added by a transcription from paper to parchment in Florence. In the same letter he asked for the *Rerum memorabilium* to be transcribed in the same manuscript. As for the works of Cicero, he begged that a number of speeches he did not have, or possessed only in a corrupted form, be copied and sent as well.

In the light of the immense difficulties confronting the literary executors of Petrarch, that Salutati's order for books was satisfied even in part was a mark of the esteem he enjoyed with the Padua circle. We know now that Lombardo found it impossible even to satisfy the demands of Petrarch's closest friends without long delays.[32] Checco da Lion, the rich Paduan courtier, had financed the initial copying of all Petrarch's works on paper, a labor that employed the energies of the available copyists for two years.[33] The task of copying was complicated by the lack of skilled hands and by the fact that Lombardo intended to edit Petrarch's works, not merely make copies of them as they were found in the library closets. To put these editions on parchment, moreover, was a very slow task. Lombardo himself made the master parchment copy of the *De viris illustribus* with his own additions included—a task completed on January 25, 1379, only five months before Salutati wrote requesting a parchment rather than a paper copy for himself.[34] That Salutati's order was finished by November 15 of the following year on parchment was a proof of Lombardo's diligence.[35] Furthermore, with

---

32. Billanovich-Pellegrin, "Una nuova lettera," pp. 215–36, discuss the circumstances surrounding the early diffusion of Petrarch's work as derived from a new letter of Lombardo dated probably 1380/81. Lombardo wrote to Dondi dall'Orologio, one of Petrarch's closest friends: "De copia dictorum librorum (Petrarch's works) habenda tibi ad presens nullo modo consulere scio, cum hic scriptorum ingens inopia sit" (ibid., p. 235).

33. Ibid., pp. 236 and 222–25.

34. *Epist.*, I, 331, n. 1. Cf. *De viris illustribus*, ed. Guido Martellotti, Edizione nazionale delle opere di Francesco Petrarca, vol. 2, pt. 1(Florence, 1964), pp. xvii–xix.

35. Ullman, *The Humanism*, p. 193, describes Salutati's codex, the *Ottob. lat.*, 1883. Lombardo copied his additions to Petrarch's work with his own hand and corrected the manuscript throughout (Ullman, *Studies*, p. 178).

the energies of the professional copyists in Padua directed to Petrarch's corpus, the delay in transcribing other books in the library is quite understandable. Nonetheless, Lombardo managed to get Salutati his *Propertius*, also on parchment, by about the same time.[36]

One request of Salutati's for a manuscript during these years met with a sharp reproof. In September 1378 Salutati had written to the Bolognese chancellor, Giuliano Zonarini, asking him to purchase a manuscript of Virgil for him in Bologna. The pious Zonarini's reply was to deliver a lecture on the dangers of reading Virgil: rather than reading this "lying seer" Salutati should be spending his time with the sacred books.[37]

If Zonarini has such fears, Salutati retorts in his response, why does he not criticize as well the study of Plato, Aristotle, Donatus, Priscian, and Cicero in the schools? On the contrary, Virgil is not only not harmful to a Christian, he is useful both for his style and the profundity of his knowledge.

> I admire the majesty of his language, the appropriateness of his words, the harmony of his verses, the smoothness of his speech, the elegance of his composition and the sweetly flowing structure of his sentences. I admire the profundity of his thought and his ideas drawn from the depths of ancient learning and from the loftiest heights of philosophy.[38]

Of course, he admits, Holy Scripture is read with greater profit than the poets, but the dispassionate judge sees that the poets both edify and support the message of Scripture.[39] He then proceeds to show that Virgil's poetry contains truth drawn from the heights of true theology. In these poems, he argues, are to be found proofs of the Trinity (*Ecl.*, VIII, 72–74), the unity of essence of Father and Son (*Aen.*, I, 664), the institution of the Church (*Aen.*, III, 409), hell (*Aen.*, VI, 616–17), and purgatory and paradise (*Aen.*, VI, 743–44). While Christians should not go to the poets to learn their faith, yet when he finds something in them consonant with truth, then, Salutati confesses, he embraces it "willingly and with happiness" (*Epist.*, I, 304). The great early thinkers of the Church, moreover, knew the poets well and learned from

---

36. Ullman, *Studies*, p. 178.

37. *Epist.*, I, 300. The quotations are taken from the English translation of the letters relating to poetry by Ephraim Emerton, *Humanism and Tyranny* (Cambridge, 1925), pp. 290–308, 312–41, and 346–77.

38. *Epist.*, I, 301–2).   39. Ibid., I, 302.

them much which was beneficial for style. Not only are modern Christians advised to use the poets to learn grammar and eloquence and for purposes of edification but also in order to read intelligently the early works of Christianity so replete with references to the pagan authors (pp. 304–5).

Salutati does not specifically claim that Virgil's poetry was in part inspired by divine revelation. It is for Zonarini to judge "whether it is characteristic of truth to emerge out of floods of falsities or whether omnipotent God wanted to reveal himself to mortals by the testimony of all sects and beliefs" (p. 302). Zonarini himself must judge how "fitting" a particular passage (*Buc.*, VIII, 72–74) is as a description of the Trinity (p. 303). After quoting various lines of Virgil suggesting possible divine inspiration, Salutati implies his own belief in God's direct influence on the poet: "but clearly it pertains to the glory of God omnipotent that even through the ignorant, those wishing to say something else and those who did not know Him, He revealed so many secrets of that which was to come" (p. 303).

That the ancient pagan poets had written their works inspired by God was a thoroughly respectable medieval position tracing its descent from the Church Fathers. Da Moglio may have expounded the thesis in his classroom and Salutati may also have heard there an exposition of Mussato's arguments justifying study of the ancient poets. However, the Florentine chancellor could not have been unaware that both Petrarch and Boccaccio had come to question such a divine influence. Significantly, Salutati omitted from his list of Virgil's predictions a citation of *Buc.*, IV, 6–7: he doubtless knew that Petrarch and Boccaccio both had not interpreted that prediction as referring to Christ. Also by this time Benvenuto da Imola might already have confided to Salutati his intention to take the same position in his partially completed commentary on Dante's *Commedia*.[40]

Zonarini's religious scruples were not allayed by this response and he wrote back citing *Buc.*, IV, 6–7 (the very passage Salutati had avoided using) to prove that Virgil believed that God's operations were eternally cyclical in contradiction to the teachings of the Faith. The Bolognese chancellor did not seem to be aware of the dispute regarding the interpretation of this passage within the ranks of the defenders of poetry themselves; rather he evidently selected these verses for criticism be-

---

40. Ronald Witt, "Coluccio Salutati and the Conception of the *Poeta theologus* in the Fourteenth Century," *Renaissance Quarterly*, 30 (1977), 548.

cause they had formed a central focus for such defenses from early Christian times.[41]

In his letter of May 5, 1379, Salutati begins his rebuttal by emphasizing the general proposition that the poets contain theological truths: "What can we expect from the songs of the poets, in which the divine spirit of truth commonly seems to resound either within the mystery of the allegories or in the very expression of the words."[42] He chooses the crucial word "resounds" carefully to allow for interpretations short of one suggesting a direct cause and effect relationship. Dealing specifically with the charge that Virgil believed in the eternal circularity of the divine activity, Salutati refers Zonarini to Eccles. 1:9–10: "There is nothing new under the sun./Is there a thing of which it is said,/'See, this is new'?" Through this passage the Holy Spirit reveals to man not the repetitive nature of God's operations but rather the circularity of natural processes and the similarity of various events in human history (pp. 325–26). Why then perversely interpret Virgil when he says the very same thing? Whether he arrived at this truth through the brilliance of his own genius or by some divine revelation or whether, inspired like Caiaphas, he spoke in ignorance, Virgil nonetheless was a prophet (p. 327). Writing after the cessation of the civil wars Virgil in these verses might be speaking of an age of justice represented by the Virgin and of peace, the "Saturnia regna." By "new offspring" he might be referring to the Platonic conception of preexistent souls lodged in the stars coming down into human bodies or, in consonance with the future Faith, to the infusion of souls created from nothing into separate bodies. But usually most interpreters take "new offspring" to refer to "Christ, God's true wisdom incarnate."[43]

---

41. *Epist.*, I, 325. It would appear from the language of this letter that Zonarini had dispatched a letter entitled "Transcursorium" in response to the above. We do not know if Salutati answered it. Domenico Silvestri, Salutati's friend, read it in any case and wrote off a bitter attack on Zonarini's position. Irritated by Silvestri's letter and probably suspecting Salutati had encouraged it, the Bolognese chancellor sent an unsigned third letter to Salutati containing Silvestri's letter in its folds. Apparently this third letter of Zonarini on poetry arrived at the beginning of April but was temporarily misplaced. A month later on May 3, 1379, however, Salutati, having found it, wrote a reply and joined to it a note of apology from Silvestri. Silvestri's attack on Zonarini has been published by Steven Marrone, "Domenico Silvestri's Defense of Poetry," *Rinascimento*, 13 (1973), 125–32.

42. *Epist.*, I, 324: ". . . quid sperare possumus de poetarum carminibus, in quibus plerumque videtur aut sub allegoriarum mysterio aut in ipso verborum propatulo certissime veritatis divinus spiritus resonare?"

43. Ibid., I, 328–29: "Quod si novam progeniem, ut plerique opinantur, Christum, veram Dei sapientiam incarnatam, velimus accipere, adhuc tamen ab illa circulationis obiectione

With this rebuttal Salutati informed Zonarini he wished to consider the discussion closed. Despite the attempt to give alternative explanations, the obvious hesitancy and sometimes ambiguous choice of words, Salutati appeared in these two letters really to have believed that at least unknowingly great pagan poets like Virgil sometimes had uttered Christian truths under the influence of divine inspiration. Like medieval defenders of poetry and Albertino Mussato at the beginning of the century, Salutati stressed a certain continuity of truth between pagan and Christian epochs as the product of the constant operations of the Holy Spirit.

To distinguish as did Petrarch and Boccaccio between the human origins of the poets' truth, even in its loftiest expressions, and the divine source of Scripture, was to emphasize the difference between the pagan and Christian worlds. But, paradoxically, this view that the poets' inspiration had been purely their own could at the same time foster a sense of affinity with the ancients founded on acceptance of a common human nature. Once Virgil's creative power, for instance, was understood in natural terms, the man and his work could become more susceptible to understanding by other men. Petrarch's letters to various ancient poets demonstrate how the process worked. For the same reason, moreover, both he and Boccaccio treated ancient and modern poetry as parts of a single art deriving its inspiration from the energy of the mind.[44] It would be many years before Salutati came to this position.

Salutati's attempts to justify poetry on the grounds that it was partially inspired by divine Providence had nothing to do with his growing interest in Christian literature during this period. In fact his *De seculo et religione* of 1381/82, which demonstrates the extent of his reading in Scripture and the Church Fathers by this time, seems totally hostile to pagan learning as a whole. Rather Salutati's arguments for poetry derived from a medieval syncretic tradition which found its most daring exponent in Mussato. On the other hand, one clear effect of the humanist's increasing religious concerns was the tendency for fortune to disappear from his letters in the 1370s. Once committed to Christianity,

---

in eo quod novam dixit et non redeuntem nonque iterandam facile purgabitur vates noster."

44. Witt, "Coluccio Salutati and the Conception of the *Poeta theologus*," pp. 542–46. To this should be added the important article of Etienne Gilson, "Poésie et vérité dans le 'Geneologia' de Boccacce," *Studi su Boccaccio*, vol. 2 (1964), 253–82. Eugenio Garin, *La cultura filosofica del Rinascimento italiano*, 2nd ed. (Florence, 1965), p. 191, deals generally with the early humanists' tendency to secularize the conception of the ancient wise men.

aware of the Augustinian critique of fortune, he gradually eliminated all references to it or specifically made it equivalent to the Will of God.[45]

He must also have made a similar examination of the idea of fate in this same decade, again helped by the succinct attack on the concept made by Augustine in the *De civitate Dei*, Bk. V. By 1378 in a letter to the Mantuan scholar, Jacopo Allegretti, who had recently been predicting a series of violent wars for Italy, Salutati was ready to deny that he had ever given credence to such prophesies. Oddly forgetting his admiration for the prophetic power of the late Paolo Dagomari, Salutati branded divination not an art but a superstition.[46] In a long poem of 199 lines appended to the letter, Salutati directed an attack against the art of divination without, however, denying other claims made by astrologers for their science.

He concedes that astrologers are able to predict natural events like earthquakes and droughts, events directly impinging on human life, but he denies that the stars govern the human mind.[47] If this were so, there could be no free will and consequently no moral responsibility for man.[48] However, Salutati continues, an examination of those writing on the stars since ancient times indicates that there is wide disagreement among the authors as to the number of heavens and the courses of the stars. If the positions of the stars at a certain hour ruled the lives of those born in that period of time, why is it that twin children can differ so greatly in their later lives?[49] Astrologers insist on claiming credit for their correct predictions but too easily forget their more numerous errors. Whatever is predicted will either be or not be and a successful prediction is a matter of chance not art: "The power to know the future," Salutati concludes, "is not a human but divine one." It belongs to God "who moves all things, who governs all things, and who never errs."[50] However, the precise relationship of fate, like that of fortune, to this all-disposing force was left for the *De fato et fortuna* to define eighteen years later.

Despite the variety of indications of a deepening religiosity in these years, the appearance of the *De seculo et religione* in 1381/82 with its condemnation of the world and severe criticism of pagan "wisdom" seems

45. Alfred von Martin, *Coluccio Salutati und das humanistische Lebensideal* (Berlin, 1916), pp. 69–70. Cf. De Rosa, *Coluccio Salutati*, pp. 145–46.

46. *Epist.*, I, 279–80: ". . . nunquam futuridicis fidem dedi . . . " For Augustine's influence on Salutati, see below, chaps. 7 and 10.

47. Ibid., I, 283.   48. Ibid., I, 282.

49. Ibid., I, 287. The influence of Augustine, *De civitate Dei*, V, 2–6, is apparent here.

50. Ibid., I, 288.

totally unexpected. How could the same author sincerely praise the ancients as the masters of the *studia humanitatis* and urge emulation of their example and in another work of the same period pronounce all their virtues sinful and their wisdom abysmal ignorance?

II

The *De seculo* was dedicated to Niccolò Lapi of Uzzano in the Valdinievole, a former canon lawyer and canon of Santa Maria del Fiore in Florence, who on February 25, 1379, joined the Camaldulensan monastery of Santa Maria degli Angeli located in the heart of the city.[51] While still in the Valdinievole Salutati had apparently known Niccolò and his family well and shortly after Niccolò entered the monastery, he visited him. In the course of the visit, Niccolò, who had taken the religious name of Jerome, prevailed on Salutati to write a treatise encouraging him to persevere in the course he had chosen.[52]

Perhaps of more immediate concern to Jerome than preoccupations about the outside world were those relating to the standards of life within Santa Maria degli Angeli. Not only was the urban monastery surrounded by the turmoil of social unrest following the *Ciompi* revolt but also the order itself was rent with internal discord. In 1380 in fact a dissident group of monks appealed to the pope against the head of the order and the *Signoria* was forced to write to the pope defending the general who had governed the Camaldulensans for almost thirty years. The following spring the urban monastery was harassed by a papal commission sent from Rome to offer prelacies to individual members of the congregation.[53] These disturbing conditions were perhaps very much on Salutati's mind when he wrote to Jerome.

The tract can be dated only approximately. In the prologue Salutati excuses his tardiness in keeping his promise. Among other things the

51. *Annales camaldulenses*, ed. G. Mittarelli and A. Costadoni, 9 vols. (Venice, 1755–73), VI, 134–35. Cf. *Epist.*, III, 10, n.4.

52. Uzzano was located less than a mile from Stignano. Salutati explains the circumstances of his writing *De seculo et religione*, ed. B. L. Ullman (Florence, 1957), p. 1.

53. *Miss.*, 19, fol. 83–83ᵛ. In an eloquent public letter, ibid. fols. 137–38, Salutati wrote the Cardinal Tommaso Frignani about the affair of the papal commision which was upsetting the whole city. The letter is published by Giuseppe Pistoni, "Un modenese amico del Petrarca, il card. Tommaso Frignani," *Atti e memorie della Accademia di sci., lett. e arti di Modena*, ser. 5, 12 (1954), 94–96. Salutati later seems to have established close ties with Santa Maria degli Angeli. His friend and correspondent Giovanni da San Miniato joined this monastery probably on Salutati's advice (*Epist.*, II, 462) and in 1402 Salutati bitterly criticized certain monks who left the monastery to found another (ibid., III, 569–84).

pressure of his duties has caused him to put off complying for a long time. Novati tentatively assigns 1381 as the date of composition and Salutati himself in a later letter to Antonio degli Alberti referred to his having written the work shortly after Jerome entered the monastery.[54] Filippo Villani, whose *De origine civitatis Florentie* was composed about 1382, refers to Salutati's manuscript *De religione et fuga* as written *nuper*.[55]

Villani's title for Salutati's work creates a problem. It is generally accepted that the B.R.F., 872, formerly in the library of Santa Maria, was the dedicatory copy. The text was corrected in Salutati's hand and his autograph letter announcing the dispatch of the manuscript to Jerome is pasted on the inside cover. The letter does not mention the manuscript expressly but refers to a gift which Salutati has been correcting recently. B.R.F., 872 bears the title *De seculo et religione*.[56] Moreover, all existing copies of the work but one, B.N.F., *Panc.*, 129, dated 1445, have that title. The latter has . . . *de contemptu mundi et* . . . *de religiositate*.[57] Nevertheless, Villani's account of Salutati's work was checked by the humanist himself, and Domenico Bandini of Arezzo, in that part of the *Fons memorabilium universi* published about 1390 and describing Salutati's writings, also called it the *De religione et fuga*.[58] Salutati referred to

54. Ibid., II, 10–11, for Novati's dating: cf. B. L. Ullman, *The Humanism*, p. 26. In *Epist.*, II, 335 (1392?), Salutati explains that he wrote it for Jerome "soon after" (*nuper*) the latter had joined the order. The date of this letter must be after 1390 because it refers to Jerome's death: (cf. ibid., II, 11, n.4 from previous page). The work could not easily have been started before early 1381 because Salutati quotes Propertius on p. 12 and that manuscript probably arrived in Florence from Padua only late in 1380 (see above, chap. 7). For psychological reasons discussed below and in the next chapter, it is likely that the work was written in 1381 rather than 1382.

55. Ibid., IV, 492. For the dating of the *De origine*, see ibid., IV, 488, and the bibliography given there. From Giuseppe Calò's discussion, *Filippo Villani e il 'Liber de origine civitatis Florentiae'* (Rocca S. Casciano, 1904), p. 81, it is clear that the date of this work as 1381/82 depends on the dating of the *De seculo* and not vice versa. My own dating for Villani's work would be 1382 at the earliest. Although no longer chancellor of Perugia, Villani was still in that city as late as May 1381: (Calò, p. 44). However, although the opening lines of his prologue to the *De origine* are subject to interpretation, it would seem that by the time he had finished that work Villani had been in retirement for some time: "Solitariae vitae secreta me iamdudum elegisse deliciarum conscientiae simplicitate confiteor" (ibid., p. 86). Villani's biography of Salutati in the *De origine* (B.L.F., *Ashb.*, 942) was corrected by Salutati with no change made in Villani's version of the title. It must be said, however, that in the second edition of the *De origine* completed in 1395/96 (*Epist.*, IV, 488), also revised after consultation with Salutati, the same title is given. Only in the Italian version of 1404/5 was the title changed to the now familiar one (ibid., IV, 500).

56. Ibid., II, 11–12.   57. *De seculo*, p. ix.

58. Ibid., IV, 503–4. Novati assigns this approximate date to Bandini's work on the grounds that the *De verecundia* (1390) is absent from Bandini's account. But Bandini makes no pretense at completeness in his list, and he may have been writing several years after 1390. In a later listing of Salutati's works compiled at least after 1396 (ibid., IV, 507), Bandini gives the title as *De seculo et religione* and includes the *De verecundia* along with other works (ibid., IV, 507). On Bandini's life, see Theresa Hankey, "Domenico di Bandini of

the treatise for the first time by name about 1392 as the *De seculo et religione* but by then he could have changed the original title.[59]

Domenico Bandini was a friend of Salutati as was Villani, and the Aretine's biography of the humanist appears to have come from conversations with Salutati himself. In his account of the life Bandini mentioned that Salutati was in the process of writing the *De laboribus Herculis*, which was to be dedicated to him, information of the sort that Salutati naturally would have given. Bandini also stated that he had decided to publish a list of Salutati's works and that he knew of no one else's doing this, a statement he would not have made had he read Villani's biography and merely copied it. Besides the *De religione*, Domenico mentioned only the *De Pyhrri bello* (written about 1388–89) and the *De laboribus Herculis*. Were he merely copying Villani's words one would expect him to have referred as well to Salutati's bucolic poetry as the earlier writer did.[60]

But if Villani and Bandini deserve to be recognized as two independent witnesses to an earlier title, what becomes of the B.R.F., 872? Could it be a second copy of the *De seculo* presented by Salutati to Giovanni da San Miniato who entered the same monastery in the mid 1390s? This volume also would have contained corrections in the author's hand. What about the autograph letter glued in the flyleaf? Might it have been found among Jerome's effects after his death and then attached to Giovanni's copy?[61]

Arezzo," *Italian Studies*, 12 (1957), 110–30, and her article "Bandini" in *Dizionario biografico degli Italiani*, vol. 5 (Rome, 1963), pp. 707–9. Also see on the manuscripts of the *Fons* the same author "Successive Revisions and Surviving Codices of the *Fons Memorabilium Universi* of Bandini, "*Rinascimento*, 11 (1960), 3–48. Bandini wrote an index of the *Genealogia deorum* of Boccaccio on Salutati's request: B.N.F., *Magl.*, VIII, 1379 (*Naz.*, II, I, 61), fol. 1. See, *Genealogie deorum Gentilium*, ed. V. Romano, Scrittori d'Italia, vols. 201–2 (Bari, 1951), II, 816–18.

59. *Epist.*, II, 335. He did this with the *De fato et fortuna* (Ullman, *The Humanism*, p. 30, n. 5).

60. Ibid., IV, 491. See above chap. 1, for the defense of Bandini's accuracy in another regard. Calò, *Filippo Villani*, p. 208, however, asserts that Bandini depends on Villani for the information in every biography except that of Petrarch. Cf. Aldo Masséra, "Le più antiche biografie del Boccaccio," *Zeitschrift für Romanische Philologie*, 27 (1903), 323.

61. Ullman, who was aware of this problem, ended by considering the B.R.F., 872 as the original copy, thereby implying that Bandini's testimony was dependent on Villani. However, no definitive solution in the matter is possible at present. The same scribe who wrote the *Ricc.* 872 was the writer of the *Vat. lat.*, 3110, fols. 1–44ᵛ, according to Ullman, *The Humanism*, pp. 189 and 268. Ullman considers the Vatican manuscript written in the early fifteenth century. Were the *Ricc.* 872 written in 1381–82, this would mean that the same scribe had been employed by the humanist for twenty years or more. We would also expect other manuscripts written by him to have been among the volumes so far recovered from the library. The absence suggests that probably the *Ricc.* 872 belongs to the 1390s at the earliest. This discussion of the B.R.F., 872 as the presentation copy of the

In any case, even if there had been a change of title, no extensive revision of the contents was involved. The title *De religione et fuga seculi* reverses the order of the two books as they now exist but then it also contradicts the order in the manuscript as Villani himself described its contents.[62]

The *De seculo et religione* forms a part of the venerable medieval traditions of ascetic literature which endeavored to condemn the sensual life of man in the world. Like previous treatments of this subject, the *De seculo* focuses on man's misuse of God's creation, which was in itself good. The error of men is that they confine their goals to achievement in this worldly sphere. While intrinsically good, the world is still of much less value than the spiritual realm and by concentrating on it men are consistently opting for an inferior rather than superior value.

As with some of his more extreme predecessors, Salutati does not always keep his distinctions clearly in the foreground.[63] Like them he appears at points to introduce Manichaean tendencies into his work. When this occurs the justification for flight from the world appears to stem not only from man's failure to orient his life according to a proper hierarchy of values but also from the fact that the world has no value at all; indeed, that it is an evil place, intolerable to anyone truly seeking God. "What is filthier? What is dirtier? What more obscene than the world?" Salutati asks. "Let us not mention how vile are the bodies amidst which we breathe, and live, of which one—that on which we happen principally to live—is by its own nature the most impure of all . . . " (p. 14).

During the 1340s Petrarch had given extensive treatment on three occasions to this same general theme of *de contemptu mundi*. But, while strongly condemning the attractions of the world, Petrarch never expressed a similar degree of pessimism. The *De vita solitaria* and the *Secretum* do not even demand that a man who would leave the world join a monastery. In general, Petrarch's modest but comfortable existence in the Vaucluse would satisfy the exigencies of solitude recommended by these works. Directed to the monks of his brother's monastery, the third treatise, the *De otio religioso*, is more properly a praise of the kind of

---

De seculo is based on a memorandum left by Prof. Ullman among his notes on Salutati's library.

62. *Epist.*, IV, 492.

63. This tendency of medieval treatises is emphasized by Robert Bultot, *La doctrine du mépris du monde, en Occident, de S. Ambroise à Innocent III*, T. 4, pts. 1 and 2: le xiᵉ siècle (Louvain-Paris, 1963–64). Such an attitude seems much less prevalent in the work of non-monastic writers like Innocent III.

withdrawal connected with the monastic life. Yet even here Petrarch offers such an encompassing and profound analysis of the human condition, enriched by contrasts between pagan and Christian culture, that the emphasis of the work falls as much on the value of the Christian life in general as it does on monasticism, its highest manifestation. On the other hand, Salutati's attack on the world seems to leave no solution to the human predicament but the monastic one.[64]

In the proemium of the work Salutati explains the diffidence he feels writing on such a theme. Not only does he know that far greater men have written on the subject in the past, but also he realizes the inappropriateness of a layman, immersed in worldly affairs, offering arguments in support of the monastic life. "What is more nauseous," he asks, "than to live sinfully and to offer oneself as a teacher of the good life to others? . . . What more ridiculous than a blind man guiding the steps of one with sight and teaching what he is known not to know?" (p. 2). Besides this, as a layman who has devoted his life to secular studies, how can he hope to treat the theme with the proper degree of religious eloquence?

Nonetheless, as a Christian he must do what he can to help his fellow man and he has made a specific promise. Perhaps in writing the author himself might be led to improve his own life or at least he might be like one who, falling into a pit from whence he is unable or unwilling to escape, calls out to others so that they avoid the same danger by taking a better path (p. 3). In any case, relying on God's grace and Jerome's prayers, he now intends to keep his promise.

The plan of the treatise is to describe in the first book the world from which Jerome has fled and then in the second to praise the way he now follows and inspire him to pursue it with enthusiasm and alacrity. In the first thirty-one chapters of Book I he describes the world as the stamping ground of the devil, the wrestling mat of temptations, the workshop of evil; the factory of vice; the bilge hole of turpitude; a treacherous snare; it is a bitter joy, false gladness, and vain exultation; the threshing floor of tribulation; a den of misery; the shipwreck of virtue; the tinder for wrong doing; it incites men to crime; it is a blinding journey. The list of accusations continues in this vein.

64. These three treatises are published with Italian translation in *Opere latine di Francesco Petrarca*, ed. A. Bufano, vol. 1 (Torino, 1975). Alfred von Martin, *Coluccio Salutati*, p. 78, expresses the difference in this way: "Seiner [Salutati] ganz mittelalterlichen Kirchenfrömmigkeit ist der Mönchsstand noch der schlechthin und absolut ideale Stand; der Seiner Zeit bereits entwachsene Petrarca sah auch hier mehr mit dem Auge des Menschen und des Ästheten."

By contrast the four final chapters (33–37) before the short summary are designed to insure "that out of my desire to condemn the world I do not dismiss this creature of God as utterly blameable." The chapter titles suggest the more positive approach: "That the world is the highway of mortals"; "that the world is a roadhouse in our travels"; "that the world supplies us with the necessities of life"; and "that the world abounds in pleasant things" (p. 4). These chapters place the blame for evil squarely on the shoulders of man. Nature itself is a guide when it comes to deciding which of the things of this world we should accept. She requires the allaying of hunger, the quenching of thirst, covering against the rain and cold, protection from the violence of winds and heat. That these few things are sufficient is shown by the simplicity of life in early times, and by that of primitive people and of sailors in the modern age. We should not deceive ourselves; by foregoing all but necessities, by subjugating our bodies, we hasten our journey to the eternal home (pp. 80–84).

Hardened sinners who ask why God put pleasures into the world to ensnare our souls can easily be answered (p. 85). God gives us intelligence; He showed Himself to our first parents and to the sacred fathers; He instructed us through the prophets and revealed Himself to us in the person of His own son. Thus, we must all believe in Him and cannot sin without secret condemnation from our conscience. We ourselves therefore admit that love of the world for pleasure's sake causes us to offend our creator and to draw away from Him. God gave us the power of desiring to abandon the world, conquer the flesh, and overcome the devil. If we feel this desire, He helps us. The more obstacles there are in our path, the more glory we attain by surmounting them. Besides, the manifold things of the world should help us to realize and admire the power of Him who created them.

Salutati's characterization of the human predicament in the first book is a traditional Christian one. As might be expected in a work dealing with the merits of monastic retreat, the predominant emphasis is on man's ability to cooperate with divine grace and merit salvation. Whereas our first parents were created by God so that they were able not to sin, we have been born in a state where we cannot not sin. But so gracious is God that he "excites our sleeping reason, subjects good will to awakened reason and makes it so that with will governing reason we elect the better path, thereby freeing us from the slavery of sin." Thus, he compensates for man's defects "provided we wish it, provided we abhor the deformity of sin and are moved through love to desire the beauty of divine justice (p. 24). Once in possession of God's grace we cannot lose it unless we want to, i.e., "when with an evil will we deviate from that governing principle of all things" (p. 86).

The mind, that part of the soul capable of contemplation and, through contemplation, of drawing near to our creator, is corrupted by knowledge of the world. If we abandon the world, we leave the devil no weapon with which to strike at us. We are able to do so if we will and we can will: "We have command of our wills so that we can turn them whither we desire and draw them whence we have focused them. For thus God moves our wills that he not impede freedom of choice and not only does he not impede but he increases the good we properly wish to do. . . . For the grace of God precedes our willing the good, it helps us willing, it cooperates with our willing and it makes our earth bring forth its fruit" (pp. 65–66). These fruits are considered merits in God's eyes and so advantageous is monastic withdrawal to a rich harvest that, as Salutati states in the proemium of the second book, while the fruits of the average Christian are multiplied thirty-fold and those of the cleric sixty, those of the monk increase a hundred fold.[65]

The second book analyzes the nature of the monastic vows and the merits gained from them, and it considers central aspects of the religious life of the monk. Jerome has bound himself to God by a three-fold oath of poverty, chastity, and obedience. Indeed the meaning of religion itself is probably derived from *religatio*, a binding of oneself to God.[66] Through his fulfillment of these vows, lust, avarice, and pride are overcome and religious perfection attained.

The one who does good works because of his vows merits more than one who does them unbound.

Who merits grace more, the one who only gave his superior the fruits of the tree but is not held to give more than he wants, or the one who gives the tree and fruits on the condition that he can never get them back again? No one doubts that he merits more who shall have given more and he bestows more who gives fruit and tree than he who offers the fruit alone; and he gives far more who gives forever in such a way that he can never get it back than he who gives so that he can stop giving if he does not wish to (pp. 111–12).

65. This statement, *De seculo*, p. 92, is repeated p. 111, and explicated in detail pp. 163–67.
66. See below, chap. 8 and n.7.

To do a good work of one's own free will without a vow is meritorious but he who vows and then does the good work does a good work twice.

Apparently he is aware of critics of monasticism—Salutati calls them "raving," "brawlers," and "prattlers"—who hold that a man gains greater merit when he performs a good deed without a vow than when bound by one.[67] These argue that we are more obligated to one who does us good freely than to one who does so because acting under an oath. Against them he maintains that the analogy will not work. First of all, we can never force God to be obligated since we owe him everything. Moreover, just as it is more sinful to leave unexecuted a vow we have made to God than to neglect the same act without a vow, so more merit accrues to the man performing an act under a vow than to someone who does the same thing free of a vow (pp. 112–13).

Salutati then cautions Jerome not to let the devil tempt him by specious reasoning into regretting the step he has taken. After a detailed treatment of the significance of the vows of chastity, poverty, and obedience (pp. 117–37), he urges Jerome to fortify himself with prayer. In a long chapter—about one eighth of the whole work (pp. 137–56)—Salutati instructs his friend on the nature and purpose of prayer. A listing of some of the beneficent results of prayer follows in three chapters concerning devotion, adoration, and humility in our attitude toward God (pp. 156–61). The treatise ends with a final exhortation to religion and a contrasting of monasticism and its vows with the evils of this world (pp. 161–67).

His concluding remarks develop the idea of the relative degree of merit attached to the lives of the layman, the cleric, and the monk. Here as elsewhere in the treatise he uses etymology extensively in an effort to explicate and justify the argument. In this case, Joseph is associated with the thirty-fold merit of the Christian lay life; Isaac with the sixty-fold merit of the cleric; and Christ with the monk's hundred-fold harvest. While conceding that laymen need not despair of salvation, Salutati argues that they must pray and struggle to preserve the merits assigned to their lot. Likewise clerics must be ever watchful to conserve the sixty allotted to them.[68] On the other hand, Jerome and other monks

67. The approach of these unidentified fourteenth-century critics of monasticism is in general strikingly like that of Valla in the *De professione religiosorum*: Charles Trinkaus, *In Our Image and Likeness*, 2 vols. (London, 1970), II, 670–71.

68. He does not exclude the possibility that clerics may increase their yield to a hundred (p. 166). I do not see how this absolute quantitative statement on the value of the life of layman, priest, and monk can be interpreted as relevant only to the circumstances in which it was written in this treatise dedicated to a monk. For this interpretation, see Re-

have only to persevere to the end in the path they have chosen to merit eternal peace and glory.

While nowhere as extensive as Petrarch's treatment in his *De otio religioso*, a secondary theme of the *De seculo* is the contrast between pagan and Christian cultures. Although occasionally using examples of ancient virtue to shame modern Christians, Salutati at the same time makes it clear that he regards even the most virtuous of the pagans as doomed men. Would that the noble, poverty-loving Cinncinatus had known Christ! (p. 126). But outside the Church there can be no salvation:

> I do not know if I speak truly, however, I dare assert with greatest devotion that all who perform virtuous acts without [consciously] obeying the divine majesty, not only do not merit but act sinfully and all who do frequent acts, for example acts of courage and of temperance, for the simple reason that they may be courageous or temperate and not merely seem so, not only know according to the flesh but do not differ from pagan philosophers (p. 134).

Directly inspired by Augustine's judgment on the pagans in the *De civitate Dei*, V, 20, Salutati's unambiguous opposition of pagan to Christian morality differs radically from the rather vague relationship between the two found in his other writings in this period.[69]

---

vilo P. Oliver's review of B. L. Ullman's edition of the *De seculo* in *Speculum*, 34 (1959), 132–35; and Robert A. Bonnell, "An Early Humanistic View of the Active and Contemplative Life," *Italica*, 43 (1966), 230–31.

69. On Augustine's severe criticism of the pagan system of values, see H. I. Marrou, *Saint Augustin et la fin de la culture antique*, 4th ed. (Paris, 1958), pp. 331–56; Harald Hagendahl, *Augustine and the Latin Classics*, 2 vols. (Göteborg, 1967), II, 408–19, 540–53 and 620–27; and Volkmar Hand, *Augustin und das klassisch römische Selbstverständnis*, Hamburger Philologische Studien, vol. 13 (Hamburg, 1970), passim, but especially, pp. 33–41. Charles Trinkaus properly focuses a portion of his analysis of the *De seculo* on Salutati's novel description of how riches led both to the downfall of the Roman Empire and the corruption of the Christian Church, uniting both a classical Roman interpretation of history (primarily that of Sallust) with a version of the Augustinian-Christian conception of the Two Cities. As Trinkaus writes, "Adhering to the monastic vow of poverty apparently offers the only substitute for a return to the pristine days of the Roman republic or the early centuries of the apostolic church" (*In Our Image*, II, 668). I do not see, however, his depiction of the dissolution of the empire through the lust for riches as an expression of "republican sentiments" (ibid., II, 667). Salutati writes: "Rem enim publicam Romanorum, quam pauper fundavit Romulus et pauperrimi principes ad tantam magnitudinem evexerunt ut imperium occeano, astris vero gloriam terminaret et eis ad occasum ab ortu solis omnia domita armis parerent, divites, L. Silla crudelis, Cinna ferox, ambitiosusque Marius, labefactaverunt, et ditiores, M. Crassus, Gn. Pompeius Magnus, ac Gaius Cesar, Lucii Cesaris filius, funditus destruxerunt. Ut in hac rerum gestarum memoria quasi quodam in speculo videre possit mortalium genus ad hanc terrenam civitatem instituendam, augendam, atque conservandam pauperes divitibus prestitisse" (p. 128). I translate "res-

Although, as we shall see, the *De seculo* is important for an understanding of Salutati's intellectual development, there is little that is original with him in this treatise. Perhaps the most novel element in the work is found in the description of Florence presented by Salutati to prove that the world is a mirror of vanities (pp. 60–61). Offering a kind of visual perspective foreign to the art of his own generation but common to the next, Salutati urges his readers to imagine Florence seen from the hill of San Miniato on the left bank of the Arno, or from the twin summits of Fiesole's mountain, or one of the other promontories high enough to behold the panorama. From such a vantage point he describes the city generally spread out below and particularly the *Palazzo della Signoria* and the cathedral, while he reflects on their glorious construction and their impermanence. The *Palazzo* is already settling on its foundations and gaping cracks are visible in its walls. The viewer's eye then falls on the private houses, many of which were destroyed in the *Ciompi* Revolt.[70] The whole scene reflects progressive decay. Whether by coincidence or design Leonardo Bruni, Salutati's closest disciple, more than twenty years later offers a similar view from the heights in his *Laudatio urbis Florentine*, but the younger man gives a much more positive assessment of the sight.[71]

Speaking generally, Salutati's main contribution to the literature in the *de contemptu mundi* tradition lay in his organization of the material into a relentless diatribe against life in the world and in favor of monastic retreat. Filippo Villani aptly characterized the work as having so many arguments "that no one could say anything more on the subject than he did."[72] For Villani the *De seculo* compared with Plato's treatment of the immortality of the soul, which had such persuasive force that many killed themselves after reading it. In the case of the *De seculo* "I do not doubt that anyone who listens to or reads the book . . . will retire to the solitary and monastic life leaving the vanities of the world behind and,

---

publica" here as "state" because its foundation is ascribed to Romulus and see the distinction simply as one between an earlier and later period of Roman history with no implication for a contrast between monarch and republic intended.

70. *De seculo*, p. 61: "Quot autem et qualia civium habitacula quotque palatia intestini dissidii civica pestis absumpsit!"

71. Hans Baron, *The Crisis of the Early Italian Renaissance*, rev. ed. (Princeton, 1966), p. 200, is of course correct in stressing that the *Laudatio* was "the first attempt . . . to discover the secret laws of optics and perspective that make the Florentine landscape appear as one great scenic structure." Could Salutati have been inspired by the powerful description given by Petrarch of the impermanence of man and his cities: *De otio religioso* in *Opere latine*, I, 706 and 708?

72. *Epist.*, IV, 492.

burning with desire for it, be totally immersed in that form of existence."[73]

Quite understandably such a treatise, composed by the chancellor of the Florentine Republic, a layman, husband, and the father of a large family raises puzzling questions about motivation. The work pronounces easily—too easily—on issues that were to trouble Salutati deeply in the last decade of his life: the relationship between the active and contemplative life and the value of ancient literature for the Christian. The *De seculo* both minimizes the merits of the ancients and denigrates life in the world. How could Salutati reconcile these conclusions with his career and his passionate love of ancient letters?

Was the *De seculo* only a kind of elaborate *declamatio*? Salutati wrote a number of these works in the form of separate speeches speaking for and against a certain proposition. But these *declamationes* were undisguised rhetorical exercises.[74] In the case of the *De seculo et religione* Salutati clearly intended the reader to interpret the work as if the author believed in the arguments presented. Of course, this could be viewed as part of the rhetorical dressing. Yet in a matter of such religious significance, this approach would have been inexcusable.[75] Salutati was a

---

73. Ibid., IV, 493. Perhaps Villani's reference to the lethal effect of Plato's *Phaedo* derives from his memory of Cleombrotus of Alexandria, who threw himself from a wall upon reading the work: Cicero, *Tusc.*, I, 34, 84; Lact., *Div. Instit.*, III, 18; and Augustine, *De civ. Dei*, I, 22. He may also have confused in mind Cato Uticensis, whom Seneca, *Epist.*, XXIV, 6, describes as reading that work before committing suicide.

74. For Salutati's declamations, see App. I.

75. Although both Berthold Ullman (*De seculo*, p. vi) and Eugenio Garin ("A proposito di Coluccio Salutati," *L'età nuova* [Naples, 1969], p. 171) regard the work as highly rhetorical, Ullman (*The Humanism of Coluccio Salutati*, p. 28) stresses Salutati's "sincerity," while Garin contends that "non sarà da credere che in quella prosa non si rispecchi un moto reale del pensiero salutatiano." In his earlier "I trattati morali di Coluccio Salutati," *Atti e memorie dell'Accademia fiorentina di scienze morali 'La Columbaria'*, n.s., 1 (1943), 60–61, Garin insists that the great emphasis placed on the human will gives the *De seculo* continuity with the humanist's other work: "La fosca presentazione della corruzione e dei pericoli del mondo non è la premessa per un invito alla fuga dal mondo, ma un incitamento alla lotta senza quartiere contro il male, lotta a cui non si sottrae, ma che anzi affronta senza limitazioni e senza compromessi proprio chi si decide alla rinuncia del chiostro?" (p. 61). But on the basis of Garin's discussion of Salutati's voluntarist position here, I find it difficult to see how it differs from that in similar treatises by medieval writers like Peter Damiani and Anselm. Garin does find, however, the "residuo medioevale . . . dominante e coscientemente assunto come centrale" (p. 59).

Trinkaus (*In Our Image*, II, 851, n. 51) makes an important point when he writes: "Salutati's very acceptance of the 'medieval' notion of the relation of lay, secular-clerical, and religious states was not in the least inconsistent with his remaining a layman and feeling himself a good Christian and admirer of monasticism." Cf. the review of Ullman's edition by Giuseppe Toffanin, "Per Coluccio Salutati," *Rinascimento*, 9 (1958), 5. Although the position on this issue expressed in the *De seculo* will be inconsistent with his later remarks on the active life (see chap. 12, this volume), it is not so within the context of his writing

born debater and loved to win arguments. But there was more involved in his motivation for writing the work.

While Salutati at the outset of the *De seculo* might honestly have been expressing his motives for writing at this time, the period of its composition (1381–82) suggests that he was also impelled by immediate personal concerns. As has been seen, the troubled political situation in Florence came to a climax in 1381 and Salutati was well aware of the threat posed to his safety by the growing ascendancy of men like Scali and Strozzi over the mobs. Even were the present regime to collapse, how would the victors treat a collaborator with the old government? His dreams of success had been satisfied far beyond his expectations; he had surrendered to an infatuation with glory and he feared the awakening was at hand. His diatribes against the world in the *De seculo* were partly motivated by the bitterness and self-recrimination he felt. He was indeed trapped in the world.

Very possibly his awareness of the precariousness of his situation in the city provoked in the middle-aged man a moral crisis of extensive proportion. Of all the many vices characterized in the *De seculo* to be shunned, the most powerful description is given to lust. "The stimulus of the flesh," he writes, "is always in us. When we are refreshed, it grows stronger; when we rest, it becomes excited; it mixes in our dreams, breaks into the midst of our prayers, forces itself into our contemplations, it stays with us when alone, it assaults those in company, it enters through the eyes, it is excited by hearing, fostered by smell, produced by taste, attained by touch, and as a rule is so violently moved by the memory of depraved delights that in one moment it can ruin the chastity of many years."[76] These are the words of one intimately acquainted with the "ferocious beast" of sex. If he himself had not actually succumbed, at least he had experienced its force and knew the consequences of making the slightest concession. Denunciation of the mon-

---

at the time. Also in a sense Trinkaus (ibid.) is right to assert that "there is a compatibility between such a so-called 'medieval' point of view as a defense of monasticism and 'humanism'." However, granting that Salutati is sincere, how are we to explain the almost totally negative depiction of ancient culture and the evils of living in the world? It is Salutati's particular way of defending monasticism which seems to me basically incompatible with his humanism and needs explanation. Armando Petrucci, *Coluccio Salutati*, Biblioteca biographica, vol. 7 (Rome, 1972), pp. 57–62, presents perhaps the most balanced characterization of Salutati's motivation. Recognizing it as "prima di ogni altra cosa (come è già stato detto dal Garin), un'opera di scuola e di retorica" (p. 58), Petrucci sees the *De seculo* partly as a response to a private moral crisis and a public one created for Salutati by the Ciompi and the aftermath of the rebellion.

76. *De seculo*, p. 118. Cited in Petrucci, *Coluccio Salutati*, p. 59. This point is based on Petrucci, pp. 59–60. See additional quotations from the *De seculo* given in Petrucci.

ster in the *De seculo* consequently served to strengthen his own resolve.

But how could the humanist not see that by extolling a life of withdrawal and by censuring ancient culture so severely, he was contradicting his own scholarly enterprise? Since 1368–69 Salutati had taken his Christianity seriously. Besides the Bible Augustine is clearly the most salient influence in the *De seculo*, but the text also shows an acquaintance with other Christian writers.[77] As has been suggested, however, while sincerely and deeply felt, his religious conceptions were quite unoriginal. In defending monasticism he proceeded with the confidence of one who connected with a well-established stream of ideas, and the intensity of his own feelings coupled with his rhetorician's desire to make a strong case pushed him toward the more extreme representatives of the tradition. In the same fashion, in writings prior to and contemporary with the *De seculo* the assumptions behind his praise of the study of ancient letters had not yet been submitted to careful scrutiny.[78] The two trends in his thought remained unreconciled.

Salutati's increasing involvement in Christian literature after 1368–69, however, had been instrumental in frustrating his efforts to finish the treatise entitled *De vita associabili et operativa*, apparently a defense of the active life. Begun in 1370–71, the writing was interrupted by the death of Caterina in 1372.[79] But if ceasing to write because depressed by her death, he did not return to the manuscript in 1373 or 1374 when his fortunes drastically changed for the better. It would seem that he found himself in these years unable, as a Christian, to make a defense of the active life. Probably Ciceronian in inspiration, the original draft would have been quite compatible with his earlier attitudes but in the Christian tradition, as he came to understand it, there were no strong arguments against the view that monasticism was the highest kind of life. In short, whereas earlier the problem of life-style had been primarily a moral one, given his increasing absorption in Christian thought, he could no longer treat this issue without paying heed to its theological implications.

77. Toffanin, "Per Coluccio Salutati," pp. 7–9; Garin, "A proposito," p. 168; and Trinkaus, *In Our Image*, II, 663. On Augustine, see chap. 10.

78. Although generally offering a positive view of antiquity, Salutati at one point in an early letter (1365) refers to pagan religion in terms which recall *De seculo*. He writes of the ancient religion as "deliratio" and as "cecitas veneficaque superstitio" (*Epist.*, I, 10). In the context it seems to be more a bow to convention than an expression of deep feeling.

79. Hans Baron, *The Crisis*, is the first to establish a link between the *De seculo* and this earlier work (pp. 106–10). Baron believes that Salutati's failure to finish the treatise stems from "a recurrent distrust of the values of this world and the recognition, from the viewpoint of religion, of the superiority of contemplation" (p. 106). The more precise chronology of Salutati's religious development offered in the preceding chapter only makes this explanation more convincing. My interpretation of the *De seculo* is basically his.

The dark pessimism of the *De seculo et religione,* however, was as temporary as the rubbled and littered sites in the center of the city where the palaces of the great Guelf leaders had stood.[80] With the changing of regimes and the reassurance that he had lost nothing, Salutati turned to his ancient scholarship with a vengeance. However, the tension was not completely dissipated: the confrontation was merely postponed. The next fifteen or sixteen years were ones devoted to *studia humanitatis.* But then followed the *De fato et fortuna* (1396), and the *De nobilitate legum et medicine* (1399). The latter especially deserves to be considered Salutati's effort to return to his earlier project of writing a *De vita associabili.* But now the author would be fortified with new insights about the role of the active life in Christianity.[81]

80. Baron, *Crisis,* p. 109.

81. A curious conflict of views is found in an exchange of sonnets between Salutati and a correspondent on the value of monastic life. The exchange consists of the correspondent's appeal to the life of withdrawal, Salutati's reply, the answer of the correspondent, and a final response by Salutati. Salutati, in this case espousing the active life, concludes at one point: "Ben giunse a quel cubile/ Petro e Paulo chè così credemo/ senza fuggir il mondo ove noi seno. . . ." The exhange was published by G. Baccini, *Zibaldone, notizie, aneddoti, curiosità e documenti, inediti o rari raccolti da una brigata di studiosi,* 1 (1888), 45–47. Baccini does not identify the other poet.

Chapter 8. IN PRAISE OF POETRY

A major change in Salutati's approach to his studies occurred in the years 1381–82. From these years the humanist devoted less energy and time to his duties as chancellor than he had earlier and avoided assuming any other offices.[1] Moreover, his letters and other personal writings reflect greater concern for philological and linguistic problems. His research and thought proceed henceforth at a more profound level.

A small incident occurring in March 1382 suggests the change taking place. On January 26, 1382, Salutati was summoned to record the deliberations of a *Consulte e Practiche* called to decide on a plan to meet an invasion of Florentine territory by hostile mercenaries. The Latin summaries of the speeches he jotted down in the official minutes were very concise, and once he had understood the argument of a particular speaker there was nothing to do but wait until the next took the floor. At one point during these hours, it occurred to him to transliterate a Latin phrase into Greek characters: "Psithacus eois nuper michi missus ab oris Indis." The phrase itself was inspired by the reading in his copy of Ovid's *Amores*, 2, 6.1–2: "Psytacus eois ales michi missus ab Indis occidit."[2] This use of Greek characters was the first proof in Salutati's existing writings that he had any direct acquaintance with the language. Taken together with other information, the doodling indicates that in these months Salutati was striving to learn the characteristics of Greek letters, their form and pronunciation. That this kind of knowledge was of immediate relevance to his etymological interests is shown by his uncompleted letter to Charles of Durazzo written in the previous fall.

When in mid-September 1381, news reached Florence of the victory of Charles of Durazzo over his enemy, Otto of Brunswick, husband of Joanna of Naples, Salutati considered it his public duty to write the new ruler of the Kingdom of Naples a panegyric to which he intended to append a long treatise on the just rule of princes. As it was, the letter was never sent nor even finished. The most likely reason for abandoning the project was that Salutati found the undertaking too great to be finished quickly. Nonetheless, he returned to the work a number of

---

1. See chap. 6.
2. Ronald G. Witt, "Coluccio Salutati and Plutarch," *Essays Presented to Myron P. Gilmore*, ed. S. Bertelli and G. Ramakus, 2 vols. (Florence, 1978), I, 335–36. For other doodlings of Salutati during meetings, see *Epist.*, II, 57.

times over a period of months, correcting and making additions.[3] The most significant of these contains the first etymological analysis found in Salutati's letters.

After praising Charles at some length for his stupendous victory and declaring that such an achievement could not have been accomplished without the aid of God, Salutati exalts Charles as the protector and asylum of the Guelfs. He then begins an elaborate treatment of the origins of the words Guelf and Ghibelline.[4] The name *gebellini* was merely another way of writing *gehennini*: "Those who, antagonistic to the Church and lacking that article of faith by which we are ordered to believe in one holy, catholic, and apostolic church, are to be plunged into hell unless they recognize their guilt." He justifies interchanging the *h* and *n* of *gehennini* with the *b* and *l* of *gebellini* in the following way:

3. Novati's original transcription of the letter was published *Epist.*, II, 11–46. It was edited without benefit of the original draft of the letter found in B.A.V., *Capp.*, 147, pp. 222–33 and 242–57. Novati was, however, able to give alternate readings and additions to his version based on the Capponi in *Epist.*, IV, 610–16. On a separate sheet of the Capponi is written: "De incoronatione regis et quid deceat reges facere. Epistola valde prolixa et quam plurimum notanda ubi est talis manus circa finem" (p. 321). This is followed by the cryptic "Pro domino Honofrio. Quinterno 7." There is no question but that this title refers to the letter to Charles in the manuscript. At the head of one fragment the title "Quid deceat regem" (p. 222) is written. Dominus Honofrius is in my opinion identical with Maestro Nofrio da S. Spirito, mentioned by ser Naddo di ser Nepo of Montecatini, *Croniche fiorentine*, Delizie degli eruditi toscani, 25 vols. (Florence, 1770–89), XVIII, 67, as serving as one of the two ambassadors to the court of Charles in 1384. Cf. B.M.E., *Campori, App.* 1252 (Busta 13[2]), where *Magister Honofrius Nicolaii sacre pagine professor ordinis hermitarum* is given as a member of an embassy sent to Charles in January 1383(4). Never dispatched to Charles, Salutati's letter was probably copied in the chancery for the ambassador and was designed as a basis for his speeches to the king.

4. The printed version of the letter, Epist., II, 28–29, contains a short historical analysis of the meaning of the terms while the additions made to the original in the Capponi, 147, fol. 246, are much more detailed as shown by Novati's transcription, IV, 612–13: " . . . cur non dicamus Gebellinos quasi Gehenninos ut pote qui contra ecclesiam sentientes et in illo deficientes articulo quo credere iubemur in unam sanctam catholicam atque apostolicam ecclesiam sint in Gehennam nisi penitendo se recognoverint demergendi? . . . Apud Grecos enim et Latinos 'l' et 'n' insimul facile commutantur. Unde et nimpham et lympham pro aqua dicimus et numerus quinquagesimus qui apud Grecos per N, apud Latinos per L litteram denotatur. Iam enim quis nescit tantam inter 'b' et 'v' consonantem fore cognationem tam in potestate quam in voce quod apud Grecos similiter sonent? Et apud Latinos una in alteram [Novati: altera] facile convertatur [Novati: communtentur canc. e *sostit.* convertantur?]. Unde in hoc nomine 'celebs' cuius [Novati considers ethimologia understood here] significatum et origo est—ğ[gratia? cum?]—teste Prisciano grammaticorum principe 'celestium vitam ducens,' 'b' pro 'v' scribitur consonante, 'v' vero consonans pro aspiratione sumi manifeste videmus. Quod enim Greci aspiratum hesperum nos vesperum dicimus. Iure igitur mutatis 'b' in 'h' et gemino 'n' in 'l' Gebellinos dicere possumus Gehenninos."

He gives a similar, if less complicated, analysis of the word *Guelf* (p. 613): [cancelled: Cur non Guelfos] quos patria unde venisse creditur nomen illud non Guelfos sed Welfos per geminum 'v' loco 'g' (in marg: scribit et proferat) cur non dictos putemus, quasi vere fos? Nam grece fos lumen est [canc: vel ignis per quem caritas figuratur]?

With the Greeks and the Latins 'l' and 'n' are mutually interchanged with ease. Whence we say both *nimpham* and *lympham* for water and the fiftieth number which is denoted by the Greeks as N, by the Latins is denoted as L. Now who does not know that there is such a relationship between 'b' and 'v' as a consonant, both in power and sound, that for the Greek they sounded alike? And with the Latins one is easily converted into the other, whence in this word *celebs* (whose signification and origin is, thanks to the authority of the prince of grammarians Priscian, 'leading the life of heavenly beings') 'b' is written for the consonant 'v', we see clearly that 'v' as a consonant is taken for an aspiration. So that we say *vesperum* for the aspirated *hesperum* of the Greek. By rights, therefore, with 'b' changed into 'h' and double 'n' into 'l' we are able to call *gebellini, gehennini.*[5]

The transliteration of Ovid's verse into Greek letters in January 1382 was a playful manifestation of the knowledge of Greek pronunciation he had acquired for more serious scholarly purposes.

A good part of Salutati's treatment of monasticism in the *De seculo et religione* relied, as has been noted, on etymological analyses. Isidore of Seville's *Etymologiae*, the *Catholicon* of Balbus, the *Lexicon* of Papias, and Uguccio Pisano's *Verborum derivationes* supplemented by St. Jerome's *De nominibus hebraicis* and Alcuin's *Interpretationes nominum Hebraicorum* provided the author with the keys to the significance both of individual words and of allegories in the Scripture.[6] Salutati's own suggestion that the word *religio* originates from *religatio* serves as the basis for his discussion of the monastic vow, while elsewhere etymological roots of words like *sentina, calamitas*, and *erumna* are given in order to show how naturally the terms describe the world.[7] There is no earlier treatise of Salutati with which to compare the *De seculo*, but the approach is without parallel in Salutati's other writings before the letter written to Charles of Durazzo in the fall of 1381.

The short characterization given in chapter 3 of Salutati's marginalia in his manuscript of Seneca indicated the concern reflected in these annotations for orthography and etymology.[8] Beginning with his letter

---

5. The passage of Priscian is found *De octo partibus orationis* (Basel, 1554), I, 3; p. 13, *De accidentibus literae*.

6. See above, chap. 7; and the footnotes to Ullman's edition, *De seculo et religione*, ed. B. L. Ullman (Florence, 1957).

7. Ibid., pp. 102–3, 14, 56, and 57. This etymology of *religio* is derived from Augustine, *De vera religione*, LV, 113. On the other hand, Cicero, *De nat. deorum*, II, 28, 72, traces it to *relegere*.

8. See above, chap. 3.

containing spelling corrections of Filippo Villani's *De origine* in 1382, Sal-utati made it a frequent subject of his private letters. To Villani, who had sent him the manuscript of his work for correction, Salutati urged greater care in orthography "since often a changed division of syllables or a joining of individual letters distorts the sense and whole meaning."[9] If not in the earlier period, at least by 1381–82 this interest in spelling was founded on the unspoken assumption that words reflected reality in their composition and that incorrect spelling would mangle truth.

The *Etymologiae* of Isidore of Seville laid the groundwork for such a belief: "When you understand the origin of a word, you more quickly comprehend its power." To grasp the origin of the word was to seize the reality it reflected.[10] This principle was reinforced in the later Middle Ages by grammarians who maintained that Latin, Greek, and Hebrew were unchanging languages. Certain of these scholars held that at least Latin and Greek were languages created by philosophers.[11] If that were the case, then the vocabularies of these languages and their syntax were consciously worked out so as to parallel and mirror things. Salutati never explicitly articulated these conceptions, but his implicit adhesion to them is proven by the tremendous energy he expended after 1381 in an effort to penetrate to the core of reality by unlocking the truth bound up in words. Only in his very late years did he have doubts about this belief.[12] Although left in fragmentary condition, the first edition of the *De laboribus Herculis* clearly went beyond the *De seculo* in its reliance on etymological analysis. This was also to be the fundamental methodolog-ical approach of the second edition of that work.

At some point in late 1381 or more probably 1382, Salutati resolved to apply the allegorical interpretation of poetry, already utilized in his con-troversy over Virgil several years before, to the tragedies of Seneca, pri-marily the *Hercules furens* and the *Hercules oeteus*.[13] Now, however, he

9. *Epist.*, II, 48. For subsequent interest in spelling in the years immediately thereafter, see ibid., II, 110–12 and 187–89.

10. Isidorus, *Etym.* I, 29. Cf. Ernst R. Curtius, *European Literature and the Latin Middle Ages*, trans. W. R. Trask (New York, 1963), p. 43; and Yves M. J. Congar, "Cephas, Cé-phalè, Caput," *Revue du moyen âge latin*, 8 (1952), 26–31.

11. On medieval grammarians' conception of language, see below, chap. 9.

12. See below, chap. 9.

13. For the date of Villani's *Liber de origine civitatis Florentie*, see chap. 7, n. 55. In Salu-tati's biography included in the second part of Villani's work, after describing the chancel-lor's letters and a number of poetic compositions, he writes: "Composuit insuper librum De laboribus Herculis, in quo persuadere conatur inexpungnabilibus locis, monstruosis terre laboribus superatis, viris fortissimis astra deberi" (*Epist.*, IV, 492). He then mentions the *De seculo et religione*—he refers to it as the *De religione et fuga seculi*—as having been written *nuper*. Novati assumed (*Epist.* IV, 492, n. 2) that, because the *De laboribus* was

would employ etymology to increase the possibilities of finding truth in the poetic allegories. In setting forth his motive for writing the treatise, Salutati explains that he and his colleague in the chancery, ser Viviano, had been perplexed about Seneca's motivation for allowing Hercules, who in *Hercules furens* was depicted as the slayer of his wife and children, to become a god in *Hercules oeteus*. Urged by ser Viviani to discuss the matter in writing, Salutati decided to dedicate his treatise on the subject to his friend's teacher of grammar, Master Giovanni da Siena, with whom ser Viviani had read Seneca.[14]

Of the eight historical tragedies by this author whom Salutati identified as the brother of Seneca, the teacher of Nero, these two, the first and the last of the series, seemed to Salutati obviously fables. To understand fully any poem, Salutati explains, one must interpret it allegorically. While poets delight the ears of the mobs with their stories, those who look deeper find the sweet taste and fragrant smell of the inner meaning. Because these particular tragedies make no pretense at depicting reality, Salutati concludes that they must, therefore, be especially profound in their message (*De lab.*, II, 585–86).

Although the poets embellish their poetry with gods, it should not be thought that they were polytheists. Recognizing that the architect of the universe operated in many different ways on nature and man, the poets gave different names to God metaphorically depending on the variety of functions and the times and places of their operations. Consequently, to grasp the poet's meaning, an etymological analysis of their language is absolutely essential. Just as man is born from the union of man and women, so the poets represented the universe as coming into being through a divine union. That they knowingly spoke of two sides of the

---

mentioned before the *De seculo*, it must have been written first. He assigned the date 1380 for its composition. My position is that it was begun after the *De seculo*, probably in 1382. First of all, there are other works of Salutati given in Villani's list out of order: the eight eclogues are cited before the *Conquestio Phyllidis* although the latter was ready for circulation in 1367 while only the first of the eclogues was polished by early 1372: see appendix I. From Villani's brief reference to the *De laboribus*, moreover, it would seem that he had only heard of the work by 1382. He mentioned it first for stylistic reasons because he wished to end his account of Salutati's writings with the elaborate description of the *De seculo*, which had so impressed him. Psychologically, the *De laboribus* fits better with the period after the fall of the democratic regime in January 1382. His Greek doodling in the register of the *Consulte e Pratiche* of that very month suggests the new turn his mind was taking after the troubles of the past few years. His etymological interests beginning in 1381 with the *De seculo*, consequently, blossomed in a very different context in the years after 1382.

14. *De laboribus Herculis*, ed. Berthold L. Ullman, 2 vols. (Zurich, 1951), II, 585. On the symbol of Hercules on the Florentine seal, see B. L. Ullman, *The Humanism of Coluccio Saluati*, Medioevo e umanesimo, vol. 4 (Padua, 1963), p. 24, n. 1.

same being and not two beings is shown by the common origin of the names for the father of the Gods and his wife: Juppiter and Juno both derive from *iuvando* or *helping* (II, 588–89).

After this introduction he briefly relates the fable of Hercules as it appears in the *Hercules furens*. In analyzing the stories surrounding Hercules, Salutati makes it clear that he is dealing with the exploits of many different men. Derived from the words *heros cleos*, that is, "strong and valiant hero," all great heroes have had that name. Indeed Varro lists forty-three different Hercules. Because it is clearly impossible "ex litterarum monumentis" to tell them apart, Salutati, invoking the precedents of Virgil and other poets, claims the right to treat them all as if they had been one man (II, 591).

At the very outset of his discussion of the allegories involved in this fable Salutati, as he did earlier for Virgil in his letters to Zonarini, implies very strongly that the work of Seneca must be seen in relation to divine forces. At least this is certain insofar as the play's allegorical presentation of the union of the body with the soul is concerned. It is a matter of faith that the human body before infusion of the soul is begotten from the male's seed in the woman's blood and that this takes place in the natural vase of the womb. After divine action, "mediante natura," causes the body to achieve an articulation of all its parts, God creates the soul and pours it into the body so that man possesses his soul while still in the uterus. At birth he emerges as a true human substance. These facts were only known to the human race with divine revelation and Salutati expresses his amazement that Seneca exhibited in the tragedy such knowledge of a process over which the philosophers of antiquity were in total disagreement (II, 592). Although he expressed belief earlier in the friendship between St. Paul and Seneca,[15] he does not rely on this relationship for an explanation here:

> But that God who overcame all the earthly fallacies and diabolical deceptions through the tongues of simple men against the wisdom and power of the world, so that the naked, the ignorant, the few, and the weak miraculously triumphed over the rich, the wise, the many and the powerful by argument, by performing miracles, and by dying subject to all kinds of torture—that God, I say, wished to reveal this truth through this poet of ours (II, 592).

If the poet really knew the truth he spoke, then God should be praised

---

15. *Epist.*, I, 150.

for inspiring him with the spirit of truth. On the other hand, if, as many think, the poet was not conscious of this but his words can be adapted to this purpose, "I give thanks to the infinite wisdom of God which made this truth available in the context of this fable." There is no need to push Salutati to a choice here, although his reference to the "certitude of truth" showing through the fictions suggests he tends to see the poet conscious of the import of his words (II, 592). However, whatever the focus of divine action, whether in the poetic inspiration or the mind of the reader, in the deepest part of the work of a poet like Seneca or Virgil, Salutati suggests, one is in contact with the ultimate source of truth and attains knowledge not discoverable by unaided reason.

That Seneca's work displays at least this divine truth becomes evident for Salutati when he submits the part of the play dealing with the conception of Yphycles and Hercules to an etymological analysis. Alcmena, daughter of Creon, had conceived two children: one to be called Yphycles, fathered by her husband, Amphytrion, and the other, Hercules, whose sire was Juppiter himself. The etymological roots of *Hercules* are various: "heros cleos"—"vir fortis et gloriosus"; "herouncleos"—"fama fortium"; "hera cleos," i.e., "terra cleos"—"gloriosus in terra," etc. Whether Hercules is interpreted as "glory of the earth," "glory of quarrels," "glory of heroes" or "glory of Juno" Salutati feels justified in seeing in the name a symbol for the soul "which is responsible for whatever is truly glorious." Alcmena, daughter of Creon, is the symbol of human flesh: "alce"—"virtus" and "mene"—"defectus." Creon himself symbolizes flesh: "creos"—"caro." Born of the flesh and flesh herself, Alcmena is wed to Amphytrion, i.e., to water, air, and fire because these three elements revolve around the earth: "amphy"—"circum" and "teron"—"volvo"; or "amphy"—"circum" and "trion"—"tres." In this union of Alcmena, flesh or earth is joined to the other three elements and Yphycles or human form is created, i.e., "yphys cleos," "gloria forme," because among all animals the human form is the most glorious. After Yphycles had already been conceived, Juppiter, induced by love for Alcmena or flesh, created Hercules, that is, soul, in the womb of Alcmena where Yphycles lay prepared for the reception of the soul (II, 591).

Patently in this instance the etymologies of the names of the individuals themselves disclose the meaning of the symbols, thus revealing the truths regarding the creation of the soul and its tie with the body. The rest of the first book explaining the allegory of Hercules' marriage to Megara and his subsequent murder of Megara with their three sons and the unfinished second book devoted to the significance of Hercules' fabled descent to the underworld proceed in the same way, with names being analyzed for their original meaning and for the truths which such identifications reveal.

Salutati basically interprets Hercules as the epitome of man "rich with all the endowments of the virtues and able to overcome all the assaults of vice" (II, 633). Referring to the myth of Hercules at the crossroads,[16] he dramatizes the struggle involved in attaining such perfection. "Thus," Salutati writes, "when at the crossroads the body was turned away by the hard and narrow way of virtue, and, with the will restrained amid earthly attractions, it was drawn to the downward way of pleasure on the left, our Hercules, electing virtue, firmly, that is, with his will, shunning that path, conquered the stimulus of the flesh and climbed" (II, 635). Not even the stars could control his actions: "Hercules, the philosopher, seeing an influence proceeding from the heav-

16. Erwin Panofsky, *Hercules am Scheidewege und andere antike Bildstoffe in der neueren Kunst*, Studien der Bibliotek Warburg, vol. 18 (Leipzig-Berlin, 1930), p. 155. Theodore Mommsen, "Petrarch and the Story of the Choice of Hercules," *Medieval and Renaissance Studies*, ed. E. Rice (Ithaca, 1959), pp. 175–96, indicates that Petrarch, not Salutati as Panofsky claimed, was the first to revive the myth of Hercules at the crossroads. For a general discussion of the Hercules motive, see, with Panofsky, B. Gaeta, "L'avventura di Ercole," *Rinascimento*, 5 (1954), 227–60; Marcel Simon, *Hercule et le Christianisme* (Paris, 1955), pp. 169 ff.; and Henri de Lubac, *Exégèse médiévale. Les quatre sens de l'écriture*, II, 2 (Paris, 1964), pp. 222–33, with its rich bibliography. I owe the Mommsen reference to Charles Trinkaus, *In Our Image and Likeness*, 2 vols. (London, 1970), II, 670, but I cannot agree with his position that Salutati did not "endorse the pagan conception but had only stated it." Salutati's analysis of the allegories of the pagan myths was designed to point out their truth content, and my reading of his treatment of the allegory suggests that he approved of what he found revealed there. It is true, as Trinkaus maintains (ibid.) that in the *De seculo et religione* "he sharply attacks what he takes to be the pagan approach to virtue," but in my view the contrast between the two works reflects Salutati's failure to integrate his classical studies and religious interests at this stage of his intellectual development. On Salutati's use of the Hercules myth, see C. Vasoli," L'estetica dell'Umanesimo e del Rinascimento," *Momenti e problemi di storia dell'estetica*, vol. 1 (Milan, 1959), p. 333. For a comparison between Salutati's *De laboribus* and *Los doze trabajos de Hercules* of Enrico de Villena, see M. Morreale, "Coluccio Salutati's *De laboribus Herculis* (1406) and Enrique de Villena's *Los doze Trabajos de Hercules* (1417)," *Studies in Philology*, 51 (1954), 95–106.

Cicero, *De off.*, I, 32, 118, is probably Salutati's prime authority for the episode. He quotes Cicero's words in full in the second edition, *De lab.*, I, 182. Because the section in the second edition includes a reference to St. Basil's account of the same story given in his *De utilitate studii in libros gentilium* (quoted by Panofsky, *Hercules*, p. 53), it would seem that this passage had to be written after Bruni did his translation of Basil sometime between 1400 and May 1403 (see chap. 10, n. 147 below). However, the reference of Basil strikes me as being a later interpolation of Salutati in the context as a whole. After quoting Cicero he writes: "Hec ille. Quod an verum fuerit aliter compertum non habeo. Miror tamen, licet hoc idem testetur maxime autoritatis Basilius, Prodici, quamvis subtilis disputator fuerit, Xenophontisque prudentiam et acumen, qui illiusce etatis tempus eligende vite nobis natura prescriptum dixerit, cum nedum vite elector sed nec moralis doctrine idoneus credatur auditor adolescens, quorum maxime sit passionibus subiacere."

ens, resisting, bore up the sky (whence it is said: 'The wise man dominates the stars'), and he has taught us that the heavens cannot so
threaten mortals that all their pressures cannot be withstood and that,
if we will fight, not concede, we can make the arduous ascent of the
virtues."[17]

In speaking of Aeneas' gold branch as representing the hero's choice
of the steep slope of virtue, Salutati, on Virgil's authority, mentions the
need of some kind of divine intervention in making the right choice (II,
622). But Hercules' decision appears primarily a product of his own will;
unaided, in the face of a series of hostile cosmic forces, he elects the
good, pursues it, and wins the prize of divinity. The same imagery of
the choice at the crossroads occurs in the second edition of the *De laboribus Herculis*, and again Hercules is presented as "of heroic virtue and a
godly man" (I, 182–83). The "pelagian" element in the demigod's moral
triumph, moreover, is similarly emphasized throughout the second version.

Such a heroic presentation of man's moral force aptly reflects Salutati's
own approach to ethical problems in his earlier writings, but lacks relevance for the life of the mature man increasingly given to meditations
on man's weakness and need for divine grace. Salutati, like his Hercules, had his own decision to make at the crossroads. By 1381–82 he
had actually made it, but years were to pass before he would show
himself capable of working out the consequences of the choice for his
thought as a whole. His earlier commitment to a medieval stoic view of
the moral athlete proved remarkably resilient.

Salutati never explained why his first edition dealing with Seneca's
plays about Hercules remained unfinished. Perhaps the work had
reached its present point when news came of Giovanni da Siena's death
in 1383. More likely, however, as he went along, Salutati considered his
discussion of poetic allegory in Seneca's tragedies too narrowly conceived. Evidently by the opening of Book II the author feels he has accomplished what he set out to do: reveal the meaning of Seneca's conception of Hercules. Now he enlarges his offering, promising the reader
an abundance of fruit after a meager repast. He henceforth intends to

---

17. *De lab.*, II, 634. I have been unable to find a passage in the *Almagest* which Ullman
cites in his note to this page as a possible source of the quotation. The Florentine physician Bernardo (see chap. XII, n. 1, below), after citing Ptolemy's *Centiloquium* in his *Questio* (Universitätsbibliotek, Wurzburg, *M. ch. f. 60*, fol. 101ᵛ), writes that Ptolemy "alibi dicit
'sapiens dominabit astris'." On the ancient uses of this theme see Hildebrecht Hommel,
"Per aspera ad astra," *Würzburger Jahrbucher für die Altertumswissenschaft*, 4 (1949), 157–65.

treat "individually" the labors of Hercules, his death, and finally his deification.[18] He probably soon came to realize that he could not simply tack such a large topic onto a discussion of Seneca's two plays about the hero. As it eventually developed, he decided to write a second expanded treatment of poetic allegory beginning with a general consideration of the origin, nature, and purpose of poetry and illustrating its conclusions with an analysis of the many fables surrounding Hercules. Boccaccio furnished him a brilliant model to follow.

In the first thirteen books of his *Genealogia deorum*, completed several years before his death in 1375, Boccaccio had summarized and explicated the allegorical significance of many of the fables surrounding the gods of antiquity. The fourteenth book of the work had been devoted to a general defense of poetry and the fifteenth to a particular defense of his book itself. Enjoying a wide circulation in manuscript in the century and a half after Boccaccio's death, the *Genealogia deorum* was one of the earliest books to be printed. By contrast the enormous second edition of the *De laboribus Herculis* survived the Renaissance in two codices and was only printed in 1951.[19]

The relative neglect of Salutati's work cannot be explained on the grounds that it was more limited in scope and less erudite than that of Boccaccio. Salutati easily matched Boccaccio in scholarship and, if formally tracing the labors of Hercules, Salutati's pursuit of allegories takes him all over the mythological map. To a degree the uncompleted state of Salutati's manuscript discouraged circulation. But more important was that whereas in Boccaccio the fable receives more prominent treatment than the truth concealed therein, for Salutati the truth content is central. Consequently, the majority of readers, who like a good story, find the *De laboribus* too abstract. After providing the barest sketch of the fable's plot, Salutati moves directly to an analysis of the hidden truth. That the method often consists of a painstaking etymological examination of key terms in the story robs the fable of its integrity. Boccaccio, on the other hand, following Petrarch, makes little use of etymological analysis.

In the introduction to the second book of the *De laboribus* Salutati describes the general contents of the whole:

18. *De lab.*, II, 612. Ullman, ibid., p. vii, ties the termination of work to the death of Giovanni da Siena.

19. See Ullman's introduction to the edition for discussion of the manuscripts, ibid., pp. viii-x.

The first book is a disputation on poetics, which remains central throughout all the other books. The second will concern the conception and birth of our subject, Hercules. . . . The third, if God grants that I may reach it, will contain the labors of Hercules. . . . The fourth, if God grants his grace, will unfold the descent to the underworld, the happenings there, the killing of his wife and sons, the interpretation of his marriages, and finally the fire on Mt. Etna, by which our Alcides was consumed and added to the number of gods . . . (I, 76).

Despite its enormous size (the printed text runs to almost six hundred pages), the work remained incomplete. There are numerous cross references and some of the sections referred to were never written. Although Salutati continued to labor at his Hercules until the end of his life, the bulk of the treatise as we have it was probably written between 1382/83 and the mid-1390s. The original plan for the work called for the last three books only, but by 1391 the first book had been added to the project and was probably already written.[20]

At the outset of the treatise Salutati feels compelled to identify the enemies of poetry. These are not only the common people but also modern philosophers who call themselves Aristotelian but know noth-

20. Salutati's original intention had been to preface a study of the labors in three books with a few introductory chapters on the nature of poetry, but as he began to write he realized the extensive nature of the subject made another book necessary (ibid., p. 76). When in 1391 he described the work as eventually to consist of four books (*Epist.*, IV, 253), it seems likely that the first book was roughly in its present state of completion (Ullman, *The Humanism*, p. 25, n. 1). In 1405 Salutati mentioned that only Book II had been completed, but even it was not corrected, while the other three books remained unfinished (*Epist.*, IV, 76). Missing at the time of his death were the following parts of the work: Book I, chap. 14; Book II has no chap. 4; and many subjects supposedly to be treated in Book IV were not written. The letter of February 1, 1405, indicates that he still intended to complete the *De laboribus* "si dederit Deus compleri," but there is no proof that he seriously worked at it thereafter.

Part of Book III had to be written after 1389/90 because there are references in it (pp. 344 and 268 respectively) to Salutati's letter to Giovanni da San Miniato composed about this time (Ullman, *The Humanism*, p. 59, n. 1) and to Salutati's *De verecundia* dated 1390 (see below, chap. 10, n. 99). His use of the *Cratylus* (II, 518) and the *Phaedo* (II, 371 and 515) means that these passages in Books III and IV could not have been written before his interest in Greek began in 1392/93 (see below, chap. 10). He did not have a copy of the Phaedo until at least 1401 (*Epist.*, III, 515). Similarly his allusion to Ptolemy's *Geography* (II, 475) provides a *terminus post quem* of early 1397 for that passage because he apparently derived what information he had about the work from Chrysoloras who only began teaching in the *Studio* in that period: Roberto Weiss, "Gli studi greci di Coluccio Salutati," *Miscellanea in onore di Roberto Cessi*, Storia e letteratura, vols. 71–73 (Rome, 1958), I, 352. Note as well, reference, *De lab.*, II, 475, to the *Anabasis*. For Basil's *De utilitate studii in libros gentilium* translated by Bruni, see chap. 10, n. 147.

ing of Aristotle. Otherwise they would know that the Greek philosopher utilized the poets in his writings. If Plato, moreover, exiled the comic poets, he did not despise the poets as a group. Ignorant of the great philosophers, the moderns devote their attention to reading the writings of the British logicians and delight in sophistic disputation (I, 3–5).[21]

As for the definition of his subject, poetry, Salutati qualifies Aristotle's conception of a poem as "a discourse of criticism or praise" and his notion that poetry utilizes fictions. These are necessary but not sufficient conditions for a poem. Orators and philosophers as well as poets occasionally resort to such discourse and utilize fictions in their work. Rather the distinguishing element of poetry is the "song" or the "metric melody"; indeed, "the poets bind all things with verses and seduce their auditors with a twofold delectation hardly comprehended." Not only is the melody of poetry sweeter than that of prose but to it belong all manner of figures: "This marvelous harmonious alteration of words, things and deeds" (I, 10). Consequently, Salutati concludes that poetry is "a power regarding praise and blame insofar as these are celebrated harmoniously in meter and figurative speech."[22]

Throughout his life Salutati insisted on the ethical value of poetry. Like history it constituted an area of study that had special power to persuade for good and against evil. With the defenders of poetry in the Middle Ages Salutati could not address himself to the problem of justifying poetry on aesthetic grounds. Also like them he tended to view poetry as a technique rather than an art as later ages understood it. Yet, especially in the *De laboribus Herculis* Salutati occasionally surrenders— as briefly in the quotation above—to the impulse to emphasize the sensual pleasure afforded by poetry, thus foreshadowing the aesthetic approach taken by late Renaissance criticism.

Despite the care with which he sets out the definition of poetry, it fits

21. Unfortunately for modern-day scholars, Salutati does not supply the names of these "Britannici". They are probably the same criticized by Bruni in his *Dialogi ad Petrum Istrum, Prosatori latini del Quattrocento*, ed. Eugenio Garin, La letteratura italiana, Storia e testi, vol. 13 (Milan-Naples, 1952), pp. 58, 60. Bruni has Niccoli attack the dialectic of the "barbarians" who live across the ocean: "Quorum etiam nomina perhorresco: Feribrigge, Buser, Occam, aliique eiusmodi, qui omnes mihi videntur a Rhadamantis cohorte traxisse cognomina." See Garin's "La cultura fiorentina nella seconda metà del 300 e i 'barbari Britanni,'" in *L'Età nuova* (Naples, 1969), 141–77; and Cesare Vasoli, "Intorno al Petrarca ed ai logici moderni," *Miscellanea mediaevalia: Antiqui und Moderni*, ed. Albert Zimmermann, vol. 9 (Berlin-New York, 1974), pp. 142–54.

22. *De lab.*, I, 14. Salutati concedes, however, that the praise or blame may not be explicit in the poem and that interpretation may be necessary to understand the work in this light (ibid., I, 69).

awkwardly with his actual discussion of poetic allegories. In origin, he writes, poetry arose intimately connected with theology. It began "with the true worship of God" after the birth of Enos, son of Seth and grandson of Adam in the two hundred thirty-fifth year after the creation of the world (I, 16 and 81–82). Nimrod was the first to command the worship of idols, and these ceremonies were celebrated in song. In time poets like Museus, Orpheus, and Linus came not only to sing of the gods but also to discuss their nature and status and those of men (I, 9).[23] Consequently, poetry deals with the whole realm of knowledge, human and divine.

The ancient pagans who made gods of men, utilized poetry to seduce the primitive minds of the people to embrace their worship (I, 7). Thus, the human nature and evil deeds of these deified men were concealed under a veil of fiction. But the use of fictions is not limited to the worshippers of false gods. Wise men who believe in the true God utilize these devices to communicate truth to the common people. But more than this, even when treating theological questions among themselves, they are forced to speak in figures, so greatly does the majesty of the ineffable God transcend our sense and intellect. For this reason the Bible includes manifold allegories (I, 15–16).

Aware of the need to differentiate the poetry of the Bible from the poetry of ancient pagan poets, Salutati distinguishes Scripture from pagan poetry with regard to the time period to which the poetic statements refer. Scripture frequently employs allegories to signify events to come as when Christ's sacrifice was prefigured in the voluntary immolation of Isaac by Abraham. The poets, on the other hand, use their allegories to signify past events. The fictitious prophecy of Anchises on the future greatness of the posterity of Aeneas was already accomplished from Virgil's point in time (I, 13–14). Oddly, he seems to have been unaware of the contradiction between this description of poetic prophecy and his defense both in this treatise and earlier in the letters to Zonarini of Virgil's poetry as predicting the coming of Christ.

23. On the poet as theologian before Salutati's generation, see Ernst R. Curtius, *European Literature*, pp. 214–27; August Buck, *Italienische Dichtungslehren vom Mittelalter bis zum Ausgang der Renaissance*, Beihefte zur Zeitschrift für Romanische Philologie, 94 (1952), pp. 67–86; Charles Trinkaus, *In Our Image and Likeness*, 2 vols. (London, 1970), II, 697–704; and my "Coluccio Salutati and the Conception of the *Poeta Theologus* in the Fourteenth Century," *Renaissance Quarterly*, 30 (1977), 538–46. Ullman provides the references for statements on the origin of poetry, I, 9 and 81. Salutati's basis for placing the birth of Seth 235 years after the creation is Gen. 4:26; and 5:3–6. For Nimrod Salutati specifically refers to Peter Comestor (*Hist. Schol. Gen.* 37 [PL 198, 1088]); for Museus, Orpheus, and Linus to Augustine, *De civ. Dei*, XVIII, 14.

Later in the same book he provides a much clearer formulation of the difference. There he maintains that in sacred Scripture not only is the inner layer of a poem true but also the outward cover as well. In the poetry of the Gentiles the exterior may contain falsehood. But lest one think that the inner meaning of secular poetry is always true, he adds quickly, "or at least it [the inner meaning] is considered as true by all nations or by some heretical group of philosophers or some nation of people." To avoid any ambiguity on this point he concludes that "even in the hidden sense one does not look for exquisite and absolutely certain truth [in the poets]."[24]

Having defined poetry, discussed its origin and explained why it is accepted by those who worship God or the gods, Salutati proceeds to discuss poetry as a synthesis of all the arts. A large place in the discussion is devoted to poetry as reflecting the earthly and celestial harmony and the relationship between this art and arithmetic—Salutati refers to the latter as arith*metrica* (I, 22–23). Relying on Boethius and Macrobius, the author attempts to explain mathematically why meter, and the hexameter in particular, has such a delightful effect on the ear (I, 23 ff). After an extremely complicated explanation he readily admits that some may criticize him for ascribing to the poets ideas of proportion of which they never dreamed (I, 34). While confessing himself unable to affirm or deny that the poets were really conscious of these principles, he nevertheless concedes that they probably developed their inventions of feet and meters by ear, and only subsequently began to analyze their discoveries. Experience makes art. Perfection is the result of experience. Aristotle (*Meta.* I, 2, 982b) traces the same kind of progress in philosophy. If such evolutions were not always underway, Salutati argues, life would be "too boring": "For the arts grow with successive and continuous additions and daily we entertain new conceptions about many things which the ancients not only could have missed but did in fact miss." This clear exposition of a doctrine of progress in the arts is without parallel in any other writing by Salutati.[25]

The thesis of the first book, that poetry is the supreme art and—by implication—superior to prose was part of the intellectual baggage inherited from the Middle Ages via his Bolognese schooling. Resting on

24. Ibid., I, 70. Cf. I, 87.
25. *De lab.*, I, 35: "Nimis etenim arida foret cuiuslibet artis speculatio si que ex arte dicta sunt adeo simpliciter posteritas recepisset quod nichil in eis duceret speculandum nisi quod inventores ipsi potuerint vel voluerint declarare. Adoleverunt equidem artes successivis et continuis incrementis, et novis in dies considerationibus multa sunt deprehensa que priscos illos nedum latere potuerunt sed sine dubio latuerunt." See chap. 9.

knowledge of the *quadrivium* and *trivium* as well as on philosophy and theology, it represents for Salutati the pinnacle of wisdom. Not only in the *De laboribus Herculis* but also in his correspondence the poet like the orator is said to have to know all things human and divine.[26] Yet these extravagant praises of poetry should be balanced with his unequivocal affirmations that prose is superior to poetry as a form of expression. While feeling compelled in 1379 to justify this position in some detail, in two letters written in the last year of his life it is stated as unquestioned truth.[27] Apparently we are confronted with two lines of thought never reconciled in his own mind: the first favoring poetry reflecting the medieval grammarian's prejudice—and the second preferring prose, an original contribution of Salutati and a fundamental tenet of Florentine humanism in the first half of the fifteenth century.

Beginning with the second book, except for occasional digressions, the rest of the *De laboribus Herculis* is one long allegory. The basic assumption behind the investigation is that generally poetic fictions contain truth either about God or created beings. In the latter case the truth regards either the nature, the effects, or the activities of these beings (I, 86). The task of the interpreter is to break the code of the poets, primarily by deciphering the allegories through an etymological analysis of the proper names involved in the fables.

At least as far as the poets were concerned, a variety of interpretations was possible.[28] Petrarch (*Seniles* IV, 5) had already expressed his belief in

26. As he writes, poetry begins "post omnes artes et ipsam artem artium, philosophiam et theologiam" (ibid., I, 20). He justifies his belief that the poet must know all things (*Epist.*, III, 493, and IV, 202; and *De lab.*, I, 18) with Cicero's *De orat.*, I, 16, 70: "Est enim finitimus oratori poeta, numeris astrictior paulo, verborum autem licentia liberior, multis vero ornandi generibus socius, ac paene par; in hoc quidem certe prope idem, nullis ut terminis circumscribat aut definiat ius suum, quo minus ei liceat eadem illa facultate et copia vagari, qua velit." Poetry's comprehensive nature makes it the supreme art: "Et ne credas ipsam utpote pauperem solum quod efficiat ab aliis mutuari, addit super omnia, quod sibi proprium est, delectationem commutationis et carminis, que quanta sit non potest facile iudicari" (p. 22). On the superiority of poetry to other disciplines, see J. R. O'Donnell, "Coluccio Salutati on the Poet Teacher," *Mediaeval Studies*, 22 (1960), 240–56.

27. In 1379 (*Epist.*, I, 338) he compares poetry to a river and prose to a sea. Riccardo Fubini cites this passage in his important review of Berthold Ullman's *The Humanism of Coluccio Salutati* in the *Rivista storica italiana*, 77 (1965), 969. For restatement of this same position in 1405–6, see *Epist.*, IV, 143 and 167.

28. This view goes back at least to Augustine, who in interpreting allegorically a scriptural passage, Gen. 1:1 writes *Conf.*, XIII, 24, 37: "In hac enim benedictione concessam nobis ante facultatem ac potestatem accipio et multis modis enuntiare, quod uno modo intellectum tenuerimus, et multis modis intellegere, quod obscure uno modo enuntiatum legerimus . . . ": cited by F. Edward Cranz, "Some Changing Historical Contexts of Allegory," lecture given at the New England Renaissance Conference, 1966, pp. 15–16. Nancy Streuver, *The Language of History in the Renaissance* (Princeton, 1970), p. 89, is somewhat

the legitimacy of a wide range of interpretations of a poetic text provided they corresponded to the literal sense of the lines. Salutati's position was much more fully developed. For him the myths belong to all.
They were left to posterity and "who would dare affirm that whoever it
was who once expounded their meaning denied others the right and
ability to interpret them?" Fulgentius among others gave his interpretations of the poets after Anaximander, Xenophanes, and Pisander had
already done so. The Church Fathers also took advantage of their right
to expound the pagan myths. If Salutati's own understanding of a fable
differs from that of his predecessors, the two positions should be judged
on their merits (I, 45–47). He even concedes that at certain points in this
very work he has given different interpretations of the same passage.
He good-naturedly invites the reader to consider the differing interpretations offered and pick the one he likes the best (II, 548–49 and 578).

There are two ways to test the accuracy of an interpretation. If the
etymologies of the proper names used in the verses support the commentator's conclusion, then "without question" the true meaning of the
author has been elicited. On the other hand, even if the proper names
do not lend themselves to the interpretation and if it seems clear that
the author never considered referring his verses to God or creatures,
nonetheless, the interpreter who makes such an application can be sure
that he has found "a far more appropriate meaning (*longe commodiorem
sensum*) than the author intended" (I, 86).

But lest this second approach suggest an arbitrary judgment on the
part of the poem's critic, Salutati adds immediately: "One should not
wonder at this. Indeed many mortals plan something for one purpose
which God, the director of creation, prepares for another." His illustration is the selling of Joseph into Egypt, which prefigures the betrayal of
Christ by Judas. Salutati's conclusion is fundamental to his methodology
of interpretation:

> The former type of poetry in Scripture, since it has as its author the
> Holy Spirit, is ordained to an infinity of meanings, nor is a truth con-
> gruent to the letter able to be conceived which was not from the be-
> ginning intended by the infinite spirit from whose throne that truth
> proceeds. The latter sort of poetry [secular poetry], however, insofar
> as it is a human invention, is so ordered to the meaning of the author

misleading when she suggests that Salutati is doing something new in interpreting the
Bible: the "interpretation of Biblical figure is no longer a matter of conforming to a single
primordial truth but an exercise of linguistic responsibility."

that sometimes it is related by God, the author of all things, to something other than what man thinks and sometimes it means only what
the man wished to express (I, 86–87).

The Holy Spirit, therefore, saw and intended all the possible "true" interpretations of Scripture, whereas the ancient poets because of some
sort of divine intervention, might express truth far greater than they
realized.

In those cases where ancient poetry contained presentiments of
Christian Revelation, the modern commentator does more than simply
impose a "far more appropriate" meaning on the verses of the poet.
Salutati's words are suggestive: "And if perchance he [Virgil] is said to
have prophesied something true, as many believe, this was not the intention of Maro but of God revealing his mysteries even through the
Gentiles and of the power of truth coming forth even out of lie" (I, 14).
If the pagans through their writings articulated divine truths—and
there is no reason to doubt that Salutati was among the "many" who
adhered to this conception—they did so unconsciously and under divine inspiration.

Returning to this matter in the second chapter of Book II, Salutati
gives several examples of prophecy from Virgil already used in his controversy with Zonarini in 1378–79. If understood "piously" the verses,
"Nate, mee vires, mea magna potentia, solus, nate, patris summi qui
tela Typhoea temnis" (Aen., I, 668–69), refer to the unity of essence and
multiplicity of persons in God. Without revelation of the divine mysteries, poets like Virgil in an attempt to extol their own false gods said
many things really fitting the true God. Similarly other verses like Ecl.,
VIII, 73–75 and Aen., I, 229–30 reveal divine mysteries unbeknownst to
their human author. According to Salutati, an attentive analysis of the
works of the poets would show that they were secretly monotheists
and that the multitude of gods which people their works were merely
names for the multiform powers, acts, and effects of the same divine
being. Nevertheless, Salutati is not inclined to grant them understanding of the truths they uttered regarding the essence of this one God (I,
82–84).

After a long discussion in the rest of Book II and in Book III of natural
and ethical truths found in ancient poetry, Salutati opens Book IV with
a consideration of the ancients' attitude toward the existence of hell.
Although to his knowledge Scripture never specifically speaks of the
eternity of souls, this truth can be inferred from various passages. The

patriarch Jacob, for instance, laments the descent of his son to hell, and, if souls did not live after death, his words would be empty. The existence of hell as a place of punishment was accepted, moreover, by the poets and thus poetry revealed a truth philosophy could not. How did the poets know this? They came to this truth not simply inspired by a certain divine spirit but, more precisely, by the inspiration of the divine will and the pure and immaculate truth. Were they really conscious of having found this truth or was it simply a poetic device for them? In Salutati's opinion they spoke of hell as of a true place, but they used the conception for their own purposes (II, 457–62).

Any attempt to be precise about Salutati's conception of the origin of the truth contained in poetry would falsify what was a very confused and fragmented attitude. There is no problem for ethical and natural truths: these were the product of human reason in which all men share. As for the theological truths, however, there can be no doubt that Salutati believed the poets were sometimes directly inspired by God, who drove them to express ideas they did not really understand. The modern commentator on the poets, he maintains, enjoys a wide range of freedom in developing his interpretation of the allegories but in certain instances he appears to be engaged in ferreting out of the fictions divine mysteries which God himself placed there. Sitting down to read a text of poetry, the intelligent reader has an expectation of encountering divine truth. Appropriately, therefore, Salutati refers to the student of poetry as "the mystic interpreter" (I, 86). While only a few passages in all of ancient poetry appeared divinely inspired because of their prophetic nature, nonetheless the belief that at some point ancient poetry bridged the gulf between natural and supranatural truth exercised a pervasive effect on Salutati's attitude toward ancient literature in general, causing him to assume a continuity between pagan and Christian culture.

The first part of the following chapter deals at length with Salutati's contribution to the history of textual criticism. Unquestionably the example of Petrarch was an important factor in arousing Salutati's interest in improving the textual tradition of ancient Latin authors. But as the foregoing discussion shows, at least in the case of poetry, by 1382 his concern for establishing the text in its integrity was also related to a belief in the value of the etymological treatment of allegories. Such an approach required both the correct word and proper spelling of the word in order to reveal the poets' meaning. At the most profound level, to penetrate the mystery of poetic allegory was to grasp the truth as the Holy Spirit inspired it in the poets.

CHAPTER 9. COMMUNION WITH THE PAST

Between 1382 and 1396 Salutati's philological and historical researches proceeded in the spirit of exuberant faith in humanism reflected in the *De laboribus Herculis*, most of which was written in these years. From the early 1380s, as his scholarly abilities developed, he demonstrated a new critical approach to ancient literature and history.[1] Paradoxically, most of Salutati's greatest achievements in scholarship came after 1396 when religious scruples beset his interests in ancient learning, bringing into question the value of the whole scholarly enterprise. In order to present Salutati's contribution to philological and historical scholarship more comprehensively, therefore, this chapter considers his work in these areas not merely in the fourteen years after 1382 but throughout his mature life. Later chapters will relate to his biography the humanist's changing views described here.

As a philologist and historian Salutati's primary concern was to understand ancient Roman culture and the relationship of his own age to it. To do this he relied upon manuscripts of the ancient authors, manuscripts he knew to be in an advanced state of corruption. To complain about the errors of the worthless scribes was traditional. Early in the thirteenth century the Bolognese rhetorician Boncompagno da Signa lamented the vices of their tribe.[2] Salutati's own statement of the predicament was darkly pessimistic: "Extensively . . . and everywhere all things are corrupted."[3] When only decades after their deaths, manuscripts containing the writings of Petrarch or Boccaccio were replete with corruptions, one could scarcely imagine how many have crept into the texts of the ancients.[4]

---

1. The first remark of Salutati regarding possible corruptions in a text actually comes in 1377 when, attempting to define a "cubit," he refers to Boethius' *Geometria*: "Qui textus fuit Boetii in Geometria, apud quem etiam non declaratur quid sit cubitus, sive scriptorum errore fuerit dimissum, sive ipse idem tanquam rem notissimam tacuerit" (*Epist.*, I, 257).

2. Boncompagno da Signa, "De artificiosa ordinatione dictionum," in his *Boncompagnus*, cited in Pio Rajna, "Per il cursus medievale e per Dante," *Studi di filologia italiana*, 3 (1932), 84.

3. This phrase forms part of the statement by Salutati summarized in the following paragraph. It is found in the *De fato et fortuna*, B.A.V., *Urb. lat.* 1184, Tr. II, 6, fol. 19–19ᵛ. For this manuscript, see chap. 11, n. 18. The passage is published in full in Berthold L. Ullman, *The Humanism of Coluccio Salutati*, Medioevo e umanesimo, vol. 4 (1963), pp. 100–101.

4. *Epist.*, III, 373, quoted by Ullman, *The Humanism*, p. 104.

Unlike his predecessors, Salutati did not limit guilt for these errors to the scribes, though surely, he maintained, the scribes are the chief of-fenders. Sometimes their minds wander and they omit parts of the text. Other times in their ignorance they change passages they do not understand or copy, as part of the text, marginal notes made by readers. But less ignorant men who read the copies also deserve some blame. Unable to understand a difficult passage, these men often jump to the conclusion that the scribe has erred. Some even make the author responsible for what seems to be a confusing passage. Consequently, they add or erase a letter, a syllable, even words, thus altering and perverting the meaning. There are others who, sensing a need to have authority to support their opinions, change a text for their own purposes. None can know how much the heretics emended Origen to serve their cause. In his own day, Salutati observes, scholars make indefensible corrections in their texts while schoolmasters order their students to erase and emend sound passages, therefore corrupting parts of the manuscripts they are currently studying.

On the whole, ignorance, not maliciousness, plays the major role in the progressive corruption of ancient writings in Salutati's view. Nor, as we shall see, does he believe these bad practices are limited to the modern age. The Romans were guilty of similar negligence and stupidity, and some corruptions go back to the ancient texts. Although stated generically, such a grasp of the genesis of corruptions clearly was of aid in his actual work in textual criticism. An understanding of how an error can occur could lead to establishing the original reading.

Salutati's ideal solution to the problem of bad manuscripts was to have copies of the works of all the ancient authors placed in public libraries and to appoint scholars to collate and edit proper texts.[5] This had been the custom in antiquity when a scholar like Callipius was entrusted with the edition of Terence's writings. However, he regarded it unlikely that such a plan could succeed because there were few scholars competent to undertake such assignments in his own day. As it was, an individual scholar was oppressed by innumerable errors in the texts and, even if he revised his own manuscripts, their limited circulation had minimal effect on the textual tradition of a particular author.

To reduce the chance of errors in manuscripts for his own library, Sa-lutati preferred an exemplar made directly on parchment rather than on paper for later transcription onto parchment. The second writing

5. *De fato*, fols. 19ᵛ–20.

only compounded the chances of corruption. Nevertheless, he was limited by circumstance. A scribe skilled enough to work accurately with expensive parchment was often hard to find. Salutati was lucky to be able to have gotten a parchment copy of Petrarch's *De viris illustribus*. But, rather than wait years for a manuscript, he was sometimes forced to take a paper copy. This apparently occurred in the case of two manuscripts of Cicero's letters (B.L.F., XLIX, 7 and 18) copied for Salutati through the kind offices of Pasquino de'Capelli. There is no indication that Salutati ever had parchment copies made from these heavily annotated paper ones.[6]

An examination of the 112 manuscripts identified as forming part of Salutati's library indicates that he made no consistent effort to emend all his books.[7] If he did extensive collation of works like the B.M.L. *Add.*, 11987 (Seneca *Trag.*) and the B.A.V., *Ottob. lat.*, 1829 (Catullus),[8] in other manuscripts his collations were limited to the first pages of a work: see, for example, B.A.V., *Vat. lat.*, 1928 (Valerius Maximus, fols. 1–7) and B.L.F., *Laur.*, XXX, 21 (Pomponius Mela, fols. 1–2). In the case of rare works where collation was impossible, like the *Laur.*, XXXVI, 49 (Propertius) and the *Laur.*, XLIX, 7 (Cicero, *Ad familiares*), he emended according to the sense of the passage.[9] He was able to collate partially *Laur.*, XLIX, 18 (Cicero, *Ad Atticum*) with the manuscript of sixty letters he had received from Broaspini, itself based on Petrarch's copy of the Verona manuscript.[10] On the other hand, many manuscripts bearing his pressmark have neither notes or variants in his hand. Because only about twenty percent or less of his library is known, some of these might be second copies left uncorrected.[11]

6. Described by Ullman, *The Humanism*, pp. 146–47.

7. Ullman, ibid., lists 111 manuscripts to which R. W. Hunt adds Bodleian MS *Auct.*, T I 27 (Books VII-XV of Pliny's *Nat. hist.*—B.N.P., *Lat.* 6798, contains Books XVI-XXXVII): "A Manuscript from the Library of Coluccio Salutati," in *Calligraphy and Paleography: Essays presented to Alfred Fairbank*, ed. A. S. Osley (London, 1965), pp. 75–79.

8. Both of these manuscripts have variants throughout in Salutati's hand which require collation with another text.

9. On Propertius, see Alice Catherine Ferguson, *The Manuscripts of Propertius* (Chicago, 1934), p. 39. Also see above, chap. 7. On Cicero's *Fam.*, see Ullman, *The Humanism*, p. 146, and the bibliography given.

10. Extensive marginal notations written in Salutati's hand but characteristic of Petrarch's style suggest that Salutati had at his disposition a copy of Petrarch's manuscript or a portion of it. He must have known another manuscript because on fol. 58, at end of the letter, he writes: "Hic deficit complementum et al' magna epistola." Most probably he was collating here with Broaspini's collection based on Petrarch's own manuscript (see above, chap. 7). Omitting several hundred lines, Salutati's text broke off I, 18, 1, at *descendimus* and went on without a break to I, 19, 11, *qualem esse*.

11. Note, for example, B.N.F., *Magl.*, XXIX, 199, fol. 41, at end of slip inserted by Sa-

With Salutati as with no other thinker of the century the modern reader observes a mind grappling with the problems of scholarship involved in establishing the genuine reading of the sources. Petrarch, the artist, hiding the wheels, never burdened his letters and treatises with references to the mechanics of scholarship. Until very recent times indeed philologists believed Petrarch's textual emendations were largely based on what he took to be the apparent sense of the passage involved.[12] Although Petrarch's skillful efforts in the area of textual criticism perhaps surpassed those of Salutati, the fact remains that the latter was the first to write about his techniques.[13] Furthermore, his written comments were doubtless paralleled by an even more extensive oral teaching to his many young followers like Loschi, Vergerio, Bruni, and Poggio, men who figured among the leaders in this discipline in the next generation.

Although he never had time to write his *De gloria* in which he intended to consider the whole problem of textual criticism at length,[14] the *De laboribus* furnishes a rich profusion of observations on emendations made in the process of interpreting specific passages in ancient writers. While many of these concern poetic texts, a number of his re-

---

lutati: "Videatur alius textus quia iste corruptus est." Cited by Ullman, *The Humanism*, p. 223.

12. G. Voigt, *Die Wiederbelebung des classischen Altertums oder das erste Jahrhundert des Humanismus*, 2 vols. (Berlin, 1893), II, 382; Pierre de Nolhac, *Petrarque et l'humanisme*, 2 vols. (Paris, 1907), I, 248, and II, 22, n. 3, and 71–72. See also A. Casacci, "Per la critica del testo nella prima metà del Quattrocento," *Reale Istituto lombardo di scienze e lettere*, Rendiconti, 59 (1926), 94–96. Giuseppe Billanovich was the leader in this revision. See his "Petrarch and the Textual Tradition of Livy," *Journal of the Warburg and Courtauld Institutes*, 14 (1951), 137–208; "Un nuovo esempio delle scoperte e delle letture del Petrarca: l'Eusebio-Girolamo-PseudoProspero,'" *Schriften und Vorträge des Petrarca-Instituts*, 3 (Cologne, 1954); and "La bibliothèque de Petrarque et les bibliothèques médiévales de France et de la Flandre," *L'Humanisme médiévale dans les littératures romanes du XIIᵉ au XIVᵉ siècle*," *Actes et colloques*, vol. 3 (Paris, 1964), pp. 205–14. E. J. Kenney, "The Character of Humanist Philology," *Classical Influences in European Culture*, A.D. 500–1500, ed. R. R. Bolgar (Cambridge, 1971), p. 122, grudgingly admits Petrarch's pioneering use of conjecture in emending texts.

13. Novati, *Epist.*, IV, 86, n. 3, called Salutati the first true restorer of textual criticism. Even with Billanovitch's research Ullman still substantially echoes Novati's opinion (*The Humanism*, pp. 105–6). But see Sesto Prete, *Observations on the History of Textual Criticism in the Medieval and Renaissance Periods* (Collegeville, 1970), p. 18.

14. *De laboribus Herculis*, ed. Berthold L. Ullman, 2 vols. (Zurich, 1951), I, 281–82: "Vellem, et est impetus, ista conqueri et nostram ab hac invidia iustis rationibus etatem excusare [originating the textual errors]. Sed alibi dabitur aptior locus, si deus dederit, sicut mens est, tractatum explicare de gloria, in quo scribendi preter epistolas soluto sermone laborem sive, ut rectius loquar, exercitium intendimus terminare." When Salutati says in Bruni's *Ad Petrum Paulum Histrum dialogus*, *Prosatori latini del Quattroncento*, ed. Eugenio Garin, La letteratura italiana, Storia e testi, vol. 13 (Milan, 1952), p. 74, that he wants to write in praise of Dante, Petrarch, and Boccaccio in another place, is this also a reference to the *De gloria*? Cf. L. Mehus, *Historia litteraria florentina*, ed. E. Kessler (Munich, 1968), p. ccxxviii.

marks are relevant for prose writings as well. Together with brief observations scattered through Salutati's other writings, the *De laboribus* gives
a good picture of Salutati's procedures.

When conflicting readings occur, Salutati prefers to rely on the oldest
codices. The distinction between *antiqui* and *novi* plays a central role in
his methodology.[15] At the same time, he is not surprised to find even
the very oldest codices (*antiquissimi*) corrupted. A case in point is a passage of the *Thebiad* in which Theseus is addressed as the murderer of
Busiris, a deed usually attributed to Hercules: "Non trucibus monstris
Busirim infandumque dedisti/Certione, et sevum velles Chyrona crematum" (XII, 576–77).[16] "Modern" codices show a great variety of readings of this passage. Most give "Busirim" but others have "Sinim," "Si-
nonem," and "Scinin," the reading Salutati later establishes as the correct
one. But even the oldest codices have a similar variety, and Lactantius
in his third-century commentary on Statius discusses the cruelty of
"Busirim" in his analysis of the passage. Obviously the error is one of
long standing. A similar variety of readings for "Certiona" and "Chy-
ron" are also found in the oldest books.

Even an outstanding ancient grammarian like Priscian was not above
lending his authority to readings which were in fact corrupted.[17] Confronted with *Aen.*, XII, 709, which in his codex read "Inter se coiisse
viros et decernere ferro," Priscian felt obliged to explain the extra syllable in the line. Priscian's suggestion was that in the ancient fashion
"viros" should be read "vir." Centuries earlier, however, citing the same
passage in his correspondence, Seneca gave the reading "cernere" not
"decernere." Here Salutati felt justified in following his rule of thumb
giving preference to the older codex. Salutati wrote in the margins of
his Priscian manuscript at this passage: "Priscian and others say 'decernere.' I think the more ancient one is the right one."[18]

---

15. See for example, *De lab.*, I, 301 and 366, and *Epist.*, III, 590. On this distinction in
the Middle Ages, see below, n. 35.

16. *De lab.*, I, 281. The Oxford edition by H. W. Garrod, 4th ed. (Oxford, 1965), gives
for these lines: "Non trucibus monstris sinin infandumque dedisti Cercyona et saevum
velles scirona crematum."

17. *De fato*, Tr. II, 6, fol. 20–20ᵛ: "Moror autem hoc crimen modernitati multos ascribere
cum inter Senece Priscianique comparerim tempora taliter Virgilium esse corruptum quod
hic ultimus talis et tantus autor alleget maroneum illum versiculum: 'Inter se coiisse viros
et decernere ferro,' volens antiquorum more quod ex illa dictione 'viros' due postreme
littere detrahantur, quo versus mensuretur legitimorum pedum debita ratione; cum tamen Seneca doceat non 'decernere' scribendum esse sed 'cernere': quod si fiat, versus illa
nulla detractione penitus indigebit."

18. B.L.F., *Ed.* 161, fol. 76: "Priscianus alii et decernere dicunt. Hunc tamen antiquiori
standum puto." The Virgil passage is cited in Sen., *Epist. ad. Lucil.*, VI, 6 (58).

The textual critic, however, should be cautious in making an emendation for fear of adding new errors to the tradition. Certain codices of Ovid's *Metamorphoses*, I, 154–55, read as follows: "Omnipotens genitor misso perfregit Olympum/fulmine et excussit subiectum Pelion Osse." Others have the reading "subiecto" rather than "subiectum," a reading suggesting at first glance that Pelion was imposed on Ossa. In this case, not only does this reading contradict the other but it also contradicts Virgil's *Eclogues*, I, 281–82: " . . . imponere Pelio Ossan scilicet, atque Osse frondosum involvere Olympum." Yet in fact this comparison does not mean that the "subiecto" reading is a corruption. If that version with "Osse subiecto" (Ossa lying under) is construed sympathetically, it relates "lying under" not to Pelion but rather to Olympus, a meaning which concords with Virgil's remark.[19] Apparently Salutati would have considered a clear contradiction with Virgil or an internal awkwardness in the imagery sufficient grounds for rejecting one reading of Ovid for another. Without this he refused to choose. The conflicting emendations of this Ovid verse by scholars down to the present bear witness to Salutati's wisdom.

The humanist frequently resorted to this practice of comparing relevant passages from other authors in an effort to establish a good reading and did so often with more positive results, at least in his own judgment. Such a comparison was essential where the reading in a single codex was in question and no collation was possible. Salutati suspected an error in the spelling of "Mariandrini" found in his one copy of Pliny's *Nat. Hist.* VI, 4—apparently the only codex available to him at the time—because it contradicted the name "Mariandyni" given by Pomponius Mela to this ancient people settled on the shores of the Euxine Sea.[20] Even the codices of Mela gave various readings. When, however, Ptolemy and Xenophon corroborated the spelling "Mariandyni," he confidently corrected the name in his Pliny codex.

In manuscripts of both prose and poetry, moreover, Salutati urged the importance of paying close attention to the possibility of insertions or alterations in the text. One of his major arguments for "Stimphalon"

---

19. *De lab.*, II, 401–2.
20. Ibid., p. 475. For variant spelling in Mela, see B.L.F., XXX, 21, fol. 9ᵛ: "In eo primum Myriandinaci urbem habitant." Although the *Summary Catalogue* of the Bodleian describes MS. *Auct.* T. 1. 27 as beginning with chapter 6 of Pliny, it begins in fact with chapter 7, and thus the spelling in Salutati's Pliny could not be checked. This information was furnished me by Cornelia Davis of the Bodleian in response to my request for a microfilm of the manuscript.

rather than "Stiphalion," as the correct spelling for the Stymphalian birds in Statius' *Thebiad*, IV, 297–98, centered on his observation of erasures of m and insertions of *i* in texts containing the second spelling.[21] Later in the *De laboribus* he also took issue with Boccaccio, this time unjustifiably, about his interpretation of a sentence in Cicero's *De natura deorum*, III, 44.[22] Unable to find in his codices of this work—note he owned several—a crucial word quoted by Boccaccio as in this passage of the text, Salutati maintained that it was in interpolation in Boccaccio's manuscript.

Certainly one of the major causes of textual errors stemmed from the failure of previous generations to learn Greek. Because the Latin Church Fathers were usually ignorant of the language, their efforts to transliterate a word from Greek into Latin could result in confusion.[23] Salutati looked to the reintroduction of knowledge of Greek in his own day as ultimately beneficial to textual emendation. While he never learned much of the language himself, the last book of the *De laboribus* indicates that perhaps in his final years the diffusion of Greek was having some effect even on the old man.[24] Most ancient codices of Virgil's *Georgics*, IV, 467–69, have the reading, "Tenarias etiam fauces, alta hostia Ditis/et caligantem nigra formidine lucum/ingressus, Manesque adiit. . . ." Especially in modern codices, Salutati writes, he finds *Tenarias* written as *Trenarus* on the false assumption that the word sounds like the Greek word for lamentations. This makes it a fitting appellation for the lower regions to which the word was applied. Obviously Salutati has the following passage of Papias' *Vocabularium* in mind here: "Trenarus mons laconiae: ubi descensus est ad inferos θρῆνος enim graece lamentatio." But, Salutati remarks, the Greek word θρῆνος is pronounced not *Trenos* but

21. *Ibid.*, I, 229–30 and 232. Also *ibid.*, II, 397. In the latter he is attempting to decide which reading is preferable for Ovid, *Meta.*, V, 329. Whereas some codices often contain the phrase "Delius in corvo est," the older codices give the reading "Delius in cervo est." He opts for the older reading but feels called on to explain the source for the error. The close association of the crow with Apollo, he believes, caused either a scribe or a teacher to alter the text of Ovid by writing "corvus" instead of "cervus."

22. *De lab.*, II, 479.

23. *Ibid.*, p. 552.

24. *Ibid.*, pp. 473–74. He gathered his knowledge on Greek pronunciation either by letter or orally from Chrysoloras. See his request for information on pronunciation (*Epist.*, IV, 269–71). Shortly after Chrysoloras' arrival Salutati wrote him requesting an analysis of Greek breathing and the proper method of pronouncing aspirated syllables. Chrysoloras graciously responded by preparing a short treatise dealing with these problems. Doubtless with the help of others Salutati did an interlinear Latin version. See Roberto Weiss, "Gli studi greci di Coluccio Salutati," in *Miscellanea in onore di Roberto Cessi*, Storia e letteratura, vols. 71–73 (Rome, 1958), I, 353.

rather *Thrinos*.[25] Furthermore, "'Tenarum' . . . not 'Trenarum' is clearly found in the Greek writers and in the ancient Latin authors. In their work 'Tenarus' is written without the letter 'r' in the first syllable and even without 'h'. This would not be if the Greeks said 'Thrinaros' and not 'Tenaros'. . . ." Curiously in this particular instance Salutati denies that the proper name hides any inner meaning. *Tenarus* is simply the name of the place. Was this obviously late discussion a suggestion of a new approach to the text, one which tended to leave behind the medieval pursuit of allegorical meanings in the etymology?

Procedures for emendation of prose manuscripts, however, are for Salutati sometimes different from those followed in working with poetry. While in poetry authors could not be depended on to maintain logical order in their thought, in prose he considers such order usual although not absolutely the rule. This principle serves him in interpreting Seneca's famous dictum, which some of the best minds of his generation endeavor to understand. According to a diversity of manuscripts Seneca's words were either: "Maxima pars vite elabitur male agentibus, magna nichil agentibus, tota vita aliud agentibus" or else "Magna pars vite elabitur male agentibus, maxime nichil agentibus, tota vita aliud agentibus." Discussing this passage of Seneca in a letter of 1398, Salutati chose the latter reading as being more logical in proceeding from "great " to "greatest" to "all."[26] From this analysis he formulated a basic rule for emendation of prose—one exactly the reverse of that followed by modern critics: "If we find a variety of readings, that which follows [logical] order is preferred to that following a disordered or confused sequence, unless some reason or circumstance justifies an inverted order." While modern editions of Seneca reject Salutati's choice of a reading, scholars as late as seventeenth century were undecided.[27]

One of the great advantages in emending poetic texts was reliance on meter. Salutati basically assumed that the poets did not make mistakes in quantities and, if occasionally they departed from the rule, they

25. The passage is cited from the Milan, 1476 edition. Salutati had doubtless heard the contemporary pronunciation of the Greek word. I am grateful to Peter Burian for this observation.

26. *Epist.*, III, 239 ff. Salutati had already treated this statement in Seneca's first letter (*Epist.*, I, 63–66). Note that in the earlier analysis he did not raise the question of defective codices. One of Salutati's later correspondents, Pietro Alboini, also glossed the passage: Theodore James, "A Fragment of an Exposition of the First Letter of Seneca to Lucilius Attributed to Peter of Mantua," in *Philosophy and Humanism. Renaissance Essays in Honor of Paul Oskar Kristeller*, ed. E. P. Mahoney (New York, 1976), pp. 531–41.

27. *L. Annaei Senecae Philosophi Epistolae*, ed. J. Lipsius and J. Gronovius (Leiden, 1649), p. 3.

rarely did so in the case of famous names. On the occasion cited above where Salutati preferred the reading "Scinin" to "Busirim" in Statius' *Thebiad* against the authority of Lactantius, his argument rested not only on the testimony of Ovid that Thesus killed "Scinin" but also on the position of the name in the verse line.[28]

Doubtless Salutati's most elaborate effort at textual criticism was not connected with establishing the allegorical meaning of the poets but rather with determining the ancient name of Città di Castello. Done in 1403 the investigation indicates the mastery Salutati had attained in this kind of research by the end of his long career. As with many of his other attempts at textual emendation, this one concerned the correct spelling of a proper name. In this case, however, the interest was purely historical and Salutati had no intention of "unlocking" the truth concealed within the word.

Having received a letter from Domenico Bandini requesting information on the original name of the town of Città di Castello, Salutati, unable to respond, decided to investigate the problem.[29] His first idea was to look for a likely name in the ancient geographers, Ptolemy, Mela, Pliny, and Solinus. Finding no help in these, he thought of the *Dialogi* of Gregory the Great where he recalled mention was made of St. Floridus, who gave his name to the cathedral of the city. He had two codices of the *Dialogi* and his hope was to find the two in agreement on the city's name. Unfortunately, in Book III, 35, one read "Floridus Trifertine Tybertine civitatis episcopus" while the other had "Floridus Tiberrine episcopus."[30] Undaunted, Salutati proceeded to consult every copy of the work he could locate in an effort to find the correct spelling, but his

28. See above, n. 16, and *De lab.*, I, 282. For similar argument for emendation on the basis of meter, ibid., I, 232–33, and II, 471–72. In the case of I, 232–33, he partially explains the particular corruptions of a text of Statius on the grounds that the ear of some readers was possibly repelled by the sound of the spondee actually written by Statius in the fifth foot of the heroic hexameter. Alice C. Ferguson, *The Manuscripts of Propertius* (Chicago, 1934), pp. 40–46, closely analyzes Salutati's corrections in his Propertius, B.F.L., XXXIII, 49. However, it is difficult to determine whether he used another manuscript for a number of his emendations or was employing techniques like meter analysis in establishing his readings. In making conjectures based on meter Salutati paralleled the work of the fourteenth-century Byzantine scholar Triclinius, who edited the plays of Euripides (G. Zuntz, *An Inquiry into the Transmission of the Plays of Euripides* [Cambridge, 1965], pp. 200–201). In Italy, however, the technique was being used as early as Lovato: Guido Billanovich, "Il preumanesimo padovano," in *Storia della cultura veneta*, vol. 2 (Vicenza, 1976), pp. 58–9.

29. *Epist.*, III, 623–27. Cf. Ullman, *The Humanism*, pp. 102–3, for his summary of the letter.

30. One of his manuscripts of Gregory, B.L.F., Marc. 566, fol. 94ᵛ appears to have "Floridus tiberine," corrected poorly to "Tibètíne" (= Tibertine?). Original may have read "Tibèrine," which Salutati took to be "Tiberrine."

examination of a total of twenty manuscripts revealed a variety of alternative spellings of the city's name.

Nevertheless, having a general idea of the name of the town, Salutati was then able to go back to his geographers for further checking. Pliny spoke of a town "Tifernum" near the Tiber River in the area where Città di Castello now stands and he also mentioned a river "Tifernus" in Apulia. Mela had the same Apulian river but called it "Trifernus." Rechecking his copy of Pliny, Salutati observed an erasure of r in the first syllable of the Apulian "Tifernus," and thus concluded that at least Pliny and Mela were in agreement on "Trifernus" as the name of the river. An examination of both Guido of Ravenna and Ptolemy showed a city of Tifernum in a location appropriate for Città di Castello. These authorities together with Pliny constituted enough evidence for him to conclude that the ancient name of the town was indeed Tifernum.[31] The correct reading of the passage in Gregory's *Dialogi* would then be Tiferna, a change of gender caused when the town (*oppidum*) became an episcopal city (*civitas*). Finally Salutati recommended that Bandini write Tifernum with an *i* instead of a *y* because he himself had seen that usage followed in a marble inscription found in the chapter house of the canons of the cathedral of St. Floridus. By this time in his life the scholar was even resorting to archeological data in his attempt to establish correct readings.[32]

As has been suggested, Salutati's intense concern for accurate manuscripts was intimately connected with his belief, essentially medieval in character, that the etymology of a word, especially of a proper noun, revealed the true meaning of the writer. If the major application of this principle was to poetic allegory, the letter to Charles of Durazzo and the *De seculo et religione* show that it could also be applied to prose. By contrast Salutati's later treatises and letters demonstrate little inclination to indulge in etymological explanations to unlock hidden truth. He endeavored to establish the spelling of *Tifernum* because he had been asked to do so by Bandini, and his clearly late discussion of the etymol-

31. *Epist.*, III, 626.
32. Irrepressible in attempting to explain errors psychologically, Salutati speculated as well that a subsequent practice grew up of referring to Tiferna as Tiberina to distinguish it from the River Tifernus in Apulia. The location of the city near the Tiber (*Tibris*) suggested the new spelling. Surprisingly he seems to have forgotten that he had just established the name of the Apulian river as being Trifernus. For archeological interests of scholars in Italy to the early fifteenth century, see Roberto Weiss, *The Renaissance of Classical Antiquity* (Oxford, 1969), pp. 1–58 (on Salutati, pp. 54–55).

ogy of the word *Tenarias* in the *De laboribus* itself was also devoid of any effort to locate a hidden truth.[33]

If a part of his original commitment to textual criticism derived from a concern for etymology, by the last years his interest in the discipline was more that of the modern scholar, not seeking to break a code but rather to establish the true readings for their own sake. As he wrote about 1405 to the young Vergerio, who had included what Salutati considered to be a corrupt reading of a Ciceronian text in his *De ingenuis moribus*: " . . . it is better to throw the whole away than to offer to the future or the present a reading which is faulty."[34]

Salutati's method of textual criticism together with his awareness of the multilayered manuscript tradition of the ancient texts he used reflects implicit notions about the nature of time. These notions are even more identifiable in his historical research. Medieval writers tended to approach the past in at least two different ways. On the one hand, they intermingled pagan with Christian cultures, thus creating for the present a two-dimensional backdrop crowded with figures and ideas available when an example or an argument was needed. On the other, they regarded the ancient past as possessing a potential for experiences very different from what was possible or at least likely in the present.[35]

As indicated in the discussion on the origins of poetry in chapter 8, Salutati displays a willingness to believe that in the very ancient past reality contained a much wider range of possibilities than in more recent times. For him earliest men had intercourse with demons and other

33. See Conclusion, this volume.

34. *Epist.*, IV, 84. In the light of the above my feeling is that Armando Petrucci, *Coluccio Salutati*, Biblioteca biographica, vol. 7 (Rome, 1972), p. 116, tends to underestimate Salutati's contribution to the development of textual criticism.

35. Richard McKeon, "Renaissance and Method in Philosophy," *Studies in the History of Ideas*, 3 (1935), 37–71; Edwin Panofsky, *Renaissance and Renascences in Western Art* (Stockholm, 1960, 2nd ed., 1965), pp. 108–13; and Peter Burke, *The Renaissance Sense of the Past* (London, 1969), pp. 1–6. Although the medieval usage of the terms *antiqui* and *moderni* implied a contrast between past and present, the conception of "past" did not have a sense of depth. For discussion of the meaning of these words, see Johannes Spörl, "Das Alte und das Neue im Mittelalter: Studien zum Problem des mittelalterlichen Fortschritts-bewusstsein," *Historisches Jahrbuch*, 50 (1930), 297–341 and 498–524; Walter Freund, *Modernus und ändere Zeitbegriffe des Mittelalters*, Neue Münstersche Beiträge zur Geschichtsforschung, vol. 4 (Cologne-Graz, 1957); Wilfried Hartmann, "'Modernus' und 'antiquus': Zur Verbreitung und Bedeutung dieser Bezeichnungen in der wissenschaftlichen Literatur vom 9. bis zum 12. Jahrhundert," *Antiqui und Moderni*, ed. A. Zimmermann, Miscellanea Medievalia, vol. 9 (Berlin, New York, 1974), pp. 21–39; Elizabeth Gössman, "'Antiqui' und 'Moderni' im 12. Jahrhundert," ibid., pp. 40–57; and G. Wolf, "Das 12. Jahrhundert als Geburtsstunde der Moderne und die Frage nach der Krise der Geschichtswissenschaft," ibid., pp. 80–84.

supernatural beings on an almost daily basis. In dealing with later time periods, however, those which his Roman sources cease to treat in fabulous terms, Salutati himself usually operates more critically, viewing the past as a continuous series of time-space sets placed one after the other down to his own experience in the present. Although the character of any one set differs from that just preceding or following, living men can appreciate the experience of men in other ages on the basis of their own experience—the possibilities at least are the same throughout.[36]

This attitude, which lies behind Salutati's research on historical problems, enables him to view another age as different but amenable to judgments based on reason and practical experience. A number of striking historical analyses result. Among other things he eventually judges the ancient poets by the same standards used to judge contemporary ones (his mature view on ancient poetry, discussed in chapter 15, shows this); develops a respectable account of the foundation of Florence (see below); and establishes the changeable character of ancient Latin while providing a periodization of ancient Latin literature (see below).

The range of his historical research seems incommensurate with his stated purpose for studying history, the pursuit of past examples and models to guide personal and public actions in the present.[37] At least as much as Petrarch, he felt a basic need to periodize and relate events to one another temporally.[38] His autobiographical remarks illustrate the

36. Eugenio Garin, *L'umanesimo italiano* (Bari, 1958), p. 10, locates the sense of historical perspective in the philological interests of humanism. On the sense of historical distance, see J. Weisinger, "Ideas of History during the Renaissance," *Journal of the History of Ideas*, 6 (1945), 415–35; August Buck, *Das Geschichtsdenken der Renaissance*, Schriften und Vorträge des Petrarca-Instituts Köln, vol. 9 (Krefeld, 1957), pp. 7 ff; W. von Leyden, "Antiquity and Authority: a Paradox in the Renaissance Theory of History," *Journal of the History of Ideas*, 19 (1958), 480–92; and Peter Burke, "The Sense of Historical Perspective in Renaissance Italy," *Cahiers d'Histoire mondiale*, 9 (1968), 615–32.

37. Salutati's most eloquent expression of history's capacity to teach by examples is found in *Epist.*, II, 290–96. Eckhard Kessler, *Das Problem des Frühen Humanismus: Seine philosophische Bedeutung bei Coluccio Salutati* (Munich, 1968), pp. 150 ff., discusses in detail the use of historical *exempla* in their relationship to Salutati's ethical ideas. See also Rüdiger Landfester, *Historia Magistra vitae: Untersuchungen zur humanistischen Geschichtstheorie des 14. bis. 16. Jahrhunderts*, Travaux d'humanisme et Renaissance, vol. 123 (Geneva, 1972), especially pp. 132, 134, 152, and 155. The work of J. T. Welter, *L'exemplum dans la littérature religieuse et didactique du Moyen Age* (Paris, 1927), remains the basic treatment of the problem of *exempla* in the Middle Ages.

38. The best example of Petrarch's need to periodize his own life is his "Posteritati," *Prose*, ed. G. Martellotti, P. G. Ricci, E. Carrara, and E. Bianchi, La letteratura italiana: Storia e testi, vol. 7 (Milan, 1955), pp. 2–18. On Petrarch's historiography, see Giuseppe Kirner, "Sulle opere storiche di Francesco Petrarca," *Annali della Scuola Normale Superiore di Pisa*, 7 (1890), 1–92; Antonio Viscardi, "Francesco Petrarca storiografo," *La cultura*, 2 (1922–23), 491–99; Carlo Calcaterra, "La concezione storica del Petrarca," *Nella selva del*

depth of this interest, which seems to have little to do with the medieval pursuit of didactic analogies. In an age when most men did not know exactly how old they were, Salutati clearly manifested a sense of his own duration in terms of a temporal sequence of events personally experienced. Occasionally he referred to his age in his letters and the distance between the present and the time since some event in his life occurred.[39] He eagerly supported the revival of the ancient custom of the birthday party, probably re-introduced in Italy at the beginning of the fourteenth century.[40] More than simply an imitation of an ancient practice, the birthday party constituted an affirmation of one's involvement in the world as a historical being. Previous centuries had been generous in their observation of religious festivals, especially the saints' days, but honoring the birthday of a living man was of a different order. It put the stamp of individuality on the flow of time and provided a measure of one's progress through the world. Oddly, this concern was more intense in the first generations of humanists than it would be among their immediate successors.

Salutati never clearly expresses the notion of an equalization of time-space sets which he utilizes in his historical writings. The closest he

Petrarca (Bologna, 1942), pp. 415–33; Guido Martellotti, "Linee di sviluppo dell'umanesimo petrarchescho," *Studi petrarcheschi*, 2 (1949), 51–82; and Eckhard Kessler, *Petrarca und die Geschichte* (Munich, 1978). Benjamin Kohl, "Petrarch's Prefaces to *De viris illustribus*," *History and Theory*, 13 (1974), 132–44, translates into English and comments on Petrarch's prefaces to his major historical work.

39. *Epist.*, IV, 352 and III, 636–37. For his precise use of *adolescens* and *iuvenis* see my "Toward a Biography of Coluccio Salutati," *Rinascimento*, 16 (1976), 21–22. For instances of use of these terms in referring to events in his life, see chap. 1 and *De lab.*, I, 215. Cf. Ullman, *The Humanism*, p. 45. For dating the life of his son, see Piero, *Epist.*, III, 401 and 417. Cf. above, chap. 7. On the chronology for the beginning of his interest in spelling, see *Epist.*, II, 279; and III, 598.

40. Poggio Bracciolini, *Epistolae*, Opera omnia, ed. Riccardo Fubini, 4 vols. (Turin, 1964–69), III, pt. 1, 305–6, writes: "Hodie, mi Nicolae, celebravi inter doctissimos viros natalem meum diem haud alias antea a me observatum; non quia magni fuerit me tantillum hominem orbi natum, sed tum ad imitationem antiquorum, quibus id moris fuit, et a Colucio nostro, expertae virtutis atque eloquentiae viro, factitatum vidimus." See the note on this passage by Phyllis Gordan, *Two Renaissance Book Hunters*, Records of Civilization, Sources and Studies, vol. 91 (New York, 1974), p. 339. Cf. her English translation, ibid., pp. 161–62. A passage in Giovanni di Conversino's *Dragmalogia* (B.N.P., *Lat.* 6494, fol. 10^{r-a}) could be interpreted to suggest that by the early fifteenth century Italian princes commonly celebrated their birthdays: "An non principum nuptie celebritates, natalia, aliave solennia sine discrimine, sine metu, sine labore, quodque detestabilius est, sine merito, milites ac per hoc dominos creant?" Within the context, however, *natalia* could be interpreted as 'saints' days'. This would be more in accord with "aliave solennia" than a birthday party would. In any case, Salutati was not the first, since the time of the Romans, to celebrate his day of birth. Decades earlier Mussato seems to have honored his birthday in some festive way: "De celebratione suae diei nativitatis fienda, vel non," *Albertini Mussati Historia augusta Henrici VII Caesaris et alia, quae extant opera* (Venice, 1636), pt. 7, 81–3.

comes to articulating a belief in "uniformitarianism" occurs in statements echoing the words of Ecclesiastes: "There is nothing new under the sun."[41] The observation is not necessarily a pessimistic comment, since the repetitive nature of history guarantees the historian predictive powers. However, while ensuring the success of his didactic enterprise, the principle, if taken seriously, would seem to undermine the historian's sense of historical depth.

In fact in Salutati's thought this affirmation of the constancy of energy from one time-set to another proves to be compatible with two contradictory tendencies. On the one hand, he can assert that "we make nothing new but like menders we patch together from pieces of richest antiquity clothes which we present as new," thus deprecating the creative efforts of the moderns;[42] and, on the other, he can point to the same inheritance of knowledge from the past as a source of gradual progress. Relying on the authority of Aristotle (see chap. 8), he argues not merely that there are changes in the arts and sciences but actual improvements. Influenced by the Epicurean theory of the advance of human society, Salutati stresses the diminution of violence in reference to the "historic progress of the human race"; the move of human beings from the wilds to cities; and the gradual development of religion from the worship of dead heroes to that of the elements, especially fire and, among fiery objects, the stars.[43]

Although both these interpretations, that of stasis and that of progress, are at least to Salutati's mind consistent with the "uniformitarianism" of time, when he speaks as a Christian he makes statements militating against the latter concept. As a Christian, Salutati realized that

41. *Epist.*, II, 293–94. Cf. ibid., IV, 136. The term *uniformitarianism* is Weisinger's ("Ideas of History," p. 428).

42. Ibid., II, 145. This can lead to a strong sense of decay: see next note below.

43. *De lab.*, I, 303; 303–5; and II, 403–4. Cicero's *De inv.*, I, 2, is probably the inspiration for his knowledge of the Epicurean conception. That Salutati's belief in limited progress of knowledge rests on flimsy grounds becomes clear in a passage in which he defends the position (*Epist.*, IV, 136). Beginning by asserting a progress in knowledge, he ends after some tortured reasoning by writing: "Cur tu et alii, quibus antiquitas ita placet, priscis et antiquissimis viris propter Platonem vel Aristotelem derogatis? An nescitis hos quicquid scribunt sive scriptum reliquerunt ab antecessoribus accepisse? Parum est quod in his laudatur, quod possint dicere suum esse; vix enim dicere potuerunt: hoc recens est." From positing an advance we are back to an assertion of the linear character of time. For medieval conceptions of progress, see Freund, "Modernus und ändere Zeitbegriffe," pp. 106–10; and E. Gössman, "'Antiqui' und 'Moderni'," pp. 50–56. Also see below, chap., 15. On the ancients' view, see Ludwig Edelstein, *The Idea of Progress in Classical Antiquity* (Baltimore, 1967), p. 92, n. 79. For Augustine (*De civ. Dei*, XII, 14) the cyclical theory was incompatible with the uniqueness of the Incarnation. See John Baille, *The Belief in Progress* (New York, 1951), pp. 75–83. The influence of Augustine on Salutati in this regard is discussed in the following paragraph.

historical time did not really have the same quality throughout. Grace could never be kept for long from asserting its claim to preeminence over the natural. Of finite significance before the Incarnation, historical action from that point on had assumed infinite importance for men. Through his activity, working in time, the Christian could earn merits of infinite consequence. Such a perspective could easily lead to a devaluation of the accomplishments of pagan culture. In fact, in his *De seculo* of 1381 Salutati used Augustine's presentation of ancient society as essentially inferior to the Christian one in arguing for the monastic life (See chap. 7). Neglected for almost two decades, this negative assessment of the pagan world reappeared in the very last years to trouble the old man's attitude toward the ancients (see chap. 15).

To the extent, however, that Augustine impressed on Salutati the difference between the mentalities of the two ages, the Church Father's work may have contributed to Salutati's incipient sense of anachronism. When a correspondent attacked Virgil on the grounds that the poet had made Aeneas a bastard in describing him as the offspring of Venus and Anchises, Salutati retorted that early men had not known matrimony and that one should not judge other ages by the laws of one's own time. His correspondent "wished to restrict the times of the Trojan War with the precepts and institutions of the Christian religion." He ought not to judge other periods "by the standards of our time."[44]

With the linear view of time qualified by the recognition of an abrupt decisive elevation in the value or consequences of human action with the advent of Christ, the two temporal segments on either side of this event became more clearly defined. When earlier writers undertook to treat pagan culture, they either piously condemned it as evil or else tended to blend it almost indiscriminately with Christian culture. In his early work Salutati very much reflected this latter tendency.[45] By contrast, in his maturity he manifested an ability to comprehend the historical difference between the pagan and Christian cultures largely because for him the natural pagan world had its own integrity and the changes wrought by the revelation of the Word could be appreciated against this

44. *Epist.*, III, 271–72. Salutati could not, however, refrain from arguing subsequently that Venus had been a real woman and the legitimate wife of Anchises (ibid., pp. 272–73).

45. Chap. 3 has shown the central role of fate and fortune in Salutati's early ethical discussions. As late as 1369 a letter of condolence to Lapo Castiglionchio on the death of the latter's nephew lacks any specific Christian element: see above chap. 4. On lack of appreciation of the distinction between Christian and pagan culture in medieval writers, see n. 35.

background. Since he could distinguish between the world of nature and that of grace, he was in a position to assign to each culture, ancient and Christian, its own character.[46]

Of course, behind Augustine's sharp distinction between pagan and Christian culture lay the vision of a God who controls everything in the universe. In Salutati's case, this theory of divine Providence, while complicating his attitudes toward the past, had little effect on his historical scholarship. Until the 1370s, influenced by his reading in pagan authors and by the Italian rhetorical tradition (see chap. 3), he ascribed a large role in human history to fate and fortune, ostensibly autonomous forces in the world. Subsequently, with these two forces solidly subordinated to the divine Will, he increasingly assigned God primacy of place in the hierarchy of causes in human history. Nonetheless, the causal power of God's will in history at the most intruded on Salutati's historical analysis as a "deeper" explanation of a series of events adequately described at another level in natural terms.[47]

In good medieval fashion there is no pre-history for Salutati. Eusebius had worked out an elaborate chronology beginning with the creation of the world and this had been supplemented by Eutropius and Orosius. Salutati follows their lead in dating events variously from the foundation of the world, the flood, the destruction of Troy, the foundation of Rome, and the birth of Christ. As with the schemes of his predecessors this integration of biblical, Greek, and Latin history can be consummated only with tremendous pushing and shoving, but Salutati seems untroubled by the disparity between various historical traditions. Depending on circumstances, the story of Adam and Eve, the legend of

46. What Aquinas accomplished for philosophy and theology by defining the limits of natural reason and working out the implications, Petrarch and Salutati did in effect for rhetoric. Although the thirteenth-century Italian *dictatores* focused on practical applications of rhetoric, they had no philosophical basis for their secularism. They never consciously faced the problem of reconciling their rhetorical interests with their religion.

47. Chap. 14 illustrates, in the case of Salutati's portrayal of Caesar's rise to power and fall, how the force of divine Providence could be imposed as an explanation on what was essentially a realistic analysis of natural causes and effects. In Salutati naturalistic tendencies were still not completely divorced from transcendental ones, but the development was well underway in his work. Louis Green, *Chronicle into History* (Cambridge, 1972), p. 146, maintains that these two were still united in Giovanni Villani but gradually bifurcated in later chronicles. As to the role of humanism in the fifteenth century, he writes: "While one might have expected the development of humanism to have been accompanied by a progressive rejection of the supernatural in all spheres of life, in fact what it appears to have brought about was rather the splitting off of the rational elements of the culture of the past from the mystical ones. This opened the way not only for a more secular conception of man's nature and destiny, but also for a more anti-natural interpretation of the action of spiritual forces" (p. 145).

the Golden Age, and the Epicurean conception of the progressive development of early man appear in his pages without Salutati making any effort to relate or reconcile them.

As suggested above, the major exception to his normal effort to assign natural causes to events occurs in dealing with earliest times. Even here he makes an attempt to reduce the scope of the supernatural. He acknowledges that, while pagan traditions interpret the stories of the gods as based on the exploits of actual men and women, Scripture considers these deities to have been demons.[48] However, his tendency in the *De laboribus* is to agree with the euhemeristic interpretation in practice.[49] Like the other gods, Hercules and the deeds surrounding his name had a basis in history. Although some of the feats reported were certainly fabulous, even those which were in some sense historical could not all have been accomplished by the same man.[50]

He is committed to the belief in giants. The Scriptures mention their existence as do pagan writers like Solinus, Pliny, and Aulius Gellius.[51] In his *Genealogia deorum* Boccaccio writes of the discovery of the statue of a giant in a cave in the neighborhood of Trapani "in our own times," and on a trip to Venice as a boy Salutati himself saw the teeth of a monstrous man said to have been Goliath.[52] Accordingly, when dealing with the legends depicting the struggles of the Titans and the Giants with the gods, Salutati looks for a foundation in reality just as he did with the stories surrounding Hercules.[53]

Salutati takes pains to explain the nature of the limitations he patently feels when writing history. History, he remarks is "that which is done but removed in memory from our age."[54] Anxious to establish what actually occurred, the historian must distinguish between the true events and those things which could have happened but did not. Of the three basic sources of human knowledge, reason, experience, and authority, the first two have minimal importance for this purpose. In historical matters proofs of logic are useless; the senses are unable to judge what is no longer present; and usually no living witnesses remain to be interrogated. Thus the historian is almost entirely dependent on the authorities who treat the incident. For this reason, the most an historian can

---

48. *De lab.*, I, 66. His assimilation of the pagan gods to demons may be his reading of Augustine, *De civ. Dei*, VIII, 14–26.

49. Ibid., II, 403.

50. Ibid., I, 165, and *Vat. lat.* 2928, Tr. III, c. 11, fol. 67ᵛ.

51. *De lab.*, II, 397, and I, 174.   52. Ibid., I, 172–73.

53. Cf. *Epist.*, III, 547 ff., on Hector.

54. *De lab.*, II, 585. He refers to Cicero, *De oratore*, II, 15, 52.

hope to attain is verisimilitude, "which is midway between fabulous fiction and certain truth."[55] When the authorities say nothing or when they differ in their accounts, reason and experience can furnish little aid.

In cases where authorities differ in describing a particular event, Salutati's practice is usually to give the various positions and conclude with a remark that the reader is to make his own judgment. But before admitting that such a disagreement actually exists, he does what he can to reconcile the authors. Perhaps the texts are corrupt or one of the authors intended his statements to be taken as allegories. Another way out is to attribute the contradictions to the different purposes the writers had in mind when referring to the event or events.[56]

Although he admits that historians who deal with anything not contemporary with themselves are likely to be unreliable,[57] he does have greater trust in some than in others. When faced on the one hand with the testimony of Solinus and Aeschylus as reported by Hyginus, and on the other by that of Pliny and Pomponius regarding the boundaries of Italy, he does not decide absolutely but admits that the "authority of Pliny and Pomponius is greater for me."[58] Between the two latter writers, however, he seems to consider the opinion of Pliny the greater, for on another occasion, when Pliny agrees with Solinus against Pomponius, Salutati decides for the first two.[59] A disagreement between Pliny and Lucan on a point of geography, moreover, provides an opportunity for Salutati to establish the principle that "the authority of the cosmographer ought to be greater than that of the poet."[60]

In the final analysis, he discredits only two supposedly ancient sources, Dares and Dictys, whom he came to consider apocryphal.[61] The

---

55. *Epist.*, IV, 125. One of his motives for rejecting the attribution of the *Octavia* to Seneca the Philosopher was that the play describes events happening after Seneca's death. That he would have known such things in advance was "veri non simile" (ibid., I, 153). See below, n. 102.

56. *De lab.*, I, 127–29.

57. Ibid., I, 79. See his interpretation of the discrepancy between Virgil and Livy in *Epist.*, III, 230.

58. *De lab.*, I, 333–34.   59. Ibid., I, 285.

60. Ibid., I, 378. Salutati does not believe that Lucan wrote in ignorance of the truth but that the poet merely wished to conceal a mystery under his words. On the whole, Ullman's statement that Salutati considered poets to be historians can only be accepted with qualification: *The Humanism*, p. 96. Cf. Alfred von Martin, *Coluccio Salutatis Traktat "Vom Tyrannen"* (Berlin, 1913), p. 93: referred to below as *De tyranno*.

61. Although he did not have much faith in their veracity in 1398 (*Epist.*, III, 311), as late as May 14, 1400, he seems to accept their authenticity (ibid., III, 389). In the summer of 1400 the *De tyranno* expresses strong doubts (*De tyranno*, p. lx). In 1401 (*Epist.*, III, 546) he is certain they were not what they claim to be. In 1387 Salutati sought a manuscript of

medieval historians, however, fare worse. Based as it is on the fictitious Dares and Dictys, the Trojan history of Petrarch's friend and patron, Guido Colonna, undergoes sharp criticism.[62] He brands the chronicles of Geoffrey of Monmouth and John of Altavilla, called Architrenius, as fabulous.[63] Jacopo da Varagine is said to have written "stupidly" in his discussion of the origin of Genoa's name.[64] Moreover, Salutati distrusts the miraculous accounts of Saba Malaspina[65] and regards the works of authors like Vincent of Beauvais and Martin of Poland as "modern garbage."[66]

In short, he despairs of the present state of the study of history and looks with nostalgia to the achievements of the ancient past. For six centuries history has been neglected and the masterpieces of the ancients have never been duplicated by subsequent writers.[67] But the decay of historical writings is merely one element of what he normally considers a general corruption. As he writes of his own age in a marginal note in his manuscript of the *Martinellus* at the point where the author laments the evils of the times: "You have not seen our age, eloquent Suplicius!"[68]

Despite the jumbled nature of these general historical conceptions and Salutati's frequent indecisiveness in evaluating conflicting opinions in his authorities, when he focused his skills on a historical problem, the results were usually impressive. His analysis of the original name of Città di Castello manifests not only his critical powers when working with manuscript sources but also his use of archeological data—a species of evidence he never discusses in his references to the nature of historical proofs. His research best known to modern scholars concerns Scipio Nasica, erroneously identified by Valerius Maximus as one per-

---

Josephus Iscanus' *De bello Trojano* (B.N.Mad., 17652 (Gay. 736), fols. 167ᵛ–168): "Vellem eciam, quia non habeo, libellum illum metricum cuius inicium est 'Iliadum lacrimas eversaque Pergama fato 'qui frigium Dareta secutus troianam historiam pertractavit. Si illos [a second manuscript is also involved] habes, mitte. Postquam enim exemplari fecerim, curabo remittere." The date is based on Salutati's statement that at the time of writing he was in his 56th year: fol. 166ᵛ. He probably eventually acquired the work (*Epist.*, III, 274).

62. *Epist.*, II, 546. Colonna's work is said to be little esteemed by most scholars and to be "carentem tam gravitate quam fide."

63. *De lab.*, II, 398.

64. *Epist.*, IV, 93. Salutati shows that Jacopo copied Solinus in his account of the origin of the name of Genoa but misunderstood his source (ibid., IV, 93–94).

65. Ibid., II, 29–30, and IV, 124–25.

66. Ibid., II, 299. Actually Salutati was of the opinion that after the times of Valentinian II (375–92) there were no great historians (*Epist.*, II, 419).

67. Ibid., II, 296.

68. B.N.F., *Conv. Sopp.*, I, VI, 18, fol. 14ᵛ: "Non vidisti nostram etatem, facunde Suplici!" See above, chap. 9, for decay motif in relation to "uniformitarianism."

son.[69] Yet his greatest achievement relates to a bigger problem, the origins of the city of Florence. The product of roughly fifteen years of investigation, his conclusions expressed in a few thousand words are published as part of his *Invectiva contra Antonium Luschum* in 1403. The methods by which he arrives at the results reveal a mastery of historical techniques unsurpassed in his century.[70]

From earliest times Florentines seem to have been conscious of their Roman origins. At least from the first surviving historical account of the city, the early thirteenth-century *Chronica de origine civitatis*, the city claimed a filial link with Rome.[71] As Giovanni Villani summarized the tradition in his *Cronica* written in the first half of the Trecento,[72] the building of Florence was related to the punitive actions undertaken by Rome against the Fiesolans, who had supported Catiline's unsuccessful conspiracy to overthrow the Republic. While initially one among many Roman generals, Caesar alone prosecuted the siege of the city to the end and accordingly deserves the credit for founding the city which grew up at the foot of the hill on which the rebellious Etruscan town had stood. But the Senate, reluctant to grant Caesar the prestige of giving his name to the city he was constructing, decided that all the captains involved in the siege should contribute to the building of the settlement: the one who finished his part first would receive the honor of naming the whole. Because all the work was completed at the same time, however, none acquired the privilege and it was finally decided to call the city "Floria" after Fiorino, a Roman captain who had lost his life in the early days of the siege.

There is no way of determining when Salutati first began to doubt the truth of the Caesar legend. Although Benvenuto da Imola already considered the Caesar foundation ridiculous in 1383,[73] it is possible that

---

69. *De tyranno*, pp. xx-xxv. Salutati believed there to have been two men, a father and son with this name. Modern historians maintain there are three. An English translation of the passage is found in E. Emerton, *Humanism and Tyranny* (Cambridge, Mass., 1925), pp. 81–85; and in Berthold L. Ullman, *The Humanism*, pp. 98–99.

70. Edited by Domenico Moreni (Florence, 1826), pp. 24–36.

71. The essential articles on early Florentine historiography are Nicolai Rubinstein, "The Beginnings of Political Thought in Florence," *The Journal of the Warburg and Courtauld Institutes*, 5 (1942), 198–227; and A. Del Monte, "La storiografia fiorentina dei secoli XII e XIII," *Bollettino dell'Istituto storico italiano per il medio evo e archivio muratoriano*, 62 (1950), 175–282.

72. Giovanni Villani, *Cronica*, ed. F. Dragomanni, 4 vols. (Florence, 1844–45), I, 55 ff.

73. Benvenuto da Imola in his *Comentum super Dantis Aldigheri Comoediam*, ed. J. P. Laciata, 5 vols. (Florence, 1887), I, 509–11, completed by 1383, criticized the Caesar foundation as ridiculous but did not substitute an alternative explanation. See discussion of Benvenuto's views in Hans Baron, *Crisis of the Early Italian Renaissance*, rev. ed. (Princeton, 1966), pp. 62–63. Filippo Villani indicated in the first edition of his *De origine civitatis Flo-*

Salutati in this period still accepted the tradition. Consequently, it is significant that, whereas in the *Missives* from 1375 on Salutati repeatedly claimed Florence's Roman origin as a title of honor for the Republic, until 1388 no description of the events surrounding Florence's foundation is to be found in these documents. For the first thirteen years of his tenure as Chancellor Salutati rarely went beyond reiterating in letters to the Romans that the Florentines were "bone of your bones and flesh from your flesh."[74] The most he asserted was that the Florentines were descendants of the Romans "as our history books tell us."[75] As presented in his pages of the *Missives*, the heritage which Florence received from Rome was always characterized as a republican one, and it is probable that Salutati consciously avoided discussion of Caesar's role in order to preserve appearances.

Beginning in 1388–89, however, there are indications that Salutati was becoming interested in the problem of the identity of the author of the city. On April 19, 1388, for the first time in the *Missives*, Salutati referred to the legend of the "circulatio": Troy was founded by Dardanus, who came from Fiesole, and Rome, the mother of Florence, was the daughter of Troy.[76] Eight months later the same theme was repeated, this time joined to the legend of a second destruction and foundation of Florence by Charlemagne.[77] Aside from the fact that these were the first references in the *Missives* speaking in any detail of the origins of Florence, from the standpoint of historiography there is nothing particularly important about the passages. But coupled with a paragraph in a letter of April 12, 1389, they should be interpreted as signs of a new concern in the events surrounding the origins of the city. In the course of this letter of April 12 warning a condottiere to refrain from making incur-

---

rentie, written in 1382, that he was aware of adverse criticism of the old legend. See Nicolai Rubinstein, "Il Poliziano e la questione delle origini di Firenze," in *Il Poliziano e il suo tempo: Atti del IV Convegno internazionale di studi sul Rinascimento* (Florence, 1957), p. 102.

74. *Miss.*, 15, fol. 86ᵛ; 17, fol. 55; 19, fols. 122 and 160.

75. *Miss.*, 16, fol. 67ᵛ.

76. *Miss.*, 21, fol. 24–24ᵛ: "Nam cum originis nostre gloria sit hanc urbem non solum a Romanis conditam sed viris romani sanguinis et traditam et repletam, debet aut potest suspicari romana maiestas nos contra maiorum nostrorum sanguinem arma moturos? Absit a nobis tantus furor, tantaque delirature mentis impietas. Ut nos, genere stirpeque Romani et illa in orbis parte positi unde Dardanus troiani sanguinis auctor, cum incolarum multitudine proficiscens Pergama condidit et vobis urbis romane parentes Eneam progenuit et Iulum, contra tot generationum seriem iunctum populum bellum plusquam civile bellumque consanguineum inferamus."

77. *Miss.*, 21, fol. 77: "Hinc equidem Dardanus Frigias penetravit ad horas a quo superbum Ylium et pius Eneas, romani sanguinis et imperii fundator et auctor. Et ex vobis hec civitas primo condita et post destructionem eius Totile perfidia factam denuo reparata. Ut hac principiorum circulatione nulla vobis civitas possit esse coniunctior."

sions on Roman soil, the Florentines reminded him of their own close link with that city. Salutati declared: "In their happier years these very Romans, meeting in a great assembly not only ordered this city to be built but, to make it an outstanding example, had it peopled with noble Roman families and citizens."[78] A letter sent to the Romans on the same day, informing them of Florence's intention to protect them, described those "happier years" of the ancient Roman Republic in more detail:

> O, would that the Divine Will decreed that this people [the Florentines] were to make the Romans again "masters of the earth" and restore "the Togaed race" to their former majesty. Thus, not only would all kings and princes fear the holy Senate of the Roman city and the power of the Italian name but, as in those happy early days— if this was really called happiness—they would shake with fear.[79]

There is no reason to believe that Salutati in these statements had discarded the old legend. It is just this, in fact, which makes the passages interesting. Instead of emphasizing the central thesis of the old story, the role of Caesar in the building of the new city, Salutati chose to exaggerate the importance of one of its more insignificant aspects, the action of the Senate in connection with both the actual construction and the organization of the colony. Rather than Caesar, it was a great assembly which was credited with the foundation: Florence was founded by republican Rome in the day of its greatness, in its "happier times." Within the limits of the old story Salutati was doing his best to republicanize his city's origins.

Six years later a public letter of Salutati indicated, however, that by this time at least he had his hands on the evidence for a new foundation theory. On March 25, 1395, in a letter to the Romans Salutati remarked at one point:

> For . . . your glorious ancestors, conquerors of the whole world, founded our city by public decree as a defense of the Roman name

78. *Miss.*, 21, fol. 96ᵛ: "Ipsi (Romani) quidem felicioribus annis magno consilio non solum iusserunt hanc urbem construi sed eam singularissimo exemplo fecerunt nobilibus romanis familiis atque civibus populari."

79. *Miss.*, 21, fol., 95ᵛ: "Scimus progenitores vestros et nostros idem genus et unum institutionis principium habuisse nobisque et nostro populo ad singularis glorie titulum reputamus genus esse romulidum quod imperium occeano et famam terminavit in astris. . . . O utinam superni dispositione numinis datum foret ut posset iste populus romanos rerum dominos gentemque togatam in prisca reponere maiestate. Ita quod sanctissimum urbis romane senatum et italici nominis potentiam nedum cuncti reges et principes vererentur sed iuxta priscorum temporum felicitatem, si illa tamen felicitas dicenda fuit, trepidi formidarent." The passage echoes Virgil, *Aen.*, I, 286.

and rule in this place because of the frequent rebellions of the Tuscans. Having confiscated lands from the Fiesolans, they sent noble
Roman citizens to inhabit the city. When Totila destroyed it, they restored the city and populated it not only with people of the lower
classes but with distinguished Roman noble families. We have always
striven to be a source of honor to our parents so that in us the dignity
of the Roman blood not degenerate through vice.[80]

The republican element was still central: Florence had been built by
public decree. The settlers were again said to have been Romans. But
for the first time reference was made to certain historical events that
indicate the influence of a classical historian.

In his *Bellum Catilinae* Sallust had written of the recruitment of soldiers by the friends of Catiline:

Meanwhile Manlius in Etruria was working upon the people, who,
because of poverty and resentment at their wrongs, were ready for
revolt. During the domination of Sulla they had lost their lands and
all their possessions. Moreover, he also contacted brigands of various
sorts who were numerous in that area and some of those from Sulla's
colonies who by prodigality and luxury had nothing left of their great
booty.[81]

He had spoken of the misery of Etruria (or Tuscia) after the civil wars
and had closely associated the founding of a colony there by Sulla with
the loss of lands and possessions on the part of the people of the region.
Was Salutati perhaps echoing Sallust's phrase in his "having confiscated
from the Fiesolans" and by the phrase "because of the frequent rebellions of the Tuscans" suggesting the period just after the civil struggle?[82]
The omission of Sulla's name as the author of the new colony in Salutati's statement is easily explained. The Florentine chancellor wanted to
claim a republican heritage for his city; he insisted that Florence had
been constructed by public decree. Sulla, on the other hand, was hardly
looked on as a republican hero by the men of the Trecento. Salutati

80. *Miss.*, 24, fol. 120: "Nam cum gloriosi progenitores vestri, victores orbis terrarum,
urbem nostram romani nominis et imperii propugnaculum hoc sub celo contra crebras
Tuscorum rebelliones decreto publico construxissent et Fesulanis agro multatis nobiles cives
romanos ad implenda menia transmiserint et destructam a Totila reparaverint suppleta
civitate non plebe solum sed insigni nobilitate romana. Semper adnixi sumus esse paren-
tibus nostris honori ne decus illud romani sanguinis in nobis per degenerationis vitium
deperiret."

81. *Bell. Cat.*, XXVIII.

82. There is no way to determine whether at this date Salutati's reference to the nobility of the settlers of Florence was influenced by Cicero, *In Catil. sec.*, IX, 20.

himself, exposing in his later *Invectiva contra Antonium Luschum* the new theory of Florence's origin in detail, wrote of Sulla's cruelty and grouped him with men of the stamp of Nero and Caligula.[83]

But besides this antipathy for Sulla, Salutati was probably reluctant at this point to commit himself further on a matter about which he was not at all certain. The words of Sallust (if Salutati was aware of their significance at this time) gave no precise details about the Sullan colonies. Salutati's uncertainty about the theory is reflected in 1398 in his letter to Donato degli Albanzani, chancellor of the Marquess of Este. In August of that year Salutati asked Donato for any information he could give about the origins of Florence.[84]

Albanzani's reply to this letter still exists. From it we know that the recently appointed chancellor of the Este believed that Florence's construction preceded the civil war between Sulla and Marius. Albanzani cited a reference in Florus to the effect that after the defeat of the Marian forces, Sulla's men sold Florence "at auction" along with other cities that had opposed them.[85] This is a view which Salutati specifically rejected later in his discussion of Florence's early history in the *Invectiva*.[86]

Also indicative of Salutati's caution in advancing a theory about which he still had reservations is the careful wording of one of his *missives* sent to Rome in the fall of this same year. He wrote: "We are Romans, I confess, since from Fiesole Dardanus accompanied by a large band of Tuscans [omission in manuscript]. Troy founded Rome and they were Romans who established this city because of the needs of the times. Therefore if someone considers this unity of origin and circularity of foundations, he can see that the Roman and Florentine peoples are one."[87] In speaking of the motive for the foundation of Florence as "because of the needs of the time," Salutati could hardly have been more ambiguous.

83. In the *Invectiva* Salutati wrote: "Possum te dicere (quis enim vetat?) assentatione Gnatorem, crudelitate Syllam, nec Syllam solummodo, sed Marium, Cinnam, Neronem sive Caligulam . . . " (p. 192). In his *De tyranno*, p. lii, he spoke of the time of Sulla's rule as "Sillanorum temporum vastitas." A bit earlier, p. xxxxvii, he warned against the dangers of murdering a ruler: "Quarum rerum metu, tolleranda potius hominis vita fuit, non Cesaris solum, qui tanta clementia sicut legitur utebatur, sed etiam Sille vel Marii, qui non poterant civile sanguine satiari."
84. *Epist.*, III, 324–25.
85. Ibid., IV, 346.
86. *Invect.*, pp. 35–36.
87. B.C.S., 5.5.8., fol. 90 (photographs of this codex are in the Archivio di Stato, Florence): "Romani, fatemur, sumus, quoniam ex Fesulis Dardanus magna sociatus Tuscorum copia Troia Romam genuit. Romanique fuerunt, qui civitatem hanc pro necessitate temporum posuerunt. Ut, siquis hanc unitatem originis et circulationem generationis consideret, videre possit romanum et florentinum populum unum esse."

By 1403 Salutati seems to have made up his mind. His discussion of the origins of Florence and of the name in the *Invectiva in Antonium Luschum* is a complete exposition of his research. Even then, on the eve of publication he sent the chapter on the origins to Domenico Bandini requesting that the Aretine scholar write him immediately if "you know more or something different."[88] We cannot determine if the finished product in the *Invectiva* reflects in any way Bandini's influence.

Salutati's account of Florence's origins was ostensibly motivated by the hostile accusation of Loschi, chancery official of the Duke of Milan, that Florence was falsely claiming to be descended from Rome. "Indeed, since you seem to deny that a Florentine is a Roman," Salutati replies at the beginning of his discussion of Florence's early history, "tell me, pray, where have you found the contrary opinion?" His opening proof of Florence's Roman origin rests on archeological remains. In one sense, in utilizing this sort of evidence Salutati is simply echoing Giovanni Villani;[89] there is, however, an important change. Salutati gives evidence of having an eye for architectural differences: the remains of the temple of Mars show that it was built "not in the Greek nor the Etruscan way . . . but clearly in the Roman" (p. 26). As for the remnants of ancient fortifications, he remarks: "The round towers still exist and the remains of the gates, which are now connected to the episcopal palace. Who has seen Rome will not only see they are Roman but will swear they are. Not only are they like the walls of Rome in their material of burned brick but also in their form" (p. 28).

After describing the traces of great Roman constructions in Florence, Salutati turned to the historical proofs: "Therefore, it is no wonder if, with so many supporting proofs, the persistent and undying tradition is that our city was a Roman creation. It clearly puts the city opposite the Fiesolans, who were opponents and enemies of the Romans, because, as we read, in the Social War Fiesole and certain other towns were destroyed." This was followed by a paraphrase of the Sallust quotation cited above. Salutati also introduced Cicero to reinforce the authority of Sallust. In his *Oratio in Catilinam secunda* Cicero had named among those implicated in the conspiracy to overthrow the Roman state "men from these colonies established by Sulla at Fiesole which I know were on the whole inhabited by the best and strongest citizens." Salutati, therefore, argues: "Since there are no traces of any colony remaining except Florence, let them believe these soldiers of Sulla took part in

---

88. *Epist.*, III, 628.   89. *Cron.*, I, 61.

the foundation of this city in order that they might resist the Fiesolans" (p. 31).

The Florentine humanist concluded his discussion of Florence's origin with a consideration of how the city obtained its name. On this matter Salutati admitted he had no information. Nevertheless, he reported that already in the time of Antoninus Pius, Ptolemy, the geographer, refers to "Florentia" among the cities of Tuscany. Pliny, on the other hand, writing a century before refers to a certain settlement that must be modern Florence under the name Fluentia: "Fluentini profluenti Arno appositi."[90] It is possible that "Fluentini" is a corruption of "Florentini," a result of the attraction of the following word "profluenti" in the mind of the scribes (p. 33). Yet Florence had been founded at the confluence of three rivers, and it is not unlikely that the original name was really Fluentia, which later generations for a variety of reasons transmuted into "Florentia." Salutati explicitly rejects the identification of Florence with the "Florentia" recorded in some of the manuscripts of Seneca ("whom certain people call Florus") to have been sold "at auction" during the civil war between Sulla and Marius. The oldest text of the *Epitome* reads "Florentina," a town located in Campania.[91]

Although contemporary scholarly opinion inclines toward the view that Florence was founded under the Second Triumvirate rather than by Sulla, Salutati's position dominated the field down to the time of Poliziano and his arguments remain eminently respectable today.[92] Bruni based his own account of the origins of the city in Book I of his *Historiarum florentini populi* published in 1415 on Salutati's findings.[93] The careful research that characterizes the whole of this first great monument of humanist historiography reflects to no small degree the long apprenticeship of its author to a great teacher.

While in his reconstruction of the founding of Florence Salutati aimed at establishing a specific historical fact, his research on the history of Latin language and literature illustrates his capacity for tracing a development over a long period. Latin was Salutati's literary language. Although recognizing the value of Greek for scholarship, he believed that the Latins had excelled the Greeks in literature, and he valued the moral tone and sobriety of the Roman writers over what he considered the

90. *Invect.*, p. 32. The passage of Pliny is III, 52. The relevant passage of Ptolemy is *Geog.*, III, under *Tuscorum: Liber geographiae* (Venice, 1511), unpaginated.

91. Florus, *Epit. rer. roman.*, II, 9 (III, 21).

92. Nicolai Rubinstein, "Il Poliziano," p. 110.

93. *Historiarum florentini populi libri XII e Rerum suo tempore gestarum commentarius*, ed. E. Santini and C. di Pierro, *R.S.I.*, vol. 19, pt. 3 (Città di Castello, 1914–26), pp. 5–6.

fickle genius of their Greek counterparts.[94] As for the modern *volgari* Salutati regarded the current interest in writing in one's mother tongue as a sign of moral degeneration. The minds of his contemporaries were too corrupted by passion to exert the powers of concentration required to master Latin.[95]

A vital interest of the humanist's mature years was in philological problems surrounding ancient Latin and patristic writings and in locating lost texts of the authors. On the basis of a passage of Lactantius, for instance, he identified the *Aratea* of Germanicus.[96] He was the first to state unequivocally that Caesar, not Julius Celsus, was the author of the *Commentarii*.[97] While he would assign no author's name, over the years he came to question the attribution of the *Epistola Valerii ad Ruffinum* either to St. Jerome or Valerius;[98] furthermore, he rejected the at-

94. Like Petrarch, Salutati refers to the Greeks as *extranei*: ibid., II, 126. He calls them *Greculi* (ibid., III, 15). Although he criticizes both *Greculi* and *Romani* for their love of glory (ibid., II, 406), he is clearly harder on the *Greculi* than on the *Romani* (ibid., II, 426). Virgil is said to be superior to Homer (ibid., III, 491).

95. *Epist.*, I, 77. He was particularly hostile to French because he believed that the French were trying to make their language the standard of civilized discourse (ibid., II, 413). Cf. I, 141 and IV, 220. His enthusiasm for Dante's work in *volgare* increased in later life, but it is unlikely that he was including Latin when he maintained in the *De fato et fortuna*, B.A.V., *Vat. lat.*, 2928, Tr. III, 11, fol. 69ᵛ, that Dante's Florentine surpassed "cunctas mundi linguas rythmicis cantibus cum elegantia dulcedineque." About 1401, in comparing the artistry of Dante with that of Homer and Virgil, he wrote: "Sentio tamen alium recte, nisi fallor, tam latiali quam greco preferendum Homero, si latine potuisset, sicut materni sermonis elegantia, cecinisse" (*Epist.*, III, 491). I agree with Rossi's interpretation of this passage that for Salutati Dante's poetry did not reach the highest perfection because he wrote in *volgare*: Vittorio Rossi, "Dante nel Trecento e nel Quattrocento," *Scritti di critica letteraria*, 3 vols. (Florence, 1930), I, 307. D. Aguzzi-Barbagli, "Dante e la poetica di Coluccio Salutati," *Italica*, 42 (1965), 119–20, points out that Rossi omitted discussing Salutati's next sentence: "Nullum tamen consumate perfectionis habitu certum est poeticam imbibisse." In the light of this second statement, he maintains that the first statement should not be viewed as a depreciation of *volgare* but rather as expressing Salutati's judgment that "qual cosa mancava alla *cultura* di Dante non alla sua *poesia* a causa della rozzezza del suo latino e ignoranza del greco." In my view the first sentence of Salutati's judgment of Dante's poetry affirms that it lacked ultimate perfection because written in *volgare*, while the second connects his remark on Dante to the general theme of this section of the letter that no poetry is perfect.

96. Berthold L. Ullman, *The Humanism*, p. 229.

97. *Epist.*, II, 299–300. Petrarch had hesitations about the medieval attribution of authorship to Julius Celsus: Giuseppe Billanovich, "Nella biblioteca del Petrarca," *Italia medioevale e umanistica*, 3 (1960), 40–46. Cf. Guido Martellotti, "Alcuni aspetti della filologia del Petrarca," *Lettere italiane*, 26 (1974), 291–96. Martellotti points out that Petrarch's own work on Caesar, *De gestis Cesaris*, in the sixteenth and seventeenth centuries was identified by philologists as the work of Celsus (pp. 295–96).

98. Berthold L. Ullman, *Studies in the Italian Renaissance*, Storia e letteratura, 2nd ed., vol. 51 (Rome, 1973), pp. 288–92, publishes an addendum to a letter dated by Ullman as late as 1392 or 1393. On p. 289 Salutati confesses his ignorance as to the author of the work he had formerly ascribed without question to Jerome (*Epist.*, I, 187), and then to a certain Valerius or Jerome (ibid., II, 374).

tribution of the medieval *Manuale sive speculum Augustini* to St. Augustine.[99] If he shared with Antonio Loschi and Pasquino Capelli the honor of bringing Cicero's *Ad familiares* from hiding,[100] he was responsible for putting the pseudo-Ciceronian *Synonyma* and *Differentiae* into circulation[101] as well as discovering Cato's *De re rustica*, Servius' *De centum metris*, Pompeius' *Commentum artis Donati*, and Maximianus' *Elegiae*.[102]

But far more important in the long run than these individual contributions was his developing a periodization of Latin prose literature which was to remain a part of the tradition of classical scholarship down to the present. At the very beginning of the fourteenth century Geremia da Montagnone distinguished between ancient and more recent authors, drawing the demarcation about the sixth century A.D.[103] Petrarch clearly sensed a profound decay in the level of Latin eloquence between the time of the late empire and his own age but he offered no precise chronology.[104] In a letter of 1395 Salutati was the first to present a fairly detailed description of a succession of literary periods from the time of Cicero down to the fourteenth century.[105] In this scheme the age of Cicero was the golden age of Latin eloquence. Along with Cicero

99. Ullman, *The Humanism*, p. 140.

100. G. Kirner, "Contributo alla critica del testo delle *Epistolae ad familiares* di Cicerone," *Studi italiani di filologia classica*, 9 (1901), 399. Cf. Remigio Sabbadini, *Le scoperte dei codici latini e greci ne' secoli XIV e XV*, 2 vols. (Florence, 1914), I, 34.

101. Ullman, *The Humanism*, pp. 224–25.

102. Sabbadini, *Le scoperte*, I, 34–35. With Boccaccio and Petrarch he correctly suspected that Seneca, the tutor of Nero, had not written the *Octavia* (*Epist.*, I, 152). But he believed erroneously that he had not authored the others traditionally ascribed to him (ibid., p. 155, and II, 99–101). On this whole problem, see Guido Martellotti, "La questione dei due Seneca da Petrarca a Benvenuto," *Italia medioevalia e umanistica*, 15 (1972), 149–69. While he appears to have had the first complete Tibullus, Lovato Lovati had at least a portion of the work: Guido Billanovich, "Il preumanesimo padovano," in *Storia della cultura veneta*, vol. 2 (Vicenza, 1976), pp. 58–9.

103. Roberto Weiss, *The Dawn of Humanism* (New York, 1970), p. 8; and Ullman, *Studies*, pp. 79–111. Geremia made a division between the ancient and later poets by defining the former as *poetae* and the latter as *versilogi*, but he made no divisions within those two categories. The first of the *versilogi* was Avianus, whom he placed chronologically after Isidore. See chap. 1, p. 8.

104. Theodore Mommsen, "Petrarch on the 'Dark Ages'," *Medieval and Renaissance Studies* (Ithaca, 1959), p. 128. See also Guido Martellotti, "Latinità del Petrarca," *Studi petrarcheschi*, 7 (1961), 219–30, esp. 220–21; and Franco Simone's important discussion of the distinction between ancient and medieval writers in Petrarch, Boccaccio, and Salutati: *Per una storia della storiografia letteraria francese*, Memorie dell'Accademia delle scienze di Torino, cl. sci., mor., stor., e filol., 4th ser., 12 (1966). Whereas Simone (pp. 63–65) emphasizes the distinction between ancient and medieval authors in Salutati's statements, I find more original his distinction between periods in ancient literature itself.

105. *Epist.*, III, 80–85. For the letter of Cardinal Oliari that provoked this discussion, see A. Campana, "Lettera del cardinale padovano (Bartolomei Oliari) a Coluccio Salutati," *Classical, Medieval and Renaissance Studies in Honor of Berthold Louis Ullman*, ed. C. Henderson, Jr., 2 vols. (Rome, 1964), II, 237–54.

flourished many other republican orators. What other age could boast Julius Caesar, Octavian, Servius Sulpicius, Marcus Cecina, Dolabella, and a host of other illustrious men? Seneca, Livy, and Valerius Maximus also seem from his account to belong to this age, although Salutati implies that there was already something of a falling off in the case of the latter. Clearly inferior to this first age of eloquence was that of Suetonius, Tacitus, Pliny the Younger, Martianus Capella, and Apuleius. On the other hand, the period of Augustine, Ausonius, Boethius, and Cassiodorus reflects something of a restoration of the former level of eloquence or "to speak more truly, a few gave a continuity to eloquence for almost a century."[106]

The writers of the next centuries "prided themselves too much on their eloquence." Ivo of Chartres, Hildebert of Lavardin, Abelard, Bernard, John of Salisbury, Richard of Pofi, and other men of their generations cannot be compared to the rhetoricians of the first age (*prisci*) or the middle age (*medii*). In his own century Salutati cautiously remarks, certain writers "raise themselves a bit" (*emerserunt parumper*): first of all Mussato and Geri of Arezzo and then Dante, Petrarch, and Boccaccio. Yet who can deny that their "capacity to speak" was inferior to the ancients? Salutati never attempted to reconcile this adverse judgment on his own time with his repeated claim that Petrarch excelled the ancients in prose and poetry.[107]

This characterization of Latin literary history reveals Salutati's capacity for integrating disparate writers and times into one overall structure. It also suggests that, although considering the writers of the eleventh to the thirteenth century vastly inferior to the ancients and below the level of the best authors of his own century, he viewed them as having some claim to literary merit and as making a positive contribution to the tradition of Latin literature.[108] His occasional appraisals elsewhere of the

106. Ibid., III, 82. After mentioning a number of authors besides these, he concludes: " . . . at alii quamplures redivivam quodammodo facundiam reduxerunt; sive, quo verius loquar, continuatam in paucis unius ferme tractu seculi tenuerunt." Significantly, Salutati presents an account of the evolution of prose writing, not of poetry. In a private communication to me Prof. Riccardo Fubini suggests that Salutati's failure to provide a chronology for poetry reflects both his sense that the greatest threat to tradition lay in the area of prose and the institutionalization of poetry in the medieval curriculum (see chap. 1), which made a comparable treatment for poetry more difficult.

107. See below, p. 266, and chap. 15, pp. 404–5.

108. This and the following paragraph are based on Richard Donovan, "Salutati's Opinion of Non-Italian Latin Writers of the Middle Ages," *Studies in the Renaissance*, 14 (1967), 185–201. Donovan's article represents a justified criticism of Berthold L. Ullman's view (*The Humanism of Coluccio Salutati*, p. 95) that Salutati had "no use for medieval and contemporary writers." For Salutati's positive attitude toward twelfth-century writers, see Donovan, "Salutati's Opinion," pp. 192–93.

work of twelfth-century writers like Abelard and Peter of Blois and his pursuit of manuscripts of their writings, primarily of their letter collections, reinforces this impression.[109] Unlike Petrarch, who ostensibly viewed the period from late antiquity to his own time as devoid of literary achievement, Salutati insisted on continuity while admitting a significant decline in stylistic excellence.[110] However, the mention of a single thirteenth-century *dictator* in the list of medieval authors, Richard of Pofi, indicates Salutati's hesitations about including authors of *dictamen* in the Latin literary tradition.[111]

He seems even more inclined to consider the late twelfth century as marking the end of the rich tradition of eloquent theological works beginning with the writings of St. Paul and running down to Anselm and Bernard. As in style so in the quality of thought he saw a decline in these later authors, but this did not mean that they "who have distinguished themselves among the greatest theologians" were not worthy of praise.[112] The discussion of Salutati's *De fato et fortuna* and the *De nobilitate legum et medicine* will show that the writings of the scholastics, while lacking style, were valued by Salutati for their intellectual merit.

Why this overall decline since the age of Cicero? As in the case of the emergence of the *volgari*, Salutati located the primary causative force for the gradual diminution of eloquence in a general moral decay. Paradigmatic of this moral decline was the practice of using the second person plural when speaking to an individual.[113] In his opinion this usage clearly arose from a wish of superiors to be flattered and from a servile hypocrisy on the part of their inferiors. His analysis of the introduction of this reprehensible custom of using *vos* instead of *tu* for individuals

109. On two occasions he urged Jean de Montreuil at the French court to obtain copies of Abelard's letters for him. See references in Donovan, p. 190. For his use of John of Salisbury, see ibid., pp. 193–94; for his admiration of Peter of Blois, ibid., 194.

110. Donovan, p. 185, cites the succinct comment of Franco Simone, *La coscienza della Rinascità negli umanisti francesi* (Rome, 1949), p. 59: "Per il Petrarca dopo la fine dell'impero romano nessun vero letterato era comparso." Cf. the comments of Mommsen, "Petrarch on the 'Dark Ages'," pp. 106–29.

111. Although Peter of Blois perhaps wrote a treatise on *dictamen*, neither his letters nor those of any of the great writers of the twelfth century properly belong to the *ars dictaminis* tradition. Rather their literary and stylistic ideals were overwhelmed in the late twelfth century when the *ars dictaminis* established its dominion over most areas of prose writing. I shall discuss this subject in a forthcoming essay. For information on the life of Richard, see K. M. Baumgarten, "Richard v. Pofi, ein Grossneffe Innocenz' III," *Neues Archiv*, 36 (1911), 743–51. For his collection of papal letters and documents, see Ernst Batzer, *Zur Kenntnis der Formularsammlung des Richard von Pofi*, Heidelberger Abhandlungen zur mittleren und neuen Geschichte, 28 (Heidelberg, 1910); and F. Bock, "Päpstliche Sekretregister und Kammerregister," *Archivalische Zeitschrift*, 59 (1963), 48–51.

112. For references, see Donovan, p. 196.

113. *Epist.*, II, 412–13.

provides another illustration of his sense of historical perspective.

Like Petrarch before him Salutati found the usage of addressing one person as several not only against the practice of ancient writers but also illogical.[114] Moreover, why when speaking of that same person to a third, does one not use the third person plural? Actually in Salutati's opinion the singular form was more complimentary than the plural in that the monad is superior to number and unity a higher form than plurality. There is some logic in utilizing the plural form when speaking to individuals who exercise public office because they indirectly represent through their position a multitude of men. Yet even this was not correct usage in Roman times.[115]

As late as 1384 he believed the medieval tradition that this corrupt use of *vos* first occurred when Julius Caesar invaded the Republic. The introduction of the plural form was just one sign of the flattering servility required for life under a tyranny.[116] By 1394, however, in the course of his correspondence with Giovanni di Conversino, the most Byzantine Latin stylist of his generation, Salutati showed that he no longer held this opinion. Giovanni had written Salutati earlier in the month, addressing him with *vos* and Salutati replied on January 25, 1394, giving many arguments against such practice.[117] As a witness to the error, Sal-

---

114. Ibid., II, 409 and 413; III, 78–79. *Francesci Petrarce Familiarum Rerum libri XXIV*, ed. V. Rossi, 4 vols. (1933–42), IV, 196. Also see *Var.*, 32, below n. 122, and *Sen.*, XV, 1, in *Opera*, II, 1046–47. Salutati specifically mentioned Petrarch's position, *Epist.*, II, 472–73. On Salutati's stand, see ibid., II, 395 and 422.

115. Ibid., II, 163, and III, 78.

116. Giuseppe Billanovich, "La première correspondance échangée entre Jean de Montreuil et Coluccio Salutati," *Italia medioevale e umanistica*, 7 (1964), 348. John of Salisbury seems to have been responsible for initiating this error from a misreading of Lucan, *Phar.*, V, 385–86: Billanovich, "La première correspondance," p. 342. Petrarch subscribed to the error: *Var.* 32, in *Epistolae de rebus et familiaribus*, ed. G. Fracassetti, 3 vols. (Florence, 1859–63), III, 380.

117. A revised chronology of the exchange of letters between Coluccio Salutati and Conversino is necessary. In publishing Giovanni di Conversino's correspondence with the Florentine humanist, Novati included the three letters known to him from the *Akad. Z.*, II, C 61, in vol. 4 of the *Epistolario*. Together with four letters of Salutati they form the following series for 1394:

Conversino: "Miratur vulgus," Jan. 4, 1394, IV, 305–8 (for corrected date see Berthold L.
    Ullman, *Studies*, pp. 221–22.
Salutati: "Dici non potest," Jan. 25, 1394 (?), II, 404–11 (Ullman, p. 225)
Conversino: "Habet hoc allocutio," Jan.–Feb. 1394, IV, 308–14
Salutati: "Multi scribis iocunda," Feb. 24, 1394, II, 411–27
Conversino: "Allata nuper tue," March 18, 1394, IV, 315–30
Salutati: "Ignitum eloquium tuum," April 1394, II, 437–39
Salutati: "Credo te miratum," Nov. 16, 1394, II, 470–80

The very long letter *Akad. Z.*, II, C 61, fols. 67/68–75ᵛ/76ᵛ ("Dulcia fautibus meis"), constitutes Conversino's response to this last letter. While continuing the argument of the re-

utati calls on Cicero, who boasts that even if the Romans of Cicero's day had lost their liberty to Caesar and flattered the patricide with the name of savior and father of the country, they never stooped so low as to address him with the plural *vos*.[118]

In his response a few weeks later, Giovanni promises henceforth to use the *tu* when writing Salutati, and, apparently ignoring Salutati's historical observation, remarks that he now recalls that no one before Caesar's conquest of the Republic used anything but the singular address for single persons.[119] This provides Salutati the opportunity in his next letter to trace his researches on the introduction of the corrupted practice of *vos*.[120] Neither Caesar nor Augustus received the *vos*, and as late as the beginning of the fifth century a writer like Sidonius always employed *tu* in speaking to individuals. If a century later Ennodius began to use *vos* in some cases, Gregory the Great by the end of the same century still kept the *tu* form in his *Pastorales*, *Dialogi*, and other works. His usage is ambiguous in his letters. Those to Bishop Augustine were written in the singular, but there are instances when the plural form was used when only one recipient is indicated. Perhaps, he postulates, this might be because the same letter was to be written to a number of individuals but only one name was provided in the rubric. Possibly, of course, Gregory may have been trying to flatter a correspondent to obtain his ends. On the other hand, even Pope Nicolas in the ninth century seems to have made exceptional use of the *vos*. While in this letter he admits his inability to establish exactly when the *vos* became common, a few months later he seems willing to say that the ancient custom of using *tu* for all individuals was "faithfully observed until a very few centuries ago," perhaps an allusion to the pivotal twelfth century when something of a break in the Latin literary tradition occurred for him.[121]

---

cent letters, it also discusses the theft of the notebook. The manuscript contains a fifth letter, "Letor et proficio," (fol. 105ᵛ/106ᵛ), dated by Remigio Sabbadini, *Giovanni da Ravenna, insigne figura d'umanista (1343–1408)* (Como, 1924), pp. 218–19, as written in January 1400. Cf. Benjamin G. Kohl, "The Works of Giovanni di Conversino da Ravenna: A Catalogue of Manuscripts and Editions," *Traditio*, 31 (1975), pp. 358–59, for the five Conversino letters. However, Kohl, p. 358, dates "Dulcia fautibus meis" as ca. 1393.

118. *Epist.*, II, 409.
119. Ibid., IV, 309.
120. Ibid., II, 415–19.
121. Ibid., II, 438. On the continuing debate on the issue of *tu* and *vos*, see T. Foffano, "La costruzione di Castiglione Olona in un opuscolo inedito di F. Pizolpasso," *Italia medievale e umanistica*, 3 (1960), 174–75. Writing a half century after Salutati, Aeneas Sylvius felt it necessary to justify his use of *tu* when writing to princely correspondents: *Der Briefwechsel des Eneas Silvius Piccolomini*, ed. Rudolf Wolkan, Fontes rerum austriacarum, vols. 61–62 and 67 (Vienna, 1909–12), I, 222–23 and 310–11. He curiously suggests that, reintro-

In 1356 Petrarch admitted to resorting occasionally to use of the plural when writing singular persons but assured his correspondent that from that moment on "whatever the subject, whatever the level of style" he would never do so again.[122] Conditions, however, made it impossible for him to keep his resolution consistently. Salutati shared this repugnance for the usage of *vos*, but he too made exceptions. He grudgingly admitted that the modern practice had more justification when addressing public officials, and his varying of *tu* and *vos* in letters to princes, popes, and cardinals suggests that he was caught between his wish to restore the old practice of *tu* everywhere and his desire to please a superior.[123]

Besides the reintroduction of the *tu*, the Latin of Salutati's private writings reflects an effort to eliminate a number of characteristics of medieval Latin in favor of ancient usage. His style at its best strikes one as reminiscent of Seneca rather than Cicero,[124] but in no sense did he make a systematic attempt to imitate any ancient author. He varied his style, moreover, depending on the subject and the audience.[125] A tract like the *De fato et fortuna* follows the rules of medieval *cursus* more closely than does the *De laboribus Herculis* or his private letters. The *De nobilitate legum et medicine* with its seventy-two conclusions resembles a scholastic treatise in its structure until the final pages when medicine takes the podium to lecture on her inferiority to law.

While apparently agreeing with Petrarch that the writer should create his own style,[126] until his very last months of life he never discussed his

---

duced by Petrarch, the use of *tu* did not become widespread until after the arrival of Chrysoloras (p. 223).

122. Var. 32, *Epistolae*, III, 381. For the dating of this letter see Ernest H. Wilkins. *Petrarch's Correspondence*, Medioevo e umanistica, vol. 3 (Padua, 1960), p. 114. For a vivid impression of the difference between Petrarch's letters as they were actually sent (with their concessions to medieval tradition) and as he later edited them for inclusion in his collection, see Armando Petrucci, *Francesco Petrarca: Epistole autografe*, Itinera erudita, vol. 3 (Padua, 1968).

123. Examples of contradiction are found in Ullman, *The Humanism*, pp. 107–8.

124. Remigio Sabbadini, *Storia del ciceronianismo e di altre questioni letterarie nell'età della rinascenza* (Torino, 1885), pp. 11–12, stresses the influence of both Seneca and Petrarch on Salutati's style. He tends to exaggerate when he writes: "Del resto il Salutati appartiene agli scrittori dello stile fiorito e pomposamente sonoro, oppresso da soverchia erudizione e troppo sentenzioso. Questo stile è una degenerazione o meglio un'esagerazione di quello del Petrarca" (p. 12).

125. Armando Petrucci, *Coluccio Salutati*, Biblioteca biographica, vol. 7 (Rome, 1972), pp. 93–94.

126. Petrarch succinctly expresses himself, *Fam.*, I, 8; I, 40–44. For Petrarch's theory of *imitatio*, see the classic article by Hermann Gmelin, "Das Prinzip der Imitatio in den romanischen Literaturen der Renaissance," *Romanische Forschungen*, 46 (1932), 118–27; and Thomas M. Greene, "Petrarch and the Humanist Hermeneutic," in *Italian Literature: Roots*

position on the matter of imitation. When he did so, it was in response to criticism of two of his young disciples, Poggio and Bruni, who insisted on observing a more classical syntax and vocabulary. By urging greater consistency in imitating ancient usage, they tended to focus on ancient Latin as a language rather than a variety of styles utilized by ancient authors. In his rebuttal of their viewpoint Salutati, while favoring the same approach to Latin, maintained that ancient Latin itself underwent change and that slavish imitation of the past was a contradiction of ancient precedent.

Salutati's conception of Latin as a mutable language assumes significance only in the context of the medieval discussions regarding the nature of human language and Latin in particular. From the twelfth century onward there had been a tendency to view human languages as accidental to a basic grammar. This grammar consisted of rules established by reason governing the determined modalities of expression in the human mind: " . . . the nature of things and their modes of being understood are the same in all men and as a consequence there are similar modes of signifying, organizing, and speaking from which grammar derives." The confection of this speculative grammar had originally been the task of the philosophers, and despite their differences, all languages must respect the rules laid down by them.[127]

The *modistae* generally considered Latin on the same par with other languages in its subordination to this speculative grammar, but since it

---

and Branches, Essays in Honor of Thomas Goodard Bergin, ed. G. Rimanelli and K. J. Atchity (New Haven and London, 1976), pp. 201–24.

127. Cited from an anonymous thirteenth-century *De modis significandi*, Bib. Sorb. Paris, 1334, fol. 131, by Charles Thurot, *Extraits de divers manuscrits latins pour servir à l'histoire des doctrines grammaticales au moyen âge* (Paris, 1863), p. 125. For manuscript, ibid., p. 46. Cf. other references, pp. 122–31. On the tendency to identify with the metalanguage, G. L. Bursill-Hall, *Speculative Grammars of the Middle Ages* (Hague, 1971), p. 38, writes: "Their conception of reality and of human reason led them to maintain that grammar must be 'one', and therefore Robert Kilwardby, one of the immediate predecessors of the Modistae, could argue that grammar can only be a science if it is one for all men; as a result of the intimacy between the reality of things and their conceptualization by the mind, grammar becomes the study of the formulation of these concepts, their actual expression being accidental, and therefore incidental to Modistic grammatical theory. Furthermore, this theory of grammar had the effect of creating the belief that the universality of things as conceived and understood by the universality of human reason could be expressed in the universal language, Latin, which was thus raised to the status of metalanguage. Minor matters such as the vernaculars had perhaps the effect of attesting differences in vocabulary, but these could be dismissed since they could not affect structure." On speculative grammar, see R. H. Robins, *Ancient and Mediaeval Grammatical Theory in Europe* (London, 1951), pp. 69–99; and J. Pinborg, *Die Entwicklung der Sprachtheorie im Mittelalter. Beiträge zur Geschichte der Philosophie und Theologie des Mittelalters*, vol. 42, pt. 2 (Münster-Copenhagen, 1967).

served as the means of expressing the analysis of the *modistae*, Latin could easily assume the status of being this speculative grammar with its characteristics. This identification occurred in the case of Dante and others of his generation who came to view Latin as a stable, consciously elaborated language. For Dante, Latin, as contrasted with the *volgari*, had "a kind of unchangeable identity of speech in different times and places." Having been invented by men and accepted by the common consent of many peoples, no one could later change it and therefore it was invariable. On the other hand, the *volgari* of Europe were always changing. Impermanent, ungoverned in their development, the *volgari* were the primary languages of men, the languages learned at their mothers' breast.[128]

The *modistae* conception of language received encouragement from the etymological tradition of Isidore codified in the word lists of the medieval lexicographers. The belief that analysing the structure of a word into its component parts allowed one to discover the component ideas hidden in the idea signified by the word easily led to a belief in language as a conscious creation of men, a creation designed to serve as a vehicle for expressing truth in all its subtleties. In interpreting the

---

128. In his *De vulgari eloquentia*, ed. A. Marigo (Florence, 1938), p. 72, Dante describes the motive for creating the *lingua artificialis* as follows: "Hinc moti sunt inventores gramatice facultatis; que quidem gramatica nichil aliud est quam quedam inalterabilis locutionis idemptitas diversis temporibus atque locis. Hec cum de comuni consensu multarum gentium fuerit regulata, nulli singulari arbitrio videtur obnoxia, et per consequens nec variabilis esse potest. Adinvenerunt ergo illam, ne propter variationem sermonis arbitrio singularium fluitantis, vel nullo modo vel saltim imperfecte antiquorum actingeremus autoritates et gesta, sive illorum quos a nobis locorum diversitas facit esse diversos." Dante's statement contrasting the *volgare* with Latin in the *Convivio*, I, v, 8 (G. Busnelli and G. Vandelli, 2 vols. [Florence, 1964], I, 33) makes the same point: "Onde vedemo ne le scritture antiche de le comedie tragedie latine, che non si possono transmutare, quello medesimo che oggi avemo; che non avviene del volgare, lo quale a piacimento artificiato si transmuta." Compare Egidius Colonna, *De reg. principum*, I, 2, pt. 2, 8, who writes: "Addiscimus per grammaticam idioma latinum, quod est idioma philosophorum: sub tali enim sermone philosophi suam scientiam tradiderunt." Ibid., pt. 2, 7: "Videntes philosophi nullum idioma vulgare esse completum et perfectum, per quod perfecte exprimere possent naturas rerum et mores hominum et cursus astrorum et alia de quibus disputare volebant, invenerunt sibi quasi proprium idioma litterale; quod constituerunt adeo latum et copiosum, ut per ipsum possent omnes suos conceptus sufficienter exprimere." Colonna is cited by G. Busnelli in Dante Alighieri, *Il Convivio*, I, 181. On Dante's conception of Latin, see Antonino Pagliaro, *Nuovi saggi di critica semantica*, 2nd ed. (Messina-Florence, 1963), pp. 219–22; and Gustavo Vinay, "Ricerche sul'De vulgari eloquentia," *Giornale storico della letteratura italiana*, 136 (1959), 236–58. For the problem of the conception of Latin in fourteenth- and fifteenth-century Italy, see the seminal article by Riccardo Fubini, "La coscienza del latino negli umanisti: 'An latina lingua Romanorum esset peculiare idioma,'" *Studi medievali*, 2nd ser., 2 (1961), 505–50, and for Dante, especially 510–16. For the influence of the *modistae* on Dante's thought, see Marigo *De vulg.*, p. 72, n. 59; and Fubini, "La Coscienza," p. 513, n. 13.

Bible, of course, the pursuit of ideas required unraveling the truths which God, not man, intended when He Himself gave names to things.[129]

Isidore (*Etymol.* I, xxix, 2) made clear that "not all names were given by the ancients according to nature but certain were arbitrarily imposed."[130] Efforts to interpret this species of vocabulary, consequently, would prove fruitless. The authority of Horace, moreover, justified the addition of new words to language, thus encouraging twelfth- and thirteenth-century Latin poets who revelled in the enterprise of creating their own vocabulary.[131] To avoid possible chaos, contemporary grammarians stressed Horace's caveat that such additions should be made with caution. Geoffrey of Vinsauf seems to have conceived of the problem of adding new words as equivalent to introducing them from other languages but confused this problem with that of accurately translating from one language into another.[132]

129. Yves M.J. Congar, "Cephas, Céphalè, Caput," *Revue du moyen âge latin*, 8 (1952), 26–36; and Etienne Gilson, *Les idées et les lettres* (Paris, 1932), 129, n. 1.

130. "Omnis enim rei inspectio etymologia cognita planior est. Non autem omnia nomina a veteribus secundum naturam inposita sunt, sed quaedam et secundum placitum, sicut et nos servis et possessionibus interdum secundum quod placet nostrae voluntati nomina damus. Hinc est quod omnium nominum etymologiae non reperiuntur, quia quaedam non secundum qualitatem, qua genita sunt, sed iuxta arbitrium humanae voluntatis vocabula acceperunt."

131. *Ars poetica*, 46–59: "In verbis etiam tenuis cautusque serendis/dixeris egregie, notum si callida verbum/reddiderit iunctura novum. si forte necesse est/indiciis monstrare recentibus abdita rerum,/fingere cinctutis non exaudita Cethegis/continget, dabiturque licentia sumpta pudenter:/et nova fictaque nuper habebunt verba fidem, si/Graeco fonte cadent parce detorta. quid autem/Caecilio Plautoque dabit Romanus ademptum/Vergilio Varioque? ego cur, adquirere pauca/si possum, invideor, cum lingua Catonis et Enni/sermonem patrium ditaverit et nova rerum/nomina protulerit? licuit semperque licebit/signatum praesente nota producere nomen."

132. John of Garland cites Horace (*Ars poetica*, 46–48) in proving that "In verbis inveniendis debemus esse cauti, quia raro licet nova verba invenire . . . ": *The Parisiana Poetria of John of Garland*, ed. T. Lawler (New Haven, 1974), pp. 26–28. Geoffrey of Vinsauf writes in his *Documentum de arte versificandi*, I, 3, ed. Edmond Faral, *Les arts poètiques du xii* et du xiii* siècle* (Paris, 1924), pp. 311–312: "Item notandum est quod docet Horatius egregie dicere sic scilicet ponendo verbum notum in nova significatione, quod nos supra plene docuimus loquendo de nominatione, pronominatione, translatione. Praedictis itaque adjiciendum est quod dicit Horatius: licet invenire nova vocabula. Quod quidam sic intelligunt, quod in una lingua licet ex una dictione aliam formare, ut ex hac dictione 'saxum' formare hanc dictionem 'saxior', ut dicatur: 'Saxior est saxo, ferrior ferro, vulpior vulpe, tigrior tigride'; sed talia nullius momenti sunt, nec illi qui hoc dicunt Horatium intelligunt. Dicit enim Horatius quod illis qui noverunt utramque linguam, scilicet graecam et latinam, licet invenire nova vocabula, scilicet transferendo de una lingua in aliam, de graeca in latinam. Translatio vero sic est facienda ad hoc, ut sit idonea et authentica, scilicet ut ipsa translatione modesta sit mutatio. Quod quidem fit, si convenientia sit in principio et differentia in fine, ut ab hoc graeco 'patyr' hoc latinum 'pater'. In hac translatione convenientia est in principio et differentia in fine. Similiter a graeco 'theos' hoc latinum 'deus'. Ibi enim convenientia est in principio et differentia in fine. Convenientiam dixi esse in principio,

In the mid-1350s, however, an unnamed physician and enemy of poetry seized on this aspect of linguistic change to argue the inferiority of
poetry to medicine.[133] Whereas both vocabulary and meters change, he
regarded science as firm and immutable. To support his arguments the
defender of medicine turned not to Horace but to Aristotle, thus apparently introducing a new text into the discussion. As Aristotle writes:
"This is shown by the state of things today, when even the language of
tragedy has altered its character. Just as iambics were adopted, instead
of tetrameters, because they are the most prose-like of all metres, so
tragedy has given up all those words, not used in ordinary talk, which
decorated the early drama and are still used by the writers of hexameter
poems" (*Rhet.*, III, 1, 1404a, 29–34).[134]

The physician's remark, at least as reported by Petrarch, who was in
correspondence with him, should not be taken as reflecting a serious
examination of the nature of language but rather as an observation designed to win the argument for medicine. Nonetheless, concerned with
vindicating the superiority of poetry over medicine, Petrarch felt obligated to defend ancient Latin as an immutable language. In the light of
the medieval discussion, he might easily have admitted that certain
words, because "arbitrarily imposed," did change whereas most—those
words signifying things "according to nature"—did not. Eager to de-

---

quia conveniunt inter se, ut dicit Priscianus, orthographia "th" et "d". Et hoc modo licet
invenire nova vocabula modeste transferenda de una lingua in aliam, sicut dixi, non ut
alii fingunt. Ecce versus Horatii testes eorum quae proposui: 'Fingere cinctutis non exaudita Cethegis/Continget dabiturque licentia sumpta pudenter/Et nova fictaque nuper habebunt verba fidem, si/Graeco fonte cadant, parce detorta . . . /Licuit semperque licebit/
Signatum praesente nota producere nomen'" [*Ars poetica*, 50–53 ad 58–59]. The problem
of linguistic changes is interpreted as one of faithful translation from one language into
another. On this issue of faithfulness, see W. Schwarz, "The Meaning of *Fidus Interpres* in
Medieval Translation," *Journal of Theological Studies*, 45 (1944), 73–78; and Agostino Pertusi, *Leonzio Pilato fra Petrarca e Boccaccio*, Civiltà veneziana, Studi, vol. 16 (Venice-Rome,
1964), pp. 434–73.

There are few indications in the Middle Ages that Latin has changed since the end of
the empire. In the ninth century Smaragdus clearly describes a Christian Latinity distinct
from "vera propriaque latinitas": see Jean Leclercq, "Smaragde et la grammaire chrétienne," *Revue du moyen âge latin*, 4 (1948), 17. In the twelfth century Alexander de Ville-
dieu's statement "cum sim Christicola, normam non est mihi cura de propriis facere, quae
gentiles posuere," found as it is in the opening lines of *Pars* III dealing with metric, perhaps applies only to that aspect of the language: *Das Doctrinale des Alexander de Villa-Dei*,
ed. Dietrich Reichling, Monumenta Germaniae paedagogica, vol. 12 (Berlin, 1893), vv.
1559–1560. But see Jean de Ghellinck, *L'essor de la littérature latine au xii*^e *siècle*, 2 vols.
(Paris, 1946), II, 46; and Christine Mohrmann, *Etudes sur le latin des chrétiens*, Storia e letteratura, vol. 87 (Rome, 1961), pp. 198–99 and 205–6.

133. *Invective contra medicum*, ed. P. G. Ricci (Rome, 1950), p. 62, suggests the argument given by the physician.

134. The translation is that of W. R. Roberts, in *Basic Works of Aristotle*, ed. R. McKeon,
13th ed. (New York, 1941), p. 1436.

stroy his opponent's case, however, he showed himself unwilling to grant any concession when it came to ancient Latin.

Petrarch begins by deceptively agreeing with his opponent that words go in and out of fashion. He illustrates the point with two instances from Roman history. The first has to do with the name Quirinus, applied to Romulus. According to Petrarch, this word came from the Sabine word *quiris* or spear, and was appropriate because the founder of Rome used a spear in battle. A second case relates to an event reported by Suetonius. Near the close of the reign of Augustus a statue dedicated to the emperor was struck by lightning and the first letter was struck off leaving *esar*. The soothsayers were consulted and they replied that the deleted *c* meant that the emperor had but a hundred days to live and the remaining letters *esar* signified that he would be placed among the Gods because the word *esar* meant God in Tuscan. Petrarch, therefore, concludes: "Go now to Tuscia and Sabina: seek out Ostia and ask what 'esar' means, what 'quiris' means and they will think you are speaking Arabic." Clearly Petrarch has deflected the criticism of the changing vocabulary of poetry to the *volgari* of ancient Italy. Latin for him is not really in question. He then analyzes Aristotle's statement: "But Aristotle, a Greek, perhaps criticized some changes in his own poets similar to the changes we see in the theologians of our own day." Again he has protected Latin by making the changes Aristotle saw in Greek similar to those corruptions wrought by medieval writers. His conclusion affirms the immutability of ancient Latin: "However in the case of the Latin poets there is no change."[135]

135. *Inv.*, p. 62: "Pauca exempli causa ponenda sunt; non tibi quidem, cervicose nescie, sed lectori. Romulus, romane urbis conditor, Quirinus dictus est. Cur? Quia hasta in preliis utebatur, que Sabinorum lingua *quiris* dicitur. Cesar Augustus, cum supremo vite tempore statua eius fulmine disiecta esset, in qua scriptum erat Cesar, et prima litera cecidisset, remanentibus quattuor sequentibus, consuluit aruspices quid sperandum sibi. Illi autem dixerunt, centum diebus victurum et non amplius: quod ea litera significaretur quam fulmen excusserat; ipsum vero post mortem in deorum numerum referendum: id enim significare quod remanserat, quoniam lingua Tuscorum, *esar* deus diceretur. Percurre nunc Tusciam ac Sabinam, quere ostiatim quid est *esar*, quid est *quiris*: arabice te locutum credent. Mille sunt talia, que sciens sileo; omnium una ratio est: mutantur verba, manent res, in quibus scientie fundate sunt. Sed Aristoteles grecus homo mutationem poetarum forte suorum aliquam reprehendebat, qualia multa hodie videmus in theologis nostris. Hec autem apud latinos poetas mutatio nulla est." Petrarch's reference to "Sabinorum lingua" and the "lingua Tuscorum" recalls Isidore of Seville's discussion of the four Latin languages, *Etymologiae*, IX, 1, 6–8: "Latinas autem linguas quattuor esse quidam dixerunt, id est Priscam, Latinam, Romanam, Mixtam. Prisca est, quam vetustissimi Italiae sub Iano et Saturno sunt usi, incondita, ut se habent carmina Saliorum. Latina, quam sub Latino et regibus Tusci et ceteri in Latio sunt locuti, ex qua fuerunt duodecim tabulae scriptae. Romana, quae post reges exactos a populo Romano coepta est, qua Na-

This rebuttal with its strange conclusion might have been more than simply a clever argument to throw off a protagonist. Petrarch might not yet have divorced himself from the notion of Latin as an "unchangeable identity of speech," at least as regards Latin in its ancient form. But in the light of a comment made by Petrarch in a letter written in the same year, the statement more probably was made for polemical purposes.

Responding to Francesco Nelli, who had written to excuse himself for misspelling a verb in the past perfect in his previous letter, Petrarch unambiguously states that ancient Latin was not always precise. Even Cicero sometimes seemed confused about the proper forms. Language, he continues, is based on "human acceptance and convention, influenced and influencing according to the dictates of language usage." Quoting the verses of Horace justifying new words: "The speech of Cato and Ennius prescribed the language of the fathers and offered new words for objects," he concludes: "There is no doubt that Cicero and Virgil altered many things and also their successors have changed or will change them by precept or habit."[136]

Whereas medieval grammarians had used these verses in relationship to the addition of new vocabulary to Latin, none before Petrarch had stressed the element of conventionality of language implicit in the ancient poet's words. Because he commented neither here not elsewhere on the significance of this conception of language as a matter of "human acceptance and conventions" for the theories of speculative grammar and the etymological tradition, one cannot be sure that this was anything more than an isolated observation. Perhaps his apparent lifelong reluctance to seek truth hidden in words through etymological analysis implies some awareness that such analysis was opposed to linguistic fact. Yet there are no sure grounds for believing that in this regard he influenced those fifteenth-century humanists culminating in Valla who, starting with an idea of a language as a common possession of a people

---

evius, Plautus, Ennius, Vergilius poetae, et ex oratoribus Gracchus et Cato et Cicero vel ceteri effuderunt. Mixta, quae post imperium latius promotum simul cum moribus et hominibus in Romanam civitatem inrupit, integritatem verbi per soloecismos et barbarismos corrumpens."

136. *Fam.*, XVI, 14 (III, 211): " . . . ut vero sic loquamur humanum placitum atque conventum, quotidiani usus imperio motum saepe movendumque; sum, ut ait Flaccus, 'lingua Catonis et Enni/Sermonem patrium ditaverit et nova rerum/Nomina protulerit,/' in quibus et Ciceronem et Virgilium sequentesque alios multa mutasse, et vel auctoritate vel consuetudine mutaturos esse non sit dubium." Could Petrarch's view of language here be the result of his rethinking his position in the *Invectiva*? While dated in the same year, the chronological relationship of the two writings is undetermined.

based on popular usages evolving over time, laid the basis for our modern approach to linguistic developments.[137]

On the other hand, Salutati very likely had a direct effect on the evolution of this conception, although he would hardly have approved of Valla's use of the idea in lashing contemporary Latin style. From what has been said, it seems paradoxical to credit Salutati with such a contribution. His penchant for etymological investigations and heavy reliance on medieval lexicons during much of his scholarly life make him appear far more old-fashioned than Petrarch. Yet, while possibly signs of a commitment to the linguistic theories of speculative grammar, more probably these traits reflect his adhesion to individual elements in the learned tradition he inherited. By contrast, the marked decline in reliance on etymologies and lexicons in the last two or three years of his life may represent a conscious rejection of the theory of language they imply.[138]

As we shall see, these last years were ones of intensive discussion between the old humanist and younger scholars in his circle, who, increasingly aware of their own merits, did not hesitate to take issue with him on a wide range of subjects. The most significant of the surviving texts illustrating the conception of language he was defending against his friendly adversaries are two letters written to Poggio Bracciolini, who had gone off to the Curia to seek his fortune. Although Poggio's letters have disappeared, something of their content can be determined from reading Salutati's answers. The old man's first letter, that of December 17, 1405, was a response to an earlier one from Poggio in which the young man, among other things, had reprehended Salutati for daring to compare Petrarch with ancient writers. Poggio had accused Petrarch of lacking *vetustas*, of failing to imitate adequately ancient style.[139]

137. Fubini, "La coscienza," pp. 531–50, deals in detail with this fifteenth-century development. See as well the discussion of the debate between Poggio and Valla in the brilliant analysis of Salvatore I. Camporeale, *Lorenzo Valla. Umanesimo e teologia* (Florence, 1972), pp. 173–92.

138. The *Epistolario* in Salutati's very last years is free of etymological analyses and references to the works of the lexicographers. See above his late discussion of "Tenarus" where strikingly in the *De laboribus Herculis* no effort is made at finding the etymological truth hidden in the word.

139. Poggio criticized Petrarch's style as lacking *vetustas* (*Epist.*, IV, 140). He attacked Petrarch not only because "reprehensibiliter vetustati contradixit" but because "in his que scripsit erravit" (*ibid.*, p. 133). To the latter criticism Salutati replied that Poggio should indicate a passage in which Petrarch's opinion contradicted the ancients and where, if it did, "quod Petrarca sensit, non sit rationabiliter preferendum." In the same months Bruni wrote Salutati criticizing the lack of *vetustas* in Salutati's method of writing proper names. Bruni's letter is published *Leonardo Bruni Aretini Epistolarum*, ed. L. Mehus, 2 vols. (Flor-

Salutati's response reveals his desire to defend not only Petrarch but also a comprehensive vision of Latin literature which would include with the great pagan writers at least the Church Fathers, if not the whole medieval literary tradition down to the late twelfth century. Having fought a lifetime against scholastic Latin and the mentality it reflected, now from within his own camp he found an equally dangerous enemy. To establish the style of pagan authors as the criterion for excellence, amounted for Salutati to breaking asunder the weld joining two cultures and proving the religious conservatives right in their suspicion of an anti-Christian bias in the new studies. Salutati's statements on the Latin language, consequently, do not derive from the quiet meditations of a scholar but from the push and shove of a debate he desperately wanted to win.[140]

Yet his own presentation of the history of Latin literature down to contemporary times made him vulnerable. In 1395 had he not pointed out the inferior "capacity to speak" of even the greatest writers of his century when compared with ancient authors? Within a year had this letter to Oliari not led Vergerio to affirm that Cicero would be his own choice for a model to imitate?[141] Doubtless well known within his Florentine circle, the master's assessment of the Latin literary tradition either inspired or at least reinforced Poggio's view that Petrarch was incomparably inferior to the pagan writers.

Among the arguments given by Salutati in rebutting Poggio's aggressive classicism is one opening with the statement: "eloquence is a varied and multifaceted thing." A bit below, elaborating on this remark, he writes: " . . . as that fountain of eloquence Cicero maintains [De orat. I, III, 12], 'the whole art of oratory lies open to view and is concerned in some measure with the common practice, custom, and speech of mankind.'"

Thus Salutati's answer on the authority of Cicero is that literary language must keep in close connection with the popular one. His judg-

---

ence, 1740–41), II, 171–74. In justification of his usage, Salutati defined the conception of creative imitation of the ancients (Epist., IV, 148). See chap. 15.

140. See Fubini's observations, "La coscienza," pp. 527–28. In his excellent review of Ullman's The Humanism of Coluccio Salutati in the Rivista storica italiana, 79 (1965), 970, Fubini writes: "In piena coerenza col carattere composito della sua cultura il S. sentiva la rinascità delle lettere meno come frattura col passato che come processo graduale e continuo . . . " Cf. Petrucci, Coluccio Salutati, pp. 108–9.

141. Vergerio, Epistolario, ed. L. Smith, Fonti per la storia d'Italia, vol. 28 (Rome, 1934), p. 178. The young Vergerio writes: "Michi vero, ut et iudicium meum audias, videtur, Ciceronem omnibus et oratoribus et poetis eloquentia prestare." Cf. Marcello Aurigemma, Studi sulla cultura letteraria fra Tre e Quattrocento (Rome, 1976), p. 64.

ment of Poggio's call for *vetustas* as a standard for modern writers returns to the same idea: "Do you not act stupidly, you and he [a like-minded friend of Poggio at Rome] and all others who so anxiously seek majesty of language in modern writers to the point that unless they surpass, or at least savour, of *vetustas* you condemn them? You criticize them because they are not guilty of the greatest vice which Cicero ascribes to those abandoning the popular kind of speech."

The whole argument concludes with a brief periodization of Latin literature prior to Cicero which shows Latin as a developing language in the centuries before Cicero: "If no changes had been made from the times of Ennius [ab Ennianis temporibus] like that which Cato the Censor accomplished, although late in life, and the changes wrought by many others after him like L. Crassus, M. Anthony, M. Varro, M. Cicero, C. Caesar, Hortensius, and many others, who cultivated the Roman language like a fertile field, the ancient crudeness of speech would have remained down to today."[142]

To confine present-day writing to standards set by ancient writers who themselves derived their eloquence from manipulating the popular forms of speech of their day is to throttle talent. Modern authors, Salutati argues, by necessity must employ the language of their own time in order to persuade their audience.[143] Consequently, eloquence assumes the appearance of a higher form of expression of the same language spoken in the streets. Contemporary popular usages govern language. Is the crucial distinction between literature or style and language really being articulated here?

The concluding lines of the argument seem to suggest not. Whereas Petrarch had used Horace's dictum on changing language merely to indicate linguistic modification in ancient times, Salutati refers to the difference between the Latin of Cato and Ennius and that of Cicero and Virgil as marking progress in literary excellence. In 1395 Salutati had outlined the failing fortunes of Latin eloquence from Cicero and his gen-

142. *Epist.*, IV, 142: "Et quoniam, ut vult fons eloquentie Cicero, omnis dicendi ratio in medio posita communi quodam in usu atque in hominum more et sermone versatur et in dicendo vitium vel maximum est a vulgari genere orationis atque a consuetudine communis sensus abhorrere, nonne inscitissime facitis tu et ille et omnes alii, qui maiestatem illam eloquii tam anxie desideratis in modernis, ut nisi vincant vel saltem redoleant vetustatem adeo mordaciter condemnetis? reprehenditis eos, quod maximo vitio, quod imponit Tullius a vulgari genere orationis discedentibus non tenentur. Si nulla mutatio ab Ennianis temporibus facta fuisset; quod accuratissime fecit, sero licet, Cato Censorius; fecerunt et alii multi post eum, ut L. Crassus, M. Antonius, M. Varro, M. Tullius, C. Cesar, Hortensius et alii plures, qui romanum eloquium, velut agrum frugiferum, coluerunt; adhuc vetus illa ruditas permaneret."

143. Fubini, "La coscienza," p. 527, comments on Salutati's "relativismo storico."

eration to the fourteenth century. Now in his correspondence with Poggio he shows that the first century B.C. constituted the high point in the evolution of Latin eloquence, which began with the earliest writers a hundred years before. Taken together, these letters sketch the contours of Latin literary history, the rise and decline of Latin literature.

Clearly, in tracing this development in terms of individual styles Salutati betrays a confusion between language and literature which he seemed anxious to avoid a sentence before. Nevertheless, even if trapped by the medieval tradition of the *auctores*, he reveals in these lines some feel for Latin as an organic whole, product of contemporary popular usage and subject to change. After all he refers not to the "language of Ennius" but to that of the "times of Ennius," while by naming the great writers of the first century B.C., Salutati intends to comprehend the language of the age in which they worked. The end result of the confusion is to place final emphasis on the relative achievements of different writers rather than on the changing character of "Romanum eloquium."

At the same time Salutati's description of the progress made in perfecting ancient Latin speech from the third to the first century actually contradicts what had been the principal motive for writing this passage. To attack Poggio's idea of requiring modern writers to imitate closely the style of the ancients and thus to free Petrarch (and himself as well) from the charge of lacking *vetustas*, Salutati had argued that, because Latin changes, true eloquence requires sensitivity to what can be achieved employing the language of one's contemporaries. But his account of the progressive development of ancient Latin to Cicero—pioneering in itself—appears to serve Poggio's purposes better than his own. Together with his earlier periodication of Latin literature in the centuries after Cicero's generation, this assessment helps to delimit that age in the evolution of Latin which offered the best models of stylistic excellence.

Salutati's periodic conception of Latin—identified, as it was, with the styles of individual authors who flourished in the various centuries—became almost immediately diffused in Florence. The remarks of Cino Rinuccini (d. 1417) in his *Invettiva contro a cierti calunniatori di Dante e di messer Francesco Petrarcha e di messer Giovanni Boccacio* suggests that the debate about the most excellent stage of the Latin language was of current interest among young scholars in the city.[144] In this work devoted

144. Printed in *Il Paradiso degli Alberti. Ritrovi e ragionamenti del 1389. Romanzo di Giovanni da Prato*, ed. A. Wesselofsky, Scelta di curiosità letterarie, vols. 86¹–88 (Bologna, 1867), II, 303–16. A new edition of the short work is found in A. Lanza, *Polemiche e berte letterarie*

to criticizing a number of intellectual groups in Florence, Rinuccini singles out one, generally considered to be the "young humanists," for special drubbing: "In order to appear well read to the mob, they shout about the piazza how many diphthongs the ancients had and why today only two are in use; and which grammar is better, that of the time of the comic Terence or the polished one of the heroic Virgil."[145] Although the work is undated, it was probably composed about 1405–6.[146] By that time, as Rinuccini witnessed to his disgust, some scholars were attempting to decide not whose style was better, that of Terence or Virgil, but rather they were evaluating the comparative excellence of the grammars of the periods when these men lived. Did Rinuccini realize that Salutati had probably furnished the fundamental idea on which these debates rested?

Half a century lay between Salutati's confused presentation of the distinction between language as composed of popular usages and literature as a superior expression of language and Valla's sharp differentiation between the two which served as the basis for his conception of

nella Firenze del primo Quattrocento, Biblioteca di cultura, vol. 27 (Rome, 1972), pp. 261–67. For bibliography on Rinuccini, see my "Cino Rinuccini's Risponsiva alla Invectiva di Messer Antonio Lusco," Renaissance Quarterly, 23 (1970), 133–49; George Holmes, The Florentine Enlightenment, 1400–1450 (London, 1969), pp. 1–6; and the important article by Giuliano Tarturli, "Cino Rinuccini e la scuola in Santa Maria in Campo," Studi medievali, 3rd ser., 17 (1976), pp. 625–74.

145. Invettiva, p. 306: "Che per parer litteratissimi apresso al vulgo gridano a piazza quanti dittonghi avenano gli antichi, e perché oggi non ne usano se non due; e qual grammatica sia migliore, o quella del tempo del comico Terenzio, o dall'eroico Virgilio ripulita. . . ." Fubini, "La coscienza," p. 510, tends to deemphasize the importance of this passage because of its presentation of grammar as a question of the style of particular authors. For my purposes the novelty of this passage consists in its accent on these authors as characterizing the nature of Latin in the period when they wrote. To what extent did Aristotle, Rhet., III, 1, 1404a, 29–34, influence another one of their interests also criticized by Rinuccini; "e quanti piedi usano gli antichi, e perché oggi non ne usano se non due. . . .?"

146. Tarturli, "Cino Rinuccini," p. 644, and I, "Cino Rinuccini's Risponsiva," p. 143, are in basic agreement that the Risponsiva was written after Bruni's Laudatio of 1403/4. See below, chap. 14, n. 48. As for the Invettiva, Tarturli, p. 651, argues with Giovanni Gentile, Storia della filosofia italiana (fino a Lorenzo Valla), ed. Vito Bellezza, Opere, XI (Florence, 1961), p. 283, and Hans Baron, The Crisis of the Early Italian Renaissance, rev. ed. (Princeton, 1966), p. 323, for a date in the first years of the fifteenth century. With them he points out that Rinuccini could not have criticized certain positions of these young humanists once Bruni had published his Laudatio (1403/4), the Second Book of the Dialogi (1405/6) and the preface to his edition of the Phaedo (1405). But when did Rinuccini, who was never an intimate of Salutati's group, know of these works? The latter two were finished by Bruni in Rome and the Laudatio, completed when Bruni was out of the city and sent to Salutati for approval via Niccoli, may not have come to Rinuccini's attention for a number of years. My own tendency is to date the Invettiva roughly around 1405/6. Baron, The Crisis, p. 290, allows the possibility that at the time of writing the Risponsiva "Cino had no knowledge that the attitude of one of the leading members of the censured circle had recently developed along the road he recommended."

grammar as inductive and posterior to language. Deriving its rules from observation of common linguistic practice, grammar in Valla's view did not consist, as medieval grammarians maintained, of deductive normative constructions. Salutati had utilized the idea of language as convention to justify the style of Petrarch and, by implication, more generally to defend the eloquence of the great Christian writers of the past. But Valla saw clearly what Salutati did not. Taking Cicero's dictum on the need to base eloquence on popular usages to its logical conclusion, he declared that in modern times Latin no longer underwent development. Contemporaries learned their Latin not as the ancient Romans did at their mothers' knees but rather from grammar books and from diligent study of the ancient authors. Latin could no longer draw life from "popular usage." A "dead" or artificial language in contemporary society, Latin must consequently conform to the usages found in the period when Latin attained its greatest heights of expression.[147]

This late controversy over language illustrates clearly the ambivalence of Salutati's humanism, the limitations on his ability to abandon certain assumptions of the medieval tradition he inherited. Dedicated to the belief in the harmony between ancient and Christian culture, he felt committed to the medieval notion of a comprehensive Latin literary tradition continuous from ancient Roman times down to his own day. In defending Petrarch's status as a writer he was in effect defending this ideal. Because of their superior knowledge, Christian writers might not only be considered comparable but even superior to the pagans.[148] He could not, however, prevent his aesthetic judgment from occasionally undercutting his cultural and religious beliefs and goals. In the last decade of his life he was motivated by his historical interest to delineate the evolution of Latin literature, and he isolated the first century B.C. as the high point of Latin eloquence, thereby laying the basis for the classicism of Poggio and Valla he so strongly opposed.

147. See the cogent observations on Valla's position on Neo-Latin made by Camporeale, *Lorenzo Valla*, pp. 187–92. Some of the clearest statements of Valla's conception emerged from his conflict with Poggio, who continued to hold largely to the stance he took against Salutati (ibid., p. 182). For Valla's analysis of Poggio's ideas on language, see ibid., p. 186.

148. This affirmation, by belittling the value of the pagan inheritance, actually poses the major threat to the harmony between ancient and Christian culture in Salutati's thought. See chap. 15.

Chapter 10. THE CITIZEN-SCHOLAR

I

The years from the restoration of patrician political domination in Florence in 1382 until the death of his wife in 1396 were the happiest of Salutati's life. His large and growing family seems to have escaped the high infant mortality rate common to all ranks of society in the century. A regime dominated by the upper classes with which he identified governed the state and his continued tenure of the chancellorship was guaranteed. Already the most famous chancellor in Europe, in the course of these years Salutati also became the leader of the humanist movement in the West and he made Florence its capital. Wealth from his office and lands provided sufficient funds to meet his needs. As the previous chapter shows, his interest in scholarship was to remain with him to the end of his life, but it was never so intense and so untroubled with religious scruples as it was in the fourteen years between 1382 and 1396.

Essentially a product of the city, raised as he was in the leading university center of Italy, gregarious, ambitious, and by constitution a hearty fellow, Salutati seems to have enjoyed fully the social life of the rich patrician families reestablished in a position of political preeminence after 1382. Although written in the late 1420s, Giovanni da Prato's *Paradiso degli Alberti* purports to be an accurate description of life in the time of the author's youth just before the First Milanese War.[1] Looking

---

1. Hans Baron, *Humanistic and Political Literature in Florence and Venice at the Beginning of the Quattrocento* (Cambridge, 1955), pp. 13–37, argues forcefully for the fictional nature of the specific details of the discussions. On the other hand, the first editor of the work, Alessandro Wesselofsky, believes the document to be "un perfetto documento storico": *Il Paradiso degli Alberti: Ritrovi e ragionamenti del 1389: Romanzo di Giovanni da Prato*, Scelta di curiosità letterarie inedite o rare dal secolo xiii al xix, disp. 86^1–88 (Bologna, 1867), I, 223. On the basis of the biographies of the individuals reported as present, Wesselofsky assigns the spring of 1389 as the only possible date. Baron's objection to the authenticity of the description is based on his opinion that some of the ideas expressed by the speakers postdate 1389 by more than a decade. An examination of the biography of one of the prominent foreigners proportedly present at the Paradiso, Marsiglio of Santa Sophia, supports Baron's argument that the account is not a historical narrative. Sometime in 1388 Marsiglio left his native university in the midst of the Carrarese war with Giangaleazzo to take up a post at Siena: Francesco Landogna, "Maestro Marsiglio di Santa Sofia e Gian Galeazzo Visconti," *Bollettino della società pavese di storia*, 33 (1933), 176–77. With his takeover of Padua, Giangaleazzo, as a part of his plan "pro reformatione novi studii patavini," called on his ally Siena to free Marsiglio from his contract so that he might return to Padua. On January 12, 1389, Siena, attempting to curry favor with Giangaleazzo, released

back nostalgically, the author claims to report a series of conversations held between the city's intelligentsia and a number of illustrious foreigners. Most of the action takes place in the gardens of the Paradiso, a great villa owned by the rich Florentine merchant Benedetto degli Alberti. While the specific events are almost certainly fictional, Giovanni probably was drawing on his memory of the kind of entertainments he had witnessed as a young man.

At the opening of the third book of *Il Paradiso* Giovanni's brief description of the luncheon given by Salutati for the renowned Paduan doctor, Marsiglio di Santa Sophia, and the natural philosopher from Parma, Biagio Pelacani, together with "a great number of doctors, artists, and other notable citizens," has, if we judge from other sources, all the marks of an accurate portrayal of the chancellor's hospitality.

> On the appointed day, the company was graciously received with a great abundance of splendid dishes and with a great supply of expensive wines, as the occasion demanded. After much music played and sung by Francesco (Landini) and his company and with the enjoyable

---

the professor "ab hodie in antea libere" (p. 179). In June 1388 Florence had elected Marsiglio to teach medicine in its *Studium* beginning in October 1389: Roberto Abbondanza, "Gli atti degli Ufficiali dello Studio fiorentino dal maggio al settembre 1388," *Archivio storico italiano*, 117 (1959), 99–100. But in June 1389 Florence had to seek a replacement for that term: see the letter of the *Signoria* to Antonio da Scarperia, *Il Paradiso*, I, pt. 1, 368–70. It is very unlikely that, having forced Siena to release Marsiglio from his contract, Giangaleazzo would then permit him to remain another four months in Tuscany and especially in Florentine territory. The Milanese lord was in fact directly responsible for Marsiglio's failure to come to the Florentine *Studio* in the fall of 1389 (*Miss.*, 22, fol. 7). A document of April 1389 indicates that by that month he was a professor at Padua. The text concerns the examination administered to Marsiglio's own son, Guglielmo, by two members of the college of medicine. Marsiglio is listed as absent: "Licentia privati examinis in medicina Mag. Guglielmi a Sancta Sophia de Padua sub Mag. Nicolao a Rido Doct. Med., et Jacopo Mag. Zanettini, Doct. Art. et Med., nominibus propriis, et nomine et vice Mag. Marsilii a S. Sophia absentis" (published in Landogna, p. 180). Marsiglio's absence from the examination should not be taken, however, to mean that he was absent from Padua but rather that he tactfully absented himself from the board interrogating his own son. In fact, not only his appointment as professor but also the festivities surrounding the graduation of his son would have kept him in Padua in the spring of 1389. Not present in Florence in 1389, he was teaching there very probably in 1396: N. Brentano-Keller, "Il libretto di spese e di ricordi di un monaco vallombrosano per libri dati e avuti in prestito (sec. XIV; fine)," *La bibliofilia*, 61 (1939), 132. In 1396, in an attempt to honor the famous doctor, the Guild of the Lana bestowed on him honorary membership: *Arti, Lana*, 99, fol. 61 (Aug. 23, 1396).

The suggestion of Graziella Federici Vescovini, *Astrologia e Scienza. La crisi dell'aristotelismo sul cadere del Trecento e Biagio Pelacani da Parma* (Florence, 1979), p. 32, that the conversations described by Giovanni took place in 1388 is equally unlikely. The manner in which Marsiglio is presented in the work suggests he is residing in Florence, when in fact in 1388 he was teaching in Siena. I would like to thank Edward Mahoney for this reference.

Because the recent edition of the work, *Il Paradiso degli Alberti*, ed. A. Lanza (Rome, 1975), was not available to me, my citations are from Wesselofsky.

meal finished, Coluccio began to speak in this fashion: "I cannot tell you how much I have to thank you for the kindness and pleasure you have given. I want very much to remind you that you should please dine here this evening. . . ."[2]

The guests return for supper and after a delightful meal—"so very joyous and full of celebration was the meal that one has never seen anything like it"—the chancellor announces the invitation given to him that afternoon for the whole company to attend a reception that evening at Benedetto degli Alberti's villa, the *Paradiso*. Joining themselves to Alberti's group, which had been awaiting their coming outside in the Piazza dei Peruzzi, Salutati and his guests move on to the gardens of the *Paradiso* for more food, wine, and entertainment.[3]

It is difficult to reconcile this picture of Salutati with the harsh critic of Francesco Bruni's simple rustic pleasures in 1377 or with the author of the *De seculo et religione*. If the attack on Bruni should be written off as primarily political, the other work cannot be dismissed as a rhetorical stunt. Salutati's learning had taught him to doubt his natural instincts. His own writings late in life presented a standard Christian-Stoic morality to which he endeavored to adhere. In moments of crisis he struggled valiantly with himself and usually his conscience prevailed. But on ordinary days, in the normal circumstances of life, the successful Florentine burgher took the place of the sage. He set a good table and enjoyed having his friends with him. A sober man, Salutati nonetheless had a taste for fine wine, and, although the vineyards of Stignano supplied a good deal of the beverages consumed in his town house, he also bought special wines on the market, such as the cask purchased after careful selection at Carmignano near Prato in 1400.[4]

Despite his frequent assertion that friends have all things in common, he was financially scrupulous. When he requested favors from friends involving expenditures, he carefully specified how reimbursement would be made. When owed money, Salutati expected in turn to be repaid. He could barely conceal his fury at a supposed friend who neglected settling his debt. If the friend repaid as he ought, he wrote in his dunning letter, he would still find Salutati a friend; if not, the lender

2. *Il Paradiso*, III, 5.
3. Ibid., III, 8 ff.
4. Ser Lapo Mazzei, *Lettere di un notaro a un mercante del secolo XIV*, ed. Cesare Guasti, 2 vols. (Florence, 1880), I, 76. In February 1391, in the same month he wrote his *volgare* war sonnet (see chap. 6, n. 39), he together with his colleague ser Viviano and the pious Guido del Palagio shared with ser Lapo a barrel of wine sent the latter by Francesco Datini (ibid., I, 8).

would try "all remedies" to have his money back. In this way "you will do with shame what you have been unwilling to do with honor."[5]

Without financial stability and a sizeable income he could not have maintained his large household, his scale of hospitality and the continuous search for books for his collection. His main source of support came from the chancery. The salary for the office was a hundred florins with an additional forty given to him to pay for helpers. He could spend all or part of the latter sum on salaries or save the whole as he did in later years when his sons served him as assistants. With fees and gifts included, the combined earnings of the chancery and the *Tratte* probably averaged about six hundred florins per year, an amount which put him in the top two percent of the Florentine income bracket.[6]

Although Salutati owned no property in Florence, he did utilize some of his revenue for the purpose of investing in land in the countryside. A commission surveying property along the Arno in the province of the Lower Arno in 1396 listed him as the owner of a fishing weir on the river at Santa Croce across the swamp of Fucecchio from Buggiano.[7]

His major interests in rural property, however, were in the Valdinievole. The fragmentary *estimo* of Stignano in 1387 shows Salutati holding a large amount of land in the communes of Buggiano, Pescia, and Uzzano.[8] In normal times he came out from Florence to his house in Stignano fairly frequently, not only for relaxation but also for supervising the operation of his fields. Some of this property doubtless came from inheritance—that of his father and brother Andrea—and Piera Riccomi must have brought some land in the Pescia area with her as a part of her dowry, but Salutati probably also purchased a good deal.[9] Moreover, in 1388 when Tomeo Balducci, his first wife's father died, the large dowry of Tomeo's deceased wife, Agnola, which the husband had con-

5. *Epist.*, III, 528. For examples of arrangements for financing book purchases, see ibid., I, 243, and III, 132.

6. Lauro Martines, *The Social World of the Italian Humanists* (London, 1963), p. 107. There may have been other small incomes like the "moggia uno di grano" given annually to the chancellor: Demetrio Marzi, *La cancelleria della Repubblica fiorentina* (Rocca San Casciano, 1910), p. 187.

7. *Dieci di Balìa, Legazioni e commissarie*, 2, fol. 2ᵛ: "Andiamo al mulino di Santa Croce. . . . A porta vilolola di ser Coluccio di verso valle o vero Cerbaia e dall'un lato le rede di Betto Saracini che v'e ¾ d'acqua e del'astricato di mattoni."

8. *Epist.*, IV, 453–61. The listing is only partial (p. 461). Although supposedly in the Archivio di Stato at Lucca in 1920 (Augusto Mancini, *Sulle tracce del Salutati* [Lucca, 1920], p. 13), it cannot now be found there.

9. That Salutati had inherited land from his brother Andrea di Piero is clear from the *estimo* of 1387 (*Epist.*, IV, 456). See above, chap. 2, n. 81. That part of Piera's dowry in money was apparently never paid (*Epist.*, IV, 545 and 571).

tinued to hold in his lifetime, was finally divided evenly between her two surviving daughters and Caterina's son, the sixteen-year-old Bonifazio. Along with a certain Leonardo di Francesco da Empoli, Salutati was named by Balducci as guardian of his minor child, a son Domenico.[10] For a time at least, Salutati had joint responsibility for managing the young man's inheritance from the father.

By the 1380's Salutati exercised a kind of patronage over the valley and its people. As a sign of his continued bond to Buggiano his name was kept in the purses of office, and he was frequently elected to a position in the local government. There was no question of his actually carrying out the duties of office.[11] When he did take part in communal politics, it was for special matters. In one instance, on April 19, 1384, he was chosen to act as a judge for Buggiano in determining the penalties to be imposed on banished citizens of the commune for failure to pay their taxes.[12] The following year he returned to discuss a proposed reform in the communal statutes with the leaders of the commune and eight men charged with the revision. The commune took the occasion of his visit to offer him an elaborate public dinner.[13]

Beginning in 1386, moreover, Salutati was appointed frequently to serve as arbiter between the Valdinievole and Florence over the matter of the tax burden of the province. Unquestionably in these last decades of the century Florence was steadily increasing the tax obligations of the Valdinievole, along with the other provinces, occasioning a good deal of protest from the taxpayers. Records of Salutati's arbitration exist not only for 1386[14] but also for 1394, 1396, and 1401.[15] Besides these instances of assistance, Buggiano individually sought Salutati's help when it could not pay its taxes to Florence in 1397. The communal government elected Giovanni di Piero, Salutati's sole surviving brother, and two of Salutati's sons, Piero and Bonifazio, to act as the commune's procurators in requesting a reduction of the impositions levied on Buggiano.[16]

---

10. A.C.B., *Delib.*, 8, fols. 333ᵛ–34.
11. Starting in late 1374 he was elected and paid for offices he could not actually exercise: A.C.B., *Delib.*, 7, fols. 229 and 8, fols. 76ᵛ, 116ᵛ, 135ᵛ, 145ᵛ, and 163.
12. Ibid., 8, fol. 132ᵛ.
13. Ibid., fol. 195ᵛ. The details of this matter and of the dinner are found in Mancini, pp. 14–15.
14. *Dipl. Pescia*, 18, June 1386: published in *Epist.*, IV, 448–52.
15. B.C.P., 1 A, 42 (146) *Raccolta di Fascicoli*, fols. 40, 14–17ᵛ, and 43.
16. On December 16, 1397, Giovanni di Piero of Stignano was sent to Florence to negotiate a loan because the communal finances were inadequate "pro solvendo communi Florentie residuum quingentorum florenorum et pagam lancearum" (*Delib.*, 9, fol. 185ᵛ). At the same time "Eligantur duo homines Florentini vel habitantes in civitate Florentie in

It was perhaps on this occasion that Salutati himself gave surety for a loan of three hundred florins from Florentine bankers so that Buggiano could pay its levies.[17] His support was also extended to Uzzano in 1394 when he acted as that commune's procurator to protest a new Florentine ruling related to the gabelle on public offices.[18]

Naturally, given the usefulness of their greatest son, the citizens of Buggiano were eager to be of help to him locally in every way. Although there are no records regarding the disposition of communal lands, it is likely that Buggiano facilitated the renting or even acquisition of such property by Salutati. The good will of the citizens was especially helpful in obtaining certain considerations on the matter of local taxes.[19] So generous was the commune when it came to aiding their powerful benefactor that when Salutati, through his son Bonifazio, requested a communal mill wheel for his own mill (probably the one he owned on the Stagnipesce), the commune consented, "having regard for the benefits formerly made in favor of the said commune by ser Coluccio."[20] Private citizens like Salvo Cei of Vellano also compensated the chancellor for services rendered on their behalf. In his testament drawn up in 1392, Cei declared that "as a sign of love in some way to repay the egregious ser Collucio Pieri, chancellor of Florence, his patron and long defender, for great services rendered to the testator himself," Salutati could have a specified piece of property in Vellano at the price he was willing to pay or, if he wished, even free of charge.[21]

Interestingly, Salutati's holdings in the *Monte commune*, the Florentine public debt, were very small for his income. Although nothing can be said with certainty about his investment overall during his thirty-two years in the city, it appears that in the first two decades he paid relatively low *prestanze*, that is, interest-bearing compulsory loans to the

---

procuratores et cohaiutatores communis Buggiani ad agendum negotia dicti communis in dicta civitate Florentie." These two were in fact Bonifazio and Piero Salutati, Salutati's sons.

17. Probably sometime during this period Salutati negotiated the loan of three hundred florins which his son Bonifazio forced the commune to pay back with interest on his father's death (*Delib.*, 10, fol. 198ᵛ).

18. A.C.U., *Deliberazioni e Partiti*, 1390–98, fol. 177. Salutati was made Uzzano's procurator in her case against a new Florentine law made for the Valdinievole "quod omnes de provincia Vallis Nebule, ituri in aliquid officium, solvant gabellam offitiorum prout solvunt cives Florentini et aliter et prout et sicut in dicta lege continetur."

19. A.C.B., *Delib.*, 9, fols. 104ᵛ–105 and *Delib.*, 10, fol. 22.

20. *Delib.*, 9, fol. 344ᵛ. His mill on the Stagnipesce is found listed in 1387: *Epist.*, IV, 458, item 32. Just before this grant of the wheel the commune also gave him the right to have his mill work even on festival days: *Delib.*, 9, fol. 344.

21. *Notarile*, L 81 (1392–99) (ser Lapo Mazzei), fols. 4ᵛ–5.

commune which were reckoned to the lender's credit and on which he received an annual interest payment. Salutati, of course, was not yet a Florentine citizen in these years and that might in some way have influenced his tax assessment. Political favoritism could also be the reason.

Whatever the explanation, it did not exempt him from paying higher taxes during the years of the Milanese Wars. On August 8, 1390, he had approximately 413 florins credit in the *Monte*, but the total of his *prestanze* for seventeen months in 1396 and 1397 alone was almost 131 florins, and in the four-year period January 1400–November 1403 he paid a little over 344 florins in compulsory loans.[22] Yet even with these larger burdens during the war years he would still not be counted as an important investor in *Monte* shares, and the income from this source was insignificant in his total revenue.

Nevertheless, *Monte* shares were well-suited to serve as collateral for debts, and in November 1391 Salutati used his *Monte* account as a guarantee of payment for at least part of his daughter's dowry.[23] While by this time some of his children were still in the cradle or toddlers, his older ones were teenagers. Dina, Salutati's only girl, was already of marriageable age, about fourteen or fifteen. Despite his personal fame, Salutati was keenly aware that his family was still "new" and this imposed a limit to his aspirations for the match. Accordingly, when Salutati cast about for a suitable alliance for his family, his choice fell on Guidetto Guidetti, member of an old but minor patrician family.

In recent times Tommaso di Mone Guidetti had brought his family into the political forefront by being elected Standardbearer of Justice three times between 1350 and 1375. Before the war with the Church Tommaso had supported measures designed to make elections to the Guelf party offices less restricted and in other ways had the appearance of being a political moderate.[24] Guidetto di Jacopo di Lando, Salutati's new son-in-law, however, came from a branch of the family enjoying no

22. Prof. Anthony Molho, who has made preliminary checks of the *Monte* records, has provided me with these figures. They are found *M.C.* 3780, fol. 70ᵛ; *M.C.* 3859, fol. 41; and *M.C.* 3863, fol. 79, respectively.

23. *Notarile*, L 81 (1392–99), fol. 14, Dec. 2, 1392, contains the reference to the financial arrangement. A notation in B.N.F., *Poligrafo Gargani*, 1728, "Salutati," refers to a lost record of the payment of the gabelle for her marriage in 1391. Cf. Marzi, p. 133, n. 7.

24. *Cronaca fiorentina di Marchionne di Coppo Stefani*, ed. Niccolò Rodolico, *RSI*, vol. 30, pt. 1 (Città di Castello, 1903–55), indice alfabetico, p. 561, under his name. Gene Brucker, *Florentine Politics and Society, 1343–1378* (Princeton, 1962), pp. 177, n. 107; 208; 210, n. 63. For the family genealogy, see Eugenio Gamurrini, *Istoria genealogica delle famiglie nobili . . .*, 5 vols. (Florence, 1668–85), IV, 150. For Guidetto Guidetti's political activity, see Gene Brucker, *The Civil World of Renaissance Florence* (Princeton, 1977), p. 519, under his name. His close association with Salutati may have helped him in his political career.

particular distinction.[25] Nonetheless, Salutati paid dearly for the alliance: the marriage contract stipulated that Dina bring as her dowry 950 florins in money and moveable wealth. The payment was partially guaranteed by a lien on Salutati's *Monte* holdings already mentioned.

This was the only match for his children actually concluded during the father's lifetime and the least illustrious. In 1409 the marriage of Bonifazio, then secretary of the *Tratte*, to the daughter of Pera di Pera Baldovinetti, one of the most active politicians in the city and head of an "Archguelf" family, was the most distinctive.[26] But Arrigo and Antonio, who married in 1416 and 1417 respectively, also did well. Arrigo espoused Margherita d'Andrea di messer Alamanno de'Medici and Antonio took the daughter of the Archguelf Guernieri de'Rossi as his wife.[27] Therefore, although Dina left her own home for that of her new husband at a fairly young age as was customary for upper-class Florentine girls, her brothers enjoyed the traditionally long male adolescence.

Salutati never spoke about life in his household—he probably spent little time in it. His professional duties gave him very few hours for the children—he often worked on holidays—and what free time he had was usually given to his books or discussions with friends. Piera made the house run and insulated her husband from the daily worries and pressures created by their large domestic establishment.

Never doubting the intellectual and physical inferiority of women, Salutati shared with his age suspicion of the dangers posed by their sexual attractiveness for the safety of the soul.[28] Unfortunately, man was

25. On Nov. 16, 1392, Salutati was listed in the books of the *Monte* (M.C. 3780, fol. 70ᵛ) as not being able to sell his shares until the end of 1394 without the permission of Guidetto di Jacopo (I am again indebted to Prof. Anthony Molho for this data on the *Monte*). Aldo Manetti, "Roberto de' Rossi," *Rinascimento*, 2 (1951), 48–49n. erroneously maintains that the Guidetti could claim as a family member a certain Cino di Francesco, a teacher of rhetoric in the school of Santa Maria in Campo: Giuliano Tanturli, "Cino Rinuccini e la scuola di Santa Maria in Campo," *Studi medievali*, 3rd ser., 17 (1976), 625 ff., has shown that the teacher was rather Cino di Francesco Rinuccini and the works ascribed to Guidetti by Manetti were actually by Rinuccini.

26. For date of marriage, see B.N.F., *Magl.*, 26, 142, fol. 10.

27. For marriage of Arrigo, see *Epist.*, IV, 396; for Antonio's marriage, ibid., IV, 405. It is, however, difficult to find any pattern of political alliances in the four marriages as a group. In contrast with the Baldovinetti and Rossi matches, those with the Medici and Guidetti suggest popular and moderate tendencies. In a way the marriages of his children reflect the ambiguous political position of the father, who had a sixth sense for picking his way between the various factions in the city.

28. On the intellectual inferiority of women, see especially *Epist.*, III, 337–41. The letter is translated in *The Earthly Republic: The Italian Humanists on Government and Society*, ed. Benjamin Kohl and Ronald Witt (Philadelphia, 1978), pp. 115–18. Also see above his affirmation in 1367 of the ancient thesis that philosophy and marriage were incompatible: chap. 2. Writing in 1392, however, he views marriage in a Christian context and positively (*Epist.*, II, 371): "Nescio cur hi matrimonium calumnientur, cur mordeant, cur irrideant,

so made that sexual intercourse was necessary for health: "For if this superfluity of sperm is retained too much, it is converted to poison and generates pernicious passions."[29] While he stressed that sexual needs must be met within marriage, Salutati could not always control his own feelings. Although he had passed through the crisis of 1380, when for a time he appeared overwhelmed with guilt about his sexual desires,[30] even as an old man he admitted to romantic inclinations probably left unsatisfied within his marriage. Nonetheless, he was genuinely fond of his wife, and they were sexually compatible as the birth of at least ten children indicates.

That Piera exercised a certain influence over her husband, who was perhaps twenty years her senior, is demonstrated in the plague summer of 1383. The plague that carried off Giovanni of Siena in Bologna was one whose effects were generally felt throughout Italy. The disease struck Florence in epidemic proportions beginning in the spring, killing many from all age groups, but the highest mortality was among the young and aged. So many citizens of means fled Florence that the *gente minuta* believed the time had finally come to destroy the regime. Although defeated in their uprising of July 21, the poor continued to pose a threat to the government until early fall when, with the diminution in mortality, those who had deserted the city returned.

Salutati was incensed at the cowardly flight of the patriciate on both political and religious grounds. To abandon the motherland in its moment of peril, he wrote his coadjutor in the chancery, ser Antonio Chelli, who had left the city, was neither just, nor courageous, nor temperate, nor prudent. Besides, since God determined who would die and who would live, our fleeing to another region made no difference.[31] This conception of the plague as the work of divine Providence represents a

---

cur reprehendant; matrimonium, inquam, Dei preceptum, Ecclesie sacramentum, legitimum generis humani principium, societatisque mortalium unitivum." He considers marriage "imperatum . . . sine dubitatione" (p. 369). On the other hand, even as late as this letter of July 1392 (in the period just before the reception of Cicero's *Ad familiares*: see below, n. 105) he clearly prizes the life of chastity over that of matrimony. Although the language is not as strong as that found in the *De seculo et religione*, ed. Berthold L. Ullman (Florence, 1957), pp. 117–21, where the vow of chastity is discussed, Salutati still maintains that the life devoted to serving God is superior to that devoted to caring for a wife (p. 371). While initially all were commanded to multiply, with this need now met the human race needs pure and immaculate intercessors for its abundant sin (p. 370). Citing Paul (1 Cor. 7:39) Salutati writes: "Igitur et qui matrimonio iungit virginem suam, bene facit; et qui non iungit, melius facit."

29. B.A.V., *Vat. Lat.* 2928, T, II, 9, fol. 23ᵛ. We might presume that the chaste monk is kept healthy by the grace of God.

30. See chap. 7.

31. *Epist.*, II, 87–98.

specific application of Salutati's developing sense of the all-powerful nature of the divine being and his rejection of pagan notions of fate and fortune discussed earlier in chapter 3. Widely diffused, his opinion became a subject of heated debate among his friends.[32]

Firmly holding this view, Salutati resolved to remain at his desk while the epidemic ran its course. The only change in his own routine was that when he went on the street he carried an aromatic in his hand, but this, as he explained to ser Antonio in a short letter, was not because he believed it efficacious against the disease but because he liked the scent. Once Salutati took such a clear position on an issue, he never admitted to changing it. Piera, however, who had just lost a sister and her father in Pescia from the disease, was not willing to face death in her family with such resignation. When Salutati referred to Piera's "advice" (*consilium*) that the family move out to the country, he was surely minimizing the amount of pressure the woman had to apply, confronting as she was her husband's firmly expressed conviction. He would not budge himself, but he reluctantly gave his permission for the others to depart.[33]

While he trusted Piera with the daily supervision of the children, Salutati can be expected to have reserved for himself the decisions on their formal education and future careers. Once his young adolescent daughter was wed and a respectable dowry transferred, he ceased to trouble himself about her, but the boys represented an ongoing concern. Though his correspondence furnishes no idea of the kind of formal education he provided for his sons, he clearly intended them to be self-supporting eventually. Very ambivalent about wealth, he spent freely in his lifetime. He could easily have afforded to buy a town house, yet he preferred to rent and the only long-term investments he considered really legitimate were those made in his homeland. Consequently, when he died, his eight surviving sons would share a relatively meager patrimony.

In the case of Boniface, his eldest son, he had no worries. Salutati never seems to have been fond of this child, the only by his first marriage, and he certainly never thought much of the boy's intellectual abilities. Fortunately Boniface had a private income from the lands he had inherited through his mother in the Valdinievole. Salutati planned that he manage the other properties of the family in the valley at the same

32. Chelli, convinced of Salutati's position, about 1400 defended it in a letter to Zabarella, who replied with a long rebuttal: *Epistolario di Pier Paolo Vergerio*, ed. L. Smith, Fonti per la storia d'Italia, vol. 74 (Rome, 1934), pp. 400–22.

33. *Epist.*, II, 96.

time. Until his late twenties, however, Boniface was allowed to enjoy the pleasures open to a bachelor in the capital. He was included in the *Tratte* for major offices in 1391 (although not a citizen) and first received the right to bear arms in 1395.[34] He only established his permanent residence in Stignano in the last part of 1399 and finally settled down to close management of the family's lands as well as his own.[35]

For a number of years Salutati vainly pursued elusive benefices for his second son, Piero, who of all the children seemed to have the greatest promise of achieving fame like that of his father. To Salutati's mind he was the best of the lot: already as a young man he was "most learned" and exhibited the capacity for eventually reaching the "height of eloquence and great fame."[36] The young man appears to have studied Greek with Chrysoloras,[37] and Salutati may personally have charged himself with his education in other disciplines. Piero never entered orders because it is unlikely that Salutati considered the reception of a benefice as the first step in an ecclesiastical career for his son. Rather a benefice was to provide a supplementary income for the youth until he could succeed his father. When the time came, Piero could resign his benefice in favor of a younger brother.

Salutati had already had some experience soliciting benefices for members of his family. By 1383 he had succeeded in obtaining a benefice in Montecatini for his nephew, Giovanni, son of his younger brother Corrado. From the official correspondence of the *Signoria*, however, it appears that the possession of the benefice was disputed.[38] The fact that Leonardo, one of Salutati's youngest sons, later held a benefice at Montecatini suggests that Giovanni won the altercation and subsequently resigned the living to his relative. Giovanni himself moved out to Buggiano in 1397 with the obvious intention of managing his deceased father's lands there.[39]

---

34. Ibid., IV, 390, n. 4; and Marzi, p. 134, n. 3.

35. A.C.B., *Delib.*, 9, fol. 343 (January 11, 1400), Bonifazio was named Buggiano's envoy to the Vicar of the Valdinievole in Pescia. A second mission followed in March (ibid., fol. 253). His name appears as counsellor in the Buggiano government in both spring and summer 1400 (fol. 360ᵛ). Bonifazio was not without some literary pretensions (*Epist.*, III, 405).

36. Ibid., III, 400–402. 37. See below, p. 306.

38. B.A.V., *Capp.*, 147, p. 160.

39. Giovanni di Corrado received his first post in Buggiano on December 1, 1397, when he was named captain of the guard of the castle of Stignano: A.C.B., *Delib.*, 9, fol. 182ᵛ. On December 16 of that year (fol. 185ᵛ) he was admitted to the purses for communal office and in 1398 was chosen for a term as defender (fol. 194ᵛ). On his family see *Epist.*, IV, 409–11. On Leonardo as "piovano di Montecatini," see ibid., IV, 269, n. 3 (from preceding page).

Negotiations for a benefice for Piero began in 1392, in the very period when Salutati was engaged in a struggle with the Curia on behalf of another nephew, Jacopo Dreucci, a cleric of the diocese of Pistoia and possibly the son of an unidentified sister of Salutati. Dreucci's problem was not unexceptional. In question was the right to hold the rectorship of the Hospital of St. Bartholomew of Prato. Originally held by a local canon lawyer, Dino di Torsiglieri, the rectorship had been turned over to Dreucci after an investigation of Torsiglieri's administration by the abbot of the monastery of Poggibonzi. Cardinal Monopolitano, official protector of the Florentine Republic at the Curia, had supported the investigation and had apparently authorized the abbot to turn the benefice over to Dreucci directly after establishing the culpability of Torsiglieri. By December 1392 Dreucci was recognized as the rightful holder of the benefice, but the canon lawyer would not concede and had collected testimony to the effect that the abbot's report of malad-ministration had been untrue.[40]

Salutati was not prepared to see Dreucci lose the living, and on December 30, 1392, he wrote to the pope begging him to refuse to receive the petition of Torsiglieri and to Bartolomeo di Meo Franchi, his friend and a papal secretary, to use his influence with Boniface IX. The cardinals of Pisa and Monopolitano were also asked to help.[41] By February 12, however, it became clear to Salutati that Torsiglieri had powerful friends in the Curia, and rumors reached Florence that he had obtained letters taking the benefice out of the hands of Salutati's nephew. By late March Dreucci was at the Curia petitioning to retain possession, and Salutati was hard at work in Florence trying to accommodate Cardinal Monopolitano's request for certain favors from the commune.[42] The eventual outcome of the case remains unknown.

Salutati's pursuit of a benefice for Piero was to prove equally frustrating. Not in orders, the young Florentine had to have a papal dispensation to qualify him for an expectancy. In all probability Ridolfi presented the petition to the Curia in December 1392, and, hearing of the favorable

40. Ibid., IV, 256–57, n. 2, for the record of the investigation. Cardinal Monopolitano seems to have been instrumental in giving the benefice to Dreucci (ibid., IV, 260–61).
41. The letters to the cardinals and to Franchi (*Epist.*, IV, 259–62) were written December 30 and 31, 1392. The letter to the pope (ibid., IV, 255–58), however, while containing material similar to that in the other letters, seems to have been dispatched only on February 11 (ibid., IV, 263, n. 1).
42. On the favor to the cardinal, see ibid., II, 432–33. The *Signoria* wrote to Monopolitano, thanking him for his services to the state and to private individuals on February 10, 1393 (B.A.V., *Capp.*, 147, p. 454).

reply, Salutati in his letter of December 30 to Franchi begged his friend's help in having the official confirmation sent as soon as possible.[43] The pope had promised verbally but Salutati required something in writing. Indicative of his sense of urgency is Salutati's use of *vos* in addressing Franchi. Three months later Salutati was able to thank Boniface IX for an expectancy just bestowed on his son: "And although a chance for promotion never occurs, however, I consider it of greatest importance to have seen your kindness, which furnishes me hope for even greater things."[44] The pope never fulfilled these hopes. A whole series of subsequent petitions to the pope supported by official embassies of the Republic failed to produce the desired result: between January and August 1396 alone the Florentine ambassadors were ordered at least four times to raise the matter of an appointment for Piero with the pope.[45]

Salutati made his last bid for ecclesiastical preferment for Piero in April 1398 when he asked for the help of another papal secretary, Francesco da Lancenigo, in promoting "a matter of personal concern."[46] Very likely Salutati knew by this time that Ottaviano di Mariotto Orlandini, a canon in the cathedral of Florence, was dying and he was out to claim the vacancy for his son. In fact, when on July 7, three months later, Orlandini died, the chapter on the following day elected Piero as his replacement. Nevertheless, within the month Salutati learned that other candidates had initiated action to gain possession of the place held by his son. As a result, early in August Salutati sent off three letters, two to friends at the Curia, Francesco Piendibeni, papal *scriptor*, and Pietro da Ascoli, the holder of a wide range of lucrative curial offices. The third went to Niccolò da Piperno, one of the claimants.[47] Despite the fact that Piero had been canonically elected and could claim a right of expectancy from the pope, on hearing of Orlandini's death, Boniface IX reserved the canonry and appointed another Florentine, son of Francesco Federighi (p. 316). Perhaps realizing the weakness of their claim, the Federighi were attempting to work out an agreement over the canonry with Niccolò to the detriment of Piero Salutati.

This time, after so many disappointed hopes, Salutati had resolved to hold the canonry for his son: "We however have possession and will protect it as far as we can" (p. 316). In his letter to Niccolò, Salutati

---

43. *Epist.*, IV, 260.　　　　　　　44. Ibid., II, 435.

45. Embassies with these instructions are mentioned by Novati (ibid., II, 434–35, n. 2) in April, June, and August. There was, however, an earlier one in January (B.C.S., 5.8.8., fol. 27).

46. *Epist.*, III, 282.

47. The letters with biographies are found in ibid., III, 312–18.

begins naively with a protestation that he has heard of his correspondent's virtue and therefore hopes for his assistance in obtaining the canonry for his son, who, he declares, was canonically elected and installed. In conclusion he informs Niccolò casually that Bartolomeo degli Alberti will speak with him of the matter as his agent (pp. 317–18). It is fair to suspect that this member of the international banking family had been instructed to offer monetary compensation in return for Niccolò's renunciation of the canonry.

The letters to Francesco Piendibeni and Pietro d'Ascoli requested help in securing the canonry but that to Pietro concerned as well a benefice in the Valdarno over which the curial official exercised some control. Apparently engaged in the efforts to capture the Florentine canonry, Salutati decided to go all-out to create a lucrative mix of benefices to insure the future prosperity of his boy.

The text of the letter to Pietro, notorious simoniac and accumulator of benefices, constitutes a mode of studied hypocrisy. Two years previous Salutati himself had authored the missive of the *Signoria* to the pope charging Pietro with the sordid crime of forgery in an effort to cheat the Alberti bank. Now (pp. 314–15,n.3) the Florentine chancellor begins by claiming the papal official as his benefactor and friend. To a friend, he reminds Pietro, nothing honestly demanded by a friend is difficult or burdensome. This brings him to the matter of the parish in the Valdarno. If it is true, as he has heard, that Pietro was responsible for creating the vacancy in the benefice, then "I pray you, sweetest brother, on behalf of whatever true friendship merits, that out of your kindness you endeavor to transfer the parish to my son, nay rather your son, for he has your name Pietro." Salutati promises to pay whatever the curial official requires short of committing simony "which I believe you abhor" (p. 315).

Despite these efforts there is no indication that Salutati emerged victorious in the campaign. Rather, from his comments following Piero's death two years later it would seem that this last hassle over the Tuscan benefices had caused him to abandon the hope and to focus solely on the young man's career in the chancery. People in Florence, according to Salutati, had already come to look on Piero as the most fitted to follow his father in the office of chancellor.[48]

These personal experiences with the Curia made a very bad impression on Salutati. When in 1400 he wrote critically of the papal adminis-

48. Ibid., III, 401.

tration, he was speaking from conviction: "It is shameful to recall and shameful to write how many and to what extent . . . lies run the length and breadth of the Roman Curia; how those seeking gain invent; how, moreover, the promoters of the ambitious tell lies even where promises already given are involved. There is nothing just, believe me, nothing sacred for those led by cupidity, the root of all evil."[49] Salutati's own conduct in these relations with the Curia, nonetheless, suggests that he was not unwilling to play the game as his contemporaries did. His bitter criticism partly stems from the fact that he frequently lost and when he won, he did so at the cost of money and time.

Salutati's efforts on behalf of a younger son, Leonardo, were in the long run more successful. Marked out for a career in the Church, the boy was perhaps already enjoying the living in Montecatini mentioned above, when in 1395, at about thirteen, he received a canonry at Padua. Salutati's elation at the easy acquisition was soon dispelled, however, when he learned that another candidate actually occupied the position. In order to vindicate his son's claim, Salutati had to invoke the assistance of Francesco Carrara and his counsellors. Leonardo's formal admission to the college of the cathedral in 1405 represented more than a decade of work on the part of the father.[50]

As for his remaining seven sons, Lorenzo was still a young adolescent when his father died, but the others would have been of age to earn their own livelihood by that time. Because of his weak health, Salutato caused his father most concern.[51] As we shall see, he would eventually find a place in the Church through the good offices of Bruni.[52] Still quite young, Andrea, apparently destined to become a notary, began helping his father in the chancery.[53] Simone, the most dashing of the boys, is mentioned on one occasion as having participated in an elegant tournament in the Piazza Santa Croce in which sixteen patrician youths jousted with one another. He later became a merchant.[54] On the other hand, Arrigo, little inclined to any profession, may have devoted his energies to running the family estates in later life after Bonifazio became notary of the *Tratte*.[55] Of Filippo's career there is no trace. By 1406 Antonio was a notary in the chancery,[56] but it is likely that his father had

49. Ibid., III, 442.
50. Ibid., IV, 268. He was still fighting for the canonry in 1400 when he sought the aid of Zabarella (ibid., III, 422).
51. See above, chap. 7, n. 7.   52. See below, chap. 15.
53. In *Epist.*, III, 138, Salutati refers to Andrea as his "socius."
54. Ibid., IV, 390.   55. Ibid., IV, 390 and 396.
56. For his matriculation, see B.N.F., *Naz*. II, IV, 397, fol. 416ᵛ.

designated him for this only subsequent to the terrible summer of 1400 which witnessed the death of both Piero and Andrea.

II

Because Salutati was by profession a busy public servant and not a university professor, he exerted his influence within the city largely in conversations with a few friends or in large informal gatherings like those held in the gardens of the *Paradiso*. The precocious Pier Paolo Vergerio, who taught dialectic in Florence between 1386 and 1388, nicely captured a typical setting for the humanist's teaching in a letter to Salutati written from Padua in 1391. Vergerio, who regarded himself as a disciple of Salutati, requesting moral guidance like a son, begged: "Write to me about virtue, a topic on which you usually discourse before a crowded group of people."[57]

Vergerio's reference to Salutati's *jocundae sermones* in this same letter recalls the description of the humanist's manner of speech as "giocoso" given in the *volgare* version of Villani's biography.[58] Such adjectives would never fit his literary style, humorless, sober, and somewhat sententious as it was. He talked to his friends but wrote for history. Composing in the shadow of the ancients, he had no place for the everyday. Esteeming sobriety in its writers, his age, untroubled by the disparity between life and style, considered Salutati a model of prose eloquence. Unfortunately for his fame, he omitted the very kind of personal material that would have made his writings attractive to a later generation.

He was a born student. As he wrote Jacopo degli Angeli in 1396 when contemplating the initiation of Greek studies in Florence:

> Oh, how much patience my silliness will demand from you and Manuel! How much and in how many ways I will daily make you laugh aloud! You know my ways; you know that I am never able to be at rest; you know how I am always pleased to teach what I know and importunately seek to learn what I do not know and how I am always happy to dispute even about things I do not understand.[59]

57. *Epistolario di Pier Paolo Vergerio*, p. 63. On Vergerio's first visit to Florence, see ibid., pref., xiv.

58. Ibid., p. 62: "Pater optime, cum in mentem venit quam iocundos sermones quamque letos dies agere tecum solitum sim. . . ." For the *volgare* Villani quotation see above, chap. 2. In the month after Salutati's death Poggio speaks of the dead man's "affabilitas" and his "festivitas" (*Epist.*, IV, 473).

59. Ibid., III, 131.

His ideas did not develop in solitude; rather he knew he functioned best when confronted with a problem posed by a correspondent or by a friend in conversation. With the exception of the second edition of the *De laboribus Herculis* and the *De fato et fortuna*, Salutati's treatises and lengthy discussions in his correspondence have an occasional quality, provoked as they were by a specific question raised or a position taken by a contemporary.[60] He clearly relished being consulted and occasionally even invited questions or literary puzzles.[61] These circumstances affecting the genesis of his thought help to explain why there is so little concern with consistency and integration of various lines of thinking. The problem and the character of the interlocutor defined the limits of the immediate discussion, and Salutati jumped in feet first.

Curious to the point of ingenuousness, willing, as we have seen, to think out loud exposing the details of the process leading to the conclusion, responsive to the personality he was addressing, Salutati was an ideal arbiter for a collective enterprise. Petrarch had been a mountain, isolated, and marvelous. Wherever he dwelt, whether in Italy or Provence, there was the center of the new cultural movement. At his death any one of the great cities of Northern Italy could have claimed hegemony. With Boccaccio dead a year after Petrarch, Florence had no obvious edge on Padua, Milan, or Bologna. That Florence by the beginning of the next century had become the leading center of humanism in Italy and remained so for almost a hundred years was largely the work of Coluccio Salutati.

Through his massive personal correspondence, he gradually made the lines of professional communication for humanists throughout Italy cross through Florence. At great personal cost he built up the largest library of ancient texts in Europe. He was without question the best humanist in Italy in his day. Yet he remained a *primus inter pares*, a leader willing to exchange information and to beg for help when he needed it. This openness, this obvious humility before the unknown, made him

60. The *De seculo, De laboribus Herculis*, 1st ed., the *De verecundia*, and the *De tyranno* were written in answer to specific requests. The *De nobilitate legum et medicine* endeavored to defend law against accusations made by a physician in a letter written to him. His *Invectiva contra Antonium Luschum* represents Salutati's response to Loschi's attack on the dignity of Florence. While formally the *De fato et fortuna* appears to be an answer to questions asked by the Abbot of Settimo to whom it is dedicated, Salutati's original decision to write the treatise came from Salutati himself: see my "Toward a Biography of Coluccio Salutati," *Rinascimento*, 16 (1976), 28–34; and below, chap. 11.

61. *Epist.*, III, 545: ". . . libere confiteri longe plura me didicisse rogatum quam studio vel doctrina. . . ."

appear to other scholars and to his disciples as a colleague in a common effort. And they responded to his guidance. By the time of his death Florence had such an accumulation of books and talent that no other city in Europe could rival it.

Salutati was not always flexible, especially once he had taken a position. When cornered he resorted to all sorts of subterfuges to escape. The debate over the status of Petrarch vis-à-vis the ancients is a classic case. To defend what he himself recognized as an exaggerated judgment, Salutati preferred sophistry to admitting that his position needed restatement.[62] Within the man there prevailed to the end an uneasy balance between pride in his opinions and achievements and his commitment to humility. He frankly admitted he loved praise.[63] But sensible to the surge of exaltation and its dangers, he usually rushed to shut it off with a pious meditation.[64] When, as he frequently did in later life, he deflected plaudits by ascribing his talents not to himself but to God, he intensely wished to believe it.[65]

At times, but then only rarely, his *amour propre* was starkly revealed. His reluctance to collect his correspondence derived from his frankly expressed fear that, were he to collect the letters now, better ones composed subsequently would be left out. Writing in August 1395 to Cardinal Oliari, who had compared Salutati to Cassiodorus and urged him to edit his letters, Salutati replied:

> My thought . . . is to leave the task of collecting the best of my public and private letters of which originals remain to my posterity, that is my adoptive sons, who avidly worship me and my works. For since my letters both public and private grow daily and these, composed in a riper age, will perhaps have more maturity and sobriety, it would not be wise to select preceding ones when it might happen that others soon to be written ought (if one judges their merit correctly) to be preferred to them. There will be time for thinking about a choice when there is nothing to add, when it will be certain that nothing is to follow which ought to be chosen before earlier writings.[66]

62. On the Petrarch debate, see above, chap. 9, and chap. 15 below. Cf. von Martin *Coluccio Salutati und das Lebensideal* (Berlin, 1916), p. 163, for his argumentativeness.

63. *Epist.*, I, 219, and III, 89.

64. *De nobilitate legum et medicinae. De verecundia*, ed. Eugenio Garin, Edizione nazionale dei classici del pensiero italiano, vol. 8 (Florence, 1943), pp. 332 and 334. *Epist.*, III, 335–37. For the positive uses of praise, see chap. 3.

65. *Epist.*, I, 300; II, 407–8; III, 439–42.

66. Ibid., III, 89–90. See above, chap. 9, for other parts of the letter.

Were he to make a selection now of those he prefers, the volume would be so large as to make it difficult for his literary heirs to add others to them. In the meantime he is keeping copies of the massive correspondence for this purpose. Before his death, however, it would appear Salutati changed his mind, at least in regard to his private letters, and began the editing and arrangement of them himself.[67]

Of his extant letters most come from the "official" collection. Because he had a hand in selecting which would survive, it can be assumed that he eliminated those revealing him in a bad light or containing material too personal for the public eye. Dozens of other letters, outside the series and presumably beyond the author's control, remain to furnish a check on the "official" selection. Interestingly, these show no clear differences in character from the others; there are no embarrassing revelations. A consummate diplomat, Salutati, ever mindful of the potential audience for his correspondence, simply avoided putting into writing what he did not wish known publicly. He took to heart his own advice to young sharp-tongued Poggio: "Believe me, dearest Poggio, because of this pride which affects all of us more than it should, there is nothing more stupid than to speak the truth, than to provoke with insults, than to speak badly of anyone at all, when you honestly can—nay I say, ought—to keep silent. . . . for this reason I admonish you, be cautious thinking, more cautious speaking, and most cautious writing. Neither say or speak what it is expedient to hide—that I not say, what you *want* to hide. Do not think only of the present but of the future. . . . Therefore keep a lock on your mouth; use your eloquence for encomiums and good words; do not delight in censuring; do not spend your efforts in insulting."[68]

Inevitably with this kind of caution in mind Salutati produced a safe correspondence but one which lacked the intimacy and wealth of personal detail sought for by the modern reader. Occasionally there are biographical remarks, but much of the correspondence is devoted to disquisitions on intellectual topics or to "encomiums and good words." As he grew older this tendency to abstractions increased: aware that through his letters he was formulating attitudes and goals for a new cultural movement, he favored introducing personal details primarily as illustrations of and reinforcement for general principles.

So attached was he to these letters that the theft of a notebook con-

---

67. Ullman, *The Humanism of Coluccio Salutati*, Medioevo e umanesimo, vol. 4 (Padua, 1963), pp. 272–76.
68. *Epist.*, IV, 129–30.

taining a number of them in prose and verse, some of which had not yet been copied for dispatch, set off a minor emotional crisis in the fall of 1394. In a letter to Giovanni di Conversino shortly after the theft, Salutati admitted that the event had disturbed and vexed him to excess.[69] Salutati's unfinished response to one of Giovanni's letters was among those taken, and he apologized to his correspondent for the delay in answering. His only consolation was that the thief, a supposed friend, might return to his senses and restore the purloined letters (p. 471).

He was only to retrieve them after the death of the robber when Leonardo Bruni located the notebook in Arezzo in 1401.[70] In another letter to Giovanni, notifying him of Bruni's discovery, he relates how over the years he "could never remember the loss without the greatest perturbation" and how with its restoration he was "filled with so much joy that I could not restrain myself from informing you just as I communicated my sadness at the theft" (p. 515).

His last letters show traces of genuine peevishness or ill-humor with his young disciples who, he suspects, have come to think him old-fashioned in ideas and style. But these are the natural groans of a moribund lion. Until then Salutati served as a magnet drawing to Florence students seeking wealth and fame through humane studies. Salutati's Florentine circle by the early 1380s consisted of a few men of high caliber, Luigi Marsili,[71] Ridolfi,[72] Domenico Bandini,[73] and a number of notaries of mediocre abilities like ser Antonio Chelli[74] and ser Domenico Silvestri.[75] By the middle of the decade, however, these were joined by three outstanding young recruits from abroad.

---

69. Ibid., II, 470–71. 70. Ibid., III, 513–14.

71. For Marsili's relationship with Salutati, see above, chap. 4 and chap. 5, and the basic treatment by R. Arbesmann, "Der Augustinereremitenorder und der Beginn der humanistischen Bewegung," *Augustiniana*, 14 (1964), 603–39, and 15 (1965), 259–69. Also see U. Mariani, *Il Petrarca e gli Agostiniani* (Rome, 1946), pp. 66–96. Since Arbesmann wrote, D. Gutiérrez has published the 1450 catalogue of Santo Spirito, "La biblioteca di Santo Spirito in Firenze," *Analecta augustiniana*, 25 (1962), 5–88, which lists five volumes in the library still remaining at that date from the bequest of Luigi Marsili, ns. 225, 226, 233, 245, and 246 (ibid., p. 10), but these volumes have not so far been identified to my knowledge.

72. See above, chap. 5, p. 140.

73. For bibliography on Bandini, see chap. 7, n. 58.

74. On Chelli, see *Epist.*, II, 80–81, n. 3; and my *Coluccio Salutati and His Public Letters* (Geneva, 1976), pp. 17–18.

75. Filippo Villani writing in 1382 (see above chap. 7, n. 55) singled out Silvestri along with Salutati as the only living poets worthy of being included in his list of illustrious Florentines considered in his *Liber de origine civitatis Florentie*. But Silvestri's name was omitted from the second edition of 1396, evidently because he failed to live up to his

Pier Paolo Vergerio of Capodistria was only seventeen or eighteen when he came to Florence in 1386 to teach rhetoric in the grammar schools. His two-year association with Salutati had, if we are to believe his own words, a tremendous moral effect on his life.[76] He returned to Florence on two other occasions, around 1394 to study civil law in the *Studio* and in 1397–99 to work on Greek with Chrysoloras.[77] He probably seized the occasion of his second visit to go through Salutati's notes on *Africa* made ten years previously in preparation for his own edition of the work which was to appear in 1397.[78]

Little is known of Salutati's relationship with Vergerio's close friend and later patron, the brilliant Francesco Zabarella of Padua. A student of canon and civil law, Zabarella arrived in Florence in 1385 and remained until 1390, working in the bishop's *curia* and teaching canon law in the *Studio*.[79] While he did not maintain a regular correspondence with Salutati after leaving Florence, news of Piero's death in 1400 moved Zabarella to write a letter of condolence to the father. Although we know from other sources that he disagreed with Salutati's stand on the celebrated issue of whether the plague could be avoided by flight, this letter and a subsequent one indicate Zabarella's sincere admiration for Salutati's character and his work.[80]

The third young scholar, Antonio Loschi of Vicenza, came to Florence specifically to work with Salutati.[81] Although forced to return home in

---

earlier promise. See references, *Domenico Silvestri: The Latin Poetry*, ed. Richard C. Jensen (Munich, 1973), pp. xv–xvi.

76. *Epistolario di Pier Paolo Vergerio*, p. 62: "Sentio plane quantum in virtute profecerim, te auctore, per id pauculum temporis, quo et videre et audire te licuit, cum ad precepta tua velut ad abundantissimum fontem sitibundus venirem." For the most recent discussions of Vergerio and his work, see Marcello Aurigemma, *Studi sulla cultura letteraria fra Tre e Quattrocento (Filippo Villani, Vergerio, Bruni)* (Rome, 1976), pp. 61–81, and David Robey, "Humanism and Education in the Early Quattrocento: The 'De ingenuis moribus' of P.P. Vergerio," *Bibliothèque d'humanisme et Renaissance*, 42 (1980), 27–58.

77. *Epistolario*, pp. 243–44, and *pref.*, pp. xv and xviii–xix.

78. See above, chap. 7, n. 31.

79. For a brief biography of Zabarella, see *Epist.*, III, 408–9. Cf. Hans Baron, "The Year of Leonardo Bruni's Birth and Methods for Determining the Ages of Humanists Born in the Trecento," *Speculum*, 52 (1977), 599 ff. Also Antonio Zardo, "Francesco Zabarella a Firenze," *Archivio storico italiano*, 5th ser., 22 (1898), 1–22.

80. *Epist.*, III, 408–22, and 456–79, for Salutati's responses. For his attack on Salutati's view about the cause of the plague, see above, n. 32.

81. V. Zaccaria, "Antonio Loschi e Coluccio Salutati, (con quattro epistole inedite del Loschi)," *Atti dell'Istituto veneto di sci., lett., ed arti*, 129 (1970–71), 346–48. For Loschi's verses of admiration sent Coluccio from Vicenza before arriving in Florence in 1386, see ibid., p. 366. On Loschi see, by the same scholar, "Le epistole e i carmi di Antonio Loschi durante il Cancelleriato visconteo (con tredici inediti)," *Atti della Accademia nazionale dei Lincei, Memorie*, ser. VIII, vol. 18, fasc. 5 (Rome, 1975), 369–443; and review article by Riccardo Fubini, *Rivista storica italiana*, 88 (1976), 865–71.

1387 after less than a year because of the destruction of the Scaglier power by Milan, the charming, eloquent young man had managed to achieve a rare degree of intimacy with Salutati and his family. After Loschi's departure, moreover, Salutati continued to nourish deep feelings for him and the younger man responded with professions of filial affection.[82] Salutati, therefore, was quite willing to help Loschi find some position in Pavia with the Milanese administration. If Salutati's letter initiated the effort, Loschi's own letter to the Milanese captain, Giacomo dal Verme, praising Visconti triumphs against the Carrara did the rest.[83] The Visconti plainly saw this talented and fiercely ambitious young man as a valuable asset and assumed tutelage of his career. By 1392 when the first war with Milan ended and Salutati was able to resume correspondence with his Milanese friends, Loschi was a canon in Padua and a confidant of the Visconti court.[84] He was to play an active role in obtaining for Salutati the manuscripts of Cicero's letters from Vercelli and Verona.

The increased budget of the *Studio* in 1385 and the years immediately after brought to Florence not only Zabarella but also many other foreign scholars, masters of their field. As the *Paradiso degli Alberti* shows, at least some of them were willing to play a role in the city's culture outside the classroom.[85] With their knowledge of current work, especially in natural sciences, metaphysics, and logic, these professors filled a gap in Florence's intellectual life which had become traditional. Encyclopedic in his interest, having little of Petrarch's disdain for the usual university subjects, Salutati found the company of these foreign scholars congenial. The impact of contact with them for his thought was subtle but pervasive.

Among local intellectuals trained in theology or natural science there were men like Ugolino da Montecatini and Luigi Marsili. Ugolino had been a friend of the humanist since their days together in the Valdinie-

---

82. While in Florence Loschi dedicated a poem to Salutati: Zaccaria, "Antonio Loschi," pp. 348 and 367–75. In March 1388 after reaching Vicenza Loschi wrote Salutati of his affection for him (ibid., pp. 375–80).

83. There can be little question that Salutati complied with Loschi's request to write a letter of recommendation to Pasquino Capelli, Giangaleazzo's chancellor: "Ac tibi, si quicquam foret cognitionis et amicicie cum Pasquino, illi me specialiter recommendes" (ibid., p. 380). G. da Schio, *Sulla vita e sugli scritti di A. Loschi vicentino, uomo di lettere e di stato. Commentarii* (Padua, 1858), pp. 189–93.

84. Zaccaria, "Antonio Loschi," pp. 352–53, n. 18; *Epist.*, II, 339 and 355.

85. Gene Brucker, "Florence and Its University, 1348–1434," in *Action and Conviction in Early Modern Europe: Essays in Honor of E. H. Harbison*, ed. Theodore Rabb and Jerrold E. Seigel (Princeton, 1969), p. 223, indicates that in these years the *Studio* had the largest income since its foundation.

vole and, although Ugolino only practiced in Florence for short periods of time, he was a frequent visitor there. The two old friends were often together: Ugolino was probably the physician with whom Salutati joked in 1383 about the cunning practices of doctors. Both Ugolino and other medical friends furnished Salutati with necessary medical advice for his researches.[86] Among his dearest and most respected friends, Marsili was Paris-trained in theology and in almost constant residence in Florence from the early 1380s until his death in 1394.

Marsili, however, was more interested in rhetorical and pietistic literature than in formal theology, and Ugolino, if a local wonder, was not among the foremost in his field. On the other hand, foreign professors in the *Studio* like the natural philosophers Biagio Pelacani and Jacopo da Forlì and the medical doctor Marsiglio da Santa Sophia were among leading Italians in their subjects. Biagio lectured in the *Studio* in 1388 and Marsiglio at least in 1394. Jacopo was in Florence in 1388–89 and for a few years in the 1390s.[87]

86. See chap. 2 above. Salutati repeatedly urged Ugolino, who practiced medicine in Pisa for twenty-five years, to establish himself permanently in Florence: F. Novati, "Maestr' Ugolino da Montecatini, medico del secolo xiv ed il suo trattato de' bagni termali d'Italia," *Memorie del r. Istituto lombardo di scienze e lettere*, cl. lett., sci. stor. e morali, 20 (1896), 147–49, publishes a letter of Ugolino to Francesco del Bene dated June 5, 1381. Salutati is probably referring to Ugolino when he remarks in 1383 (*Epist.*, II, 89–90): ". . . ipsorum [of these doctors] unus, quem aliquando visitatorem habui, hominem, iudicio meo, tum scientificum tum iocundum, verum dixit, suis acquiescentes consiliis nunquam ad sanitatem devenire permittant. . . ." He taught at the Studio in Florence between 1393 and 1395 and seems to have practiced medicine in the city sometime between 1402 and 1406: Novati, "Maestr' Ugolino," pp. 150 and 152–53. Also see "Consiglio medico di Maestr' Ugolino da Montecatini ad Averardo de' Medici," ed. F. Baldasseroni and G. Degli Azzi, *Archivio storico italiano*, 4th ser., 38 (1906), 140–52. Salutati refers to Tommaso del Garbo in *De laboribus Herculis*, ed. Berthold L. Ullman, 2 vols. (Zurich, 1951), I, 134, but Maestro Tommaso was already dead by 1382: see Filippo Villani, *Liber de civitatis Florentiae famosis civibus*, ed. Gustavus C. Galletti (Florence, 1847), p. 29, and a more accurate edition of these passages in Talbot R. Selby, "An Edition of Filippo Villani's 'De viris illustribus Florentinis'" (Ph.D. Diss., University of North Carolina at Chapel Hill, 1956), pp. 112–14. On the basis of his conversations with his professional friends and his reading in ancient medical writings, Salutati did not hesitate to offer his own explanation of medical problems like baldness (*Epist.*, III, 450–51) and of the nature of conception and growth of the fetus (*De lab.*, I, 108–37). He was an honorary member of the *Arte dei medici e speziali* before 1386 as were his children Bonifazio, Arrigo, and Antonio in later years: *Arte medici e speziali, Matricole*, 7, fols. 44ᵛ (Salutati), 32ᵛ (Bonifazio), 10 (Arrigo), and 10ᵛ (Antonio).

87. On Marsiglio, see n. 1 above. On Pelacani, see Graziella Federici Vescovini, "Problemi di fisica aristotelica in un maestro del XIV: Biagio Pelacani da Parma," *Rivista di filosofia*, 51 (1960), 181; see also her "'Le Questioni di perspectiva' di Biagio Pelacani da Parma," *Rinascimento*, ser. 2, 1 (1961), 163–243, and *Astrologia e scienza*. Cf. Edward Grant, "Blasius of Parma," *Dictionary of Scientific Biography* (New York, 1970), II, 192–95; and my "Salutati and Contemporary Physics," *Journal of the History of Ideas*, 38 (1977), 669. For additional bibliography, see Vescovini, "Il problema dell'ateismo di Biagio Pelacani da Parma," *Rivista critica di storia della filosofia*, 28 (1973), 123. Important for an understanding of Pelacani's general cultural significance is Anneliese Maier, "Der Widerruf des Blasius von Parma,"

The rejuvenation of the *Studio* also accelerated the rate of book-buying and copying and favored introduction of new works. The list of manuscripts acquired or lent by the Vallombrosan monk, Giovanni di Baldassaro, during the last years of the fourteenth century indicates the existence in the city of a variety of fourteenth-century works of logic, natural philosophy, and theology:[88] the commentaries on Lombard by Gregory of Rimini (145 and 157), by Pietro da Candia (142, 147, 148, 157, and 158), and by William of Ockham (146); a variety of treatises by Biagio Pelacani (143, 150, and 153); the *Calculationes* of Suiset (151); and a large number of logical and philosophical writings by John Buridan, Albert of Saxony, William Heytsbury, Walter of Burley, Marsiglio of Inghen, and other unspecified authors.

Already widely read in ancient and medieval writings in medicine and natural sciences, especially astronomy and astrology,[89] Salutati, through conversing with these foreign professors and reading the books they brought with them, became aware of new developments in logic and natural sciences occurring in Northern Europe. Ever distrustful of the logicians' effort to establish their discipline as the master science, by 1398 he was at least acquainted with problems of signification, supposition, and appellation, which were very much the focus of fourteenth-century logicians.[90] He was so taken with current theories of natural science that he borrowed conceptions like *impetus*, as well as *intensio* and *remissio*, for his discussion of theology and ethics. The *De fato et*

Die Vorläufer Galileis im 14. Jahrhundert (Rome, 1949), 279–99. A discussion of the work of Jacopo is found in Marshall Clagett, *Giovanni Marliani and Late Medieval Physics* (New York, 1941), passim. Also see on Jacopo, Roberto Abbondanza, "Gli atti Ufficiali dello Studio fiorentino dal maggio al settembre 1388," *Archivio storico italiano*, 117 (1959), 90, 102 (appt. for 1388–89).

88. N. Bretano-Keller, "Il libretto di spese," pp. 129–58. The numbers in the text here refer to pages of this article where the particular manuscripts are described.

89. Salutati's knowledge of astronomy is evident from this poem dedicated to Jacopo Allegretti: *Epist.*, I, 281–88 (1383?). In the *De seculo* he cites, evidently first-hand, Aristotle's *De caelo* and *Meterologica*, Chalcidius' translation of the *Timaeus*, Campanus, and Alfraganus: *Colucii Salutati de seculo et religione*, ed. Berthold L. Ullman (Florence, 1957), pp. 75–76 and 35. In his correspondence there are references to Albertus Magnus, *De mineralibus* (*Epist.*, II, 44); Chalcidius' version of the *Timaeus* (II, 144); the *Parisinae Tabellae*, the *Toletanae Tabellae*, and the *Alphunsinae Tabellae* (I, 286); Alfraganus (I, 258); Avicenna, *Liber canonis* (IV, 297); Boethius, *Geometria* (I, 257); and Campanus (I, 258). In Book I of the *De laboribus*, most probably completed before 1391, he cites Aristotle's *De mundo* (II, 47), and again the Latin *Timaeus* (I, 12–13).

90. Witt, "Salutati and Contemporary Physic'" p. 667. He knew enough about the *moderni* more than ten years earlier to know that they were the enemies of poetry: chap. 8, n. 21. On the meaning of these words in late medieval logic, that is, the meaning of the *proprietates terminorum*, see William and Martha Kneale, *The Development of Logic* (Oxford, 1962), pp. 246–74. For a general treatment of late medieval logic, see Philotheus Boehner, *Medieval Logic: An Outline of its Development from 1250 to 1400* (Chicago, 1952).

fortuna (1396) employs the idea of *impetus* to distinguish between God's immediate action, which must be present for any movement to take place, and the resident quality of movement imparted by God to the creature. He found the conceptions of *intensio* and *remissio* useful in 1401 when debating whether or not two contrary passions could be present in the same individual at the same moment.[91]

But much more important, Salutati's contact with first-rate minds trained in natural philosophy had the effect of stimulating him to read more extensively in Aristotle, search for Plato's surviving writings, and explore the works of recent theologians like Thomas and Scotus.[92] What theological conceptions Salutati had had previously were in large part derived from Augustine. Salutati cites Augustine for the first time in 1377, and over the next decade and a half his references manifest a growing knowledge of the Saint's writings.[93]

Augustine, however, never was for him the pervasive influence he had been for Petrarch. Salutati never related to the Saint as a personality: for example, he mentions the *Confessions* only twice and then in his last letters.[94] While he saw Augustine within a historical context, he made no effort to grasp him as a rounded individual. As he did with other writers, excepting possibly Cicero in the *De tyranno*,[95] Salutati tended to consider Augustine an authority, a source of facts and wisdom but not a personality.

As an authority Augustine furnished Salutati with the sharp differentiation between Christian and pagan cultures which figured prominently in the *De seculo et religione*.[96] The Saint was also the source of

91. "Salutati and Contemporary Physics," pp. 671–72.

92. Although Salutati apparently had studied Aristotle's treatises on astronomy before 1390 (see n. 89), his knowledge of the metaphysical and ethical writings of the philosopher was weak before this time. His allusion to the *De anima*, I, 5, 409b–411b, was almost certainly based on the discussion of the work found in the treatise of the correspondent to whom he was writing (*Epist.*, I, 34 [1367]). His references to the *Metaphysics* in Book I of the *De laboribus* are only concerned with the nature of poetry (I, 35 and 65). For the *Nic. Eth.*, see below, n. 104. For his search for a Latin translation of Plato, see below, p. 303. The *De verecundia* presents the first indications that he is aware of the theological writings of Thomas and Scotus. In the year of the publication of the *De verecundia* he praises Thomas' exposition on Job (*Epist.*, II, 240).

93. Ibid., I, 247. Novati, ibid., IV, 677–78, provides a listing of the works of Augustine cited in the correspondence and the pages where the references can be found.

94. Ibid., IV, 191 and 225. He owned at least one complete copy of the *Confessions*, which he heavily annotated and a second partial copy; Ullman, *The Humanism*, pp. 134–40 and 162.

95. See below, chap. 14, and the *De tyranno: Coluccio Salutatis Traktat vom Tyrannen*, Alfred von Martin (Berlin, 1913), pp. xxxiv–xxxxi. His approach to Cicero in this work reflects the inspiration of Petrarch, *Sen.*, XIV, 1 (Opera, I, 419).

96. See chap. 7.

Salutati's position on the relationship between fate, fortune, free will, and divine Providence, which underlay his stand on the proper attitude toward the plague.[97] Augustine's neo-Platonic definition of evil as nonbeing by 1390 appeared in Salutati's analysis of the contrast between virtue and vice.[98]

This last discussion came at a time when Salutati was increasingly concerned to present his ideas on man and human destiny in a metaphysical and theological framework. Otherwise an insignificant little treatise, the *De verecundia* of 1390 provides the earliest evidence of a new philosophical sophistication in the rhetorician, which was to become more obvious with time. On the eve of the first war with Milan, a physician of Faenza, Antonio Baruffaldi, wrote Salutati asking his opinion on the nature of modesty, whether or not it was to be considered a virtue. The question intrigued Salutati, and, although the letters of Baruffaldi had only been sent on January 20, by February 2 the humanist had penned a reply.[99] He also considered the composition a liberation "from the labyrinth of public duties with which I am involved and burdened continually" (p. 278).

The *De verecundia* is essentially a scholastic *quaestio* following closely in content Thomas' treatment of the same issue in *Summa theologica* II, II, q. 144.[100] Salutati's argument in brief is that, while for the Greeks modesty or blushing was regarded as a passion because essentially a fear of shame, for the Romans it was seen as a virtue. An analysis of the sources reveals that the difference in conception between the two groups of writers stems from the fact that they meant different things by the word. While drawing heavily on Thomas' arguments and au-

97. See chap. 7.

98. *Epist.*, II, 274. On Augustine's conception of evil as privation of good or being, see R. Jolivet, "Le problème du mal chez s. Augustin," *Archives de philosophie*, 7, 2 (1930), 1–104, with extensive bibliography, pp. 102–4; and Etienne Gilson, *The Christian Philosophy of St. Augustine* (New York, 1960), pp. 144–45 and 314, no. 7.

99. *De verecundia* in *De nobilitate legum et medicinae. De verecundia*, ed. Eugenio Garin, Edizione nazionale dei classici del pensiero italiano, vol. 8 (Florence, 1947), pp. xxxiv–xxxv; 277 and 336 for dates. Although in epistolary form, Salutati considered the work a treatise (*Epist.*, II, 267 and III, 184). In 1397 Baruffaldi sent Salutati his own treatise, a defense of the precedence of the male sex organ in reproduction (ibid., III, 189). While confessing himself ignorant in the matter, Salutati declares that Baruffaldi has apparently demonstrated his position to be true. Was Salutati's own account of the reproductive process in the *De laboribus*, I, 108–37, written after or before reception of the treatise from the physician of Faenza? With the exception of the quotation from Dante's *Purg.*, XXV, 37 ff., the authorities mentioned in the *De laboribus* and those discussed by Salutati as appearing in Baruffaldi's work (*Epist.*, III, 189–91) are different. Moreover, Salutati seems to have a more balanced view of the contribution of women to the reproductive process in his analysis than Baruffaldi (*De lab.*, I, 115).

100. *De verecundia*, p. 365 (notes).

thorities, Salutati gives evidence that he had gone through Aristotle's relevant writings himself. Moreover, for the first time in his extant writings he stresses that the will has precedence over the intellect in the human personality. He specifically opposes Thomas in making the will the seat of the habitus of virtue (p. 304). Rich throughout in quotations from and allusions to ancient literature, the *De verecundia* represents a curious blend of scholasticism and humanism which became so characteristic of much of Salutati's work in later years.

From 1392 he utilized a rather general conception of the Ideas or Forms, distinguishing as he did in a letter of that year the *species* in God from the *species* in things.[101] His first-dated discussion of a theory of cognition was in 1394.[102] At least by the last year of his life he knew

101. *Epist.*, II, 367–68: "Et quoniam individua quelibet hominum, sicut habent ortum et principium sui esse, sic et naturaliter habent occasum et ut desinant esse quod sunt, ordinavit summus rerum omnium opifex Deus continua generatione individua sibi humana succedere, quo posset hec sublimior creaturarum corporalium species permanere. Si nullus siquidem homo sit, potest humane speciei ratio certa subsistere, que solum, cum ipsa Deus non sit, illi divine menti, cuius noticia rerum est causa, presens erit et cognita; species autem ipsa non erit, licet subsistat eius ratio sive idea, ad cuius limites et exemplum hanc formam sive speciem, que homo dicitur, necessarium est fluxisse. Nec mirum; supra rerum enim omnium que sunt numerum, licet plura numerabilia non subsistant, infinitas numerorum esse rationes, aliquis, qui recte sentiat, non negabit; quas solus infinite essentie, bonitatis, vigoris et intelligentie Deus cognoscit et capit. Ut subsistat igitur actualiter humanum genus, necessaria generatio fuit, per quam, cum eternaliter in temporaneis corruptibilibusque individuis conservari non possit, interminabilis, imo potius finiende individuorum successionis beneficio persevereet." The most that can be said of this confusing account is that Salutati has some knowledge of a doctrine of divine ideas. I wish to thank Edward P. Mahoney for giving me his assessment of this passage. On the doctrine generally, see H. Pinard, "Création," *Dictionnaire de théologie chrétienne*, 3.2 (Paris, 1938), pp. 2150–63; Heinrich Rüssmann, *Zur Ideenlehre der Hochscholastik* (Freiburg-in-B., 1938); and A. Carlini, "Idea," *Enciclopedia filosofica*, 4 vols. (Venice, 1957–58), II, 1169–81.

102. "Pudeat, mi Peregrine, talia dicere vel sentire: alta res mens est et, ut ita loquar, divina et que transcendat adeo sensus, quod coniuncta corpori nichil possit corporeum per se et principaliter intueri. Recipiuntur enim obiectorum species a sensibus corporis; distinguuntur a sensu communi, abstrahuntur a phantasia et, cum per ipsam fuerint intellectui representata, possibili lumine quodam, quem intellectum agentem vocant, reducente possibilitatem in actum, creatur in anima intellectio, que primus actus est intellectus humani; ut hac ratione videre possis hunc totum anime nostre discursum per plura media mentem, hoc est intellectum vel vim memorativam, a qua mens dicta est, attingere. Cuius mentis opus est abstrahere ab istis singularibus communia quedam, dividere atque componere; que nunquid facias, cum Iohannam admiraris et vides, an solum oculos pascas et sensibus condelecteris, quod nobis est commune cum belluis, tibimet volo respondeas" (*Epist.*, III, 28). The account here is so imprecise that any assignment of a source of influence is difficult. Edward P. Mahoney, to whom I am again indebted for his help in analyzing this passage, suggests the punctuation ". . . representata possibili, lumine . . ." in the first sentence instead of that proposed by Novati given above. In any case, among other things, the text indicates awareness on Salutati's part of a doctrine of the internal senses and of abstraction.

In the *De nobilitate*, p. 110, he describes the act forming the universal as a process involving a *collectio*: "Ex individuorum enim, communi quaedam ratione, specifice differen-

enough of the position of the *moderni* that *esse* and *essentia* were identical *realiter* to reject it.[103] Even in the case of a standard work like Aristotle's *Nicomachean Ethics*, there is no solid proof that he read the work before 1390.[104]

Certainly some of this new philosophical interest developed in the course of his efforts to decipher poetic allegories for the *De laboribus*. But more imortant was the stimulation created by the reanimated *Studio*. In his discussion with eminent professional philosophers and scientists he encountered a bracing intellectual rigor, a flood of new ideas, and was forced to submit his own positions to the criticisms of these men. From these contacts Salutati's thought emerged with larger dimensions and, while the point should not be exaggerated, became better structured. The following three chapters demonstrate the extent to which he endeavored to place some of his earlier ethical and religious ideas within a broader theological and philosophical context.

Despite Salutati's growing awareness of the importance of scholastic thought for his own work, the whole period from 1382 to 1396 should be viewed as the period of his life when his appreciation for ancient Roman literature and history was at its height. No addition to his library pleased him more than did that of *Ad familiares*, made possible through

---

tie colliguntur, et ex differentiis ratio Platonis et Socratis speciem hominis facit. . . ." This may be taken from Boethius, *In Isagogen Prophyrii commenta, PL*, 64, p. 85.

103. *Epist.*, IV, 179–80.

104. Excluding passages from this work found in the *De laboribus*, Books II, III, and IV, where dating of specific sections is difficult, there are three possible indications of Salutati's direct knowledge of the *Nic. Eth.* before the late 1380s. In a letter written in October 1386, Salutati states: "Is est profecto qui amico apud amicum solet—imo sum amicus sit alter ipse ut inquid Aristotiles in Ethicis . . . " (B.N.Mad., 17652 [*Gay.* 736], fol. 166ᵛ). The dating of this unpublished letter is based on Salutati's remark that he is nearing 56 years of age (ibid., 166ᵛ). In the opening lines he writes that his correspondent sent him the letter ten months before or two days after Christmas (fol. 166). Since Salutati was born in 1331, a date in October 1386 is certain. He had at least two manuscripts containing the Aristotle passage (*Nic. Eth.*, IX, 4, 1166a, 31). B.N.F., *Conv., sopp.*, I, V, 21, fol. 183ᵛ, reads: "Est enim amicus alius ipse." B.A.V., *Vat. lat.*, 2996, fol. 49, gives same reading except ips*e* in the Vatican manuscript is ips*i*. My opinion is that Salutati in 1386 was probably quoting Aristotle second-hand.

Besides this reference there is an anecdote possibly taken from the *Nic. Eth.*, III, 10, referred to in the *De seculo*, p. 28. He uses the same anecdote again in 1383? (*Epist.*, II, 70). But the story of *Nic. Eth.* appears also in the *Problem.*, 28, 7, and *Eud. Eth.*, III, 2, 12. A possible third reference to the *Nic. Eth.* prior to 1388/89 depends on the dating of a letter: see chap. 13, n. 6.

However, after 1390 and especially from the time of the *De nobilitate legum et medicine* citations and references to the *Nic. Eth.* are legion in the correspondence. By 1404 Salutati knew at least ten commentaries on the work (*Epist.*, IV, 37–38). Without mentioning the chronology, Richard B. Donovan, "Salutati on Non-Italian Writers," *Studies in the Renaissance*, 14 (1967), 199, observes "of all Aristotle's works this is the one he quotes most frequently."

the good offices of Capelli and Loschi in 1392. In his letter of thanks to Capelli he expressed undying gratitude, hardly restraining himself for joy. Through this correspondence, he writes, he can finally see Cicero as an entire person engaged in his day-to-day life and appreciate his stature among the men of his time. One of Salutati's remarks must have made the Milanese chancellor wince: "By your gift I have seen the bases of the civil wars and how that ruler of the whole world plunged from popular liberty into the servitude of monarchy."[105] Salutati could not refrain from teasing his friend in attacking the rule of princes on the basis of historical evidence furnished by Capelli himself. The latter was doubtless wise not to engage in an epistolary exchange with the clever Florentine.

But Salutati was also serious in this remark. Just as in 1377 at a particularly dark period of the war against the Church he had been led to make several extreme, republican statements condemning not simply tyranny but any one-man rule, so now under the influence of Cicero's letters he articulated for the first time in his private writings a similar judgment. This time, however, there are indications that the vivid impressions created by Cicero's words caused this political "notion" to have greater endurance. A missive of 1395, for instance, renders a severe judgment on the establishment of the empire of the Caesars, the only reference to this event in the public letters since 1377.[106] Had there been open warfare with Giangaleazzo in the years immediately after 1393, it would have been interesting to observe how far Salutati might have gone—always restrained as he was by the complexion of Florence's system of alliances. As it was, when hostilities resumed in 1397, Salutati had already passed into a new phase, one which his missives accurately reflect.

Devotion to his scholarship coupled with the demands of his official position did not prevent Salutati from continuing his abiding interest in writing poetry in Latin and *volgare*. In 1388 or 1389 he even embarked on a literary project which rivaled his *Bucolics* in its ambitious propor-

---

105. *Epist.*, II, 389. The Vercelli manuscript was doubtless brought to Florence by the Visconti embassy, which arrived in Florence in September 1392 (*Miss.*, 23, fol. 48). Besides Andreasio Cavalcabò and Ruggiero Cane there was Pietro Filargo, Bishop of Novara, otherwise known as Pietro da Candia (see above, chap. 10). His personal secretary, the middle-aged scholar Ub. Decembrio, met Salutati for the first time while on this embassy with his master. Decembrio's two letters to Salutati are published by Novati, "Aneddoti viscontei, *Archivio storico lombardo*, 35 (1908), 196–200 and 200–201. For a correction of Novati's dating of these letters, see A. Corbinelli, "Appunti sull'umanesimo in Lombardia," *Bollettino della società pavese di storia patria*, 16 (1916), 120–22.

106. See chap. 6.

tions. On a January day in one of these two years, Salutati stopped at
the public baths—probably those in the via delle Terme—on his way
home after work. For some reason, this particular evening the baths
were deserted and he could take his steam bath in solitude. As he pon-
dered the dangers of going to war with Milan, his mind drifted to
thoughts on the difficulties involved in describing a battle actually in
progress. Lucan's indirect manner of depicting the battle of Thessalia
came to mind. He remembered Lucan's description of the battle in the
form of a vision as being artless and arid. Virgil alone of the poets seemed
to him to have been successful in this task. The heat of the bath stimulated his thoughts and he resolved to attempt to write about a battle in
verse.

While the bathman was giving him his rubdown, the rush of warlike
images was being arranged in hexameters in his mind. Before he left
the baths, Salutati had more than twenty lines in his head. Returning
home, he called for pen, paper, and ink and, while the servants set the
table for dinner, he wrote these down. The battlelines described, Salutati by bedtime had finished verses detailing the action of the slingers.
It was not, however, until the following day that the idea occurred to
apply his scene to a particular event. His choice fell on the battle waged
by King Pyrrhus in 279 B.C., near Ascoli with the Romans under C.
Fabricius Luscinus. In the succeeding days the work went on until it
reached the length of one book of the *Aeneid*. At that point, with the
initial stages of battle not yet finished, he laid the work aside. As he
related five or six years later, he felt intimidated when he compared his
own work to that of the ancients.[107]

If daunted by the task of writing an epic, he was still willing to undertake lesser poetic compositions. In the spring of 1392 the arrival of a
Latin poem from the Genoese notary, Giovanni della Stella, written in
celebration of the signing of the peace and of the peacemakers, inspired the humanist to respond in kind. In dedicating his own verses
to praising the young writer's talents, Salutati, either insincere or curiously forgetful of his recent attempt at writing an epic, presented himself as "returning to youthful studies."[108] Shortly after this he acknowledged a poem by Bartolomeo di Napoli with a long poetic reply including
a similar statement. Salutati wrote, "you call me back to the studies of

107. *Epist.*, III, 59–61. This work is considered lost. As he explained his reason for
halting his writing (*Epist.*, III, 61): "Hoc autem carmen acephalum et sine determinatione
dimisi: non enim adeo michi placeo, quod ipsum ab antiquorum maiestate plurimum dis-
cedere non cognoscam."
108. Ibid., II, 313.

my youth."[109] Nevertheless, these two poems of 1392 appear to have been his last in Latin and no *volgare* poem can be dated after this time.

On the other hand, the years 1391–92 marked the beginning of Salutati's interest in Greek literature. While he had had a smattering of elements of Greek earlier in his life, Salutati had until this time never made a serious effort either to learn the language or even to collect Latin translations of Greek writers.[110] A copy of Pilato's translation of Homer was the only work of Greek literature in his library for many years.[111] Then in 1390–91 one of his young friends, Roberto Rossi, met two Greek scholars in Venice on embassy from the Eastern emperor. On his return to Florence Rossi's report of his conversation with Manuel Chrysoloras and Demetrius Cydones must have caused a good deal of excitement in Salutati's circle. Rossi's admiration for the two learned Greeks and his account of the reported riches of Greek literature had a profound effect on Salutati. He was especially desirous of obtaining copies of the works of Plutarch, one of Chrysoloras' favorite authors.[112] Until then Salutati had known only the brief spurious passage quoted and attributed to him by John of Salisbury.[113]

His interest in Plutarch led him to write to a number of friends, among them Cardinal Pietro Corsini at Avignon, requesting knowledge of the whereabouts of Latin translations of the Greek author's work. Corsini obliged by sending a translation of Plutarch's *De cohibenda ira* he himself had commissioned in 1373. Disturbed by the awkward Latin of the translator, Simon Atumano, Archbishop of Thebes, Salutati sat down to rework the Latin and on May 15, 1392 or 1393, he dispatched Atumano's work together with his own to Avignon for the cardinal to compare the results. In his accompanying letter he expressed his desire for any other works of Plutarch that might be available.[114]

Corsini must have put him in contact with Juan de Heredia, Master of the Knights of Jerusalem, who was known to have commissioned an

---

109. Ibid., II, 343.

110. Chap. 8, for Salutati's early knowledge of Greek.

111. Ibid., I, 267 (1377) cites the *Odyssey*. It is difficult to know when he became acquainted with the *Iliad*, but he probably had read it some years before 1393 when he urged Loschi to make a new version of the work (ibid., II, 354 ff.).

112. Ronald Witt, "Salutati and Plutarch," *Essays Presented to Myron P. Gilmore*, ed. Sergio Bertelli and Gloria Ramakus, 2 vols. (Florence, 1978), I, 336–37 and 342.

113. *Epist.*, II, 482. For the beginning of Greek studies in the early Renaissance in Europe and particularly in Venice, see the account by Deno J. Geanakoplos, *Greek Scholars in Venice* (Cambridge, Mass., 1962), pp. 1–40.

114. The problems surrounding the dating of this letter are discussed in "Salutati and Plutarch," pp. 336–42.

Aragonese translation of the *Parallel Lives*. When Salutati wrote Heredia on February 1, 1393/94, he already had in hand a partial list of the rubrics of the translation, probably sent by Corsini. Eager to have a copy of the manuscript, he offered Heredia his manuscript of Pilato's *Odyssey* which he knew the grand master sought.[115] For some reason unable to comply with Salutati's request, Heredia referred him to his fellow countryman, Cardinal de Luna, soon to become Pope Benedict XIII, who also had a copy in his possession. This led to a series of negotiations, probably ending sometime in 1395 with Salutati's reception of the desired work.[116]

At the same time as the search for Plutarch translations was in progress, Salutati on another front was urging Antonio Loschi to do a new translation of the Homeric epics in the same manner as he had himself reworked the *De ira*.[117] His growing philosophical preoccupation led him in 1393 to request a Latin translation of Plato's *Phaedo*. Having heard of its existence in an unspecified Dominican library, Salutati urged one of his friends with access to the library to furnish him with a manuscript.[118]

Yet in the course of these four years from 1391 to 1395, as he came more and more to see the vital necessity of having better knowledge of Greek literature for humanistic studies and to realize the poor quality and inadequate number of existing translations, Salutati became convinced that Western scholars could use the Greek heritage only by learning Greek themselves. He consequently encouraged the thirty-five-year-old Jacopo degli Angeli in his intention to go to Constantinople in 1395 to study with Chrysoloras. One day, he hoped, a native Florentine would be in a position both to teach Greek in his native city and make available the riches of Greek thought in Latin translations. More immediately, however, he together with his circle of friends nourished the

---

115. *Epist.*, II, 301–2.   116. "Salutati and Plutarch," p. 343.

117. *Epist.*, II, 354–56, dated July 21, 1393, and 398–99, dated September 29, 1392. On the dating of these letters, see Berthold L. Ullman, *Studies in the Italian Renaissance*, Storia e letteratura, 2nd ed., vol. 51 (Rome, 1973), pp. 219–20, and Zaccaria, "Antonio Loschi," pp. 353–57.

118. *Epist.*, II, 444. Revilo P. Oliver, "Salutati and Plato," *Transactions and Proceedings of the American Philological Association*, 71 (1940), 315–34, discusses the sources of Salutati's knowledge of Plato. He was still seeking a copy about 1401 when he wrote to Giovanni di Conversino asking for the *Phaedo* along with the *Timaeus* and the commentary of Chalcidius (*Epist.*, III, 515). Salutati's manuscript (*Vat. Lat.*, 2063) containing Chalcidius' translation of the *Timaeus* and the *Phaedo* translated by Aristippus is probably taken from Conversino's copy: B. L. Ullman, *The Humanism*, pp. 186–87 and 246. On the basis of Salutati's citations from the *Phaedo*, Oliver (p. 320) suggests that Salutati had the manuscript in hand by about 1402.

hope that through Angeli Chrysoloras might be lured to Florence to give lessons.

Arriving in the city in the autumn of 1395, despite the siege of the Turks, Angeli met both Cydones and Chrysoloras and obtained the latter's consent to become his student. The first letters from Angeli reached Florence in February 1396, accompanied by letters from the two Greeks addressed to Rossi. That from Chrysoloras also contained a short note for Salutati. These communications only stimulated Salutati to greater efforts to obtain an attractive appointment from the government to draw Chrysoloras to Florence. By the second week of March, in fact, a dispatch was sent off for Constantinople containing a letter from Salutati, written on February 15 to Cydones and another to Chrysoloras on March 8.[119] In the latter Salutati notified Chrysoloras of his appointment to a professorship in the Florentine *Studio*.[120]

The official letter offering the Greek scholar the position, however, was only ready by March 28.[121] Although impatient to give Chrysoloras official notification of the election, Salutati had to wait until the terms of the appointment had been worked out by the *Studio* officials in order to draft the formal offer. As presented in the *Studio*'s letter of March 28, Chrysoloras would receive an annual salary of one hundred florins, and the duration of the appointment was for ten years. In addition to his courses in the *Studio*, he was expected to offer private instruction free to anyone requesting it; but, if the students wished to give something in payment, he could accept it without diminution of salary. Although structured in the official mode of the chancery, the letter's use of *tu* rather than *vos* gave the document a humanistic touch resembling closely the letter composed forty-six years before by Boccaccio inviting Petrarch to teach in the *Studio*.[122]

Three days before the official document Salutati composed a personal

---

119. Apparently neither Salutati nor Rossi noticed which of the letters from the Greeks contained the note to Salutati and Salutati mistakenly wrote to Cydones on February 15 acknowledging the communication. Before dispatching the letter, however, he wrote another to Chrysoloras correcting what he now realized to be his error but stating that the contents of the letter to Cydones were applicable to both the scholars (ibid., III, 119–20).

120. Ibid., III, 122–25.

121. Giuseppe Cammelli, *Manuele Crisolora: I dotti bizantini e le origini dell'umanismo*, 3 vols. (Florence, 1941–54), I, 34–5, n. 2.

122. Alessandro Gherardi, *Statuti della Università e Studio fiorentino dell'anno MCCCLXXXVII seguiti da un' appendice di documenti dal MCCCXX al MCCCCLXXII*, Documenti di storia italiana, vol. 7 (Florence, 1881), pp. 283–86. The background and style of this letter are discussed in Ginetta Auzzas, "Studi sulle 'Epistole': I. L'invito della Signoria fiorentina al Petrarca," *Studi sul Boccaccio*, vol. 4 (Florence, 1967), pp. 203–40.

letter to Angeli probably designed to accompany it. Salutati urged his friend to do his utmost to have the Greek accept the Florentine offer and to have him come quickly to fulfill "our expectation and hunger."[123] Angeli must also buy books: histories, poetry, mythology, works on metrics, and dictionaries. He especially emphasizes his desire to have all of Plato, Plutarch, and Homer, the last "in big letters on parchment"—it seems the old man with weakening sight hoped eventually to be able to read the Homeric poems in the original. If Chrysoloras needs money, Angeli is to obtain it in Salutati's name from the Bilotti brothers in Constantinople. The chancellor was obviously prepared to make every effort to induce the famous Greek to accept Florence's offer. To Angeli, who had perhaps complained in his letter of the difficulties encountered in mastering Greek, Salutati gave warm encouragement to continue, and a few suggestions for organizing his study of the language. His warning to Angeli that he was doggedly determined to follow the lessons to be given in Florence has already been quoted earlier.

Nevertheless, Salutati was forced to wait for almost a year before Chrysoloras' arrival in the city. Angeli together with Chrysoloras and Cydones actually reached Venice by late October or early November, but Angeli and Chrysoloras did not proceed on immediately to Florence. Apparently the Greek was not fully satisfied with the terms of the contract offered by the *Studio*, and once in Venice, he hesitated. Desperate to have him, Salutati managed to obtain a new offer, which on December 11 was embodied in a letter sent to Venice. By the new terms Florence was prepared to offer 150 gold florins, that is, a fifty percent increase in salary, to limit the contract to only five years, to free Chrysoloras from any teaching in the *Studio*, and to permit him to give his lessons in his own home. He was still required to give free teaching to any Florentine, but from non-Florentines he could demand a fee.[124] The more favorable arrangement finally decided Chrysoloras and the long-awaited teacher presented himself to the *Signoria* on February 2, 1397.

The brilliant group of young and middle-aged men who met at Chrysoloras' house in Florence for Greek lessons was almost coextensive with Salutati's own circle. According to Bruni's later observation there were Roberto Rossi, Palla Strozzi, Vergerio, Jacopo Angeli, and "molti con-

123. The letter is found *Epist.*, III, 129–32.
124. Cammelli, pp. 39–42 and 47–49. Cf. Roberto Weiss, "Lo studio del greco a Firenze," *Medieval and Humanist Greek*, ed. R. Aversani, G. Billanovich, and G. Pozzi, Medioevo e umanesimo, vol. 8 (Padua, 1977), pp. 234–36.

disciepoli," probably those somewhat less successful in their studies.[125] Almost certainly Niccolò Niccoli, whom Bruni referred to at one point as "my colleague and helper in learning Greek," was among these latter as was Salutati's talented but very busy son, Piero.[126]

Nothing is known of Salutati's relationship with the immensely wealthy intellectual dilettante Palla Strozzi, whose name never appears in Salutati's writings, but there are varying amounts of detail regarding his link to the others. Salutati and the cynical Niccoli were not very close. Although there is no reason to suspect Poggio's later identification of Niccoli as a disciple of Luigi Marsili, Niccoli was a strange intellectual heir for the pious Augustinian friar.[127] Leonardo Bruni's depiction of him in the *Dialogi ad Petrum Istrum* as the irreverent, clever protagonist of the discussion was doubtless accurate.[128] An esthete with a bad tongue and worse morals—he lived openly with a mistress—he may have charmed younger men with his gossip and iconoclastic wit, but Salutati never trusted the man.[129]

Like Strozzi and Niccoli, Rossi was a wealthy patrician but with a more professional bent. Somewhat older than the other two, he was in his mid-forties by the time of Chrysoloras' arrival.[130] Rossi had known Salutati since his early days as chancellor but, as in Niccoli's case, Luigi

125. Cammelli, pp. 51–52.

126. Cammelli discounts Niccoli's knowledge of Greek (ibid., pp. 72–75). Among references to Niccoli's relationship to Greek learning he omits the words of Bruni in his dedication of Xenophon's *De tyranno* to Niccoli ("Praefatio in libellum Xenophontis de tyranno traductum per L. Aretinum," in Hans Baron, *Leonardo Bruni Aretino. Humanistisch-Philosophische Schriften*, Quellen zur Geistesgeschichte des Mittelalters und der Renaissance, vol. 1 [Leipzig, 1928; repr. Wiesbaden, 1969], p. 100): ". . . in Graecis ipsis addiscendis socius mihi adiutorque fuisti." Although not mentioned by Bruni as a student of Chrysoloras, it is almost certain that Piero, Salutati's talented son, would have followed the courses. In fact, he is named together with Angeli, Rossi, and Strozzi as Chrysoloras' procurators after his departure from Florence in 1400 (Cammelli, p. 106, n. 1). Ognibene Scola, close friend of Vergerio, also studied with Chrysoloras for a time in Florence: G. Cogo, "Di Ognibene Scola umanista padovano," *Nuovo archivio veneto*, 2nd ser., 8, 1 (1894), 117.

127. Poggio Bracciolini, "In funere Nicolai Nicoli civis florentini," *Opera omnia*, ed. Riccardo Fubini, 4 vols. (Torino, 1964–69), I, 271. The letters of Poggio to Niccolo have been translated into English by Phyllis G. Gordan, *Two Renaissance Book Hunters*, Records of Civilization, Sources and Studies, vol. 91 (New York, 1974). Cf. Vespasiano da Bisticci, *Le vite*, ed. Aulo Greco, 2 vols. (Florence, 1970–76), II, 225–26; and Weiss, "Lo studio del greco," pp. 247–48.

128. *Ad Petrum Paulum Histrum Dialogus*, ed. Eugenio Garin in *Prosatori latini del Quattrocento*, La letteratura italiana, vol. 13 (Milan-Naples, 1952), pp. 44–99.

129. The only monograph on Niccoli is Giuseppe Zippel, *Niccolò Niccoli* (Florence, 1890). Also see Lauro Martines, *The Social World of the Italian Humanists* (Princeton, 1963), passim. On his mistress and character, Zippel, pp. 37–40; and Martines, pp. 257–58.

130. The bibliography on Rossi is published together with some of Rossi's writings by Aldo Manetti, "Roberto de' Rossi," pp. 33–55. Cf. G. Cammelli, pp. 61–64.

Marsili had a more formative influence on him. For a time he studied with Giovanni Malpaghini, the brilliant child prodigy become disappointed adult.[131] In 1367 Malpaghini had abruptly left Petrarch's service to pursue a dream of studying Greek in Southern Italy but got only as far as Pisa before turning back destitute and footsore.[132] Perhaps inspired by his teacher's example and certainly provided with more ample means, Rossi had gone to Venice in 1390–91 to learn Greek from Chrysoloras and Cydones.[133] Only family responsibilities prevented him from accompanying Angeli to Constantinople in 1395. Once having acquired a knowledge of the language he devoted the rest of his life to teaching Greek in Florence.

Apart from his concern with Greek, it is difficult to determine how committed Rossi was to the new studies. He seems to have been passionately interested in logic and the one translation from Greek definitely his was a Latin translation of Aristotle's *Posterior Analytics*.[134] Bruni described him as playing host to the first day's discussion in the *Dialogi* but not taking an active role in the exchange of ideas.[135]

On the other hand, Salutati seems to have had a closer relationship with fellow provincials like himself. From a relatively affluent family of Scarperia, Jacopo Angeli spent his adolescence in Florence where he established an intimate contact with Salutati.[136] Encouraged by the older man, Jacopo spent over a year in Constantinople with Chrysoloras and served as intermediary for negotiations between the Greek scholar and the Florentine government. He also executed Salutati's charge to bring

131. Roberto Weiss, "Jacopo Angeli da Scarperia (c. 1360–1410/11)," *Medieval and Humanist Greek*, ed. R. Avesani, G. Billanovich, and G. Pozzi, Medioevo e umanesimo, vol. 8 (Padua, 1977), p. 258.

132. Petrarch, *Seniles*, V, 5 and 6. The incident is treated in detail by Arnaldo Foresti, "Giovanni da Ravenna e il Petrarca," *Commentari dell' Ateneo di Brescia per l'anno 1923* (1924), 165–201. Malpaghini left Petrarch definitely in 1368. His residence in Florence probably dates from the years around 1390. Sabbadini dates his birth about 1346: *Giovanni da Ravenna insigne figura d'umanista (1343–1408)* (Como, 1924), p. 242. He had clearly been in Florence, living in close contact with Salutati some years before a rift occurred between the two men. Salutati's letter to Malpaghini trying to patch the matter up is dated 1392/93 (Ullman, *Studies*, p. 230). Rossi probably studied privately with Malpaghini before going to Venice in 1390/91. Malpaghini's first recorded appointment in the Florentine *Studio* is 1394.

133. R. J. Loenertz, *Correspondance de Manuel Calécas*, Studi e Testi, vol. 152 (Vatican City, 1950), p. 64.

134. Manetti, "Roberto de'Rossi," pp. 33–34. See interesting observations of Roberto Weiss, "Lo Studio del greco," pp. 246–47.

135. *Dialogus*, p. 46. For Roberto's civic offices, see Martines, *The Social World*, pp. 154–59. Gene Brucker, *The Civic World of Renaissance Florence* (Princeton, 1977), illustrates Rossi's central role in the councils of state. See, for example, pp. 286; 291, n. 209; and 293.

136. Roberto Weiss, "Jacopo Angeli da Scaperia," p. 257.

back with him from Constantinople the nucleus of a Greek library.[137] After spending the summer of 1400 helping Bonifazio care for six of Salutati's younger sons in Stignano, two of whom fell sick with plague, he left Florence for Rome in the fall. From this year until his death in 1410/11 a stream of Latin translations poured from his pen.[138]

Of all the young Florentine scholars Salutati had greatest hopes for Leonardo Bruni, who became like a son to him after the death of Piero. Born in Arezzo and attending grammar school there, Bruni came to Florence to study civil law about 1392/93 and apparently abandoned these studies in 1397 to give himself wholeheartedly to learning Greek with Chrysoloras.[139] Unlike Rossi and Jacopo, who were essentially translators, Bruni showed himself capable of applying his Greek learning in the creation of original work. However, his first surviving composition, a poem entitled *Carmen de adventu imperatoris* written at the outset of his Greek studies about 1397/98 was too early to reflect such influence.[140]

In many ways the old and the young man were very different. Bruni had none of Salutati's encyclopedic interests, his mystical tendencies. He was quite content to restrict himself to the realm of natural reason where he felt the rhetorician's interest properly belonged. A better grasp of Latin grammar gave him a tight, crisp style quite in contrast with the meandering, distended quality of Salutati's prose. Bruni was more politically minded, more secular, and if he was devout, he kept it to himself. The leader of Florentine humanism after Salutati's death, Bruni set the tone for the movement in the city for the next forty years.

Salutati did not feel it beneath his dignity to sit with these younger men on the benches of the schoolroom in Chrysoloras' house learning his lessons in the unfamiliar tongue. He tried at least. Shortly after Chrysoloras' arrival, the new teacher graciously prepared at Salutati's request the short treatise on Greek breathing already mentioned.[141] In a letter written later in his sojourn in the city, Chrysoloras still spoke optimistically of the humanist's possibilities of mastering the language.[142] Yet Salutati's knowledge of Greek never advanced much beyond a very

137. *Epist.*, III, 131–32.
138. Weiss lists his translations and other publications, "Jacopo Angeli," pp. 272–76.
139. Hans Baron, "The Year of Leonardo Bruni's Birth," p. 609.
140. Hans Baron, *The Crisis of the Early Italian Renaissance*, rev. ed. (Princeton, 1966), pp. 329–30, and *Crisis*, Appendices, 1st ed., p. 575.
141. For the circumstances surrounding the writing of this small treatise, see Roberto Weiss, "Gli studi greci di Coluccio Salutati," Miscellanea in onore di Roberto Cessi, Storia e letteratura, vols. 71–73 (Rome, 1958), I, 353. Cf. Agostino Pertusi, "Le prime grammatiche greche a stampa," *Italia medioevale e umanistica*, 5 (1962), 348.
142. *Epist.*, IV, 343; and Weiss, "Gli studi," I, 353.

rudimentary stage, and to the end of his life he was unable to translate the most simple Greek texts.

His failure to learn Greek despite the presence of a truly great teacher was in part the fault of old age. But more than this, the first part of Chrysoloras' teaching paralleled the period of the Second Milanese War, and Salutati's official responsibilities were heavy. Throughout the whole period, moreover, deeply committed to a number of other scholarly endeavors, he was unable to pursue Greek studies with any consistency. Gradually, it seems, he came to feel that with so few years before him, it was better to obtain what he needed in Greek either from queries put to Chrysoloras or from his own disciples as they gained mastery of the language. After Chrysoloras' departure in March 1400, Bruni and Angeli were especially helpful to him. Even after their respective departures for the *Curia*, they dispatched him their Latin translations and responded generously to his request for information from Greek sources.

In the fall of 1399 Chrysoloras like many Florentine citizens fled the city in the face of an increasing death rate from the plague.[143] He remained at a villa belonging to Palla Strozzi in the Casentino until the spring, when he left to join the entourage of the Eastern emperor, who had come to Italy to seek troops and money to defend his diminishing territories. Chrysoloras never returned to fulfill the rest of his contract. With the instruction halted and Florence daily becoming more dangerous, Vergerio also left for the North.[144] By fall, moreover, Angeli was on his way to seek employment in the Curia. But a tradition had been established.

Shortly before he left the city, Angeli produced the first fruits of the new Greek learning, Plutarch's *Vita Bruti*, a biography, which must have been of special interest to Salutati because of its close relationship to the crucial period in Roman history at the very end of the Republic.[145] In the following year in Rome he completed a second life, the *Vita Ciceronis*, whose choice was perhaps similarly dictated by its focus on the late Republic.[146] Leonardo Bruni's production of translations began with Basil's *De utilitate studii in libros gentilium*, dedicated to Salutati, who had requested the work, and this was followed by Xenophon's *De tyranno*.[147]

143. Cammelli, pp. 105–6. Cf. Weiss, "Lo studio del greco," pp. 237–38.

144. *Epistolario di Pier Paolo Vergerio*, pp. xviii–xix.

145. Weiss, "Jacopo Angeli," pp. 261, 272.

146. Ibid., p. 273.

147. Hans Baron, *Leonardo Bruni Aretino*, pp. 99–101. Weiss, "Lo studio del greco," p. 252, suggests the translation was directly inspired by Salutati's *De tyranno* of 1400.

Both these works were finished before May 1403, but Salutati lived to see at least two other translations from his greatest disciple, the *Phaedo* of Plato and Plutarch's *Vita M. Antonii*, the latter again dedicated to Salutati but probably completed after Bruni was at the Curia.[148]

By the time of Bruni's departure for Rome in the late winter of 1405, only Strozzi, Niccolì and Rossi remained in the city of those Florentines who can be identified as studying with Chrysoloras. Although Niccolì's Greek was weak, he together with Strozzi was responsible for increasing the accessibility of Greek works in Florence,[149] while Rossi, who devoted himself full-time to the teaching of Greek, was in the process of preparing a new generation of students trained in the second ancient language. Despite Florence's losses to Rome and his own apprehension that Florence would lose its cultural lead,[150] Salutati at the end of his life could count as one of his greatest accomplishments the restoration of Greek studies to the Western world.

---

148. Baron, *Leonardo Bruni Aretino*, pp. 3–4 and 102–4. Weiss maintains there may have been other translations done while he was in Florence: "Lo studio del greco," pp. 244–45, n. 117, and 254.

149. Cammelli, pp. 57–58 and 74, n. 2. Salutati, however, mentions Vanni di Montecuccoli as a student of Greek (see below, chap. 15).

150. *Epist.*, IV, 119–20.

PART IV. THE FINAL DECADE

CHAPTER 11. THY WILL BE DONE

In the very days when Salutati was trying to persuade the Florentine government to invite Chrysoloras to the city, Piera Salutati died. She fell ill on February 15: "She suffered with a great enduring pain; for fourteen days she fought with death."[1] Piera died on the 28th and was buried the next day.[2] In the four letters relating the details of her death and describing his feelings, Salutati spoke of the grief without consolation he had felt while watching her die: "I prostrated myself in sorrow before God, I shouted, I prayed. I demanded that God might spare her on account of my tears."[3] Realizing at her death that God's will had been done, he bent his own will to necessity: "I dried my tears, I ended my weeping and, giving thanks to God, I composed myself with his assistance so that, feeling the loss, I was made absolutely insensible to the pain."

He described her death as having occurred not by fortune but by divine decree: "I struggled with the greatest grief, believe me," he wrote to his friend Zambeccari in June, "and although it oppressed my senses, my reason conquered and is now conquering; for not only at this time but often even now and then grief tests me."[4] Thus, finding consolation in the thought that Piera was mortal, from the hour of her death, because "of reason" and "God's grace", he felt the strength to resume his normal life. The day of her burial falling on the same day as the swearing in of the new priorate, Salutati left the funeral to administer the oaths according to the duties of his office.[5]

This last demonstration of fortitude impressed his contemporaries; no doubt Salutati intended it to. Even in deep grief there is a struggle not to exploit the sudden attention from others.[6] But on the day after her death he was in fact truly relieved, not only because she was out of her agony but also because he had not lost control. Years before when Caterina died he had experienced months of physical and mental breakdown. When in 1393 he had upbraided ser Andrea da Volterra

---

1. *Epist.*, III, 137.
2. For her burial, see ibid., III, 126, n. 1.
3. Ibid., III, 138.
4. Ibid., III, 140.
5. Ibid., III, 142.
6. Salutati denies too easily any interest on his part in receiving applause for his fortitude (ibid., III, 142). This should not be taken as agreeing with von Martin, *Coluccio Salutati und das humanistische Lebensideal* (Berlin-Leipzig, 1916), pp. 171 ff., who essentially describes Salutati as unfeeling.

about his continued mourning for the sudden death of his wife and all his children, Salutati could not have helped wondering whether he would have been strong enough to bear such a loss.[7] His reaction to Piera's death proved that he could follow his own teachings. His appearance at the induction ceremony of the priors was as much a testimony for himself as it was for others. In replying to a letter of sympathy from the same ser Andrea whom he had consoled three years before, Salutati must have felt relieved that the power of God had indeed brought comfort to his heart.[8]

Salutati's exchange of letters in 1396 with ser Andrea reveals a new intensity in the humanist's interest in Dante. He had always had a deep respect for the poet's work. In 1374, even while ranking Dante's poetry below that of the recently deceased Petrarch, he referred to Dante as a "truly divine man."[9] Twenty-one years later in 1395 he went further. In his letter to Cardinal Oliari in which he compared the ancients to the moderns, Salutati characterized Dante as "that highest honor of *volgare* eloquence to whom no one who flourished in our time nor anyone in ancient times is to be compared in terms of knowledge and genius."[10]

Until 1396, however, there was little indication that Dante's writings had much effect on Salutati's thinking. On two occasions, once in 1374 and again in 1383, in response to requests by correspondents, he had explicated certain passages of the *Divina commedia* and in one of these cases defended Dante's judgment.[11] Around 1392/93 there was one instance and possibly a second when Salutati utilized Dante as an authority in the course of a discussion.[12] Nevertheless, in the days of Piera's illness and immediately thereafter, Dante's thought took on a

7. Ibid., II, 439–44.

8. This letter of Salutati is lost but its existence is known from a reference to it in the letter to Zambeccari (ibid., III, 140–41). Salutati writes of this letter: "Ego me, quid inquam ego?, imo Deus me invictum et insensibilem reddidit (to grief); ut, sicut ad Vulterranum Andream, alterum fratrem meum, scripsi, dicere potuerit tunc anima mea, dicereque possit et nunc flentibus quibuscunque tales casus . . . " and the translation of Dante cited below follows.

9. Ibid., I, 183.   10. Ibid., III, 84.

11. Ibid., II, 76–79; and 101–3. In the latter he defends Dante's geographical as well as his historical judgment. For the date 1374 for the first letter, see Berthold L. Ullman, *Studies in the Italian Renaissance*, Storia e letteratura, 2nd ed., vol. 51 (Rome, 1973), pp. 213–14.

12. In Book II of the *De laboribus Herculis*, ed. Berthold L. Ullman, 2 vols. (Zurich, 1951), I, 108 and 112, Salutati incorporates portions of Dante's *Divina commedia*, *Purg.*, XXV, 37 ff., into his account of human conception: cf. above, chap. 10, n. 99. Although the chronology of his writing this book cannot be established with certainty, my impression is that, if Book I was almost completed by 1391, this section was probably written in large part soon after. Moreover, if Novati's reconstruction of line 12, *Epist.*, III, 504 (1392/93), is correct, Salutati cited a phrase of Dante as an endorsement of his criticism of gossip. For the dating of this letter, see above, chap. 10, n. 132.

vital significance for him as he attempted to find solace in the pages of the *Divina commedia*. His lost metric response to ser Andrea's letter of sympathy included a Latin translation of portions of Dante's poem in which he found beautifully expressed the emotion of resignation to God's will he felt in himself. In a letter to Pellegrino Zambeccari he quotes again a portion of the translation.[13] Dante's Beatrice has descended into Limbo to commission Virgil to lead Dante from error. To Virgil's amazement that she has dared to descend from heaven to such a frightening depth she responds:

> Io son fatta da Dio, sua mercè, tale
> che la vostra miseria non mi tange,
> nè fiamma d'esto incendio non m'assale   (*Inf.*, II, 91–93)

which Salutati translated:

> Sum summi factura Dei; merces sua talis,
> Quod miserum vestre me non contingit erumne,
> Meque nec invadunt huiusce incendia flamme.

From this time to his death Dante was to be the single most pervasive intellectual influence in his life.

The *De fato et fortuna*, written within a year of his wife's demise, was probably the immediate outcome of Salutati's struggle to accept Piera's death as reflecting the decree of a just and loving God. His letter to Zambeccari in June 1396 mingles intimate expressions of feeling with philosophical and theological meditations suggesting that Salutati was deeply concerned at the time with understanding in larger terms the significance of his recent encounter with death.

Piera is not mentioned in the treatise, and perhaps Salutati was not even conscious of a connection. For years he had discussed the effect of divine Providence on human life in piecemeal fashion, primarily in connection with the narrow issue of the plague. Since 1374, when he had first formulated his position, he had returned on a number of occasions to defend his belief that, because God decrees the hour of our death, flight from the plague makes no sense.[14] Now, having been forced to reexamine his position in a time of crisis and successfully having triumphed over his own weakness and doubts, he resolved to present

13. See above, n. 8.
14. *Epist.*, I, 170–71, and II, 80–98. Also see *Epist.*, II, 99, 105–9, 224–27, 230–37, 238–44, 318–27. Daniela De Rosa, "Il concetto della storia nel pensiero di Coluccio Salutati," *Sapienza*, 32 (1979), 466, cites an instance of Salutati's use of this concept in the public letters.

the whole problem in a synthetic fashion as he had never done before.

Composing at a rapid rate, he was ready by July to send Books I and II entitled *De fato* to his French correspondent Jean de Montreuil for criticism. The *De fortuna*, consisting of Books III and IV, was perhaps already completed by the end of 1396, when an opportunity presented itself for giving the work better focus. The Abbot of Settimo in Perugian territory wrote Salutati about this time asking him to explain the cause of the bloody internecine warfare which was destroying the civil peace of Perugia. Adding a short introduction dedicating the work to the abbot and a final chapter dealing specifically with the Perugian situation, Salutati had the treatise in final form by late 1396 or early 1397.[15]

The work, while important as an indication of Salutati's intellectual life in this period, had nothing new to say on the problem of the relationship of an all-powerful God to man's moral responsibility. The humanist's position on fate and fortune as manifestations of divine Providence, his reconciliation of free will with necessity, and his adoption of the conception of evil as nonbeing, were based on Augustine's analysis in Book V of the *De civitate Dei*. His views on predestination could have been derived from any number of theologians from Augustine down to fourteenth-century writers like Scotus. He relied heavily on distinctions developed in Aristotle's *Physics*, 2, 4–6, for his characterization of chance and fortune.[16]

Occasionally the author gives indications that he is speaking within the context of current philosophical and theological debates. In the course of arguing that fortune is a real cause of certain effects, Salutati reflects an acquaintance with recent criticism of the principle of causation.[17] To one who maintains that because fortune cannot be observed it must be a mere name, Salutati retorts:

> But what else, pray, do you see but effects in those things which are generated, nourished, and grow naturally? You see the seed whether

15. Ronald Witt, "Toward a Biography of Coluccio Salutati," *Rinascimento*, 17 (1976), 23–34. Salutati prided himself on his ability to compose quickly (*Epist.*, I, 307).

16. W. Rüegg, "Entstehung, Quellen und Ziel von Salutatis de Fato et Fortuna," *Rinascimento*, 5 (1954), 151–77, analyzes Salutati's sources in detail. On the earlier influence of Augustine on Salutati's writings, see chapt. 10.

17. Julius R. Weinberg, *Nicholas of Autrecourt, A Study in 14th-Century Thought* (Princeton, 1948), pp. 31–50. Occam and his close followers generally opposed Autrecourt's denial of natural causality. For a brief discussion of the problem and bibliography, see William Courtney, "Covenant and Causality in Pierre d'Ailly," *Speculum*, 46 (1971), 94–102. Ernest A. Moody, "Ockham, Buridan, and Nicolas of Autrecourt," *Studies in Medieval Philosophy, Science and Logic* (Berkeley, 1975), pp. 127–60, sketches a range of issues on which Ockham and Autrecourt disagree. There is, however, no specific evidence that Salutati knew either Ockham or Autrecourt.

it be the fruit or a dried particle of it; you see the earth and the peasant working and preparing it like the womb of a mother with plow-
ing and raking and by digging trenches so that he might throw or
plant the seed or set the plants in a row; you do not see the crop born
but rather you see it already born and behold the top of the shoot
rising from the spreading softness of the leaves and from a certain
solidity of nodules new leaves generated as if from the fibrous first
roots; you judge rather than see, that the roots have moved the plants
and the shoots, and that after a sufficient time they grew; you see the
peasant carrying out the rules of agriculture, thinning the plants and
watering the seedlings. Tell me, since you see so many things, and
so many actions and so much growth, where do you see nature producing all these things? . . . You do not see nature or fortune. . . .
Nature hides and fortune hides![18]

Although making no general statement applicable to all causes, Salutati
maintains here that at least in regard to these natural effects the relationship between cause and effect is never observed but inferred from
the regularity of a specific series of events. On the other hand, a few
pages earlier he seems to suggest that the causal principle is innate in
the human mind.[19] In any case he has no wish to challenge its reality.
His particular argument, in fact, depends on every effect having a cause.
But his point like that of other critics is that we cannot have certain
proof of a connection.

　　While he never gives enough detail, he may also have had something in mind approaching Scotus' vision of God's *potentia absoluta*—
Salutati refers once to God's *"absoluta potentia."*[20] "For God is free," he
writes, "subject in his actions to no law whatsoever."[21] What gives a

18. I have used wherever possible B.A.V., *Vat. lat.*, 2928, corrected by Salutati, for my
text of the *De fato et fortuna*. Where this text has *lacunae* the very accurate B.A.V., *Urb. lat.*,
1184, was utilized. *Vat. lat.*, 2928, Tr. III, 7, fol. 57ᵛ: "Et quia vides, obsequor, preter effectum in his que naturaliter generantur, nutriuntur, augentur? Vides semen sive sit fructus
sive desecta quedam particula; vides humum et ipsam exercentem agricolam preparan-
temque quasi matris gremium tum sulcis et porculis, tum scrobium defossionibus ut sem-
ina iaciat vel serat ponatque vel in ordine plantas; vides non nasci sed natam segetem et
de foliorum sparsa mollicie surgere fistulatum culmen et a quadam nodulorum soliditate
nova folia quasi de prime radicis fomite generari; sentis potiusquam videas radices egisse
plantas et surculos et post aliquid legitimi temporis adolevisse; vides agriculture preceptis
astantem colonum purgantem segetes plantulasque rigantem. Dic michi, cum tot videas
res, tot actiones totque videas incrementa, ubi vides naturam illa omnia producentem?
. . . Nec naturam vides nec fortunam . . . Latet natura latetque fortuna."
19. Ibid., fol. 56ᵛ: "Verum quia mentibus hominum communis inhesit opinatio cuncta
fieri ab aliquo. . . ."
20. Ibid., Tr. II, 10, fol. 26ᵛ.
21. Ibid., Tr. II, 9, fol. 22ᵛ. In ibid., Tr. II, 7, fol. 8ᵛ: "Potest fateor dei omnipotentia

Scotist rather than an Ockhamist tendency to his statements on God's freedom in creating the universe is his insistence that were we to see the whole of creation in its causes and effects, we would judge God's work just and good, thus suggesting that there had been a standard, presumably his essence, to which God adhered in making the world.[22]

Furthermore, in the light of the controversy dividing the Dominicans and Franciscans on the relative superiority of will and intellect, Salutati seems to side with the Dominicans in the treatise when he character-izes the intellect as the supreme human power[23] and asserts that the will cannot but choose the *summum bonum* when confronted with it.[24]

---

cuncta que vult." Scotus' definition of *potentia absoluta* could very well be in his mind: ". . . absoluta est respectu cuiuslibet quod non includit contradictionem. . . . Potentia or-dinata Dei . . . est illa quae conformis est in agendo regulis praedeterminatis a divina sapientia, vel magis a divina voluntate" (Op. Ox., II, d. 7, q. unica, 18). Because of the apparent limitation on God's power in creation (see n. 22), Salutati is probably not using a nominalist definition.

22. *Vat. lat.*, Tr. II, 10, fol. 26: "O si posses, inquam, ista videre, crede mihi, cum cau-sas coniunctas effectibus et res sociatas rebus aspiceres sic agi debere iudicares ut agitur. Nec in divine iusticie splendore damnares permissa, mirareris peccata vel doleres adversa sed in omnibus divinam intuens bonitatem abundantemque misericordiam congauderes benignitati gratie. Nec renitere posses ordinationi iusticie, nichilque prorsus appareret in-dignum, nichilque penitus non laudandum." On the nominalistic conception of *potentia absoluta*, see Heiko Oberman, *The Harvest of Medieval Theology* (Cambridge, Mass., 1963), pp. 30–47. Also see Charles Trinkaus, *In Our Image and Likeness*, 2 vols. (London, 1970), I, 79–80, who suggests that Salutati's conception of God's absolute power resembles that of Nominalists. For Scotus, God's will is His essence and He acts in accord with it in creat-ing: Etienne Gilson, *Jean Duns Scot, Introduction à ses positions fondamentales* (Paris, 1952), p. 307.

Specifically regarding God's justice, Scotus maintains that, while the divine will is the cause of all good (*Rep. Par.*, I, d. 48, q. unica), the moral law is not arbitrary. The ten commandments are not simply valid because God commanded them (*Rep. Par.*, II, d. 22, q. unica, 3). While Scotus appears to hold that God could dispense with some of the commandments in the second table, he apparently could not do so with others in that group or with any in the first table (*Op. Ox.*, III, d. 37, q. unica, 5–8).

23. He refers in *Vat. lat.*, Tr. II, 8, fol. 12ᵛ, to the "nobilissima . . . virtutum anime quam intellectum dicimus." For voluntarism of Scotus, see Walter Hoeres, *Der Wille als Vollkom-menheit nach Duns Scotus* (Munich, 1962). For debate over will and intellect generally, see Paul O. Kristeller, *Medieval Aspects of Renaissance Learning*, ed. and trans. Edward P. Ma-honey, Duke Monographs in Medieval and Renaissance Studies, vol. 1 (Durham, 1974), pp. 81–89.

24. Ibid., Tr. III, 8, fol. 60ᵛ: "Quoniam agentia libera et voluntaria preter quam respectu finis ultimi, qui est suprema beatitudo quam neminem contingit nolle, libere possunt velle et nolle quicquid sibi quod voluntate fieri debeat proponatur." Scotus admitted a natural inclination to beatitude but he believed that the will often pursued it as a goal. However, he rejected the idea that will was necessitated in this regard: Lawrence D. Roberts, "The Concept of Human Freedom," in *Deus et Homo ad mentem I. Duns Scoti*, Studia Scholastico Scotistica, vol. 5 (Rome, 1972), p. 325. Salutati's language is so imprecise as to make his own view unclear except that "neminem contingit" suggests a preference for Thomas: *ST*, Ia, IIae, q. 5, a. 4, *ad* 2. The passage that follows the above, stressing the attraction of the will for the good presented to it by the intellect, is equally ambiguous (fols. 60ᵛ–61): "Nam quamvis quanto res plus habuerit de ratione boni tanto magis appetibilis sit et in ipsam

Within a year or so the *De nobilitate legum et medicine* would unquestionably uphold the will's superiority.[25] Does this then mean that in 1396–97 Salutati was consciously on the other side and then switched or had he simply not yet thought through his stand before writing the *De nobilitate?* On the issue of the will versus intellect as well as on others regarding the principle of causality and the *potentia absoluta* of God, the *De fato* simply does not elaborate enough for us to catch more than subtle reverberations of his contact with scholastic writers and teachers in the *Studio.*[26]

In the opening chapters of the *De fato et fortuna* Salutati explains that his work is designed to show how the order of causes "proceeds by fixed and immutable reason" in obedience to God's decrees while the human will remains free and contingencies exist in the universe.[27] Recognizing as he did a certain causative power in the stars for natural and human events, Salutati also wished to present the celestial forces as obedient instruments of God's Providence and to refute any implica-

---

voluntas nostra tanto feratur ardentius quanto meliorem sciverit vel opinetur intellectus, quia tamen semper voluntas sit libera et quantum in se est velle possit et nolle ad utrumlibet dici debet."

25. In 1390 he had already made the will rather than the intellect the seat of the habitus of virtue (chap. 10). The *De nobilitate* takes up and develops this theme from the earlier work.

26. The only nominalist theologian, however, whom Salutati is known to have met is Pietro da Candia. The latter came twice to Florence as ambassador of Giangaleazzo. The first embassy is mentioned in chap. 10, n. 105. The second occurred in February, 1393: Francesco Novati, "Aneddoti viscontei," *Archivio storico lombardo*, 35 (1908), 203–5. The embassy stayed ten days (B.N.F., *Panc.*, 158, fol. 172). Incidentally, Decembrio accompanied Pietro on the second as well as on the first trip. The second time he probably carried with him Loschi's poem, "Sextus hiperboreum iam versat aquarius annum," written the previous month for Salutati: V. Zaccaria, "Antonio Loschi e Coluccio Salutati (Con quattro epistole inedite dal Loschi)," *Atti dell'Instituto veneto di sci., lett., ed. arti.*, 129 (1970–71), 360–62, discusses the date for the poem and publishes it (ibid., pp. 380–87).

To judge from the library list of Giovanni di Baldassaro, Pietro's commentaries on *The Sentences* circulated widely in Florence (see chap. 10). The only extensive treatment of Pietro da Candia is that of F. Ehrle, *Der Sentenzenkommentar Peters von Candia* (Münster, 1925), but there is no obvious influence of Pietro's thought as presented by Ehrle on Salutati's theological position. A complete study of Pietro, however, is badly needed. Buridan, in fact, is the only nominalist thinker who clearly influenced him through his writings: see chap. 12, n. 36.

27. *Vat. lat.*, *Proem.*, fol. 1ᵛ. On the *De fato et fortuna*, see Alfred von Martin, "Die Popularphilosophie d. florentiner Humanisten Coluccio Salutati," *Archiv für Kulturgeschichte*, 11 (1913), 411–54; Luigi Gasperetti, "Il 'De fato' del Salutati," *Rinascita*, 4 (1941), 555–82; Eugenio Garin, "I trattati morali di Coluccio Salutati," *Atti e memorie dell'Accademia fiorentina di scienze morali "La Colombaria,"* n.s. 1 (1943–46), 62–66; Walter Rüegg, "Entstehung," pp. 143–90; Nicola Badaloni, "Discussioni umanistiche su fato e libertà," *Critica storica*, 1 (1962), 269–77; Trinkaus, *In Our Image*, I, 76–102; and Ronald Witt, "Toward a Biography of Coluccio Salutati," *Rinascimento*, 17 (1976), 28–34. Although my own presentation differs in details from that of Charles Trinkaus, his constitutes the fundamental interpretation of this work.

tions of astral determinism of human destiny.[28] His intention ultimately was to achieve a total conception of the universe in which God had decreed the complete order of causes and effects from all eternity but yet where God remained responsive to human decisions and deeds.

God as first cause of all beings and their operations is not immediately responsible for all effects. Rather, He created a vast series of causes, each endowed with particular qualities suited to producing specific effects in specific situations. Thereby from eternity He provided those effects which have in fact been produced.[29] Nothing can happen other than God's all-powerful will ordains; in this sense all things happen necessarily. Fate is defined as "necessity flowing from God's Providence directing and governing all things which exist and are produced in the universe."[30] At one point he describes this "fatal necessity" as a kind of universal energy "urging matter that it desire the form which it lacks."[31]

While all things in the created order happen necessarily in the sense that all the chains of causes and effects have been ordained from eternity, this order is nonetheless completely contingent. Dependent as created causes and effects are on place, time, on the particular nature of matter and, in the case of voluntary causes, on freedom of action, the necessity of the whole created order is only relative.[32] Even the heavenly bodies operating with unchanging regularity have a qualified necessity because they, like every other created thing, had a beginning and God was able either not to make them or once in existence to cause them to cease to be.[33]

28. B.A.V., *Vat. lat.*, *Proem.*, fol. 1.

29. B.A.V., *Vat. lat.*, Tr. II, 7, fol. 9: "Non cogitemus igitur deum providentia sua precise solum effectus quos cernimus ordinasse, sed omnino suis coniunctos providisse cum causis, nec alterius nature causam preparare quam eius que propter effectum requiritur producendum. Ut quecumque fluat a divine providentie infallibilitate necessitas non immediate vel simpliciter coniungatur effectui sed mediantibus causis quas ad illum producendum voluit vel oportuit adhiberi."

30. B.A.V., *Urb. lat.*, Tr. II, 1, fol. 9: "Ut fatum sit necessitas a dei providentia fluens cuncta dirigens et gubernans, que sub celo sunt et efficiuntur."

31. B.A.V., *Vat. lat.*, Tr. II, 6, fol. 7^v: "Materiam urgens ut formam que deficit concupiscat."

32. This definition of contingency as residing in the determinate character of essence and operation makes Salutati's approach Scotistic. For Thomas the difference between necessary and contingent lay in the fact that in the latter essence is separate from existence. For this difference between Scotus and Aquinas, see Luigi Lammarrone, "Contingenza e creazione nel pensiero di Duns Scoto," *Deus et homo*, p. 465.

33. B.A.V., *Vat. lat.*, Tr. III, 9, fol. 63–63^v; also, Tr. II, 11, fol. 28: "Est etiam intuendum summaque memoria fixeque recolendum quod, licet omnia eterna necessaria sint, si tamen habent factionis initium et creata de nichilo vel ex aliquo facta sunt, quoniam fuerint a voluntate dei, contingentia esse consequens et necessarium est. Potuit enim deus illa

Salutati sometimes uses the scholastic term *necessitas suppositionis* to describe this relative necessity.[34] If one thing is necessarily caused by another thing and that prior cause exists, the first thing will follow of necessity as an effect. If God determines an effect to be and orders the causes so as to bring it into being, the effect is necessarily produced "by supposition of causes and order." By contrast, God is absolutely necessary in that He cannot not be. In His creation of the world, however, He operated voluntarily and contingently because He was under no constraint: nothing existed before Him or together with Him to impose limits on his actions.[35]

All created or rather secondary causes can be divided into the natural and the voluntary; they are distinguished on the basis that the former operate from natural inclinations and the latter from conscious decision.[36] Although demons and angels are counted among the voluntary causes, the *De fato et fortuna* is primarily concerned with the human will. By its very nature this will must be free: "Indeed it is fated and necessary that the will, which is by its essence free, does nothing except freely and, whatever condition is proposed to us, the will cannot be coerced."[37] The essence of every existent requires that nothing es-

---

non facere, potuerunt etiam et de sui natura postquam a sola dei et prime cause libera voluntate procedunt omnino non esse. Ut quicquid arguatur de infallibilitate divine providentie vel naturalis necessitatis aut etiam ad causarum concursum de necessitate provenientibus effectibus, nullo tamen modo pura necessitas inferatur."

34. Ibid., Tr. II, 6, fol. 6ᵛ: "Est autem et necessarium suppositionis, ut cum aliquo presupposito necessarium quiddam infertur ut, si infallibiliter aliquid futurum est, necessario fiet et erit cuius existentia pendet ex veritate suppositionis." For this term in Aquinas see *ST*, 1, q. 19, a.3, *ad* 6 and a.8 *ad* 1 and 3; q. 23, a.3, *ad* 3. Scotus uses *necessitas consequentis* or *consequentiae* with the same meaning: *Exposit. in Metaph. Arist.*, XI, 5, 2, 2, 36. Just as in ontology absolute necessity contrasts with *necessitas suppositionis*, in logic the absolute necessity characteristic of a metaphysical demonstration contrasts with the demonstration *ex suppositione finis* of physics and ethics: William A. Wallace, *The Role of Demonstration in Moral Theology*, Texts and Studies, vol. 2 (Washington, 1962), pp. 19, 31, 50–54, and 98–99. On *suppositio* generally, see Philotheus Boehner, *Medieval Logic: An Outline of its Development from 1250 to c. 1400* (Chicago, 1952), pp. 27–51; and W. Kneale and M. Kneale, *The Development of Logic* (Oxford, 1962), pp. 247–74; L.M. de Rijk, *Logica Modernorum. A Contribution to the History of Early Terminist Logic*, vol. 2.1 (Assen, 1967).

35. B.A.V., *Vat. lat.*, 6ᵛ: "Est igitur necessarium non solum quod impossibile est aliter se habere sed quod impossibile est non esse." Necessity (God) is defined as that "cui nulla vi resisti potest" (fol. 6). He is citing Cicero, *De inv.*, II, 57.

36. Ibid., Tr. III, 6, fol. 54ᵛ; and Tr. III, 10, fol. 65ᵛ–66.

37. Ibid., Tr. II, 6, fol. 7ᵛ: "Fatale quidem et necessarium est voluntatem, que de sui essentia libera est, nichil agere nisi libere et omnino cogi non posse, quecumque nobis conditio proponatur." Compare Scotus, *Rep. Par.*, I, d. 10, q. 3, 4: "Et sicut quamlibet entitatem consequitur modus essendi eius proprius, ita et quamlibet formam activam consequitur immediate sicut modus agendi. Propterea sicut non est alia causa quare voluntas vult, nisi quia voluntas est voluntas, ita non est alia causa, quare voluntas vult sic necessario vel contingenter, nisi quia voluntas est voluntas. . . ." Also cf. *Op. Ox.*, IV, d. 49, q. 10, 10.

sential to its existence and nature be lacking.[38] Just as fire ceases to be fire if it is deprived of heat, so the will ceases to be will if it does not have the freedom to choose.

Another way of classifying created causes is to distinguish between causes on the basis of degrees of contingency. Contingent in the sense that their existence is not identical with their essence, heavenly bodies have a necessary cause unlike the rest of creation because no internal nor external elements impede their regular operations. Eclipses of the sun and moon and the motion of the stars in the heavens "always maintain themselves in the same uniform fashion."[39] By contrast, in the sphere beneath the moon the concatenation between causes and effects is not absolutely regular. Even here, however, there are varying degrees of contingency. Many effects are produced "often, frequently, or in many cases." A second group are labeled *ad utrumlibet* because of the indeterminacy of their effects. These consist of some natural causes and all voluntary causes "which, as if in a certain middle ground, almost equally regard being and nonbeing. . . ."[40] Sperm in the vagina, for example, is so balanced between masculine and feminine producing tendencies that either male or female offspring can result. In the case of the human will, despite the fact that the will seeks an object with an intensity proportionate to the good which the intelligence recognizes it to possess, nevertheless, "the will is always free, and, insofar as it is able in itself to will or not to will, it ought to be called *ad utrumlibet*."[41]

The free operation of the human will is built into the hierarchy of causes and, in acting, freely accomplishes its part in the universal design. The will freely decides to follow a course of action that has been ordained by God from all eternity and prepared for by his provision of all the prior elements appropriate to eliciting the specific response.

38. Ibid., Tr. II, 8, fol. 12ᵛ.   39. Ibid., Tr. III, 8, fol. 59.

40. Ibid., Tr. III, 8, fol. 60ᵛ: "Vult ergo philosophus quod omnes effectus qui sepe, frequenter, vel in pluribus fiunt in eo quod producuntur nec ad casum pertineant nec fortunam quamvis inter contingentia reponantur. Potius autem vel causaliter vel fortuito quod rarum est ea dicimus impediri. Sicut e contra dicendum est in his que diximus fieri raro. Non habent enim a casu vel fortuna quod impediantur et non fiant, sed potius hoc quod fiant. Contingentia autem ad utrumlibet illa sunt que quasi quodam medio ferme equaliter et esse respiciunt et non esse, ut aliquem sedere vel non sedere." The reference to Aristotle is to *Physics*, II, 5, 196b.

41. Ibid., Tr. III, 8, fol. 61: ". . . semper voluntas sit libera et, quantum in se est, velle possit et nolle ad utrumlibet dici debet." The term *ad utrumlibet* used to describe the contingency of the human will in Lombard's *Sent.*, II, d. 25, is not employed by Scotus in his commentary on that passage. Scotus prefers related phrases like *ad alterutrum, ad unum illorum* or *in utrumque* (*Op. Ox.*, II, d. 25, q. unica, 22). On the other hand, Thomas follows Lombard's usage (*In IV lib. Sent.*, II, 25, q. 1, a. 1).

Truly if the first cause concurs, the heavens influence, the combinations assist, the first movement of the will urges, nothing resists and all things are disposed for the act, and if at length the election of the will follows and its fixed command ensues, what prevents it from being said that in this order and necessary disposition of causes the effect occurred which was intended?[42]

In fact so eager is Salutati to stress the predominant role played by God in the human act, that it is difficult to see what is left for the free will: "For it is written that God operates in us will and execution. Nay, rather, since he is first cause of all things, he influences the acts of our wills far more than the will itself does; so that not only because prior in eternity and time but even because of greater activity, the whole ought to be attributed and ascribed to God."[43] Yet Salutati repeatedly asserts that the human will is by its nature free to will or not to will.

Basic to his conception of the relationship of the divine absolute will to its creation is the position that necessity and contingency can cohere in the same created object at the same time. Salutati confesses frankly that this is a "mirabile quiddam."[44] While created objects are necessarily produced in obedience to the decrees of divine Providence and in their turn necessarily give rise to particular effects, they still act in themselves in accord with their own essences. Causes *ad utrumlibet* are in their essence undetermined in their operation as to a specific result, and man not only feels his will to be free but by its very nature is free.

How does fortune affect human action? As has been seen in preceding chapters, even while rejecting his earlier conception that fortune was blind and savage, Salutati never believed that fortune was "an empty name." Rather, he became accustomed to conceiving of it as equivalent

42. Ibid., Tr. I, 3, fol. 3: "Verumtamen si concurrat prima causa, influat celum, assistat complexio, instet primus voluntatis motus, nil resistat omniaque disposita sint ad actum, demumque sequatur voluntatis electio, et eius fixum subsequatur imperium, quid fateri vetat in hoc causarum ordine et dispositione necessario effectum qui intenditur provenire?" Cf. Augustine, *De civ. Dei,* V, 9.

43. Ibid., Tr. II, 6, fol. 5ᵛ: "Scriptum est enim Deum operari in nobis velle atque perficere, immo cum ipse sit prima causa rerum omnium, longe plus influit in nostrarum voluntatum actus quam ipsa voluntas. Ut non solum per prius eternitatis et temporis sed etiam per plus activitatis totum Deo debeat tribui et ascribi." Also see, *Epist.,* II, 236.

44. Ibid., Tr. II, 7, fol. 9: ". . . latius et strictius extenditur ista necessitas quam fatalem seu divine providentie dicimus quam ut solum necessariis conjungatur velut cuncta necessitet. Necessitat enim cuncta que de nihilo produxit ut sint. Sed ut necessaria vel contingentia sint et qualia fuerint proxime agentia vel qualis effectuum natura requirat talia sint non ab ipsa solum provenit sed ab aliis causis etiam cum quibus perficitur quod illa providit. Ut mirabile quiddam eveniat quod simul coeant necessitas et contingentia."

to God's Providence. In the *De fato* his tendency is to speak of fortune in relationship to voluntary causes and of chance when referring to natural phenomena.[45] Fortune is identified with "the hidden and accidental cause of a rare, notable, and unexpected effect happening in a way other than intended by the agents"; while chance becomes "the accidental and hidden cause of a natural effect happening rarely and contrary to the inclination of nature." Accordingly, fortune and chance do not apply to all the many "surprises" encountered in the course of daily experience but only to those which are rare and noteworthy. In the case of fortune specifically the occurrence must have enough significance for the individual affected to regard it as a product of good or evil for himself.

Both fortune and chance emerge as manifestations of God's Providence, which in obedience to God's commands utilizes the indeterminacy or potentialities of created substance to accomplish God's purposes.

> Therefore, if one considers and understands the matter properly, one should not be reluctant to give the names 'arbiter,' 'mistress goddess,' to this Divine Providence, to which it is right to refer both chance and fortune in as much as it does those things which we do not intend and those things which happen against the principle of nature (certainly using wills and nature not as active causes but rather as instruments of human events and of those things which are done on account of men).[46]

Naturally his strongest evidence for the existence of fortune and chance are the miracles recounted in the Bible, such as the transformation of the wife of Lot into a pillar of salt and the escape of the three young men from Nebuchadnezzar's fiery furnace. In the former instance, when Lot's wife refused to obey the commandment not to look back on the doomed city, God "using no external matter" turned the woman into a pillar of salt.[47] In the other case divine power prevented the natural processes of the fire from taking effect, i.e., the "quality and condition"

45. Ibid., Tr. III, 6, fol. 54–54ᵛ.
46. Ibid., Tr. III, 11, fol. 69: "Hanc igitur divinam providentiam in quam casum referre par est atque fortunam postquam ipsam agere que non intendimus queve preter nature rationem fiunt, certum est utentem voluntariis et natura non velut agentibus causis, sed potius ut instrumentis rerum humanarum et eorum que propter hominem facta sunt, arbitram et dominam deam dicere a veritatis ratione, siquis recte respiciat saneque intelligat, non abhorret."
47. B.A.V., *Urb. lat.*, Tr. I, 3, fol. 7.

by which it would quickly have consumed the three bodies.[48] What occurred in these kinds of situations was that God or a spiritual instrument of God acted immediately, breaking the normal series of cause and effect relationship, and producing an extraordinary result. Although no effect can be produced without a sufficient or "legitimate" cause, the first cause and its spiritual agents are always "legitimate" at any level of the hierarchy of causes and effects.[49]

What Salutati wants to prove by this insistence on the existence of fortune and chance is that there is an area of contingency in nature. Especially he seeks to demonstrate that those created beings that act *ad utrumlibet* are so contingent that potentially they can produce a variety of different effects. Recognition of such indeterminacy facilitates depicting a universe where at any stage in a causal series supernatural powers can intervene either to hinder the normal causal relationship from taking place or positively to actualize the hidden potential of a created object in an unexpected manner. The reality of fortune and/or chance (as Salutati defines the concepts) not only exalts the absolute freedom of God but also, by guaranteeing the existence of contingency, enhances the argument for the freedom of the human will.

One of the major preoccupations of the *De fato* is to refute the astrological doctrines of Ptolomaic Arab astronomy which pose a threat to Salutati's convictions regarding the existence of contingency in the universe and the freedom both of man and God. He does not deny that the stars affect human lives, but he questions the possibility that man can understand what the constellations portend both because of the vast network of stellar phenomena and because of the defective nature of human measuring instruments. At the same time Salutati does not doubt that the stars, seen as subordinate to God in the series of causes and absolutely dependent on His disposition, have an effect on natural events and on the human soul. It is unthinkable for him that God would have created the enormous number of stars He did merely to ornament the heavens and to hide Himself from man's view. Nor is it sufficient to explain the existence of the tenth sphere merely as a lodging place for the *beati*; as spirits they had no need of such vast spaces. Rather the heavens were doubtless created to effect "the generation, the conservation, and governance of inferior beings."[50] The fatal necessity that is

---

48. B.A.V., *Vat. lat.*, Tr. I, 1, fol. 2ᵛ.
49. Ibid., Tr. III, 5, fol. 51ᵛ: "Omnia ergo sive naturalia sive voluntaria suam et legitimam causam habent non solum qua sunt hoc ens, sed etiam qua sunt tale ens."
50. Ibid., Tr. III, 1, fol. 34.

defined as God's Providence "is first in the heavens and then in inferior causes not only inhering and existing in them but directing them and maintaining them that they not pass away, so that these things produce the wanted effects."[51] Fate or the influence of the stars, therefore, is a part of the chain of cause and effect leading from God's will down to the most insignificant terrestial effect.

As he had already maintained in his poem to Jacopo Allegretti, written in 1378 and included in this treatise, the position of the stars affects man not only by causing natural disasters, favorable or unfavorable climatic conditions, healthy or deformed bodies, but also by impinging on human conduct itself. The heavens exert power over the complexion of the humours in the body predisposing individuals to act in certain general ways. But these astral forces do not operate unimpeded. Not only do chance and fortune interfere with their effect on inferior objects but inferior objects themselves also limit astral activity because of their own natures.[52]

Although recognizing the influence of the stars as a manifestation of the divine will, Salutati does not feel completely comfortable with the idea. He assumes that on the whole astral forces are hostile to man's best interests. The Promethean image of his younger days still fascinates the old man. To surrender to the urging of the stars is to become a slave of natural forces. Like other natures under the stars, man's nature modifies their effects, but in man's case Salutati seems to be advising active resistance: "In vain . . . do the heavens pour out the madness of war if princes and peoples are unwilling. Thus it is said; 'The wise man will dominate the stars.' "[53]

Similarly, despite fortune's identification with divine Providence, by the end of the work Salutati's early antagonism toward fortune insinuates itself into his moral instructions. It must be "fickle fortune" he has in mind when he writes: "And since our power of foresight (*providentie nostre facultas*) thus considers all things that it might avoid infinite chance and, if it is not able to exclude chance, delay and foreknow it; and since nothing foreknown is able to be accidental, it results that where there is much widsom there is a minimum of fortune."[54] These attacks

---

51. B.A.V., *Urb. lat.*, Tr. II, 1, fol. 9: "Sed quia necessitas ista fatalis, prout a dei providentia est, prius est in celo et exinde est in interioribus causis, non solum eis inherens et in ipsis existens, sed ipsas dirigens et continens ne fluant ut in debitos ferantur effectus. . . ." Cf. Augustine, *De civ. Dei*, V, 8.

52. B.A.V., *Vat. lat.*, Tr. III, 1, fol. 36ᵛ.

53. B.A.V., *Vat. lat.*, Tr. IV, fol. 36ᵛ. Cf. chap. 8, n. 17.

54. B.A.V., *Vat. lat.*, Tr. IV, fol. 78ᵛ: "Ex quo corollarie possumus et debemus inferre,

on his former enemies, fate and fortune, however, are mere lapses in a general theological and philosophical discussion which strives to explain the pain and anxiety of life as a part of the universal divine plan.

With this plan described in terms of the various kinds of causes involved in its realization and the existence of an area of contingency established in which man's free will can function, the special nature of the relationship between God and man can now be understood. Because by the very necessity of his nature man must be free in willing, he must also accept responsibility for his choices. Man's moral freedom, moreover, makes him capable of doing either good or evil.

But what can be the cause of evil in a universe where everything is created by God? If the source of evil is found in the human will, how is it that God, who is present in the will, is not also partly responsible? Salutati's answer is to define evil as the deformity of an act and, as such, a pure privation of being, i.e., of good. Insofar as deformity inheres in the act, man, not God, is at fault because God "does not work the deformity of acts which is defect, not effect, nor does deformity have an efficient cause but a deficient one."[55] Deformity is a product of impotency just as blindness is a privation of sight or colorlessness a privation of color.[56] Man is ordered by God to obey His commandments and, if our acts are not in accord with these, they are deficient.

Salutati's verbal formulation of the problem suggests the negative quality of the evil he strives to depict: "If we do not direct to God that which we do, we render imperfect the good act we do, not because we act but because we do so deficiently. So that sin is in no way committed by doing but rather by not doing whatever we fail to do."[57] Further, no

---

cum humanis actibus admixti sint infinitis et incogitatis modis casus atque fortuna, de quibus nulla possit haberi certitudo, quibusque variantur et prohibentur tam voluntatum nostrarum opera quam nature, celumque sic influat quod iuxta patientium qualitatem et dispositionem operetur, stultissimam esse fluctuantem incertam et inanem omnem astrologorum scientiam qua de futuris audent aliquam polliceri vel tradere veritatem. Quandoquidem incursu casualium et fortuitorum totius influentie vis differri variarique valeat et elidi. Et quoniam providentie nostre facultas sic cuncta considerat quod infinitos casus excludat, vel si prohibere non possit, tardet et presciat et nullum previsum possit esse fortuitum, consequens est quod, ubi plurimum sit sapientie, minimum debeat esse fortune." See chap. 13, n. 22.

55. Ibid., Tr. II, 9, fol. 18: "Non . . . operatur actuum deformitatem, que defectus est, non effectus, nec efficientem causam habet, sed deficientem." Cf. Augustine, *De lib. arb.*, II, 19–20 [50–54].

56. Ibid., Tr. II, 9, fol. 17ᵛ.

57. Ibid., fol. 20: "Si non dirigimus enim in deum id, quod facimus. . . . delinquimus et actum bonum quem facimus, deficiendo, non agendo, reddimus imperfectum. Ut nullum omnino, sicuti premisimus, peccatum faciendo committatur sed non faciendo quicquid delinquimus contrahatur.

man can be saved on the basis of his good deeds. In himself everyone acts defectively and is worthy of damnation.[58] Since the fall of our first parents the human will is so corrupted that meritorious acts of salvific importance are beyond human power. Only those who have been pre-destined to receive divine grace are capable of doing good works; the rest are damned. But whereas God predestines the good from all eter-nity to heaven, the evil are damned on the basis of God's foreknowl-edge—they are the *presciti*. Through this distinction between the *pres-citi* and *predestinati* Salutati feels able to present God both as merciful and just.

There is nothing in any man which compels God to bestow His grace on one rather than another: otherwise grace would lose its character and become a just reward for merit. Why God predestines some to eternal life by infusing the grace necessary to work acts of merit cannot be determined by us. The creator could have chosen to save all men in this way, so unlimited is His power, but just as His predestination to eternal life demonstrates His mercy, so His punishment of sinners dis-plays His justice.[59] In any case, He asks, can man, who does not under-stand why he himself acts, dare question God's motives?[60] We only know that God permits Judas to commit his sins and justly condemns him as one of the *presciti*, while Peter, who without grace would also be lost, is granted the immutable privilege of predestination and cannot in fact not be saved.[61]

Complete reliance on the efficacy of God's grace for personal salva-tion does not lead him to despair on the one hand nor to passivity on the other. If no one is saved because of his works, at the same time no one will be saved without them. Works constitute for the humanist the measure according to which retribution will be made "since divine mercy will make a place for each one according to the merit of his works."[62]

58. Ibid., Tr. II, 10, fol. 23: "Nullus ex operibus quidem salvus fit, sed prorsus ex gra-tia."

59. Ibid., Tr. II, 10, fols. 23ᵛ–24; and *Epist.*, II, 325. Perhaps Trinkaus, *In Our Image* I, 93, is correct in stating that Salutati derived this distinction between the *presciti* and *pre-destinati* from Egidio Romano's *Tractatus de predestinatione, prescientia, paradiso, purgatorio et inferno*. While to my knowledge he never cited Egidio by name, he appears to owe him the particular distinction between *esse* and *essentia* he embraced in later life: see my, "Col-uccio and Contemporary Physics," *Journal of the History of Ideas*, 38 (1977), 668. On the other hand, he easily could have taken it from Scotus (*Op. Ox.*, I, d. 41, q. unica, 13). See discussion of Scotus' position in Paul Vignaux, *Justification et prédestination au xivᵉ siècle* (Paris, 1934), pp. 23–31.

60. Ibid., fol. 25ᵛ.   61. Ibid., Tr. III, 11, fols. 28ᵛ–29.

62. Ibid., Tr. II, 10, fol. 24–24ᵛ: "Non ergo damnabitur aliquis vel salvabitur absque operibus, quandoquidem reddit deus unicuique secundum opera sua, quamvis nemo ex propriis operibus salvus fiat."

We are admonished to do good works because they are good and because God commands them. For the predestined they determine the degree of the soul's glory in heaven, and for the *presciti* they help diminish the extent of punishment. Despite the fact that God saves and damns men in an eternal now, the actions of men's free will still have significance on the outcome of the judgment. How such contingency and necessity cohere in the same actions appears "a marvelous secret indeed."[63]

Salutati borrowed his conceptions of evil and predestination almost *en bloc* from previous writers, yet his having nothing original to say did not indicate a lack of intensity in his convictions. He believed in them devoutly, and the moral and educational theories he developed in the last decades of his life must be seen in this general theological context. The moral struggle was primarily depicted by the mature Salutati as a conflict between man's basically sinful will and the merciful yet just God, who strove by various means to lead the errant sinner back to Him. Malignant forces play no role in the cosmic struggle because the universe is essentially kind, and it is principally man misusing his God-given freedom who upsets the beneficient order.

Nonetheless, the *De fato* indicates that Salutati has not entirely abandoned the heroic moral conceptions of his youth which saw man, seemingly unaided by divine power, forced to struggle against supernatural forces threatening to subject him. In regard both to astral influences and fortune some of this vision remained. In the last thirty years of his life the dynamic of Salutati's moral doctrines derived largely from his conviction that "we can be certain that grace will never desert us in our actions if we take care to regulate the will by the rule of right reason."[64] Nonetheless, occasionally he lapses into expressions that reflect his earlier, very different belief in the ability of the wise man to "dominate the stars."

Of all the sources of inspiration identifiable in the pages of the *De fato* the *Divina commedia* is the most pervasive. On three occasions in discussing the all-powerful nature of God and the identification of fortune with divine Providence Salutati quotes passages from the poem in his own Latin translation.[65] A large segment of Book IV is devoted to de-

---

63. Ibid., fol. 24ᵛ.
64. Ibid., Tr. II, 11, fol. 31ᵛ: "Certique simus nunquam gratiam nobis in agendo deficere si cura fuerit voluntatem recte rationis regula temperare."
65. B.A.V., *Urb. lat.*, Tr. I, 3, fol. 7ᵛ (*Purg.*, XVI, 70–72); B.A.V., *Vat. lat.*, Tr. III, 11, fol. 69ᵛ (*Inf.*, VII, 73–96); and ibid., 12, fol. 72ᵛ (*Purg.*, XVI, 58–83). The two long passages are edited in Eugenio Garin, "Dante nel Rinascimento," *Rinascimento*, 7 (1967), 26–28. Erik

fending Dante against the criticism of the astrologer Cecco d'Ascoli, who in 1326 attacked the poet for his views on fate and fortune. But Dante's influence is not limited to seconding the humanist's already formed views. The poet plays a decisive role in this work in shaping Salutati's interpretation of the past.

In previous discussions relating the plague to the will of God, Salutati had occasionally cited historical events, mostly drawn from biblical history, as examples of divine intervention in human history. But in no sense did he present a conception of history as reflecting the unfolding of a divine plan.[66] The potential for such a view was there but before the *De fato* the use of history was essentially anecdotal. Even many of the historical examples found in the *De fato*, such as Joshua at the battle of Jericho and the murder of the gifted Marcellus, serve only as individual illustrations of God's power. The analysis of the civil strife at Perugia pictures the bloodshed as a discreet instance in the relationship between God's absolute will and human evil without setting the event in the context of a general divine plan for the universe.[67]

By contrast, in his treatment of the murder of Caesar in the *De fato* a partial outline of God's design for human history begins to emerge. Inspired by Dante's grand interpretation of this event, Salutati characterizes Brutus as the voluntary instrument of the divine will, which intended at this precise time to terminate the Republic and establish the empire. Nonetheless, in the *De fato* the presentation remains fragmentary and contradictory. Only four years later, under the growing influence of Dante, will Salutati produce a clear statement on how and why a new age was brought about, an explanation that was to have immense repercussions on Salutati's view of the relationship between pagan and Christian society. Consequently, to understand the significance of Salutati's remarks on Brutus in the *De fato* for his vision of Providence in history, it seems best to postpone discussion until the analysis of the *De tyranno* in chapter 14.

Petersen, "Some Remarks on Coluccio Salutati's De Fato et Fortuna," *Institut du moyen-âge grec et latin*, 18 (1976), 5–17, emphasizes the extent to which *De fato* is an effort to clarify Dante's notion of *fortuna*. Dott[essa] Daniela De Rosa was kind enough to draw my attention to Petersen's article.

66. For examples from the Bible, see *Epist.*, II, 106–7, 118, and 236. He frequently explained the plague as a punishment for sin. Similarly, he saw the Schism as a punishment for the worldly ambitions of the papacy and the Ciompi as God's penalty for Florence moving arms against the Church (ibid., 122–28).

67. The historical events are mentioned in *Vat. lat.*, 2928, Tr. III, 9, fol. 62–62ᵛ; ibid., Tr. III, 7, fols. 55–56ᵛ; and ibid., Tr. V, fols. 78ᵛ–81.

CHAPTER 12. THE CHRISTIAN CITI-ZEN

In appearance an occasional work, the *De nobilitate legum et medicine* fits naturally into place after the *De fato* with its vindication of the freedom of the will. Finished in August 1399, the treatise was inspired by a Florentine physician, identified only as Bernardo Fiorentino, who had written a work claiming to establish that medicine had both greater certitude and dignity than law.[1] As has been observed, Salutati had something more than a superficial interest in medicine, and he enjoyed good relationships with members of the profession.[2] Unlike Petrarch, who firmly believed that a physician had no need of eloquence, Salutati praised the efforts of medical men to cultivate the art of rhetoric, and he did his best to put a favorable interpretation on Petrarch's obvious antipathy to them.[3] The *De nobilitate* was not motivated by a basic hostility to medicine but by irritation at the arrogance of a particular physician, who claimed that his art was superior to the law. Salutati, who had previously opposed the choleric Bernardo in conversations on this is-

1. For the date and manuscripts of this work, see the edition of the work by Eugenio Garin, *De nobilitate legum et medicinae. De verecundia*, ed. Eugenio Garin, Edizione nazionale dei classici del pensiero italiano, vol. 8 (Florence, 1947), pp. xxxii and lvi. Garin's scholarly notations to the text demonstrate the significance of thirteenth- and fourteenth-century scholastics for Salutati's position. On the law vs. medicine debate in the fifteenth century, see Lynn Thorndike, *Science and Thought in the Fifteenth Century* (New York, 1929), pp. 24–58 and 261–64, and his "The Debate for Precedence between Medicine and Law: Further Examples from the Fourteenth to the Seventeenth Century," *Romanic Review*, 27 (1936), 185–90; E. Garin, *La disputa delle arti nel Quattrocento*, Edizione nazionale dei classici del pensiero italiano, vol. 9 (Florence, 1947); and Clodomiro Mancini, "Coluccio Salutati e la medicina del '400," in *La medicina genovese nel '400*, ed. G. del Guerra, Scientia veterum, ser. 5, vol. 47 (Pisa, 1963), pp. 39–53.

Novati identified Salutati's opponent, Bernardo Fiorentino, with Bernardo di ser Pistorio (*Epist.*, III, 390, n. 3). In 1959 Giulio F. Pagallo, in his article "Nuovi testi per la'Disputa delle Arti' nel Quattrocento: La *Quaestio* di Bernardo da Firenze e la *Disputatio* di Domenico Bianchelli," *Italia medioevale e umanistica*, 2(1959), 467–68, identified the tract to which Salutati was responding as Universitätsbibliotek, Wurzburg, *M.ch. f. 60*, fols. 96–109. Bernardo's tract begins: "Quaestio quam nunquam ab aliquo determinatam vidi proponitur disputanda. Que scienciarum vel arcium nobilitate prefulgeat, an medicine an legis?"

2. See above, chap. 10. He warmly praised Marsilio da Santa Sophia after his death and wrote his epitaph: Berthold L. Ullman, *Studies in the Italian Renaissance*, Storia e letteratura, vol. 51 (Rome, 1955), 300–1.

3. According to Salutati, Petrarch was only joking when he wrote this in his *Rerum senilium*, III, 8 (*Opera*, pp. 860–61); *De nobilitate*, p. 280. Bernardo took Petrarch's critique seriously (*Questio*, *passim* but especially fols. 96ᵛ–97, 104–104ᵛ and 107). He employed Boccaccio's remarks against lawyers in the *Genealogie deorum gentilium*, chap. XV (ed. Vincenzo Romano, Scrittori d'Italia, 2 vols. [Bari, 1951], pp. 687–88) to prove his case (see especially fols. 97, 102 and 108).

sue, knew that his own treatise would not convince the physician, but Bernardo's tract furnished him the occasion to organize his thoughts on the general question of the relationship of will to intellect.[4]

In presenting the case for medicine, Bernardo, expressly avoiding theological arguments, aimed at establishing his case through natural reason.[5] For him the contrast between medicine and law was really one between two styles of life, the speculative and the active. He clearly wished to avoid the question of the relative superiority of the intellect to the will while utilizing Aristotle's claims for theoretical knowledge as the goal of man's pursuit of felicity. Salutati, however, insisted on presenting the debate in a larger context, identifying Bernardo along with Aristotle as defending the intellect and himself as favoring the will.[6] He also refused to abide by Bernardo's limitation on proof, and his rebuttal mixed arguments drawn from theology with others based on reason.[7]

The debate, however, is essentially *ad hominem* from Salutati's standpoint. Without discussing the relative value of the contemplative life traditionally associated with the powers of the intellect, there can be no thorough assessment of the relationship of the intellect and will, and Salutati expressly excludes the contemplative life from consideration. There is for him no continuity between the speculative and the contemplative life; the first is a function of intellect in its natural operations and the other of intellect infused with grace. Whereas speculation is "the simple investigation of the true," contemplation serves as "the end

4. He also sensed that the logicians, for whom he cared little, were also in agreement with Bernardo's attack (ibid., p. 2). Although apparently speaking of the approach to debating of physicians in general, he probably had Bernardo particularly in mind when he wrote (ibid., p. 24): "Nec ut fieri solet in disputationibus vestris, vos in clamores et insaniam commoveatis."

5. Ibid., p. 12: "Principio quidem, licet divina dimittas et solum, ut ais, humana consideres, quoniam homo Dei imago est, necesse fit quod humana similitudinem habeant divinorum." Salutati is referring to *Questio*, fol. 100ᵛ: "Unde Ysidorus dicit jus civile est quod quisque populus sive civitas sibi proprium humana divinaque causa [manuscript has *cum*] constituet. Divina dimittimus; de humana disputamus quae Ysidoro ibidem teste constant iamque discrepant, quoniam alie aliis querentibus placent." The reference is to Isidor's *Etym.*, V, 2 & 5.

6. Aristotle's position in *Nic. Eth.*, X, 7–8, 1177a–1178b, is mentioned in *De nobilitate*, pp. 30, 164, and 270. Also see ibid., p. 180. Bernardo expressly refuses to consider the issue of superiority (*Questio*, fol. 107ᵛ): "Nolo hic expendere sermones quae alcior sit potentia an scilicet intellectus an voluntas licet sit libera."

7. In the sphere of natural reason Cicero is doubtless Salutati's major authority. *De nobilitate*, p. 16, illustrates the two levels of truth at which Salutati argues: "Videsne quantum nature tribuit noster Arpinas? Nec id volo nunc scrutari verumne sit, nos ex puris naturalibus in ultimam posses beatitudinem pervenire, quoniam satis constet donum illud ex gratia gratis dari; sicut ea que dirigunt et ordinantur in ipsum ex gratia scimus gratum faciente prodire. Sed auctoritate tanti viri (Cicero) constat hec principia, que sunt rationis atque virtutis, naturaliter nobis inesse."

of all actions and the eternal perfection of joys never attainable on earth but attained in the homeland where God will be all in all and we will not see as in a mirror darkly."[8] He unhesitatingly admits that this form of life is superior to the active but, apparently untroubled by his implicit endorsement of the intellect's superiority, he proceeds to argue for the will's preeminence.[9]

Salutati's analysis in the *De nobilitate*, stressing as it does the powers of the will in the natural and theological spheres in contrast with those of the intellect limited only to the former, could not fail to convince any Christian who accepted his premises. Despite the fragility of his organization of categories, this scholastic elaboration of seventy-one conclusions for the superiority of the law (some of which are derisory) is Salutati's most original treatise. In it for the first time Salutati works out a defense for the priority of the will to the intellect and relates it to his own civic commitment.

Bernardo's treatise proclaiming the nobility of medicine bristled with a variety of subconclusions and corollaries but the author insisted on eight major points which are not always clearly distinguished from one another.

1. Law is not a science since it can prescribe nothing with certitude nor prove its principles in a scientific manner. Because medicine has these attributes, it is a science. (*Questio*, fols. 100^v–101^v).

2. Medicine studies those things which always or frequently act in the same way, while the subject of law is subject to change. (Ibid., fols. 101^v–102).

3. Medicine like natural science in general has only less certitude than mathematics. (Ibid., fol. 102).

4. Medicine excels not only law in the certitude of its principles but ethics as well. The principles of that which it knows lie in natural things. The principles of law and ethics are found in us and therefore are subject to change by an act of will. (Ibid., fol. 102).

5. Medicine deals with natural entities created by God, while law and ethics have as their subject entities created by ourselves. (Ibid., 102).

6. While the end of medicine is contemplative happiness, that of law is political felicity or an extrinsic good. (Ibid., fol. 102^v).

8. Ibid., pp. 36–38. The distinction between the two corresponds with Augustine's division between *sapientia* and *scientia* (ibid., p. 190).

9. Rather than outlining Bernardo's major points at the outset, Salutati saves them until the end when he summarizes his rebuttal (ibid., pp. 240–48). On p. 240 he includes the question of certainty in the third point of Bernardo but on p. 242 treats it as if it had been a separate point.

7. All morality is practical and cannot in any way be considered science. (Ibid., fols. 102ᵛ–103).

8. Medicine is not practical but theoretical, because "the end intended for it is only knowledge, not effect." (Ibid., fol. 103).

Salutati's often confusing response to these conclusions stems in part from his opponent's wide claims for medicine, making it coextensive at times with physics and at others with the whole of speculation. Correspondingly, Salutati attacks medicine, now as a practical application of physics, denying it qualities he grants to the science; now as identical with physics. In the second case he deems all natural science inferior to law.[10] Moreover, in those passages where Salutati establishes the superiority of will, he clearly assumes under intellect not only natural sciences but all theoretical knowledge insofar as it derives from natural reason.

The *De nobilitate* begins with a definition of nobility as "not a thing in itself but inhering in something else, that is, a quality which indicates something exceptionally good existing in the thing called noble by which it is preferred to other things."[11] Subsequently, Salutati defines law and medicine, their origin and nature, their focus and what they accomplish. After a comparison of the merits of both, he then undertakes to refute Bernardo's attacks against law. Finally, he introduces medicine herself to summarize the argument, admonish Bernardo for his extravagant claims in her behalf, and to award the victory to law.

Salutati's answer to Bernardo revolves around five basic arguments. The first is directed against the physician's contention that whereas the rules of medicine are the same everywhere, law varies with circumstances and is essentially arbitrary. Salutati's response is founded on Cicero *De legibus*, I, 6, 19: the laws of human society are specific formulations of natural laws found in the minds of men. These in turn reflect the rules governing the proper activity of man's essence in the divine mind. Salutati uses the metaphor of birth to describe the process of lawmaking: "So that their origin (of the laws) is from the seat of divinity from which, in something like birth, they come forth with the aid of natural reason and human promulgation."[12] His image suggests that

---

10. See ibid., pp. 32, 86, 116–18, and 266. Bernardo had written (*Questio*, fol. 102ᵛ): "Speculativas scientias ponit philosophus solum esse tres principales, scilicet, metaphysicam, id est, divinam, mathematicam et phisicam, id est, naturalem quae includit medicinam."

11. Ibid., p. 8.

12. Ibid., p. 76. For various definitions of law summarized above, see for example, pp. 14, 16, 18, 170 and 178. His definition on p. 18 reads: "Est igitur lex, prout humana est,

through our inner experience of the law human beings have contact with the will of their creator, who instilled his commandments there. Medicine, on the other hand, takes its beginning from contact with created objects and is hence inferior.

Not only does law have more nobility because of the source whence its principles derive but, secondly, it excels medicine in the kind of good which it produces. Medicine aims at natural good while the law generates moral good. Echoing the *Nicomachean Ethics*, I, 31, 1102a, Salutati maintains that, whereas medicine focuses on man as a good of nature, i.e., as a body among other bodies, the law envisages him from the moral standpoint, that aspect of his being which truly distinguishes him from the lower creatures. While speculation is essentially passive in its study of the operations and nature of bodies, law endeavors to realize the peculiar potential of man's essence as a free cause, that is, his capacity as a moral being to work for the common good. Aiming at a higher form of good, consequently, law has greater dignity than medicine.[13]

Salutati's third major position is that the benefits of speculation in general and medicine in particular are limited to individuals. The physician aims at curing his patient. If he is clumsy or works on an erroneous theory, the result affects only himself and the patient. The rewards of speculation may be fame and wealth or perhaps simply the joy of learning what one did not know. Nonetheless, the good produced is singular and whether it is produced or not is of little significance.

On the other hand, Salutati holds with Aristotle and Cicero that the legislator seeks a universal end, the attainment of the common good. "The laws," he writes, "in their final purpose, which is to pronounce a just sentence in individual cases, are devoted to and aim at the particular goal of justice in such a way that before everything they may protect the universal good of the city, of the kingdom and of the whole society

---

communis quedam preceptio rationis eterne inclinationisque nature, quam ille promulgat qui communitatis legitimam curam habet." Garin, ibid., p. 355, note to p. 76, emphasizes the generally Thomistic shading of Salutati's statement on the origin of the law. On natural law in Thomas, see Thomas E. Davitt, *The Nature of Law* (St. Louis and London, 1951), pp. 125–47; Odon Lottin, *Morale fondamentale*, Bibliothèque de théologie, Théologie morale, vol. 1 (Tournai, 1954), esp. 105–228; and Hans Meyer, *Thomas von Aquin* (Paderborn, 1961), pp. 586–653. For Cicero's conception of law, see F. Cauer, *Ciceros politisches Denken* (Berlin, 1903), pp. 14–38; and R. W. and A. J. Carlyle, *History of Medieval Political Theory in the West*, 2nd ed., 6 vols. (London, 1928), I, 1–18. For Cicero's political thought generally, see the Introduction to *Marcus Tullius Cicero, On the Commonwealth*, trans. with Intro. by G. H. Sabine and S. B. Smith (New York, 1929), pp. 39–99; and H. Strasburger, *Concordia Ordinum: Eine Untersuchung zur Politik Ciceros* (Amsterdam, 1956).

13. *De nobilitate*, pp. 50, 94, 100, and 266–68. Cf. Matteo Iannizzotto, *Saggio sullf filosofia di Coluccio Salutati* (Padua, 1959), pp. 120–22, on natural and moral good in Salutati.

of man."[14] Like Aristotle, Salutati regards politics as the master science—Salutati calls it "architectonica"—thus implying that political science orders the other sciences taught in the state with an eye to serving its comprehensive goal, the good of men.[15] Consequently, whereas the life devoted to speculation serves at best individuals, the active life benefits many, at times the whole community.

Although Aristotle's characterization of man as a political animal—set as it is in a philosophy in which speculation holds the first place in human activity—can have only qualified effect on Salutati, Cicero's discussion of the active life has no such limitations.[16] Quoting from the *De oratore*, I, 8, 32, Salutati lauds the work of the lawyer, who guards both individuals and the city from injustice and dangers.[17] The *Tusculan Disputations*, V, 2, 3, provides him with an encomium on the function of ethics which for Salutati is one with the law:

> O philosophy, guide of life, explorer of virtue, liberator, without you what would become of us and of all human life? You raised cities; brought dispersed men together in a common life; you joined them first together by residence, then by marriage through the communication of words and letters; you, inventor of laws, mistress of custom and of disciplines![18]

Yet, even when the Ciceronian source is not specific, the influence of Cicero's stress on the active life in the *De nobilitate* may be assumed at work in such passages as the following:

> I am always busy with activity, aiming at the final goal so that whatever I do is advantageous to me, my family, my relatives and what is before everything, my friends and the homeland. I act so that I can live in such a way as to help the whole of human society by my example and with my works. . . .[19]

14. *De nobilitate*, p. 134. He specifically cites Aristotle, *Nic. Eth.*, I, 13, 1102a 2, to prove this point (*De nobilitate*, pp. 102 and 104).

15. Ibid., pp. 168 and 244, based on *Nic. Eth.*, I, 1, 1094a. Salutati feels compelled to justify his making law equivalent to politics (pp. 168 and 170). Cf. as well, pp. 198 and 200.

16. See Introduction of Sabine and Smith, cited in n. 12, pp. 47–48.

17. *De nobilitate*, pp. 142 and 162.

18. Ibid., pp. 230 and 232. Bernardo had quoted the same passage in his work but used it to show that, while the establishment of principles of justice was ultimately the task of the philosopher, legislation was the task of the practical intellect (*Questio*, fol. 100ᵛ).

19. Ibid., p. 180. See as well p. 36, where, beginning with Cicero's definition of duty (*De off.*, I, 3, 7–8), Salutati ends with a praise of the active life.

The greatest benefactors of man are not the speculative thinkers but the law givers who instituted their societies in justice and so provided guidance for their communities for generations after their death.

Salutati's fourth general argument in the controversy regards Bernardo's statement that principles of medicine have greater certitude than those of law. Bernardo built his argument on Grosseteste's distinction of three levels of certitude depending on whether the object is necessary as in mathematics, whether it occurs always or frequently as in natural sciences, or whether the object is contingent and fortuitous. Bernardo had defined law, based as it was on the human will, with the first, and medicine with the second and to an extent the third kind of certitude.[20]

Salutati counters this by separating the certitude of the thing in itself from the certitude of the knower. Knowing is not an operation of the object but rather of the apprehending subject and properly all true knowledge derives from knowing universals or species.[21] Because the unchanging eternal species, not singular members of the species, are the object of a particular science, it makes no difference for certitude if the singulars are themselves unchanging or accidental. Although human laws depend on a decree of the will, the universal principles expressed in the laws are eternal. Thus, laws are no more products of an arbitrary, mutable human will, than are the conclusions of physics or medicine.[22]

Indeed, human laws are more certain than the principles of medicine in that the former are more in contact with their source of knowledge than medicine with its source. The doctor must work with an infinite number of changing singular objects in nature in an effort to define specific essence. In the cases of human bodies, men differ from one an-

20. *De nobilitate*, pp. 38–40. Garin cites the relevant passage from Grosseteste, pp. 352–53. Neither he nor Bernardo (*Questio*, fol. 101–101ᵛ) appears to be quoting Grosseteste word for word. Cf. the analysis of Salutati's commentary on Grosseteste by M. Iannizzotto, *Saggio*, pp. 70–78.

21. Ibid., p. 40: " . . . non autem scientia potest esse, que solum est universalium, que sunt generales et specifice singularium rationes." Also see p. 112. Salutati appears to believe that the mind abstracts the species from the sense experience (p. 186). Also see pp. 42–44. In the same work and elsewhere his language is so imprecise that he seems to suggest that the *species* in the mind is a *collectio* (p. 110 and above chap. 10, n. 102). Despite these latter references, it is almost certain that Salutati believed there to be *species* of things and ideas of *species* in God's mind: see my, "Coluccio Salutati and Contemporary Physics," *Journal of the History of Ideas*, 38 (1977), 667–68, n. 2. At one point in his writings he describes the *phantasia* as abstracting the *species* from the *sensus communis* (chap. 10, n. 102).

22. *De nobilitate*, p. 46.

other, and even the same man varies with circumstance. Herbs and po-
tions all have infinite numbers of properties which render the pursuit of
their specific forms impossible.[23] Accordingly, while all sciences are
equal in that they rest on knowledge of the eternal species ultimately
found in the divine essence, the difficulty of grasping the species that
concern the medical profession forces doctors to rely on conjecture in
their work.[24] Whereas medicine is a *scientia quia* or one working from
effect to cause, law is a *scientia propter quid* because it proceeds in the
reverse direction.[25] Certain of his principles, the legislator has the task
of applying them to circumstances. There are essentially three such
rules: (1) do to others as we would have them do to us; (2) do not do to
others what we would not have them do to us; and (3) the same law
applies to all men. No one, in any society, no matter how barbarian or
ignorant, would deny the truth of these injunctions.[26]

Much of what Salutati says about the uncertainty of medicine would
seem to undermine the certainty of physics as well. In contrast to metaphysics, which considers eternal, incorporeal reality, physics is limited
to studying the operations of forms in connection with material bodies.[27]
Like medicine, physics approaches its objects through sense perception
and would seem to encounter the same difficulties in establishing the
specific nature of forms, infinite in number and with infinite properties
depending on space and time. In the words of Aristotle, "like the eyes
of bats in the light of day so is our intellect to those things which are by
nature the clearest of all."[28] However, Salutati appears reluctant to attack the certitude of the master science physics. He obviously believes
that the degree of certitude connected with principles of natural science
varies: we are more certain of conclusions made about bodies like the
stars than about the workings of different drugs.

The *De nobilitate* carries further Salutati's critique of the cause and effect relationship initiated in the *De fato*. In this treatise as in the earlier

---

23. Ibid., pp. 112–22 and 260.   24. Ibid., p. 114.

25. Ibid., p. 84. He draws the distinction from Aristotle's *Metaphysics*, I, 1, 981a-b. Also,
De nobilitate, pp. 262 and 264. There is no indication that Salutati knew any commentaries
on either the *Metaphysics* or the *Posterior Analytics*.

26. Ibid., p. 44.

27. Ibid., pp. 116–18: "Nonne pars illa philosophie, que de perpetuis et incorporalibus
agit, quales sunt hominum anime, qualiaque sunt earum, et omnium que incorporea fuerint,
universalia, que proprie sub scientia cadunt, altior est atque sublimior quam que circa
corpora fluxibilia versatur et agit?"

28. Ibid., p. 114. As an example of the difficulties of physics in finding certainty, Salutati points up the problems involved in establishing that ninth and tenth spheres exist
when only eight can be observed. The existence can only be proven "ratione verisimili"
(p. 128).

one he has no intention of questioning the validity of the causal principle but rather of pointing up the lack of certainty in the conclusions of
natural science: "The causes of both nature and fortune hide."[29] Or, as
he writes in the *De nobilitate*: "It is not enough to have principles of
nature and to know that they cannot change. . . . To generate certainty
you must know what your natural principles are!"[30] In large part the
critique serves a dialectical purpose: in the *De fato* he defends the reality
of fortune, in the *De nobilitate* he stresses the certitude of the law against
the arrogance of the natural scientist. Aware of current discussions
about the causal relationship, Salutati is willing to go only so far in his
questioning. Considering his medical adversary beaten on the grounds
of the certitude of medicine, he pursues him into his place of refuge,
the domain of physics, but having raised the spectre of the damage he
can do there, he withdraws, content with having established that the
principles of the law are more certain than those of either medicine or
physics.

The discussion of the respective degrees of certitude attainable in
natural science and in law serves the purpose of providing a vivid contrast between the world of nature and the world of man.[31] As a result,
Salutati significantly reinforces the consciousness of man's uniqueness
in the universe and justifies the claims of law and related disciplines to
be properly human sciences. Up to this point he has established his case
relying on natural reason alone. When, however, he takes up his final
principal argument and moves into the sphere of supranatural truth,
his defense of the law and of the active as against the speculative life
assumes its fullest significance.

The human intellect not only is defective in being unable to have certain knowledge of the essences of natural objects, but it can never attain
fulfillment of its final end. Aristotle's view that man's happiness lies in
speculation is erroneous and merely condemns man to frustration. The
individual can never know the infinite number of truths nor can he have
perfect knowledge of God whose essence is infinite.[32] The proper end of
man is not to know God's essence but rather to enjoy him eternally, and
this enjoyment is properly a function of the will inspired by divine

29. See chap. 11.
30. *De nobilitate*, p. 114. Medicine, however, was more vulnerable to Salutati's attack
because "fallax rerum experimentum" (p. 78) was its essential source, whereas physics
was presumably more abstract and rational: "Quotiens enim ab experimento discesserint,
in physicam transeunt relinquentes limites medicine" (p. 86).
31. Garin makes this point very effectively in his notes (ibid., pp. 353, 357, and 359).
32. Ibid., pp. 164–66.

grace. This perfect state is termed beatitude because having as its direct object God, in whom are unified all the individual goods of the universe, the will completely satisfies its desire. However, Revelation tells us that no one will be saved without works and that our reward in heaven will be commensurate with the amount of good works to our credit. Accordingly, we must act here on earth to attain felicity, and the law is the rule and measure of human action. To live by the law is to live justly and to work both for one's personal salvation and for the good of the whole body of citizens. The role of law is twofold: it fosters earthly felicity by making the citizenry virtuous, thus giving peace to the state, while at the same time guiding them toward their eternal beatitude.[33]

Salutati, however, grants speculation a role in the determination of the laws and the conduct of the active life. The principles of the law are necessarily established by rational inspection of the human soul and its powers. We use our intellectual faculties to know (*scire*) our soul and its attributes not for that knowledge in itself but in order to utilize (*dirigere*) our powers for performing virtuous works.[34] This kind of speculative activity aims at the enjoyment of the good, the moral improvement of men, and the conservation of society, whereas the speculation praised by Bernardo is limited to knowledge without affecting the quality of men's lives. Understood in its practical and speculative aspects, therefore, law becomes equivalent to practical wisdom, which Salutati defines as "an intellectual virtue, a habit concerned with governing all conduct."[35]

The relative superiority of the will to the intellective power in this relationship comes out clearly in Salutati's description of their joint functioning. As distinguished from the unconscious inclination of the natural object or the natural appetite of the sensitive creature, the human will is the *motus animi* of the rational creature. Unwilling to postulate a real division between intellect and will, Salutati presents them as

33. Ibid., pp. 98 and 166. On p. 166 he writes succinctly: " . . . ad felicitatis adeptionem tam moralis quam ultime necessarias esse leges. . . ."

34. Ibid., p. 36.

35. Ibid., p. 214. Shortly before, Salutati uses Bernardo's own expressions to define *justitia legalis* as the virtue containing all the virtues and the "perfecte virtutis usus" (p. 210). In his correspondence, however, he implies that *justitia legalis* is only that part of *prudentia* concerned with our public actions (ibid., III, 95 and 184). As he writes in 1396 (III, 95): "Nam legalis iusticia non solum unica virtus est, sed omnes virtutes, que cunctos mortalium actus in bonum publicum; quod longe divinius est quam privatum; dirigit et intendit." A bit below this (p. 96) he defines "iuris prudentia" as "legalis agibilium ratio." Nowhere in his works does Salutati indicate an awareness of the difference between the Stoic and Peripatetic schools on this issue of prudence and justice. For references, see Klaus Heitman, *Fortuna und Virtus*, Studi italiani, vol. 1 (Graz, 1958), pp. 98–150.

two aspects of the same human act: the passive aspect is the intellective element, the active, the volitional.[36] Chronologically prior to the first movement of the intellect and setting that faculty in motion is the desire to know. This originates in the will.[37] In the first movement the possible intellect, passive insofar as it has received the species of exterior objects through the operations of the sensitive organs of the body, presents these intellections of external objects to the will.[38] Because these objects are not only beings but also goods, the will commands the intellect to contemplate these objects, to understand not only what they are but also in what manner they are. At this point the will determines what things will be chosen or pursued among that which is knowable. In making this choice, Salutati emphasizes, the will is perfectly free to choose or not to choose, and its object is not the mental conception presented to it by the intellect but rather the good it finds in the thing known.[39] Throughout the process, Salutati concludes, the intellect has functioned as the servant of the will in that, in obedience to its command, the intellect furnishes the material necessary for the will's proper functioning.

In relationship to the final end of man, moreover, the will influenced by divine grace again has precedence over the intellect. Only through

---

36. *De nobilitate*, p. 188. The two faculties are one "realiter" and can be distinguished only "ratione": "Ut cum voluntas et intellectus propter unitatem anime realiter unum sint, sic ratione differant quod illa dominetur, iste serviat." Salutati curiously cites Aristotle, *Nic. Eth.*, X, 7, 1177b, in proof that the intellect is in reality joined with the will: " . . . Philosophi verba, si recte voluerim intelligere, non dividunt ab intellectu voluntatem, sed ea sine dubitatione coniungunt." Salutati's position that the human will and intellect are only rationally distinct probably derives from his reading of Buridan's commentary on Aristotle's *Nic. Eth.*, *Quaestiones Joannis Buridani super decem libros* (Paris, 1513), VI, q. 3 (Tertio, quaeritur utrum potentie anime sint ab anima realiter distincte?): fols. 110–11. Also see his discussion of same problem, III, q. 3: fol. 62–62ᵛ. Ullman, *The Humanism of Coluccio Salutati*, Medioevo e umanesimo, vol. 4 (Padua, 1963), p. 220, incorrectly reading a remark of Salutati (*Epist.*, III, 391: May 7, 1400), writes that Salutati possessed only two questions of the ninth book of this commentary. In fact, Salutati says that he possessed a manuscript of the work up to the second question of the ninth book: "Questionis optimi Buridani ultra duas questiones noni libri, licet Parisius super hoc scripserim, nunquam potui reperire. Dicuntque peritiores eum ulterius non processisse." On the wide diffusion in fourteenth-century Italy of Buridan's commentary, see Graziella Federici Vescovini, "A propos de la diffusion des oeuvres de Jean Burdian en Italie du XIVᵉ au XVIᵉ siècles," *The Logic of John Buridan: Acts of the 3rd European Symposium on Medieval Logic and Semantics, Copenhagen 16–21, November 1975*, ed. Jan Pinborg (Copenhagen, 1976), pp. 21–45 and especially for Florence in the late fourteenth century, pp. 25–26. Throughout her *Astrologia e scienza: La crisi dell'aristotelismo sul cadere del Trecento e Biagio Pelacani da Parma* (Florence, 1979), Vescovini stresses the importance of Buridan for Pelacani.

37. Ibid., p. 192.   38. Ibid., p. 186. See below, n. 49.

39. Ibid., pp. 186 and 192. Again, the will's freedom is proclaimed in relationship to the goods presented it by the intellect, but he says nothing of the will when confronted with the final beatitude (see above, chap. 11).

the action of grace on the will can this faculty realize its true goal which is to love God. Insofar as the intellect is concerned, its operation is limited to contemplating God as infinite beatific good loved by the will under divine inspiration: "The act of understanding is fulfilled when it understands that infinite beatific good. It is fulfilled; nay, it cannot go beyond this."[40]

Seen against this theological background the claim of the will to surpass the intellect is irresistible. Indeed, implicitly in the climax of this discussion the puny speculative intellect has been left behind, and we seem to be contrasting an intellect informed by divine grace with a will similarly moved. Even then it is chiefly on the will that God focuses his grace to bring men to him: through this faculty men will enjoy God eternally. Moreover, in such a Christian context the capacity of human beings to create their own form of good through action constitutes, when fully realized, an excellence that makes them equal to the angels: "By means of this goodness, mortals ascend above themselves and by the merits of one man, that is, the mediator between God and men, Jesus Christ, and of the Virgin Mary and perhaps of others, they have outdistanced all the angels in glory."[41] When in the final analysis Salutati formulates the arguments in favor of the law, he has in mind a sense of justice or prudence not limited by the natural powers of the individual but guided by an awareness of the true end and proper activity of men. Ultimately, it is the claim of law understood in this Christian sense which Salutati vindicates in the face of Bernardo's brief for medicine.

By means of fair laws the legislator establishes a political felicity for his people which is continuous with that eternal one in heaven. Citing Prov. 29:18, "Blessed is he who protects the law," Salutati comments: "Blessed indeed is he while we live in this world with hope; and, after living by the law, truly blessed is he in reality."[42] Although in the *De*

40. Ibid., p. 190: "Verum quoniam verus et extremus hominis finis non est cognoscere sive scire, sed illa suprema beatitudo, que videre est Deum, sicuti est, visoque frui, visumque diligere illique et eternaliter coherere per dilectionem que sic unit diligentem atque dilectum quod qui per illam adheret Deo unus spiritus est cum eo, nec hoc adipsci possumus scientia vel speculatione humana sed Dei gratia per virtutes et operationes, certum est ad illam veram felicitatem activam vitam, cuius voluntas principium est, non speculativam pertinere, que perficitur intellectu, et in ea ipsa beatitudine nobilior et formalior est voluntatis actus, qui dilectio est, quam actus intellectus, qui contemplatio sive visio dici potest. Terminatum est enim intelligere quotiens infinitum illud bonum beatificum comprehendit, terminatum est equidem nec potens est ulterius proficisci."

41. Ibid., p. 202. Also p. 220.

42. Ibid., p. 166. He perhaps did not wish to use *caritas* in this work because he kept most of his discussion of the law in the realm of natural reason and it was more consistent for him to use *justitia* or *prudentia* than to describe the dedication to the common good in terms of a theological virtue.

nobilitate Salutati speaks of our love of God in eternity as *dilectio* and of our desire to serve the common good on earth as *prudentia* or *justitia legalis*, more normally in his writings he describes this activity of the human will infused with divine grace as *caritas*.

In his mature writings Salutati defined *caritas* in the usual Christian sense as "love (*dilectio*) of God and of one's neighbor."[43] According to God's eternal law, he wrote in the *De fato*, we must love God on account of Himself and our neighbor on account of God, for apart from God nothing is to be loved for itself. Consequently, "our acts must be ordered as reason demands toward God and to our neighbor on account of God,"[44] This orientation of love is created in us by God (*caritas creata*) and by it we merit possession of God (*caritas increata*) in heaven.[45] Of the theological virtues it alone remains after the individual soul has left the body.[46]

Although in his early correspondence, as has been seen, (chap. 3) patriotism was equivalent to *caritas* but without any theological implications, from the first years of his chancellorship, patriotism as *caritas* assumed a Christian character. And, by the time of his writing the *De nobilitate*, the concept of a specifically Christian patriotism, which had been a secondary aspect of the moral ideas of a theologian like Aquinas, came to the forefront of Salutati's religious thought. By nature men have a sense of their bond with other men and an affection for them that determines all mankind to be political and social creatures. Not only is it against nature to hurt other men, it is also inhuman not to go to their aid when necessary. Furthermore, Christians have an even higher responsibility to love their fellow men because they are told to love one another as themselves and to extend this love even to their enemies.[47]

Nevertheless, our obligation to love all men as brothers does not mean that we are obligated to all in the same degree. We owe more to our family and fellow citizens by reason of proximity than to strangers. The devotion to the common good is rightly felt most strongly within the boundries of the homeland. Even Christ had this sense of homeland in that he left Egypt to return to Israel to suffer martyrdom there.[48] Thus, not only do Christians have a greater responsibility to serve others but

43. *De seculo et religione*, ed. Berthold L. Ullman (Florence, 1957), p. 27. Also see, *Epist.*, I, 247, and II, 319. For Salutati's earlier use of *caritas*, see chap. 3.

44. B.A.V., *Vat. lat.*, 2298, Tr. II, 7, fols. 19ᵛ–20.

45. *De seculo*, p. 27.

46. *Epist.*, I, 247. Cf. Aquinas, who separates *justitia* from *caritas*, see: ST IIa, IIae, 58, aa. 5–6.

47. *Epist.*, I, 253–54 and 318.   48. Ibid., I, 311.

the example of Christ indicates that this responsibility is greatest in regard to the *patria*.

The significance of the *De nobilitate* in this matter is that it provides the theological justification for concluding that, just as Christians have more responsibility to be better citizens, so they have a better opportunity for fulfilling their obligations. Because they are aware of the proper ordering of goals in the light of divine revelation and because God through his influence on their souls helps them to perform the good works that will earn them eternal beatitude, Christians make better citizens. Had Aristotle seen the true end of man as Christians do, he would never have believed that speculation rather than the active life was the best for man.[49]

Salutati's Christian conception of the active life came to constitute an important aspect of his growing sense of the gulf between the ancient and the Christian eras and of the essential inferiority of the culture of the pagan world which lived without the truth. Whereas the *De fato* maintained that God had willed the destruction of city-state republicanism and had established the empire which was to last down to Salutati's own time, the *De nobilitate* provided the means whereby the patriotism of the ancient world, untouched by Christian *caritas*, could be considered basically human selfishness. The antipagan attitudinizing of the *De seculo* was in the last years becoming the dominant tendency of Salutati's thought. By 1404, for example, he was insisting that the advent of Christ made fulfillment of our natural obligation to cherish other men more possible. Rejecting as applicable to Christians Aristotle's doctrine that one could not have many friends, he explained that, while true of pagan times, the coming of Christ had changed the situation. It is possible for a whole society to be friends among themselves.

> But one might object that nowhere and never was there such a society. I believe that the pagans perhaps did not experience this benefit (friendship) on a wide scale, although sometimes one reads of a cohort happily giving its life for the safety of the whole army. But that true love (*vera caritas*) had not yet descended from heaven about which we read: "Now the company of those who believed were of one heart and soul." It happened in this way, as the golden words of Jerome truly say: "For this is the true relationship with Christ as the connecting tie. . . ." It is accomplished by the perfection of Christian teaching if we do what we are commanded; for we are ordered to love our

49. *De nobilitate*, p. 270.

neighbor as ourselves and Christ does not command impossible things of us. Who can prevent a truly perfect society and total friendship from existing founded on this basic belief common to all Christians?[50]

The tone of the De nobilitate is in striking contrast with that of the De fato. In the earlier treatise the freedom of the human will was affirmed, but the emphasis in the work fell on the omnipotence of an all-powerful, all-disposing God. Like the De fato, the De nobilitate reflects Salutati's concern with distinguishing the operations of a world of nature from the realm of human freedom, but the De nobilitate confidently presents this free will as a dynamic force for good.

According to his own statement, in defending the superiority of the will over the intellect, Salutati was aligning himself with the Franciscans against the Dominicans.[51] Unfortunately, except for Thomas, he never mentions any scholastic thinkers in this text or elsewhere, thus making it impossible for us to be certain of influences. Nor do his conceptions and terminology help much in identifying precise Franciscan sources. Garin's excellent commentary to his edition suggests a heavy reliance on Thomas throughout, while possible Scotistic ideas can be located only in the sections dealing with the priority of the will over the intellect.[52]

50. Epist., IV, 20. The quotations are taken respectively from Acts, 4:32 and Jerome's Epist., 53, ad Paulinum in PL 22, 540.

51. Epist., III, 524–25. Sending a copy of the work to ser Pietro di ser Mino, Salutati asks him to advise a possible critic that "cuncta ponderet diligentique digerat examine nec ferat super hoc nimia voluntate sententiam fratrumque minorum consulat scolam et inveniet hanc opinionem, quam verissimam arbitror, apud illorum optimos constantissime retineri, licet Dantes noster et Predicatorum sententia contradicat."

52. Essentially in pp. 182–96; and notes 362–65. However, one of the basic characteristics of Scotus' thought, the distinctio formalis, is not to be found in Salutati. Whereas the theologian distinguishes between the human intellect and will with this distinction (Op. Ox. II, d. 16, q. unica, 17), Salutati uses a "distinctio rationis." See above, n. 36. Less significant perhaps is Salutati's apparent disagreement with Scotus, who insisted that the first cognition of the intellect was independent of the will. Salutati held that even this could not occur "sine consensu vel imperio voluntatis." See Wilhelm Kölmel, "Wille und Freiheit in der Lehre des Duns Scotus und des 'Humanismus,'" in Deus et Homo ad mentem I. Duns Scoti, Studia Scholastico Scotistica, vol. 5 (Rome, 1972), p. 352, n. 1. Garin (De nobilitate, p. 364, n. to p. 192 suggests that St. Bernard, whom Salutati cites in this section on the superiority of the will to reason, may have been his source. Bernard, De gratia et libero arbitrio, II, PL 182, 1003, refers to reason as "data voluntati ut instruat illam, non destruat. Destrueret autem, si necessitatem ei ullam imponeret. . . ." While acknowledging the possible link with the thought of Augustine and Scotus, Garin suggests that Bernard may have induced Salutati to make the exaggerated claim for the power of the will. This passage of the De nobilitate, however, might better be seen in conjunction with a similar statement made in his correspondence about the same time—Novati, Epist., III, 437–38, assigns it a date of 1400?—which reads: "Intellectus enim adeo segnis est et iners, quod per semetipsum semper iacet. Nam primus eius actus est, quem [text obviously should read que] a sensibus speciebusque sensibilium excitatur, quod omnino patientis

The humanist was not a philosopher. When he borrowed philosophical ideas, he did so with great liberty and often in imprecise language. While there is no reason to doubt Franciscan inspiration in his defense of the prerogatives of the will, the influence was probably generic. His knowledge of Franciscan ideas may even have been limited to information gleaned from conversation. But at the very least, general awareness of the position gave him a degree of assurance in expressing his own sense of the will's importance in both ethical and theological terms.

Given the preeminence of the will, Salutati was able to transform Cicero's conception of the active life into a Christian ideal: that of the patriot in a Christian commonwealth. Thomas doubtless furnished Salutati great assistance through his own analysis of human nature and law, which draws heavily on Aristotelian ideas but sets them in a Christian context.[53] Because of his belief in the preeminence of the intellect, Thomas like Aristotle is logically forced to give the life of the citizen second place after that of the contemplative. Salutati's preference for the will, on the other hand, afforded a basis for vindicating the priority of the active life of the Christian citizen absorbed in serving the common good of the community. "Clearly in it (the highest virtue)," one commentator writes, "the Aristotelian tendency of the political nature

---

est. Secundus autem est compositionis rationisque discursus, quod facere non potest, nisi voluntas imperaverit et semper astiterit discurrenti; ut quotiens voluntas non precipiat vel ab urgendo desistat, intellectus noster penitus nichil agat. Nam et obiectum sensibile parum agit, nec per se potest intellectum possibilem actuare, si voluntas iubens semper intellectui non assistat; que si mentem fixam ad aliquid teneat, nichil preter illud intelligere valeat vel sentire, quod patris Augustini constat exemplo. Refert enim in libris De Civitate Dei se vidisse quendam devotissimum sacerdotem, qui, cum oraret, adeo rapiebatur, quod stimulis ad sanguinis effusionem usque confossus nullum omnino signum ostenderet sentientis" (pp. 445–46). In contrast with the treatise, Salutati maintains in the letter that the intellect has a first act preceding the operation of the will. Through the senses and the sensible *species* the intellect is aroused "parum"—he wishes to minimize the role of the former acting on the latter in order subsequently to magnify the power of the will. The second act of the intellect, the discursive, ratiocinative operation of the intellect, is initiated by an act of the will. It would seem from his words here, "compositionis rationisque discursus," that this second stage begins with the ideas of sense objects already formed in the first. But this does not seem to be the case from what follows, for an act of will is said to be needed for the actualization of the possible intellect. Although the language and the doctrine of the passivity of the soul in sense experience are quite un-Augustinian, Salutati's basic image of the cognitive act is determined by his somewhat inaccurate recollection of Augustine's anecdote in the De civ. Dei, XIV, 24. In my view the exaggerated voluntarism of the passage in the De nobilitate reflects this same view. For Augustine's theory of sensation see Étienne Gilson, *The Christian Philosophy of St. Augustine*, trans. L. E. M. Lynch (New York, 1960), pp. 44–111; and M. A. I. Gannon, "The Active Theory of Sensation in St. Augustine," *The New Scholasticism*, 30 (1956), 154–80.

53. See above n. 12. On Thomas' political theory, see Thomas Gilby, *The Political Thought of Thomas Aquinas* (Chicago, 1958), pp. 90–332; and Gilson, *Le Thomisme, Introduction à la philosophie de Saint Thomas d'Aquin*, 6th ed. (Paris, 1965), pp. 375–405.

of man, the Roman public ethic and Christian charity come together."[54]

Salutati made no effort to reconcile these voluntarist conclusions with his unambiguous affirmation of the superiority of the contemplative to the active life made earlier in the *De nobilitate*.[55] Very probably he neglected to do so because Bernardo himself wanted to avoid the term *contemplation* with its theological implications and because Salutati was surer of winning the argument if his opponent was defending speculation. Seventeen or eighteen years before in the *De seculo* Salutati had, of course, actually quantified the relative merits of the contemplative and the active life: he had assigned a hundred-fold harvest to the monk leading the former and thirty to the Christian layman, living the active life in the world.

Nevertheless, at least six years prior to the publication of the *De nobilitate* Salutati had already considerably altered that judgment. His letter of 1393 to ser Andrea of Volterra, mentioned in the last chapter as written when ser Andrea had suddenly lost his wife and all his children, indicates that a reevaluation was underway.[56] In response to ser Andrea's statement that he now was thinking of entering a monastery, Salutati advised his friend that taking religious vows as a result of suffering worldly adversity was a bad motive. While he did not use the terms active and contemplative life, they were in fact the subject of discussion. Salutati insisted that

> different people come to God in different ways. Some choose the secret and solitary life, like the hermits and anchorites or like the cenobites we read about; and I know that many come to God's glory following the busy life in society. The great riches of Abraham did not corrupt his son Isaac nor his grandson Jacob. High position did not harm Moses or Aaron or those who followed them in power, Joshua and many others whom the Old and New Testaments consider holy men. For although the solitary life is considered safer, it is not so; for to engage (*vacare*) in honest activity honestly is as holy and perhaps more so than to give oneself (*ociari*) to the solitary life. Indeed, holy seclusion is of advantage only to oneself, as he [St. Jerome] says. But

54. Ianizzotto, *Saggio*, p. 123.

55. Salutati's hesitations in this work and elsewhere make questionable Giuseppe Sciacca's affirmation (*Il concetto di tiranno dai Greci a Coluccio Salutati* [Palermo, 1953], p. 90) that "tutta la produzione Salutatiana costituisce un vero e proprio inno alla vita attiva nella sua contrapposizione con la contemplativa." Similarly Eugenio Garin's description of Salutati as a voluntarist (*L'umanesimo italiano* [Bari, 1958], p. 34) can only be accepted with reservations. See further ambiguity below in this regard.

56. See above, chap. 11.

holiness in the affairs of the world edifies many because it is available to many and because it furnishes an example to many and brings many along with it to the gates of heaven.[57]

Ser Andrea should not, therefore, desert the world because of fear of its turmoil, but only out of love (*caritas*), that is, because God has touched him.

A letter written in the same years—between March 9, 1388, and March 9, 1394—places similar stress on dangers of life in the monastery and the need to examine one's motivations before taking the monastic vow.[58]

57. *Epist.*, II, 453. Both the verbs *vacare* and *otiari* were commonly used to express the activity of the monk, who was free to devote his time to pious contemplation. The reference to Jerome is taken from *Epist.*, 53, *ad Paulinum* in *PL* 22, 542.

58. This letter dated March 9 of some unknown year was edited by Lucia Gai, "Frammenti di un codice sconosciuto di Coluccio Salutati," *Motivi di riformi tra '400 e '500*, Memorie domenicane, n.s. 3 (1972), 304–5. Gai suggests provisorily that it was written in the last decade of the Trecento "dato che l'argomentazione addotta è molto simile, ma più coerentemente svolta, rispetto a quella presenta in lettere composte entro l'ultimo decennio del '300" (p. 302, n. 1). Copied with this letter and Salutati's brief treatise on punctuation is a sermon by Francesco da Empoli dated October 19, 1404. Establishing a precise chronology for this letter will probably prove impossible, but dating can be done within certain limits.

Although the specific formulation of the rubric containing the address (which follows the text of the letter, p. 305) is the work of an early amanuensis, it is doubtless based on the original: "Ser Colucius Pyeri de Salutatis Cancellarius Florentinus compilavit epistulam suprascriptam: et eam transmisit domino Anthonio de Forolivio scribe domini Benedicti abbatis Vallisumbrose, desideranti heremiticam vitam eligere, consulens ei." Because Antonio is referred to as *dominus* and because Salutati himself in the text greets him as "venerabilis in Christo pater" (p. 304) and in the conclusion asks him for his prayers in the mass (p. 305), we can affirm that Antonio was a priest. Thus, on March 9 of an unidentified year Salutati was writing to a priest, serving as scribe of the Abbot of Vallombrosa, Benedetto. The priest had written Salutati to request his advice about joining the monastery.

A registry of letters and other documents for Vallombrosa under the government of three successive abbots, Simone, Benedetto, and Bernardo, indicates that Benedetto was abbot of the monastery as early as 1387: B.N.F., *Conv. sopp.*, G 6 (1502), fol. 71—the date at top reads "MCCCLXXXVII" followed by "Lictere transmisse in forma publica et patenti tempore domini Benedicti Abbatis Vallisumbrose que registrande venerunt." This suggests that he only entered into his functions after March 25, 1387. His successor began his duties in June 1401 (ibid., fol. 84) although Benedetto was already dead before December 22, 1400 (*Dipl.*, Vallombrosa, December 22, 1400). The last date accordingly provides an absolute *terminus ante quem* for the letter. When Antonio first appears in the registry on January 14, 1389 (*Conv. sopp.*, fol. 78–78ᵛ), he appears with the same attributions as in the address of Salutati's letter: *dominus* and *scriba* of the Abbot Benedetto. His brother, Neri, whose name is found in the registers from February 2, 1384 (ibid., fol. 46), is apparently the notary of the monastery and is so designated in a document of November 1395 (*Dipl.*, Vallombrosa [day unknown] November 1395). Unfortunately for dating Salutati's letter to Antonio, Abbot Benedetto's register contains a lacuna from March 10, 1390 (*Conv. sopp.*, fol. 80ᵛ) to September 20, 1394 (fol. 81). But when it resumes, Antonio in the subscription to a letter of February 14, 1395 (fol. 82), identifies himself as the writer of the letter, this time adding to his titles that of *monachus*: "Per dominum Antonium Bernardi monachum,

With its emphasis on the superior virtues of life in the world, however, this second letter actually amounts to a disparagement of the life of withdrawal. It was a response to a letter written by a priest, a certain Antonio di Bernardo da Forlì, who since at least January 14, 1389, had been a scribe for the abbot of Vallombrosa. He had probably joined the *familia* of the recently elected abbot, Benedetto, through the efforts of his own brother, Neri di Bernardo, the monastery's notary since as early as February 2, 1384. Not only his brother's residence there but also the monastery's reputation for sanctity attracted the obviously devout Antonio. To judge from Salutati's reply, Antonio was seriously contemplating joining the monastery—perhaps he had already become a novice[59]— and wanted to have the opinion of the learned humanist about the wisdom of his decision.

While acknowledging that he "would not dare not praise the pious intention (of Antonio)," Salutati immediately warns that to leave the world appears to be deserting one's neighbor, "who in my opinion cannot be sufficiently helped by our prayers and example alone but who needs the assistance of daily admonishment, affectionate personal contact and continuous diligent attention" (p. 304). Shut in a cell one can help only oneself: "No one can persuade me that the merit of the hermit Paul and that of the bishop Augustine were equal: the former profited himself and perhaps a few others; the latter both himself and an

scribam nostrum." The inference to be drawn from this altered title is that at some point between January 1389 and February 1395 Antonio became a monk.

Somewhat greater precision is possible. This register of the abbots contains in the last section a list of those entering the monastery from February 5, 1371 (fol. 120), to September 28, 1389 (fol. 134)—a few registrations for 1418–21 follow on fol. 134, but nothing subsequently. Because Antonio's name is nowhere enumerated as joining the monastery, it seems fair to maintain (assuming the list is complete) that he did not become a brother until after September 28, 1389. It must also be added that after February 14, 1395, in the rare subscriptions where Antonio identifies himself, he is not consistent. In the one other subscription where his name occurs during the abbacy of Benedetto (June 1400: fol. 92), he still calls himself *scriba* and *monachus*. But, working as scribe under Benedetto's successor, he varies, signing as scribe and monk in fols. 85, 87, 87ᵛ, 90 (twice), 92, and as scribe in fols. 88, 89, and 91. If, as the lists of entrances into the monastery suggests, Antonio did not join Vallombrosa until after September 28, 1389, then his first signature on February 14, 1395, as *monachus* indicates a change in status, whereas the absence of the term in later years suggests merely that he had no fixed practice in referring to himself in subscriptions. On these grounds I would assign a date to Salutati's letter of March 9 to some year between 1388—the first March 9 during the abbacy of Benedetto—and 1394, the last March before February 14, 1395, when Antonio appears as a monk.

59. Giovanni di Michele of Florence, who became a monk of Vallombrosa on April 15, 1376, relates that his novitiate lasted sixteen months (B.A.V., *Chigi*, C VIII 191, fol. 181). Antonio may well have taken this first step before writing Salutati and was hesitating about the final profession.

infinite number of others not only in his own time but in all generations."[60] Salutati goes so far as to identify the monk with the servant of
Matt. 25:14–30, who, because he did not use it profitably, was deprived
of the talent given him by his lord. While "there is no method, status
or degree of living worthily with which and from which the ascent to
God is impossible," nonetheless, he affirms, more kings, priests, and
popular leaders reached beatitude than anchorites and hermits. The last
statement, similar to one made in the letter to ser Andrea but modified
there with a "forte," is here given without qualification.

Salutati also lays greater stress in this letter to Antonio on the dangers of solitude and the temptations to self-indulgence in withdrawal.
Is Antonio sure that he does not seek solitude primarily out of the desire for peace, security, and freedom from the commands of a prelate?
To withstand the temptations of such a life Antonio must give himself
to unsparing tears, fasts, prayers, self-inflicted beatings, and sorrowing
for past sins. Once committed, Antonio cannot honorably abandon his
choice: "Persuade yourself that you will not be alone if you focus your
mind on the crucified Christ, for you will only feel yourself deserted
and abandoned if you stop thinking of him" (p. 305). In the event, having received Salutati's opinion, Antonio considered the challenge, examined his conscience, and joined the monastery.

Written in the years when Salutati was hard at work on the *De laboribus Herculis*—perhaps after September, 1392 in the period of intense enthusiasm following his reading of Cicero's correspondence—this letter
seeks to convince a correspondent that the best Christian life is led in
society.[61] Almost diametrically opposed to the conclusion of the *De seculo et religione*, like that treatise it makes no effort to rivet its thesis into
a theoretical structure in which the will emerges superior to the intellect. Consequently, one still suspects weakness at the basis of the confident defense of the active life.

To lay firm foundations for the active life was one of the tasks of the
De nobilitate in 1399. Yet the espousing of now the contemplative now
the active life as *the* superior life style in different parts of that work
frustrates any effort to derive a clear picture of their real relationship to
one another. A letter written by Salutati to his friend Zambeccari a year

60. Salutati here refers to Paul of Thebes, who died in 341 after living ninety years as
an anchorite.
61. As late as June/July 1392, Salutati still urged those wanting to save their souls to
flee the world (*Epist.*, II, 329.).

before the publication of this treatise, however, probably represents Salutati's most balanced judgment on the conflicting life styles and their relationship to the human faculties of reason and will.

The letter of May 23, 1398, was the final one in a series to the Bolognese chancellor concerning his colleague's wild infatuation with a Bolognese girl.[62] Ostensibly Zambeccari's confession of error made in a recent letter proved the success of Salutati's vigorous campaign to convince the desperate lover to cease his pursuit of Giovanna, his beloved. But, as Salutati implies, Zambeccari's changed attitude was in fact a product of his sorrow at having been abandoned by the young woman, who left Bologna to follow her husband in exile. Knowing well the mercurial Zambeccari, Salutati cannot take seriously the lover's emotional profession of a newly found religious faith and his intention to leave his family and official position in order to become a hermit. Although not without a note of humor—rare in Salutati's writing—the letter moves from an analysis of Zambeccari's particular motivations to a consideration of the whole problem of the active and contemplative life.

Salutati introduces the general problem by pointing out to his correspondent that, unless he has really given up his earthly passion for Giovanna, solitude will offer Zambeccari no relief; it may even intensify his desires. On the other hand, if his emotions are under the control of his will, Zambeccari can find tranquility of mind living in the midst of crowds. Often men living in the world lead more Christian lives than anchorites in their solitude. Indeed the active citizen, serving his family and the state, imitates closely the work of divine Providence which acts for all creation.[63]

From this point on, however, Salutati's presentation bristles with ambiguities caused by his own essentially ambivalent feelings. The contemplative life, he continues, is admittedly more perfect in that its direct object is God. Those in the active life, while acting with a view to God as their final object, still serve imperfect creatures. Furthermore, because the object of the contemplative is eternal, such a life is less dependent on outward things; it is more peaceful; has greater continuity with life after death; and is more noble because it exercises the intellect, "the nobler faculty of the soul, which among all living things

62. Ibid., III, 285–308. This letter is published in English translation in *The Earthly Republic: The Italian Humanists on Government and Society*, ed. Benjamin Kohl and Ronald Witt (Philadelphia, 1978), pp. 93–114.

63. *Epist.*, III, 303.

is alone the property of man."[64] Based on an election of the will to rise above the needs of the body, the contemplative life is more elevated than the active life devoted to necessities.

Having conceded the inferiority of the active life to one devoted to intellectual contemplation of divine truth, Salutati swerves in almost the opposite direction. If linked to the acquisition of necessary elements of human existence, the active life is still concerned with virtue; it too opens a way to heaven. As in the *De nobilitate*, where he uses the argument in favor of the superiority of the will to the intellect, Salutati then depicts the final beatitude of man as an act of loving and enjoying, which are functions primarily of the will:

> . . . eternal beatitude is an act, not a possession, and is devoted to loving, viewing and enjoying (frui), and all discursive operations of speculation and contemplation cease in it. Furthermore, when we die, we will see the truth as it is. Would it not, therefore, be appropriate to say that the active life follows the contemplative after death just as the active life precedes it in act while we are alive, since the former produces and begets the latter.[65]

If on earth the active life is inferior to the contemplative in that it deals primarily with daily necessities, after death, when all discursive activities of the mind cease, it is superior. For then we possess God eternally by an act of love.

In practice, however, the two forms of life cannot be sharply separated. The progress of contemplation itself consists in a movement from act to act. The contemplative cannot eschew certain necessary actions of life nor, as a Christian, refuse to help his neighbor work for salvation. Nor should he strive to be without feeling; after all, Christ himself wept. At the same time the Christian devoted to the active life cannot be so absorbed in doing things for God's sake that "he entirely lacks a contemplative element." Salutati cites the careers of Augustine and Jerome to demonstrate that the contemplative life must inevitably be mixed with action, but he stops short of providing a definite conclusion.[66] Rather, as if ignoring all that he said in defense of the active life, in the last lines of the letter he abruptly confesses, "I hope that, if you leave the world in this way, you not abandon me 'in this confused world, attempting to flatter everyone' [the words Zambeccari had used to describe Salutati's situation] as you threaten. The latter words you spoke

64. Ibid., III, 305.   66. Ibid., III, 306.
65. Ibid., III, 305–6.

with great anger. In this case, since I have confidence in you, induce me to follow you or, if I would remain behind, force me by violence to stay with you."[67]

As in the *De fato* the intellect of man remains in this letter the nobler faculty of man, despite the fact that the will now appears to be the dominant force both in human psychology and in the individual's effort to attain salvation. If the final phrases of the letter are dismissed as being more rhetorical than sincerely meant, it would seem that Salutati's last word on the subject of the merit of the two life-styles was that for a Christian they can never exist isolated one from the other but that even the greatest saint has to combine the two. His own life was a demonstration of this flexible position. Historically, however, Salutati was the first European thinker to provide the theoretical framework by which the active life understood as the lay life devoted to public service could be regarded as of at least equal merit with the contemplative life and therefore worthy of pursuit by good Christians.[68] As he wrote to Zambeccari in this letter of 1398:

> Clearly, your fleeing the world can draw your heart from heavenly things to earth and I, remaining in earthly affairs, will be able to raise my heart to heaven. And you, if you provide for and serve and strive for your family and your sons, your relatives and your friends, and your state (which embraces all), then you cannot fail to raise your

67. Ibid., III, 308.

68. By stressing the combination of the two lives, Salutati returns here to Augustine's conception of action and contemplation as two aspects of the same life (*De civ. dei*, VIII, 4). Cf. Robert Bonnell, "An Early Humanistic View of the Active and Contemplative Life," *Italica*, 43 (1966), 225. Gregory the Great's various discussions of the problem could also be interpreted as stressing an integration of the two: J. Leclercq, F. Vandenbroucke, and Louis Bouyer, *A History of Christian Spirituality*, trans. Benedictines of Holmes Eden Abbey, Carlisle, vol. 2 (London, 1968), pp. 10–12.

The Middle Ages tended to conceive of the "active" life within a clerical or monastic context. For example, the problem of the two modes of life was a real one for monastic superiors who had to an extent to engage in action: Jean Laclercq, *Otia monastica*, Studia anselmiana, vol. 51 (Rome, 1963), pp. 96–102. For Aquinas and certainly for others the tendency was to view a mixing of the active and contemplative life as more perfect than the contemplative life alone. In the "mixed life" the individual actively preached and taught those things learned in contemplation. Such a life demonstrated "abundantiam contemplationis:" *ST*, III, q. 40, a. 1 *ad* 2; also IIa, IIae, q. 188, a. 6 *resp*. On this problem in Thomas, see James A. Weisheipl, *Friar Thomas d'Aquino: His Life, Thought, and Work* (New York, 1974), pp. 261–63; and Thomas Gilby, *The Political Thought of Thomas Aquinas* (Chicago, 1958), pp. 164 and 230. Cf. St. Bernard, *Sermones in cantica*, IX, 8, and XLI, 4, 5. Only rarely is the active life discussed as primarily the life of the layman, and then it is found to be clearly inferior to the contemplative life. John Newell, "The Dignity of Man in William of Conches and the School of Chartres in the Twelfth Century" (Ph.D. Diss. Duke, 1978), pp. 148–54, presents William as having a lay conception of the active life although recognizing its inferiority to the contemplative.

heart to heavenly things and please God. Indeed, devoted to these things, you are perhaps more acceptable since you not only claim for yourself the coexisting presence of the first cause: but striving as hard as you can for things necessary to your family, pleasing to your friends, and salubrious for the state, you work together with that same cause that provides for all.[69]

Thus in leading the active life the Christian becomes the willing instrument of divine Providence.[70]

---

69. Ibid., III, 304–5. Note another balancing of the merits of intellect and will, ibid., III, 445–47.

70. This idea is also suggested in the *De nobilitate*, pp. 12 and 14, where Salutati develops the idea of man as *imago Dei*. Widar C. Sforza, "Osservazioni sul 'De nobilitate legum' di Coluccio Salutati," in *Umanesimo e scienza politica*, Atti del congresso internazionale di studi umanistica, ed. E. Castelli (Rome-Florence, 1949), pp. 69–74, maintains that Salutati's conception of law was essentially Thomistic and intellectualist. Thus, he was unable to assert unambiguously the superiority of the active life. In Sforza's opinion, without a voluntaristic view of law that accepted "la realtà effettuale del mondo politico, dove non di rado le ragioni degli uomini, specialmente quelle degli uomini che comandano, contraddicono al modello razionale del bene" (p. 73) there is no solid basis for affirming the superiority of action over contemplation and of will over reason.

Chapter 13. CHRISTIAN ARISTOTELIANISM

In the very month when the *De nobilitate* began to circulate a wave of hysterical piety swept over Florence. Salutati and his family were caught up in the religious fervor connected with the movement of the *Bianchi*, which affected not only Florence but much of Northern Italy.[1] In the beginning of August *Bianchi* coming from Genoa, where the movement was already underway, preached in the city of Lucca. They were to dress in white and for nine days to go in procession, calling aloud for mercy and peace, while forgiving all personal grievances and arbitrating those of other men. As Salutati wrote on August 25, for nine days the penitents were to sleep outside on the ground; eggs and meat were forbidden and only bread and cheese allowed (*Epist.*, III, 358). He had been on hand when the procession, three thousand strong, arrived from Lucca to begin the conversion of Florence. These were "not lowly people, but leaders and notable merchants of that city, all wearing sacred ropes [around their necks] and marked with the crucifix, walking barefooted behind the banner of the cross which they held erect, brandishing in their own hands a whip made of knotted ropes for their own shoulders . . . " (III, 356).

In Florence shops were closed, the churches full and all were busy preparing "sacks for clothes, cords for belts, and ropes for whips" (III, 357). Salutati himself sounded exalted. Only his official duties kept him from leaving through the gate of San Niccolò on August 28 with a mass of Florentine Bianchi under the leadership of the bishop of Fiesole for a nine-day procession to Arezzo and back. On August 30 he reported the occurrence of miracles: "Indeed the blind see, the lame walk, the deaf hear and, except for the grace of resurrection, whatever is read in the Scriptures is as if renewed (*renovatur*). Among other things in four places within our territory the images of the cross shed living blood."[2]

---

1. On the Bianchi, see bibliography in notes of *Epist.*, III, 356–58 and 362–64; for recent bibliography, see Gene Brucker, *Renaissance Florence* (New York, 1969), p. 292; and Vincenzo Lacitra, "Gerardo Anechini cantore dei Bianchi," *Studi medievali*, 10, no. 2 (1969), 399.

2. *Epist.*, III, 362. Francesco Datini, the Merchant of Prato, joined the *Bianchi* at Prato: Iris Origo, *The Merchant of Prato* (London, 1957), pp. 316–19; and David Herlihy, *Medieval and Renaissance Pistoia* (New Haven, 1967), pp. 250–53. Domenico Vittorini, "Salutati's Letters to the Archbishop of Canterbury," *Modern Language Journal*, 36 (1952), 373–77, provides several translations from Salutati's letters on the *Bianchi* written to Thomas Arundel.

Although no direct link between the *Bianchi* movement and the outbreak of the plague in the last half of 1399 has been established,[3] certainly in retrospect the *Bianchi* must have appeared as God's final inducement to sinners to repent before the onslaught of the holocaust that would sweep them to death. Already by the fall of 1399 the plague was raging in Bologna where Pietro da Moglio's widow died of the disease. As Salutati explained to Bernardo da Moglio in a letter of consolation on his mother's death: "As to fear of the plague, I would not say that God plays with us nor is he angry, but rather that, unmoved, untroubled, and tranquil, he punishes our sins" (III, 368). Early in the following year the plague began to take its toll in Florence as well, and the exodus to the country began. As the summer drew on, the *Signoria* found it necessary to hire additional soldiers to protect the almost empty city from surprise attack. But the ravages of the disease were not limited to the capital; smaller towns and the countryside as well suffered heavy losses.

By the beginning of 1400 Bonifazio was already living in the Valdinievole, but the rest of the family remained in Florence. In February Salutati wrote to his friend Pietro Turchi, chancellor of Malatesta dei Malatesta, reporting that his family was well but adding that in any case there was no need to worry: "The plague, which now begins here, makes me feel secure and without fear, not because I am unaware that it might strike me, but since, if it is the will of God, I am certain that I shall be left untouched. If, however, he has perchance decreed it, I know that I would prepare flight and all remedies in vain" (III, 379). During the plague of 1390 Salutati remarked that by that time he had seen five general plagues and one local one (II, 226). As it happened, he and his family survived that of 1390 without incident, but the epidemic of 1400 was not to spare Salutati's house.

On May 23, Salutati requested the privilege to carry weapons for Piero; by the end of May the young man was dead of plague.[4] The father describes his feelings when he first realized that Piero was seriously ill:

3. Alfonso Corradi, *Annali delle epidemie occorse in Italia dalle prime memorie fino al 1850 compilati con varie note e dichiarazioni*, 5 vols. (repr. ed., Bologna, 1973), IV, 96–99, however, suggests such a connection. Salutati himself, months after the *Bianchi* and before the plague struck Florence, ascribed it to God's inspiration (*Epist.*, III, 381–82): "Deus autem vel ad excitandos peccatores vel admonendos vel ad confundendum obstinationem eorum, licet quomodo vel quo consilio; quoniam infinitos habet; id fecerit, sit incertum, auctor vere fuit tante novitatis et devotionis, quam spero bonam et salutiferam tandem fore bonis, licet tante rei nondum videri possit effectus." Although at this point he seemed somewhat sceptical of the value of the movement, the events of the next few months cannot fail to have convinced him that the *Bianchi* were God-inspired and related to the plague.

4. Piero obtained this right on November 22, 1399 (*Tratte*, 315, fol. 19ᵛ), and again on May 23, 1400. For the date of Piero's death, see *Epist.*, III, 396, n. 1.

"the mind, presaging evil, soon saw what was to be and, out of grief and anxiety caused by the magnitude of the imminent evil, prostrated itself before God with a sorrow I have never felt before. I sought piously and humbly that that cup might pass from me" (III, 416). His sense of loss seems absolute: "My Piero, my hope, my delight, my help and the alleviator of my labors, my glory, the support of threatening old age, the column of home and family, on whom this most celebrated city cast its eyes with an almost incredible affection. . . ."

The old man's grief was even more profound than it had been four years before. He searched in vain for consolation in the maxims of the philosophers. Only the Bible finally gave him the peace of mind and the hope he searched for (III, 416 ff.). Summoned to Piero in the final hour, Salutati gave the young man his benediction, without tears or emotion, admonishing him to accept the will of God. Piero responded that, if necessary, he was prepared to die. Extreme unction was administered. Salutati encouraged his assembled family not to resist the will of God and to accept His decree. At Piero's bedside in the moment before death, Salutati writes: " . . . Unmoved I drank in the last breath." With others weeping, Salutati straightened up, closed the eyelids of the corpse, shut the lips together, and composed the arms in the shape of a cross. Then, "looking on his face undistubed by fear, I left the room, I will not say happy, but clearly neither mournful or sad. Praise be to God, who made me act such as I had not thought possible" (III, 421). Less than a month after the death of Piero, Salutati was able to write to his friend, Domenico Bandini, in Arezzo that "not with a sad face but with a sober one, which becomes my age and reputation, I hide not my sorrow but my great joy . . . " (III, 398).

In this second tragedy within four years Salutati had again demonstrated to himself not only the healing power of God's Word but also his own moral stamina. After years of reading and self-discipline he had found in himself the strength he had hoped to have. Rather than collapsing ignominiously in his grief as he had done once before and thus giving the lie to his whole philosophy of life, Salutati felt confirmed in his beliefs. He could surmount any crisis; he was free of fear. Salutati's equanimity in the face of Piero's death became a source of admiration for his own generation to the extent that thirty years after his death Gianozzo Manetti in his eulogy of the chancellor concluded his remarks by narrating Salutati's reaction to this loss in detail, utilizing the incident to illustrate Salutati's "marvelous constancy" (IV, 513).

It was probably at this point that Salutati took the precaution of sending some of his children to the country, keeping only Filippo with him. He gives no justification for moving his family out of the city in the light of his position on the inevitability of divine decrees.[5] Jacopo Angeli went along with them to Stignano to escape the danger of infection and to help Bonifazio and the older children supervise the younger ones. When in July Bonifazio was away from Stignano and Arrigo fell ill, Angeli was there to keep Salutati informed of the condition of his son by daily letters (III, 403–4). Fortunately, Arrigo recuperated but within days Andrea was down with the same disease. By the beginning of August Andrea was dead in Stignano and Filippo in Florence was gravely ill (III, 406). Like Arrigo, however, Filippo survived.

The death of Piero forced Salutati to reexamine some of his traditional notions about death and consolation, virtue and emotion. Actually over the previous decade he had been working toward some of the positions that were ultimately crystallized by this experience of intense grief. Salutati's curious lack of real knowledge of Aristotle's *Nicomachean Ethics* before about 1390 may help to explain in part the Stoic bias of his previous ethical observations.[6] As he came to understand the Peripatetic positions on morality, he felt increasingly attracted by the less heroic demands of an ethic that put the acquisition of virtue within the normal possibilities of man. In his later years Salutati appears to have moved toward formulating some sort of harmonization of Christian and Peripatetic ethics.

The first datable comparison between Stoic and Peripatetic ethics in Salutati's writings appears in a letter written about 1392. The analysis is a product of Salutati's attempt to answer the question of a correspondent as to whether or not anger was a sin.[7] Salutati curiously introduces

5. Ibid., III, 397. He might have justified their move to Stignano on the grounds that the family normally went to the country for the summer.

6. See above, chap. 10, n. 104. The first mention to my knowledge of Aristotle's doctrine of virtue as a medium between two extremes is found in *Epist.*, II, 184, in a letter dated by Novati 1383/89. A date 1388/89 would seem consistent with frequent appearance of this conception in the year immediately after this time: *De verecundia* in *De nobilitate legum et medicinae: De verecundia*, ed. Eugenio Garin, Edizione nazionale dei classici del pensiero italiano, vol. 8 (Florence, 1947), p. 304. Also Salutati's general interest in the Aristotelian conception of virtue only starts with 1390. Subsequently see *Epist.*, III, 431 and 565; and *De nobilitate*, p. 138.

7. My tendency is to relate these remarks on anger to Salutati's concern with obtaining Atumano's Latin translation of Plutarch's *De ira* from Cardinal Corsini in Avignon. In my article "Salutati and Plutarch," *Essays Presented to Myron P. Gilmore*, ed. Sergio Bertelli and Gloria Ramakus, 2 vols. (Florence, 1978), I, 336 ff., I dated his reworking of Autumano's text as finished by May 1392 or 1393. Because the present letter (*Epist.*, II, 307–12) makes no mention of Plutarch's opinions, I would assume it was written before Salutati had received the Plutarch. Unfortunately the letter can only be dated approximately.

the topic with an interpretation of St. Paul's letter to the Ephesians 4:26: "Be angry but do not sin; do not let the sun go down on your anger. . . ."[8] As Salutati understands Paul, there is no sin if one is moved to anger for the sake of justice. Moreover, if angered by a personal offense and one is able to suppress the passion, no mortal sin is committed. He then turns to the difference between the Stoic position, including that of Cicero and Seneca, and the view of Aristotle and his followers.

The Stoics abhor anger together with all other passions as being against reason. When one has perfect virtue, there is in their opinion no struggle with the emotions. Passions simply are not felt. On the other hand, Aristotle maintains that the justification for anger depends on time, place, and other circumstances. Not to show anger when appropriate is to him foolishness (II, 310). As Salutati sees the two positions, the morality of Aristotle is more appropriate for the average man. Denying the possibility of lofty detachment, the Peripatetics accept the likelihood of a struggle between the appetite and the will preceding the performance of virtuous acts. As for the attainment of the Stoic conception of virtue, Salutati avers that perhaps only Jesus Christ possessed this degree of virtue. Nonetheless, simply ignoring the statement of St. Paul, which he represents as fairly close to the views of Aristotle, Salutati concludes: "Thus we are able to say that these [the Peripatetics] spoke according to the common condition and manner of human behavior but that those [the Stoics] came closest to the truth" (II, 311).

In his earlier years Salutati vacillated between endorsing an ethical ideal of apathy and one that admitted at least momentary confusion, even of philosophers, when confronted with an unexpected event. In the former case the virtuous life was one of complete inner peace while in the latter the virtuous man was never quite beyond an occasional struggle with his passions.[9] In one letter of 1382 he implied that in the case of the death of loved ones, such a struggle was a reflection of our nature as human beings, but he merely touched the point incidentally and went on incongruously to define moral perfection as constituted by emotional independence from every external thing.[10] The letter of 1392

8. *Epist.*, II, 310.   9. See chap. 3.
10. Echoing Cicero, *Tusc. disp.* III, 14, 28–31, Salutati writes: "Illam remotam a sensibus nostris fortitudinem seu constantiam, sive, ut verius loquar, inhumanitatem et duriciam semper exhorrui" (*Epist.*, II, 55). While this seems to suggest that Stoic demands are against human nature, the following sentence implies that we have the passions in order that we might become virtuous fighting against them: "Nam si in nobis multum non possent illi primi motus et precipue qui sunt virtuti proximi, non esset tam arduis virtutibus

opts for this more rigorous attitude toward virtue and reinforces its affirmations by making Christ the ideal impassible Stoic sage.

The significance of the letter of 1392, however, lies in the fact that for the first time Salutati was undeniably aware that passions like anger could be approached positively. Both St. Paul and Aristotle maintained that in certain circumstances anger was a justifiable reaction and not simply to be tolerated within limits as an aspect of the weakness of the flesh. Still unable to accept such a positive assessment of a passion, Salutati's response was to dismiss it with the illogical argument that the Peripatetics—St. Paul is forgotten—were providing an ethic appropriate for the common run of mankind.

Repeatedly in these years Salutati expressed his high esteem for Stoic morality as opposed to the more moderate demands of the Peripatetics, who recognized health and affluence as secondary goods. While in Book III of the *De laboribus Herculis* he rejected two of the four leading ancient ethical philosophies, that of the Academics and the Epicureans, and was noncommital about Aristotle's position, he praised the Stoics "who beyond all the others get to the essence of true virtue by sharp arguments and define virtues in themselves rather than seeing them insofar as they relate to man."[11] The Peripatetics, on the other hand, embrace a moral theory that follows common practices more closely and "They admit some passions which all the Stoics detest." In 1393 in writing to Juan Heredia he concedes that the "rigid" morality of the Stoics aims at "a perfection never to be found."[12] But, as has been seen, its impossibility did not deter Salutati from considering it the true conception.

His reference to Christ in his letter to Zambeccari in the spring of 1398 gives an indication that some kind of reevaluation of his ethical views was in progress. In the course of his efforts to encourage Zambeccari not to enter a monastery, Salutati attacked the notion that the contemplative should strive to reach a state of indifference to everything but God.

> Will he be a contemplative so completely devoted to God that disasters befalling a dear one or the death of relatives will not affect him and the destruction of his homeland not move him? If there were such a person, and he related to other people like this, he would

---

locus, quarum maximus splendor est contra difficilia niti." On p. 56 he appears to embrace the rigid Stoic idea of apathy as a goal.

11. *De laboribus Herculis*, ed. Berthold L. Ullman, 2 vols. (Zurich, 1951), I, 311–12.

12. *Epist.*, II, 292.

show himself not a man but a tree trunk, a useless piece of wood, a hard rock and obdurate stone, nor would he imitate the mediator of God and man who represents the highest perfection. For Christ wept over Lazarus and he cried abundantly over Jerusalem, in these things as in others, leaving us an example to follow.[13]

Salutati had written about the patriotism of the sage from the time of his first extant letters and had repeatedly acknowledged the need to tolerate passionate first responses to the onslaughts of fortune.[14] What he had never done before was to recognize the passionate character of the life of Christ. The Son of God became now not the Stoic sage but the lover, emotionally committed to mankind. This vision of Christ, "the highest perfection," served as a focus for Salutati's hesitations about Stoic ethics.

The *De nobilitate* with its emphasis on the centrality of the will in its relationship to *caritas* also played a role in this reevaluation of ethics. Although the word *caritas* appeared countless times in Salutati's work prior to the writing of this work, after its publication *caritas* in its emotional aspect came more to the foreground.[15] Love was recognized as a passion as well as a virtue. Friendship, which Salutati had consistently identified as an aspect of *caritas*, now became a passion as well, one intimately connected with virtue (III, 464).

All of these elements in a new conception of the role of the passions appearing in the 1390s come together in the meditations of the grieving father attempting to understand his own reactions to Piero's death and testing his conclusions against his long-held beliefs. The results of his thinking are revealed in the course of two letters written in August 1400 and February 1401 to Francesco Zabarella, who in an effort to console Salutati had urged him to remember that death was not an evil, that it befell all men, and that it was inevitable.[16] In answering such basically

13. Ibid., III, 305–6; also see *The Earthly Republic. The Italian Humanists on Government and Society*, ed. B. Kohl and R. Witt (Philadelphia, 1978), p. 112.

14. See above, chap. 3.   15. *Epist.*, III, 430.

16. Zabarella wrote two letters to Salutati. The first must have been written in the middle of the summer of 1400 (*Epist.*, IV, 347–49). Salutati's reply, *Epist.*, III, 408–22 (August 30, 1400), was followed by a second letter from Zabarella (*Epist.*, IV, 353–61). Salutati's second letter was written February 21, 1401 (III, 456–79). Cf. summary of contents of Salutati's letters as presented by Alberto Tenenti, *Il senso della morte e l'amore della vita nel Rinascimento (Francia e Italia)* (Turin, 1957), pp. 55–58. Tenenti characterizes Salutati's admission of the legitimacy of feeling fear of death as "un aspetto di tutta una sensibilità in formazione che avrebbe ben presto costituito una base sufficiente per gli uomini che amavano la vita." For Alfred von Martin, *Coluccio Salutati und das humanistische Lebensideal* (Berlin-Leipzig, 1916), p. 88, in this break with the Stoa comes "die ganze innere Unvereinbarkeit

Stoic arguments these letters do not construct an alternative ethical system. But quite clearly, taken together, they demonstrate a tendency in Salutati's thought to move away from Stoicism and toward a more Christian approach to ethics, one heavily buttressed by Peripatetic ideas.

Without essentially changing his often stated opinion on death as a natural, not a moral evil, Salutati was now prepared to argue what he had always strenuously denied: that death, if not a sin and only limited to the natural aspect of the human being, was nonetheless to be feared. Marking as it did the dissolution of man as a composite of soul and body, it was the greatest of natural evils.[17] Despite his previous countless efforts to console others with the doctrine of Cicero and the Stoics that death was not an evil, the old humanist surprisingly confided that he had never considered this doctrine of any value for that purpose.[18] To support his new position, Salutati cited Aristotle *Nic. Eth.* III, 6, 1115a 27–28: "Now death is the most terrible of all things for it is the end. . . ." To require as the Stoics did that this privation of life be neither feared nor lamented was to ask the impossible: "The authority of Aristotle and the moderation of the Peripatetics are of greater validity than that severity, nay that hardness and inaccessible zeal of the Stoics" (III, 463).

Zabarella's first thesis that there can be no good but virtue and no bad but evil furnishes the old humanist with an opportunity to attack this basic Stoic premise as erroneous. Heavenly beatitude, Salutati points out, is certainly a good and the goal of virtue and yet does not itself constitute a virtue (III, 464). Similarly, political security, the aim of justice, is a good without being a virtue. Again, the operation of virtue which the indwelling *habitus* of virtue produces is itself not virtuous but still must be counted among good things. What of friendship? According to Aristotle it is a passion not a virtue but is produced by virtue and coexists with virtue.[19]

---

antiker Innerweltlichkeit und christlicher Überweltlichkeit zum Ausdruck." Nonetheless, as in the case of the death of Salutati's wife (see above, chap. 11, n. 6) von Martin does not think the humanist felt very deeply about his son's death (*Coluccio Salutati*, pp. 175 ff.). Rather he maintains (p. 173) that Salutati demonstrates a "Mangel an tieferem Gefühl und weicheren Empfindungen."

17. *Epist.*, III, 417–18 and 460–63.

18. Ibid., III, 417. In fairness to Salutati it is difficult to know whether he means that he never considered this kind of consolation possible in the early stages of grief or not at all effective. In his earlier letters he appears to think that grief is really weakness and his consolation was intended to work immediately.

19. For Aristotle's conception of friendship, see J. J. Joachim, *Aristotle: The Nicomachean Ethics* (Oxford, 1951), pp. 241–61; and William F. R. Hardie, *Aristotle's Ethical Theory* (Oxford, 1968), pp. 317–35.

He recalls in both letters the figure of Christ, already used against Zambeccari in 1398, to demonstrate his point dramatically. Christ's weeping for Lazarus appears now as only the most significant example of a biblical pattern (III, 413 and 465). Christ's tears were foreshadowed by Adam mourning the death of Abel, Jacob bewailing the loss of Joseph, and David weeping over the body of the perfidious Absalom (III, 413 and 469). When Christ himself was confronted with death, Salutati writes "with what sadness of soul" he prayed God that the cup might pass from him, "for my soul is sad unto death" (III, 464–65). If death was not truly an evil, why was it then that Christ, who had no fear of the second death, broke into a sweat at the thought of his future passion?

As for Zabarella's second point that, because death happens to all, there is no cause for sorrow at personal losses, Salutati responds that death in fact is not equal in that it comes to men at different ages and in different circumstances, nor is meditation on death the same as the confrontation with death itself. Again the example of Christ shows that thinking about imminent death does not produce relief but sadness: "Remember Christ, the greatest of all philosophers [omnium philosophorum maximus] to whom no human being is comparable. As I mentioned above, when he thought about death he broke out in a sweat of blood nor did his sadness disappear."[20] Furthermore, does this method of consolation not imply that we should feel better because others are also suffering? (III, 472). Is it not true that when others are suffering together with us individual grief is compounded by universal misery?

The Stoic insistence on superhuman virtue is no longer a mark of its truth but rather of its falsity. No mortal has ever satisfied such standards of conduct and to do so would make man a stone (III, 468). Cicero's critique of more rigid Stoic doctrine supplies Salutati with some of his most striking statements: "their wisdom is invidious and obscure" (ibid.). "For we have in our hearts," Salutati writes in his first letter quoting Cicero, "something tender and fragile which has never learned to obey reason"[21]

Salutati finds more substance to Zabarella's third point: that it is foolishness to abandon oneself to grief when nothing can be done to change

---

20. *Epist.*, III, 470. As examples of unrestrained weeping despite frequent contact with death Salutati cites Hecuba and Niobe (ibid., III, 469).

21. Ibid., III, 413. Cf. M. Iannizzotto, *Saggio sulla filosofia di Coluccio Salutati* (Padua, 1959), p. 117. Cicero serves frequently in these letters as a support for Salutati's attack on the Stoics, but Cicero's own ambivalence toward the Stoic position made his role in the reevaluation secondary to that of Aristotle among the philosophers.

matters. Initially Salutati responds by pointing out that when a loss is irreparable the grief is greater, not less. This and the other consolations of philosophy simply do not achieve their end. Only time can heal, and it cures even the greatest sufferings without need of philosophic precepts. He subsequently embraces this position but only after approaching it from the supernatural level: "Truly my consolation, which is only in God, who governs all things and disposes them kindly and tenderly and wisely, nay in the wisest possible way—my consolation is prepared aforehand and is felt at the time. Afterwards, moreover, the previous experience is fortified by the constancy of faith."[22] The knowledge that God provides in his infinite wisdom for all things makes it easier to accept one's loss. Nothing can be done about what has occurred, but we should have no wish to have it otherwise: "It is of no consequence or moment whether we die late or soon, since the goal of life is to return to that highest source. Thus it is appropriate to congratulate the dying, not pity them and especially those who are taken away more quickly by a briefer span of life" (III, 478).

In a sense it must seem that Salutati has returned by a different route to his former conclusion about not weeping for the dead or fearing death. Nevertheless, the context in which he urges his remedies for grief has changed. The tension no longer lies between the Stoic standards of moral perfection and the weakness of the flesh but between the Christian belief in an all-disposing God, who extends the glories of paradise to his elect, and the suffering, loving Christ, who asks that the chalice of death pass from him. The range of permissible feelings has been vastly expanded.

Despite its rationalistic basis, Aristotelian ethics had influenced the transition. Salutati's willingness to recognize the legitimacy of certain passions was closely connected with his questioning of the claim of the monastic life to superior value. While the life of withdrawal had traditionally been linked with Stoic thought, Aristotle offered an ethic for laymen, involved with their families and committed to their society. His was an ethic that sought to deal with the emotional aspect of humanity by channeling rather than destroying it. Salutati's ethical conceptions in the last decade of his life, centered as they were on Christian *caritas*, operated at a different level from those of a naturalistic philosophy, but

22. *Epist.*, III, 477–78. His conception of virtue as struggling against forces of fate and fortune is still in *De fato et fortuna*.

they were essentially adapted to the lay life and thus congenial to some of the tendencies of Peripatetic morality.[23]

The correspondence of the last five years significantly contains no letters of consolation, and the previously frequent statement of the view that death was not an evil never recurs.[24] In this same period, moreover, Salutati seems ready to question another Stoic view, one he had unswervingly held throughout his mature life. The Christian tendency of his ethical thought is even more evident here in that Aristotle agreed with the Stoics in their view that without all the virtues one could not

23. I can in no way agree with Luigi Borghi, "La doctrina morale di Coluccio Salutati," *Annali della R. Scuola Normale Superiore di Pisa*, lett. stor. e filos., 2nd ser., 3 (1934), 89, who concludes a long discussion on Salutati's change of attitude toward death as follows: "La virtù, come si è visto, è per Coluccio, cospicua opera umana, che si conquista da noi senza l'influsso nè del fato nè di Dio, nè della natura." Borghi's attempt to ascribe to Salutati the belief that morality is a production of the human spirit with "ogni vestigio soprannaturalistico . . . bandito" (p. 92) is incompatible with Salutati's conservative religious tendencies. I see no basis for Borghi's voluntaristic interpretation of Salutati's morality as "decidedly heterodox and revolutionary" (ibid.).

24. His last letter of consolation was written between the two letters to Zabarella on September 9, 1400, to his young friend ser Pietro di ser Lorenzo da Montevarchi (*Epist.*, III, 422–33). In the awkwardly formulated letter Salutati appears very indecisive about how to go about his task of consoling the young man. First of all, he makes very clear as he says in the second letter to Zabarella that time must pass after a loss for reason to be restored (*Epist.*, III, 426). His basic argument is that because death is not a moral evil it cannot harm the good. It serves rather as a punishment for the bad and should only be feared by them. Although he says nothing about its being a natural evil, the conclusion follows a similar argument in his second letter to Zabarella: " . . . mortem naturaliter malum esse, moraliter vero bonam, si contingat bonis . . . malamque malis . . . " (*Epist.*, III, 462–63). The letter to ser Piero attacks the Stoic dictum that it would have been best not to have been born (*Epist.*, III, 431) but embraces the *meditatio mortis* for its efficacy in reducing fear of death. While he had spoken briefly against this kind of consolation in the first letter to Zabarella (*Epist.*, III, 418–19), he dealt with its ineffectiveness at length in the second (*Epist.*, III, 466–75). Although one cannot maintain that a clearly formulated anti-Stoic morality emerges from the Zabarella letters, it is fair to say that such a tendency is at work. This letter to ser Pietro, consequently, represents a kind of transition period when Salutati is really unsure of the value of consolatory letters as he had been writing them. I cannot accept the view of Jerrold Seigel (*Rhetoric and Philosophy in Renaissance Humanism* [Princeton, 1968], p. 73) that this letter to ser Pietro is "in total contradiction to what he (Salutati) had written ten days earlier, and would repeat five months later. . . ." Von Martin's position is essentially that of Seigel (*Coluccio Salutati*, p. 165). Nor do I agree with Seigel's conclusion that "Salutati could embrace or reject philosophical doctrines as the occasion demanded." Armando Petrucci (in *Coluccio Salutati*, Bibliotheca biographica, vol. 7 [Rome, 1972], p. 80), however, is literally correct when he remarks that the letters to Zabarella constitute an "isolato accenno" to the new view on death since Salutati never returns to the subject in later letters.

Of course, in his official capacity Salutati continued to dictate consolatory letters after 1400. See the passage of the letter sent to Antonio Visconti Manovello di Appiano in 1404 on the death of Gherardo Leonardo d'Appiano cited by Daniela De Rosa, "Il concetto della storia nel pensiero di Coluccio Salutati," *Sapienza*, 32 (1979), 474. The essential message is that we must believe that God wills what is best for us.

be truly virtuous and that such a status of virtue was attainable by man.[25]

In a letter written during his last years Salutati avers that the attainment of prudence, which requires possession of all the virtues, is possible only through the action of God's grace. Not only Christ but also the holy fathers and martyrs inspired by divine grace attained this perfection: "Not only did they bear torments patiently but . . . they fearlessly awaited death despite its terrible aspect; nay, what is more, they voluntarily rushed to it since they were not called upon to die and could have fled" (III, 660). However, just at this point where a Christian Stoicism is emerging, not the figure of the weeping Christ but that of St. Paul comes to mind: "However, just as I would not deny that perfect virtue was in them, I would not affirm that they possessed the virtues consummately when the greatest of the apostles wrote of himself: 'I am carnal, sold under sin.' And a little afterwards: 'For I delight in the law of God in my inmost self, but I see in my members another law at war with the law of my mind.'" Certainly this condition is not that of one who ought to be regarded as consummately "virtuous." Therefore, speaking of the virtue of virtues he concludes, either consummate prudence is a product of divine grace or it cannot be attained by man in this life. Salutati himself leans toward the latter alternative:

> For who is so endowed with the eyes of the lynx and of such a perspicacious and powerful intellect that he knows how to give form to present events on the basis of the past or establish rules for future ones? We are, however, able to be more or less participants in this virtue [that is, prudence] and thus it happens that one man is considered more prudent than another (III, 660).

If tone be emphasized rather than specific coincidence on a wide range of doctrines, Salutati was working out his own brand of Christian Aristotelianism in his last years. Furthermore, his growing respect for Aristotle's ethics since the early 1390s had a striking effect on at least one of

---

25. *Epist.*, III, 657–61 (January 15, 140?). Also see ibid., III, 560–61, on the necessity of divine grace for perfect virtue. For Aristotle's position, see *Nic. Eth.*, I, 13, 1102b 13–26; III, 12, 1119b 15–16. Without all the virtues, man for Aristotle was only continent. It is very possible, however, that Salutati did not understand Aristotle's position on this issue. On the two passages of Aristotle, see the commentary in Réné Gauthier and Jean Jolif, *L'éthique à Nicomaque: Introduction, Traduction et Commentaire*, 2 vols.-in-3 (Louvain-Paris, 1958–59), II, 1:95–96 and 1:250. For the general position of Aristotle on the issue of moral weakness, see James J. Walsh, *Aristotle's Conception of Moral Weakness* (New York-London, 1963) and William F. R. Hardie, *Aristotle's Ethical Theory* (Oxford, 1968), 258–93.

his disciples, Leonardo Bruni, and perhaps on others. Bruni's approach to Aristotle's ethical doctrine, however, was very different. He regarded it as a natural system appropriate for the lay life and divorced from the theological superstructure into which it had been incorporated piecemeal by Salutati. Precisely this self-imposed limitation to the natural world constituted the fundamental distinction between Trecento and Quattrocentro Florentine humanism. Yet this very ability to distinguish the theological from the natural realm was a result in part of Salutati's own work.

Chapter 14. POLITICS, HISTORY, AND THE SANCTITY OF MEDIEVAL TRADITIONS

The messenger who brought Salutati's first letter of August 31, 1400, to Zabarella in Padua, carried with him the short treatise, *De tyranno*, dedicated to a certain Antonio da Aquila, a student in the Paduan *Studio* and very likely a disciple of Zabarella.[1] Probably written in summer when the ravages of the plague brought official business almost to a halt and Salutati's duties in the chancery were few, the treatise was the kind of constructive assignment he needed while recovering from the loss of Piero and Andrea. Sitting in the study of the almost deserted house, the noises of the burial carts rising from below through the open windows, Salutati composed his reply to questions contained in a letter from Antonio, who for all he knew had already fallen victim in Padua to an epidemic which in Florence almost matched the mortal intensity of the plague of 1348.

Antonio had asked two questions.[2] The second was, Were Antenor and Aeneas traitors to Troy? The nature of the first was not specifically stated, but according to the structure of Salutati's reply it most probably was, Were Cassius and Brutus traitors to Rome? (*De tyranno*, p. viii). Like the second the first question concerned the problem of treason, but, unlike the second, it involved a very delicate issue for a Florentine, Was Dante right or wrong to place the two murderers of Caesar in the

---

1. Throughout this book I have utilized Alfred von Martin's edition of the *De tyranno: Coluccio Salutatis Traktat vom Tyrannen* (Berlin, 1913). A second edition was made by F. Ercole, *Tractatus de tyranno von Coluccio Salutati* (Berlin, 1914). Also found in Ercole's *Coluccio Salutati. Il trattato De tyranno e lettere scelte* (Bologna, 1942) with Italian translations. An English translation of the work was done with introduction by E. Emerton in his *Humanism and Tyranny, Studies in the Italian Trecento* (Cambridge, Mass., 1926). For further bibliographical information on the text, refer to Hans Baron, *The Crisis of the Early Italian Renaissance*, rev. ed. (Princeton, 1966), p. 497. The analysis of the *De tyranno* in this chapter is substantially taken from my article, "The *De Tyranno* and Coluccio Salutati's View of Politics and Roman History," *Nuova rivista storica*, 53 (1969), 434–74. At the end of his letter to Zabarella he refers to the work (*Epist.*, III, 422). Antonio appears to have died before the treatise arrived in Padua (ibid., III, 479). Where English translations are given in the text, I provide the pagination of both von Martin's edition and the Emerton translation.

2. At the conclusion of the treatise, Salutati refers to his answer "super utraque dubitatione" (*De tyranno*, p. lxi). That the second question concerned Antenor and Aeneas is clear from the text: "Postremo nunc restat quod de Antenore dubitas et Enea, paucis, sicut promisimus, expedire" (ibid., p. lix).

lowest depths of Hell? Furthermore, to judge the act of Cassius and Brutus and hence the opinion of Dante, one must first determine whether Caesar had been the father of his country or merely a tyrant. If the father of his country, then Caesar was unjustly killed and his murderers justly damned. If, on the other hand, he had been a tyrant, then before acquitting Brutus and Cassius of murder, one had still to decide whether tyrannicide was justified. Even preliminary to this discussion, a definition of tyranny was required. Consequently, in reply to the Paduan student's questions on treason, Salutati first directed himself to a consideration of the problem of tyranny, a procedure doubtless influencing his choice of title for the treatise.

Essentially the *De tyranno* is a literary work designed as a defense of the immortal Dante's reputation.[3] Salutati wrote both as a lover of the poet's work and as a Florentine citizen who felt one of the great glories of his city under attack. But to defend Dante Salutati realized he must justify the poet's assessment of Caesar's career, a topic of intense controversy in the Middle Ages. Also involved was contradicting some of his own earlier statements about the Roman dictator.

Thinkers of the thirteenth and fourteenth centuries felt highly ambivalent about the figure of Caesar. His military prowess, his intelligence, his clemency made him very attractive. As founder of the empire under which, ideally at least, Europe still lived and as the immediate predecessor of Augustus in whose reign Christ was born, Caesar seemed to the men of these centuries an instrument of God. Realistic thinkers, moreover, could look back to the corruption of the republican state and regard Caesar as having offered the only hope for Rome. Yet considered as the author of the civil wars, which took the lives of hundreds of thousands of citizens, and as the dictator who by dubious means rose to supreme power in the state, Caesar was certainly objectionable to the medieval mind.[4]

---

3. Ercole arrived at the conclusion that the primary purpose behind the work was to establish the "legittimità e la opportunità del guidizio dantesco." See his "Coluccio Salutati e il supplizio dantesco di Bruto e Cassio," *Bulletino della Società dantesca italiana*, n.s., 21 (1914), 128. Baron, *The Crisis*, p. 164, makes the same judgment. Armando Petrucci, *Coluccio Salutati*, Biblioteca biographica, vol. 7 (1972), p. 91, while admitting that it is in part a defense of Dante, argues that the defense of Caesar's rise to power must be seen in relationship with the oligarchic character of Florentine government in 1400. For Petrucci Salutati wished to "rivendicare la legittimità e la provvidenzialità di un regime politico che, in una qualsiasi legale forma istituzionale, garantisce la concordia fra i cittadini, il rispetto della legge, l'ordinata ed indiscussa prevalenza nell' ordinamento dello Stato dei 'boni viri'."

4. My "The *De tyranno*," 443–45, provides bibliography for ancient and medieval sources critical of Caesar to supplement the largely favorable accounts of the "mantle of Caesar"

When Dante chose to place Brutus and Cassius in the depths of *Inferno* and Caesar in the highest region, therefore, he was taking sides on an issue of long standing. Indeed, occasionally in remarking on the various passages involving Caesar (like *Inf.*, IV, 123, *Inf.*, XXXIV, or *Par.*, VI) Trecento commentators on the *Divina commedia* themselves reflect various adverse opinions in their remarks. The partially completed commentary of Boccaccio, in fact, appears to have been the immediate source of Antonio da Aquila's doubt about the wisdom of Dante's assignment of places in *Inferno* to the dictator, his murderers, and Aeneas and Antenor.

Unfortunately, Boccaccio's analysis of the *Commedia*, made at the very end of his life, was not set down beyond the close of Canto XVI of the *Inferno*.[5] His comment on the central passage, Canto XXXIV, consequently, is not known and perhaps was never made. What remains of the work, however, is sufficient to permit us to say that, while in other works expressing either a favorable or ambivalent attitude toward the Roman dictator,[6] Boccaccio in the *Commento* is clearly no friend of Caesar. In his comment on *Inf.*, II, Boccaccio identifies Caesar as "he who violently seized all the government of the state."[7] Commenting on *Inf.*, IV, 123, after describing the circumstances of Caesar's origin, the great qualities he possessed (courage, military ability, eloquence, the gift of poetry, and the virtue of clemency), and his great vice of lust, Boccaccio goes on to describe how Caesar "seized the state and against the laws of Rome made himself perpetual dictator."[8] He also demanded the right to wear the laurel wreath continually (Boccaccio sarcastically says this was to cover up his baldness). Because Caesar wanted to become king, he was slain by a conspiracy in the Senate.

A few pages later Boccaccio faces up to the question of why Caesar and some of the others mentioned in *Inf.*, IV, were placed in such respectable quarters in Hell:

> And within the castle he places Aeneas, who, according to Virgil's testimony, lived for some time with Dido with little honor, and who

found in A. Graf, *Roma nella memoria e nelle immaginazioni del Medio Evo*, 2 vols. (Torino, 1882–83), I, 248 ff.; E. G. Parodi, "Le storie di Cesare nelle letteratura italiana del primo secolo," *Studi di filologia romanza*, 4 (1889), 237–503; and F. Gundolf, *Caesar, Geschichte seines Ruhms* (Berlin, 1925).

5. *Il comento alla Divina Commedia*, ed. D. Guerri, Scrittori d'Italia, vols. 84–86 (Bari, 1918). For adverse opinions on Caesar in earlier Dante commentators, see my "The 'De tyranno,'" pp. 445–46.

6. In his *De casibus illustrium virorum* (Paris, 1539), fol. 67ᵛ, Boccaccio refers to the murder of Caesar as a "parricidium."

7. *Il commento*, I, 205.   8. Ibid., II, 49.

besides in the opinion of most people plotted with Antenor the betrayal of Ilion, his city (a deed not only foul but also most sinful). There he also places Caesar, who, as has been shown, was incestuous, basely deflowered many women, robbed and emptied the Roman public treasure and, what is more, tyrannically seized the government of the state and held it while he lived.[9]

Boccaccio then proceeds to question the reason for the presence of Lucretia and Saladin, individuals also guilty of great sins, in this region of *Inferno*.

How to resolve what appears to be a contradiction in Dante's arrangement? Boccaccio's answer is that Dante chose these famous figures because they were known to all men as having certain definite virtues. The poet placed them where he did to symbolize these virtues and for artistic purposes he forgot the vices of which they were guilty.[10]

While this justification of Dante's decision might have saved the poet from some criticism, it was not sufficient to quiet the concern of those interested in knowing whether or not Caesar in fact had been a tyrant and whether both Antenor and Aeneas had been traitors. Boccaccio clearly seems to say that the real individuals were actually traitors. Twenty years later Antonio da Aquila, probably struck by the disparity between the views of Dante and those of his most famous commentator, wrote to Salutati to resolve his doubts about Dante's judgment.

Perhaps outspoken criticism of Dante's judgment on Caesar was in circulation decades before Salutati took up his pen to defend the great Florentine poet. Benvenuto da Imola, Boccaccio's disciple, in his own commentary on *Inf.*, XII, might be alluding to specific accusations when he writes: "Come now and prefer Alexander to Caesar if you can; or ask why Dante did not place Caesar here (in the Seventh Circle, place of the violent against God), who besides his many other great virtues was a very sober man. . . ."[11] The justification of Alexander's fate for Benvenuto seems to be that not only was he violent to his enemies but also, when drunk, he raged against his friends. Caesar, Benvenuto is saying,

9. Ibid., II, 87.   10. Ibid., II, 87–88.

11. Benvenuto da Imola, *Commentum super Dantis Aldigherii Comoediam*, ed. J. P. Lacaita, 5 vols. (Florence, 1887), I, 407. The question of Caesar's tyranny here might have been raised because of the implications of Pietro d'Alighieri's commentary on *Inf.*, XII. Although Pietro does not accuse Caesar of tyranny, nonetheless, in speaking of violent tyrants, he quotes lines from Lucan's *Pharsalia*, II, 439–40: "Caesar, in arma furens, nullas nisi sanguine fusco / Gaudet habere vias . . .": *Pietri Allegherii, Super Dantis ipsius genitoris comoediam commentarium*, ed. V. Nannucci (Florence, 1845), p. 153. It would have been natural for some critic reading Pietro's commentary to ask why Caesar was not put in the circle of the violent.

was not a drunkard or a violent man and should not be compared with Alexander. Possibly Benvenuto, aware that a charge has been made against Dante for his failure to place Caesar in this circle together with Alexander, is attempting to defend Dante's decision.

His own attitude to Caesar is, nevertheless, as ambiguous as that of most of his contemporaries. While emphasizing at various points in his analysis the idea that God ordained the creation of the Roman monarchy and that Caesar's death was "most unworthy," at others he expresses opposite feelings just as strongly.[12] Speaking of Caesar's assault on the state, for example, Benvenuto writes: " . . . but the arms of Caesar, up to this point magnificent and glorious, now became impious and unjust because nothing can excuse their use against the motherland" (*Commentum*, IV, 438). A few pages later he continues his indictment of Caesar:

> Just as Livy says of Hannibal, Caesar had vices equal to his great virtues and he did many terrible things because of his desire to rule. In his consulate, having expelled his colleague Bibulus with force, he did all things according to his will and before this he had tried to alter the state of things in the city in many ways that he might come to power. He alone was the defender of the conspirators of Cataline; he was the refuge of all the guilty ones when he said that such things were natural in civil wars. Twice he despoiled the treasury of Rome, the first time fraudulently, the second time by force. He bought the high priesthood for a great sum of money; he made himself perpetual dictator, nay, as Lucan says, all things belonged to Caesar (IV, 446).

Earlier in the *Purgatorio* Benvenuto explains that Metellus, the tribune who barred the way to Caesar into the treasury, is called "the good" "because he dared to thwart Caesar, the violator of liberty" (II, 272). Benvenuto, moreover, is ostensibly pained to have to identify as Marcus Brutus that Brutus who is between the jaws of Satan, for Marcus Brutus was a man of great soul and literary genius: "However, to me it seems that this ought to be understood as Decimus Brutus" (II, 560).

This then is the background against which Salutati's own remarks on Caesar are to be judged. Like every other writer of the Middle Ages, Salutati never wavered in his condemnation of many of the Roman emperors as tyrants: Caligula and Nero especially were branded along with

12. See references in Hans Baron, *The Crisis* pp. 153–55.

Dionysius and Tarquin as paradigms of tyranny. In the case of Caesar, however, Salutati displayed the usual ambivalence. Although in the War of the Eight Saints he might have criticized the Caesars as a group,[13] he made no direct criticism of Caesar as an individual. Characteristic of Salutati's mixed sentiments of admiration and disapproval is a reference to Caesar in a letter written to Francesco Guinigi of Lucca in December 1374:

> Caesar himself, who criminally invaded the Republic . . . never attained such a great and undisputed glory from an infinity of victories as he acquired from the clemency shown to his conquered enemies, despite danger to himself, and from his conservation of citizens' lives. For this reason he was called first father of the homeland [*primus pater patrie*]: for this reason his clemency was said to have conquered victory itself.[14]

In this passage there seems to be no incongruity between Caesar's having usurped power in the Roman state and his rightful claim to the title of *pater patriae*.

In much the same way a second passage taken from a letter written nine years later gives evidence of a confusion of attitudes. "But the dictator Caesar," Salutati writes, "whose goal, like that of other Romans, was love of the homeland and an immense desire for praise, after the Gauls had been conquered, Pompey vanquished and killed and the Senate overcome, and after the state and the homeland had been subjected, . . . is said to have frequently stated—as if he were tired of living—'I have done with nature and have enough glory.' "[15] Salutati seems to feel no inconsistency involved in ascribing a love of country to Caesar at the same time as he describes his destruction of the Roman state. Obviously Salutati was pulled in two directions by his recognition on the one hand of Caesar's outstanding personal qualities and on the other of the great ambition of the dictator which led him to try to overthrow the much admired Republic.

The manner in which Salutati's rediscovery of the *Epistolae familiares* in 1392 stirred up republican feelings in the humanist has already been mentioned in chapter 10. His republican fervor also found its way into Florentine propaganda when in 1394 in a public letter to Genoa he severely criticized Caesar together with Augustus: both are presented as

13. "The 'De tyranno,' " p. 452.   15. Ibid., II, 195.
14. *Epist.*, I, 197.

marking "the beginning of perpetual servitude."[16] Salutati used the reference to warn Genoa of the evils of civil disturbances and the possible outcome in tyranny.

Connected with his branding of the Principate as introducing Rome to servitude and his criticism of Caesar as the "patricida patrie" was Salutati's first mention of details surrounding the assassination of Caesar.[17] Up to this time he had never even mentioned the names of Brutus and Cassius, his murderers. In a letter assigned by Novati to 1392–94, in the process of justifying Cicero's participation in politics, Salutati referred to Cato and Brutus as having committed themselves to the Civil War but on opposing sides. Brutus had fought faithfully for Caesar against Pompey, but "it is clear that with the victory inclining to Caesar at Emathia, Brutus thought of encompassing his murder, inasmuch as he saw that the one whom he was unable either by advice or force to restrain from being a tyrant, he might at least impede by the knife." Salutati's conclusion, however, was that Brutus' goal was to be frustrated. Quoting Virgil (Aen., VIII, 334), he writes: "'Omnipotent fortune and ineluctable fate' as the events showed, stood in the way."[18]

Not only was this the first time that Salutati had mentioned the murder of the Roman, but it was also the first occasion on which he had introduced into his remarks on Caesar a suggestion that supernatural forces influenced his career. The source behind Salutati's statement on the fateful career of Brutus was obviously Lucan, whose Pharsalia he quoted twice in the discussion.[19] Nonetheless, when Salutati again referred to Caesar's murder a few years later, the pagan ideas of fate and fortune had been Christianized, and Brutus' designs were shown to have been impeded by the Christian God. This was Dante's influence.

On two previous occasions Salutati himself asserted the Roman domination of the world to have been ordained by God, but he had not associated that rule specifically with the creation of the office of emperor nor had he tried to elucidate God's purpose in granting the Romans such power.[20] It was unquestionably Dante's brilliant poetic ren-

16. Miss., 23, fol. 180ᵛ: "Quid enim fuerunt Cesaris vel Octavii dominatus nisi principium perpetue servitutis."

17. See chap. 10.   18. Epist., III, 26.

19. Salutati believed that Lucan's verses in Phar. referred to Decimus rather than Marcus Brutus (see n. 22 below). Particularly important in Lucan's presentation of Brutus as a figure marked by destiny is Phar., VII, 586–96.

20. In a missive written in 1378 (B.R.F., 786, fol. 142), Salutati had written to the Romans: "In exaltationem Romani nominis et augmentum fidey Christiane infinita illa sapientia increata, que celestia, terrestia et inferna gubernat, immensa sua bonitate dispo-

dering of a tradition going back to Orosius in the fifth century, together with his own dramatic additions, which was in time to provide Salutati with an interpretation of the significance of the murder.[21] Dante's vision of Brutus and Cassius writhing with Judas in the mouths of Satan and of the imperial eagle soaring in Paradise was by stages to become Salutati's own.

The *De fato* represents the first stage in this development. In Book I Salutati introduces the murder of Caesar in connection with a discussion of the existence of spiritual powers like angels and demons. As an illustration Salutati cites the tradition that two angels or *genii* are assigned to each man, one encouraging the individual to good, the other to evil. Referring to ancient historians—actually Lucan's *Pharsalia* remains a prime source for him—the author offers the example of Decimus Brutus, who in the middle of the night was confronted with a terrifying apparition which identified itself as Brutus' evil genius. This encounter supposedly occurred at the very time Brutus was contemplating the murder of Caesar. Salutati consequently implies that Brutus' plan was inspired by an evil force. Brutus embarked upon a plan which would backfire, in that thinking by the death of Caesar to remove tyranny from the state, he opened the way to an introduction of tyranny.[22]

---

suit ut urbs Romana, quam armorum viribus sibi prefecerat, sedis apostolice sedes esset, ut sicut ab ea temporaliter omnia regebantur sic in eadem urbe universa fidelium multitudo ecclesie sancte caput cum devotione requireret et, ydolorum superstitione ac abominatione sublata, verum deum humiliter adoraret." In his *De seculo et religione*, ed. Berthold L. Ullman (Florence, 1957), p. 18, Salutati writes: " . . . cum Romanis, inquam, quorum auspiciis, ut gentili utar vocabulo, dominatus orbis dispositione celestis numinis debebatur. . . ." These general references to divine influence on the Romans are suggestive of Augustine's analysis in the *De civitate dei*, Bk. V, but Salutati's belief that the Roman Empire was a part of God's holy scheme for establishing and diffusing the Faith is either ultimately borrowed from Orosius' *Historiarum adversum paganos*, VI, 22, Corpus scriptorum ecclesiasticorum latinorum, vol. 5 (Vienna, 1882), pp. 426–28, or reflects a misunderstanding of Augustine. See Robert A. Marcus, *Saeculum: History and Society in the Theology of St. Augustine* (Cambridge, 1970), pp. 45–71, for a discussion of Augustine's desacralization of Roman history. Although Augustine believed divine Providence governed human history, he saw no direct connection between developments in Roman history and God's plan for the salvation of the world through Christ.

21. For a discussion of the origins of the legend that the foundation of the imperial office was decreed by God as fitting preparation for the advent of Christ, see Charles T. Davis, *Dante's Idea of Rome* (Oxford, 1957), pp. 57–68. Davis' analysis contrasts Orosius' conception of the role of Rome with that of Augustine and traces the legend in its development to the time of Dante.

22. *Vat. lat.*, 1184, Tr. I, 2, fol. 5: "Volebant etiam duos cuilibet homini traditos angelos, quos etiam genios appellabant; quorum unus hortaretur ad bonum, alter autem inclinaret in malum. Unde et gentilium testantur hystorie, vigilanti Decimo Bruto, qui morte Cesaris tollere tyrannidem de re publica cogitans, successioni tyrannidis aditum patefecit, horrendam noctu se imaginem obtulisse, cuius aspectu perterrito, cum interrogasset quisnam foret, respondisse dicitur 'genium tuus malus' et ex vestigio disparuisse."

The same historical event reappears in Tract II, this time in illustrating the congruency between divine omnipotence and man's free will. God had foreseen and willed from the beginning of time that Brutus would slay Caesar. Yet at the same time Brutus' resolve to kill him and his execution of the plot were acts of Brutus' free will. His action was not forced but was voluntary. Salutati's discussion of free will in the *De fato* was, moreover, only one aspect of the larger problem of the existence of contingency in the universe, and in the matter of the murder he argues that not only was Brutus' will contingent but it was possible for Caesar to have died in other ways. Someone else besides Brutus could have struck the fatal blow; Caesar might have died of sickness or on the battlefield. Of course, God not only determined that Caesar would die, but how and when; nonetheless, Salutati maintains, in a sense these alternatives were still possible if unrealized.[23]

But can Salutati really intend to argue that God wanted to establish a tyranny, a conclusion abhorrent to the minds of medieval men? Without facing up to the issue directly, he implies an answer to this question in Tract IV. After a long quotation from Dante regarding the all-powerful force of God's Providence, the humanist analyzes the battle of Thessalia in these terms.[24] While it is true, he writes, that those who utilize their reason to provide for eventualities are generally less subjected to fortune than those who do not, nevertheless, there are times when, despite all efforts made, men's plans are upset by the will of God, called fortune or Providence. In the battle of Thessalia Brutus and Cassius had the largest forces and were the most likely to win the struggle. Yet, because of what seemed chance happenings, their army was defeated and their cause lost to Anthony and Octavian. Salutati's comment on the victory of the latter restates, within the context of his general discussion of fate, fortune, and chance, a traditional medieval view and one taken directly from Dante:

> But with the divine will deciding that at the coming of the true king, His son, the world would be under one prince of princes and, since the disposition of God was the power behind the attention of worldly affairs—about which our Dante says: "Your wisdom has no means of countering her; she foresees, judges, and pursues her reign, no less god, than the gods who reign elsewhere"—I say this disposition of God ordained all matters of the civil war toward the goal of a future

23. *Vat. lat.*, 2928, Tr. II, 7, fols. 10ᵛ–11ᵛ and Tr. II, 8, fols. 13–14.
24. Ibid., Tr. III, 12, fols. 72ᵛ–73ᵛ.

monarchy so that by chance and beyond the intention of the actors those things occurred that led to the end of the senatorial regime.[25]

To judge from the conclusion of the passage, Brutus' murder of Caesar opened the door not to tyranny but to legitimate monarchy, and the way was thus clear for defending God from the charge of having punished a hero trying to protect the world from tyranny. But Salutati does not develop this approach. Rather the *De fato et fortuna* in 1396 leaves the problem unresolved: Brutus' reputation as the defender of republican liberty remains untarnished at the same time as the Christian God appears to have utilized the human actors to bring into being a one-man rule of the world state.

Over the next four years the influence of Dante on Salutati continued to increase. In 1399 his correspondence indicates that the Florentine humanist was in search of a more accurate copy of the *Commedia* than was available in Florence. On October 2, 1399, in a letter to Niccolò di Tuderano, at the time in the service of the Polenta of Ravenna, Salutati requested his correspondent to locate a manuscript of Dante once in the possession of Menghino Mezzani, Cardinal of Ravenna, who had been a protector of the poet.[26] Although the works of Petrarch and Boccaccio, recently deceased, were already filled with errors of the amanuenses, he wrote, the *Commedia* was far worse because written in the *volgare* and open to distortion by more unskilled people. He also hoped to be able to have a commentary of the poem supposedly written by the cardinal himself. Because Mezzani's library had been taken over by the Polenta, Salutati hoped that Niccolò could locate the volumes he wanted.

In the spring of the following year he again corresponded with Niccolò, this time partly to express his pleasure that Niccolò had offered to undertake the investigation: " . . . if you accomplish this and it is what I think, I will count it not among the least gifts of happiness, since I do not know what more pleasurable thing can happen to me."[27] At the very

25. Ibid., fol. 73ᵛ: "Sed, decernente divini numinis voluntate, quod in adventu veri regis filii sui mundus sub uno principum principe regeretur et esset dei dispositio mundanarum rerum versatrix de qua noster Dantes inquit: illi nulla quidem sapientia vestra resistit. Hec iubet; hecque suum diiudicat exequiturque regnum prout alii moderamina tradita divi. Hec, inquam, dei dispositio cuncta illa bella civilia in future monarchie fastigium ordinavit ut illa fortuito et preter agentium intentionem contingerent quibus senatorius desineret principatus." For the Dante citation (*Inf.*, VII, 85–87), see above chap. 11, n. 65. See the excellent discussion of Daniela De Rosa, "Il concetto della storia nel pensiero di Coluccio Salutati." *Sapienza*, 32 (1979), 471–73.

26. *Epist.*, III, 371–75.   27. Ibid., III, 383.

end of the letter he returned to remind Niccolò of the importance of the two manuscripts for him. There can be no mistaking the passion with which the words are expressed: "Finally, however, I beg you again and again about Dante. If you knew and could see my feeling, you would perceive how my whole being burns, nor would you be long in furnishing me aflame the liquid of hoped-for grace. 'Quam michi cum dederis cumulata morte remittam!'"[28] There is no indication that Salutati's wishes were satisfied, but by that summer he was again writing a second more extensive defense of Dante in the *De tyranno*.

The continuing rise of Caesar's stature in the humanist's eyes related intimately to Salutati's growing attachment after 1396 to the figure and the writings of Dante. In a letter to Astorgio Manfredi written in February 1398, Salutati gave evidence of a definite shift in his interpretation of Julius Caesar and this paved the way for a solution of the conflicting interpretations of the events surrounding Caesar's murder voiced in the *De fato*.[29] While Salutati refers to Caesar as having attained the *dominium* in Rome "with the native country granting power," he speaks of his murder as "the sacrilege of Brutus."[30] Moreover, Salutati adds, Caesar did many good things for the citizens including his ungrateful slayers. Apparently by this time Salutati is moving toward a position that would allow him to justify Caesar's rule as legitimately established and which, consequently, would rob Brutus' act of its dignity. This was the approach of the *De tyranno*.

The treatise is divided into six parts, each designed to answer a different problem: (1) Who is a tyrant? (2) Is it lawful to kill a tyrant? (3) Was Caesar a tyrant? (4) Was Caesar justly killed? (5) Was Dante justified in placing the murderers of Caesar in Hell? (6) Were Antenor and Aeneas traitors to Troy?

A statement on the nature of tyranny from the *Magna moralia* of Gregory the Great occupies a central place in Salutati's effort to arrive at a definition of tyranny, and in it he distinguishes two general types of tyranny, the one of character, the other of action:

> Properly speaking a tyrant is one who rules a state without the forms of law (*non jure*), . . . but everyone who rules arrogantly (*superbe*) exercises a tyranny of his own sort. Sometimes a person may practice this in a state through an office which he has received, another in a province, another in a city, another in his own house, and another

28. Ibid., III, 388. The quotation is a version of Virgil, *Aen.*, IV, 436.
29. *Epist.*, III, 260–62.   30. Ibid., III, 260.

through concealed malignity, within his own heart. God does not ask how much evil a man does, but how much he would like to do.[31]

Salutati is careful to specify that he is concerned only with the second sort of tyranny, that of action. Obviously for him tyrannical impulses of the heart that remain unexpressed in action transcend the categories of law and politics. Then follows a discussion of Gregory's views on tyrannical action. According to Salutati, Gregory suggests the existence of three forms of tyranny, each corresponding to one of the three legitimate forms of government, the royal, the constitutional or the political, and the despotic: "Now in these several forms of government, the arrogant ruler becomes a tyrant, and that is the meaning of these words of Gregory . . . " (De tyranno, p. xiii: p. 77).

The next sentence is important for its contrast with Salutati's position on monarchy later in the treatise: "For he describes first the legitimate royal power in a state, then the constitutional in a province or a city and then the despotic in one's own house." Attributing definite forms of governments to the various levels of political life, Salutati assigns the royal to the level of the respublica, the political or constitutional to that of the province or the city, and the despotic to the level of the house. Interestingly, there is nothing in Gregory's words to suggest that he had such a distinction in mind: Gregory speaks of levels of government but not of appropriate constitutions for each. One can assume that revealed in this gloss is Salutati's own categorization of political structures imposed on Gregory's words. This is done incidentally, instinctively, but for this very reason such a categorization should be regarded as much a part of Salutati's thought as his notion of a "best" form of government expressed in Part IV of his work.

Having given his gloss of Gregory's statement on tyranny, Salutati observes that a tyrant is the prince who does not rule according to law.[32]

---

31. Von Martin, De tyranno, p. xi; Emerton p. 76. Emerton translates superbe as "autocratically." I prefer "arrogantly." For smoothness of translation I have rendered it as an adverb in English.

32. In the first and especially the second part of the work Salutati is to an extent patterning his analysis after Bartolus of Sassoferrato's De tyrannia, published forty years before: Consilia quaestiones et tractatus (Venice, 1578), fols. 117–19ᵛ. See summary of the discussion on the relationship of Salutati's work to that of Bartolus in first edition of Hans Baron, The Crisis of the Early Italian Renaissance, 2 vols. (Princeton, 1955), II, 500–501. Also see my "The 'De tyranno'," p. 436, n. 7. The work of Bartolus was published posthumously: see B.N.F., Naz., II, IV, 108, fol. 34, where the explicit of the treatise reads: "Explicit tractatus tirampnidis per dominum Bartolum de Saxoferrato, legum doctorem, juris commentatorem ac etiam comitem palatinum, quem non publicavit, morte proventu, sed publicavit post eius mortem, dominus Nicolaus Alexandri de Perusio, legum doctor, eius

Either he does not have legal title to rule and is a *tyrannus ex defectu tituli* or, while possessing legal title, he rules *superbe* and is a *tyrannus ex parte exercitii* (p. xv). Part II of the treatise is devoted to the problem of tyrannicide in respect to the two different situations. Salutati obviously considers usurpation of public power as one form, the most serious, of usurpation in general. If by Roman law individuals are authorized to kill usurpers of private property, they have an even greater right to kill those attempting to occupy the state.

But it is possible for a *tyrannus ex defectu tituli* to legitimize his power (pp. xxvii-xxviii).[33] In cases where the community has no overlord, the usurper must obtain popular approval either implicitly or explicitly; in communities where there is an overlord he needs both this approval and the overlord's sanction. If this overlord lives abroad and does not assert his authority (obviously the case of many of the political unities in Italy), then the election is probably valid until the overlord declares to the contrary. But until the *tyrannus ex defectu tituli* has a title and consequently ceases to be a tyrant on these grounds, he is nothing but a dangerous criminal and can be killed by anyone.

In regard to the *tyrannus ex parte exercitii* the problem of tyrannicide is quite different.[34] This is the case of the ruler who, although he has legitimate title to rule, abuses his power. According to Salutati, if the community has an overlord and that overlord sanctions his deposition or punishment, there is no question that the community may act to dispose of the tyrant. If the community has no superior, it is empowered to punish its legitimate lord turned tyrant if it so decides (pp. xxviii-xxix). But private citizens cannot take matters into their own hands. The ruler's title has the sanction of the community and of the overlord (where this is necessary) and only by the action of the duly constituted authorities can such a ruler be deposed (p. xxxiv).

With Part III begin those lively sections of the work of greatest interest for Salutati's own thought. Both John of Salisbury and Cicero have accused Caesar of being a tyrant. Salutati's procedure is to focus on Cic-

---

gener, sub anno domini MCCCLVII, die xi, mense novembris et dixitur quod ideo ipsum non publicavit quia non perfecerat ipsum."

33. *De tyranno*, p. xvii. The discussion of the *tyrannus ex defectu tituli* is interrupted pp. xx-xxv, by the extensive historical excursus on the figure of Publicus Scipio Nasica discussed above in chap. 9.

34. In the light of Salutati's text, I am unable to follow Giuseppe Sciacca's argument that Salutati recognized only one kind of tyranny, that of *ex defectu tituli: Il concetto di tiranno dai Greci a Coluccio Salutati* (Palermo, 1953), p. 101.

ero and to disprove his criticism of Caesar by the remarks of Cicero himself. While Caesar lived, Salutati begins, Cicero praised him and accepted benefits from his hand. Even when allied with Pompey, Cicero realized that the struggle between Pompey and Caesar was "not as to whether some one man should rule and be the supreme dictator of the state, but which of the two it should be" (p. xxxix: p. 98). It was, Salutati says, an act of God that caused Caesar to triumph in this struggle. Even Cicero admits that once in power Caesar "atoned for the horrors of civil strife, than which nothing can be more cruel, by his wonderful magnanimity" (p. xxxx: p. 99). All supported his rule: "So that, with the approval of the citizens, all kinds of honors were heaped upon this one man: statues around the temples, in the theatre a pointed crown, a raised seat in the Senate, a decorated gable for his house, his name given to a month of the year; besides these the titles of "Father of the Fatherland" and "Perpetual Dictator"; finally—whether by his own consent or not is uncertain—the insignia of royalty offered him publicly by Anthony as consul."[35]

Judging from the arguments used by Salutati to prove Caesar's legitimacy as ruler of Rome at the time of his death, it could be said that, although initially without title, he became monarch through universal recognition. And yet this does not seem to be Salutati's conclusion. "Can a man raised to power constitutionally and through his own merits," Salutati claims, "a man who showed such a humane spirit, not to his own partisans alone but also to his opponents because they were his fellow citizens—can he properly be called a tyrant . . . ? We may, therefore, conclude with this proposition: that Caesar was not a tyrant, seeing that he held his principate in a commonwealth, lawfully and not by abuse of law" (p. xxxxi: p. 100). But Salutati has not, of course, shown us that Caesar was "raised to power constitutionally for his own merits." In what way then has he proven that Caesar "held his principate in a commonwealth, lawfully and not by abuse of law?" At least at the beginning of his analysis he suggests that Caesar came to power through force alone. The problem imposes itself: by making logical leaps in his argument is Salutati attempting to distort the historical facts of Caesar's rise to power in order to justify Caesar's rule as legitimate from its very inception?

The possibility of distortion becomes more definite from the very out-

---

35. Ibid., p. xxxxi: pp. 99–100. This is a quotation from Florus, *Epit.*, II, 13, 90.

set of Part IV, the section designed to answer the question, Was the murder of Julius Caesar justified? Here again Salutati sees Caesar raised to power by the gratitude of his fellow citizens:

> Since, therefore, Caesar cannot properly be accounted a tyrant, seeing that he was raised by the gratitude of his fellow citizens to that height whence other princes, whom no one considers as tyrants, were carried on to the imperial succession, who can maintain that his murder was justified? (p. xxxii: pp. 100–101).

Immediately after this assertion he directs his attention to the murderers. Did they not accept offices at his hands? Did not the Senate confirm all his acts and carry out even his unaccomplished projects after his assassination? Did they not recognize his legitimacy by these very things? (p. xxxii) Would the Roman people have so favored a dead tyrant? Not only was this murder displeasing to men but it was also a heinous act in the eyes of the gods. Within three years all the conspirators perished violently. Is this not a sign of divine displeasure? (p. xxxvi).

Then follows a long series of justifications for his power based on counsels of prudence: the conditions of the empire given the civil strife required the rule of one man. Revolution against the man who was attempting to bind up the wounds of the state was a crime. Revolution in any case is a dangerous thing: "There never was anyone possessed of power so great or prudence so divine that a revolution could realize his true intention" (p. xxxxvii: p. 105).

In connection with this emphasis on the magnanimity of Caesar toward his enemies and his efforts to bring peace and justice to the state, Salutati launches into a defense of monarchy as the ideal form of government. Do not all authorities agree, Salutati asks, "is it not sound politics, approved by the judgment of all wise men, that monarchy is to be preferred to all other forms of government, provided only that it be in the hands of a wise and good man?" (p. l: p. 108). Just as the heavens are ruled by one God, so human affairs are better managed the nearer they imitate this divine order.[36] Where many command "there will be not one government but several." If there had been monarchical rule in Rome, there would never have been a civil war. The aristocratic government was "wholly unsuited to the times." Proof of this is what hap-

---

36. He echoes here a favorite medieval justification of monarchy. Salutati's use of the idea may be based directly on Giles of Rome's *De regimine principum*, III, 2, 3, of which he owned at least two copies: Ullman, *The Humanism*, pp. 167–68 and 180–81.

pened after the murder of Caesar. The civil war that broke out again could only be ended when Octavian united the imperial power in the hands of one man.

One would assume that Salutati is arguing that Caesar's rule, originally *ex defectu tituli*, became legitimate through the tacit or express consent of the community: its worth was proven *ex parte exercitii* and the conditions of the times led the Roman people to sanction it. This, however, is definitely not the conclusion Salutati draws. At the opening of Part V before taking up the work of Dante, Salutati gives us specifically the conclusion that he has been aiming at throughout his analysis of Caesar's rule: "Since then Caesar, as has been most abundantly proved, was not a tyrant by defect of title, seeing that the grateful country freely chose him for its prince, nor by reason of *superbia*, since he ruled with clemency and humanity, it is clear that his murder was a most accursed crime" (p. liv: p. 111). Salutati's position is unambiguous. The Florentine humanist's justification of Caesar is that he was neither a *tyrannus ex defectu tituli* nor a *tyrannus ex parte exercitii* and therefore was treacherously and unjustly murdered. According to all his definitions, Caesar, for Salutati, ought to have been a *tyrannus ex defectu tituli* who removed his illegitimacy through the beneficence of his rule and consequently ceased to be a tyrant. But Salutati has no intention of justifying tyranny in any way. Admittedly there is a gap, a *non sequitur* between evidence and conclusion. He specifically makes Caesar a legitimate monarch without any stain on his title.

Thus, by vindicating Caesar Salutati can in Part V free Dante completely from the charge of error in placing the murderers in the lowest depths of Hell. Dante was entirely right in his judgment. Here again Salutati infers that the power of Caesar was above reproach both as to use and title:

> And who can criticize Dante for thrusting into the depths of hell and condemning to extreme punishment those abandoned men who sinned so grievously in treacherously murdering Caesar, the father of his country, while he was administering with such clemency the government which the Senate and people of Rome had conferred upon him in a desperate crisis to put an end to the evils of civil war? (p. lvii: p. 113).

Thus, Salutati explains Caesar's rise to power with the justification that the Senate and people of Rome called him to become their ruler and to bring an end to the civil war.

Just as Judas betrayed the God-man, so his companions in the mouth of Satan betrayed Caesar, "the image as it were, of divinity in the rightfulness of his rule," the defender of the fatherland and their own benefactor. Dante's judgment, moreover, is supported (1) by the authority of Virgil, (2) by the fact that the conspirators were defeated, and (3) by the manifestation of the will of God, who with Augustus brought the world under the rule of one man:

> And so we may conclude that our Dante, in this matter as in others, made no mistake either theologically or morally, and still less poetically, in condemning Brutus and Cassius in the way he did—nay, not only that he made no mistake, but that without any question he rendered a just judgment (p. lix: pp. 114–15).

The last section of the De tyranno, Part VI, is a mere appendage to the treatise. In answer to the question of whether or not Antenor and Aeneas were traitors to Troy, Salutati replies that the old histories are at variance and no definite judgment can be drawn. The matter of Aeneas and Antenor is, however, not completely unconnected with the central problem of the work. Dante placed Aeneas in the most comfortable quarters of the Inferno and Antenor in the terrible Ninth Circle, which was reserved for traitors.[37] Very probably the question of Aeneas and Antenor was raised along with that of Caesar's murderers in connection with the validity of Dante's assessments in the Divina commedia. Yet criticism of his judgment on Aeneas and Antenor must not have been very violent for Salutati was willing to leave the matter of their guilt in doubt. The judgment, of course, was not susceptible to historical proof and their position in the Inferno was much less central to the basic structure of the work than was that of Caesar and his murderers. Whatever the explanation, Salutati was prepared to leave open the matter of the guilt of the two Trojans.

Looked at from one direction the De tyranno is patently a polemic. A very perceptive analysis of how Caesar rose to power and why, it is utilized not for the purposes of historical truth but for winning an argument. If Dante is to be vindicated, Caesar both in his rise to power and in his administration of office must be exonerated of any illegitimacy. But from another standpoint Salutati's favorable interpretation of Caesar and the beginning of the Roman monarchy fits well with what he had been writing over the past five years. Only in this tract Salutati's

---

37. Aeneas has a place in the first circle (Inf., IV, 122): Antenor's punishment is described in Inf., XXXII, 88.

doubts about Caesar's position have been erased. The hesitations about Caesar's rise to power, which Salutati had nourished throughout most of his life and even in these very years around the turn of the century, are barely perceptible in the *De tyranno*. Carried away by the need to defend Dante and by his conviction of the justice of Dante's general position, Salutati was led to simplify an attitude that was fundamentally more complex for him.[38]

In his pro-monarchical work there is no question that Salutati intended to endorse tyranny. He expended a good deal of effort trying to prove that in no sense was Caesar a tyrant. Moreover, his assignment, at the very outset of the treatise, of certain constitutions to certain levels of government—the monarchical for the state, the political or republican for the province, and the despotic for the family—suggests that when he speaks of monarchy as the best form of government he is not being a disloyal Florentine. In the legal language of the day Florence like Milan and other Italian city-states was a *provincia* or *civitas* within the *respublica* of the Holy Roman Empire, and Salutati specifically considers a political or republican regime appropriate at this level.[39]

Salutati's defense of monarchy focuses on the empire, and his analysis of the establishment of the imperial office with Caesar and Augustus aims at proving that this office was willed by God. Salutati's concern in this account is not really political but rather religious. Endowed with a sharper historical sense than Dante, his acceptance of the guilt of Brutus and the providential creation of the imperial office led him to interpret the murder of Caesar as the political dividing line between pagan and Christian history. Intimately related to the advent of Christ, the principate of Augustus initiated a historical epoch of far greater significance than the preceding one. The passage from the ancient to the modern world, moreover, not only was willed by God but was also accom-

---

38. Peter Herde, "Politik und Rhetorik in Florenz am Vorabend der Renaissance," *Archiv für Kulturgeschichte*, 47 (1965), 209–10, tends in my opinion to exaggerate the rhetorical element in Salutati's writings as a whole.

39. Ernst Walser, *Gesammelte Studien zur Geistesgeschichte der Renaissance*, ed. Schnyder von Wartensee (Basel, 1932), p. 31, writes: "Wenn er diese Macht aber theoretisch einem Weltkaiser zugestand, so war er völlig anderer Meinung, wenn es sich praktisch um Florenz und den Herzog von Mailand handelte, dessen Streben gerade darauf ging, den Florentinern und ganz Italien das Glück einer monarchischen Staatsform zuteil werden zu lassen." Daniela De Rosa, *Coluccio Salutati: Il cancelliere e il pensatore politico*, Biblioteca di storia, vol. 28 (Florence, 1980), pp. 144 ff., stresses the political realism of Salutati in this work. She highlights Salutati's recognition that the Roman people in late republican times, having lost their taste for liberty, needed a strong ruler to keep order. Thus, the rise of the monarchy under Caesar and later Augustus was for the humanist a historical necessity.

plished by a legal transmission of power. As font of justice, God would not have operated in any other fashion.

The fervor of piety created by the *Bianchi*, coupled with his intense awareness of God's presence in a city racked with a divinely inflicted epidemic, stimulated Salutati's religious sensibilities to their highest point in the months when he was writing the *De tyranno*. Only the tremendous architecture of Dante's vision could fulfill the need he felt to interpret his experience in image and thought.

Although Dante's conviction that the empire was God-willed and legitimate remained with Salutati until the end, the period of crisis passed and some of Salutati's old hesitations about Caesar himself returned. As he wrote in 1405:

> There was in Gaius Caesar the dictator, son of Lucius Caesar, a marvelous and extraordinary clemency, there was also enormous ambition and in the same man was a sobriety even praised by his enemies and a lustful desire criticized by his friends. Whence Cato is said to have remarked that no one ever invaded the state while sober except for Caesar.[40]

This attempt to balance the great vices and virtues of Caesar was another manifestation of the humanist's usual feeling of ambivalence toward the figure of the great conqueror. Bruni's presentation of Salutati in the second book of the *Dialogi ad Petrum Paulum Histrum*, written a few years after this statement, also lends support to the suspicion of a movement away from the extreme position of 1400 on Caesar. True, Bruni has Salutati say that he has never been able to criticize Caesar as a parricide (this is literally true because Cicero had spoken the words "patricida patrie" in his letter of 1392) but the whole tone of the speech is one of uncertainty in the overall assessment of Caesar's career and personality.[41] Still alive at the time of writing, Salutati would certainly have objected to this interpretation of his views had it been a misrepresentation.

Salutati's political propaganda as chancellor of the Florentine state cannot of course be seen in isolation from the political circumstances in which it functioned. Yet, as chapter 6 shows, the Florentine *missives* in the last ten years of his life fit surprisingly well with the evolution of his

40. *Epist.*, III, 443. Novati, p. 437, n. 1, assigns the date Nov. 3, 1400? to this letter. Salutati's other references to Caesar during these last years suggest neither praise or blame (ibid., III, 552 and IV, 156 and 234).

41. *Ad Petrum Paulum Histrum Dialogus*, ed. E. Garin, *Prosatori latini del Quattrocento*, La letteratura italiana, Storia e testi, vol. 13 (Milan, 1952), p. 78.

personal outlook. From 1396 and the *De fato et fortuna* Salutati increasingly approached intellectual problems from a Christian standpoint, and in seeking ways of formulating and resolving them Christian precedents were of more importance than pagan ones. At the same time the war against Milan was not represented as a struggle between Romans and barbarians, the daughter of Rome defending her liberty against a tyrant, but rather as a phase of the medieval Guelf-Ghibelline struggle. After 1400, moreover, this theme was seconded by another reflecting Salutati's concern for legitimacy in the *De tyranno*. While liberty had always been closely connected with law in Salutati's thought, in the last five years of his chancery the war of Florence and her allies against Milan was conceptualized as a battle between legitimate and illegitimate powers where the nature of the specific constitutional regime was ignored.

Elements of this theme in Salutati's political thinking in this last phase of his life are brought together in his *Invectiva contra Antonium Luschum* written in 1403.[42] According to Salutati's letter of September 11, 1403, to Pietro Turchi, chancellor of Carlo Malatesta, Pietro had sent him a copy of an invective against Florence written by Salutati's former student and friend, Antonio Loschi, and begged him to answer Loschi's charges.[43] However, Salutati had hesitated: "For I said: what will you do, Lino Coluccio? You are in your seventies (in February I shall be seventy-three). Will you, who up to this time has never attacked anyone in your private capacity except in jest, begin now to rave? Will you abandon a habit of long standing?" (III, 636–37). Finally, Salutati confides, he realized that his duty required a response and with this letter to Pietro he was sending both the invective of Loschi and his own.

If we are to take Salutati at his word, it was at Pietro's urging he undertook the labor of writing his *Invectiva contra Antonium Luschum*, and he began his work when he was in his seventies, that is, at some time after February 16, 1401. Judging from Salutati's reference to himself as presently seventy-two in connection with making the decision, one could presumably say that the work was begun after February 16, 1403. Although he does not specifically credit Turchi with bringing Loschi's work to his attention, he makes him responsible for suggesting the project.[44]

42. *Invectiva in Antonium Luschum Vicentinum*, ed. Domenico Moreni (Florence, 1826), pp. 1–198.

43. *Epist.*, III, 634 and 638.

44. Ibid., III, 636–37: "Dicebam enim: quid, Line Coluci, facies? an septuagenarius; februarius enim mensis septuagesimum et tertium adducet annum; qui neminem hucusque

Apart from Salutati's *Invectiva*, where it is quoted in sections, each followed by a detailed refutation, Loschi's *Invectiva in Florentinos* survives in only four manuscripts and did not apparently have a wide diffusion. Written in March or April 1397 several months after the outbreak of the Second Milanese War, the work constitutes a bitter attack on the Florentines as the principal threat to the peace of Italy.[45] Not only were the rulers of Florence tyrants but they were allied with three other tyrannical powers, the Gonzaga, the Carrara, and the Este of Ferrara, against Giangaleazzo, the defender of Italian liberty.[46] Florence's alliance with the French king was a special object of Loschi's critique (pp. 108–18). As he presents it, the Florentines were so terrified of Milan that they were willing to promise the French domination of Italy in exchange for help against their enemy. He scoffs at the Florentine claim to be descendants of the Romans; rather they are the "feces" of Italy (pp. 18–19 and 108).

To all appearances Salutati's response to Loschi was preceded by another composed by Cino Rinuccini, the Florentine merchant-rhetorician.[47] If in fact some of the point by point rebuttal of Loschi, found in Rinuccini's *Risponsiva alla invectiva di messer Antonio Luscho*, was written in 1397, the work itself was not published until after 1406.[48] By creating

---

tuo nomine nisi iocose leseris, incipies, discedens ab habitu tam longe consuetudinis, insanire?" For dating of work, see appendix 2.

45. The dating of Loschi's tract has been convincingly established by Hans Baron, *Humanistic and Political Literature in Florence and Venice* (Cambridge, 1955), pp. 38–47. For the manuscripts, see Ronald Witt, "Cino Rinuccini's *Risponsiva alla Invettiva di Messer Antonio Lusco*," *Renaissance Quarterly*, 23 (1970), 138, n. 22.

46. *Invectiva*, p. 82.

47. Hans Baron, *Humanistic and Political Literature*, p. 49, suggests that it was written in the late spring or early summer of 1397. The work was published by Moreni in the same volume with Salutati, *Invectiva*, pp. 199–250. On Cino, see chap. 10.

48. Salutati is described as if already dead: Witt, "Cino Rinuccini's *Risponsiva*," p. 143; and Giuliano Tanturli, "Cino Rinuccini e la scuola di Santa Maria in Campo," *Studi medievali*, 3rd. ser. 17 (1976), 633. Whereas I have argued for a completion date for the work as late as 1436, Tanturli (pp. 633–44) convincingly shows that the passage on which my argument rests is nonspecific as far as chronology is concerned. I also accept his evidence for Rinuccini's total authorship, which a completion date of 1436 would have made impossible.

If, however, we accept 1406 and 1417 as the *terminus post quem* and *terminus ante quem* respectively for the completion of the *Risponsiva*, we must still determine when the work was begun. Contrary to Tanturli's interpretation of my article (p. 640), I nowhere state that a "prima stesura," "sicuramente databile," was written in April–June 1397. Indeed in my article (p. 146) I recognize the possibility that Rinuccini wrote the *Risponsiva* as a response to a reedition of Loschi's work "in later years." My basic conclusion on the dating of the *Risponsiva* was that we must recognize "the inability to present a convincing solution to the problem of dating the composition." Tanturli's excellent discussion raises even more questions (pp. 642–43) about establishing a *terminus post quem* for the beginning of the work. In analyzing what he considers datable portions of the *Risponsiva*, Tanturli points

the illusion that the *Risponsiva* was contemporary with Loschi's tract, the Florentine teacher of rhetoric was able to increase the dramatic quality of his work, while inclusion of historical and theoretical arguments made originally by Bruni in the *Laudatio* gave it added depth and cogency.

Although Salutati's *Invectiva* probably preceded Rinuccini's *Risponsiva*, it does not appear to have been written until six years after Loschi's very topical work and circumstances described by Loschi had generally changed. To respond effectively Salutati had a problem. To attack Loschi on the basis of hindsight meant ignoring most of what his opponent had said as no longer relevant. Giangaleazzo was dead, his empire crumbling and Loschi himself had already probably left Milan for Vicenza. Writing at the outset of the Second Milanese War, Loschi had attacked allies who had long since left the Florentine camp. He had delivered threats to Florence's security which from the safety of 1403 were recognized to have been empty.

On the other hand, Florentine honor in a particular period of the Republic's existence had been assaulted and Salutati burned to justify Florentine conduct throughout the Milanese wars. He also wished to preserve the dramatic effect of responding point by point to his adversary. At the same time he felt the need of reminding his readers of how the whole struggle came out. Accordingly, he settled on the idea of working within two time-frames simultaneously. Essentially rebutting Loschi in terms of political and military circumstances prevalent in 1397, he occasionally interjected statements that brought the discussion up to date. The different time periods reflected in Salutati's discussion, therefore, were vital ingredients in a work designed as propaganda but structured as a refutation of a topical diatribe written years before.

The most significant scholarly aspect of the *Invectiva* is Salutati's presentation of the results of his brilliant researches into the origins of Florence, already discussed in chapter 9. For the purposes of political propaganda in this work, however, Salutati made very limited use of his discovery that Florence had had a Roman foundation in the time of

---

to a statement by Rinuccini which could not have been written before July 1402 (pp. 642–43): "Né dè nostri fratelli Bolognesi, i quali, maldicente, ora con vizio ricordi, isperiamo né ci disperiamo, conciosiacosaché nostre forze sieno potentissime per difendere la libertà, e ancora crediamo che, come grati, per nostra virtù ristituta, insino a ora conservata, di loro libertà si ricordino" (p. 215). But, one may ask, would Rinuccini have written this passage after October of the same year? Because the portion referring to Salutati as dead must have been written after 1406, the work appears to have been composed over a period of years.

Sulla. As compared with Bruni, who contemporaneously utilized the theory of the republican foundation of the city to enhance and explain Florence's republican heritage, Salutati merely pointed to his historical arguments as proof that Florence was indeed the daughter of Rome.

Within the context of the *Invectiva* as a whole a republican emphasis would have been quite out of place. The political and historical associations that predominate in the work are medieval; Salutati attacks the tyranny of Giangaleazzo not as a republican but rather as a jurist. As in the *De tyranno* Salutati assumes the existence of an imperial constitutional order with the emperor "our natural lord, our Caesar" at the top (p. 140), capping the edifice of power and endorsing its legitimacy either by explicit authorization or tacit recognition of inferior rulers.[49] The essence of the liberty that the Visconti lord threatens is the rule of law: "The sweet bridle of liberty which is to live according to the law" (p. 53). To Loschi's charge that Florence was allied with three tyrants, Salutati responds by making the three rulers as respectable as he can. The Este have ruled for nine generations and have been famous five generations before the time of Frederick II. As for Francesco Carrara, this prince has governed justly for a number of years and is beloved by his subjects. Apparently unable to say much about the Gonzaga on this score, Salutati changes his approach when he comes to that prince: "Why do you call tyrants these men [Este and Carrara] and that noble lord of Mantua whom you count the third tyrant, when your own lord calls them lords, sons and brothers?" Loschi plainly contradicts Giangaleazzo on this point. Is the Visconti prince lying or is Loschi? (p. 105).

Bothered that the imperial investiture of Giangaleazzo as duke of Milan exempts him from charges of tyranny at least on the grounds of *ex defectu tituli*, Salutati writes:

> But you say: was he [Giangaleazzo] not made duke of Milan and count of Pavia by imperial authority. He was so made, I confess, if counts and dukes are made among foaming cups and a crowd of lords and nobles reeling with wine, and if they are created to the prejudice and ruin of the empire for foul gain not because of race, virtue or merits. Yes, if one who established a tyranny and lives constantly as

49. Although I do not agree entirely with his note to this passage, I think Alfred von Martin, *Salutati und das humanistische Lebensideal* (Berlin-Leipzig, 1916), p. 133, aptly describes the tendency of the *De tyranno* when he writes: "Diese Überordnung der religiös und moralisch fundierten Rechtsstaatsidee über das Freiheitsideal bedingt notwendig eine verhältnismässige Gleichgültigkeit gegen die Frage der Staatsform: ob Republik oder Monarchie, diese Frage wird als mehr oder weniger nebensächlich betrachet."

a tyrant nor first ceases to be a tyrant can be made a legitimate count or duke. Yes, if title and words suffice and habits and merits are not required for this (pp. 105–6).

Utilizing his powers obtained from Caesar, the Visconti prince transformed "the just rule of the sacred Empire into a cruel tyranny" (p. 147).

As for the French, Salutati continues, they like the Florentines abominate servitude. It is a characteristic of this people to enjoy liberty under their monarch (*regia libertate*) (p. 84). As frequently before, Salutati credits the French with being "our founders." Charlemagne reestablished the city after the population had been dispersed by the ravages of Totila, and from that time to the present the Florentines have been devoted to the French and to their common Guelf allegiance. "Wherefore," Salutati concludes at one point, "cease wondering about the devotion of the Florentines to the sacred house of France for this glorious race has always had a peculiar concern for this its people [of Florence]" (p. 171).

The *Invectiva* is unquestionably "a solemn hymn to triumph":[50] Florence had vanquished its bitter enemy and the Republic was saved. Yet, as in Salutati's official propaganda, the ideological framework in which this triumph was conceived seems strikingly medieval. While the Guelf character of the allies is less prominent in this work than in the public letters, the conception of the struggle against the Visconti as primarily one between the forces of law and order and those of lawless ambition was common to both. A theme frequently found in Salutati's early public letters, by 1400–1401 it became the dominant definition of liberty. The medieval political prejudices had never been far from center stage in Salutati's mind but, reinforced by Dante's religious interpretation of history, they now preempted his thought.

As an old man Salutati was perhaps even a more fervent Florentine patriot than he had been thirty years before, but at the theoretical level the ordered world of a universal Christian monarchy—in which Florence had its place—exercised an irresistible appeal to one who felt the whole of created reality informed and moved by the eternal Providence of the Christian God. Immersed in this essentially religious vision of politics as he was, the republican experience of the ancient world appeared to him irrelevant and insignificant. The transformation of Salutati's attitude to antiquity, however, was not limited to his approach to politics but affected other central aspects of his thought as well.

---

50. *Epist.*, III, 636, n. 1 (continued from previous pages).

CHAPTER 15. THE OLD HUMANIST AND CHANCELLOR: A NEW GENERATION

With Piero and Andrea gone Salutati had to alter plans for his children. Bonifazio was thirty but not particularly gifted for the notarial profession. Yet he seemed the most likely among the boys to succeed to the chancery. Immediately recalled from Stignano, Bonifazio officially enrolled in the Guild of Judges and Notaries on October 29, 1400. Rather than go to live in his father's house, however, Bonifazio decided to find a place of his own across town in the *gonfalone* of the *Leone nero* in the quarter of Santa Maria Novella.[1] When Giovanni di Currado returned to Florence sometime later, he joined his cousin in the new apartment.[2] Arrigo Salutati, a young man in his early twenties, also chose these bachelor quarters over a room in his father's house. Documents of the *Tratte* for the Council of the People over the next few years list the three as representing the *Leone nero* in that body.[3]

Although the listing of Bonifazio in 1391 as eligible for the major offices had been the result of an error,[4] the regular appearance of the Salutati family in the purses of the *tratte* after 1400 was not. On November 26, 1400, ignoring the provisions of the law of 1379, which required thirty years residence and taxpaying in the city for citizenship, in the case of men originating from the Valdinievole the Republic made Salutati and all relatives of his male line citizens of Florence.[5] Salutati himself had been personally exempted by the law of 1379 from the restrictions against noncitizens holding lucrative notarial appointments in the gov-

1. *Tratte*, 62, fols. 369ᵛ–70. He is registered as being from the quarter of Santa Maria Novella. On fol. 369ᵛ his original registration was given as Santa Croce and then cancelled. His only known literary work is a sonnet (*Epist.*, III, 405).
2. Ibid., fol. 369ᵛ and for the same quarter. Giovanni did not join the guild until 1403 according to these records. But B.N.F., *Naz.*, II, IV, 397, fol. 410, gives the date May 1401 for his matriculation.
3. Evidence that Arrigo lived together with Bonifazio and Giovanni in the *Leone nero* section of Santa Maria Novella is found in elections to this body: *Tratte*, 147, ad an. Cf. Demetrio Marzi, *La cancelleria della Repubblica fiorentina* (Rocca San Casciano, 1910), p. 133, n. 7.
4. Marzi, p. 135, n. 7, and above, chap. 10. It is unfortunate that a number of observations made in Marzi's note are inaccurate or cannot be found in the references. Most serious are the statements calling Piero "ser" and referring to Bonifazio and Antonio as notaries in the 1390s.
5. Marzi, p. 147.

ernment, but after November 1400, his children who were notaries were eligible for these as well. By 1406 not only Bonifazio but also Giovanni di Currado and Antonio had joined the notarial guild and were consequently able to enjoy such appointments. Very possibly Salutati had made the request for citizenship himself. The plague of 1400 had made him realize the need to establish his family in Florence while he was still alive. Not only would citizenship make it easier for his sons in the notariate to earn a living but his other children would also have access to the public offices so necessary for a family's prestige and protection against enemies. He also wished to die a Florentine citizen.

Both Bonifazio and Giovanni went to work in the chancery as Salutati's helpers.[6] But neither had sufficient experience to be Salutati's coadjutor as Piero had been. For this reason Salutati hired ser Lapo Mazzei, the pious notary who had worked for him in this position at least once decades before.[7] Facing up to the truth of what he already felt, that Bonifazio did not have the capacity to succeed him, Salutati endeavored to have the *Tratte* divided from the chancellorship as it had been for a year in 1376–77. Although it entailed a good deal of detailed work and required a reputation for honesty, this post did not demand much intellectual acumen from its holder. On June 1, 1405, Salutati succeeded in having Bonifazio installed in the position of secretary of the *Tratte* at a salary of eighty florins per year.[8] Bonifazio named his brother Antonio as his coadjutor and both appeared to have served in their offices until the *Tratte* was reunited with the Laws at Bonifazio's death in 1413.[9]

After steadfastly refusing to accept any office besides the chancellorship and the *Tratte* for twenty years, Salutati now held office in the Guild

6. In 1404 Bonifazio also acted as notary of the *Entrata*: ibid., p. 150. The document dated July 28, 1378, mentioned by Marzi as copied by Bonifazio as "coadjutor" of Salutati must certainly have been written by him after 1400 and not in 1378 as Marzi implies (ibid., p. 139, n. 6). Cf. *Capitani di Parte*, 794, fol. 114.

7. Ronald Witt, *Coluccio Salutati and His Public Letters* (Geneva, 1976), p. 16, n. 35.

8. Marzi, p. 148.

9. Antonio aided Bonifazio but did not become a notary until 1406: B.N.F., *Naz.*, II, IV, 397, fol. 416ᵛ. He was not yet a notary on May 27, 1406, when he approved the addition to the Uzzano statutes of 1389 in his capacity as coadjutor of the *Tratte*: S.C.S., Uzzano, 904, fol. 81. B.L. Ullman, *The Humanism of Coluccio Salutati*, Medioevo e umanesimo, vol. 4 (Padua, 1963), p. 8, n., misunderstands the meaning of the signatures of Salutati and his sons on the revisions of these statutes of the *comuni soggetti*. In the decade after his death the burlesque *Lo Studio d'Atene* (ed. Ludovico Frati, Scelta di curiosità letterarie inedite o rare dal secolo XII al XVII, disp. 203 [Bologna, 1884], pp. 113–17) speaks of the four "scholars" among the surviving brothers, that is, ser Bonifazio, ser Antonio, messer Leonardo, and messer Salutato, as moving like "quattro ombre" and "prive d'ogni sentimento" one after the other, the three behind holding the hem of the cloak of the one before: "Il vostro padre, buon messer Coluccio,/se ne portò di quel ch'assai vi mancha/et che sonar vi fa sotto l'chappuccio."

of Judges and Notaries four times in the five years before his death.[10] His willingness to serve so frequently reflects not so much a late blooming desire for civic honors as it does his hope that in this position he might be able to influence the lists of those notaries eligible for government offices and consequently enhance the careers of his sons and their cousin.

Did the transfer of Bonifazio, his brother, and cousin to another part of town indicate a rift in the decimated family? The two older young men worked together with Salutati in the chancery daily and had there been deep animosity between them such a situation would have become intolerable in time. More likely, the move of the bachelors to new lodgings reflected a degree of financial independence and a desire to have a measure of freedom impossible in their father's house. In the last years the old man enjoyed an almost total triumph over the desires of his body. Of course, enormous success and age itself had made the victory easier. Salutati now followed his convictions with a consistency which must have proven oppressive to those close to him. Furthermore, despite the resignation expressed in his letters, he probably could not overcome impatience with his surviving children. The best had died with Piero, and he seemed to expect little from the remaining sons.

To a degree, however, the move of his sons to another quarter of the city stemmed from Salutati's failure to purchase a family seat in the city around which the children could settle after their own marriages. Salutati and Piera had raised their whole family in the Piazza dei Peruzzi but had never purchased the house. Thus, unlike other upper-class Florentine families the Salutati had no center. Nor was the move of Bonifazio, Giovanni, and Arrigo to the *Leone nero* permanent. The catasto of 1427 shows Arrigo and Antonio both dwelling in the *gonfalone* of the *Vipera* in the same quarter.[11]

Salutati's failure to buy his own house in Florence had no economic cause nor was it a product of uncertainty that he might lose his official post and be forced to leave the city. Rather to purchase a house in the city to serve as a center of dynastic ambitions seemed to tie him too obviously to the world. On the other hand, it appeared perfectly legitimate to round out his ancestral holdings in the countryside. He had a duty to provide his children with sufficient capital and training so that they could earn their own livelihood. Unfortunately, the fortunes of war

10. He was elected proconsul of the guild in 1402 and served as councillor in 1401, 1404, and 1405 (*AGN*, 26, fols. 3ᵛ, 15ᵛ, 16ᵛ, and 17).

11. *Epist.*, IV, 521 and 549.

in the Valdinievole coupled with the stagnation of the rural economy in the early fifteenth century ultimately frustrated his intentions.[12]

Given his high earnings Salutati could have left a large fortune, but he would not devote himself to amassing riches, justifying his own greed with the excuse that he was saving for his children's future. He spent generously for books and his own and his family's comforts. Very possibly in the last years he gave substantial anonymous gifts to religious institutions. His philosophy of expenditure was best summed up in a letter in 1390 to Pellegrino Zambeccari, who had complained of his own inability to save money: "It is better to spend for good reasons everything inherited from one's parents or what relatives and friends bestow either by liberality or testamentary bequest or what fortune provides or industry accumulates—than to build up a huge fortune."[13] His goal was to use the things of this world rather than love them. That the next generation of Salutati declined considerably in fortune was partially because of the father's failure to endow his surviving sons with sufficient wealth to compensate for their own lack of ability to earn it.

Just as Salutati doubtless understood the desire of his older sons to seek the independence of a separate apartment across town, so he appreciated the wish of some of the best scholars in his circle to seek their fortunes in Rome as he had done himself. At the same time, he could not help but have a certain sense of being abandoned in his old age and his letters to his young friends in Rome display the ambivalence he felt. Jacopo da Scarperia was the first to leave in the fall of 1400 after the cessation of the plague. Initially employed in the household of a cardinal, he was officially named an apostolic *scriptor* on July 25, 1401.[14] In his letter of congratulation to the new papal official Salutati mentions his desire to have a translation of the *Vita Ciceronis*, the second of Jacopo's efforts at Latin translation of Greek. (*Epist.*, III, 522). Salutati was to utilize this translation four years later in his debate with Poggio over the merits of Petrarch (IV, 129).

Poggio Bracciolini, urged by Bruni, was the next member of Salutati's circle of young scholars to leave. The young provincial with the marvel-

12. See chap. 10 for indication of his land holdings. Novati (*Epist.*, IV, 573) notes the destruction of Stignano in 1430 by Francesco Sforza which ruined the Salutati houses there. On the gradual impoverishment and depopulation of the Florentine *contado* generally from the last decades of the fourteenth century, see Anthony Molho, *Florentine Public Finance in the Early Renaissance, 1400–1435*, Harvard Historical Monographs, vol. 65 (Cambridge, 1971), pp. 23–45. Also cf. above, chap. 2.

13. *Epist.*, II, 222. He never was able to accept Aristotle's view that a certain degree of material comfort is necessary for happiness (ibid., IV, 117).

14. Ibid., III, 523.

ous calligraphy and the caustic wit, honed by resentment of his dire poverty, had been in Salutati's employ at least since early in 1401.[15] Salutati had known Poggio's shiftless father and had tried to help Poggio by giving him work, but he never felt completely comfortable with him.[16] Nevertheless, informed by Poggio of his wish to go to the Curia, Salutati wrote his powerful friend, the papal secretary, Francesco Piendibeni, praising Poggio in the highest terms.[17]

Having arrived in Rome by November or early December 1403, Poggio like Jacopo first found employment in the household of a cardinal (III, 653–54). In the very first days in the city Poggio began what was to become one of the major concerns of his scholarship, the collection of Roman inscriptions. Salutati's answer of December 23 to Poggio's letter announcing his arrival in Rome expressed thanks to Poggio for his having included a list of inscriptions with the communication (III, 655). Apparently the young notary was still executing a copying assignment for Salutati, a manuscript of a complete edition of Cicero's *Philippica*, which Jacopo had recently discovered.

Poggio's advancement was even more rapid than that of Jacopo, who was twice his age. Francesco di Piendibeni did his work well and within a few months of his arrival Poggio was raised to the rank of papal *scriptor* (IV, 6–7). Not quite certain of Poggio's future comportment in his new post, Salutati included in his letter of congratulations to Poggio a rather condescending exhortation to the young man to be obedient to his superiors. However, he revealed nothing of his uneasiness about Poggio's ability to control his tongue in his letter to Francesco thanking him for the honor he had shown Poggio and Salutati personally: "He was educated and, if there is something to learn, I know that he will be easily taught" (IV, 5).

Despite the lure of Rome and the reception accorded his two friends Bruni did not immediately follow. He seems to have found life in Florence too congenial as his *Laudatio urbis Florentinae* and his *Dialogi* (1401–6), clearly inspired by the Florentine milieu, show. The tie between Salutati and Bruni was very close. Filial concern had motivated Bruni in

15. Ernest Walser, *Poggius Florentinus: Leben und Werken* (Leipzig, 1914), p. 2, n. 3. Cf. Poggio Bracciolini, *Epistolae miscellaneae* in *Opera omnia*, ed., Riccardo Fubini, 4 vols. (Turin, 1964–1969), IV, 581–82. For Poggio's work as an amanuensis for Salutati, see Berthold L. Ullman, *The Origin and Development of Humanistic Script*, Storia e letteratura, vol. 79 (Rome, 1960), pp. 21 ff.

16. *Epist.*, III, 555, n. 1. The letter, dated by Novati as October 18, 1401, was written in 1402 or after because of the title "ser" given to Poggio. Walser has shown that Poggio did not become a notary until 1402 (*Poggius Bracciolini*, doc. 7, p. 327).

17. *Epist.*, IV, 4.

1401 to seek and recover in Arezzo the copybook containing many of the old humanist's letters purloined years before and much lamented ever since. Having mastered Greek, the young man placed himself continuously on call to help Salutati when he needed help in that language. In his *Dialogi ad Petrum Istrum*, Bruni affectionately depicts Salutati at the center of a literary discussion similar to that in which he frequently engaged. While respectful of the venerable scholar, the younger participants in the talk not only expressed their own opinion freely but were encouraged to disagree by Salutati himself.

Late in 1404, however, one of the papal secretaries died and Bruni was nominated for the post. The promised rewards of such a high position were too much for him, and in March 1405 he travelled south, arriving at the gates of Rome on March 25.[18] As a move to win papal favor, Bruni dedicated his new translation of the *Phaedo* to Innocent VII. Amazed at the youthful appearance of the Florentine, Innocent hesitated and this gave time for Jacopo Angeli, pushed forward by his friends, to submit his name as a rival candidate for the post. Innocent VII took advantage of the arrival of a long letter on the schism from the duke de Berry to test the ability of the two contenders. Both were to formulate a response and the appointment would be given to the better writer. Bruni emerged the victor and was appointed secretary late in April.[19] Receiving news of this in early August, Salutati wrote off a letter to the pope, fulsome in its praise for the new appointee. Only subsequently did he learn of Jacopo's unseemly rivalry. His response was to entrust Bruni with delivering a letter of reproach to the loser, a commission Bruni for various reasons chose not to execute.[20]

With Bruni gone, Salutati began to think anxiously about the future of humanism in Florence. Poggio, Leonardo, and Jacopo were in Rome, perhaps permanently. Of those scholars remaining Salutati thought only Roberto dei Rossi and Vanni di Montecuccoli worthy of singling out (IV, 119). But he knew Roberto to be indifferent to drawing disciples to study the *humanitatis artes*, and in any case the two men together would not have sufficed. Interestingly, he does not mention Poggio's *alter ego*, Niccoli. Presumably, he considered the aesthetic patrician too much of a diletante to accomplish significant work in literary studies. In

18. Ibid., IV, 99, n. 3 (from previous page), and *Leonardi Bruni Arretini Epistolarum Libri VIII*, ed. L. Mehus, 2 vols. (Florence, 1741), I, 3. Our understanding of the epistolary exchange between the two men is complicated not only by the loss of a number of their letters in 1405 but also by the fact that some of the letters sent never arrived at their destinations or did so only with great delay (*Epist.*, IV, 99–100).

19. *Leonardi Bruni*, I, 3–4.   20. *Epist.*, IV, 110–13.

the last months of his life the old humanist acknowledged his fear that a veritable *translatio studiorum* to Rome was taking place. Although the work of these Florentines would still serve the advancement of learning generally, he regretfully predicted "an enormous decline" of scholarship in Florence itself, one "which even Cicero could scarcely remedy."

Despite his genuine affection for these younger men in Rome, there is no question that Salutati's written exchanges with them reflect a steady deterioration in the friendship. Partly this stems from his per-haps unconscious resentment that they had abandoned him and Flor-ence for more lucrative circumstances. But there was a more important reason for this development. In his daily contacts with them in Flor-ence, Salutati's relationship with Poggio, Leonardo, and Jacopo had been the natural and easy one depicted by Bruni in his *Dialogi*. He wanted these younger men to have a good measure of freedom to think and dispute. But once forced to communicate with them in writing, Sal-utati tended to sound more rigid and condescending. He had become a sage in the eyes of the world and was well aware that the letters to his friends in Rome would rapidly come to the attention of the literary pub-lic. At the same time the disciples in Rome had become the cynosure of attention. Having attained high positions in the curial bureaucracy with surprising rapidity because of their merits, they naturally smarted at the sententious remarks of the old man. Knowledge that many of the letters exchanged would eventually be widely distributed—if not by them-selves, at least by Salutati—only made their sense of annoyance worse.

That Salutati might write a letter to Jacopo castigating him for his com-portment in the matter of the papal secretaryship is understandable but that he would insist that it should be delivered to the vanquished Jacopo by Bruni, the victor, reflects a serious lack of sensitivity in dealing with his disciples. Salutati's epistolary exchanges with Poggio, moreover, contain explicit admonitions to the young man to watch his tongue. Such warnings easily became tiresome to Poggio, as Poggio's last letter to Salutati in early 1406 demonstrated. Poggio's statement that he would henceforth not speak his mind in his letters to Salutati but would rather resort to flattery was certainly not designed to reduce friction.

By this time Salutati's relationship with Bruni had also badly deterio-rated. In August 1405 Bruni had fallen ill in Viterbo and for twenty days struggled with a high fever. In a letter to Salutati, written in mid-Sep-tember, the convalescing Bruni described to his old master the discom-forts of being ill in a war-wracked city like Viterbo where there were no good doctors and a dearth of spices and drinkable wine.[21] Salutati acknowledged the receipt of Bruni's letter on October 8 but delayed answering it in detail until November 6.[22] The letter took the form of a diatribe against Bruni's morality. Bruni was not merely sick in body but in soul as well. In time of severe illness rather than meditate on his relationship with his maker, Bruni had his thoughts on doctors, wines, and spices, the preoccupations of Epicureans. Salutati exhorted the young man to put aside these thoughts and to speak "not as a human being but as a man; not as one of the mob but as a wise man" (IV, 118–19).

Salutati had already irritated Bruni unwittingly by his letter of August 11 to Jacopo, which had apparently been open so that Bruni could read it before delivery. From the contents it is clear that Salutati had understood that prior to summoning Bruni to Rome, the pope had offered the post of secretary to Jacopo, who had refused. His censure of Jacopo focused on Angeli's sudden change of heart once he understood that Bruni was to be appointed. Perhaps Bruni's failure to deliver the message was motivated not by his desire to spare Jacopo's feelings but because the depiction of events was so unflattering to him personally. Wounded that Salutati could have believed that Jacopo had been preferred to him, Bruni assertively corrects the error and then with peevishness adds: "If you, however, wish to write things properly, correct this part of the letter as well as the construction at the beginning since it is incorrect and inelegant."[23] There is no way of knowing if Salutati had received this letter of August 15 before writing his own of November 6. However, he probably needed no incentives to inspire him to attack sharply Bruni's complaining of his physical wants in the latter's letter of September.

Already ruffled by Salutati's letter to Jacopo, Bruni was enraged by what he regarded as an uncalled-for assault in that of November 6. As he wrote to Niccoli: "For when I complained to him as to a parent that sick with fever I found neither wine, nor doctors, nor anything else fit for sick people in this city, he seized this occasion—as if he were Zeno

21. Ludwig Bertalot, "Forschungen über L. B. Aretino," *Archivum romanum*, 15 (1931), 321–23: now in his *Studien zum italienischen und deutschen Humanismus*, ed. Paul O. Kristeller, Storia e letteratura, vol. 130 in two (Rome, 1975), II, 417–19.

22. *Epist.*, IV, 105 and 113 ff.

23. Ibid., IV, 112. The letter (I, 3) is found in Mehus' edition p. 6 with this passage deleted. Novati identifies the letter as I, 6 in error. Bruni here, as later in November/December, seems to be attacking, among other things, Salutati's manner of writing proper names.

or Diogenes—and began to flail me as mad that I was afflicted with corporeal desire."[24] Feeling unable to control his anger if he tried to rebut Salutati's charges, Bruni, either in November or December, opted for the same means of expressing his hostility as in August. He criticized Salutati's letter for its style and grammar.[25]

Salutati's answer of January 9 was dignified but conciliatory. Bruni had hurt him by suggesting that he probably now regretted the strong letter of recommendation written on Bruni's behalf to the pope. Infinitely more painful, however, was the insinuation that he was unsure of Latin grammar. Salutati had for some time suspected that his young friends in Rome were agreed on this, but the letter of Bruni confirmed the suspicions of the old man whose preeminence as a Latin stylist had heretofore been unassailed.

Nonetheless, Salutati realized that he and Bruni were close to a rupture, and he wanted to avoid this more than to triumph in an altercation and to vindicate his style. Consequently, the letter is a model of self-control. It is a calm, effective defense against a specific charge that he has not followed ancient usage in writing first and family names. He also takes up incidental matters designed to relieve the tension and to highlight the casual intimacy of the two men's relationship. At the very close Salutati binds Bruni by promising to send him a volume of his collected writings on the Schism as soon as they are copied.[26] Bruni, penitent, did not know how to answer this letter. Since a papal commission taking him to the Romagna offered an opportunity to see his mentor face to face in Florence, he postponed writing. Bruni was already in the Romagna when on May 11 news reached him that Salutati was dead.[27]

Bruni, however, redeemed himself. On the eve of Bruni's departure for Rome, Salutati had implored him to obtain a benefice for Salutato, whose only hope of livelihood was in the Church. Salutati also re-

---

24. *Leonardi Bruni*, I, 20.   25. Ibid., II, 171–74 and *Epist.*, IV, 375–78.
26. Ibid., IV, 157.

27. Ibid., IV, 470. Salutati's criticism of Vergerio's *De ingenuis moribus*, which the author had sent him for approval, led to a cooling of relations with the young northern humanist as well. Vergerio's overtly courteous response to Salutati's letter pointing out errors in the work barely masked his irritation at having received a mixed review from the principal authority (ibid., IV, 78–86 and 365–70). To Salutati's criticism of his spelling, Vergerio replied flippantly: "Nam quid in eo genere laudis contendam, que sit cum cartis peritura? Nemo enim nunc aut Ciceronem aut Virgilium aut ullum prorsus antiquorum de orthographia vel laudat vel reprehendit" (p. 369). On Vergerio, see chap. 10. For a recent discussion of Vergerio's *De ingenuis moribus*, see David Robey, "Humanism and Education in the Early Quattrocento: The *De Ingenuis Moribus* of P. P. Vergerio," *Bibliothèque d'Humanisme et Renaissance*, 42 (1980), 27–58.

minded him of the request by letter once Bruni was at the Curia. Boni-fazio's trip to Rome in summer 1405 was probably connected with this matter.[28] Eventually through Bruni Salutato was to receive not one but two benefices, a canonry in Florence and another in Fiesole. Asking the benefices for himself from the pope, Bruni then unselfishly resigned them in favor of Salutati's sickly, weak-eyed son, thereby fulfilling his debt to his now deceased master.[29]

While the most obvious sources of tension between Salutati and the younger generation of scholars were emotional, he was also divided from them by a series of intellectual issues. Until relatively late in life Salutati had managed to keep his Christian sentiments in isolation from his scholarly concerns. From his earliest letters he had occasionally ac-knowledged the "blindness" or "ignorance" of the pagans, but these were affected judgments, formal obeisances to Christianity, which left his deep admiration for the ancients untouched. The *De seculo et religione* displayed Salutati's awareness of a number of themes, which together deprecated the natural knowledge on which antiquity prided itself. Yet, while his religious sentiment in the circumstances was genuine, there seem to have been no great depths to the feelings sufficient to force him to reevaluate his commitment to humanistic studies. He only initiated this process in the mid-1390s in the course of writing the three tracts, *De fato et fortuna*, *De nobilitate legum et medicine*, and *De tyranno*. Although each of the three had a separate principal focus, all represented in vari-ous ways an effort to come to grips with the problem of appraising his experience and learning from a Christian standpoint. However, the achievement of the pagans came off badly when submitted to criteria derived from Christian Revelation and, as the process of osmosis oc-curred, his enthusiasm for antiquity and its achievements diminished.

On the other hand, Salutati's younger friends were not driven by the same compulsion to see their scholarship in a theological framework, and they found tedious the old man's efforts to belittle the value of pa-gan learning on such grounds. Although they were like Salutati, com-mitted to utilizing eloquence for moral improvement of themselves and others, they intended to focus primarily on the natural, not the Chris-tian man. Curiously in their secular tone Florentine humanists of the

28. *Leonardi Bruni*, I, 7.

29. Ibid., I, 47, and Salvino Salvini, *Catalogo cronologico de' canonici della chiesa metropoli-tana fiorentina* (Florence, 1782), p. 32, n. 287, under the year 1409, describes Salutato as being the curate of S. Maria di Figline and of S. Martino a Brozzi and a canon of Bologna in addition to having the two benefices given him by Bruni.

first half of the fifteenth century were closer to the rhetoricians of the thirteenth century than their immediate predecessors. They were out to close a door opened by Petrarch and Salutati in the fourteenth century. Nonetheless, the self-consciousness and consistency of their approach owed much to the distinction between the secular and the divine established by the pioneers of the humanist movement.

In the last decade of Salutati's life, as religious scruples came to dominate his view of ancient culture, there were still frequent points at which his feeling for antiquity was very positive. For instance, in 1396 in Book II of the *De fato* Salutati had included a long section on Socrates, who preferred to die in prison for the truth rather than escape.[30] He favorably compared the pagan to St. Peter, who fled Rome to escape persecution. In 1401 Socrates still received very high marks as the founder of moral philosophy. In what was the humanist's most elaborate statement on the nature of eloquence, Salutati urged the need for the future orator to be well-schooled in Cicero and Seneca and in the ethical thought of Aristotle "because ethics, which Socrates created, are those matters for which all adornment and fluency of speech are prepared" (III, 604). The relationship of ancient moral thought, the cornerstone of eloquence, to Christianity was also affirmatively stated:

> Do not, however, think that I want you so to devote yourself to that Socratic moral thought without conjoining with it those things pertaining to Christian perfection, not in such a way as to become an adherent of the preachers of our time but so that in living wisely and in writing soberly you might embrace that perfection of morality by which without doubt the doctrine of Christ is fulfilled.[31]

Although Christianity is superior, there is a continuity between its teachings and those of ancient morality.

Nevertheless, the stress on the inferiority of ancient wisdom to Christian truth becomes more insistent with the death of Piero. Salutati's attack on Stoic moral principles as a basis for consoling those bereaved by the death of loved ones is symptomatic of the emergence of decidedly condescending attitudes toward the pagans. Similarly, because he recognizes the foundation of the Roman monarchy now as a product of God's design, republican sentiments have to find a place within a framework of political thinking which accepts the emperor as the fount of secular order and justice in Christian society. In eschatological terms,

---

30. *De fato et fortuna*, Tr. II, 8: B.A.V., *Vat. Lat.*, 2928, fol. 16.
31. *Epist.*, III, 605.

moreover, the only significant history becomes that which follows the advent of Christ—always excepting of course the saga of the Jews in which God foreshadows his ultimate intentions. Finally, Salutati's justification of the active life of the citizen as superior to the speculative life, while partly inspired by Aristotle and Cicero, is comprehensible only within the context of Christian theology, which sees final beatitude as an act primarily of the will rather than the intellect.

After 1400 he aggressively sought opportunities to deflate the reputation of the ancients. The pagan belief in prophecy was attacked as "stupid and vain" (*Epist.*, IV, 14); the ancient religion was "foolishness" (IV, 52); and its conception of the life of the soul "wild imagination" (III, 460). His earlier recognition that the Greek and Roman heroes craved glory now becomes a ringing condemnation. This "preoccupation of the Gentiles" is unfavorably contrasted with that of the Christians, whose duty was not to live for fame and perhaps not even for eternal life but for God alone "who is the end of all things" (III, 471). The error of the ancient pagans was the error of corrupt flesh before the revelation of divine truth (III, 472). The denial by the ancients that one could have many friends indicates the inadequacy of the pagan conception of love. Christian love by contrast enables many to be linked by a mutual tie of friendship as happens in the relationship between men living in a large monastery (IV, 20).

Salutati's exchange with Poggio in the winter of 1405–6 revealed the extent to which the old humanist was ready to forsake his commitment to ancient literature when he felt the preeminence of Christian truth questioned. The two disagreed primarily about Petrarch's literary stature in comparison with that of the ancients.[32] Salutati viewed Poggio's insistence that modern writers were so far inferior in learning that they could not even be compared to the ancients as an attack on Christian culture generally. If Poggio meant by the ancients Church Fathers like Jerome, Augustine, Chrysostom, and Ambrose, Salutati began in the first letter, then they were in agreement because they and other early Christian writers were supreme. Among these, moreover, Augustine deserved recognition as the apex of learning.[33]

But in considering the ancient pagan and modern Christian writers, he continues, one must remember that learning consists of two elements, wisdom and eloquence. On these grounds, then, "benefitting from the doctrine of the Christian faith, not only Petrarch but even the

---

32. See above, chap. 8 and chap. 9.   33. *Epist.*, IV, 131.

most poorly educated person of our time excels the Gentiles: Cicero, Varro, and all the Romans; Aristotle, Plato, and the Greeks" [IV, 134–35]. These ancients indulged in impossible beliefs about the eternity of the world and a universe ruled by necessity. In ethics they erred in thinking that pleasure, or virtue, or a harmonious human society, or meditation on death or speculation could be the end of man. Certainly Petrarch excelled all these writers of antiquity because of his faith and possession of the truth.[34]

If not wiser, Salutati asks, should we at least concede that the ancients were more eloquent than Petrarch and other moderns? According to Cicero, "No one can be an orator worthy of the highest praise unless he has attained knowledge of all the greatest subjects and arts. For speech must flower and exude this knowledge, and if the orator is unaware or ignorant of it, his speech has a certain empty and childish character. So it must be admitted that everyone who excels someone in wisdom also excels him in eloquence" (III, 137). Salutati's astounding conclusion to this argument is as follows: "But you say: will you drive me mad? Will you force me to confess that the theologians of our time and those who have flourished for almost three hundred years are eloquent? These are in the number of those who, in the words of Augustine, tell true things in such a way that it is tedious to listen, difficult to understand, and finally not easy to believe. I know, dearest Poggio, that just as our theologians surpass the Gentiles in knowledge of the truth, so the latter outdistance ours, not in skill and majesty of expression (which without knowledge of the truth is childish), but in that form of speech which, as Horace says, is "void of thought, and but sonorous trifles" (IV, 137).

Salutati's second letter, that of March 26, repeats in substance the principal arguments of the first but appears to put still more stress on the inferiority of the pagans. Even the badly educated Christian is superior to the best of the Gentiles: "Not a single teaching of any of them can survive" (IV, 163–64). Every ancient thinker "deviated from the truth which you hold most certain." Nor were they able to be virtuous.

34. Petrarch was capable of making a stark contrast between Christian and pagan knowledge, but he did not question the ancients' claim to eloquence. As he wrote in his *De ignorantia sui ipsius et multorum* (*Opera*, II, 1162–63): "Si mirari autem Ciceronem, hoc est Ciceronianum esse, Ciceronianus sum. Miror enim nempe, quin etiam non mirantes illum miror, si qua haec ignorantiae nova confessio videri potest, hoc sum animo fateor, hoc stupore. At ubi de religione, idem de summa veritate, et de vera foelicitate, deque aeterna salute cogitandum incidit, aut loquendum, non Ciceronianus certe, aut Platonicus, sed Christianus sum. . . . Caeterum multum hac in parte plus fidei apud me habiturus fuerit, prius quisque Catholicus, quamvis indoctus, quam Plato ipse vel Cicero."

Even if in other respects an act may appear good, it is imperfect when done for the wrong final end. For instance, were love of country the final goal of virtuous action, then Brutus' sacrifice of his sons would not be reckoned as virtuous because he acted as much out of desire for personal glory as for patriotism. Now the true ultimate goal of man is God himself: " . . . this God, who is the object of the beatific vision, the subject of love, and that beatitude which is made up of the vision or awareness or love of this being, cannot be applied to anything else but Himself nor can this truly final end be altered in any way, or sought for any other reason but for itself." He then concludes: "The Gentiles and writers on ethics did not see this [the true end of man] and for this reason they could not discourse properly or in a fashion worthy of imitation either on humanity or on moral science or ethics, which is the same thing" (IV, 164). His condemnation in these two letters of the worthlessness of ancient eloquence and moral thought seems equivalent to a denial of the humanistic enterprise.

Characteristically, Salutati overreacted to Poggio's threat, falling into a wholesale condemnation of the pagans championed by the younger man. As suggested in chapter 9, Poggio's position on the incomparable superiority of the ancients to Petrarch brought into question Salutati's insistence on the continuity of the literary tradition from ancient times to the present. However, the evolution of his thought in the last years provided Salutati some strong arguments for superceding his earlier view and matching Poggio's dogmatism with his own. If the two literatures, pagan and Christian, were incomparable, then, Salutati argued, the superiority lay with the Christian. He died before having to face the consequences of his statement for his life's work.[35]

Beset in his last years by critics with secularist and classicizing tendencies, Salutati at the same time faced a serious, more traditional challenge from another direction. Since at least 1378 Salutati had occasionally been called on to defend the reading of ancient poetry from the attacks of those pious Christians who forbade its study. His De laboribus had been designed as a massive justification of poetry and an explication of poetic allegory, but his views on the nature of poetry in recent years had subtly changed, and from the mid-1390s he had worked on the manuscript only in a desultory fashion. Indeed, the defense of poetry found in Salutati's private correspondence in the last decade and a

35. I cannot agree with von Martin's rather stark conclusion that the debate between Salutati and Poggio is a conflict between faith and reason: *Coluccio Salutati und das humanistische Lebensideal* (Berlin, 1916), p. 62.

half of his life differs significantly from his treatment in the *De laboribus Herculis*.

The most extensive discussions are found in three letters to Giovanni da San Miniato, originally a devotee of the Muses, who abandoned the literary for the military profession, only to desert that in turn for the spiritual joys of monasticism. Of the three, one was written about 1389/ 90, another in September 1398/99, and the last and longest, on January 25, 1404/5. Two other letters written toward the end of the humanist's life treat the same subject. One composed in 1398 dealt with the reported destruction of the statue of Virgil in Mantua by Carlo Malatesta and the other, unfinished at the time of Salutati's death, constituted a general response to the attack on secular letters by fra Giovanni Dominici in his *Lucula noctis* published in 1405.[36]

As in the letters to Zonarini and the *De laboribus Herculis*, Salutati refers in these five letters to the Church Fathers, first, as authorities recognizing the legitimacy of studying the poets and, secondly, as evidence that such knowledge can enrich a Christian's own writing.[37] Again he repeatedly emphasizes the figurative nature of poetry and the necessity of speaking in allegories when dealing with matters of which our intellect can form no conception.[38] Poetry is "a divine not a human invention." As we know from dreams and portents, when God Himself communicates with men, he utilizes figurative language like the poets to express his message (IV, 181). Moreover, Scripture stands out as "the most holy and perfect poem of celestial and salutary things" (III, 231). Given by God, Scripture offers in its early books the first expressions of poetry. Echoing the account of the *De laboribus Herculis* in his letter of 1404/5, Salutati identifies the Hebrews, Enoch, Noah, Abraham, and

36. Letters to Giovanni da San Miniato are found *Epist.*, III, 221–31; 539–43; and IV, 170–205. For the dating of the letters, see Berthold L. Ullman, *Studies in the Italian Renaissance*, Storia e letteratura, 2nd. ed., vol. 51 (Rome, 1973), pp. 227, and 248–49; also *The Humanism*, pp. 59–60. I accept Ullman's dates of *circa* 1389 for *Epist.*, III, 221–31; 1398/99 for III, 539–43; and 1404/5 for IV, 170–205. On *Lucula noctis* see Ullman, *The Humanism*, pp. 63–65, and notes. Salutati also wrote two defenses of Virgil, defending him from charges of error and immorality: *Epist.*, III, 264–76, dated by Novati as 1398(?) and by Ullman about 1378 (*The Humanism*, p. 55, n. 2); and III, 232–38, dated by Novati 1397(?). Because these are not defenses of poetry but rather refutations of specific mistakes, they do not concern this discussion. Vergerio's attack on Malatesta is found *Epistolario di Pier Paolo Vergerio*, ed. Leonard Smith, Fonti per la storia d'Italia, vol. 74 (Rome, 1934), pp. 189–202. Another defense by an unidentified writer is published by D. J. B. Robey, "Virgil's Statue at Mantua and the Defense of Poetry: An Unpublished Letter of 1397," *Rinascimento*, 9 (1969), 191–203. For the earlier discussion, see above, chap. 7.

37. *Epist.*, III, 290–91 and 542; and IV, 182.

38. Ibid., III, 226, and IV, 176 ff.

♦

Moses as the first poets.[39] This mode of speaking was then "usurped" from these divinely inspired poets by the Gentile poet-theologians and by all those who "spoke piously and rationally about God." The Christians derived it from "all the prophets and sacred writings and found it mingled with the Holy Gospel by our Saviour Himself."

There are, however, certain elements in these letters which stand in marked contrast with Salutati's position on poetry expressed in all his earlier works. Taken together these letters indicate that Salutati's view of poetry altered in his later years to such an extent that, while maintaining a significant difference in tone, he drew much closer to the "naturalistic" conception of poetic creativity identified with Petrarch and Boccaccio.[40]

In none of the five letters concerned does he cite verses from the poets to demonstrate their power to utter truths known only by Revelation to Christians. He also makes no claim for any action of the Holy Spirit on the poets. Rather, he explicitly denies such contact by specifying that the poets' knowledge was of human origin. In the first letter to Giovanni da San Miniato, dated 1389/90, he explains how the poets aimed to express in figures "that secret of the highest divinity, which they perceived, celebrated, and represented according to their reason, or rather, since it was before God's revelation, by their estimative power."[41] What Virgil thought about the final end of man is said to have been "according to the understanding of the Gentiles" (III, 231). In dealing in 1398 with the destruction of Virgil's statue, while still endorsing the principle that Scripture differs from pagan poetry because it is true at both levels of meaning, Salutati makes it clear that the two differ also because of the source of the truths expressed in each.

> It is characteristic of divine poetry to use truth for a sign by which another truth lurking mysteriously beneath might be hidden so that the second truth like a companion can then come forth. However,

39. Ibid., IV, 180–81. It should be emphasized here that no "secret tradition" is involved. Salutati sees the poets taking over the allegorical poetic form ("quem morem") and not the content of Hebrew poetry.

40. See chap. 7.

41. Ibid., III, 226. The passage in context reads: "Et quia tam arduam rem eloqui, que sensum omnem transcendebat, ut pure intelligerentur, non poterant, figuras quasdam excogitaverunt, quibus illud summe divinitatis arcanum, quod ratione vel potius ante Dei revelationem extimatione perceperant, celebrarent atque referrent, et quanto sublimius loquendi genus etiam excultorum hominum ingenia reperire potuerunt, sive natura sive arte sive quodam usu et exercitatione dicendi, huic mysterio, quo maior adderetur auctoritas, dicaverunt."

although it can use a truth to signify other things, it is appropriate for human poetry, which does not immediately spring from the pure truth, not to reject fictions and other foolish devices although its aim is to lead to and produce the truth.[42]

Salutati's third letter to Giovanni da San Miniato of 1404/5 makes this distinction between the two different sources of truth, rather than stressing, as did the *De laboribus*, the truth content of the external level, which is in that work the basic criterion for separating Scripture and pagan poetry. One of Salutati's longest letters (IV, 170–205), it was written partly to silence Giovanni, who had boasted in a letter sent to one of Salutati's young admirers, Antonio Corbinelli, that in the debate on poetry with Salutati in 1398/99, he, Giovanni, had emerged the winner.[43] It would seem that, during one of those two previous years, upon receiving Salutati's rebuttal of his attack on poetry, Giovanni had written a reply left unanswered by Salutati, who was either preoccupied with other matters or perhaps bored by the correspondence. The fact that five or six years later Giovanni considered that silence as recognition of defeat, however, galvanized Salutati into action.

In this letter of January 25, 1404/5, Salutati quotes extensively from the Church Fathers, including St. Basil, who was recently translated from Greek by Bruni, and defines both the similarity and difference between Scripture and poetry.[44] Scripture like poetry hides truth "under a covering of falsity." Among the examples of outward fictions in the Bible cited are the Song of Solomon and the parables of Christ. The language of Scripture in referring to God's actions is also largely figurative. When God is said to "see" or "repent," such words cannot be taken in their normal meaning. But if both Scripture and pagan poetry are alike in that they sometimes contain fictions, a new distinction between the

42. Ibid., III, 292. August Buck, *Italienische Dichtungslehren vom Mittelalter bis zum Ausgang der Renaissance*, Beihefte zur Zeitschrift für Romanische Philologie, vol. 94 (1952), p. 87, appears to me to distort Salutati's meaning here when he explicates the passage as meaning "Die allegorische Interpretation wird dann auch wieder mit der theologischen Poetik in Verbindung gebracht: Jede Dichtung ist letzten Endes göttlichen Ursprungs: auch aus heidnischen Dichtern, die den christlichen Gott nicht kannten, leuchtet oft der Strahl der göttlichen Wahrheit."

43. Berthold L. Ullman publishes the letter of Giovanni to Corbinelli in *Studies*, pp. 249–53. This paragraph is based on Theodore F. Rich, "Giovanni da Sanminiato and Coluccio Salutati," *Speculum*, 11 (1936), 386–90; and Ullman, *Studies*, pp. 248–49. Unless otherwise indicated, quotations given in the text for the letter to Giovanni da San Miniato and Giovanni Dominici are taken from the English translation of the *Letters* by Ephriam Emerton, *Humanism and Tyranny* (Cambridge, 1925), pp. 312–41 and 346–77.

44. *Epist.*, IV, 178–80. Salutati had previously spoken of the figurative language of Scripture without branding it falsehood: see for example, *De lab.*, I, 8–9, and 15–16.

two is necessary. Whether or not Salutati consciously realizes this, he subtly shifts in the course of this letter to a new formulation of the distinction by emphasizing that Scripture is divinely inspired while poetry is strictly of human origin:

> But, I pray you, who would say that any portion of Scripture is really a poem, though it be composed in verse, even though the narrative be in poetic form, that is, hiding truth under a false covering of words. A poem is one thing, a narrative in poetic form is another. A poem is man's invention, a fiction or the relation of something fictitious; but Holy Scripture is not of human invention, is neither fiction nor related as something fictitious, but is absolute truth even though in a perverted or inappropriate form of speech (IV, 199–200).

In some sense as a compensation, immediately after denying such inspiration to poetry, Salutati insists on the ultimately divine origin of all truth. Salutati's very language suggests the philosophical direction of his interests in these last years:

> That the process not be infinite, all truth must be brought back (*reducere*) from truths to *the* Truth, the end and origin of all truths. This is God alone, not simply *the* Truth, but as I wrote you at the time, every real and infinite and genuine truth, the source, that is, the seed and origin of all truth, not only preceding all truth, which is what is, but manifesting and declaring all truth, which is correct functioning (*rectitudo*) of the mind, that is, the conformity of things with the intellect (*rerum scilicet adequatio cum intellectu*), which in a certain way is all things. For the mental concept, which teaches and reveals that which is, is not God but may more properly be said to be from God. Perhaps you do not take this to be God but when it is carried back (*reducere*) to God, it is without doubt in substance (*realiter*) God, differing in the way of signifying (*modo significandi*) and not in that which is signified (*in re*). Wherefore, if truth is found in the prophets and in other sacred writings, whether of the Gentiles or of the faithful, or in the songs of the poets, which you abhor, it makes no difference. The truth is God and from God, as you see, so that, when you find it where you least expected, you should joyfully embrace it (IV, 200 [my translation]).

Earlier in the letter Salutati writes much the same thing: "Since the truth [of the poets] is true, it has a marvelous harmony with theological truth, nor is it to be excluded from the sanctuary of theology. Between truths and truths there is no dissension, nothing which makes them mutually destructive or exclusive" (IV, 184 [my translation]). Yet this recognition that all truth is in the final result derived from God and that through human reason the poets discovered certain theological truths is not at all equivalent to the belief that these truths were implanted directly in the poet's mind by the Holy Spirit.

The belief in some kind of divine inspiration acting on the poets, expressed in the letters to Zonarini and in the *De laboribus Herculis*, was essentially incompatible with Salutati's new distinction between Scripture and poetry. In those earlier discussions the crucial factor was the truth value of the literal meaning in Scripture. Behind Salutati's shift to the new criterion lay his abandonment of the belief in poetic inspiration as at times influenced by divine agency.

To distinguish thus between the human origins of the poet's truth, even in its loftiest expressions, and the divine source of Scripture, was to emphasize the difference between the pagan and Christian worlds. In Petrarch and Boccaccio this view that the poets' inspiration was purely their own could foster a sense of affinity with the ancients founded on acceptance of a common human nature. Once Virgil's creative power was understood as natural, the man and his work could become more susceptible to understanding in human terms. Petrarch's letters to various ancient poets demonstrate how the process worked. For the same reason, moreover, both he and Boccaccio treated ancient and modern poetry as parts of a single art deriving its inspiration from the energy of the human mind. On the other hand, this desacralization of the poets was for Salutati one more motive to question the value of pagan letters for a Christian. Such thinking was of course potentially disastrous for a humanist.

Early in 1406, in the same period when he was writing to Poggio branding the ethical writings of the pagan philosophers as useless to Christians and their rhetoric as empty sound, Salutati was forced for at least the fifth time since 1389 to defend the ancients. However, his opponent was far more formidable than Giovanni da San Miniato and on this occasion Salutati was far more ambivalent toward the pagans than he had ever been.[45] Fra Giovanni Dominici, born in Florence in 1355/56,

---

45. The essential details of the life of fra Giovanni Banchini are found in Stefano Orlandi, *Necrologio di S. Maria Novella*, 2 (Florence, 1955), II, 77–108. Cf. G. Cracco, "Banchini, Giovanni di Domenico," *Dizionario biografico degli italiani*, vol. 5 (Rome, 1963), pp. 657–64. Also see Lia Sbriziolo, "Note su Giovanni Dominici," *Rivista di storia della Chiesa in Italia*, 24 (1970), 4–30, and 29 (1975), 1–11; Michael Contrada. "Fra Giovanni Dominici in

was widely known in Italy for his learning and his eloquent preaching. Salutati doubtless knew him as early as 1385/87, when he served as prior of Santa Maria Novella in Florence. Subsequently, he held various administrative positions in the Dominican Order in the Veneto, rising in 1393 to become vicar general of the Reformed Dominican convents in Italy. Like Salutati he had been deeply affected by the *Bianchi* movement in 1399 and had led a procession through Venice against the express command of the Venetian government. This resulted in his exile from Venetian territory and probably caused the annulment of his appointment as vicar general in March 1400.

After leaving Venice Dominici returned to Santa Maria Novella in Florence, where, with frequent absences, he resided for the next seven years. In addition to teaching the Bible in the *Studio*, Dominici frequently preached, especially during the weeks of Lent. Attracted to the friar both because of his eloquence and his pious life, Salutati added his personal efforts to those of the *Signoria* to make certain that Dominici would not be transferred elsewhere.[46] Feeling himself unable to meet the challenge posed by Salutati's letter of 1404/5, fra Giovanni da San Miniato turned to Dominici to take up the challenge. Fra Giovanni Dominici obliged by writing in 1405 an enormous work entitled the *Lucula noctis*, dedicating it to Salutati.

Dominici's work is highly scholastic in its presentation, first giving the arguments favoring the other side and then discussing those which militate against it.[47] One of the significant aspects of Dominici's position is that whereas previously both in the writings of fra Giovanni da San Miniato and in those of Salutati's other correspondents the problem of Christianity versus pagan culture had been limited to the value of reading the poets, now the study of the whole pagan corpus of writings was in question. Dominici admitted that for minds well-established in faith reading of the ancient poets and philosophers is permissible but not for the young or those not yet secure in their Christian convictions.

Salutati read the volume carefully, probably in the last months of 1405

Florence" (Senior Diss., Harvard Univ., 1972), and *Giovanni Dominici (+ 1419): Saggi e Inediti*, Memorie Domenicane, n.s. 1 (1970).

46. *Epist.*, IV, 8–9.

47. *Iohannis Dominici Lucula noctis*, ed. E. Hunt (Indiana, 1940). For an outline of the work, see Hunt's introduction. Also see Berthold L. Ullman," The Dedication Copy of Giovanni Dominici's *Lucula noctis*," in *Studies*, pp. 255–75; and his, *The Humanism*, pp. 63–64. The *Lucula noctis* demonstrates the author's extensive knowledge of Greek culture as it came through Latin sources: Roberto Weiss, "Lo studio del greco a Firenzo," *Medieval and Humanist Greek*, Medioevo e umanesimo, vol. 8 (1977), pp. 242–43.

or early 1406, and made numerous annotations on the pages of the manuscript. His intention was to write an elaborate answer befitting Dominici's extensive treatment, but only a portion of the work was finished before his death. The existing fragment throughout is pervaded by a tone of deep piety. Salutati opens his rebuttal of Giovanni with an extended profession of his Christian faith:

> Indeed I engage in this argument with you the more freely in that it would not be, I think, to affirm anything opposed to or proposed against faith, because if perchance it were [against faith], I would immediately recall and condemn it. For God gave his servant this grace that never in anything have I felt opposed to faith or even lightly hesitated concerning it, though human reason might seem to be in contrast. How should my intellect presume to disagree with the Holy Scriptures or to doubt in those matters which the community of the faithful has determined? I don't know about others. As far as I am concerned I have always been most firmly persuaded—even when I was a little boy and even more now when by the grace of God through my age I have seen more and perhaps know more—that no doctrine is more powerful than our faith and the Scriptures and that whatever contradicts it is most false, whatever departs from it, mad. I have always considered it the height of stupidity and an excess of intellectual presumption to deviate in any way from the precepts of Jesus, from the teachings of Paul or from the counsels of either, which Jerome insisted on and translated, Ambrose treated, Gregory expounded and Augustine disputed, or to be unwilling to agree in everything with men of such great sanctity and erudition. Let the crowd of would-be philosophers follow Aristotle or Plato, let them follow the poisonous Averroes, or a better man if they have one—I do not care to wander through their names. Jesus Christ alone pleases me, and He, crucified for the salvation of the faithful, Who, though studies were flourishing in Greece and Italy, . . . made the wisdom of this world folly. Folly indeed, not by the wisdom of the wise or the power of the mighty but by the foolishness of preaching and the cross, through fishermen and not through philosophers, through men of humble condition and not through the powerful of this world.[48]

Salutati proceeds by justifying each of the seven liberal arts within this framework. With a rare touch of humor, the old man illustrates the

---

48. *Epist.*, IV, 214–15. The translation follows closely that of Charles Trinkaus, *In Our Image and Likeness*, 2 vols. (London, 1970), I, 55.

need for better spelling by citing examples taken from Dominici's *Lucula noctis*.[49] Unfortunately, the work breaks off just before the point where, after stressing the poetic quality of Scripture, Salutati would have to offer a distinction between it and poetry. Nevertheless, by describing the "outward layer" of the Song of Songs as "erotic and lascivious" and the language of Scripture as "departing from the proper and usual meaning," Salutati appears to be preparing the way for a distinction drawn along lines found in the letter of 1404/5.[50] The cautious approach taken to the arts in the sections written gives no indication that he intended to treat poetry with great exuberance.

As he assesses the value of each of the *trivium* and *quadrivium*, it becomes clear that Salutati was endeavoring to assign the arts strictly anciliary roles in the service of the faith. While it can be argued that the discussion was conditioned by the quality of his correspondent and the specific issue—whether secular letters should form a part of the education of the young Christian—none of his other letters in defense of pagan authors, including his last one to fra Giovanni da San Miniato a year or so earlier, had had such a subdued tone. It seems more probable that this attitude was the product of the coalescence of a variety of Christian tendencies that had led him in the previous months to assail the value of imitating the ancients. A lover of argument to the end, Salutati would not allow himself to admit his doubts in his correspondence with Dominici. Nonetheless, it appears that his own faith in the enterprise of humanism was in question and that he could bring himself to do no more in its defense than to stress the importance of secular letters in the early stages of a Christian education.

Until the last year of his life Salutati was rarely sick. An illness in 1405, however, must have been quite serious.[51] Ser Lapo Mazzei's undated letter to Francesco Datini referring to ser Coluccio's illness probably belongs to this year.[52] Ser Lapo frankly admits he is unhappy at being tied to the office because of the chancellor's ill health, but, he informs Datini, "ser Coluccio is getting well quickly and so will be restored to health." The illness occurred in the spring and in July Salutati

---

49. Ullman, *Studies*, pp. 259–75, analyzes these errors in detail.
50. *Epist.*, IV, 236 ff.
51. He was sick in the spring of 1405 (ibid., IV, 92). His only other reference to illness in his letters are ibid., I, 335 and II, 183. In the latter letter he writes of being seriously ill three times in the winter of 1384. For the date, see Ullman, *Studies*, pp. 216–17. We would not, however, expect him to say much about his health given his ethical position.
52. *Lettere di un notaro a un mercante del secolo XIV con altre lettere e documenti*, ed. Cesare Guasti, 2 vols. (Florence, 1880), II, 25.

describes to Bruni the rigors of taking the waters at the Baths of Morba located in the Val di Cecina, where he seems to have had a long cure.[53]

The details of Salutati's final weeks are lacking. Perhaps the illness of the previous year struck again only more virulently. Death must have come quickly because the chancellor was working in the office up to the last days of April. The last missive in his hand in the registers was written on April 23; the last missive in this register belonging to his term was sent to the Roman pope on April 30.[54] Perhaps he composed the rough draft, but the register copy is in another's hand.

In his very last days the *Signoria*, as a gesture of honor to the dying man, placed his name in the purses for a variety of notarial offices. Accordingly, in what must have been a rigged extraction Salutati's name was drawn for the first time in his life for the post of notary of the *Signoria* for the two months May-June. On May 12, a week after Salutati's death, a *provvisione* approved by the councils of the Republic noted in its authorization to substitute Giovanni Currado for Salutati in the post—that Salutati himself had requested it. The same provision recognized that an automatic substitution would be made for Salutati by ser Giovanni and ser Antonio every time the late chancellor's name was drawn.[55] In effect this kept the two men well-employed with notarial offices until the last purse containing Salutati's name was exhausted in 1413.[56]

Death came to him on May 4, a Tuesday, in the evening.[57] On the following morning his friendly opponent in the last controversy in which he participated, fra Giovanni Dominici, preached a sermon in the Piazza dei Peruzzi before the Salutati house. A chronicler wrote of Dominici's eulogy: " . . . and he said many things and enumerated his great accomplishments among which he said that Salutati had written ten books except the sixth, which was not finished."[58] At the thirteenth hour his close friend and colleague, ser Viviano di Neri "with the greatest dignity" placed the laurel crown of the poet on the dead man's head. Before the assembled populace, including the priors, the Twelve, and

53. *Epist.*, IV, 101–3.
54. *Miss.*, 26, fols. 151ᵛ and 152.
55. *Epist.*, IV, 466–70.
56. For elections to public offices, see *Tratte*, 114, under "ser Coluccius" and *Tratte*, 78, fols. 162ᵛ, 178, 183ᵛ, 189ᵛ, 205, and 269. Salutati's successor in the chancery was ser Benedetto Fortini. For information on Fortini, see Marzi, *La cancelleria*, pp. 153–56; and Witt, *The Public Letters*, pp. 16–17 and 40–41.
57. As Marzi notes (*La cancelleria*, p. 148, n. 3), his death was recorded in the *Libri dei Morti* "in scrittura molto più chiara ed elegante del solito."
58. "Diario florentino de Bartolommeo di Michele del Corazza," *Archivio storico italiano*, 5th ser., 14 (1894), 241.

the Sixteen, together with the knights and doctors of the city, ser Viviano eulogized the dead man: "He was indeed an outstanding man of great learning, wise in practical things, of the best nature, upright and God-fearing."[59] He had prepared himself a place near his second wife and their children in S. Romolo near the house, but the Republic decreed otherwise. After a solemn procession through the street, Salutati's catafalque was deposited in the cathedral with an elaborate ceremony.

On Sunday, May 2, the news of the illness and its gravity had reached Buggiano. On that day the assembly provided that "since the esteemed man, ser Coluccio Piero of Stignano, Florentine chancellor, is at the end of his life and, as it seems, has few days left on this earth, [it is proposed] that, if almighty God will take him away, his body be honored as much as this commune has means to do."[60] On the 5th when the procession of dignitaries accompanied the corpse to its place of burial, among their number were representatives from Buggiano and the banner of his commune of origin was draped across the coffin along with the colors of the Florentine Republic and those of the Judges and Notaries and the Wool Guild.[61]

His eight surviving children did not have a great fortune to divide. True in the end to his belief that material possessions were to be used but not loved, he left no will. This omission for a notary could only have been intentional.[62] It symbolized the cutting of his tie with earth and permitted him to carry away only that which was truly his own.

---

59. This passage from the *Priorista del Palazzo*, ad an., is quoted by Marzi together with the other sources on the burial (*La cancelleria*, pp. 148–49). On Salutati's burial and his iconography, see *Epist.*, IV, 167–70, n. 1, 389, and 559–65. Cf. Giuseppi Conti, *Fatti e aneddoti di storia fiorentina secoli XIII-XVIII* (Florence, 1902), pp. 130–33.

60. A.C.B., *Delib.*, 10, fol. 146ᵛ.

61. Marzi, *La cancelleria*, p. 149. On May 12, 1406 (*Delib.*, 10, fol. 147) another grant of money was made available by Buggiano for the purpose of honoring Salutati.

62. *Notarile*, F 298 (ser Filippo di Cristofano, 1418–19), fol. 95ᵛ (March 14, 1420) refers to the inheritance as follows: "Venerabilis et honestus vir dominus Salutatus olim domini Coluccii Pieri, canonicus florentinus, sciens et cognoscens hereditatem dicti olim domini Coluccii eius patris sibi esse pro sexta parte ab intestato delatam et ipsam hereditatem sibi fore et esse potius utilem et lucrosam quam inutilem vel dapnosam, ideo dictam hereditatem adivit etc. Rogans etc." I would like to thank Dr. Gino Corti of Florence for this reference.

Tradition has it that he left almost no liquid wealth, but clearly the remark of the seventeenth-century chronicler Marmi is a bit of hagiographic foolishness. According to Marmi, the account books of ser Coluccio showed that he had "né casa, né altra possessione che le paterne, et non si gli trovò più che fiorini 40 di oro:" B.N.F., *Magl.* XXV, 64, fol. 110ᵛ; Marzi, *La cancelleria*, p. 150. Cf. *Epist.*, IV, 569.

CHAPTER 16. CONCLUSION

Between Petrarch and Boccaccio and the generation of Bruni and Poggio, Coluccio Salutati held the unrivaled leadership of Italian humanism, towering above other figures like Francesco da Fiano, Benvenuto da Imola, and Giovanni di Conversino. The bleakness of alternative leadership suggests the precarious quality of the Petrarchan legacy. Through his prestige as chancellor and the fame of his public letters, his vast network of private correspondence, his eagerness to relate classical studies to moral and religious problems of his day, his effort to encompass within a continuous tradition the ancient Latin authors, the Fathers, and the medieval rhetoricians, and his successful introduction of Hellenic studies into the Latin West, Salutati elevated humanism from the stage of pioneering, isolated genius to that of a major movement in European cultural and intellectual life.

Salutati's provincial origins obscure the fact that he passed his childhood and early youth in Bologna, the traditional center of Italian learning. His early formation in the school of Pietro da Moglio, himself disciple of Giovanni del Virgilio, one of the forerunners of humanism, prepared him for reception of Petrarch's teachings but also determined to an extent the manner in which he exploited them. The stylistic and conceptual innovations of the group of scholars to which Giovanni belonged along with Lovato Lovati and Albertino Mussato developed primarily in poetry. Except in the area of historical writing, the later thirteenth- and early fourteenth-century reformers posed no challenge to the rule of *ars dictaminis* over the domain of literary prose. Furthermore, in their secularism and the unexamined character of their use of pagan themes and symbols, they were indeed very much one with the thirteenth-century *dictatores*.

The most distinctive contribution of Petrarchan humanism lay in its conscious endeavor to take seriously the traditional link between ethical teaching and rhetoric and to emphasize the role of eloquence in serving the faith. But this achievement was intimately connected with Petrarch's refusal to accept the authority of *dictamen* over prose. His *Epistolae de rebus familiaribus*, begun in 1345 after the discovery of a collection of Cicero's private letters, amounted to a declaration of war against the stylistic tradition of almost two centuries. Acknowledging implicitly the rationale perpetuating the supremacy of *ars dictaminis* in the composition of official corespondence, he insisted that at least in the private sphere an end should be made to the use of set phrases, a rigorous *cursus*, and slavish obedience to the Horatian dictum of brevity, all of which set carefully constructed limits on expression of one's personality and ideas in general.

To his last years Salutati remained influenced by his early training in Bologna, where during his school days the heavy burden of a successful medieval rhetorical tradition was at best mitigated by aspirations for a deeper understanding of ancient sources and a more informed imitation of ancient poetical work. His early correspondence reflects the assumption of a century of Italian *dictatores* that ancient eloquence could best be rivalled by dealing with themes preferred by the pagans themselves. These letters play continuously upon the topics of fate, fortune, friendship, and heroic virtue, illustrated in the grand manner of *stilus rhetoricus* by reference to ancient examples.

Other residual effects of his Bolognese experience appear when, after 1381, Salutati resolves to devote his principal energies to scholarship. His unexamined acceptance of poetry as superior to prose embodied in his *De laboribus Herculis*, his commitment to pursuing truth through study of pagan poetic allegories—some of which presumably conceal truths made known by divine revelation—his tireless examination of etymologies to unlock the truth bound up in words betray the inspiration of the medieval grammarians. His commitment to etymologies, moreover, led him to an endless exploitation of the oftentime fantastic fruits of medieval lexicography.

Nevertheless, from his first datable productions—his two letters, to Nelli in 1359/61, and to da Moglio in 1360—Salutati's prose shows that he has already detached himself from the yoke of *dictamen* manuals and, rather than striving for effect by stringing together a succession of brilliant periods, demonstrates on occasion a willingness to develop an integrated moral argument. In time, Petrarch's letters would convince him that Christian eloquence had the capacity to match that of ancient rhetoric. This discovery, contemporaneous with a deepening of his religious faith, gradually led to the enrichment of Salutati's writings and the impressment of pagan cultural achievements into the service of Christian goals.

When compared with Petrarch, Salutati seems to have experienced a steady intellectual growth up to the end of his life. To an extent Petrarch's notorious penchant for endlessly retouching and bringing up to date his past masked real changes in his thought. While he is not "without a history," that history is very difficult to write. Fortunately for the biographer, Salutati suffered his work to stand once written. Such tolerance for one's own past is remarkable in the case of a writer like Salutati, who, very reluctant to admit a mistake or a change of heart, might easily have "adjusted" the past to suit his present position. Perhaps the press of his daily occupations rather than policy allowed the survival of traces of his intellectual journey. But the impression of significant long-term evolution in Salutati is not merely the result of the existence of his letters in their original form. Less independent minded than Petrarch and more deeply imbued with the scholarly tradition, Salutati had much further to develop.

Also less subtle than Petrarch, whose thought was often multilayered in significance and consciously ambiguous, Salutati developed and expressed his ideas dialectically. This contrast stemmed partly from the different milieus in which each did his thinking. Petrarch usually kept his own counsel, announcing the results in his writing, whereas Salutati worked out many of his ideas in conversation. But Salutati's circumstances only reinforced what was an essential cast of mind. He tended to conceive of the pursuit of truth occurring within the context of a trial or debate between proponents of two sides. When engaged in championing his side, Salutati's aim was to win conviction by every means available. In the process he was often neither fair to his opponent's position nor entirely representative of his own thought and feelings. At points in the arguments the reader can pick out "soft spots" reflecting his personal hesitations, but Salutati's intention was to leave the reader or listener with such a monolithic, massive wall of proofs of his stand that no doubt of their validity could be entertained.

This dialectical character of Salutati's thought might easily lead to the suspicion that his writings do not accurately reflect his own views. A major current of Salutati scholarship in fact maintains that the chancellor's expression of different ideas on the same subject at different times should not be taken as reflecting real change in his thought but as a calculated response to altered situations.[1] The facts of his life provide solid grounds for rejecting the belief that Salutati had at his disposition from the time of his earliest works the whole warehouse of ideas he

1. This view has been most cogently expressed by Peter Herde, "Politik and Rhetorik in Florenz am Vorabend der Renaissance: Die ideologische Rechtfertigung der Florentiner Aussenpolitik durch Coluccio Salutati," *Archiv für Kulturgeschichte*, 7 (1965), 141–220; and Jerrold Seigel, *Rhetoric and Philosophy in Renaissance Humanism* (Princeton, 1968), pp. 63–98 and 249 ff. Herde focuses primarily on Salutati's sincerity in his political utterances while Seigel's is a more general questioning of Salutati's intellectual honesty.

eventually used and that he simply made an objective, emotionally detached selection from among them as the need arose. While allowance must be occasionally made for rhetorical exaggeration in his statements, the account of his thought in relationship with the details of his life makes it clear that he experienced a genuine development in his thinking over the years.

A closely related criticism focusing on Salutati's status as a professional rhetorician presents him as an ambitious, selfish individual skillful at manipulating fine words and thoughts for his own interests.[2] That he was eager for success lies beyond question. He desperately begged and flattered his way from Tuscany to Rome and back, experiencing dissatisfaction and misfortune the length of the route. With the fiasco of Lucca in mind, once in Florence he kept his head low, his integrity unblemished, his conversation guarded, and his smile for everyone. His reward was to survive the Ciompi period and the birth pangs of the new regime of 1382. Gradually, having made himself an indispensible fixture of the Florentine state, he felt less reluctance to speak out on public issues, but he never ceased using his ability to stay with the winners which he so painstakingly cultivated in his early years in the city. His task after 1382 was facilitated by the evolution of a large center group of upper-class families who sought political stability by removing with death or exile potential threats to the *status quo* from the extremes. His entrance into Florentine service and rapid rise to the chancellorship were admittedly accomplished by ethically dubious means. A keenly felt embarrassment lies concealed in his mendacious affirmation to Marsili that he had been totally ignorant of the imminent dismissal of Monachi, whose position he assumed. But from 1375 on success blessed his enterprises and, fortunately for his reputation, removed the need for ruthlessness. To his credit he basked in his good fortune and limited his ambition to holding on to what he had gained. There is no trace of further egregious compromises of his integrity for personal advantage.

The basic thrust of the criticism that Salutati was a supreme egotist, however, stands refuted by his demonstrated capacity for friendship. His professions of love for men with whom he was barely acquainted or whom he never met must be taken as a literary conceit, but the roster of his real friends is impressive. Ugolino da Montecatini, ser Domenico Silvestri, ser Antonio Chelli, ser Lapo Mazzei, and Luigi Marsili, to name but a few, were obviously linked to Salutati by strong ties of mutual

2. This is essentially the viewpoint of Alfred von Martin, *Coluccio Salutati und das humanistische Lebensideal* (Berlin-Leipzig, 1916). See especially pp. 142 ff.

feeling. If his immediate affection for the young Loschi was perhaps misplaced, the fault was not Salutati's. But his relationships with Bruni, Vergerio, and Jacopo da Scarperia were ones of obviously reciprocal love.

Much has been made of the style and content of his various letters written on the occasion of the death of his wife and favorite son. The twentieth-century critic easily sees the studied language, the citations, and the use made of the deaths themselves for broad philosophical and theological ruminations as revealing a lack of deep human feeling.[3] To do so raises the whole question of the relationship between literature and life. Salutati was well aware when he wrote these lines on the death of his loved ones that his letters would circulate from hand to hand, possibly (he hoped) for centuries. But that he endeavored to structure the description of his feelings neither cheapens them nor means they did not exist. The changes wrought in his intellectual life by the death first of the woman and then of the young man testify to the depths of the loss he felt. Every age, including our own, finds it difficult not to write "formally" about its grief. Writing within a literary tradition in a primarily literary language like Latin, Salutati can hardly be expected to have abandoned himself to the incoherency that is the direct expression of sorrow.

Although disputatious, didactic, and somewhat self-satisfied, Salutati with his gregarious, affectionate, open nature and his spirit of enterprise brought humanism "out of the closet" into the forum. The Florentine chancellor, an organizer and entrepreneur, was the ideal leader of the movement at that moment. Petrarch taught primarily through the example of his finished products. Salutati, on the other hand, offered up his half-formed ideas for consideration and divulged his scholarly recipes to the first comer. Largely through the training he provided, Florence became the seat of a group of brilliant scholars, who guaranteed their city's dominant role in the humanist movement until the mid-fifteenth century.

That Salutati wrote almost entirely in Latin reflects his prejudice against the *volgare*. Although he came to appreciate its beauty and utility only late in life, he always granted ancient Greek the same preeminent status as Latin on the basis of reputation. Once seriously impressed by its virtues, Salutati brought all his influence to bear on establishing the teaching of Greek in the city. On the other hand, in his

3. Von Martin, ibid., pp. 171–82, views the evidence of these letters as decisive proof of Salutati's egotism.

eyes the carelessness and sloth of recent generations were typified in the spread of *volgare* literature—he never reconciled this attitude with his devotion to the *Divina commedia*. His patriotic bias combined with his general disapproval of the *volgare* to make his judgment on French as a literary language totally hostile.

Among the arduous tasks imposed on the would-be Latin author Salutati placed a premium on attention to detail. His concern for proper punctuation actually was not original: almost every *ars dictaminis* included a little treatise on the subject as part of its instruction. But this was not true of spelling where Salutati pioneered in demanding rigorous conformity to correct usage, some of which he himself helped to define. Petrarch had demonstrated some reforms in his works but Salutati made correct orthography a pet project. He also never wearied of emphasizing the necessity of paying heed to signification and etymology in fitting one's vocabulary to one's thought. These teachings contributed to the evolution of the more exacting standards for correct expression characteristic of the next generation.

Throughout his lifetime his immense library remained at the disposal of his friends and correspondents, who were allowed to borrow books for reading, for copying, and for correcting their own manuscripts. Thus, Salutati's marginal notes and corrections became part of the manuscript tradition of many important ancient works. Salutati may have received some oral instruction from Boccaccio and learned from contact with a few of Petrarch's manuscripts, but the methodology for textual emendation he freely taught and wrote about seems to have been largely his own creation.

This concern for corrected ancient texts, so characteristic of Renaissance humanism, was in Salutati's case motivated in part by medieval attitudes toward etymology and allegory. Believing as he did that etymology unlocked the truth hidden in a word, it became imperative to establish the correct reading (and spelling naturally) of the word or words in order for the etymological analysis to begin. This need was particularly felt in regard to texts containing pagan poetic allegories. To his mind these allegories expressed hidden truth, some of which had been inspired by God. In certain instances submitting an accurate text to etymological analysis led to recovering wisdom directly imparted by the Holy Spirit. While such truth always found its counterpart in Christian Revelation, the duplication in a pagan author was useful for apologetic purposes.

Although the humanist's motivation for textual emendation remained until very late in life confused with these old-fashioned strands of thought, the methodology unquestionably heralded the future. His rules for ferreting out errors in the texts were predicated on the assumption that the psychology of error remains the same over the centuries. Because of this common psychology, every text has a history of errors going back almost to the beginning, and it falls to the emendator to reach back to the original by comparing various manuscripts of the texts in an effort to identify the interloping elements and replace them with the true readings. In his last years, with no visible effect on his search for correct emendations, he discarded his belief in allegory as sometimes containing divinely revealed truth and possibly also gave up his faith in the ability of etymology to unlock the hidden truth of the word. By this time textual emendation had become a pursuit of truth set down by the ancient writers not as sometime prophets of the Word, but as exceptional human beings.

His earlier view granting divine inspiration to certain pagan poetic allegories as well as to those of Scripture localized the primary difference between the two categories of texts in the veridic character of Scripture both in its literal and hidden meaning as opposed to pagan poetry which was true at the inner level but false on the surface. His later realization that Scripture occasionally shared the use of deceptive figurative language with pagan poetry forced him to shift his definition of the difference. Consequently, he ultimately found Scripture to differ from pagan poetry in its being directly inspired by God while the writers of poetry derived inspiration from their own creative powers. Already undermined by a practical methodology of textual emendation treating poetry as an historical artifact, the quasi-sacred status of ancient poetry fell before an approach considering the poets as gifted but earthbound beings whose lives and works were accessible to the understanding of other human beings.

The absence of etymological analysis and of references to the medieval lexicographers in his last writings indicate a tardy renunciation of the assumption that Latin was an artificially created language. Perhaps his excursions into the history of Latin style and his final pronouncements on the nature of language explain the change. In his polemic with Poggio, Salutati ennunciated a stylistic doctrine that every age had its own linguistic character, that is, peculiarities of vocabulary and syntax derived from current popular usage which the orator must manipulate to achieve literary excellence in his own time. While the ultimate effect of this position was to open up language and style to historical analysis, the conflict of religious convictions and literary goals with aesthetic judgments made Salutati's interpretation of its significance highly ambivalent.

Inconsistently, Salutati proved to be both an ancient and a modern. Through his analysis of the vicissitudes of the second person singular form of the Latin verb he demonstrated how such historical investigations could be conducted. Applying his view of the ancient writers as creative historical beings to prose, he attacked the medieval view of these writers as a sort of monolithic block, thus providing the first account of the evolution of Latin literature through a comparison of prose styles. That such excursions into literary history inevitably contained value judgments not only exalting the age of Cicero over other periods of ancient literature but also asserting the basic superiority of pagan over Christian writers made him understandably uneasy. Consequently, when threatened by Poggio's classicism, he found himself arguing that not only was modern literature equal to the ancient on the basis of changing standards of linguistic eloquence but even superior given its access to higher truth.

Implicit both in his chronology of Latin literary development and his defense of Christian eloquence against Poggio's attack was a belief that Latin from the beginning down to modern times formed a continuity. With the possible exception of the thirteenth century, no age was without some claim to Latin eloquence. Unlike Petrarch, who saw himself isolated from the ancient rhetoricians by a millenium of linguistic decadence, Salutati perceived only a brief hiatus between the eloquent writers of the twelfth century and the works of Geri d'Arezzo and Mussato. More catholic in his tastes, Salutati felt less estranged from the more recent past and less reluctant to learn from it.

To an extent Salutati's commitment to the integrity of the Latin literary tradition merely presented with greater clarity and detail a basic assumption of the medieval approach to literature. If he occasionally contradicted it for religious and aesthetic motives, nevertheless the assumption, embodied as it was in his writings in the form of literary history, had real merit. While the immediate future belonged to the proponents of the "Dark Ages" thesis of medieval literature, centuries later insistence on continuity would find wide acceptance among scholars, and medieval writings would be appreciated for their eloquence.

The basic influence of Salutati's mature thought in his textual criticism, his late approach to allegory and poetry in general, his view of language, and his chronology of the Latin literary tradition all served to desanctify ancient history, thus making it possible for scholars to apply to the past criteria of experience and logic learned and utilized in the present. In historical research, application of the lessons of experience and rules of rationality to the writings of ancient authorities allowed him to produce a splendid study of the origins of Florence and offered a realistic presentation of Caesar's rise to power in the Roman state. With these short essays he demonstrated to the younger generation how secular history was to be written—literary and nonliterary sources should be exploited for discovering the answer to specific questions asked of the past.

He shared responsibility with Petrarch for establishing the clear distinction between Christian and pagan history and culture. What Aquinas accomplished for philosophy and theology by defining the limits of natural reason and working out the implications, Petrarch and Salutati did in effect for rhetoric. Although the Italian *dictatores* and French humanists of the twelfth century like John of Salisbury and Peter of Blois focused on practical applications of rhetoric, they had no sharp awareness of the differences between the Christian and pagan cultures and never consciously faced the problem of reconciling their rhetorical interests with their religion.

Although endeavoring to prove the integrity of the literary tradition, Salutati came to be deeply conscious of the differences between the natural culture of the pagan world and the Christian culture illuminated by divine revelation. As a historian, he gradually grew to appreciate the changes wrought by Christ's word in various aspects of society. Although he could not forebear placing value judgments on these differences, his delineation of the two spheres of culture contributed to the rise of a concept of anachronism basic to the modern mentality. If his immediate followers were in a sense similar to the *dictatores* of the thirteenth century in their interest in the secular world, they differed from the latter in being mindful of the limits separating the world of nature from that of grace.

Salutati's mature writings demonstrate a willingness to place his ideas on ethics within a theological and philosophical framework. Less fastidious, more ecumenical than his predecessor, Salutati willingly sought help wherever he could find it, betraying no reluctance to using terminology, ideas, and at times even the words of eminent scholastics. The increasing dimensions of his thought can partly be explained by his intensive contact after 1385 with those outstanding representatives of late scholasticism who came to teach in the reformed Florentine *Studio*. Indeed, from the 1390s his writings became philosophically respectable. He willingly confronted crucial issues like the relative superiority of the intellect or will and the merits of the active versus the contemplative life, issues which Petrarch had never faced squarely in his writings. True to the dialectician's style, however, he often took unequivocal positions which concealed his own hesitations. The same work could contain passages insidiously qualifying the absolute statements highlighted in the conclusion.

When Salutati ceased to accept the intellect as superior to the will and the contemplative life as superior to the active cannot be determined with precision. Although his own way of life demonstrated a prejudice for activity over contemplation and Cicero early on furnished him with arguments for defining man as a political animal, his challenging of the medieval tradition on the intellectual level came relatively late. He had learned from Augustine to consider the human will the focus of the soul's struggle for salvation, and Petrarch taught him the close ties among rhetoric, ethics, and volition. But Augustine's Platonism and Petrarch's ambivalence undercut the effectiveness of their writings as countervailing forces against the medieval preference for the contemplative life and the acknowledged superiority of the intellect.

Contemporary Franciscan thought provided him with the weapons he needed for the attack. If the final meeting of the soul with God consists of an act of love and not of an intellectual vision, then the human will assumes first place in the hierarchy of faculties. Salutati's originality lay in linking this theological conclusion to a defense of the active life of the citizen. Such an existence offers optimal occasion for realizing our capacity for loving while on this earth. Within this theological framework Cicero's arguments for the active life of the citizen assume validity. Indeed because it is now informed with knowledge of the proper end of man, the active life can attain a higher degree of perfection than in pagan times.

However, even the De nobilitate legum et medicine, the most elaborate presentation of these arguments, betrays Salutati's reservations. While affirming the superiority of the will over the intellect and of the active life over the speculative, he prefaces the whole discussion by specifying that the prerogatives of the contemplative life are not in question. His final judgment on the question of styles of life in his writings appears to be a compromise of the extremes: while the active life is superior to the contemplative generally, the individual must devote himself to both at different times. Unenlightened by contemplation, the will can go astray, while without the diligence of the will the good known cannot be realized in practice.

Nevertheless, despite the qualifications and vacillations, the overall tendency of Salutati's thought was to affirm that he who combines in one the roles of husband, father, friend, citizen, and devout Christian finds favor in God's eyes. If he has eloquence as well, then as orator he maximizes the effectiveness of his love and concern for the common good, thereby fulfilling the demands of Christian *caritas*. In effect Salutati, who dared to characterize Christ as a Jewish patriot, was the first European thinker to provide a justification for the superiority of the life of the Christian citizen to that of the cleric or monk. And yet it must be admitted that he never consciously worked out a general approach to morality consistent with his espousal of the active life. Acquainted with the Aristotelian doctrine of *mediocritas* from the late 1380s, Salutati initially rejected it for its lack of heroic proportions. Until 1400 his basic allegiance remained with the brittle medieval Stoic doctrine of indifference to external events, one which played such a major role in the moral teachings of twelfth-century humanists and thirteenth-century Italian *dictatores* alike and survived as a strong ethical current in Petrarch.

The reversal of Salutati's opinion ostensibly had nothing to do with any awareness of disparity between various strands of ideas in his thought but rather resulted from the shock of Piero's death, which disclosed the contradiction between Stoic moral precepts and the demands of human nature. By the testimony of his heart he convicted Stoicism of inhuman rigidity. He found Aristotle's concession to the flesh more valid. Christ himself showed that fear of death was legitimate. Virtuous conduct was not a matter of denying feelings but rather of holding a mean between two extremes of action and thus of properly channelling emotion.

The move toward a Christian Aristotelianism stopped at this. He made no effort to weld the scattered borrowings of the *De nobilitate* from Aristotle's statements on civic obligation and the philosopher's general remarks on the nature of virtue into a burgher ethic. While Bruni's mature, secular morality would have been questionable for Salutati, Bruni's republican political theory seems an obvious consequence of the older man's view of man as a political animal and of the active life as the superior mode of human existence. In Salutati's own writing, however, the civic ethic remains a body without a head. During the years when his ethical ideas reached their fullest development, Salutati's republican sentiments appear strangely dulled.

Despite occasional flights of enthusiasm motivated by exceptional circumstances, he had never been totally a theoretical republican. He cherished the communal form of government directed by the better people, but he could not visualize its existence independent of the imperial structure in which it was legally locked. Discussion of alternative theories of government could only arise when the empire lost its reality and autonomous powers within the old structure were considered independent. Until then political questions were generally reducible to legal formulation and remained in the province of the lawyers. Salutati's scattered expression of republican ideas, which were not developed in his own thought, had significance when those ideas recurred in the work of the next generation of Florentines whose allegiance the empire had lost.

His vigorous defense in 1400 of monarchy as the best form of government and of Caesar's role in its creation, however, went beyond a mere recognition of the empire as a fact of Italian political life. Together with other of his political and historical opinions, these views reflect the evolution of a new standard of values based on a Christian perspective that saw the pagan culture as intrinsically inferior to the Christian because, deprived of the Truth, it was essentially a product of human pride and ignorance. As a matter of fact, the *De seculo et religione* of 1381 had already utilized this perspective in an effort to denigrate the accomplishments of natural man. Nevertheless, like the rest of the treatise, this argument has an air of exaggerated pessimism. While more than a display of his ability to outdo his predecessors in depicting life in the world as odious and human achievements as squalid, the *De seculo* exposes a Christianity not yet internalized. Salutati's condemnation of pagan culture is little more than a facile borrowing from Augustine, not a conclusion produced by his own earnest if vain effort to fuse his studies of the ancients with faith.

In the years after the publication of the *De seculo*, when he was plunged into scholarship and captivated by his growing understanding of ancient life, Salutati felt no compulsion to integrate the two halves of his intellectual life. In 1396, however, brought up short by his need to "explain" his wife's death, he forced himself to come to grips with the task of fashioning his own version of Christian humanism. Whereas Petrarch managed to the end to keep a delicate balance between his Christian devotion and his reverence for antiquity, in Salutati the mixture remained unstable.

Having developed by 1396 a certain capacity for religious exaltation, confronted over the next few years by a series of frustrating, anxiety-provoking occurrences—a never-ending war, a deepening schism in the Church, and a murderous plague heralded by miracle-working *Bianchi*—Salutati felt his religious imagination soar. The spectacular sights and divine music of Dante's *Commedia* stimulated in him the vision of an immense, multi-layered universe obedient in every part to the awesome will of God. He felt no obligation to accept Dante's authority on the supremacy of the human intellect but, when the poet led him where Salutati himself would go, he followed. From the dizzying heights of God's eternity, the soteriological question became preeminent and the hierarchy of values was rearranged. The disparity between the knowledge and the potential destiny of even the simplest Christian and those of the wisest and best pagan was overwhelming. Augustine's verdict on the pagans assumed pictorial form in Dante's poem.

In his last years this theological perspective increasingly intruded itself on his discussions of ancient and modern culture. The *De tyranno* aptly illustrates the abruptness with which this can occur. After a detailed legalistic analysis of tyranny and a realistic account of Caesar's rise to and fall from power, Salutati launches into a ringing defense of monarchy and a condemnation of Caesar's murderers. Beneath the polemical motivation of these later sections lay a deeply felt urge to tie these momentous events to the mysterious workings of Providence. Caesar and the monarchy whose foundations he laid formed a vital part of God's design for redeeming the sinful world.

Almost everywhere in his last days when Christian culture is compared with that of the ancients, antipagan prejudice irresistibly determines the judgment. Possessed of true knowledge of the good, how can the Christian not have a greater potential for achieving friendship, for serving his country, etc.? By the end, questioning in his own mind the educational credentials of the pagans, the humanist was ill-equipped to do battle with Dominici. His best efforts were to produce the emasculated apologetic on their behalf.

Had they known of the fable of Hercules at the crossroads, the Italian rhetoricians of the thirteenth and early fourteenth centuries would have had no difficulty in agreeing with the ancients that it accurately represented the nature of the basic human problem. The two directions confronting Hercules were on the one hand that of virtue and on the other that of lust and pleasure. While the decision required courage to make and execute, Hercules had the power in himself to accomplish the task. When Salutati employed the tale in his *De laboribus Herculis*, he too was convinced of the meaning of the choice, of the innate power of man to take the right road and of the reward: "The wise man dominates the stars!" But as he aged, he came to see that the road plan was far more complicated. From deep within arose the suspicion that the Christian homeland did not lie along the same path, just beyond the pagan virtues. Then, finally, in the dusk, the issue lost its importance. One way only was sure underfoot and that was Christ's.

Unlike the heirs of one's worldly goods, those who inherit an intellectual legacy are more selective about what they will accept. Salutati's disciples willingly appropriated many of the key treasures from his endowment but on the whole they did not accept his religious superstructure, believing it an encumbrance. Although some members of this group, for example Poggio and Manetti, occasionally show religious concerns in their work, secular themes predominate in Florentine thought in the first half of the fifteenth century. While Salutati would no doubt have objected to this state of affairs, he would perhaps have found even more distasteful the trends of the next fifty years after the revival of the Platonic and neo-Platonic corpus. These works contributed to the development of a climate of thought, mystical and syncretistic in nature, which not only reacted against the secular currents of Bruni's day but which threatened to confuse the distinctions between pagan and Christian culture, between nature and grace, so painstakingly established by the fourteenth-century humanists.

APPENDIX I. THE MINOR WORKS OF SALUTATI

In addition to his humanistic treatises and his official and personal correspondence, Salutati authored a wide variety of minor works, some of which we know only by references in his letters or by surviving fragments. His earliest extant Latin poem is one of 28 lines dedicated to Pietro da Moglio in 1360/1 and published by Berthold L. Ullman, *Studies in the Italian Renaissance*, Storia e letteratura, 2nd ed., vol. 51 (Rome, 1973), pp. 296–97. See above, chap. 1. Doubtless his most popular Latin poetic work was the *Conquestio Phyllidis*, ed. Richard C. Jensen ("Coluccio Salutati's Lament of Phyllis," *Studies in Philology*, 65[1968], 116–23), and finished by October 1367 (see above, chap. 4, n. 23). Another poem published by Jensen together with Marie Bahr-Volk, *Fabula de vulpe et cancro* ("The Fox and the Crab: Coluccio Salutati's Unpublished Fable," *Studies in Philology*, 73[1976], 162–75), cannot be assigned any date.

Petrarch inspired Salutati to write at least two Latin poems. The *Metra Colutii Pyerii ad Petrarcham incitatoria ad Africe editionem* (*Epist.*, 231–41) was designed to lead Petrarch to publish the *Africa*. Salutati mentioned it as complete in his letter to Roberto di Battifolle in April 1374 (ibid., I, 184). He referred to it again in a letter to Broaspini in November 1375 (ibid., I, 222). For a new manuscript of the work see Giuseppe Billanovich and Elizabeth Pelligrin, "Una nuova lettera di Lombardo della Seta," *Studies in Honor of Berthold Louis Ullman*, ed. Charles Henderson, Storia e letteratura, vols. 93–94 (Rome, 1964), II, 219, n. 2. See above, chap. 3. In a letter of December 1375, Salutati explained that a poem on Petrarch's death, *De Petrarche interitu*, had grown longer than he originally intended and was not yet finished (*Epist.*, I, 224). However, there is no reason to doubt, as Novati does, that the work was not completed eventually. Even if Manetti's mention of the work (ibid., IV, 512) depended entirely on the Italian version of Villani's biography (ibid., IV, 500), it is arbitrary for Novati to dismiss the vulgarizer's reference to the "Della morte del Petrarcha" as "tutto vago." The title simply occurs in a list of Salutati's works and is not more "vague" than any other reference. Mehus claimed to have seen the work in a Vallombrosa codex (ibid., I, 224).

Only fragments of Salutati's *Bucolics* remain (ibid., I, 163, and possibly 323; II, 191; IV, 118, 508 and probably 506). The first and sixth eclogues were in finished form by 1372 (according to ibid., I, 157) and by 1382, if Villani is to be trusted (ibid., IV, 491), the original plan for eight was realized. The Latin poems, however, could not have been widely known if Bernardo da Moglio, who had been in contact with Salutati at least since 1383, did not know them in 1390 (ibid., II, 266). A brief discussion of Salutati's bucolic poetry including the *Conquestio Phyllidis* is found in E. Carrara, "Le vestigia bucholiche di Coluccio Salutati," *Studi petrarcheschi ed altri scritti* (Turin, 1959), pp. 205–17.

Novati's edition of Salutati's correspondence contains three of Salutati's other Latin poetic compositions in their entirety: a criticism of lovers written in 1382/3 as a response to Alberto degli Albizzi's complaint of unrequited love (*Epist.*, II, 57–64 and IV, 287–90, respectively); a poem on the Muses sent to Maestro Bartolomeo da Regno on July 16, 1392(?) (ibid., II, 345–54); and one against divination for Jacopo Allegretti sent on July 12, 1378 (ibid., I, 281–88). Incidentally, Salutati inserted this last poem in his *De fato et fortuna*: B.A.V., *Vat. Lat.* 2928, Tr. III, 1, fols. 37–40. Salutati's war sonnet, *Invectiva Florentinorum contra arma domini Comitis Virtutum transmissa per ser Colucium domino Henghiramo de Brachis*, and de Bracci's response are published by L. Mehus, *Historia litteraria florentina*, ed. E. Kessler (Münich, 1968), p. cccxii. Both belong to the first Milanese war 1390–1392. See above, chap. 6, n. 39. Salutati's most ambitious poetic work, *De bello Pyrrhi habito cum Romanis*, dealing with the Roman war against Pyrrhus, was apparently destroyed by Salutati himself. Other Latin poetry or references to Latin poetry authored by Salutati are found in *Epist.*, I, 5–6, 44–51, 67; II, 313, 327; III, 214.

Salutati's Italian poetry has never been systematically collected. Francesco Flamini, *La lirica toscana del Rinascimento anteriore ai tempi del Magnifico* (Pisa, 1891), pp. 731–33, identifies manuscripts and editions of seven of Salutati's sonnets including two composed in a mixture of Latin and *volgare*. For these two see above, chap. 7, n. 81. Flamini republishes one of the seven sonnets he identifies, the immensely popular war poem, "O scacciato dal ciel da Michael" (p. 60). Also see chap. 6, n. 39, and above.

In addition to the seven published Italian sonnets mentioned in Flamini, there are at least three others still unpublished: (1) "Se voi star sano": B.N.F., *Naz.*, II, VIII, 39, fol. 15ᵛ; (2) "Pronto all'ufficio": B.M.V., *Ital.*, IX, 204, fol. 80; B.L.F., 90, 103, fol. 172; B.R.F., 1156, fol. 2ᵛ; and (3) "Sanza riposo": B.N.F., *Naz.*, II, II, 40, fol. 214. The index of the last codex identifies this poem as Salutati's work.

Throughout his mature life Salutati was called on to compose Latin epitaphs for tombs. A variety of these are found *Epist.*, I, 94; II, 131, 220; IV, 247; and L. Mehus, *Historia*, pp. cccxiii-cccxv. For Salutati's Latin epigrams beneath paintings of worthies, done for the Palazzo della Signoria, see Theresa Hankey, "Salutati's Epigrams for the Palazzo Vecchio," *Journal of the Warburg and Courtauld Institutes*, 22(1959), 363–65.

Salutati obviously enjoyed translating from Italian into Latin. His Latin translation of two sonnets of Petrarch is published by A. Zardo, *Il Petrarca e i Carraresi* (Milan, 1887), pp. 306–07. The B.N.P., *Lat.*, 8731, fols. 77ᵛ–78, is a more accurate version than the B.N.F., *Pal.* 185, fol. 122, used by Zardo for his edition. Latin translations of portions of Dante's *Divina commedia* are found *Epist.*, III, 141; and B.A.V., *Vat. lat.*, 2928, Tr. III, 11 and 12, fols. 69ᵛ, 72ᵛ and 73ᵛ. Salutati's revision of Simon Atumano's Latin translation of Plutarch's *De cohibenda ira* is discussed by Giuseppe di Stefano, "La découverte de Plutarque en Occident," *Memoria dell'Accademia delle scienze di Torino*, cl. sci., mor., stor., e filol., ser. 4, 18 (1968).

While Salutati can be expected to have delivered numerous orations during his career as chancellor of the Florentine Republic, only two of these survive. The *Sermo Colucii Pyerii de Stignano, Cancellarii Florentini habitus . . . ad Phylippum de Alenconio . . .* , dated June 1381 (B.A.V., *Capp.*, 147, pp. 35–7; and *Epist.*, IV, 506, n. 3); and the *Oratoribus Regis Francorum. Responsio facta per dominum Colucium pro parte Colligatorum et Communis Florentie*, written in 1382 (B.A.V., *Capp.*, 147, pp. 7–8 and 400–02; *Epist.*, IV, 506, n. 3). The *Exhortatio facta per ser Colucium cancellarium florentinum per modum arenghe sive sermonis defendendo civitatem bononiensem contra Comitem Virtutem*, attributed by Novati to Salutati and dated 1389 (*Epist.*, IV, 507) is not his. See similar attribution in L. Frati, "Una miscellanea umanistica della r. Biblioteca Universitaria di Bologna," in *Miscellanea di studi in onore di Attilo Hortis*, 2 vols. (Trieste, 1910), 2: 324; and Ullman, *The Humanism*, pp. 34–35. The Milanese lord referred to as "dominus B." (B.A.V., *Vat. lat.*, 3121, fol. 187) is clearly Bernabo Visconti and the events mentioned in the oration are related to Albornoz' attempt to protect Bologna from the Visconti in the last half of 1360 and 1361. The most recent event mentioned as occurring before the speech ("novissime") involved "arcem Bononie volentes prodere pecunia corrupti custodes": fol. 185. This probably refers to an incident in August 1361: *Cronica di Matteo Villani*, ed. F. Dragomanni, 2 vols. (Florence, 1846), II, 368–69.

The *Congratulatio florentinissime civitatis Florentie ad fidos Anconitanos de expugnatione fortissime ac dure sue arcis et libertatis restitutione*, dated January 19, 1383/1382, is without doubt by Salutati, but Ullman (*The Humanism*, pp. 34–5) incorrectly considers it an *arenga*. The work is a missive sent by the *Signoria* to Ancona and probably was recorded in the appropriate volume of *Missive* since disappeared. The work has been published by C. Ciavarini, *Collezione di doc. stor. antichi inediti ed editi vari della città e Terre marchigiane*, 5 vols. (Ancona, 1870–84), I, 145–47.

Of the Florentine humanist's three extant declamations the most famous was his *De Lucretia*, of which there are three modern editions: H. Müller in *Blätter f. d. bayer. Gymn-und Realschulwesen*, 14 (1878), 371–374; M. Korelin, *Rannij italjanskij gumanism i ego istoriografia*, Moscow University, Otdel istorikofilologicheskij, Uchenyin Zapiski, vols. 14–15 (Moscow, 1892), II, Append., pp. 7–12; and Enrico Menesto, *Coluccio Salutati: Editi e inediti latini dal Ms. 53 della Biblioteca comunale di Todi*, Res Tudertinae, vol. 12 (Todi, 1971), pp. 35–43. Cf. *Epist.*, IV, 253–54, n. 4.

The other two are *Declamatio quod melius regnum sit successivum quam electivum*, ed. by Berthold L. Ullman in "Coluccio Salutati on Monarchy," *Mélanges Eugène Tisserant*, Studi e Testi, vols. 231–37 (Città del Vaticano, 1964), V, 402–06; and *Questio est coram Decemviris*, ed. Andrew McCormick in "Freedom of Speech in Early Renaissance Florence: Salutati's *Questio est coram Decemviris*," *Rinascimento*, 2nd. ser., 19(1979), 237–40.

Finally, two small works attributed to Salutati are the *Ratio punctandi*, ed. by Lucia Gai, "Frammenti di un codice sconosciuto di Coluccio Salutati," *Motivi di riforma tra '400 e '500*, Memorie domenicane, n.s., 3(1973), 306; and *Epitome Statii Achilleidos*. For both texts see Ullman, *The Humanism*, pp. 35–6.

Appendix II. THE DATING OF THE *INVECTIVA IN ANTONIUM LUSCHUM VICENTINUM*

In his *Humanistic and Political Literature in Florence and Venice* (Harvard, 1955), pp. 51–60, Hans Baron examines in detail the problem of dating Salutati's *Invectiva in Antonium Luschum Vicentinum*, ed. Domenico Moreni (Florence, 1826). On the basis of a close analysis of the text he proposes that Salutati's work was written in two or three stages: one belonging to late 1397, another to the period immediately after the fall of Bologna, and the third to 1403, after Giangaleazzo's death. Baron notes passages that justify Florence's policy of building a coalition of allies, a situation characteristic of the period 1397–98 but not of 1402 when Florence stood alone (p. 53). These passages indicate the formation of alliances "which identifies the time before the Truce of Pavia in May 1398." Salutati goes to great lengths in defending Florence's alliance with France, an alliance abruptly terminated by the truce. Moreover, Salutati refers to "this second war," i.e., the war that began in March 1397 and ended in March 1400 with the Peace of Venice (p. 55). Baron finally notes "side by side with Salutati's confident assertions that Florence's long established friendship with Bologna was so natural and inevitable that it could not be undermined, there are sneers against this sister-republic referring to suspected machinations with Milan of some Bolognese citizens in the autumn of 1397, and laments over Bologna's defection and her subjection to Giangaleazzo's tyranny in June and July of 1402." Thus, we have a multilayered work consisting of sections and even individual sentences written at different periods. For instance, when Salutati writes (*Invectiva*, p. 106): "Credis ne quod oblitus sit illustris dominus Marchio, licet, ut secundum tempora, quibus loqueris, nos loquamur, adhuc puer sit . . . ," Baron comments after *quibus loqueris*, "*loquamur* is obviously an editorial insertion from the time of publication" (*Humanistic and Political Literature*, p. 54, n. 9).

Berthold L. Ullman in his *The Humanism of Coluccio Salutati*, Medioevo e umanesimo, vol. 4 (1963), 33–34, n. 2, strongly disagrees with Baron: "He [Baron] would have Coluccio begin his book in 1397 and finish it in 1402–3 and speaks of 'first draft,' 'final version,' 'two strata,' etc. There is no shred of evidence for this. As Novati shows, Loschi wrote his invective in 1397–98 after the outbreak of the second war between Florence and Milan (spring, 1397). On account of the war Coluccio did not see a copy for some time (Novati suggests two or three years after its appearance, which would take us to 1399–1401). Actually Coluccio's letter to Pietro Turchi . . . written September 11, 1403, makes clear that Coluccio was nearing his seventy-third birthday (February 16, 1404) when he received Loschi's treatise from Turchi. He says, furthermore, that he is returning Loschi's invective and enclosing his reply, written therefore—all of it—in the summer of 1403."

Baron's reply to Ullman (*Crisis*, rev. ed., pp. 484–87) contained a number of astute observations on Salutati's letter to Turchi which he felt Ullman had misinterpreted. First of all, Salutati does not say that before receipt of Turchi's letter he had been unaware of Loschi's work. Secondly, Salutati's phrase in the September letter that he was nearing his seventy-third birthday cannot mean that, as Ullman writes, "Coluccio was nearing his seventy-third birthday *when he received Loschi's treatise from Turchi*" (the italics are Baron's). For Baron, Turchi's letter probably came nearer to February 16, 1403, and as early as July Salutati had a chapter in a form capable of being read by a friend.

On the other hand, Salutati's letter does furnish persuasive evidence that he only began writing the *Invectiva* after receiving Turchi's letter and implies that Salutati had not seen Loschi's work before. When Turchi "commanded" Salutati to reply to Loschi, Salutati writes: " . . . cum viderem rebus magnum, oratione longum obiurgandique necessitate fecundum . . . steti dubius quidnam facturus essem" (III, 634–35). He also tells us clearly that his decision to compose an invective occurred when he was in his seventies, i.e., after February 16, 1403, and his immediate reference to his next birthday suggests that that decision was made in 1403. To question Salutati's statements here amounts to considering them falsehoods.

The appearance of different time layers in Salutati's work, to my mind, can easily be explained by the fact that Salutati was attacking a document full of charges that were no longer current while attempting to make his response an effective piece of writing. The kind of procedure Salutati adopted is illustrated by the passage cited by Baron and given above (*Invectiva*, p. 106, and *Humanistic and Political Literature*, p. 54, n. 9). In this passage Salutati declares to Loschi "that we will speak in the time period in which you spoke." In my opinion this is not, as Baron holds, an insertion, but an explanation for Salutati's method of debating Loschi. Consequently, when he speaks in the same passage of "hoc bello," i.e., the Second Milanese War, Salutati is purposely speaking "in

the time period in which you spoke" (secundum tempora, quibus loqueris).

Furthermore, my reading of the work does not suggest to me that
Salutati really "says that things that did happen would never happen"
(*Crisis*, p. 485). Rather, defending Florentine judgments, he tends to
obfuscate and avoid admitting errors. His remarks on the Gonzaga alliance, which ultimately collapsed, is a case in point. While he assures
Loschi that Este and Carrara will remain loyal to their alliances, all he
says of Gonzaga is "demens erit, quod se deserat, vel sociorum defen-
sionem, quae sui sit, omittat" (*Invectiva*, p. 107). I am not aware that he
anywhere threatens Loschi with an imminent French invasion which,
were he writing in 1397, he would be expecting.

As the text of this chapter implies, the only significance of dating the
Invectiva as written in 1403 is that this helps to point up Salutati's tendency after 1400 to emphasize the theme of political legitimacy as a de-
sideratum and to join that to the theme of Guelfism taken over from
the Second Milanese War.

INDEX

442

Burley, Walter of, 295
Bursill-Hall, G. L., 260n

Caesar (Gaius Julius), 255, 257, 258, 268, 386; controversy concerning, 164, 242n, 330, 368–78, 380–85, 424, 427, 428; debate over, as founder of Florence, 246–48; identified by Salutati as author of *Commentarii*, 253
Caesar, Lucius, 386
Calamari, Giuseppe, 26n
Caligula (Roman emperor), 250, 272
Callipius, 228
Calò, Giuseppe, 196n, 197n
Camaldulensan monastery, 195, 196
Camaldulensans, 195
Cambi, Giovanni, 141–42
Cambini, ser Giovanni, 100n
Cambio da Poggibonzi, 61n
Camera d'Arme, 111
Cammelli, Giuseppe, 306n
Campania, 252
Campanus, Johannes, 295n
Cane, Ruggiero, 300n
Capelli, Pasquino, 160–62, 229, 254, 293n, 300
Capitoli (Florentine territorial laws), 26n, 31–33, 49
Caritas, 342n, 343–44, 347, 348, 361, 364, 426; as pagan *caritas patrie*, 74–75n
Carlo di Calabria, 61n
Carmignano, 274
Carrara, Francesco, the Younger, 158, 160, 165, 286, 390, 437
Carrara family, 58, 157, 162, 293, 388
Carrarese war, 272n
Carro, gonfalone of, 181n
Casentino, 118, 309
Casini, Bruno, 57
Cassiodorus, 255, 289
Cassius (Gaius Longinus). *See* Brutus
Castelfranco, 32n
Castellani, Vanni, 144, 146
Castello, Città di, 129; original name of, 235–36, 245
Castiglionchio, Lapo, 57, 59, 61n, 62, 87, 101, 122, 132n, 137, 139, 241n
Castiglionchio, Simone, 87, 101
Castracani, Castruccio (duke of Lucca), 3, 4, 5
Casucchi, fra' Niccolò da Girgenti, 130
Catiline, 246, 249, 372
Cato, the Censor, 265, 268; *De re rustica*, 254; *Distichs*, 14
Cato, Uticensis, 205n, 374, 386
Catullus, manuscript of, 184, 185–86, 229

Causation: as fate and fortune, 63–65, 66n, 71, 73–74, 87–88, 101, 193–94, 241n, 242, 281, 297, 417, 316–30 *passim*, 339, 364n, 374, 376; and grace, 71, 87–88, 199–201, 210, 217, 241, 328, 329, 332, 339–47, 366; and principle of contingency, necessity, 316–19, 338–39, 376; and Providence, 54, 87–88, 163, 193, 194, 242, 280, 297, 313–30, 351, 354, 356, 357, 364, 374–86 *passim*, 391, 402–3, 429; as source of ascetic inspiration, 190–93, 213–26 *passim*, 421; as source of eternal species, 337–38; as source of human law and will, 334–35; as source of Scripture, 406–7, 409, 433; as source of truth, 409–10, 427. *See also* Astrology, astrologers; Will
Cavalcabo, Andreasio, 300n
Cecco d'Ascoli, 330
Cecina, Marcus, 255
Cecina, Val di, 414
Cei, Salvo da Vellano, 277
Celle, Giovanni delle, 131
Celsus, Julius, 253
Cenci, ser Domenico da Buggiano, 29n
Cesana, 132
Cessionis, via, 171, 174. *See also* Schism of 1378
Chabod, Federico, 112n
Chalcidius, 295n, 303n
Chancellor: of *Anziani* of Lucca, 92–93, 99; of Commune of Lucca, Salutati as, 86–100; and notary of legislation of Todi, Salutati as, 47–48, 78–81; of Republic of Florence, 46, 112, 115–17, 120, 121, 122–23, 124–25, 137, 140–42, 165, 393, 394
Chancery: Florentine, 112, 113n, 118n, 125, 393, 414; Lucchese, 92; Milanese, 113n, papal, 113n
Charlemagne, restoration of Florence by, 247, 391
Charles IV (emperor), 76, 90, 91n
Charles VI (king of France), 173, 176, 388
Checco da Lion, 189
Chelli, ser Antonio, 115, 139, 148, 183, 188, 280–81, 291, 419
Chittolini, Giorgio, 27n
Christendom, 128, 170, 174
Christianity, Salutati's attitude towards: in late 1360s, 63–64; 1369–95, 66, 71–72, 74–75, 85–86, 87–88, 101, 164, 190–91, 193, 199, 203, 205, 207–8, 225, 226, 240–42, 271, 274, 279n, 296; from 1396, 330, 342–47, 350–54, 358–66, 374, 377, 385, 391, 401–5, 406, 407, 410–13, 417, 421–29; and paganism, 62, 203, 207, 226, 240–42, 271, 296, 344, 401–5, 410–13, 427–29
Chronica de origine civitatis, 246

Ronald G. Witt is Professor of History, Duke University. In addition to many articles in scholarly journals, Professor Witt has published *Coluccio Salutati and His Public Letters* and is co-editor of *The Earthly Republic of the Italian Humanists* and *Cultural Roots and Continuities*.